SECURE DATA SCIENCE

SECURE DATA SCIENCE
Integrating Cyber Security and Data Science

Bhavani Thuraisngham, Murat Kantarcioglu, and
Latifur Khan

CRC Press
Taylor & Francis Group
Boca Raton London New York

CRC Press is an imprint of the
Taylor & Francis Group, an **informa** business

First edition published 2022
by CRC Press
6000 Broken Sound Parkway NW, Suite 300, Boca Raton, FL 33487-2742

and by CRC Press
2 Park Square, Milton Park, Abingdon, Oxon, OX14 4RN

© 2022 Taylor & Francis Group, LLC

CRC Press is an imprint of Taylor & Francis Group, LLC

ISBN: 978-0-367-53410-3 (hbk)
ISBN: 978-1-032-21257-9 (pbk)
ISBN: 978-1-003-08184-5 (ebk)

DOI: 10.1201/9781003081845

Typeset in Times
by MPS Limited, Dehradun

Dedication

We dedicate this book to all those who have lost their brave battle to COVID-19 and have motivated us to continue with our research and education activities on Data Science, Security, and Privacy during these difficult days.

Contents

PART I Supporting Technologies for Secure Data Science

PART II Data Science for Cyber Security

PART III   Security and Privacy-Enhanced Data Science

PART IV   Access Control and Data Science

Preface

BACKGROUND

Recent developments in information systems technologies have resulted in computerizing many applications in various business areas. Data has become a critical resource in many organizations, and therefore, efficient access to data, sharing the data, extracting information from the data, and making use of the information has become an urgent need. As a result, there have been many efforts on not only integrating the various data sources scattered across several sites, but extracting information from these databases in the form of patterns and trends and carrying out data analytics has also become important. These data sources may be databases managed by database management systems, or they could be data warehoused in a repository from multiple data sources.

The advent of the World Wide Web (WWW) in the mid-1990s has resulted in even greater demand for managing data, information, and knowledge effectively. During this period, the services paradigm has conceived which has now evolved into providing computing infrastructures, software, databases, and applications as services. Such capabilities have resulted in the notion of cloud computing. Over the past five years, developments in cloud computing have exploded and we now have several companies that provide infrastructure software and applications computing platforms as services.

As the demand for data and information management increases, there is also a critical need for maintaining the security of the databases, applications, and information systems. Data, information, applications, the web, and the cloud have to be protected from unauthorized access as well as from malicious corruption. The approaches to secure such systems have come to be known as cyber security.

The significant developments in data management and analytics, web services, cloud computing, and cyber security have evolved into an area called big data management and analytics (BDMA) as well as big data security and privacy (BDSP). The US Bureau of Labor and Statistics (BLS) defines *big data* as a collection of large datasets that cannot be analyzed with normal statistical methods. The datasets can represent numerical, textual, and multimedia data. Big data is popularly defined in terms of five Vs: Volume, Velocity, Variety, Veracity, and Value. BDMA requires handling huge volumes of data, both structured and unstructured, arriving at high velocity. By harnessing big data, we can achieve breakthroughs in several key areas such as cyber security and healthcare, resulting in increased productivity and profitability. Not only do the big data systems have to be secured but also the big data analytics have to be applied for cyber security applications such as insider threat detection.

Managing and analyzing massive amounts of data utilizing statistical reasoning and machine learning has resulted in an area called *data science*. That is, data science integrated big data management with statistics and machine learning. Data science techniques have been applied to many areas including healthcare, finance, marketing, and cyber security. On the other hand, the data science techniques could be attacked by malicious processes. That is, while data science can be applied to solve cyber security problems such as insider threat detection, the data science techniques have to be secure. This has resulted in an area called *secure data science*. This book will focus on various aspects of secure data science. In particular, this book will discuss both the foundational technologies for secure data science such as data science and cyber security as well as discuss the applications of data science for cyber security, securing data science and some emerging directions in secure data science including data privacy.

We have written two series of books for CRC Press on data management/data mining and data security. The first series consists of ten books. Book #1 (*Data Management Systems: Evolution and Interoperation*) focused on general aspects of data management and also addressed interoperability and migration. Book #2 (*Data Mining: Technologies, Techniques, Tools, and Trends*) discussed data mining. It essentially elaborated on Chapter 9 of Book #1. Book #3 (*Web Data Management and Electronic Commerce*) discussed web database technologies and discussed e-commerce as an application area. It essentially elaborated on Chapter 10 of Book #1. Book #4 (*Managing and Mining Multimedia Databases*) addressed both multimedia database management and multimedia data mining. It elaborated on both Chapter 6 of Book #1 (for multimedia database management) and Chapter 11 of Book #2 (for multimedia data mining). Book #5 (XML, Databases and the Semantic Web) described XML technologies related to data management. It elaborated on Chapter 11 of Book #3. Book #6 (*Web Data Mining Technologies and Their Applications in Business Intelligence and Counter-Terrorism*) elaborated on Chapter 9 of book #3. Book #7 (*Database and Applications Security:Integrating Information Security and Data Management*) examines security for technologies discussed in each of our previous books. It focuses on the technological developments in database and applications security. It is essentially the integration of Information Security and Database Technologies. Book #8 (*Building Trustworthy Semantic Webs*) applies security to semantic web technologies and elaborates on Chapter 25 of Book #7. Book #9 (*Secure Semantic Service-Oriented Systems*) is an elaboration of Chapter 16 of book #8. Book #10, (*Building and Securing the Cloud*) is an elaboration of Chapters 5 and 25 of Book #9.

Our second series of books consists of six books. Book #1 is on the *Design and Implementation of Data Mining Tools*. Book #2 is on the *Design and Implementation of Data Mining Tools for Malware Detection*. Book #3 is on *Secure Data Provenance and Inference Control with Semantic Web*. Book #4 is on *Analyzing and Securing Social Media*. Book #5 is on *Big Data Analytics with Applications in Insider Threat Detection*. Finally, Book #6 (which is this book) is on *Secure Data Science: Integrating Cyber Security and Data Science*. For this series, we are converting some of the practical aspects of our work with students into books. The relationships between our texts will be illustrated in this book's Appendix.

ORGANIZATION OF THIS BOOK

This book is divided into four parts, each describing some aspect of the technology that is relevant to secure data science. The major focus of this book will be on data science for cyber security as well as securing data science. In addition, we will also discuss some of the experimental systems we have developed and provide some of the challenges involved.

This book is divided into four parts, each describing some aspect of the technology that is relevant to data science and cyber security. Part I, consisting of four chapters, will describe supporting technologies for secure data science, including data security and privacy, data mining for cyber security, cloud computing and semantic web and big data security and privacy. These supporting technologies provide the background information for secure data science. Part II, consisting of four chapters, provides a detailed overview of the data science techniques we have developed for cyber security. In particular, scalable data science techniques for malware analysis and stream analytics for insider threat detection will be discussed. Part III, consisting of five chapters, will discuss security and privacy-enhanced data science, including attacks to data science, adversarial machine learning, and privacy-aware policy-based data management. We also discuss how our work can be applied to a specific applications and that is the COVID-19 pandemic. Part IV discusses access control and data science and consists of five chapters. It describes secure cloud query processing, policy-based information sharing, access control framework based on semantic web for social media data, inference controller for semantic web-based big data. We also discuss how some of our work could be applied to an application such as the Internet of Transportation systems.

DATA, INFORMATION, AND KNOWLEDGE

In general, data management includes managing the databases, interoperability, migration, warehousing, and mining. For example, the data on the web has to be managed and mined to extract information and patterns and trends. Data could be in files, relational databases, or other types of databases such as multimedia databases. Data may be structured or unstructured. We repeatedly use the terms data, data management, and database systems and database management systems in this book. We elaborate on these terms in this book's Appendix. We define data management systems to be systems that manage the data, extract meaningful information from the data, and make use of the information extracted. Therefore, data management systems include database systems, data warehouses, and data mining systems. Data could be structured data such as those found in relational databases, or it could be unstructured such as text, voice, imagery, and video.

There have been numerous discussions in the past to distinguish between data, information, and knowledge. In some of our previous books on data management and mining, we did not attempt to clarify these terms. We simply stated that data could be just bits and bytes or it could convey some meaningful information to the user. However, with the web and also with increasing interest in data, information, and knowledge management as separate areas, in this book we take a different approach to data, information, and knowledge by differentiating between these terms as much as possible. For us, data is usually some value like numbers, integers, and strings. Information is obtained when some meaning or semantics is associated with the data such as John's salary is 20K. Knowledge is something that you acquire through reading and learning and, as a result, understand the data and information and take actions. That is, data and information can be transferred into knowledge when uncertainty about the data and information is removed from someone's mind. It should be noted that it is rather difficult to give strict definitions of data, information and knowledge. Sometimes we will use these terms interchangeably also. Our framework for data management discussed in this book's Appendix helps clarify some of the differences. To be consistent with the terminology in our previous books, we will also distinguish between database systems and database management systems. A database management system is that component which manages the database containing persistent data. A database system consists of both the database and the database management system.

FINAL THOUGHTS

The goal of this book is to explore the applications of data science for cyber security as well as securing the data science techniques. We will discuss various concepts, technologies, issues and challenges for secure data science. In addition, we also present several of the experimental systems in secure data science that we have designed and developed at the University of Texas at Dallas. We have used some of the material in this book together with the numerous references listed in each chapter for graduate level courses at The University of Texas at Dallas on "Big Data Analytics" as well on "Big Data Security and Privacy."

It should be noted that the field is expanding very rapidly with several open sources tools and commercial products for managing and analyzing big data. Therefore, it is important for the reader to keep up with the developments of the various big data systems. However, security cannot be an afterthought. Therefore, while the technologies for big data are being developed, it is important to include security at the onset.

Acknowledgments

We thank the administration at the Erik Jonsson School of Engineering and Computer Science at the University of Texas at Dallas for giving us the opportunity to conduct our research. We also thank Ms. Rhonda Walls, our project coordinator, for proofreading and editing the chapters. Without her hard work this book would not have been possible. We thank many people who have supported our work or collaborated with us.

- Dr. Cliff Wang from the Army Research Office for funding our research on Adversarial Machine Learning.
- Dr. Victor Piotrowski from the National Science Foundation for funding our capacity building work on assured cloud computing and big data security and privacy.
- Dr. Robert Herklotz (retired) from the Air Force Office of Scientific Research for funding our research on insider threat detection as well as several of our experimental systems.
- Dr. Ashok Agrawal formerly of National Aeronautics and Space Administration for funding our research on stream data mining.
- Prof. Jiawei Han and his team from the University of Illinois at Urbana Champaign as well as Dr. Charu Agrawal from IBM Research for collaborating with us on stream data mining.
- Prof. Elisa Bertino (Purdue University), Prof. Maribel Fernandez (Kings College, University of London), Prof. Elena Ferrari and Prof. Barbara Carminati (both from the University of Insubria, Italy), and for their collaborations with us on Access Control.
- The following people for their technical contributions: Dr. Mehedy Masud for his contributions to Chapters 6, 7, and 8; Dr. Pallabi Parveen for her contributions to Chapter 9 (part of Dr. Parveen's PhD thesis); Dr. Yan Zhou and Dr. Bowie Xi for their contributions to Chapter 10; Dr. Yan Zhou for her contributions to Chapter 11; Dr. Li Liu for her contributions to Chapter 12 (part of Dr. Liu's PhD thesis); Dr. Elisa Bertino, Dr. Maribel Fernandez and Dr. Jonathan Bakdash for their contributions to Chapter 13; Dr. Farhan Husain and Dr. Arindam Khaled for their contributions to Chapter 15 (part of Dr. Husain's PhD thesis); Dr. Tyrone Cadenhead, Dr. Vaibhav Khadilkar and Dr. Jyothsna Rachapalli for their contributions to Chapter 16; Dr. Raymond Heatherly, Dr. Barbara Carminati and Dr. Elena Ferrari for their contributions to Chapter 17 (part of Dr. Heatherly's PhD thesis); and Dr. Tyrone Cadenhead for his contributions to Chapter 18 (part of Dr. Cadenhead's PhD thesis).

Acknowledgements

[text largely faded and illegible]

Permissions

Chapter 6: Data Science for Malicious Executables

Masud, M.M., Khan, L. & Thuraisingham, B. *A Scalable Multi-Level Feature Extraction Technique to Detect Malicious Executables. Inf Syst Front* **10,** 33–45 (2008). Reprinted/adapted by permission from Springer Nature. © 2008.

Chapter 7: Stream Analytics for Malware Detection

Masud, M.M., Gao, J., Khan, L., Han, J., Thuraisingham, B. (2009) *Integrating Novel Class Detection with Classification for Concept-Drifting Data Streams.* Reprinted/adapted by permission from Springer Nature: Springer eBook. Machine Learning and Knowledge Discovery in Databases. ECML PKDD 2009. Lecture Notes in Computer Science, vol 5782. Buntine, W., Grobelnik, M., Mladenić, D., Shawe-Taylor, J. (eds) © Springer-Verlag Berlin Heidelberg 2009.

Chapter 8: Cloud-Based Data Science for Malware Detection

Mohammad M. Masud, Tahseen M. Al-Khateeb, Kevin, W. Hamlen, Jing Gao, Latifur Khan, Jiawei Han, and Bhavani Thuraisingham. 2011. *Cloud-Based Malware Detection for Evolving Data Streams.* © 2011. Republished with permission from ACM (Association for Computing Machinery), from *ACM Trans. Manage. Inf. Syst.* 2, 3, Article 16 (October 2011), 27 pages.

Chapter 9: Stream Analytics for Insider Threat Detection

P. Parveen, J. Evans, B. Thuraisingham, K. W. Hamlen and L. Khan, *Insider Threat Detection Using Stream Mining and Graph Mining,* © 2011 IEEE. Reprinted, with permission, from *2011 IEEE Third International Conference on Privacy, Security, Risk and Trust and 2011 IEEE Third International Conference on Social Computing,* 2011, pp. 1102–1110, doi: 10.1109/PASSAT/SocialCom.2011.211

P. Parveen, N. McDaniel, V. S. Hariharan, B. Thuraisingham and L. Khan, *Unsupervised Ensemble Based Learning for Insider Threat Detection,* © 2012 IEEE. Reprinted, with permission, from the Proceedings of *2012 International Conference on Privacy, Security, Risk and Trust and 2012 International Conference on Social Computing,* 2012, pp. 718–727, doi: 10.1109/SocialCom-PASSAT.2012.106.

Pallabi Parveen, Nathan McDaniel, Zackary Weger, Jonathan Evans, Bhavani, M. Thuraisingham, Kevin, W. Hamlen, Latifur Khan, *Evolving Insider Threat Detection Stream Mining,* Republished with permission of World Scientific Publishing Co., Inc. *International Journal on Artificial Intelligence Tools* Vol. 22, No. 5 (2013) 1360013 (24 pages). © 2013; permission conveyed through Copyright Clearance Center, Inc.

Chapter 10: Adversarial Support Vector Machine Learning

Yan Zhou, Murat Kantarcioglu, Bhavani Thuraisingham, and Bowei Xi. 2012. *Adversarial Support Vector Machine Learning.* © 2012. Republished with permission of ACM (Association of Computing Machinery), from the *Proceedings of the 18th ACM SIGKDD International Conference on Knowledge Discovery and Data Mining* (KDD '12), New York, NY, USA, 1059–1067. DOI:https://doi-org.libproxy.utdallas.edu/10.1145/2339530.2339697

Chapter 11: Adversarial Learning Using Relevance Vector Machine Ensembles

Y. Zhou, M. Kantarcioglu and B. Thuraisingham, *Sparse Bayesian Adversarial Learning Using Relevance Vector Machine Ensembles*, © 2012 IEEE. Reprinted, with permission, from *IEEE 12th International Conference on Data Mining*, 2012, pp. 1206–1211, doi: 10.1109/ICDM.2012.58.

Chapter 12: Privacy Preserving Decision Trees

Li Liu, M. Kantarcioglu and B. Thuraisingham, *Privacy Preserving Decision Tree Mining from Perturbed Data*, © 2009 IEEE. Reprinted, with permission, from *42nd Hawaii International Conference on System Sciences*, 2009, pp. 1–10, doi: 10.1109/HICSS.2009.353.

Chapter 13: Towards a Privacy Aware Quantified Self Data Management Framework

Bhavani Thuraisingham, Murat Kantarcioglu, Elisa Bertino, Jonathan, Z. Bakdash, and Maribel Fernandez. 2018. *Towards a Privacy-Aware Quantified Self Data Management Framework.* © 2018. Reprinted with permission of the authors from the *Proceedings of the 23nd ACM on Symposium on Access Control Models and Technologies (SACMAT '18)*. Association for Computing Machinery, New York, NY, USA, 173–184.

Chapter 14: Data Science, COVID-19 Pandemic, Privacy, and Civil Liberties

B. Thuraisingham, *Data Science, COVID-19 Pandemic, Privacy and Civil Liberties* © 2020 IEEE. Reprinted, with permission, from *IEEE International Conference on Big Data (Big Data)*, 2020, pp. 2634–2638, doi: 10.1109/BigData50022.2020.9377966.

Chapter 15: Secure Cloud Query Processing Based on Access Control for Big Data Systems

M. Husain, J. McGlothlin, M. M. Masud, L. Khan and B. M. Thuraisingham, *Heuristics-Based Query Processing for Large RDF Graphs Using Cloud Computing.* © 2011 IEEE. Reprinted, with permission, from," in *IEEE Transactions on Knowledge and Data Engineering*, vol. 23, no. 9, pp. 1312–1327, Sept. 2011, doi: 10.1109/TKDE.2011.103

Thuraisingham, B. et al. (2012) *Cloud-Centric Assured Information Sharing.* Reprinted/adapted by permission from Springer Nature: Springer eBook, PAISI 2012. Lecture Notes in Computer Science, vol 7299. Chau, M., Wang, G.A., Yue, W.T., Chen, H. (eds) Intelligence and Security Informatics. © Springer-Verlag Berlin Heidelberg 2012.

A. Khaled, M. F. Husain, L. Khan, K. W. Hamlen and B. Thuraisingham, *A Token-Based Access Control System for RDF Data in the Clouds*, © 2010 IEEE. Reprinted, with permission, from Proceedings of *2010 IEEE Second International Conference on Cloud Computing Technology and Science*, 2010, pp. 104–111, doi: 10.1109/CloudCom.2010.76.

Chapter 16: Access Control-Based Assured Information Sharing in the Cloud

Thuraisingham, B. et al. (2012) *Cloud-Centric Assured Information Sharing.* Reprinted/adapted by permission from Springer Nature: Springer eBook, PAISI 2012. Lecture Notes in Computer Science, vol 7299. Chau, M., Wang, G.A., Yue, W.T., Chen, H. (eds) Intelligence and Security Informatics. © Springer-Verlag Berlin Heidelberg 2012.

Cadenhead, T., Kantarcioglu, M., Khadilkar, V., Thuraisingham, B. (2012) *Design and Implementation of a Cloud-Based Assured Information Sharing System.* In: Kotenko, I., Skormin, V. (eds) Computer Network Security. MMM-ACNS 2012. Lecture Notes in Computer

Science, vol 7531. Springer, Berlin, Heidelberg. https://doi-org.libproxy.utdallas.edu/10.1007/ 978-3-642-33704-8_4. Reprinted/adapted by permission from [Springer Nature]. Lecture Notes in Computer Science, vol 7531. by Cadenhead, T., Kantarcioglu, M., Khadilkar, V., Thuraisingham, B. © 2012

Chapter 17: Access Control for Social Network Data Management

Barbara Carminati, Elena Ferrari, Raymond Heatherly, Murat Kantarcioglu, and Bhavani Thuraisingham. 2009. *A Semantic Web Based Framework for Social Network Access Control.* © 2009. Republished with permission of from ACM (Association for Computing Machinery), from *Proceedings of the 14th ACM symposium on Access control models and technologies (SACMAT '09).* Association for Computing Machinery, New York, NY, USA, 177–186; permission conveyed through Copyright Clearance Center, Inc.

Barbara Carminati, Elena Ferrari, Raymond Heatherly, Murat Kantarcioglu, Bhavani Thuraisingham, *Semantic Web-based Social Network Access Control.* © 2011. Republished with permission of Elsevier Science & Technology Journals, from Computers & security, Volume 30, Issues 2–3, 2011, Pages 108–115, ISSN 0167–4048; permission conveyed through Copyright Clearance Center, Inc.

Chapter 19: Emerging Applications for Secure Data Science: Internet of Transportation Systems

B. Thuraisingham, *Cyber Security and Artificial Intelligence for Cloud-based Internet of Transportation Systems, 2020 7th IEEE International Conference on Cyber Security and Cloud Computing (CSCloud)/2020 6th IEEE International Conference on Edge Computing and Scalable Cloud (EdgeCom),* 2020, pp. 8–10. © 2020 IEEE. Reprinted with permission from *2020 7th IEEE International Conference on Cyber Security and Cloud Computing (CSCloud)/2020 6th IEEE International Conference on Edge Computing and Scalable Cloud (EdgeCom)*

Authors

Dr. Bhavani Thuraisingham is the Founders Chair Professor of Computer Science at The University of Texas, Dallas (UTD) and the Founding Executive director of UTD's Cyber Security Research and Education Institute (2004–2021). Her current research is on integrating cyber security, cloud computing and data science. Prior to joining UTD, she worked at the MITRE Corporation for 16 years including a three-year stint as a Program Director at the NSF. Prior to MITRE, she worked for the commercial industry for six years including at Honeywell. She has experience developing commercial products as well as transferring technology to operational systems. She is a Fellow of the ACM, IEEE, AAAS and NAI and the recipient of numerous awards from IEEE and ACM. More details of her work can be found at http://www.utdallas.edu/~bxt043000/

Dr. Murat Kantarcioglu is the Ashbel Smith Professor of Computer Science and Director of Data Security and Privacy at UTD. He received his Ph.D. in Computer Science from Purdue University. Dr. Kantarcioglu is Fellow of IEEE and AAAS, an ACM Distinguished Scientist and has received prestigious awards including the IEEE Technical Achievement Award for Intelligence and Security Informatics and the and the Homer R. Award from AMIA. Dr. Kantarcioglu is also the recipient of an NSF CAREER award He is an ACM Distinguished Scientist. His current research interests include Adversarial Machine Learning and Data Privacy. More details of his work can be found at http://www.utdallas.edu/~muratk/

Dr. Latifur Khan is a Professor of Computer Science and Director of Big Data Analytics at UTD. He is also a Co-Director of the Women in Data Science Center. He received his Ph.D. in Computer Science from the University of Southern California. Dr. Khan is an IEEE Fellow, an ACM Distinguished Scientist and has received prestigious awards including the IEEE Technical Achievement Award for Intelligence and Security Informatics and the IEEE Big Data Security and Privacy Senior Research Award. He is also a Fellow of the British-based IET and BCS. His research focuses on big data management and analytics and machine learning for cyber-security. More details of his work can be found at http://www.utdallas.edu/~lkhan/

1 Introduction

1.1 OVERVIEW

The collection, storage, manipulation, analysis, and retention of massive amounts of data have resulted in serious security and privacy considerations. Various regulations are being proposed to handle big data so that the privacy of the individuals is not violated. For example, even if personally identifiable information is removed from the data, when data is combined with other data, an individual can be identified. While collecting massive amounts of data causes security and privacy concerns, big data analytics applications in cyber security are exploding. For example, an organization can outsource activities such as identity management, intrusion detection, and malware analysis to the cloud. The question is, how can the developments in big data analytics and data science techniques be used to solve security problems? Furthermore, how can we ensure that such techniques are secure and can adapt to adversarial attacks? Before we answer these questions, we need to ask the question, "What is data science?" According to www.oracle.com, "Data science combines multiple fields including statistics, scientific methods, and data analysis to extract value from data." Since data science includes many fields, it has been used interchangeably with big data analytics and machine learning. Therefore, unless otherwise stated, we will use the terms data science, machine learning, and big data management and analytics interchangeably. They all deal with extracting useful nuggets from massive amounts of data using a variety of techniques including statistical reasoning, pattern recognition, and learning.

Data science techniques have been used extensively for cyber security applications over the past two decades. These applications include intrusion detection, insider threat detection, and malware analysis. While data science techniques have many applications in cyber security, they also result in privacy violations. This is because it is now possible to use various machine learning tools and analyze massive amounts of data rapidly and extract information that could be highly sensitive or private. Furthermore, the data science techniques could be subject to cyber-attacks. Therefore, we may not be able to trust the results produced by data science/machine learning. This book describes both aspects. That is, it first describes a variety of data science applications in cyber security. It will describe the application of data science including stream data analytics and novel class detection for cyber security applications such as insider threat detection. Next it will discuss both security and privacy-enhancing data science techniques. It will discuss the trends in areas such as adversarial machine learning that take into consideration the attacker's behavior in developing machine learning techniques. It will also discuss how privacy-enhanced techniques may be incorporated into data science. Furthermore, it provides an overview of access control for data science and big data management. That is, it describes various policy enforcement techniques for controlling access to massive amounts of data. It will also discuss some applications of secure data science to assured information sharing, cloud data management, and social media. The reader will get an understanding of the following: (i) Security and privacy issues for data science. (ii) How data science techniques can be applied to cyber security problems. (iii) Ways to modify machine learning techniques that take into consideration the behavior of the attackers. (iv) Privacy-enhanced techniques for big data analytics. (v) The applications of security techniques (e.g., access control) for data science applications such as securing social media and cloud-centric assured information sharing.

This chapter details the organization of this book. The organization of this chapter is as follows. Concepts such as big data analytics, data science, and machine learning are discussed in

DOI: 10.1201/9781003081845-1

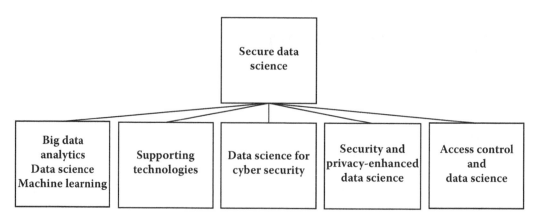

FIGURE 1.1 Concepts discussed in this chapter.

Section 1.2. Supporting technologies for secure data science will be discussed in Section 1.3. Data science techniques for cyber security problems will be discussed in Section 1.4. Security and privacy-enhanced data science such as the attacks to data science techniques as well as ensuring privacy for data science techniques are discussed in Section 1.5. Access control and data science will be discussed in Section 1.6. Organization of this book will be given in Section 1.7. We conclude this chapter with useful resources in Section 1.8. It should be noted that the contents of Sections 1.3 through 1.6 will be elaborated in Parts I through IV of this book. Figure 1.1 illustrates the contents covered in this chapter.

1.2   BIG DATA ANALYTICS, DATA SCIENCE, AND MACHINE LEARNING

We have heard the terms big data analysis, data science and machine learning used in several applications and in this book we have used them interchangeably. However, there are some key differences. While they all focus on analyzing data to extract the nuggets, big data analytics is about analyzing massive amounts of heterogeneous data. Data science also analyzes data using data mining and statistical reasoning techniques. Machine learning is also about data analysis but focuses on learning techniques including deep learning. In this section, we will explore these terms further.

The US Bureau of Labor and Statistics (BLS) defines *big data* as a collection of large datasets that cannot be analyzed with normal statistical methods. The datasets can represent numerical, textual, and multimedia data. Big data is popularly defined in terms of five Vs: Volume, Velocity, Variety, Veracity, and Value. Big Data Management and Analytics (BDMA) requires handling huge volumes of data, both structured and unstructured, arriving at high velocity. By harnessing big data, we can achieve breakthroughs in several key areas such as cyber security and healthcare, resulting in increased productivity and profitability. Big data spans several important fields: business, e-commerce, finance, government, healthcare, social networking, and telecommunications, as well as several scientific field such as atmospheric and biological sciences. BDMA is evolving into a field called data science that not only includes BDMA, but also machine learning, statistical methods, high-performance computing, and data management.

Data scientists aggregate, process, analyze, and visualize big data in order to derive useful insights. BLS projected both computer programmers and statisticians to have high employment growth during 2012–2022. It was reported by IBM that there were around 2.7 million data science jobs available in 2020 [IBM]. The demand for data science experts is on the rise as the roles and responsibilities of a data scientist are steadily taking shape. Currently, there is no debate on the fact that data science skillsets are not developing proportionately with high industry demands.

Therefore, it is imperative to bring data science research, development and education efforts into the mainstream of computer science. Data is being collected by every organization regardless of whether it is industry, academia, or government. Organizations want to analyze this data to give them a competitive edge. Therefore, the demand for data scientists including those with expertise in BDMA techniques is growing by several folds every year.

While BDMA is evolving into data science with significant progress over the past five years, Big Data Security and Privacy (BDSP) is becoming a critical need. With the recent emergence of the *Quantified Self* (QS) movement, personal data collected by wearable devices and smartphone apps is being analyzed to guide users in improving their health or personal life habits. This data is also being shared with other service providers (e.g., retailers) using cloud-based services, offering potential benefits to users (e.g., information about health products). But such data collection and sharing are often being carried out without the users' knowledge, bringing grave danger that the personal data may be used for improper purposes. Privacy violations could easily get out of control if data collectors could aggregate financial and health-related data with tweets, Facebook activity, and purchase patterns. In addition, access to the massive amounts of data collected has to be stored. Yet few tools and techniques exist for privacy protection in QS applications or controlling access to the data.

While securing big data and ensuring the privacy of individuals are crucial tasks, BDMA techniques can be used to solve security problems. For example, an organization can outsource activities such as identity management, email filtering, and intrusion detection to the cloud. This is because massive amounts of data are being collected for such applications and this data has to be analyzed. Cloud data management is just one example of big data management. The question is: how can the developments in BDMA be used to solve cyber security problems? These problems include malware detection, insider threat detection, intrusion detection, and spam filtering.

Machine learning focuses on learning from prior experience and making predictions. The learning techniques may include neural networks, decision trees, and support vector machines. Machine learning is considered to be a branch of Artificial Intelligence (AI). AI also includes planning systems, agents, and expert systems. Figure 1.2 illustrates the various concepts in big data analytics, data science, and machine learning. As stated earlier in this book, we have used the terms interchangeably.

1.3   SUPPORTING TECHNOLOGIES

We will discuss several supporting technologies for secure data science. These include (i) data security and privacy; (ii) data mining for security applications; (iii) cloud computing, semantic web, and social networks; and (iv) big data security and privacy. Figure 1.3 illustrates the supporting technologies discussed in this book.

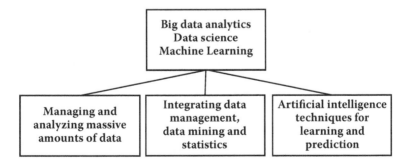

FIGURE 1.2   Big data analytics, data science, and machine learning.

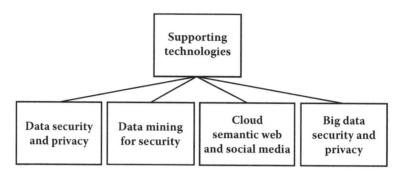

FIGURE 1.3 Supporting technologies.

With respect to data security and privacy, we will describe database security issues, security policy enforcement, access control, and authorization models for database systems, as well as data privacy issues. With respect to data mining, which we will also refer to as data analytics, we will introduce the concept and provide an overview of the various data mining techniques to lay the foundations for some of the techniques to be discussed in Parts II, III, and IV. With respect to data mining applications in security, we will provide an overview of how some of the data mining techniques discussed may be applied for cyber security applications. With respect to cloud computing, semantic web, and social networks, we will provide some of the key points including cloud data management and technologies such as RDF (Resource Description Framework) for representing and managing large amounts of data. We will also discuss aspects of analyzing and securing social networks. With respect to big data security and privacy, we will discuss the concepts and the challenges such as big data analytics for cyber security, attacks to big data analytics, privacy enhanced big data analytics, and access control for big data. These technologies will provide the foundations for the concepts to be discussed in Parts II, III and IV.

1.4 DATA SCIENCE FOR CYBER SECURITY

Malicious insiders, both people and processes, are considered to be the most dangerous threats to both cyber security and national security. For example, employees of a company may steal highly sensitive product designs and sell them to the competitors. This could be achieved manually or often via cyber espionage. The malicious processes in the system can also carry out such covert operations.

Data mining techniques have been applied for cyber security problems including insider threat detection. Techniques such as support vector machines and supervised learning methods have been applied. Unfortunately, the training process for supervised learning methods tends to be time-consuming and expensive and generally requires large amounts of well-balanced training data to be effective. Also, traditional training methods do not scale well for massive amounts of insider threat data. Therefore, we have applied data science techniques for cyber security applications such as malware analysis, novel class detection and insider threat detection.

We have designed and developed several data science techniques for detecting malicious insiders. In particular, we have adapted our stream data analytics techniques to handle massive amounts of data and detect malicious insiders in Part III of this book. We have also designed cloud-based implementations for scalable malware detection. The concepts addressed in Part III are illustrated in Figure 1.4.

1.5 SECURITY AND PRIVACY ENHANCED DATA SCIENCE

One of the challenges we are faced with when using data science and machine learning techniques is that these techniques could be attacked. The adversary usually learns about our models and the

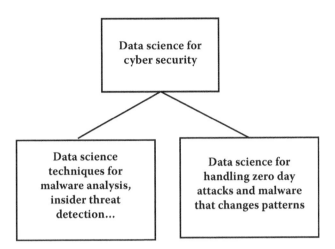

FIGURE 1.4 Data science for cyber security.

data we use and will try and poison the data and thwart the models. We have to be several steps ahead of the adversary and adapt our models. This area has come to be known as *adversarial machine learning* (or *adversarial data mining*). Another problem with data science is that it is now possible to link different pieces of data together and infer highly private or sensitive information. In some other cases it is important to publicize the results of machine learning (e.g., preventing the spread of disease) but keep the personal data private (a particular individual having the disease).

Part III will address techniques to handle attacks to data science as well as privacy-enhanced data science. We discuss techniques such as adversarial support vector machine learning to handle cyber-attacks to the machine learning techniques. With respect to privacy, we give an example of privacy aware decisions trees. We will also discuss a privacy aware policy-based data management framework for quantified self-applications. Finally we will discuss a concrete application for privacy and that is the COVID-19 pandemic. The chapters in Part III will give the reader some understanding of how to deal with cyber-attacks to machine learning techniques as well as ensure privacy while carrying out machine learning. Figure 1.5 illustrates security and privacy enhanced data science.

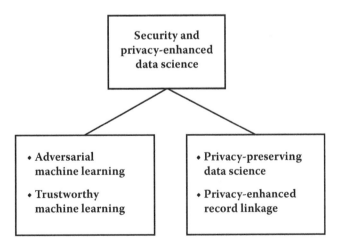

FIGURE 1.5 Security and privacy-enhanced data science.

1.6 ACCESS CONTROL AND DATA SCIENCE

The data science systems, such as the big data management systems, have to be secure. That is, the access to the data must be controlled according to the policies. The policies we will examine are rooted in access control policies. These policies not only control access to the data but may also be used to control data sharing as well as controlling unauthorized inferences.

Part IV will discuss the various cloud-based systems we have developed to control access to the big data systems. We first discuss secure cloud query processing systems based on access control that we have developed utilizing the Hadoop/MapReduce framework. Our system processes massive amounts of semantic web data. In particular, we have designed and developed a query optimizer for the SPARQL query processor that functions in the cloud. We have also developed an assured information sharing system that operates in the cloud. Here, different organizations share data according to the policies. In addition, we discuss a semantic web-based access control framework for social media data. We consider social media systems to be an application of big data technologies. Finally, we discuss inference control for big data systems. While access control policies control access to the data directly, the inference control policies control access to the data indirectly through inference. Finally, we will discuss how some of our technologies may be applied to an emerging application and that is the Internet of Transportation (an aspect of the Internet of Things) systems. Figure 1.6 illustrates some of the experimental cloud systems that we have developed.

1.7 ORGANIZATION OF THIS BOOK

This book is divided into four parts, each describing some aspect of the technology that is relevant to data science and cyber security. Part I, consisting of four chapters, will describe supporting technologies for secure data science. In Chapter 2, data security and privacy issues are discussed. In Chapter 3, an overview of various data mining techniques for cyber security applications is provided. Cloud computing and semantic web technologies are discussed in Chapter 4. Finally, some of the emerging technologies such as big data security and privacy are discussed in Chapter 5. These supporting technologies provide the background information for secure data science.

Part II, consisting of four chapters, provides a detailed overview of the data science techniques we have developed for cyber security. Chapter 6 focuses on the data science techniques for malware analysis. Stream data analytics for novel class detection is discussed in Chapter 7. Chapter 8 discusses the use of cloud for scalable data science techniques for malware analysis. Finally, we discuss stream data analytics for insider threat detection in Chapter 9.

Part III, consisting of five chapters, will discuss security and privacy-enhanced data science. Chapter 10 discusses attacks to data science systems and describes our approach to adversarial machine learning in general and support vector machine learning in particular. Chapter 11 describes adversarial relevance vector machine learning. Privacy-enhanced data science with decision trees as an example is discussed in Chapter 12. Finally, our work on a privacy-aware policy-based data management framework for the quantified self-applications is discussed in Chapter 13. Finally, in Chapter 14, we discuss how our work can be applied to a specific application and that is the COVID-19 pandemic.

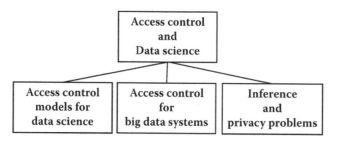

FIGURE 1.6 Access control and data science.

Part IV discusses access control and data science and consists of five chapters. Chapter 15 describes a secure cloud query processing system based on access control for big data. Chapter 16 describes policy-based information sharing system we have developed that operates in a cloud. Our information sharing policies are rooted in access control policies. An access control framework based on semantic web for social media data, which we consider to be a form of big data, is discussed in Chapter 17. We describe the inference controller we have developed based on access control for semantic web-based big data in Chapter 18. Finally, we discuss how some of our work could be applied to an application such as the Internet of Transportation system in Chapter 19.

Each part begins with an introduction and ends with a conclusion. Furthermore, Chapters 2 through 17 each start with an overview and ends with a summary and references. Chapter 20 summarizes this book and discusses future directions. This book's Appendix provides an overview of data management and discusses the relationship between the texts we have written. This has been the standard practice with all of our books.

We have essentially developed a four-layer framework to explain the concepts in this book. This framework is illustrated in Figure 1.7. Layer 1 is the Supporting Technologies layer and covers the

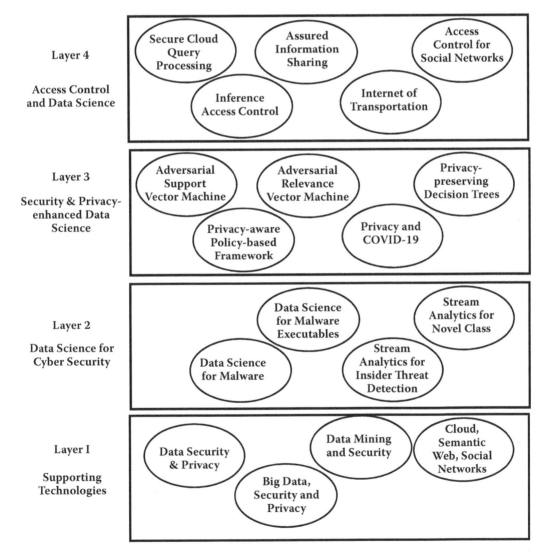

FIGURE 1.7 Layered framework.

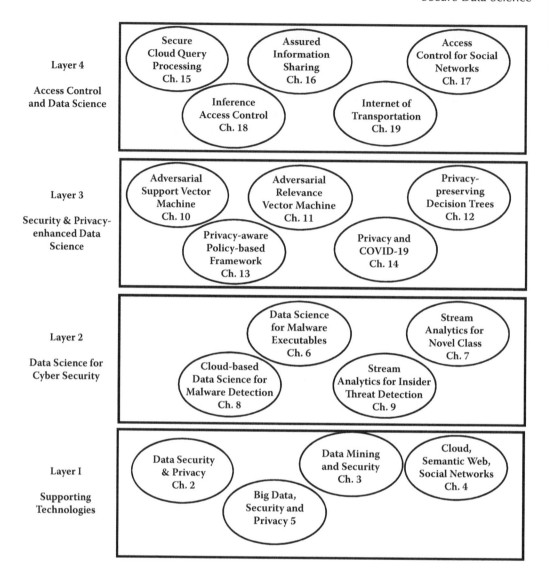

FIGURE 1.8 Contents of this book with respect to the framework.

chapters in Part I of this book. Layer 2 is the Data Science for Cyber Security layer and covers the chapters in Parts II. Layer 3 is the Security and Privacy-enhanced Data Science Layer and covers the chapters in Part III. Layer 4 is the Access Control and Data Science layer and covers the chapters in Part IV. The relationship between the various parts of this book is given in Figure 1.8.

1.8 NEXT STEPS

This chapter has provided an introduction to this book. We first provided a brief overview of secure data science and then discussed concepts such as big data analytics, data science, and machine learning. Next, we discussed data science for cyber security. This was followed by a discussion of security and privacy enhanced data science. Then a discussion of access control and data science was given. One of the main contributions of this book is describing how data science and cyber security can support each other to develop secure and private systems. We have also given numerous references throughout this book.

Several new data science, cloud computing and big data conferences have emerged in recent years. These include IEEE Computer Society's Cloud Computing Conference held in conjunction with the Services Computing Conference as well as CloudCom. In addition, the IEEE Computer Society has launched a conference on Big Data. Also, traditional database management, data mining, and machine learning conferences have focused on big data analytics, while the cyber security conferences now have a major focus on integrating cyber security and data science/machine learning. There is also a conference devoted to data science (e.g., IEEE/ACM joint conference).

We strongly believe that the future of computing is with cloud computing and the future of data is with data science. Cloud computing and data science will have applications in numerous fields in order to provide scalable data analytics solutions. Integrated with machine learning, they will provide not only scalable data analytics solutions but also technologies that can learn from experiences and make predictions. The challenge is to put various services and components together and build scalable and secure data science and machine learning systems. In addition, systems that manage massive amounts of data securely while ensuring the privacy of individuals will become one of the major challenges we will be faced with for the next several decades.

REFERENCE

[IBM] IBM, https://www.forbes.com/sites/louiscolumbus/2017/05/13/ibm-predicts-demand-for-data-scientists-will-soar-28-by-2020/?sh=7c4fe5d67e3b.

Part I

Supporting Technologies for Secure Data Science

Introduction to Part I

Part I, consisting of four chapters, will describe supporting technologies for secure data science. In particular, (i) data security and privacy; (ii) data mining for cyber security applications; (iii) cloud, semantic web, and social media; and (iv) big data security and privacy issues will be discussed.

Chapter 2 will describe security technologies. In particular, we will discuss various aspects of data security and privacy, including access control models and data privacy issues. In Chapter 3, we will provide some background information about data mining techniques also discuss ways of applying data mining for cyber security such as intrusion detection and insider threat detection. In Chapter 4, we will provide an overview of cloud computing, semantic web, and social network technologies. This is because the experimental systems we have discussed in Part IV utilize various aspects of cloud, semantic web and social network technologies. In addition, these techniques are some of the foundational technologies for big data management and analytics. In Chapter 5, we will discuss big data security and privacy issues including the developments and challenges in big data for cyber security and attacks to big data. The chapters in Part I lay the foundations for the discussions in Parts II, III, and IV.

DOI: 10.1201/9781003081845-3

2 Data Security and Privacy

2.1 INTRODUCTION

As we have stated in Chapter 1, secure data science technologies integrate big data/data science technologies with security technologies. In this chapter, we will discuss security technologies. In particular, we will discuss various aspects of data security and privacy aspects of cyber security. An aspect of data science technologies such as data mining technologies as well as cloud and semantic web technologies will be discussed in Chapters 3 and 4. Big data security and privacy issues will be discussed in Chapter 5.

Since much of the discussion in this book is on big data analytics/data science and security, we will provide a fairly comprehensive overview of security for data management systems. In particular, we will discuss security policies as well as enforcing the policies in database systems. Our focus will be on discretionary security policies. We will also discuss data privacy aspects. More details on secure data management can be found in [FERR2000] and [THUR2005a].

The most popular discretionary security policy is the access control policy. Access control policies were studied for operating systems back in the 1960s and then for database systems in the 1970s. The two prominent database systems, System R and INGRES, were the first to investigate access control for database systems (see [GRIF1976] and [STON1974]). Since then, several variations of access control policies have been reported including role-based access control and attribute-based access control [NIST]. Other discretionary policies include administration policies. We also discuss identification and authentication under discretionary policies. Note that much of the discussion in this chapter will focus on discretionary security in relational database systems. Many of the principles are applicable to other systems such as object database systems, distributed/federated database systems, and cloud data management systems (see, e.g., [THUR1994]).

Before one designs a secure system, the first question that must be answered is what is the security policy to be enforced by the system? Security policy is essentially a set of rules that enforce security. Security policies include mandatory security policies and discretionary security policies. Mandatory security policies are the policies that are "mandatory" in nature and enforced by the systems. Discretionary security policies are policies that are specified by the administrator or the owner of the data. Mandatory security policies are part of non-discretionary security policies. Role-based access control policies are also considered to be non-discretionary security policies [SAND1996].

By policy enforcement, we mean the mechanisms to enforce the policies. For example, back in the 1970s, the relational database system products such as System R and INGRES developed techniques such as the query modification mechanisms for policy enforcement (see, e.g., [GRIF1976] and [STON1974]). The query language SQL (Structured Query Language) has been extended to specify security policies and access control rules. More recently languages such as XML (eXtensible Markup Language) and RDF (Resource Description Framework) have been extended to specify security policies (see, e.g., [BERT2002] and [CARM2004]). We also discuss privacy concerns in data management and privacy-enhanced data management techniques. We also include a discussion of privacy-enhanced data mining.

The organization of this chapter is as follows. In Section 2.2, we introduce discretionary security including access control and authorization models for database systems. We also discuss role-based access control systems. In Section 2.3, we discuss ways of enforcing discretionary security including a discussion of query modification. We also provide an overview of the various commercial products. Data privacy considerations will be discussed in Section 2.4. Section 2.5

DOI: 10.1201/9781003081845-4

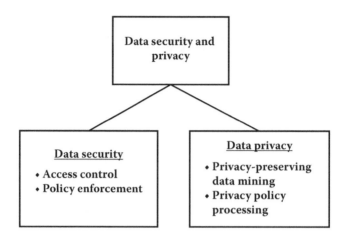

FIGURE 2.1   Data security and privacy.

summarizes this chapter. Figure 2.1 illustrates the concepts discussed in this chapter. We assume that the reader has some knowledge of data management. For more details on this topic, we refer the reader to some texts such as [DATE1990] and [THUR1997].

2.2   SECURITY POLICIES

The organization of this section is as follows. In Section 2.2.1, we will provide an overview of access control policies. Administration policies will be discussed in Section 2.2.2. Issues in identification and authentication will be discussed in Section 2.2.3. Auditing a database management system will be discussed in Section 2.2.4. Views as security objects will be discussed in Section 2.2.5. Figure 2.2 illustrates various components of discretionary security policies discussed in this section.

2.2.1   ACCESS CONTROL POLICIES

Access control policies were first examined for operating systems. The essential point here is that can a process be granted access to a file? Access could be read access or write access. Write access could include access to modify, append, or delete. These principles were transferred to database systems such as INGRES and System R. Since then, various forms of access control policies have been studied. Notable among those are the role-based access control policies which are now implemented in several commercial systems. Note that access control policies also include mandatory policies. Figure 2.3 illustrates the various types of access control policies.

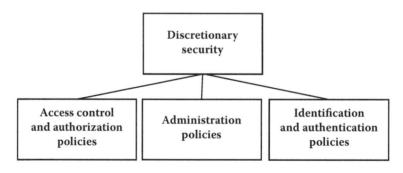

FIGURE 2.2   Discretionary security policies.

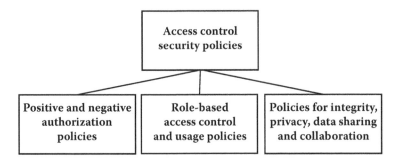

FIGURE 2.3 Access control security policies.

2.2.1.1 Authorization-based Access Control Policies

Many of the access control policies are based on authorization policies. Essentially what this means is that users are granted access to data based on authorization rules. In this section, we will discuss various types of authorization rules. Note that in the book chapter by Ferrari and Thuraisingham [FERR2000], a detailed discussion of authorization policies is provided.

2.2.1.1.1 Positive authorization

Early systems focused on what is now called positive authorization rules. Here, user John is granted access to relation EMP or user Jane is granted access to relation DEPT. These are access control rules on relations. One can also grant access to other entities such as attributes and tuples. For example, John has read access to attribute *salary* and *write* access to attribute *name* in relation EMP. Write access could include append, modify, or delete access.

2.2.1.1.2 Negative authorization

The question is if John's access to an object is not specified, does this mean John does not have access to that object? In some systems, any authorization rule that is not specified is implicitly taken to be a negative authorization while in other systems negative authorizations are explicitly specified. For example, we could enforce rules such as John does not have access to relation EMP or Jane does not have access to relation DEPT.

2.2.1.1.3 Conflict resolution

When we have rules that are conflicting then how do we resolve the conflicts? For example, we could have a rule that grants John read access to relation EMP. However, we can also have a rule that does not grant John read access to the salary attribute in EMP. This is a conflict. Usually a system enforces the least privilege rule in which case John has access to EMP except for the salary values.

2.2.1.1.4 Strong and weak authorization

Systems also enforce strong and weak authorizations. In the case of strong authorization, the rule holds regardless of conflicts. In the case of weak authorization, the rule does not hold in case of conflict. For example, if John is granted access to EMP and it is a strong authorization rule and the rule where John is not granted access to salary attribute is a weak authorization, there is a conflict. This means the strong authorization will hold.

2.2.1.1.5 Propagation of authorization rules

The question here is how do the rules get propagated? For example, if John has read access to relation EMP, then does it automatically mean that John has read access to every element in EMP? Usually this is the case unless we have a rule that prohibits automatic propagation of an authorization rule. If we have a rule prohibiting the automatic propagation of an authorization rule, then we must explicitly enforce authorization rules that specify the objects that John has access to.

2.2.1.1.6   Special rules

In our work on mandatory policies, we have explored extensively the enforcement of content and context-based constraints. Note that security constraints are essentially the security rules. Content and context-based rules are the rules where access is granted depending on the content of the data or the context in which the data is displayed. Such rules can be enforced for discretionary security also. For example, in the case of content-based constraints, John has read access to tuples only in DEPT D100. In the case of context or association-based constraints, John does not have read access to names and salaries taken together; however, he can have access to individual names and salaries. In the case of event-based constraints, after the election, John has access to all elements in relation EMP.

2.2.1.1.7   Consistency and completeness of rules

One of the challenges here is ensuring the consistency and completeness of constraints. That is, if the constraints or rules are inconsistent, then do we have conflict resolution rules that will resolve the conflicts? How can we ensure that all of the entities (such as attributes, relations, elements, etc.) are specified in access control rules for a user? Essentially what this means is, are the rules complete? If not, what assumptions do we make about entities that do not have either positive or negative authorizations specified on them for a particular user or a class of users?

We have discussed some essential points with respect to authorization rules. Some examples are given in Figure 2.4. Next, we will discuss some popular access control models and they are role-based access control, which is now implemented in commercial systems and attribute-based access control implemented in web-based systems.

2.2.1.2   Role-based Access Control

Role-based access control has become one of more popular access control methods (see [SAND1996]). This method has been implemented in commercial systems including Trusted Oracle. The idea here is to grant access to users depending on their roles and functions.

The essential idea behind role-based access control also known as RBAC is as follows. Users need access to data depending on their roles. For example, a president may have access to information about his/her vice presidents and the members of the board while the chief financial officer may have access to the financial information and information on those who report to him. A director may have access to information about those working in his division while the human resources director will have information on personal data about the employees of the corporation.

Authorization rules:

- John has read access to employee relation
- John does not have write access to department relation
- Jane has read access to name values in employee relation
- Jane does not have read access to department relation

FIGURE 2.4   Authorization rules.

Essentially, role-based access control is a type of authorization policy, which depends on the user role and the activities that go with the role.

Various research efforts on role hierarchies have been discussed in the literature. There is also a conference series called SACMAT (Symposium on Access Control Models and Technologies) that evolved from role-based access control research efforts. For example, how does access get propagated? Can one role subsume another? Consider the role hierarchy illustrated in Figure 2.5. This means if we grant access to a node in the hierarchy, does the access propagate upwards? That is, if a department manager has access to certain project information, does that access get propagated to the parent node, which is a director node? If a section leader has access to employee information in his/her section does the access propagate to the department manager who is the parent in the role hierarchy? What happens to the child nodes? That is, does access propagate downward? For example, if a department manager has access to certain information, then do his subordinates have access to that information? Are there cases where the subordinates have access to data that the department manager does not have? What happens if an employee has to report to two supervisors, one his department manager and the other his project manager? What happens when the department manager is working on a project and has to report to his project leader who also works for him?

Role-based access control has been examined for relational systems, object systems, distributed systems, and now some of the emerging technologies such as data warehouses, knowledge management systems, semantic web, e-commerce systems, and digital libraries. Furthermore, object models have been used to represent roles and activities (see, e.g., proceedings of the IFIP

FIGURE 2.5   Role hierarchy.

Database Security Conference series and more recently the Proceedings of the ACM Conference series on Data and Applications Security and Privacy).

2.2.1.3   Usage Control

More recently Sandhu et al. has developed yet another access control-like model and that is the Usage Control Model, which he refers to as UCON (see, e.g., the work reported in [PARK2004]). The UCON model attempts to incorporate some additional features into role-based access control including attribute mutability and obligations.

2.2.1.4   Attribute-based Access Control

Due to the fact that roles are not uniform across organizations, it was felt that role-based access control was not sufficient for web-based systems. Around the same time, web services and service-oriented architectures and cloud-based systems gained popularity and are now widely used. Therefore, an access control model based on claims was developed for such an environment. This model is attribute-based access control. Here, a user makes certain claims about him or her. These claims are then verified by the organization that wants to give the user access to the resources. If the user's claims are valid, then the policies are checked as to whether such a user has access to the resources. Attribute-based access control has become extremely popular in the last decade [NIST].

2.2.2   ADMINISTRATION POLICIES

While access control policies specify access that specific users have to the data, administration policies specify who is to administer the data. Administration duties would include keeping the data current, making sure the metadata is updated whenever the data is updated, and ensuring recovery from failures and related activities.

Typically, the database administrator (DBA) is responsible for updating, say, the metadata, the index and access methods, and also ensuring that the access control rules are properly enforced. The System Security Officer (SSO) may also have a role. That is, the DBA and SSO may share the duties between them. The security-related issues might be the responsibility of the SSO while the data-related issues might be the responsibility of the DBA. Some other administration policies being considered include assigning caretakers. Usually owners have control of the data that they create and may manage the data for its duration. In some cases, owners may not be available to manage the data, in which case they may assign caretakers (i.e., custodians).

Administration policies get more complicated in distributed environments, especially in a web environment. For example, in web environments, there may be multiple parties involved in distributing documents including the owner, the publisher, and the users requesting the data. Who owns the data? Is it the owner or the publisher? Once the data has left the owner and arrived at the publisher, does the publisher take control of the data? There are many interesting questions that need to be answered as we migrate from a relational database environment to a distributed and perhaps a web environment. These also include managing copyright issues, data quality, data provenance, and governance. Many interesting papers have appeared in recent conferences on administration policies. Figure 2.6 illustrates various administration policies.

2.2.3   IDENTIFICATION AND AUTHENTICATION

For the sake of completion, we discuss identification and authentication as part of our discussion on discretionary security. By identification we mean users must identify themselves with their user ID and password. Authentication means the system must then match the user ID with the password to ensure that this is indeed the person he or she is purporting to be. A user may also have multiple identities depending on his/her roles. Identity management has received a lot of attention especially with the advent of web services (see [BERT2006]).

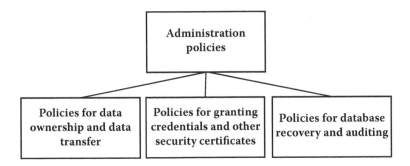

FIGURE 2.6 Administration policies.

Numerous problems have been reported with the password-based scheme. One is that hackers can break into the system and get the passwords of users and then masquerade as the user. In a centralized system, the problems are not as complicated as in a distributed environment. Now, with the World Wide Web and e-commerce applications, financial organizations are losing billions of dollars when hackers masquerade as legitimate users.

More recently biometrics techniques are being applied for identification and authentication. These include face recognition, fingerprint recognition, and voice recognition techniques to authenticate the user. These techniques are showing a lot of promise and are already being used. We can expect widespread use of biometric techniques as face recognition technologies advance.

2.2.4 AUDITING A DATABASE SYSTEM

Databases are audited for multiple purposes. For example, they may be audited to keep track of the number of queries posed, the number of updates made, the number of transactions executed, and the number of times the secondary storage is accessed so that the system can be designed more efficiently. Databases can also be audited for security purposes. For example, have any of the access control rules been bypassed by releasing information to the users? Has the inference problem occurred? Has privacy been violated? Have there been unauthorized intrusions?

Audits create a trail and the audit data may be stored in a database. This database may be mined to detect any abnormal patterns or behaviors. There has been a lot of work in using data mining for auditing and intrusion detection. Audit trail analysis is especially important these days with e-commerce transactions on the web. An organization should have the capability to conduct an analysis and determine problems like credit card fraud and identity theft.

2.2.5 VIEWS FOR SECURITY

Views as a mechanism for security have been studied a great deal both for discretionary security and mandatory security. For example, one may not want to grant access to an entire relation especially if it has, say, 25 attributes such as healthcare records, salary, travel information, personal data, etc. Therefore, the DBA could define views and grant users access to the views. Similarly, in the case of mandatory security, views could be assigned security levels.

Views have problems associated with them including the view update problem (see [DATE1990]). That is, if the view is updated, then we need to ensure that the base relations are updated. Therefore, if a view is updated by John and John does not have access to the base relation, then can the base relation still be updated? That is, do we create different views for different users

EMP			
SS#	Ename	Salary	D#
1	John	20K	10
2	Paul	30K	20
3	Mary	40K	20
4	Jane	20K	20
5	Bill	20K	10
6	Larry	20K	10
1	Michelle	30K	20

Rules:
John has Read access to V1
John has Write access to V2

V1. VIEW EMP (D#=20)		
SS#	Ename	Salary
2	Paul	30K
3	Mary	40K
4	Jane	20K
1	Michelle	30K

V2. VIEW EMP (D#=10)		
SS#	Ename	Salary
1	John	20K
5	Bill	20K
6	Larry	20K

FIGURE 2.7 Views for security.

and then the DBA merges the updates on views as updates on base relations? Figure 2.7 illustrates views for security.

2.3 POLICY ENFORCEMENT AND RELATED ISSUES

The organization of this section is as follows. SQL extensions for security are discussed in Section 2.3.1. In Section 2.3.2, we discuss query modification. Impact of discretionary security on other database functions will be discussed in Section 2.3.3. Note that we will focus on relational database systems. Figure 2.8 illustrates the various aspects involved in enforcing security policies. These include specification, implementation and visualization (where visualization tools are being used for the visualization of the policies).

Policy enforcement Mechanisms:

Query modification algorithm

Rule processing to enforce the access control rules

Theorem proving techniques to determine if policies are violated

Consistency and completeness checking of policies

FIGURE 2.8 Policy enforcement.

2.3.1 SQL EXTENSIONS FOR SECURITY

This section discusses policy specification. While much of the focus will be on SQL extensions for security policy specification, we will also briefly discuss some of the emerging languages. Note that SQL was developed for data definition and data manipulation for relational systems. Various versions of SQL have been developed including SQL for objects, SQL for multimedia and SQL for the web. That is, SQL has influenced data manipulation and data definition a great deal over the past 30 years (see [SQL3]).

As we have stated, SQL is a data definition and data manipulation language. Security policies could be specified during data definition. SQL has GRANT and REVOKE constructs for specifying grant and revoke access to users. That is, if a user, John, has read access to relation EMP, then one could use SQL and specify something like "GRANT JOHN EMP READ" and if the access is to be revoked, then we need something like "REVOKE JOHN EMP READ." SQL has also been extended with more complex constraints such as granting John read access to a tuple in a relation and granting Jane write access to an element in a relation.

In [THUR1989], we specified SQL extensions for security assertions. These assertions were for multi-level security. We could use similar reasoning for specifying discretionary security policies. For example, consider the situation where John does not have read access to names and salaries in EMP taken together, but he can read names and salaries separately. One could specify this in SQL-like language as follows:

GRANT JOHN READ
EMP.SALARY
GRANT JOHN READ
EMP.NAME
NOT GRANT JOHN READ
Together (EMP.NAME, EMP.SALARY).

If we are to grant John read access to the employees who earn less than 30K, then this assertion is specified as follows:

GRANT JOHN READ
EMP
Where EMP.SALARY < 30K

Note that the assertions we have specified have been incorporated into any standards. These are some of our ideas. We need to explore ways of incorporating these assertions into the standards. SQL extensions have also been proposed for role-based access control. In fact, products such as Oracle's Trusted database product enforce role-based access control. The access control rules are specified in an SQL-like language.

Note that there are many other specification languages that have been developed. These include XML, RDF, and related languages for the web and the semantic web. Semantic web is essentially an intelligent web. SQL-like languages have been specified for XML and RDF. For example, XML-QL was developed for XML, which then evolved into a language called XQuery. SPARQL is now the query language for RDF (see [THUR2007]). We will use such languages in our systems to be discussed in Part IV. Figure 2.9 illustrates specification aspects for security policies.

2.3.2 QUERY MODIFICATION

Query modification (now known as query re-writing) was first proposed in the INGRES project at the University of California at Berkeley (see [STON1974]). The idea is to modify the query based on the constraints. We have successfully designed and implemented query modification for

Policy Specification:

SQL extensions to specify security policies

Rule-based languages to specify policies

Logic programming languages such as
Prolog to specify policies

FIGURE 2.9   Policy specification.

mandatory security (see [DWYE1987], [THUR1987], [THUR1993]). However, much of the discussion in this section will be on query modification based on discretionary security constraints. We illustrate the essential points with some examples.

Consider a query by John to retrieve all tuples from EMP. Suppose that John only has read access to all the tuples where the salary is less than 30K and the employee is not in the security department. Then the query

Select * from EMP
Will be modified to
Select * from EMP
Where salary < 30K
And Dept is not Security

Where we assume that the attributes of EMP are, say, *name, salary, age,* and *department.*

Essentially what happens is that the "where" clause of the query has all the constraints associated with the relation. We can also have constraints that span across multiple relations. For example, we could have two relations EMP and DEPT joined by Dept #. Then the query is modified as follows:

Select * from EMP
Where EMP.Salary < 30K
And EMP.D# = DEPT.D#
And DEPT.Name is not Security

We have used some simple examples for query modification. The detailed algorithms can be found in [DWYE1987] and [STON1974]. The high level algorithm is illustrated in Figure 2.10.

2.3.3   DISCRETIONARY SECURITY AND DATABASE FUNCTIONS

In Section 2.3.2, we discussed query modification which is essentially processing security constraints during the query operation. Query optimization will also be impacted by security constraints. That is, once the query is modified, then the query tree has to be built. The idea is to push selections and projections down in the query tree and carry out the join operation later.

Other functions are also impacted by security constraints. Let us consider transaction management. Bertino et al. have developed algorithms for integrity constraint processing for transactions management (see [BERT1989]). We have examined their techniques for mandatory security constraint processing during transaction management. The techniques may be adapted for

```
┌────────────────────────────────────────────────────────────┐
│                                                              │
│   Query Modification Algorithm:                              │
│                                                              │
│   Input: Query, security constraints                         │
│   Output: Modified Query                                     │
│                                                              │
│   For constraints that  are relevant to the                 │
│   query, modify the where clause of                          │
│   the query via a negation                                   │
│                                                              │
│   For example: If salary should not be released to           │
│   Jane and if Jane requests information from employee,       │
│   then modify the query to retrieve information from         │
│   employee where attribute is not salary                     │
│                                                              │
│                                                              │
│                                                              │
│   Repeat the process until all relevant constraints          │
│   are processed                                              │
│                                                              │
│   The end result is the modified query                       │
│                                                              │
└────────────────────────────────────────────────────────────┘
```

FIGURE 2.10   Query modification algorithm.

discretionary security constraints. The idea is to ensure that the constraints are not violated during transaction execution.

Constraints may be enforced on the metadata. For example, one could grant and revoke access to users to the metadata relations. Discretionary security constraints for metadata could be handled in the same way they are handled for data. Other database functions include storage management. The issues in storage management include developing appropriate access methods and index strategies. One needs to examine the impact of the security constraints on the storage management functions. That is, can one partition the relations based on the constraints and store them in such a way so that the relations can be accessed efficiently? We need to develop secure indexing technologies for database systems. Some work on secure indexing for geospatial information systems is reported in [ATLU2004]. Databases are audited to determine whether any security violation has occurred. Furthermore, views have been used to grant access to individuals for security purposes. We need efficient techniques for auditing as well as for view management.

In this section, we have examined the impact of security on some of the database functions including query management, transaction processing, metadata management, and storage management. We need to also investigate the impact of security on other functions such as integrity constraint processing and fault tolerant computing. Figure 2.11 illustrates the impact of security on the database functions. It should be noted that some of the discussions in this section have been extended for big data management. Details are provided in [THUR2017].

2.4   DATA PRIVACY

Data privacy is about protecting sensitive information of individuals. While different definitions of privacy have been proposed, the most common definition is that a person decides what information is to be released about him or her. While data privacy has been studied for decades, especially with statistical databases, with the advent of the World Wide Web and the

Secure database functions:

Query processing: Enforce access control rules during
query processing; inference control; consider security
constraints for query optimization

Transaction management: Check whether security
constraints are satisfied during transaction execution

Storage management: Develop special access methods and
index strategies that take into consideration the security
constraints

Metadata management: Enforce access control on metadata;
Ensure that data is not released to unauthorized individuals
by releasing the metadata

Integrity management: Ensure that integrity of the data is
maintained while enforcing security

FIGURE 2.11   Security impact on database functions.

efforts on applying data mining for counter-terrorism applications, there has been an increasing
interest in this topic over the past 15 years. Much research has been reported on balancing the
need between privacy and security. The first effort on privacy-preserving data mining was
reported in [AGRA2000]. Several other efforts on this topic followed since the early 2000s
[KANT2004]. In addition, treating the privacy problem as a variation of the inference problem
was studied in [THUR2005b].

With the developments in big data technologies, there is significant interest in data privacy. For
example, a National Science Foundation workshop on Big Data Security and Privacy was held in
September 2014 and the results have been reported in [NSF2014]. With advancements in technology such as data analytics and the interest in data privacy among the policy makers, lawyers,
social scientists, and computer scientists, we can expect significant developments in protecting the
privacy of individuals as well as ensuring their security.

2.5   SUMMARY AND DIRECTIONS

In this chapter, we have provided an overview of discretionary security policies in database systems. We started with a discussion of access control policies including authorization policies and
role-based access control. Then we discussed administration policies. We briefly discussed identification and authentication. We also discussed auditing issues as well as views for security. Next,
we discussed policy enforcement. We also discussed SQL extensions for specifying policies as
well as provided an overview of query modification.

There is still a lot of work to be done. For example, much work is still needed on role-based
access control and attribute-based access control for emerging technologies such as the cloud and
IoT (Internet of Things). We need administration policies to manage multi-party transactions in a
web environment. We also need biometric technologies for authenticating users. Digital identity is
becoming an important research area especially with cloud systems.

Security policy enforcement is a topic that will continue to evolve as new technologies emerge.
We have advanced from relational to object to multimedia to web-based to cloud-based data

management systems. Each system has some unique features that are incorporated into the security policies. Enforcing policies for the various systems will continue to be a major focus. We also need to carry out research on the consistency and completeness of policies. Policy visualization may help toward achieving this. Policy management in the cloud and big data is an active area of research. Our work includes access control as well as policy-based information sharing in the cloud. The experimental systems we have developed on security policy enforcement in the cloud are discussed in Part IV.

REFERENCES

[AGRA2000] R. Agrawal, Ramakrishna Srikant: Privacy-preserving Data Mining, *SIGMOD Conference*, ACM SIGMOD Record, 292000, 439–450.

[ATLU2004] V. Atluri, S. Chun, An Authorization Model for Geospatial Data, *IEEE Transactions on Dependable Secure Computing*, Volume 1, #4, 2004, 238–254.

[BERT1989] E. Bertino, D. Musto, Integrity Constraint Processing during Transaction Processing, Acta Informatica, Volume 26, #1-2, 1988, 25–57.

[BERT2002] E.Bertino, B.Carminati, E. Ferrari, Access Control for XML Documents, Data and Knowledge Engineering, Volume 43, #3, 2002.

[BERT2006] E. Bertino, Digital Identity Management and Protection. *Proceedings of the 2006 International Conference on Privacy, Security and Trust*, Ontario, Canada, 2006.

[CARM2004] B. Carminati, E. Ferrari, B. Thuraisingham, Using RDF for Policy Specification and Enforcement B, *Proceedings of the DEXA Conference Workshop on Web Semantics*, Zaragoza, Spain, August 2004.

[DATE1990] C. Date, An Introduction to Database Systems, Addison-Wesley, 1990.

[DWYE1987] P. Dwyer, G. Jelatis, B. Thuraisingham, Multilevel Security for Relational Database Systems, Computers and Security, Volume 6, #3, 1987, 245–251.

[FERR2000] E. Ferrari, B. Thuraisingham, Secure Database Systems, *Advances in Database Management*, Artech House (Editors: M. Piatini, O. Diaz), 2000.

[GRIF1976] P. Griffiths, B. Wade, An Authorization Mechanism for a Relational Database System, ACM Transactions on Database Systems, Volume 1, #3, 1976, 242–255.

[KANT2004] M. Kantarcioglu, Chris Clifton: Privacy-preserving Distributed Mining of Association Rules on Horizontally Partitioned Data. IEEE Transactions on Knowledge and Data Engineering, Volume 16, #9, 2004, 1026–1037.

[NIST] Guide to Attribute Based Access Control (ABAC) Definition and Considerations, NIST Special Publication 800-162, 2014. https://csrc.nist.gov/publications/detail/sp/800-162/final

[NSF2014] National Science Foundation Workshop, http://csi.utdallas.edu/events/NSF/NSF-workhop-Big-Data-SP-Feb9-2015_FINAL.pdf

[PARK2004] J. Park, R. Sandhu, The UCON Usage Control Model, ACM Transactions on Information and Systems Security, Volume 7, #1, 2004, 128–174.

[SAND1996] R. Sandhu, E. Coyne, H. Feinstein, C. Youman, Role-based Access Control Models, IEEE Computer, Volume 29, #2, 1996, 38–47.

[SQL3] American National Standards Institute https://datacadamia.com/data/type/relation/sql/ansi

[STON1974] M. Stonebraker, E. Wong, Access Control in a Relational Database Management System by Query Modification, *Proceedings of the ACM Annual Conference*, ACM Press, NY, 1974.

[THUR1987] B. Thuraisingham, Security Checking in Relational Database Management Systems Augmented with Inference Engines, Computers and Security, Volume 6, #6, 1987, 479–492.

[THUR1989] B. Thuraisingham, P. Stachour, SQL Extensions for Security Assertions, Computer Standards and Interface Journal, Volume 11, #1, 1989, 5–14.

[THUR1993] B. Thuraisingham, W. Ford, M. Collins, Design and Implementation of a Database Inference Controller, Data and Knowledge Engineering Journal, Volume 11, #3, 1993, 5–14.

[THUR1994] B. Thuraisingham, Security Issues for Federated Database Systems, Computers & Security, Volume 13, #6, 1994,509–525.

[THUR1997] B. Thuraisingham, Data Management Systems: Evolution and Interoperation, CRC Press, Boca Raton, FL, 1997.

[THUR2005a] B. Thuraisingham, Database Security, Integrating Database Systems and Information Security, CRC Press, 2005.

[THUR2005b] B.M. Thuraisingham, Privacy Constraint Processing in a Privacy-enhanced Database Management System, Data & Knowledge Engineering, Volume 55, #2, 2005, 159–188.

[THUR2007] B. Thuraisingham, Building Trustworthy Semantic Webs, CRC Press, 2007.

[THUR2017] B. Thuraisinghan, P. Pallabi, M. Masud, L. Khan, Big Data Analytics with Applications in Insider Threat Detection CRC Press, 2017.

3 Data Mining and Security

3.1 INTRODUCTION

Data mining (as well as machine learning) can be considered to be a key aspect of data science. We have used data mining and analytics techniques in several of our efforts for various applications such as intrusion detection systems and social media systems. For example, in our previous book [THUR2016] we discussed algorithms for location-based data mining that will extract the locations of the various social media (e.g., Twitter) users. These algorithms can be extended to extract other demographics data. Our prior research has also developed data mining tools for sentiment analysis as well as for cyber security applications. For example, in one of our previous books, we discuss data mining tools for malware detection [MASU2011]. In this chapter, we provide some background information about general data mining techniques as well as their applications to cyber security so that the reader can have an understanding of the field. In addition, we will also discuss aspects of attacks to the data mining techniques as well as privacy considerations.

Data mining outcomes (also called tasks) include classification, clustering, forming associations as well as detecting anomalies. Our tools have mainly focused on classification as the outcome and we have developed classification tools. The classification problem is also referred to as supervised learning in which a set of labeled examples is learned by a model, and then a new example with unknown labels is presented to the model for prediction.

There are many prediction models that have been used such as Markov model, decision trees, artificial neural networks (ANN), support vector machines (SVM), association rule mining (ARM), among others. Each of these models has its strengths and weaknesses. However, there is a common weakness among all of these techniques, which is the inability to suit all applications. The reason that there is no such ideal or perfect classifier is that each of these techniques was initially designed to solve specific problems under certain assumptions.

In this chapter, we discuss the data mining techniques that have been commonly used. Specifically, we present the Markov model, SVM, ANN, ARM, the problem of multi-classification as well as image classification, which is an aspect of image mining. In our research and development, we have designed hybrid models to improve the prediction accuracy of data mining algorithms in various applications, namely, intrusion detection, social media analytics, WWW prediction and image classification [AWAD2009].

Data mining has many applications in security, including in national security (e.g., surveillance) as well as in cyber security (e.g., malware detection). The threats to national security include attacking buildings, destroying critical infrastructures such as power grids and telecommunication systems [BOLZ2005]. Data mining techniques are being investigated to find out who the suspicious people are and who is capable of carrying out terrorist activities [THUR2003]. Cyber security is involved with protecting the computer and network systems against corruption due to Trojan horses and viruses. Data mining is also being applied to provide solutions such as intrusion and malware detection and auditing [MASU2011]. In this chapter, we will focus mainly on data mining for cyber security applications.

The organization of this chapter is as follows. In Section 3.2, we provide an overview of data mining. We start with a discussion of data mining tasks in Section 3.2.1 and then provide some details on data mining techniques that we have utilized in our work. Some of these techniques are also utilized in Parts II and III of our book (e.g., support vector machines, decision trees). In particular, we discuss various data mining techniques such as SVM, Markov models, ARM, and

FIGURE 3.1 Data mining and security.

decision trees which will be described in Sections 3.2.2 through 3.2.6. In Section 3.3, we will discuss data mining for cyber security applications. In particular, we will discuss cyber threats and applications of data mining to detect such threats. Attacks to the data mining techniques as well as the privacy implications of data mining will be discussed in Section 3.3.4. Section 3.4 summarizes this chapter. Figure 3.1 illustrates the concepts in this chapter.

3.2 DATA MINING TECHNIQUES

3.2.1 OVERVIEW

Before we discuss data mining techniques, we provide an overview of some of the data mining tasks (also known as data mining outcomes). Then we will discuss the techniques. In general, data mining tasks can be grouped into two categories: predictive and descriptive. Predictive tasks essentially predict whether an item belongs to a class or not. Descriptive tasks, in general, extract patterns from the examples. One of the most prominent predictive tasks is classification. In some cases, other tasks such as anomaly detection can be reduced to a predictive task such as whether a particular situation is an anomaly or not. Descriptive tasks, in general, include making associations and forming clusters. Therefore, classification, anomaly detection, making associations, and forming clusters are also thought to be data mining tasks.

Next, the data mining techniques can either be predictive or descriptive or both. For example, neural networks can perform classification as well as clustering. Classification techniques include decisions trees, SVM as well as memory-based reasoning. ARM techniques are used, in general, to make associations. Link analysis that analyzes links can also make associations between links and predict new links. Clustering techniques include K-means clustering. An overview of the data mining tasks (i.e., the outcomes of data mining) is illustrated in Figure 3.2. The techniques (e.g., neural networks, support vector machines) are illustrated in Figure 3.2. Sections 3.2.2 through 3.2.6 discuss some of the data mining techniques we have used in our work. More details of our data mining techniques (Figure 3.3) can be found in our previous books (e.g., [AWAD2009, MASU2011, THUR2017]).

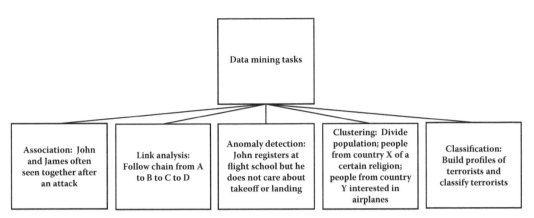

FIGURE 3.2 Data mining tasks.

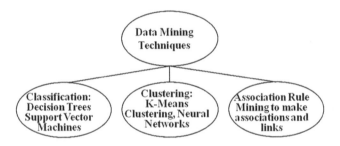

FIGURE 3.3 Data mining techniques.

3.2.2 ARTIFICIAL NEURAL NETWORKS

ANN is a very well-known, powerful, and robust classification technique that has been used to approximate real-valued, discrete-valued, and vector-valued functions from examples [MITC1997]. ANNs have been used in many areas such as interpreting visual scenes, speech recognition, and learning robot control strategies. An ANN simulates the biological nervous system in the human brain. The nervous system is composed of a large number of highly interconnected processing units (neurons) working together to produce our feelings and reactions. ANNs, like people, learn by example. The learning process in the human brain involves adjustments to the synaptic connections between neurons. Similarly, the learning process of ANN involves adjustments to the node weights. Figure 3.4 presents a

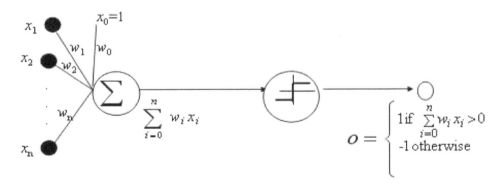

FIGURE 3.4 The perceptron.

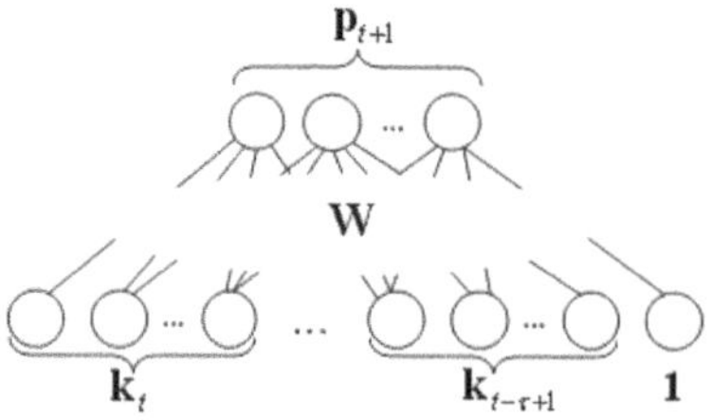

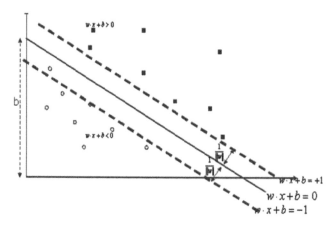

FIGURE 3.5   Artificial neural network.

simple neuron unit, which is called a perceptron. The perceptron input, x, is a vector or real-valued inputs. w is the weight vector, in which its value is determined after training. The perceptron computes a linear combination of an input vector x.

Learning the perceptron involves choosing values for the weights. Initially, random weight values are given to the perceptron. Then the perceptron is applied to each training example updating the weights of the perceptron whenever an example is misclassified. This process is repeated many times until all training examples are correctly classified.

The computation power of a single perceptron is limited to linear decisions. However, the perceptron can be used as a building block to compose powerful multi-layer networks. In this case, a more complicated updating rule is needed to train the network weights. In this work, we employ an ANN of two layers and each layer is composed of three building blocks (see Figure 3.5). We use the back-propagation algorithm for learning the weights. The back-propagation algorithm attempts to minimize the squared error function.

3.2.3   SUPPORT VECTOR MACHINES

SVM are learning systems that use a hypothesis space of linear functions in a high-dimensional feature space, trained with a learning algorithm from optimization theory. This learning strategy introduced by Vapnik et al. [CRIS2000, VAPN1995, VAPN1998, VAPN1999] is a very powerful method that has been applied in a wide variety of applications. The basic concept in SVM is the hyper-plane classifier, or linear separability. In order to achieve linear separability, SVM applies two basic ideas: margin maximization and kernels, that is, mapping input space to a higher dimension space, feature space.

For binary classification, the SVM problem can be formalized so that we find a linear separating hyper-plane classifier. Furthermore, we want this hyper-plane to have the maximum separating margin with respect to the two classes (see Figure 3.6). The functional margin, or the margin for

FIGURE 3.6   Linear separation in SVM.

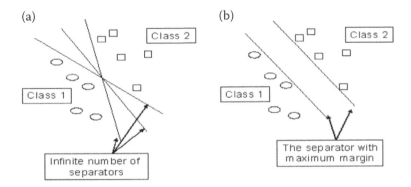

FIGURE 3.7   The SVM separator that causes the maximum margin. (a) Infinite Number of Separators (b) Separators with Maximum Margin.

short, is defined geometrically as the Euclidean distance of the closest point from the decision boundary to the input space. Figure 3.7 shows an intuitive explanation of why margin maximization gives the best solution of separation. In Figure 3.7(a), we can find an infinite number of separators for a specific dataset. There is no specific or clear reason to favor one separator over another. In Figure 3.7(b), we see that maximizing the margin provides only one thick separator. Such a solution proves to achieve the best generalization accuracy, that is, prediction for the unseen [VAPN1995, VAPN1998, VAPN1999].

Only those points that lie closest to the hyper-plane give the representation of the hypothesis/classifier (Figure 3.8(a)). These most important data points serve as support vectors. Their values can also be used to give an independent boundary with regard to the reliability of the hypothesis/classifier [BART1999]. Figure 3.8(a) shows two classes and their boundaries, that is, margins. The support vectors are represented by solid objects, while the empty objects are non-support vectors. Notice that the margins are only affected by the support vectors, that is, if we remove or add empty objects, the margins will not change. Meanwhile any change in the solid objects, either adding or removing objects, could change the margins. Figure 3.8(b) shows the effects of adding objects in the margin area. As we can see, adding or removing objects far from the margins, for example, data

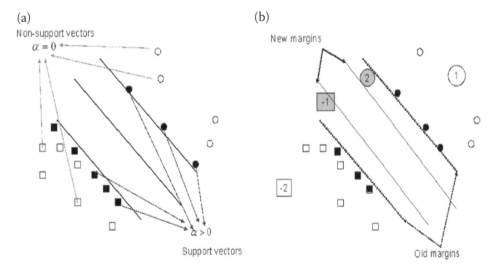

FIGURE 3.8   (a) The values of for support vectors and nonsupport vectors. (b) The effect of adding new data points on the margins.

point 1 or −2, does not change the margins. However, adding and/or removing objects near the margins, for example, data point 2 and/or −1, has created new margins.

3.2.4 MARKOV MODEL

Some recent and advanced predictive methods for web surfing are developed using Markov models [PIRO1996, YANG2001]. For these predictive models, the sequences of web pages visited by surfers are typically considered as Markov chains, which are then fed as input. The basic concept of the Markov model is that it predicts the next action depending on the result of previous action or actions. Actions can mean different things for different applications. For the purpose of illustration, we will consider actions specific for the WWW prediction application. In WWW prediction, the next action corresponds to prediction of the next page to be traversed. The previous actions correspond to the previous web pages to be considered. Based on the number of previous actions considered, Markov models can have different orders. In the following, we present an illustrative example of different orders of Markov model and how it can predict.

3.2.4.1   Example

Imagine a website of six web pages: P1, P2, P3, P4, P5, and P6. Suppose we have user sessions as in Table 3.1. Table 3.1 depicts the navigation of many users of that website. Figure 3.9 shows the *first-order Markov model*, where the next action is predicted based on only the last action performed, that is, last page traversed, by the user. States S and F correspond to the initial and final states, respectively. The probability of each transition is estimated by the ratio of the number of times the sequence of states was traversed and the number of times the anchor state was visited. Next to each arch in Figure 3.9, the first number is the frequency of that transition, and the second number is the transition probability. For example, the transition probability of the transition (P2 to

TABLE 3.1

Collection of user sessions and their frequencies

Session	Frequency
P1, P2, P4	5
P1, P2, P6	1
P5, P2, P6	6
P5, P2, P3	3

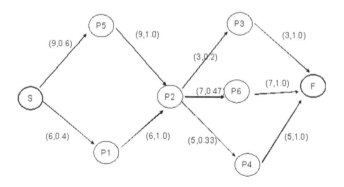

FIGURE 3.9   First-order Markov model.

P3) is 0.2 because the number of times users traverse from page 2 to page 3 is 3 and the number of times page 2 is visited is 15 (i.e., 0.2 = 3/15).

Notice that the transition probability is used to resolve prediction. For example, given that a user has already visited P2, the most probable page she visits next is P6. That is because the transition probability from P2 to P6 is the highest.

Notice that that transition probability might not be available for some pages. For example, the transition probability from P2 to P5 is not available because no user has visited P5 after P2. Hence, these transition probabilities are set to zeros. Similarly, the Kth-order Markov model is where the prediction is computed after considering the last K^{th} action performed by the users. In WWW prediction, the Kth-order Markov model is the probability of user visits to P_k^{th} page given its previous k-1 page visits.

Figure 3.10 shows the second-order Markov model that corresponds to Table 3.1. In the second-order model, we consider the last two pages. The transition probability is computed in a similar fashion. For example, the transition probability of the transition (P1, P2) to (P2, P6) is 0.16 = 1 × 1/6 because the number of times users traverse from state (P1, P2) to state (P2, P6) is 1 and the number of times pages (P1, P2) is visited is 6 (i.e., 0.16 = 1/6). The transition probability is used for prediction. For example, given that a user has visited P1 and P2, she most probably visits P4 because the transition probability from state (P1, P2) to state (P2, P4) is greater than the transition probability from state (P1, P2) to state (P2, P6). The order of Markov model is related to the sliding window. The Kth-order Markov model corresponds to a sliding window of size K-1.

3.2.5 Association Rule Mining (ARM)

Association rule mining is a data mining technique that has been applied successfully to discover related transactions. The association rules technique finds the relationships among itemsets based on their co-occurrence in the transactions. Specifically, association rule mining discovers the frequent patterns (regularities) among those items sets. For example, what are the items purchased together in a superstore? In the following, we briefly introduce ARM. For more details, see [AGRA1993] and [AGRA1994]. There are several efficient algorithms proposed to find association rules such as AIS algorithm [AGRA1993, AGRA1994], SETM algorithm [HOUT1995], and AprioriTid [LIU1999].

In the case of web transactions, we use association rules to discover navigational patterns among users. This would help to cache a page in advance and reduce the loading time of a page. Also, discovering a pattern of navigation helps in personalization. Transactions are captured from the clickstream data captured in web server logs.

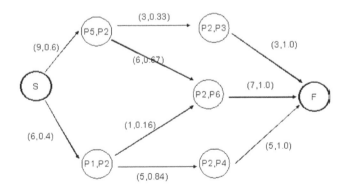

FIGURE 3.10 Second-order Markov model.

In many applications, there is one main problem in using ARM. First, a problem with using global minimum support (*minsup*), because rare hits, that is, web pages that are rarely visited, will not be included in the frequent sets because it will not achieve enough support. One solution is to have a very small support threshold; however, we will end up with a very large frequent itemsets, which are computationally hard to handle. Liu et al. [LIU1999] propose a mining technique that uses different support thresholds for different items. Specifying multiple thresholds allow rare transactions, which might be very important to be included in the frequent itemsets. Other issues might arise depending on the application itself. For example, in case of WWW prediction, a session is recorded for each user. The session might have tens of clickstreams (and sometimes hundreds depending on the duration of the session). Using each session as a transaction will not work because it is rare to find two sessions that are frequently repeated (i.e., identical); hence, it will not achieve even a very high support threshold, *minsup*. There is a need to break each session into many subsequences. Mobasher et al. [MOBA2001] propose a recommendation engine that matches an active user session with the frequent itemsets in the database and predicts the next page the user most probably visits.

3.2.6 Decision Trees

As its name implies a decision tree is essentially a tree consisting of different types of nodes: the root node, the intermediate nodes, and the leaf nodes. A question is asked at each root or intermediate node and depending on the answer a branch is selected. The process ends when all the leaf nodes are reached. A question could be of the form "Is gender male or female" or "Is age greater than 50." The challenge is to select the right features such as gender and age. Training data is used to train the model and the model is subsequently tested against the test data.

One could ask, what is the challenge with constructing the decision tree? One of the major challenges is to determine when to stop splitting the tree. Several algorithms have been developed over the past decades in coming up with different ways to construct the tree. In Part III of this book, we consider one such decision tree and examine privacy aspects. More details can be found in [HAN2000].

3.2.7 Multi-class Problem

Most classification techniques solve the binary classification problem. Binary classifiers are accumulated to generalize for the multi-class problem. There are two basic schemes for this generalization, namely, one-vs-one, and one-vs-all. To avoid redundancy, we will present this generalization only for SVM.

3.2.7.1 One-vs-One

The one-vs-one approach creates a classifier for each pair of classes. The training set for each pair classifier $(i,)$ includes only those instances that belong to either class i or j. A new instance x belongs to the class upon which most pair classifiers agree. The prediction decision is quoted from the majority vote technique. There are $n(n-1)/2$ classifiers to be computed, where n is the number of classes in the dataset. It is evident that the disadvantage of this scheme is that we need to generate a large number of classifiers, especially if there are a large number of classes in the training set. For example, if we have a training set of 1,000 classes, we need 499,500 classifiers. On the other hand, the size of the training set for each classifier is small because we exclude all instances that do not belong to that pair of classes.

3.2.7.2 One-vs-All

One-vs-all creates a classifier for each class in the dataset. The training set is pre-processed such that for a classifier j instances that belong to class j are marked as class $(+1)$ and instances that do not belong to class j are marked as class (-1). In the one-vs-all scheme, we compute n classifiers, where n is the number of pages that users have visited (at the end of each session). A new instance x is predicted by assigning it to the class that its classifier outputs the largest positive value (i.e., maximal marginal).

The advantage of the one-vs-all scheme, compared to the one-vs-one scheme, is that it has fewer classifiers. On the other hand, the size of the training set is larger for one-vs-all than for a one-vs-one scheme because we use the whole original training set to compute each classifier.

3.3 DATA MINING, CYBER SECURITY, AND PRIVACY

We first discuss the various cyber security threats in Section 3.3.1 and then discuss how data mining may be applied to handle these threats in Section 3.3.2. Finally, we discuss the attacks to the data mining techniques in Section 3.3.3.

3.3.1 CYBER SECURITY THREATS

This section discusses the various cyber threats, including cyber-terrorism, insider threats, and external attacks. Figure 3.11 illustrates the various types of cyber security threats.

3.3.1.1 Cyber-Terrorism, Insider Threats, and External Attacks

Cyber-terrorism is one of the major terrorist threats posed to our nation today. As we have mentioned earlier, there is now so much of information available electronically and on the web. Attacks on our computers as well as networks, databases, and the Internet could be devastating to businesses. We are hearing almost daily about the cyber-attacks to businesses. It is estimated that cyber-terrorism could cost billions of dollars to businesses. For example, consider a banking information system. If terrorists attack such a system and deplete accounts of the funds, then the bank could lose millions and perhaps billions of dollars. By crippling the computer system, millions of hours of productivity could be lost and that equates to money in the end. Even a simple power outage at work through some accident could cause several hours of productivity loss and as a result a major financial loss. Therefore, it is critical that our information systems be secure. We discuss various types of cyber-terrorist attacks. One is spreading malware that can wipe away files and other important documents; another is intruding the computer networks.

Note that threats can occur from outside or from the inside of an organization. Outside attacks are the attacks on computers from someone outside the organization. We hear of hackers breaking into computer systems and causing havoc within an organization. These hackers infect the computers with malware that can not only cause great damage to the files stored in the systems but also spread to other systems via the networks. But a more sinister problem is the insider threat problem. People inside an organization who have studied the business practices develop schemes to cripple the organization's information assets. These people could be regular employees or even those working at computer centers and contractors. The problem is quite serious as someone may be

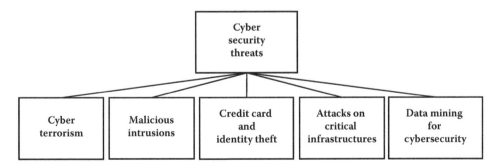

FIGURE 3.11 Cyber security threats.

masquerading as someone else and causing all kinds of damage. Malicious processes in the system can also masquerade as benign processes and cause damage. Data mining techniques have been applied to detect various attacks. We discuss some of these attacks next.

3.3.1.2   Malicious Intrusions

Malicious intrusions may include intruding the systems, the networks, the web clients and servers, and the databases and applications. Many of the cyber-terrorism attacks are due to malicious intrusions. We hear much about network intrusions. What happens here is that intruders try to tap into the networks and get the information that is being transmitted. These intruders may be human intruders or malicious processes. Intrusions could also happen on files. For example, a malicious individual can masquerade as an employee and log into the corporation's computer systems and network and access the files. Intrusions can also occur on databases. Intruders pretending to be legitimate users can pose queries such as SQL queries and access the data that they are not authorized to know.

Essentially cyber-terrorism includes malicious intrusions as well as sabotage through malicious intrusions or otherwise. Cyber security consists of security mechanisms that attempt to provide solutions to cyber-attacks or cyber-terrorism. When we discuss malicious intrusions or cyber-attacks, it would be useful to think about the non-cyber world and then translate those attacks to attacks on computers and networks. For example, a thief could enter a building through a trap door. In the same way, a computer intruder could enter the computer or network through some sort of a trap door that has been intentionally built by a malicious insider and left unattended through perhaps careless design. Another example is a thief entering the bank with a mask and stealing the money. The analogy here is an intruder masquerading as a legitimate user takes control of the information assets. Money in the real world would translate to information assets in the cyber world. More recently we are hearing about ransomware where hackers are not only stealing the data but also holding the data ransom by encrypting the data. Then the owner of the data has to pay a ransom, usually in the form of bitcoins, and then retrieve his/her data. That is, there are many parallels between what happens in the real world and the cyber world.

3.3.1.3   Credit Card Fraud and Identity Theft

Credit card fraud and identity theft are common security problems. In the case of credit card fraud, others get hold of a person's credit card numbers through electronic means (e.g., when swiping the card at gas stations) or otherwise and make all kinds of purchases; by the time the owner of the card finds out, it may be too late. A more serious problem is identity theft. Here one assumes the identity of another person, say by getting hold of the social security number and essentially carries out all the transactions under the other person's name. This could even be selling houses and depositing the income in a fraudulent bank account. By the time the owner finds out, it will be far too late. It is very likely that the owner may have lost millions of dollars due to the identity theft. We need to explore the use of data mining both for credit card fraud detection as well as for identity theft. There have been some efforts on detecting credit card fraud [CHAN1999]. However, detecting identity theft still remains a challenge.

3.3.1.4   Attacks on Critical Infrastructures

Attacks on critical infrastructures could cripple a nation and its economy. Infrastructure attacks include attacking the telecommunication lines, the power grid, gas pipelines, reservoirs, and water and food supplies and other basic entities that are critical for the operation of a nation. Attacks on critical infrastructures could occur due to malware or by physical means such as bombs. For example, one could attack the software that runs the telecommunication systems and close down all the telecommunications lines. Similarly, software that runs the power grid could be attacked. Infrastructures could also be attacked by natural disaster such as hurricanes and earthquakes. Our main interest here is the attacks on infrastructures through malicious attacks. While some progress has been made on developing solutions to such attacks, much remains to be done. One of the directions we are pursuing is to examine the use of data mining to detect such infrastructure attacks.

3.3.2 Data Mining for Cyber Security

Data mining is being applied for problems such as intrusion and malware detection and auditing. For example, anomaly detection techniques could be used to detect unusual patterns and behaviors. Link analysis may be used to trace the viruses to the perpetrators. Classification may be used to group various cyber-attacks and then use the profiles to detect an attack when it occurs. Prediction may be used to determine potential future attacks depending in a way on information learned about terrorists through email and phone conversations. Also, for some threats, non-real-time data mining may suffice while for certain other threats such as for network intrusions, we may need real-time data mining. Many researchers are investigating the use of data mining for intrusion detection [AWAD2009]. While we need some form of real-time data mining where the results have to be generated in real time, we also need to build models in real time. For example, credit card fraud detection is a form of real-time processing. However, here, models are usually built ahead of time. Building models in real time remains a challenge. Data mining can also be used for analyzing web logs as well as analyzing the audit trails. Based on the results of the data mining tool, one can then determine whether any unauthorized intrusions have occurred and/or whether any unauthorized queries have been posed [MASU2011].

Other applications of data mining for cyber security include analyzing the audit data. One could build a repository or a warehouse containing the audit data and then conduct an analysis using various data mining tools to see if there are potential anomalies. For example, there could be a situation where a certain user group may access the database between 3 and 5 am in the morning. It could be that this group is working the night shift, in which case there may be a valid explanation. However, if this group is working between, say, 9 am and 5 pm, then this may be an unusual occurrence. Another example is when a person accesses the databases always between 1 and 2pm, but for the last two days he/she has been accessing the database between 1 and 2am. This could then be flagged as an unusual pattern that would need further investigation.

Insider threat analysis is also a problem both from a national security as well from a cyber security perspective. That is, those working in a corporation who are considered to be trusted could commit espionage. Similarly, those with proper access to the computer system could insert malicious code that behaves like benign code until an opportunity arrives to steal the data. Catching such terrorists is far more difficult than catching terrorists outside of an organization. One may need to monitor the access patterns of all the individuals of a corporation even if they are system administrators, to see whether they are carrying out cyber-terrorism activities. However, this could result in privacy violations. Our approach to applying data mining for insider threat detection as well as some other cyber security threats such as malicious executables and novel malware detection is discussed in Part II. Figure 3.12 illustrates some of our applications of data mining for cyber security. For more details on a high-level overview, we refer to [THUR2004] and [THUR2005].

3.3.3 Security and Privacy-Enhanced Data Mining

This section first discusses attacks on data mining techniques and then will provide an overview of privacy enhanced data mining. The chapters in Part III focus on security and privacy-enhanced data mining. Figure 3.13 illustrates the concepts.

Learning tasks, such as intrusion detection and spam filtering, face adversarial attacks. Adversarial exploits create additional challenges to existing learning paradigms. Generalization of a learning model over future data cannot be achieved under the assumption that current and future

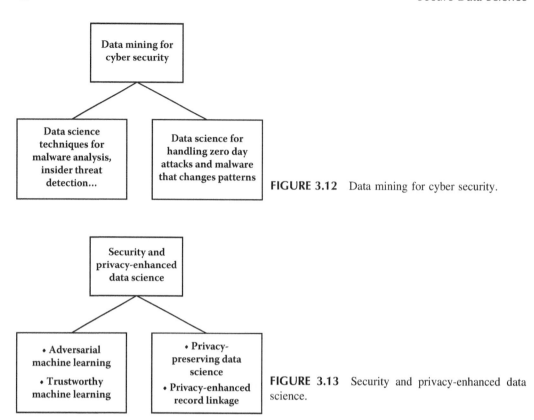

FIGURE 3.12   Data mining for cyber security.

FIGURE 3.13   Security and privacy-enhanced data science.

data share identical properties, which is essential to the traditional approaches. In the presence of active adversaries, data used for training in a learning system is unlikely to represent future data the system would observe. The difference is not just simple random noise which most learning algorithms have already taken into consideration when they are designed. What typically flunk these learning algorithms are targeted attacks that aim to make the learning system dysfunctional by disguising malicious data that otherwise would be detected. Therefore, the learning algorithms have to adapt themselves to handle the adversarial attacks. This has come to be known as adversarial machine learning. In Part III of this book, we will discuss such adversarial machine learning techniques.

Another focus of this book is data privacy that results due to data mining. Data mining techniques (which have now evolved into machine learning and data science techniques) are used to derive patterns from massive amounts of data [THUR1998]. However, such techniques could extract nuggets that are previously known. These nuggets could violate individual privacy [THUR2002]. Due to increasing concerns related to privacy, various privacy-preserving data mining techniques have been developed to address different privacy issues [THUR2005]. These include privacy preserving association rule mining techniques and privacy preserving decision trees [AGRA2000, LIU2009]. The idea behind privacy preserving data mining is to randomize and/or perturb the data and then carry out data mining. This way the sensitive data could be kept private.

Privacy-preserving data mining techniques usually operate under various assumptions and employ different methods. The previous works mainly fall into two categories: perturbation and randomization-based approaches and secure multi-party computation-based approaches. In the case of perturbation-based approaches, the data is perturbed so that the sensitive data could be kept private. In the case of the randomized approach, random values are introduced to the data. In the case of secure multiparty computation-based approaches, the idea is for each party to encrypt its secret. Privacy-preserving data mining is carried out on the encrypted secrets. The final results are divulged to the parties. However, each party's secret is only known to that party.

The earlier perturbation and randomization approaches have a step to reconstruct the original data distribution. More recent research in this area adopts different data distortion methods or modifies the data mining techniques to make it more suitable to the perturbation scenario. Secure multi-party computation approaches, which employ cryptographic tools to build data mining models, face high communication and computation costs, especially when the number of parties participating in the computation is large.

3.4   SUMMARY AND DIRECTIONS

In this chapter, we first provided an overview of the various data mining tasks and techniques and then discussed some of the techniques that we have used in our work. These include ANN, SVM, decision trees, and ARM. We have utilized a combination of these techniques together with some other techniques in the literature as well as our own techniques to develop data analytics techniques for very large databases. Some of these techniques are utilized in Parts II, III, and IV (e.g., decision trees, SVM).

Numerous data mining techniques have been designed and developed and many of them are being utilized in commercial tools. Several of these techniques are variations of some of the basic classification, clustering, and association rule mining techniques. One of the major challenges today is to determine the appropriate techniques for various applications. We still need more benchmarks and performance studies. In addition, the techniques should result in fewer false positives and negatives.

Next, we provided an overview of data mining for cyber security applications. In particular, we discussed the threats to computers and networks and described the applications of data mining to detect such threats and attacks. Finally, we discuss the security and privacy attacks to data mining, for example, we discuss attacks to data mining techniques and how we may adapt them to combat the threats. We also discuss privacy problems that would result due to its data mining and discuss solutions such as privacy-aware data mining.

Data mining, cyber security, and privacy is a very active research area. Various data mining techniques, including link analysis and association rule mining, are being explored to detect abnormal patterns. Because of data mining, users can now make all kinds of correlations. In addition, in the past ten years massive amounts of data are being collected. We need big data analytics techniques to detect potential security violations. This also raises privacy concerns. More details on privacy can be obtained in [THUR2002]. More recently there has been a lot of focus on adversarial data mining/machine learning. Much of the contents in this book is based on data mining/machine learning as they relate to cyber security and privacy.

REFERENCES

[AGRA1993] R. Agrawal, T. Imielinski, A. Swami, Mining Association Rules between Sets of Items in Large Database, *Proceedings of the ACM SIGMOD Conference on Management of Data*, Washington, DC, May 1993, pp. 207–216.

[AGRA1994] R. Agrawal, R. Srikant, Fast Algorithms for Mining Association Rules in Large Database, *Proceedings of the 20th International Conference on Very Large Data Bases*, San Francisco, CA, 1994, pp. 487–499.

[AGRA2000] R. Agrawal, R. Srikant, Privacy-Preserving Data Mining, *ACMSIGMOD Conference*, Volume 29, #2, 2000, pp. 439–450.

[AWAD2009] M. Awad, L. Khan, B. Thuraisingham, L. Wang, Design and Implementation of Data Mining Tools, CRC Press, 2009.

[BART1999] P. Bartlett, J. Shawe-Taylor, Generalization Performance of Support Vector Machines and Other Pattern Classifiers, *Advances in Kernel Methods – Support Vector Learning*, MIT Press, 1999, pp. 43–53.

[BOLZ2005] F. Bolz, K. Dudonis, D. Schulz, The Counterterrorism Handbook: Tactics, Procedures, and Techniques, 3rd ed. (Practical Aspects of Criminal & Forensic Investigations), CRC Press, 2005.

[CHAN1999] P. Chan, W. Fan, A. Prodromidis, S. Stolfo, Distributed Data Mining in Credit Card Fraud Detection, IEEE Intelligent Systems, Volume 14, #6, 1999, pp. 67–74.

[CRIS2000] N. Cristianini, J. Shawe-Taylor, *Introduction to Support Vector Machines*, 1st ed., Cambridge University Press, 2000, pp. 93–122.

[HAN2000] J. Han, M. Kamber, J. Pei, Data Mining: Concepts and Techniques, Morgan Kaufmann, 2000.

[HOUT1995] M. Houtsma, A. Swanu, Set-Oriented Mining of Association Rules in Relational Databases, *Proceedings of the Eleventh International Conference on Data Engineering*, Washington, DC, 1995, pp. 25–33.

[LI2007] C. Li, L. Khan, M. Bhavani, M.H. Thuraisingham, S. Chen, F. Qiu, Geospatial Data Mining for National Security: Land Cover Classification and Semantic Grouping, *Proceedings of ISI*, New Brunswick, NJ, 2007.

[LIU1999] B. Liu, W. Hsu, Y. Ma, Association Rules with Multiple Minimum Supports, *Proceedings of the Fifth ACM SIGKDD International Conference on Knowledge Discovery and Data Mining*, San Diego, CA, 1999, pp. 337–341.

[LIU2009] L. Liu, M. Kantarcioglu, B.M. Thuraisingham, *Privacy Preserving Decision Tree Mining from Perturbed Data*, HICSS, 2009, pp. 1–10.

[MASU2011] M. Masud, L. Khan, B. Thuraisingham, Data Mining Tools for Malware Detection, CRC Press, 2011.

[MITC1997] T.M. Mitchell, *Machine Learning*, McGraw Hill, 1997.

[MOBA2001] B. Mobasher, H. Dai, T. Luo, M. Nakagawa, Effective Personalization Based on Association Rule Discovery from Web Usage Data, *Proceedings of the ACM Workshop on Web Information and Data Management (WIDM01)*, 2001, pp. 9–15.

[PIRO1996] P. Pirolli, J. Pitkow, R. Rao, Silk from a Sow's Ear: Extracting Usable Structures from the Web, *Proceedings of 1996 Conference on Human Factors in Computing Systems (CHI-96)*, Vancouver, British Columbia, Canada, 1996, pp. 118–125.

[THUR1998] B. Thuraisingham, Data Mining: Technologies, Techniques, Tools and Trends, CRC Press, 1998.

[THUR2002] B. Thuraisingham, Data Mining, National Security, Privacy and Civil Liberties, SIGKDD Explorations, New York, NY, Volume 4, #2, December 2002.

[THUR2003] B. Thuraisingham, Web Data Mining Technologies and Their Applications in Business Intelligence and Counter-terrorism, CRC Press, 2003.

[THUR2004] B. Thuraisingham, Managing Threats to Web Databases and Cyber Systems, Issues, Solutions and Challenges, Kluwer (Editors: V. Kumar, J. Srivastava, Al. Lazarevic), 2004.

[THUR2005] B. Thuraisingham, Database and Applications Security, CRC Press, 2005.

[THUR2016] B. Thuraisingham, S. Abrol, R. Heatherly, M. Kantarcioglu, V. Khadilkar, L. Khan,Analyzing and Securing Social Networks, CRC Press, 2016.

[THUR2017] B. Thuraisingham, P. Praveen, M. M. Masud, L. Khan, Big Data Analytics with Applications in Insider Threat Detection, CRC Press, 2017.

[VAPN1995] V.N. Vapnik, The Nature of Statistical Learning Theory, Springer, 1995.

[VAPN1998] V.N. Vapnik, Statistical Learning Theory, Wiley, 1998.

[VAPN1999] V.N. Vapnik, The Nature of Statistical Learning Theory, Springer-Verlag, 1999.

[YANG2001] Q. Yang, H. Zhang, T. Li, Mining Web Logs for Prediction Models in WWW Caching and Prefetching, *The 7th ACM SIGKDD International Conference on Knowledge Discovery and Data Mining KDD*, ACM, San Francisco, CA, August 26–29, 2001, pp. 473–478.

4 Big Data, Cloud, Semantic Web, and Social Network Technologies

4.1 INTRODUCTION

Chapters 2 and 3 discussed concepts in data security and privacy, data mining for cyber security as well as attacks to data mining. These supporting technologies are part of the foundational technologies for the concepts discussed in this book. For example, Part II describes data science for cyber security, while Part III describes security and privacy aware data science. In addition to data security and privacy as well as data mining and security, big data technologies, cloud and semantic web are some of the foundational technologies that we have utilized in our work on secure data science. This chapter discusses these foundational technologies.

Over the past ten years or so, numerous big data management and analytics systems have emerged. In addition, various cloud service providers have also implemented big data solutions. In addition, infrastructures/platforms for big data systems have also been developed. Notable among the big data systems include MongoDB, Google's BigQuery, and Apache HIVE. The big data solutions are being developed by cloud providers including Amazon, IBM, Google, and Microsoft. In addition, infrastructures/platforms based on products such as Apache's Hadoop, Spark, and Storm have been developed.

Selecting the products to discuss is a difficult task. This is because almost every database vendor as well as cloud computing vendors together with analytics tools vendors is now marketing their products as big data solutions. When we combine the products offered by all vendors as well as include the open-source products, then there are hundreds of products to discuss. Therefore, we have selected the products that we are most familiar with by discussing these products in the courses we teach and/or using them in our experimentation. In other words, we have only selected the service providers, products, and frameworks that we are most familiar with and those that we have examined in our work. Describing all of the service providers, products, and frameworks is beyond the scope of this book. Furthermore, we are not endorsing any product in this book.

We utilize the cloud platform for managing and analyzing large datasets. We will see throughout this book that cloud computing is at the heart of managing large datasets. Cloud computing has emerged as a powerful computing paradigm for service-oriented computing. Many of the computing services are being outsourced to the cloud. Such cloud-based services can be used to host the various cyber security applications such as insider threat detection and identity management. Google has now introduced the MapReduce framework for processing large amounts of data on commodity hardware. Apache's Hadoop Distributed File System (HDFS) is emerging as a superior software component for cloud computing combined with integrated parts such as MapReduce [DEAN2004, GHEM2003, HDFS]. Clouds such as HP's Open Cirrus Testbed are utilizing HDFS. This, in turn, has resulted in numerous social networking sites with massive amounts of data to be shared and managed. For example, we may want to analyze multiple years of stock market data statistically to reveal a pattern or to build a reliable weather model based on several years of weather and related data. To handle such massive amounts of data distributed at many sites (i.e., nodes), scalable hardware and software components are needed. The cloud computing model has emerged to address the explosive growth of web-connected devices, and

DOI: 10.1201/9781003081845-6

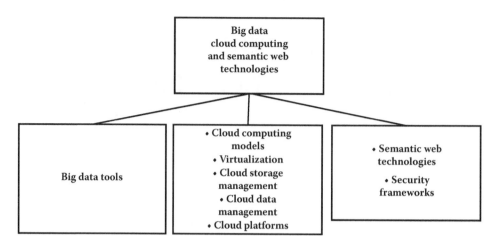

FIGURE 4.1   Big data, cloud computing, and semantic web technologies.

handle massive amounts of data. It is defined and characterized by massive scalability and new Internet-driven economics.

Another concept that is being used for a variety of applications is the notion of the semantic web. A semantic web is essentially a collection of technologies to produce machine-understandable web pages. These technologies can also be used to represent any type of data, including schema for big data and malware data. We have based some of our analytics and security investigation for data represented using semantic web technologies. In particular, we have represented social networks using semantic web technologies and subsequently applied our analytics techniques to extract useful relationships. We have also examined security and privacy for social network represented using semantic web technologies.

The organization of this chapter is as follows. Section 4.2 discusses big data management and analytics tools. Cloud computing concepts are discussed in Section 4.3. Concepts in semantic web are discussed in Section 4.4. Analyzing and securing social networks is discussed in Section 4.4. Section 4.5 concludes this chapter. Figure 4.1 illustrates the concepts discussed in this chapter. More details of the tools and technologies discussed in this chapter are given in [THUR2007], [THUR2013], and [THUR2017].

4.2   BIG DATA MANAGEMENT AND ANALYTICS TOOLS AND TECHNOLOGIES

We discuss various classes of big data management and analytics tools, including infrastructure tools and big data management and analytics tools. The tools discussed are illustrated in Figure 4.2 [THUS2010].

4.2.1   INFRASTRUCTURE TOOLS TO HOST BIG DATA SYSTEMS

In this section, we will discuss various infrastructure products that host various big data systems. These are: Apache's Hadoop, Spark, Storm, Flink and Kafka and the MapReduce programming model [WHIT2015] . These infrastructure tools can also be considered to be cloud computing tools.

4.2.1.1   Apache Hadoop

Hadoop is an open-source distributed framework for processing large amounts of data. It uses the MapReduce programming model that we will discuss next. Its storage system is called the Hadoop Distributed File System (HDFS). It is hosted on clusters of machines. A file consists of multiple

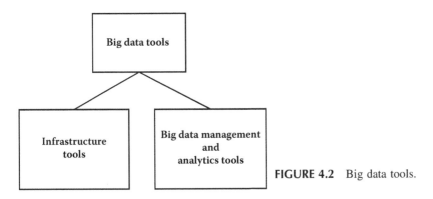

FIGURE 4.2 Big data tools.

blocks and the blocks of a file are replicated for availability. It supports the parallel processing of the data for performance. JobTracker is a part of Hadoop that tracks the MapReduce jobs. These jobs are submitted by the client application. Most of the big data systems as well as the cloud applications are hosted on Hadoop. More details of Hadoop can be found in [HDFS].

4.2.1.2 MapReduce

MapReduce is a programming model and an associated implementation that takes the client requests and transforms them into MapReduce jobs. These jobs are then executed by Hadoop. The main feature of the programming model is the generation of jobs. The MapReduce model has two components: (i) Map and (ii) Reduce. As stated in [MAPR], "a MapReduce job usually splits the input dataset into independent chunks which are processed by the map tasks in a completely parallel manner. The framework sorts the outputs of the maps, which are then input to the reduce tasks. Typically, both the input and the output of the job are stored in a file system. The framework takes care of scheduling tasks, monitoring them and re-executes the failed tasks." More details of the MapReduce model are given in [MAPR].

4.2.1.3 Apache Spark

Apache Spark is an open-source distributed computing framework for processing massive amounts of data. The application programmers use Spark through an interface that consists of a data structure called the Resilient Distributed Dataset (RDD). Spark was developed to overcome the limitations in the MapReduce programming model. The RDD data structure of Spark provides the support for distributed shared memory. Due to the in-memory processing capabilities, Spark offers good performance. Spark [SPAR] has interfaces with various NoSQL-based big data systems such as Cassandra and Amazon's cloud platform. Spark supports SQL capabilities with Spark SQL.

4.2.1.4 Apache Pig

Apache Pig is a scripting platform for analyzing and processing large datasets. Apache Pig enables Hadoop users to write complex MapReduce transformations using simple scripting language called Pig Latin. Pig converts Pig Latin script to a MapReduce job. The MapReduce jobs are then executed by Hadoop for the data stored in HDFS. Pig Latin programming is similar to specifying a query execution plan. That is, the Pig Latin scripts can be regarded to be an execution plan. This makes it simpler for the programmers to carry out their tasks. More details on Pig can be found in [PIG].

4.2.1.5 Apache Storm

Apache Storm is an open source distributed real-time computation system for processing massive amounts of data. Storm is essentially a real-time framework for processing streaming data and real-time analytics. It can be integrated with the HDFS. It provides features like scalability, reliability, and fault tolerance. The latest version of Storm supports streaming SQL, predictive modeling and integration with systems such as Kafka. In summary, Storm is for real-time processing and Hadoop is for batch processing. More details on Storm can be found in [STOR].

4.2.1.6   Apache Flink

Flink is an open-source scalable stream processing framework. As stated in [FLIN], Flink consists of the following features: "(i) provides results that are accurate, even in the case of out-of-order or late-arriving data, (ii) is stateful and fault-tolerant and can seamlessly recover from failures while maintaining exactly-once application state, and (iii) performs at large scale, running on thousands of nodes with very good throughput and latency characteristics." Flink is essentially a distributed data flow engine implemented in Scala and Java. It executes programs both in parallel and pipelined modes. It supports Java, Python, and SQL programming environments. While it does not have its own data storage, it integrates with systems such as HDFS, Kafka, and Cassandra.

4.2.1.7   Apache Kafka

Kafka was initially developed by LinkedIn and then further developed as an open-source Apache project. It is also implemented in Scala and Java and is a distributed stream processing system. It is highly scalable and handles massive amounts of streaming data. Its storage layer is based on a pub/sub messaging queue architecture. The design is essentially based on distributed transaction logs. Transaction logs are used in database systems to recover from the failure of the transactions. More details on Kafka can be found in [KAFK].

4.2.2   BIG DATA MANAGEMENT AND ANALYTICS TOOLS

In this section, we will discuss the various Big Data Management and Analytics (BDMA) systems and tools. We first provide big data systems that are based on SQL. These are Apache Hive and Google BigQuery. Then we discuss NoSQL (non-SQL) databases in general. This is followed by a discussion of example NoSQL systems such as Google BigTable, HBase, MongoDB, Cassandra, CouchDB, and the Oracle NoSQL Database. This will be followed by a discussion of two data mining/machine learning systems for big data and they are Weka and Apache Mahout.

4.2.2.1   Apache Hive

Apache Hive is an open-source SQL-like database/data warehouse that is implemented on top of the Hadoop/MapReduce platform. It was initially developed by Facebook to store the information related to Facebook data. However, later it became an open-source project and a trademark of Apache. Hive manages very large datasets and functions on top of the Hadoop/MapReduce storage model. It provides an SQL-like query language, which is called HiveQL. That is, SQL-like queries are supported by Hive. However, since Hadoop is implemented in Java, the queries are also implemented in Java. This way, there is no need to have a low-level Java API to implement the queries. The Hive engine essentially converts the SQL queries into MapReduce jobs that are then executed by Hadoop. More details on Apache Hive can be found in [HIVE].

4.2.2.2   Google BigQuery

BigQuery is essentially a data warehouse that manages petabyte scale data. It runs on Google's infrastructure and can process SQL queries or carry out analytics extremely fast. For example, terabyte data can be accessed in seconds while petabyte data can be accessed in minutes. The BigQuery data is stored in different types of tables: native tables store the BigQuery data, views stores the virtual tables, and external tables store the external data. BigQuery can be accessed in many ways such as command line tools, RESTful interface or a web user interface, and client libraries (e.g., Java, .NET, Python). More details on BigQuery can be found at [BIGQ].

4.2.2.3   NoSQL Database

NoSQL database is a generic term for essentially a non-relational database design or scalability for the web. It is known as a non-relational high-performance database. The data models for NoSQL databases may include graphs, document structures, and key-value pairs. It can be argued that the databases that were developed in the 1960s such as IBM's IMS and those based on the network data model are NoSQL databases. However, other object-oriented data models that were developed in the 1990s led the way to develop NoSQL databases in the 2000s. What is different from the NoSQL databases and the older hierarchical, network, and object databases is that the NoSQL databases have been designed with the web in mind. That is, the goal is to access massive amounts of data on the web rapidly.

The most popular NoSQL database model is the key value pair. While relational databases consist of a collection of relations where each relation has a collection or attributes, these attributes are labeled and included in the schema. NoSQL databases have tables that have two columns: Key and Value. Key could be anything such as a person's name or the index of a stock. However, the value could be a collection of attributes such as the name of the stock, the value of the stock, and other information such as whether to buy the stock and if so, the quantity recommended. Therefore, all the information pertaining to a stock can be retrieved without having to perform many joins. Some of the popular NoSQL databases will be discussed in this section (e.g., MongoDB and HBase). For a detailed discussion of NoSQL databases, we refer the reader to [NOSQ]. More details are also given in [CATT2011].

4.2.2.4   Google BigTable

BigTable is one of the early NoSQL databases running on top of the Google File System (GFS). It is now provided as a service in the cloud. BigTable maps the row key and the column together with a time stamp into a byte array. That is, it is essentially a NoSQL database that is based on the key value pair model. It was designed to handle petabyte-sized data. It uses compression algorithms when the data gets too large. Each table in BigTable has many dimensions and may be divided into what is called tablets to work with GFS. BigTable is used by many applications, including Google's YouTube, Google Maps, Google Earth, and Gmail. More details on BigTable can be found in [BIGT].

4.2.2.5   Apache HBase

HBase is an open-source non-relational distributed database that was the first table developed for the Hadoop/MapReduce platform. That is, HBase is a NoSQL database that is based on a column-oriented key value data store model. It is implemented in Java. The queries are executed as MapReduce jobs. It is somewhat similar to Google's Big Table and uses compression for in-memory storage. HBase is scalable and handles billions of rows with millions of columns. It also integrates multiple data stores in different formats as well as facilitates the storage of sparse data. More details on HBase can be found in [HBAS].

4.2.2.6   MongoDB

MongoDB is a NoSQL database. It is a cross-platform open-source distributed database. It has been used to store and manage documents. That is, it is mainly a document-oriented database. The documents are stored in a JSON-like format [CROC2006]. It supports both field and range queries as well as regular expression-based searches. It supports data replication and load balancing, which occurs through horizontal scaling. The batch processing of data as well as aggregation operations can be carried out through MapReduce. More details of MongoDB can be found at [MONG] and [CHOD2010].

4.2.2.7 Apache Cassandra

Cassandra is a NoSQL distributed database [HEWI2010]. It was first developed at Facebook to power the Facebook applications and then became an Apache foundation open software initiative. It was designed with no single point of failure in mind. It supports clusters that span multiple data centers. All the nodes in a cluster perform the same function. As a result, there is virtually no single point of failure. It supports replication and is highly scalable. It is also fault tolerant and is integrated with Hadoop with support for MapReduce. The query language supported by Cassandra is Cassandra Query Language (CQL), which is an alternative to SQL. It can also be accessed from programs such as Java, C++, and Python. More details of Cassandra can be found at [CASS].

4.2.2.8 Apache CouchDB

As stated in [COUC], CouchDB enables one to access data by implementing the Couch Replication Protocol. This protocol has been implemented by numerous platforms from clusters to the web to mobile phones. It is a NoSQL database and implemented in a concurrent language called Erlang. It uses javaScript object notation (JSON) to store the data and JavaScript for the query language. More details on CouchDB can be found in [COUC] and [ANDE2010].

4.2.2.9 Oracle NoSQL Database

Oracle is one of the premier relational database vendors and they have marketed relational database products since the late 1970s. They offered object-relational database products in the 1990s and more recently the NoSQL database. The NoSQL database is based on the key value paid model. Each row has a unique key and has a value that is of arbitrary length and interpreted by the applicant. Oracle NoSQL database is a shared-nothing system and is distributed across what are called multiple shards in a cluster. The data is replicated in the storage nodes within a shard for availability. The data can be accessed via programs such as those written in Java, C, Python as well as RESTful web services. More details on the Oracle NoSQL database can be found at [ORAC].

4.2.2.10 Weka

Weka is an open-source software product that implements a collection of data mining techniques from association rule mining to classification to clustering. It has been designed, developed, and maintained by Mankato University in New Zealand. Weka 3, a version of Weka, operated on big datasets. While earlier versions of Weka required the entire datasets to be loaded into memory to carry out say classification, the big data version carried out incremental loading and classification. Weka 3 also supports distributed data mining with Map and Reduce tasks. It also provides wrappers for Hadoop and Spark. More details on Weka can be found at [WEKA].

4.2.2.11 Apache Mahout

The Apache Mahout provides an environment to implement a collection of machine learning systems. These systems are scalable and implemented on top of Hadoop. The machine learning algorithms include classification and clustering. The instructions of the machine learning algorithms are transformed into MapReduce jobs and executed on Hadoop. Mahout provides Java libraries to implement the mathematics and statistical techniques involved in machine learning algorithms. The goal is for the machine learning algorithms to operate on very large datasets. In summary, as stated in [MAHO], Mahout provides the following three features: "(i) a simple and extensible programming environment and framework for building scalable algorithms, (ii) a wide variety of premade algorithms for Scala + Apache Spark, H2O, and Apache Flink, and (iii) Samsara, a vector math experimentation environment with R-like syntax which works at scale." More details on Mahout can be found at [MAHO].

4.3 CLOUD COMPUTING

4.3.1 CLOUD COMPUTING MODELS

As stated in [CLOUD], cloud computing delivers computing as a service while in traditional computing it is provided in the form of a product. Therefore, users pay for the services based on a pay-as-you-go model. The services provided by a cloud may include hardware services, systems services, data services, and storage services. Users of the cloud need not know where the software and data are located; that is, the software and data services provided by the cloud are transparent to the user. NIST has defined cloud computing to be the following [NIST]:

> Cloud computing is a model for enabling ubiquitous, convenient, on-demand network access to a shared pool of configurable computing resources (e.g., networks, servers, storage, applications, and services) that can be rapidly provisioned and released with minimal management effort or service provider interaction.

The cloud model is composed of multiple deployment models and service models. These models are described next.

4.3.1.1 Cloud Deployment Models

There are multiple deployment models for cloud computing. These include the public cloud, community cloud, hybrid cloud, and the private cloud. In a public cloud, the service provider typically provides the services over the World Wide Web (WWW) that can be accessed by the general public. Such a cloud may provide free services or pay-as-you-go services. In a community cloud, a group of organizations get together and develop a cloud. These organizations may have a common objective to provide features such as security and fault tolerance. The cost is shared among the organizations. Furthermore, the cloud may be hosted by the organizations or by a third party. A private cloud is a cloud infrastructure developed specifically for an organization. This could be hosted by the organization or by a third party. A hybrid cloud consists of a combination of public and private clouds. This way in a hybrid cloud an organization may use the private cloud for highly sensitive services, while it may use the public cloud for less sensitive services and take advantage of what the WWW has to offer. Kantarcioglu and his colleagues have stated that the hybrid cloud is deployment model of the future [KHAD2012a]. Figure 4.3 illustrates the cloud deployment models.

4.3.1.2 Service Models

As stated earlier, cloud computing provides a variety of services. These include Infrastructure as a Service (IaaS), Platform as a Service (PaaS), Software as a Service (SaaS), and Data as a Service (DaaS). In IaaS, the cloud provides a collection of hardware and networks for use by

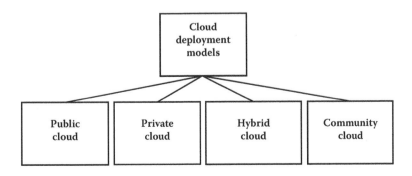

FIGURE 4.3 Cloud deployment models.

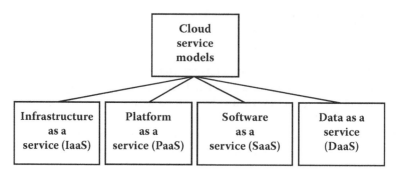

FIGURE 4.4 Cloud service models.

the general public or organizations. The users install operation systems and software to run the applications. The users will be billed according to the resources they utilize for their computing. In PaaS, the cloud provider will provide to users the systems software such as operating systems and execution environments. The users will load applications and run them on the hardware and software infrastructures provided by the cloud. In SaaS, the cloud provider will provide the applications for the users to run. These applications could be billing applications, tax computing applications, and sales tools. The cloud users access the applications through cloud clients. In the case of DaaS, the cloud provides data to the cloud users. Data may be stored in data centers that are accessed by the cloud users. Note that while DaaS used to denote Desktop as a Service, more recently it denotes Data as a Service. Figure 4.4 illustrates the services models.

4.3.2 Virtualization

Virtualization essentially means creating something virtual and not actual. It could be hardware, software, memory, and data. The notion of virtualization has existed for decades with respect to computing. Back in the 1960s, the concept of virtual memory was introduced. This virtual memory gives the application program the illusion, which has contiguous working memory. Mapping is developed to map the virtual memory to the actual physical memory.

Hardware virtualization is a basic notion in cloud computing. This essentially creates virtual machines hosted on a real computer with an operating system. This means while the actual machine may be running a Windows operating system, through virtualization it may provide a Linux machine to the users. The actual machine is called the host machine while the virtual machine is called the guest machine. The term "virtual machine monitor," also known as the hypervisor, is the software that runs the virtual machine on the host computer.

Other types of virtualization include operating system (OS) level virtualization, storage virtualization, data virtualization, and database virtualization. In OS level virtualization, multiple virtual environments are created within a single operating system. In storage virtualization, the logical storage is abstracted from the physical storage. In data virtualization, the data is abstracted from the underlying databases. In network virtualization, a virtual network is created. Figure 4.5 illustrates the various types of virtualizations.

As we have stated earlier, at the heart of cloud computing is the notion of a hypervisor or the virtual machine monitor. Hardware virtualization techniques allow multiple operating systems (called guests) to run concurrently on a host computer. These multiple operating systems share virtualized hardware resources. Hypervisor is not a new term; it was first used in the mid-1960s in the IBM 360/65 machines. There are different types of hypervisors; in one type the hypervisor runs on the host hardware and manages the guest operating systems. Both VMware and XEN, which are popular virtual machines, are based on this model. In another model, the hypervisor runs within a

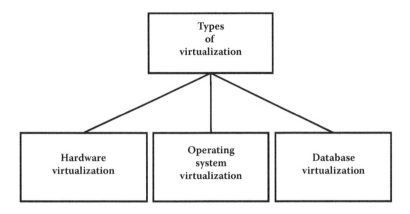

FIGURE 4.5 Types of virtualization.

conventional operating system environment. Virtual machines are also incorporated into embedded systems and mobile phones. Embedded hypervisors have real-time processing capability. Some details of virtualization are provided in [VIRT].

4.3.3 CLOUD STORAGE AND DATA MANAGEMENT

In a cloud storage model, the service providers store massive amounts of data for customers in data centers. Those who require storage space will lease the storage from the service providers who are the hosting companies. The actual location of the data is transparent to the users. What is presented to the users is virtualized storage; the storage managers will map the virtual storage with the actual storage and manage the data resources for the customers. A single object (e.g., the entire video database of a customer) may be stored in multiple locations. Each location may store objects for multiple customers. Figure 4.6 illustrates cloud storage management.

Virtualizing cloud storage has many advantages. Users need not purchase expensive storage devices. Data could be placed anywhere in the cloud. Maintenance such as backup and recovery are provided by the cloud. The goal is for users to have rapid access to the cloud. However, due to the fact that the owner of the data does not have complete control of his data, there are serious security concerns with respect to storing data in the cloud.

A database that runs on the cloud is a cloud database manager. There are multiple ways to utilize a cloud database manager. In the first model, for users to run databases on the cloud, a *virtual machine image* must be purchased. The database is then run on the virtual machines. The second model is the database as a service model; the service provider will maintain the databases. The users will make

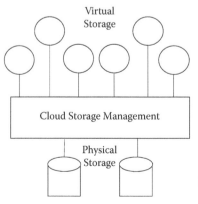

FIGURE 4.6 Cloud storage management.

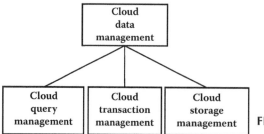

FIGURE 4.7   Cloud data management.

use of the database services and pay for the service. An example is the Amazon relational database service, which is a SQL database service and has a MySQL interface [AMAZ]. A third model is the cloud provider, which hosts a database on behalf of the user. Users can either utilize the database service maintained by the cloud or they can run their databases on the cloud. A cloud database must optimize its query, storage, and transaction processing to take full advantage of the services provided by the cloud. Figure 4.7 illustrates cloud data management.

4.3.4 CLOUD PLATFORMS

In this section, we will discuss how some cloud service providers are supporting big data management. In particular, we discuss Amazon's DynamoDB and Microsoft's Cosmos DB. Then we discuss the cloud-based big data solutions provided by IBM and Google.

4.3.4.1 Amazon Web Services' DynamoDB

Dynamo is a NoSQL database, which is part of Amazon Web Services (AWS) product portfolio. It supports both document and the key value store models. High performance and high throughput are the goals of DynamoDB. With respect to storage, DynamoDB can expand and shrink as needed by the applications. It also has an in-memory cache called Amazon DynamoDB Accelerator that can provide millisecond responses for millions of requests per second. More details on DynamoDB can be found at [DYNA].

4.3.4.2 Microsoft Azure's Cosmos DB

Cosmos DB is a database that runs on Microsoft's cloud platform, Azure. It was developed with scalability and high performance in mind. It has a distributed model with replication of availability. Its scalable architecture enables the support for multiple data models and programming languages. As stated in [COSM],

> the core type system of Azure Cosmos DB's database engine is atom-record-sequence (ARS) based. Atoms consist of a small set of primitive types e.g., string, Boolean, number, etc. Records are structs and sequences are arrays consisting of atoms, records or sequences.

Developers use the Cosmos DB by provisioning a database account. The notion of a container is used to store the stored procedures, triggers, and user-defined functions. The entities under that database account include the containers as well as the databases and permissions. These entities are called resources. Data in containers is horizontally partitioned. More details of the Cosmos DB can be found in [COSM].

4.3.4.3 IBM's Cloud-Based Big Data Solutions

IBM is a leader in cloud computing including managing big data in the cloud. It has developed an architecture using a collection of hardware and software that can host a number of big data systems. IBM offers database as a service and provides support for data management as well as data analytics. For example, Cloudant is a NoSQL data layer. The dashDB system is a cloud-based data analytics system that carries out analytics. ElephantSQL is an open source database running in the cloud. In addition, the IBM cloud also provides support for a number of data management capabilities, including for stream computing and content management. More details on IBM's cloud big data solutions can be found in [IBM].

4.3.4.4   Google's Cloud-Based Big Data Solutions

The Google cloud platform is a comprehensive collection of hardware and software that enables the users to obtain various services from Google. The cloud supports both the Hadoop/MapReduce as well as the Spark platforms. In addition to the users accessing the data in BigTable and BigQuery, Google also provides solutions for carrying out analytics as well as accessing systems such as YouTube. More details on Google's cloud platform can be found in [GOOG].

4.4   SEMANTIC WEB

4.4.1   SEMANTIC WEB TECHNOLOGIES

As we have mentioned earlier in this chapter, some of our experimental big data systems we have developed have utilized cloud and semantic web technologies. While cloud computing was the subject of Section 4.3, in this section we will provide an overview of semantic web technologies.

While the current web technologies facilitate the integration of information from a syntactic point of view, there is still a lot to be done to handle the different semantics of various systems and applications. That is, current web technologies depend a lot on the "human-in-the-loop" for information management and integration. Tim Berners Lee, the father of the WWW, realized the inadequacies of current web technologies and subsequently strived to make the web more intelligent. His goal was to have a web that would essentially alleviate humans from the burden of having to integrate disparate information sources as well as to carry out extensive searches. He then came to the conclusion that one needs machine-understandable web pages and the use of ontologies for information integration. This resulted in the notion of the semantic web [LEE2001]. The web services that take advantage of semantic web technologies are semantic web services.

A semantic web can be thought of as a web that is highly intelligent and sophisticated so that one needs little or no human intervention to carry out tasks such as scheduling appointments, coordinating activities, searching for complex documents, as well as integrating disparate databases and information systems. While much progress has been made toward developing such an intelligent web, there is still a lot to be done. For example, technologies such as ontology matching, intelligent agents, and markup languages are contributing a lot toward developing the semantic web. Nevertheless, one still needs the human to make decisions and take actions. Since the 2000s, there have been many developments on the semantic web. The World Wide Web Consortium (W3C) is specifying standards for the semantic web [W3C]. These standards include specifications for XML (eXtensible Markup Language), RDF (Resource Description Framework), and interoperability (see also [AKIV2012, ALIP2010a, ALIP2010b, KHAN2002, KHAN2004, and PART2011]).

Figure 4.8 illustrates the layered technology stack for the semantic web. This is the stack that was developed by Tim Berners Lee. Essentially the semantic web consists of layers where each layer takes advantage of the technologies of the previous layer. The lowest layer is the protocol layer and this is usually not included in the discussion of the semantic technologies. The next layer is the XML layer. XML is a document representation language. While XML is sufficient to specify syntax, semantics such as "the creator of document D is John" is hard to specify in XML. Therefore, the W3C developed RDF, which uses XML syntax. The semantic web community then went further and came up with a specification of ontologies in languages such as OWL (Web

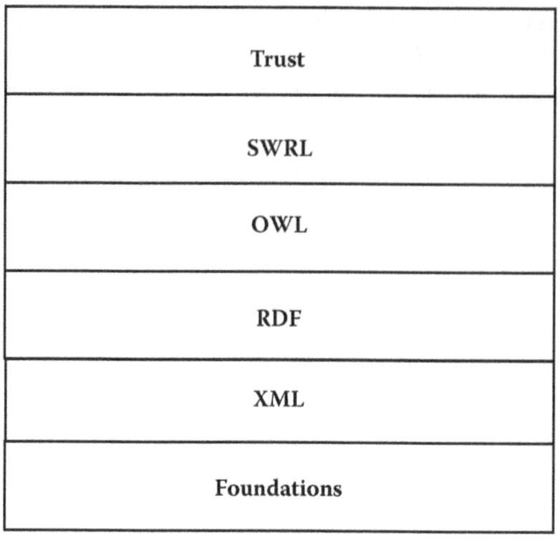

Trust
SWRL
OWL
RDF
XML
Foundations

FIGURE 4.8   Technology stack for the semantic web.

Ontology Language). Note that OWL addresses the inadequacies of RDF. In order to reason about various policies, the semantic web community has come up with web rules language such as SWRL (Semantic Web Rules Language). Next, we will describe the various technologies that constitute the semantic web.

4.4.1.1   XML

XML is needed due to the limitations of HTML (Hypertext Markup Language) and complexities of SGML (Standard Generalized Markup Language). XML is an extensible markup language specified by the W3C and designed to make the interchange of structured documents over the Internet easier. An important aspect of XML used to be Document Type Definitions (DTDs), which define the role of each element of text in a formal model. XML schemas have now become critical to specify the structure of data. XML schemas are also XML documents [BRAY1997].

4.4.1.2   RDF

The RDF is a standard for describing resources on the semantic web. It provides a common framework for expressing this information so it can be exchanged between applications without loss of meaning. RDF is based on the idea of identifying things using web identifiers (called Uniform Resource Identifiers, or URIs), and describing resources in terms of simple properties and property values [KLYN2004].

RDF has a formal semantics, which provide a dependable basis for reasoning about the meaning of an RDF graph. This reasoning is usually called entailment. Entailment rules state which implicit information can be inferred from explicit information. In general, it is not assumed that complete information about any resource is available in an RDF query. A query language should be aware of this and tolerate incomplete or contradicting information. The notion of class and operations on classes are specified in RDF through the concept of RDF Schema [ANTO2008].

4.4.1.3   SPARQL

SPARQL (Simple Protocol and RDF Query Language) [PRUD2006] is a powerful query language. It is a key semantic web technology and was standardized by the RDF Data Access Working Group of the W3C. SPARQL syntax is similar to SQL, but it has the advantage whereby it enables queries to span multiple disparate data sources that consist of heterogeneous and semi-structured data. SPARQL is based around graph pattern matching [PRUD2006].

4.4.1.4 OWL

The Web Ontology Language (OWL) [MCGU2004] is an ontology language that has more expressive power and reasoning capabilities than RDF and RDF Schema (RDF-S). It has additional vocabulary along with a formal semantics. OWL has three increasingly expressive sub-languages: OWL Lite, OWL DL, and OWL Full. These are designed for use by specific communities of implementers and users. The formal semantics in OWL is based on description logics (DL), which is a decidable fragment of first-order logics.

4.4.1.5 Description Logics

Description logics (DL) is a family of knowledge representation (KR) formalisms that represent the knowledge of an application domain [BAAD2003]. It defines the concepts of the domain (i.e., its terminology) as sets of objects called classes, and it uses these concepts to specify properties of objects and individuals occurring in the domain. Description logic is characterized by a set of constructors that allow one to build complex concepts and roles from atomic ones.

4.4.1.6 SWRL

The Semantic Web Rule Language (SWRL) extends the set of OWL axioms to include horn-like rules, and it extends the horn-like rules to be combined with an OWL knowledge base [HORR2004]. The proposed rules are of the form of an implication between an antecedent (body) and a consequent (head). The intended meaning can be read as: whenever the conditions specified in the antecedent hold, the conditions specified in the consequent must also hold. Both the antecedent (body) and consequent (head) consist of zero or more atoms. An empty antecedent is treated as trivially true (i.e., satisfied by every interpretation), so the consequent must also be satisfied by every interpretation. An empty consequent is treated as trivially false (i.e., not satisfied by any interpretation), so the antecedent must not be satisfied by any interpretation. Multiple atoms are treated as a conjunction, and both the head and body can contain conjunction of such atoms. Note that rules with conjunctive consequents could easily be transformed (via Lloyd-Topor transformations) into multiple rules each with an atomic consequent.

4.4.2 Semantic Web and Security

We first provide an overview of security issues for the semantic web and then discuss some details on XML security, RDF security, and secure information integration, which are components of the secure semantic web. As more progress is made on investigating these various issues, we hope that appropriate standards would be developed for securing the semantic web. Security cannot be considered in isolation. Security cuts across all layers.

For example, consider the lowest layer. One needs secure TCP/IP, secure sockets, and secure HTTP. There are now security protocols for these various lower layer protocols. One needs end-to-end security. That is, one cannot just have secure TCP/IP built on untrusted communication layers; we need network security. The next layer is XML and XML schemas. One needs secure XML. That is, access must be controlled to various portions of the document for reading, browsing, and modifications. There is research on securing XML and XML schemas. The next step is securing RDF. Now with RDF not only do we need secure XML, we also need security for the interpretations and semantics. For example, under certain contexts, portions of the document may be *unclassified* while under certain other contexts the document may be *classified*.

Once XML and RDF have been secured, the next step is to examine security for ontologies and interoperation. That is, ontologies may have security levels attached to them. Certain parts of the ontologies could be *secret* while certain other parts may be *unclassified*. The challenge is how does one use these ontologies for secure information integration? Researchers have done some work on the secure interoperability of databases. We need to revisit this research and then determine what else needs to be done so that the information on the web can be managed, integrated, and exchanged securely. Logic, proof, and trust are at the highest layers of the semantic web. That is, how can we trust the information that the web gives us? Next we will discuss the various security issues for XML, RDF, ontologies, and rules.

4.4.2.1 XML Security

Various research efforts have been reported on XML security (see, e.g., [BERT2002]. We briefly discuss some of the key points. The main challenge is whether to give access to all the XML documents or to parts of the documents. Bertino et al. have developed authorization models for XML. They have focused on access control policies as well as on dissemination policies. They also considered push and pull architectures. They specified the policies in XML. The policy specification contains information about which users can access which portions of the documents. In [BERT2002], algorithms for access control as well as computing views of the results are presented. In addition, architectures for securing XML documents are also discussed. In [BERT2004] and [BHAT2004], the authors go further and describe how XML documents may be published on the web. The idea is for owners to publish documents, subjects request access to the documents, and untrusted publishers give the subjects the views of the documents they are authorized to see. W3C is specifying standards for XML security. The XML security project is focusing on providing the implementation of security standards for XML. The focus is on XML-Signature Syntax and Processing, XML-Encryption Syntax and Processing, and XML Key Management. While the standards are focusing on what can be implemented in the near-term, much research is needed on securing XML documents (see also [SHE2009]).

4.4.2.2 RDF Security

RDF is the foundation of the semantic web. While XML is limited in providing machine understandable documents, RDF handles this limitation. As a result, RDF provides better support for interoperability as well as searching and cataloging. It also describes contents of documents as well as relationships between various entities in the document. While XML provides syntax and notations, RDF supplements this by providing semantic information in a standardized way [ANTO2008].

The basic RDF model has three components: they are resources, properties, and statements. Resource is anything described by RDF expressions. It could be a web page or a collection of pages. Property is a specific attribute used to describe a resource. RDF statements are resources together with a named property plus the value of the property. Statement components are subject, predicate, and object. So, for example, if we have a sentence of the form "John is the creator of xxx," then xxx is the subject or resource, property or predicate is "creator," and object or literal is "John." There are RDF diagrams very much like, say, the entity relationship diagrams or object diagrams to represent statements. It is important that the intended interpretation be used for RDF sentences. This is accomplished by RDF schemas. Schema is a sort of a dictionary and has interpretations of various terms used in sentences.

More advanced concepts in RDF include the container model and statements about statements. The container model has three types of container objects and they are bag, sequence, and alternative. A bag is an unordered list of resources or literals. It is used to mean that a property has multiple values but the order is not important. A sequence is a list of ordered resources. Here the order is important. Alternative is a list of resources that represent alternatives for the value of a property. Various tutorials in RDF describe the syntax of containers in more detail. RDF also provides support for making statements about other statements. For example, with this facility one can make statements of the form "The statement A is false," where A is the statement "John is the creator of X." Again, one can use object-like diagrams to represent containers and statements about statements. RDF also has a formal model associated with it. This formal model has a formal grammar. The query language to access RDF document is SPARQL. For further information on

RDF, we refer to the excellent discussion in the book by Antoniou and van Harmelen [ANTO2008].

Now to make the semantic web secure, we need to ensure that RDF documents are secure. This would involve securing XML from a syntactic point of view. However, with RDF, we also need to ensure that security is preserved at the semantic level. The issues include the security implications of the concepts resource, properties, and statements. That is, how is access control ensured? How can statements and properties about statements be protected? How can one provide access control at a finer grain of granularity? What are the security properties of the container model? How can bags, lists, and alternatives be protected? Can we specify security policies in RDF? How can we resolve semantic inconsistencies for the policies? What are the security implications of statements about statements? How can we protect RDF schemas? These are difficult questions and we need to start research to provide answers. XML security is just the beginning. Securing RDF is much more challenging (see also [CARM2004]).

4.4.2.3   Security and Ontologies

Ontologies are essentially representations of various concepts in order to avoid ambiguity. Numerous ontologies have been developed. These ontologies have been used by agents to understand the web pages and conduct operations such as the integration of databases. Furthermore, ontologies can be represented in languages such as RDF or special languages such as web ontology language (OWL). Now, ontologies have to be secure. That is, access to the ontologies has to be controlled. This means that different users may have access to different parts of the ontology. On the other hand, ontologies may be used to specify security policies just as XML and RDF have been used to specify the policies. That is, we will describe how ontologies may be secured as well as how ontologies may be used to specify the various policies.

4.4.2.4   Secure Query and Rules Processing

The layer above the Secure RDF layer is the Secure Query and Rule processing layer. While RDF can be used to specify security policies (see, e.g., [CARM2004]), the web rules language developed by W3C is more powerful to specify complex policies. Furthermore, inference engines developed to process and reason about the rules (e.g., the Pellet engine developed at the University of Maryland). One could integrate ideas from the database inference controller that we have developed (see [THUR1993]) with web rules processing to develop an inference or privacy controller for the semantic web. The query processing module is responsible for accessing the heterogeneous data and information sources on the semantic web. Researchers are examining ways to integrate techniques from web query processing with semantic web technologies to locate, query and integrate the heterogeneous data and information sources.

4.4.3   Cloud Computing Frameworks Based on Semantic Web Technologies

In this section, we introduce a cloud computing framework that we have utilized in the implementation of our systems for malware detection as well as social media applications, some of which are discussed in this book. In particular, we will discuss our framework for RDF integration and provenance data integration.

4.4.3.1   RDF Integration

We have developed an RDF-based policy engine for use in the cloud for various applications, including social media and information sharing applications. The reasons for using RDF as our data model are as follows: (i) RDF allows us to achieve data interoperability between the seemingly disparate sources of information that are catalogued by each agency/organization separately. (ii) The use of RDF allows participating agencies to create data-centric applications that make use of the integrated data that is now available to them. (iii) Since RDF does not require the use of an explicit schema for data generation, it can be easily adapted to ever-changing user requirements. The policy engine's flexibility is based on its accepting high-level policies and executing them as rules/constraints over a directed RDF graph representation of the provenance and its associated data. The strength of our policy engine is that it can handle any type of policy that could be represented using RDF technologies, horn logic rules (e.g., SWRL) and OWL constraints. The power of these semantic web technologies can be successfully harnessed in a cloud computing environment to provide the user with capability to efficiently store and retrieve data for data intensive applications. Storing RDF data in the cloud brings a number of new features such as scalability and on-demand services, resources and services for users on demand, ability to pay for services and capacity as needed, location independence, guarantee quality of service for users in terms of hardware/CPU performance, bandwidth, and memory capacity. We have examined the following efforts in developing our framework for RDF integration.

In [SUN2010], the authors adopted the idea of Hexastore and considered both RDF data model and HBase capability. They stored RDF triples into six HBase tables (S_PO, P_SO, O_SP, PS_O, SO_P, and PO_S), which covered all combinations of RDF triple patterns. They indexed the triples with HBase-provided index structure on row key. They also proposed a MapReduce strategy for SPARQL Basic Graph Pattern (BGP) processing, which is suitable for their storage schema. This strategy uses multiple MapReduce jobs to process a typical BGP. In each job, it uses a greedy method to select join key and eliminates multiple triple patterns. Their evaluation result indicated that their approach worked well against large RDF datasets. In [HUSA2009], the authors described a framework that uses Hadoop to store and retrieve large numbers of RDF triples. They described a schema to store RDF data in the HDFS. They also presented algorithms to answer SPARQL queries. This made use of Hadoop's MapReduce framework to actually answer the queries. In [HUAN2011], the authors introduced a scalable RDF data management system. They introduced techniques for (i) leveraging state-of-the-art single node RDF-store technology, and (ii) partitioning the data across nodes in a manner that helps accelerate query processing through locality optimizations. In [PAPA2012], the authors presented H2RDF, which is a fully distributed RDF store that combines the MapReduce processing framework with a NoSQL distributed data store. Their system features unique characteristics that enable efficient processing of both simple and multi-join SPARQL queries on virtually unlimited number of triples. These include join algorithms that execute joins according to query selectivity to reduce processing, and include adaptive choice among centralized and distributed (MapReduce-based) join execution for fast query responses. They claim that their system can efficiently answer both simple joins and complex multivariate queries, as well as scale up to three billion triples using a small cluster consisting of nine worker nodes. In [KHAD2012b], the authors designed a Jena-HBase framework. Their HBase-backed triple store can be used with the Jena framework. Jena-HBase provides end users with a scalable storage and querying solution that supports all features from the RDF specification. More details of HBase can be found in [HBASE] and [GEOR2011].

4.4.3.2   Provenance Integration

While our approach for assured information sharing in the cloud for social networking applications is general enough for any type of data including cyber security data, we have utilized provenance data as an example. We will discuss the various approaches that we have examined in our work on provenance data integration. More details of our work can be found in [THUR2014].

In [IKED2011], the authors considered a class of workflows which they call generalized map and reduce workflows (GMRWs). The input datasets are processed by an acyclic graph of map and reduce functions to produce output results. They also showed how data provenance (lineage) can be captured for map and reduce functions transparently. In [CHEB2013], the authors explored and addressed the challenge of efficient and scalable storage and querying of large collections of provenance graphs serialized as RDF graphs in an Apache HBase database. In [PARK2011], they proposed RAMP (Reduce and Map Provenance) as an extension to Hadoop that supports provenance capture and tracing for workflows of MapReduce jobs. The work discussed in [ABRA2010] proposed a system to show how HBase Bigtable-like capabilities can be leveraged for distributed storage and querying of provenance data represented in RDF. In particular, their ProvBase system incorporates an HBase/Hadoop backend, a storage schema to hold provenance triples, and a querying algorithm to evaluate SPARQL queries in their system. In [AKOU2013], the authors' research introduced HadoopProv, a modified version of Hadoop that implements provenance capture and analysis in MapReduce jobs. Their system is designed to minimize provenance capture overheads by (i) treating provenance tracking in Map and Reduce phases separately, and (ii) deferring construction of the provenance graph to the query stage. The provenance graphs are later joined on matching intermediate keys of the Map and Reduce provenance files.

4.5 ANALYZING AND SECURING SOCIAL NETWORKS

4.5.1 INTRODUCTION TO SOCIAL NETWORKS

Online Social Networks (OSNs) have gained a lot of popularity on the Internet and become an important research topic attracting many professionals from diverse areas. Since the advent of OSNs sites like Facebook, Twitter, and LinkedIn, OSNs continue to impact and change every aspect of our lives. From politics to business marketing, from celebrities to newsmakers, everyone is hooked on the phenomenon. Facebook is used to connect with friends and share various personal and professional data as well as photos and videos; LinkedIn is entirely a professional network that is used to connect to colleagues. Google+ is similar to Facebook while Twitter is a free social networking and micro-blogging service that enables users to send and read messages known as tweets. Tweets are text posts of around 140 characters displayed on the author's profile page and delivered to the author's subscribers who are known as *followers*. Each network has its own set of advantages and the networks make money mainly through advertising since the services they provide are largely free of charge unless of course one wants to get premium service in networks such as LinkedIn.

Much of our work on social media analytics has focused on analyzing tweets. In particular, we have analyzed tweets for detecting suspicious people as well as analyzing sentiments. Also, many of the experimental systems we have developed have focused on social media data represented using semantic web technologies. Our work has also examined Facebook and studied the information people post and determined whether one could extract sensitive attributes of the users. We have also used semantic web-based representations of social networks in our work on social network access control. We discuss social media analytics applications and then discuss security and privacy issues. Part IV will discuss a system that we have developed for analyzing and securing semantic web-based social media systems. Figure 4.9 illustrates aspects social media analytics, security and privacy. The key points will be elaborated in Sections 4.6.2 through 4.6.4. More details can be found in [THUR2016].

4.5.2 SOCIAL MEDIA ANALYTICS APPLICATIONS

4.5.2.1 Applications Extracting Demographics

In this task, the social media data are analyzed and demographics data such as location and age are extracted. If a social media user has already specified his or her location, then there is no further work to do here. Otherwise, one simple way to extract location is to check the locations of one's friends and then determine the location with the assumption that one lives near one's friends. The age attribute can be extracted by checking LinkedIn to see when a person graduated and then compute the age. It should be noted that there could be deviations from the norm and so there is a potential for false positives and negatives.

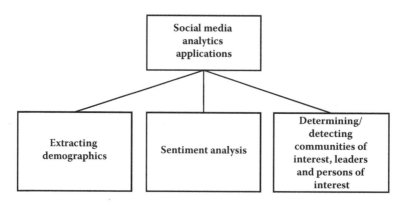

FIGURE 4.9 Social media analytics, security, and privacy.

4.5.2.2   Sentiment Analysis

Here one analyzes the tweets and extracts words such as "I like Pizza" or "I dislike chocolates." The idea here is to analyze the tweets of the various individuals and determine what the sentiments are toward a particular item such as pizza or chocolate or a topic such as sports or music.

4.5.2.3   Detecting Communities of Interest

Certain people in a network will have similar goals and interests. Therefore from the posts in Facebook, one can connect the various people with similar interests so that they can form a community. The analysis here will be to extract the individuals of similar interests and connect them.

4.5.2.4   Determining Leaders

In this application, one analyzes the network to see three numbers of connections that a person has and also the strength of the relationships. If many people are connected to a person or follow a person, then that person will emerge as a leader. There are obvious leaders such as celebrities and politicians and non-obvious leaders who can extract by analyzing the network.

4.5.2.5   Detecting Persons of Interest

If, say, communicating with a person from a particular country makes a person suspicious, then that person could be a person of interest. This way the person can be investigated further. Often persons of interest are not straightforward to find like communicating with a person from a particular country. Therefore, the challenge is to extract the hidden links and relationships through data analytics techniques.

4.5.2.6   Determining Political Affiliation

The idea here is to determine the political affiliations of individuals even though they have not specified explicitly whether he or she is a liberal or a conservative. In this case, one can examine the political leaders they admire (e.g., Margaret Thatcher or Hillary Clinton) and whether they go to church or not and make a determination as to whether the person is a liberal or a conservative.

The above examples are just a few of the applications. There are numerous other applications such as determining gender biases, detecting suspicious behavior, and even predicting future events. These SNA (Social Networks Analysis/Analytics) techniques use various analytics tools that carry out association rule mining, clustering, classification, and anomaly detection among others. We discuss how the various data mining techniques are applied for SNA in the next section.

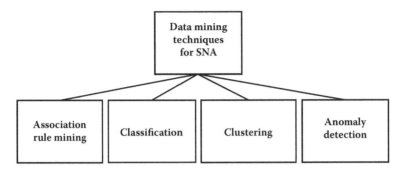

FIGURE 4.10   Data mining techniques for SNA.

4.5.3   Data Mining for Social Networks

Chapter 3 provided an overview of some of the data mining techniques that we have used in our work as well as some other techniques that have been proposed for SNA. In this section, we will examine how various data mining techniques are being applied for SNA. The objective of these techniques is to extract the nuggets for the various applications such as determining demographics and detecting suspicious behavior. Figure 4.10 illustrates the various data mining techniques that are being applied for SNA.

4.5.3.1   Association Rule Mining

Association rule mining techniques extract rules from vast quantities of information. These rules determine items that are purchased together or people who are seen together. Therefore, within the context of SNA, association rule mining techniques will extract rules that specify the people who have a strong relationship to each other.

4.5.3.2   Classification

Classification techniques will determine classes from a set of predefined criteria. Appling such techniques for SNA, one can form communities of interest. For example, one community may consist of the individuals who like tennis, while another community may consist of individuals who like golf. Note that there is a predefined criterion where a person likes sports if he/she plays the sport and he/she also watches the sport.

4.5.3.3   Clustering

Clustering techniques will form groups when there are no predefined criteria. Therefore by analyzing the data, one extracts patterns such as people who live in the northeast smoke mostly cigarettes while people who live in the southwest smoke mostly cigars.

4.5.3.4   Anomaly Detection

Anomaly detection techniques determine variations to the norm. For example, everyone in John's social network likes watching spy movies except Paul and Jane.

4.5.3.5   Web Mining

Web mining techniques have a natural application for SNA. This is because the WWW can be regarded to be a network where the nodes are the web pages and links are the links between the web pages. Therefore, web structure mining determines how the web pages are connected to each other while web content mining will analyze tube contents of the WWW. Web log mining will analyze the visits to a web page. Similarly, one can mine the social graphs and extract the structure of the graph. The contents of the graphs (that is, the data) can be mined to extract the various patterns. One can also mine the visits to, say, a Facebook page, which is analogous to web log mining.

4.5.4 Security and Privacy

Due to data mining, users can access information about the various members of social networks and extract sensitive information. This could include financial data, health data, and travel data, which an individual may want to keep private. Additional sensitive information that can be extracted includes political affiliations and gender preferences as well as drinking and smoking habits. In our previous work we examined various privacy violations that occur in social media data due to data mining and analytics. We have applied various data analytics techniques and have shown how private information can be inferred [ABRO2016].

Another aspect of security is confidentiality. That is, access to the sensitive information in social media has to be controlled. Users should have the option to grant access to only certain friends. Furthermore, one may place more trust on some friends. We have examined access control for social networks represented using semantic web technologies. We also developed experimental systems including inference control in social networks as well as cloud-based assured information sharing

4.6 SUMMARY AND DIRECTIONS

In this chapter, we have discussed three types of big data systems. First, we discussed what we call infrastructures to host big data systems. These are essentially massive data processing platforms such as the Apache Hadoop, Spark, Storm, and Flink. Then we discussed various big data management systems. These included SQL-based systems and NoSQL-based systems. This was followed by a discussion of big data management and analytics systems. We have experimented with several of these systems. They include Apache Hadoop, Storm, MapReduce, Hive, MongoDB, and Weka.

We believe that big data technologies have exploded over the past decade. Many of the systems we have discussed in this chapter did not exist just 15 years ago. We expect the technologies to continue to explode. Therefore, it is important for us to not only keep up with the literature but also experiment with the big data technologies. As progress is made, we will have a better idea as to what system to use when, where, why, and how.

Next, we introduced the notions of the cloud and semantic web technologies. We first discussed concepts in cloud computing including aspects of virtualization. We also discussed the various service models and deployment models for the cloud and provided a brief overview of cloud functions such as storage management and data management. In addition, some of the cloud platforms, especially as they relate to big data technologies, were also discussed. Next, we discussed technologies for the semantic web, including XML, RDF, Ontologies, and OWL. This was followed by a discussion of security issues for the semantic web. Finally, we discussed cloud computing frameworks based on semantic web technologies. More details on cloud computing and semantic web can be found in [THUR2007] and [THUR2014].

Our discussion of cloud computing and semantic web will be useful in understanding some of the experimental systems discussed in Part IV of this book. For example, we have discussed experimental secure very large data processing systems that function in a cloud. We have also discussed assured information sharing in the cloud where the data is represented using semantic web technologies. Big data, cloud, and semantic web are some of the foundational data science technologies needed for the discussions in Part IV.

REFERENCES

[ABRA2010] J. Abraham, P. Brazier, A. Chebotko, J. Navarro, A. Piazza, Distributed Storage and Querying Techniques for a Semantic Web of Scientific Workflow Provenance, *Proceedings Services Computing (SCC), 2010 IEEE International Conference on Services Computing*, 2010, Miami, FL, 178–185.

[AKIV2012] N. Akiva, M. Koppel, Identifying Distinct Components of a Multi-author Document, *EISIC*, 2012, 205–209.

[AKOU2013] S. Akoush, R. Sohan, A. Hopper, HadoopProv: Towards Provenance as a First-Class Citizen in MapReduce, *Proceedings of the 5th USENIX Workshop on the Theory and Practice of Provenance*, 2013, Lombard, IL.

[ALIP2010a] N. Alipanah, P. Parveen, S. Menezes, L. Khan, S. Seida, B.M. Thuraisingham, Ontology-Driven Query Expansion Methods to Facilitate Federated Queries, *SOCA*, Perth, Australia, 2010, 1–8.

[ALIP2010b] N. Alipanah, P. Srivastava, P. Parveen, B.M. Thuraisingham, Ranking Ontologies Using Verified Entities to Facilitate Federated Queries, *Web Intelligence*, 2010, 332–337.

[AMAZ] Amazon Relational Database Service, http://aws.amazon.com/rds/.

[ANDE2010] C. Anderson, J. Lehnardt, N. Slater, CouchDB: The Definitive Guide: The Definitive Guide, O'Reilly Media, 2010.

[ANTO2008] G. Antoniou, F. Van Harmelen, Semantic Web Primer, MIT Press, 2008.

[BAAD2003] F. Baader, The Description Logic Handbook: Theory, Implementation, and Applications, Cambridge University Press, 2003.

[BERT2002] E. Bertino, E. Ferrari, Secure and Selective Dissemination of XML Documents, ACM Transactions on Information and System Security (TISSEC), Volume 5, #3, 2002, 290–331.

[BERT2004] E. Bertino, G. Guerrini, M. Mesiti, A Matching Algorithm for Measuring the Structural Similarity between an XML Document and a DTD and Its Applications, Information Systems, Volume 29, #1, 2004, 23–46.

[BHAT2004] R. Bhatti, E. Bertino, A. Ghafoor, J. Joshi, XML-Based Specification for Web Services Document Security, Computer, Volume 37, #4, 2004, 41–49.

[BIGQ] BigQuery, https://cloud.google.com/bigquery/.

[BIGT] BigTable, https://cloud.google.com/bigtable/.

[BRAY1997] T. Bray, J. Paoli, C.M. Sperberg-McQueen, E. Maler, F. Yergeau, Extensible Markup Language (XML), World Wide Web Journal, Volume 2, #4, 1997, 29–66.

[CARM2004] B. Carminati, Elena Ferrari, Bhavani M. Thuraisingham, Using RDF for Policy Specification and Enforcement, DEXA Workshops, 2004, 163–167.

[CASS] Cassandra, http://cassandra.apache.org/.

[CATT2011] R. Cattell, Scalable SQL and NoSQL Data Stores, ACM SIGMOD Record, Volume 39, #4, 2011, 12–27.

[CHEB2013] A. Chebotko, J. Abraham, P. Brazier, A. Piazza, A. Kashlev, S. Lu, Storing, Indexing and Querying Large Provenance Data Sets as RDF Graphs in Apache HBase, IEEE International Workshop on Scientific Workflows, Santa Clara, CA, 2013, 1–8.

[CHOD2010] K. Chodorow, M. Dirolf, MongoDB: The Definitive Guide, O'Reilly Media, 2010.

[CLOUD] What is Cloud Computing? https://aws.amazon.com/what-is-cloud-computing/.

[COSM] Microsoft Azure Cosmos, https://azure.microsoft.com/en-us/blog/a-technical-overview-of-azure-cosmos-db/.

[COUC] CouchDB, http://couchdb.apache.org/.

[CROC2006] D. Crockford, The Application/JSON Media Type for Javascript Object Notation (JSON), 2006. https://datatracker.ietf.org/doc/html/rfc4627.

[DEAN2004] J. Dean, S. Ghemawat, MapReduce: Simplified Data Processing on Large Clusters, http://research.google.com/archive/mapreduce.html

[DYNA] DynamoDB, https://aws.amazon.com/dynamodb/.

[FLIN] Flink, https://flink.apache.org/.

[GEOR2011] L. George, HBase: The Definitive Guide, O'Reilly Media, 2011.

[GHEM2003] S. Ghemawat, H. Gobioff, S.-T. Leung, The Google File System, ACM SIGOPS Operating Systems Review, Volume 37, #5, 2003, 29–43.

[GOOG] Google, https://cloud.google.com/solutions/big-data/.

[HBASE] HBase, https://hbase.apache.org/.

[HEWI2010] E. Hewitt, Cassandra: The Definitive Guide, O'Reilly Media, 2010.

[HDFS] Apache Hadoop, http://hadoop.apache.org/.

[HIVE] Apache HIVE, https://hive.apache.org/.

[HORR2004] I. Horrocks, P.F. Patel-Schneider, H. Boley, S. Tabet, B. Grosof, M. Dean, SWRL: A Semantic Web Rule Language Combining OWL and RuleML, W3C Member submission, 2004. https://www.w3.org/Submission/SWRL/ - W3C Member Submission 21.

[HUAN2011] J. Huang, D.J. Abadi, K. Ren, Scalable SPARQL Querying of Large RDF Graphs, *Proceedings of the VLDB Endowment*, Volume 4, #11, 2011.

[HUSA2009] M.F. Husain, P. Doshi, L. Khan, B. Thuraisingham, Storage and Retrieval of Large RDF Graph Using Hadoop and MapReduce, Cloud Computing, LNCS 5931, Springer-Verlag, 2009, pp. 680–686.

[IBM] IBM, https://www-01.ibm.com/software/data/bigdata/.

[IKED2011] R. Ikeda, H. Park, J. Widom, Provenance for Generalized Map and Reduce Workflows, Stanford InfoLab, 2011. http://ilpubs.stanford.edu:8090/985/.

[KAFK] Kafka, http://kafka.apache.org/.

[KHAD2012a] V. Khadilkar, K.Y. Octay, M. Kantarcioglu, S. Mehrotra, Secure Data Processing over Hybrid Clouds, IEEE Data Engineering Bulletin, Volume 35, #4, 2012, 46–54.

[KHAD2012b], V. Khadilkar, M. Kantarcioglu, P. Castagna, B. Thuraisingham, Jena-HBase: A Distributed, Scalable and Efficient RDF Triple Store, 2012, technical report: http://www.utdallas. edu/~vvk072000/Research/Jena-HBase-Ext/tech-report.Pdf.

[KHAN2002] L. Khan, F. Luo. Ontology Construction for Information Selection. *ICTAI*, 2002, pp. 122–127.

[KHAN2004] L. Khan, D. McLeod, E.H. Hovy, Retrieval Efectiveness of an Ontology-Based Model for Information Selection. *VLDB J*, Volume 13, #1, 2004, 71–85.

[KLYN2004] G. Klyne, J.J. Carroll, B. McBride, Resource Description Framework (RDF): Concepts and Abstract Syntax, W3C Recommendation 10, 2004. https://www.w3.org/TR/rdf-concepts/.

[LEE2001] T.B. Lee, J. Hendler, O. Lasilla, The Semantic Web, Scientific American, Volume 284, # 5, May 2001, 34–43.

[MAHO] Mahut, http://mahout.apache.org/.

[MAPR] MapReduce, https://hadoop.apache.org/docs/r1.2.1/mapred_tutorial.html.

[MCGU2004] D.L. McGuinness, F. Van Harmelen, OWL Web Ontology Language Overview, W3C Recommendation, 2004. https://www.w3.org/TR/owl-features/.

[MONG] MongoDB, https://www.mongodb.com/.

[NIST] Definition of Cloud Computing, National Institute of Standards and Technology, http://csrc.nist.gov/publications/nistpubs/800-145/SP800-145.pdf.

[NOSQ] NoSQL, http://nosql-database.org/.

[ORAC] Oracle, https://www.oracle.com/big-data/index.html.

[PAPA2012] N. Papailiou, I. Konstantinou, D. Tsoumakos, N. Koziris, H2RDF: Adaptive Query Processing on RDF Data in the Cloud, *Proceedings of the 21st International Conference Companion on World Wide Web*, Lyon, France, 2012, 397–400.

[PARK2011] H. Park, R. Ikeda, J. Widom, Ramp: A System for Capturing and Tracing Provenance in MapReduce Workflows, VLDB Endowment, Volume 4, #12, 2011, 1351–1354.

[PART2011] J. Partyka, P. Parveen, L. Khan, B.M. Thuraisingham, S. Shekhar, Enhanced Geographically Typed Semantic Schema Matching, *Journal of Web Semantics*, Volume 9, #1, 2011, 52–70.

[PIG] Apache Pig, https://pig.apache.org/.

[PRUD2006] E. Prud'hommeaux, A. Seaborne, SPARQL Query Language for RDF, W3C Working Draft, 2006. https://www.w3.org/2001/sw/DataAccess/rq23.

[SHE2009] W. She, I.L. Yen, B. Thuraisingham, E. Bertino, The SCIFC Model for Information Flow Control in Web Service Composition, *IEEE International Conference on Web Services (ICWS) 2009*, Los Angeles, CA, 2009, 1–8.

[SPAR] Apache Spark, http://spark.apache.org/.

[STOR] Apache Storm, http://storm.apache.org/.

[SUN2010] J. Sun, Q. Jin, Scalable RDF Store Based on HBase and MapReduce, *Proceedings 3rd International Conference on Advanced Computer Theory and Engineering, Chengdu, China*, Volume 1, 2010, 633–636.

[THUR1993] B. Thuraisingham, W. Ford, M. Collins, J. O'Keeffe, Design and Implementation of a Database Inference Controller, Data and Knowledge Engineering Journal, Volume 11, #3, 1993, 271–297.

[THUR2007] B. Thuraisingham, Building Trustworthy Semantic Webs, CRC Press, 2007.

[THUR2013] B. Thuraisingham, Developing and Securing the Cloud, CRC Press, 2013.

[THUR2014] B. Thuraisingham, Secure Data Provenance and Inference Control with Semantic Web, CRC Press, 2014.

[THUR2016] A. Satyen, B. Thuraisingham, S. Abrol, R. Heatherly, M. Kantarcioglu, V. Khadikar, L. Khan, Analyzing and Securing Social Networks, CRC Press, 2016.

[THUR2017] B. Thuraisingham, P. Praveen, M.M. Masud, L. Khan, Big Data Analytics with Applications in Insider Threat Detection, CRC Press, 2017.

[THUS2010] A. Thusoo, J.S. Sarma, N. Jain, Z. Shao, P. Chakka, N. Zhang, S. Antony, H. Liu, R. Murthy, Hive – A Petabyte Scale Data Warehouse Using Hadoop, *Proceedings Data Engineering (ICDE), 2010 IEEE 26th International Conference on Data Engineering (ICDE)*, Los Angeles, CA, 2010.

[VIRT] Virtualization and Cloud Management, http://www.vmware.com/solutions/virtualization-management/index.html.

[W3C] World Wide Web Consortium, www.w3c.org.

[WEKA] Weka, http://www.cs.waikato.ac.nz/ml/weka/bigdata.html.

[WHIT2015] T. White, Hadoop: The Definitive Guide: Storage and Analysis at Internet Scale, O'Reilly Media, Inc., 2015.

5 Big Data Analytics, Security, and Privacy

5.1 INTRODUCTION

While Chapters 2, 3, and 4 have discussed some foundational technologies for integrating data science and cyber security, this chapter describes the some of the challenges in big data security and privacy (BDSP) that have formed the basis for this book. In particular, we provide a summary of the discussions at the National Science Foundation sponsored workshop on Big Data Security and Privacy) held in Dallas, Texas, on September 16–17, 2014. Our goal is to build a community in BDSP to explore the challenging research problems. We also presented the results of the workshop at the National Privacy Research Strategy meeting in Washington DC to set the directions for research and education on these topics.

Recently, a few workshops and panels have been held on BDSP. Examples include the ACM CCS workshop on big data security, ACM SACMAT, and IEEE Big Data Conference panels. These workshops and panels have been influenced by different communities of researchers. For example, the ACM CCS workshop series is focusing on big data for security applications, while the IEEE Big Data Conference is focusing on cloud security issues. Furthermore, these workshops and panels mainly address a limited number of the technical issues surrounding BDSP. For example, the ACM CCS workshop does not appear to address the privacy issues dealing with regulations or the security violations resulting from data analytics.

To address the above limitations, we organized a workshop on BDSP on September 16–17, 2014 in Dallas, Texas, sponsored by the National Science Foundation (NSF) [NSF]. The participants of this workshop consisted of interdisciplinary researchers in the fields of higher performance computing, systems, data management and analytics, cyber security, network science, healthcare, and social sciences who came together and determined the strategic direction for BDSP. NSF has made substantial investments both in cyber security and big data. It is therefore critical that the two areas work together to determine the direction for big data security. We made a submission based on the workshop results to the National Privacy Research Strategy [NPRS]. We also gave a presentation at the NITRD (The Networking and Information Technology Research and Development) Privacy Workshop [NITRD]. This document is the workshop report that describes the issues in BDSP, presentations at the workshop and the discussions at the workshop. We hope that this effort will help toward building a community in BDSP.

The organization of this chapter is as follows. Section 5.2 describes the issues surrounding BDSP. Research challenges are discussed in Section 5.3. Figure 5.1 illustrates the topics discussed in this chapter.

5.2 ISSUES IN BIG DATA SECURITY AND PRIVACY

5.2.1 BACKGROUND FOR THE WORKSHOP

This section describes issues in BDSP that were given to the workshop participants to motivate the discussions. These issues include both security and privacy for big data as well as big data management and analytics for cyber security. While big data has roots in many technologies, database management is at its heart. Therefore, in this section we will discuss how data management has evolved and will then focus on the BDSP issues.

DOI: 10.1201/9781003081845-7

FIGURE 5.1 Research issues in BDSP.

Database systems technology has advanced a great deal during the past four decades from the legacy systems based on network and hierarchical models to relational and object database systems. Database systems can now be accessed via the web, and data management services have been implemented as web services. Due to the explosion of web-based services, unstructured data management and social media and mobile computing, the amount of data to be handled has increased from terabytes to petabytes and zetabytes in just two decades. Such vast amounts of complex data have come to be known as *big data*. Not only must big data be managed efficiently, such data also has to be analyzed to extract useful nuggets to enhance businesses as well as improve society. This has come to be known as big data analytics.

Storage, management, and analysis of large quantities of data also result in security and privacy violations. Often data has to be retained for various reasons including for regulatory compliance. The data retained may have sensitive information and could violate user privacy. Furthermore, manipulating such big data, such as combining sets of different types of data, could result in security and privacy violations. For example, while the raw data removes personally identifiable information, the derived data may contain private and sensitive information. For example, the raw data about a person may be combined with the person's address, which may be sufficient to identify the person.

Different communities are working on the big data challenge. For example, the systems community is developing technologies for massive storage of big data. The network community is developing solutions for managing very large networked data. The data community is developing solutions for efficiently managing and analyzing large sets of data. Big data research and development is being carried out both in academia, industry, and government research labs. However, little attention has been given to security and privacy considerations for big data. Security cuts across multiple areas, including systems, data, and networks. We need the multiple communities to come together to develop solutions for BDSP.

This section describes some of the issues in BDSP. An overview of big data management and analytics is provided in Section 5.2.2. Security and privacy issues discussed at the workshop are given in Section 5.2.3. Our goal toward building a community is discussed in Section 5.1.

5.2.2   Big Data Management and Analytics

Big data management and analytics research is proceeding in three directions. They are as follow:

i. Building infrastructure and high performance computing techniques for the storage of big data;
ii. Data management techniques such as integrating multiple data sources (both big and small) and indexing and querying big data; and
iii. Data analytics techniques that manipulate and analyze big data to extract nuggets.

We will briefly review the progress made in each of the areas. With respect to building infrastructures, technologies such as Hadoop and MapReduce as well as Storm are being developed for managing large amounts of data in the cloud. In addition, main memory data management techniques have advanced so that a few terabytes of data can be managed in main memory. Furthermore, systems such as Hive and Cassandra as well as NoSQL databases have been developed for managing petabytes of data.

With respect to data management, traditional data management techniques such as query processing and optimization strategies are being examined for handling petabytes of data. Furthermore, graph data management techniques are being developed for the storage and management of very large networked data.

With respect to data analytics, the various data mining algorithms are being implemented on Hadoop- and MapReduce-based infrastructures. Additionally, data reduction techniques are being explored to reduce the massive amounts of data into manageable chunks while still maintaining the semantics of the data.

In summary, big data management and analytics techniques include extending current data management and mining techniques to handle massive amounts of data as well as developing new approaches, including graph data management and mining techniques for maintaining and analyzing large networked data.

5.2.3   Security and Privacy

The collection, storage, manipulation, and retention of massive amounts of data have resulted in serious security and privacy considerations. Various regulations are being proposed to handle big data so that the privacy of the individuals is not violated. For example, even if personally identifiable information is removed from the data, when data is combined with other data, an individual can be identified. This is essentially the inference and aggregation problem that data security researchers have been exploring for the past four decades. This problem is exacerbated with the management of big data as different sources of data now exist that are related to various individuals.

In some cases, regulations may cause privacy to be violated. For example, data that is collected (e.g., email data) has to be retained for a certain period of time (usually five years). As long as one keeps such data, there is a potential for privacy violations. Too many regulations can also stifle innovation. For example, if there is a regulation that raw data has to be kept as is and not manipulated or models cannot be built out of the data, then corporations cannot analyze the data in innovative ways to enhance their business. This way innovation may be stifled.

Therefore, one of the main challenges for ensuring security and privacy when dealing with big data is to come up with a balanced approach toward regulations and analytics. That is, how can an organization carry out useful analytics and still ensure the privacy of individuals? Numerous techniques for privacy-preserving data mining, privacy-preserving data integration, and privacy-preserving information retrieval have been developed. The challenge is to extend these techniques for handling massive amounts of often networked data.

Another security challenge for big data management and analytics is to secure the infrastructures. Many of the technologies that have been developed, including Hadoop, MapReduce, Hive, Cassandra, PigLatin, Mahout, and Storm, do not have adequate security protections. The question is, how can these technologies be secured and at the same time ensure high performance computing?

Next, the big data management strategies such as access methods and indexing and query processing have to be secure. So the question is how can policies for different types of data such as structured, semi-structured, unstructured, and graph data be integrated? Since big data may result from combining data from numerous sources, how can you ensure the quality of the data?

Finally, the entire area of security, privacy, integrity, data quality, and trust policies has to be examined within the context of big data security. What are the appropriate policies for big data? How can these policies be handled without affecting performance? How can these policies be made consistent and complete?

This section has listed some of the challenges with respect to security and privacy for big data. We need a comprehensive research program that will identify the challenges and develop solutions for BDSP. Security cannot be an afterthought. That is, we cannot incorporate security into each and every big data technology that is being developed. We need to have a comprehensive strategy so that security can be incorporated while the technology is being developed. We also need to determine the appropriate types of policies and regulations to enforce before big data technologies are employed by an organization. This means researchers from multiple disciplines have to come together to determine what the problems are and explore solutions. These disciplines include cyber security and privacy, high performance computing, data management and analytics, network science, and policy management.

While the challenges discussed above deal with securing big data and ensuring the privacy of individuals, big data management and analytics techniques can be used to solve security problems. For example, an organization can outsource activities such as identity management, email filtering, and intrusion detection to the cloud. This is because massive amounts of data are being collected for such applications and this data has to be analyzed. Cloud data management is just one example of big data management. The question is: how can the developments in big data management and analytic techniques be used to solve security problems? These problems include malware detection, insider threat detection, intrusion detection, and spam filtering. Another emerging challenge is what happens if the big data analytics techniques are attacked. This also includes answering questions such as what happens if the data science (also machine learning and artificial intelligence) techniques are attacked. Many industries for healthcare to transportation to finance to retail are relaying on data science techniques. If the data science technologies are attacked then one cannot rely on the results. We will discuss these aspects and more in the next section.

5.3 RESEARCH CHALLENGES FOR BIG DATA SECURITY AND PRIVACY

5.3.1 WORKSHOP OBJECTIVES

This section provides a summary of the discussions on BDSP at the NSF workshop. The workshop consisted of keynote presentations, presentations by the participants, and workgroup discussions. We organized two workgroups: one on BDSP led by Dr. Elisa Bertino and the other on big data analytics for cyber security led by Dr. Murat Kantarcioglu. While the major focus of the workshop was on privacy issues due to big data management and analytics, we also had some stimulating discussions on applying big data management analytics techniques for cyber security. Therefore, this section provides a summary of the discussions of both workgroups.

The organization of this section is as follows. The philosophy behind BDSP is discussed in Section 5.3.2. Privacy-enhanced techniques are discussed in Section 5.3.3. A framework for big data privacy is discussed in Section 5.3.4. Research challenges and interdisciplinary approaches to big data privacy are discussed in Section 5.3.5. An overview of big data management and analytics techniques for cyber security is provided in Section 5.3.6. Attacks on big data/data science are discussed in Section 5.3.7.

5.3.2 Philosophy for Big Data Security and Privacy

As discussed by Bertino [BERT2014], technological advances and novel applications, such as sensors, cyber-physical systems, smart mobile devices, cloud systems, data analytics, and social networks are making it possible to capture and to quickly process and analyze huge amounts of data from which to extract information critical for security-related tasks. In the area of cyber security, such tasks include user authentication, access control, anomaly detection, user monitoring, and protection from insider threat [BERT2012]. By analyzing and integrating data collected on the Internet and web, one can identify connections and relationships among individuals that may, in turn, help with homeland protection. By collecting and mining data concerning user travels and disease outbreaks, one can predict disease spreading across geographical areas. And those are just a few examples; there are certainly many other domains where data technologies can play a major role in enhancing security.

The use of data for security tasks is, however, raising major privacy concerns [THUR2002]. Collected data even if anonymized by removing identifiers such as names or social security numbers, when linked with other data, may lead to re-identifying the individuals to which specific data items are related to. Also, as organizations such as governmental agencies often need to collaborate on security tasks, datasets are exchanged across different organizations, resulting in these datasets being available to many different parties. Apart from the use of data for analytics, security tasks such as authentication and access control may require detailed information about users. An example is multi-factor authentication that may require, in addition to a password or a certificate, user biometrics. Recently proposed continuous authentication techniques extend user authentication to include information such as user keystroke dynamics to constantly verify the user identity. Another example is location-based access control [DAMI2007] that requires users to provide to the access control system information about their current location. As a result, detailed user mobility information may be collected over time by the access control system. This information, if misused or stolen, can lead to privacy breaches.

It would then seem that in order to achieve security, we must give up privacy. However, this may not be necessarily the case. Recent advances in cryptography are making possible to work on encrypted data, for example, for performing analytics on encrypted data [LIU2014]. However, much more needs to be done as the specific data privacy techniques to use heavily depend on the specific use of data and the security tasks at hand. Also, current techniques are not still able to meet the efficiency requirement for use with big datasets.

In this document, we first discuss a few examples of approaches that help with reconciling security with privacy. We then discuss some aspects of a framework for data privacy. Finally, we summarize research challenges and provide an overview of the multi-disciplinary research needed to address these challenges.

5.3.3 Examples of Privacy-Enhancing Techniques

Many privacy-enhancing techniques have been proposed over the last 15 years, ranging from cryptographic techniques such as oblivious data structures [WANG2014] that hide data access patterns to data anonymization techniques that transform the data to make it more difficult to link specific data records to specific individuals; and we refer the reader for further references to specialized conferences, such as the Privacy-Enhancing Symposium (PET) series (https://petsymposium.org/2014/) and journals, such as Transactions on Data Privacy (http://www.tdp.cat/). However, many such techniques either do not scale to very large datasets and/or do not specifically address the problem of reconciling security with privacy. At the same time, there are a few approaches that focus on efficiently reconciling security with privacy and we discuss them as follows:

- *Privacy-preserving data matching:* Record matching is typically performed across different data sources with the aim of identifying common information shared among these sources. An example is matching a list of passengers on a flight with a list of suspicious individuals. However, matching records from different data sources is often in contrast with privacy requirements concerning the data owned by the sources. Cryptographic approaches such as secure set intersection protocols may alleviate such concerns. However, these techniques do not scale for large datasets. Recent approaches based on data transformation and mapping into vector spaces [SCAN2007] and combination of secure multiparty computation (SMC) and data sanitization approaches such as differential privacy [KUZU2013] and k-anonymity [INAN2008, INAN2012] have addressed scalability. However, work needs to be done concerning the development of privacy-preserving techniques suitable for complex matching techniques based for example on semantic matching. Security models and definitions also need to be developed supporting security analysis and proofs for solutions combining different security techniques, such as SMC (secure multiparty computation) and differential privacy.
- *Privacy-preserving collaborative data mining:* Conventional data mining is typically performed on big centralized data warehouses collecting all the data of interest. However, centrally collecting all data poses several privacy and confidentiality concerns when data belongs to different organizations. An approach to address such concerns is based on distributed collaborative approaches by which the organizations retain their own datasets and cooperate to learn the global data mining results without revealing the data in their own individual datasets. Fundamental work in this area includes: (i) techniques allowing two parties to build a decision tree without learning anything about each other's datasets except for what can be learned by the final decision tree [LIND2000]; (ii) specialized collaborative privacy-preserving techniques for association rules, clustering, k-nearest neighbor classification [VAID2006]. These techniques are, however, still very inefficient. Novel approaches based on cloud computing and new cryptographic primitives should be investigated.
- *Privacy-preserving biometric authentication:* Conventional approaches to biometrics authentication require recording biometrics templates of enrolled users and then using these templates for matching with the templates provided by users at authentication time. Templates of user biometrics represent sensitive information that needs to be strongly protected. In distributed environments in which users have to interact with many different service providers, the protection of biometric templates becomes even more complex. A recent approach addresses such an issue by using a combination of perceptual hashing techniques, classification techniques, and zero-knowledge proof of knowledge (ZKPK) protocols [GUNA2014]. Under such approach, the biometric template of a user is processed to extract from it a string of bits which is then further processed by classification and some other transformation. The resulting bit string is then used, together with a random number, to generate a cryptographic commitment. This commitment represents an identification token that does not reveal anything about the original input biometrics. The commitment is then used in the ZKPK protocol to authenticate the user. This approach has been engineered for secure use on mobile phones. Much work remains, however, to be done in order to reduce the false rejection rates. Also, different approaches to authentication and identification techniques need to be investigated based on recent homomorphic encryption techniques.

5.3.4 Multi-objective Optimization Framework for Data Privacy

Although there are attempts at coming up with a privacy solution/definition that can address many different scenarios, we believe that there is no one size fits all solution for data privacy. Instead, multiple dimensions need to be tailored for different application domains to achieve practical solutions. First of all, different domains require different definitions of data utility. For example, if we want to build privacy-preserving classification models, 0/1 loss could be a good utility measure. On the other hand, for privacy-preserving record linkage, F1 score could be a better choice. Second, we need to understand the right definitions of privacy risk. For example, in data sharing scenarios, the probability of re-identification given certain background knowledge could be considered the right measure of privacy risk. On the other hand, $\varepsilon = 1$ could be considered an appropriate risk for differentially private data mining models. Finally, the computation, storage, and communication costs of given protocols need to be considered. These costs could be especially significant for privacy-preserving protocols that involve cryptography. Given these three dimensions, one can envisage a multi-objective framework where different dimensions could be emphasized:

- *Maximize utility, given the risk and costs constraints:* This would be suited for scenarios where limiting certain privacy risks are paramount.
- *Minimize privacy risks, given the utility and cost constraints:* In some scenarios (e.g., medical care), significant degradation of the utility may not be allowed. In this setting, the parameter values of the protocol (e.g., ε in differential privacy) are chosen in such a way that we try to do our best in terms of privacy given our utility constraints. Please note that in some scenarios, there may not be any parameter settings that can satisfy all the constraints.
- *Minimize cost, given the utility and risk constraints:* In some cases, (e.g., cryptographic protocols), you may want to find the protocol parameter settings that may allow for the least expensive protocol that can satisfy all the utility and cost constraints.

To better illustrate these dimensions, consider the privacy-preserving record matching problem addressed in [INAN2012]. Existing solutions to this problem generally follow two approaches: sanitization techniques and cryptographic techniques. In [INAN2012], a hybrid technique that combines these two approaches is presented. This approach enables users to make trade-offs between privacy, accuracy, and cost. This is similar to the multi-objective optimization framework discussed in this chapter. These multi-objective optimizations are achieved by using a blocking phase that operates over sanitized data to filter out pairs of records, in a privacy-preserving manner, that do not satisfy the matching condition. By disclosing more information (e.g., differentially private data statistics), the proposed method incurs considerably lower costs than those for cryptographic techniques. On the other hand, it yields matching results that are significantly more accurate when compared to the sanitization techniques, even when privacy requirements are high. The use of different privacy-parameter values allows for different cost, risk, and utility outcomes.

To enable the multi-objective optimization framework for data privacy, we believe that more research needs to be done to identify appropriate utility, risk, and cost definitions for different application domains. Especially defining correct and realistic privacy risks is paramount. Many human actions ranging from oil extraction to airline travel, involve risks and benefits. In many cases, such as trying to develop an aircraft that may never malfunction, avoiding all risks are either too costly or impossible. Similarly, we believe that avoiding all privacy risks for all individuals would be too costly. In addition, assuming that an attacker may know everything is too pessimistic. Therefore, coming up with privacy risk definitions under realistic attacker scenarios are needed.

5.3.5 MULTIDISCIPLINARY APPROACHES

Comprehensive solutions to the problem of security with privacy for big data require addressing many research challenges and multidisciplinary approaches. We outline significant directions in what follows:

- *Data confidentiality:* Several data confidentiality techniques and mechanisms exist, the most notable being access control systems and encryptions. Both techniques have been widely investigated. However, for access control systems for big data we need approaches for the following:
  - *Merging large numbers of access control policies:* In many cases, big data entails integrating data originating from multiple sources; these data may be associated with their own access control policies (referred to as "sticky policies") and these policies must be enforced even when the data is integrated with other data. Therefore, policies need to be integrated and conflicts solved.
  - *Automatically administering authorizations for big data and in particular for granting permissions:* If fine-grained access control is required, manual administration on large datasets is not feasible. We need techniques by which authorization can be automatically granted, possibly based on the user digital identity, profile, and context, and on the data contents and metadata.
  - *Enforcing access control policies on heterogeneous multi-media data:* Content-based access control is an important type of access control by which authorizations are granted or denied based on the content of data. Content-based access control is critical when dealing with video surveillance applications which are important for security. As for privacy, such videos have to be protected. Supporting content-based access control requires understanding the contents of protected data and this is very challenging when dealing with multimedia large data sources.
  - *Enforcing access control policies in big data stores:* Some of the recent big data systems allow users to submit arbitrary jobs using programming languages such as Java. For example, in Hadoop, users can submit arbitrary MapReduce jobs written in Java. This creates significant challenges to enforce fine-grained access control efficiently for different users. Although there is some existing work [KHAN2014, ULUS2014] that tries to inject access control policies into submitted jobs, more research needs to be done on how to efficiently enforce such policies in recently developed big data stores.
  - *Automatically designing, evolving, and managing access control policies:* When dealing with dynamic environments where sources, users, and applications as well as the data usage are continuously changing, the ability to automatically design and evolve policies is critical to make sure that data is readily available for use while at the same time ensuring data confidentiality. Environments and tools for managing policies are also crucial.
- *Privacy-preserving data correlation techniques:* A major issue arising from big data is that in correlating many (big) datasets, one can extract unanticipated information. Relevant issues and research directions that need to be investigated include:
  - *Techniques to control what is extracted and to check that what is extracted can be used and/or shared.*
  - *Support for both personal privacy and population privacy:* In the case of population privacy, it is important to understand what is extracted from the data as this may lead to discrimination. Also, when dealing with security with privacy, it is important to understand the trade-off of personal privacy and collective security.

- *Efficient and scalable privacy-enhancing techniques:* Several such techniques have been developed over the years, including oblivious RAM, security multi-party computation, multi-input encryption, homomorphic encryption. However, they are not yet practically applicable to large datasets. We need to engineer these techniques, using for example parallelization, to fine tune their implementation and perhaps combine them with other techniques, such as differential privacy (like in the case of the record linkage protocols described in [SCAN2007]). A possible further approach in this respect is to first use anonymized/sanitized data, and then depending on the specific situation to get specific non-anonymized data.
- *Usability of data privacy policies:* Policies must be easily understood by users. We need tools for the average users and we need to understand user expectations in terms of privacy.
- *Approaches for data services monetization:* Instead of selling data, organizations owning datasets can sell privacy-preserving data analytic services based on these datasets. The question to be addressed then is: how would the business model around data change if privacy-preserving data analytic tools were available? Also, if data is considered as a good to be sold, are there regulations concerning contracts for buying/selling data? Can these contracts include privacy clauses be incorporated requiring, for example, that users to whom this data pertains to have been notified?
- *Data publication:* Perhaps we should abandon the idea of publishing data, given the privacy implications, and rather require the user of the data to utilize a controlled environment (perhaps located in a cloud) for using the data. In this way, it would be much easier to control the proper use of data. An issue would be the case of research data used in universities and the repeatability of data-based research.
- *Privacy implication on data quality:* Recent studies have shown that people lie especially in social networks because they are not sure that their privacy is preserved. This results in a decrease in data quality that then affects decisions and strategies based on these data.
- *Risk models:* Different types of relationship of risks with big data can be identified: (a) big data can increase privacy risks; (b) big data can reduce risks in many domains (e.g., national security). The development of models for these two types of risk is critical in order to identify suitable trade-off and privacy-enhancing techniques to be used.
- *Data ownership:* The question about who is the owner of a piece of data is often a difficult question. It is perhaps better to replace this concept with the concept of stakeholder. Multiple stakeholders can be associated with each data item. The concept of stakeholder ties well with risks. Each stakeholder would have different (possibly conflicting) objectives and this can be modeled according to multi-objective optimization. In some cases, a stakeholder may not be aware of the others. For example, a user about whom the data pertains to (and thus a stakeholder for the data) may not be aware that a law enforcement agency is using this data. Technology solutions need to be investigated to eliminate conflicts.
- *Human factors:* All solutions proposed for privacy and for security with privacy need to be investigated in order to determine human involvement, for example, how would the user interact with the data and his/her specific tasks concerning the use and/or protection of the data, in order to enhance usability.
- *Data lifecycle framework:* A comprehensive approach to privacy for big data needs to be based on a systematic data lifecycle approach. Phases in the lifecycle need to be identified and their privacy requirements and implications need to be identified. Relevant phases include:

- *Data acquisition:* We need mechanisms and tools to prevent devices from acquiring data about other individuals (relevant when devices like Google glasses are used); for example, can we come up with mechanisms that automatically block devices from recording/acquiring data at certain locations (or notify a user that recording devices are around). We also need techniques by which each recorded subject may have a say about the use of the data.
- *Data sharing:* Users need to be informed about data sharing/transferred to other parties.

Addressing the above challenges requires multi-disciplinary research drawing from many different areas, including computer science and engineering, information systems, statistics, risk models, economics, social sciences, political sciences, human factors, and psychology. We believe that all these perspectives are needed to develop effective solutions to the problem of privacy in the era of big data as well as to reconcile security with privacy.

5.3.6 BIG DATA ANALYTICS FOR CYBER SECURITY

To protect important digital assets, organizations are investing in new cyber security tools that need to analyze big data ranging from log files to email attachments to prevent, detect, and recover from cyber-attacks [KAR2014]. As a part of this workshop, we explored the following topics:

- *What is different about big data management analytics (BDMA) for cyber security?* The workshop participants pointed out that BDMA for cyber security needs to deal with adaptive and malicious adversaries who can potentially launch attacks to avoid being detected (i.e., data poisoning attacks, denial of service, denial of information attacks, etc.). In addition, BDMA for cyber security needs to operate in high volume (e.g., data coming from multiple intrusion detection systems and sensors) and high noise environments (i.e., constantly changing normal system usage data is mixed with stealth advanced persistent threat related data). One of the important points that came out of this discussion is that we need BDMA tools that can integrate data from hosts, networks, social networks, bug reports, mobile devices, and Internet of Things sensors to detect attacks.
- *What is the right BDMA architecture for cyber security?* We also discussed whether we need different types of BDMA system architectures for cyber security. Based on the use cases discussed, participants felt that existing BDMA system architectures can be adapted for cyber security needs. One issue pointed out was that real-time data analysis must be supported by a successful BDMA system for cyber security. For example, once a certain type of attack is known, the system needs to be updated to look for such attacks in real time, including re-examining the history data to see whether prior attacks have occurred.
- *Data sharing for BDMA for cyber security:* It emerged quickly during our discussions that cyber security data needs to be shared both within as well as across organizations. In addition to obvious privacy, security, and incentive issues in sharing cyber security data, participants felt that we need common languages and infrastructure to capture and share such cyber security data. For example, we need to represent certain low-level system information (e.g., memory, CPU states, etc.) so that it can be mapped to similar cyber security incidents.
- *BDMA for preventing cyber-attacks:* There was substantial discussion on how BDMA tools could be used to prevent attacks. One idea that emerged is that BDMA systems that can easily track sensitive data using the captured provenance information can potentially detect attacks before too much sensitive information is disclosed. Based on this observation, building provenance-aware BDMA systems would be needed for cyber-attack prevention. Also, BDMA tools for cyber security can potentially mine useful attacker

information such as their motivations, technical capabilities, modus operandi, etc. to prevent future attacks.

- *BDMA for digital forensics:* BDMA techniques could be used for digital forensics by combining or linking different data sources. The main challenge that emerged was identifying the right data sources for digital forensics. In addition, answers to the following questions were not clear immediately: What data to capture? What to filter out (big noise in big data)? What data to link? What data to store and for how long? How to deal with machine-generated content and Internet of Things?

- *BDMA for understanding the users of the cyber systems:* Participants believe that BDMA could be used to mine human behavior to learn how to improve the systems. For example, an organization may send phishing emails to its users and carry out security re-training for those who are fooled by such a phishing attack. In addition, BDMA techniques could be used to understand and build normal behavior models per user to find significant deviations from the norm.

Overall, during our workshop discussions, it became clear that all of the above topics have significant research challenges and more research needs to be done to address them. Furthermore, regardless of whether we are using BDMA for cyber security or for other applications (e.g., healthcare, finance), it is critical that we need to design scalable BDMA solutions. These include parallel BDMA techniques as well as BDMA techniques implemented on cloud platforms such as Hadoop/MapReduce, Storm, and Spark. In addition, we need to explore the use of BDMA systems such as HBase and CouchDB for use in various applications.

5.3.7 Cyber Security for Big Data Analytics

One of the challenges we are faced with when using data science and machine learning techniques is that these techniques could be attacked. The adversary usually learns about our models and the data we use and will try and poison the data and thwart the models. We have to be several steps ahead of the adversary and adapt our models. This area has come to be known as *adversarial machine learning* (or *adversarial data mining*).

Learning tasks, such as intrusion detection and spam filtering, face adversarial attacks. Adversarial exploits create additional challenges to existing learning paradigms. Generalization of a learning model over future data cannot be achieved under the assumption that current and future data share identical properties, which is essential to the traditional approaches. In the presence of active adversaries, data used for training in a learning system is unlikely to represent future data the system would observe. The difference is not just simple random noise which most learning algorithms have already taken into consideration when they are designed. What typically fail these learning algorithms are targeted attacks that aim to make the learning system dysfunctional by disguising malicious data that otherwise would be detected. Existing learning algorithms cannot be easily tailored to counter this kind of attack because there is a great deal of uncertainty in terms of how much the attacks would affect the structure of the sample space. Despite the sample size and distribution of malicious data given at training time, we would need to make an educated guess about how much the malicious data would change, as sophisticated attackers adapt quickly to evade detection. Attack models, that foretell how far an adversary would go in order to breach the system, need to be incorporated into learning algorithms to build a robust decision surface.

5.4 SUMMARY AND DIRECTIONS

This chapter has explored the issues surrounding BDSP as well as applying big data management and analytics techniques for cyber security. As massive amounts of data are being collected, stored, manipulated, merged, analyzed, and expunged, security and privacy concerns will explode. We need to develop technologies to address security and privacy issues throughout the lifecycle of the data. However, technologies alone will not be sufficient. We need to understand not only the societal impact of data collection, use, and analysis, we also need to formulate appropriate laws and policies for such activities. Our workshop explored the initial directions to address some of the major challenges we are faced with today. We need an interdisciplinary approach consisting of technologists, application specialists, social scientists, policy analysts, and lawyers to work together to come up with viable and practical solutions.

This chapter has described the security and privacy issues for big data as well as discussed the issues that need to be investigated for applying BDMA techniques for cyber security. We have also provided summaries of the workshop presentations and discussions. We made a submission to the National Privacy Research Strategy on October 16, 2014 that was based on the workshop summary. We also participated in the National Privacy Research Strategy Conference in Washington, DC February 18–20, 2015 and gave a presentation of the workshop summary at this event. Our goal is to build a community in BDSP. In addition, the National Institute of Standards and Technology (NIST) has also developed a report on the security and privacy for big data [NIST1]. This report is published by NIST's BDSP Working Group, which is part of NIST's [NIST2] Big Data Working Group. Furthermore, NIST is also developing a framework called NICE (National Initiative for Cyber Security Framework) for cyber security education. We need to incorporate BDSP as well as BDMA for cyber security topics into this framework. Therefore, it is important for the different agencies to continue to work together and develop strategies not only for research but also for education in BDSP as well as on applying BDMA for cyber security.

REFERENCES

[BERT2012] E. Bertino, Data Protection from Insider Threats, Morgan & Claypool, 2012.

[BERT2014] E. Bertino, "Security with Privacy – Opportunities and Challenges" Panel Statement, *COMPSAC*, Anchorage, Alaska, 2014, 436–437.

[DAMI2007] M. Damiani, E. Bertino, B. Catania, P. Perlasca, GEO-RBAC: A Spatially Aware RBAC, *ACM Transactions on Information and System Security*, Volume 10, #1, 2007, 2–42.

[GUNA2014] H. Gunasinghe, E. Bertino, Privacy Preserving Biometrics-Based and User Centric Authentication Protocol for Mobile Devices, *Proceedings of 2014 Network and System Security (NSS2014)*, Xi'an, Chi-na, October 15–16, 2014.

[INAN2008] A. Inan, M. Kantarcioglu, E. Bertino, M. Scannapieco, A Hybrid Approach to Private Record Linkage, ICDE, 2008, 496–505.

[INAN2012] A. Inan, M. Kantarcioglu, G. Ghinita, E. Bertino, A Hybrid Approach to Private Record Matching, IEEE Transactions on Dependable Secure Computing (TDSC), Volume 9, #5, 2012, 684–698.

[KAR2014] S. Kar, Gartner Report: Big Data Will Revolutionize Cyber Security in the Next Two Years, CloudTimes.Org, February 12, 2014.

[KHAN2014] L. Khan, K. Hamlen, M. Kantarcioglu, Silver Lining: Enforcing Secure Information Flow at the Cloud Edge, IC2E, Boston, MA, 2014, 37–46.

[KUZU2013] M. Kuzu, M. Kantarcioglu, A. Inan, E. Bertino, E. Durham, B. Malin, Efficient Privacy-Aware Record Integration, *Proceedings of Joint 2013 EDBT/ICDT Conferences, EDBT'13*, ACM, Genoa, Italy, March 18–22, 2013.

[LIND2000] Y. Lindell, B. Pinkas, Privacy Preserving Data Mining, *Advances in Cryptology*, Springer-Verlag, August 20–24, 2000.

[LIU2014] D. Liu, E. Bertino, X. Yi, Privacy of Outsourced K-Means Clustering, *Proceedings of the 9th ACM Symposium on Information, Computer and Communication Security*, Kyoto (Japan), June 4–6, 2014.

[NIST1] https://bigdatawg.nist.gov/.

[NIST2] https://www.nist.gov/itl/applied-cybersecurity/nice.

[NITRD] http://csi.utdallas.edu/events/NSF/NPRS%20Workshop%20Presentation.pdf.

[NPRS] https://www.nitrd.gov/cybersecurity/nprsrfi102014/BigData-SP.pdf.

[NSF] http://csi.utdallas.edu/events/NSF/NSF%20workshop%202014.htm.

[SCAN2007] M. Scannapieco, I. Figotin, E. Bertino, A. Elmagarmid, Privacy Preserving Schema and Data Matching, *Proceedings of 2007 ACM SIGMOD International Conference on Management of Data, Beijing, China,* 2007, pp. 653–664.

[THUR2002] B. Thuraisingham, Data Mining, National Security, Privacy and Civil Liberties, SIGKDD Explorations, Volume 4, #2, 2002, 1–5.

[ULUS2014] H. Ulusoy, M. Kantarcioglu, E. Pattuk, K. Hamlen, Vigiles: Fine-Grained Access Control for MapReduce Systems, *2014 IEEE International Congress on Big Data (BigData Congress)* Anchorage, Alaska, USA, 2014, pp. 40–47.

[VAID2006] J. Vaidya, Y. Zhu, C. Clifton, Privacy Preserving Data Mining, *Advances in Information Security* 19, Springer, 2006, pp. 1–121.

[WANG2014] H.X. Wang, K. Nayak, C. Liu, E. Shi, E. Stefanov, Y. Huang, Oblivious Data Structures, IACR Cryptology ePrint Archive, 2014, 185.

Conclusion to Part I

Part I, consisting of four chapters described supporting technologies for secure data science. In Chapter 2, we provided an overview of discretionary security policies in database systems. We started with a discussion of access control policies, including authorization policies and role-based access control policies. Then we discussed administration policies. We briefly discussed identification and authentication. We also discussed auditing issues as well as views for security. Next, we discussed policy enforcement as well as SQL extensions for specifying policies as well as provided an overview of query modification. Finally, we provided a brief overview of data privacy aspects. In Chapter 3, we provided an overview of data mining for cyber security applications. In particular, we discussed various data mining techniques and described their applications to detect intrusion detection and insider threat detection. Chapter 4 introduced the notions of the cloud, semantic web, and social network technologies. This is because some of the experimental systems discussed in Part IV utilize these technologies. We first discussed concepts in cloud computing, including aspects of virtualization, deployment models, and cloud functions. We also discussed technologies for the semantic web, including XML, RDF, Ontologies, and OWL. Finally, we discuss social network analytics and security. In Chapter 5, we discussed big data security and privacy. First, we discussed security and privacy issues and then discussed some of the research challenges.

As previously stated, the chapters in Part I lay the foundations for the discussions in Parts II, III, and IV. Data science for cyber security will be discussed in Part II. Security and privacy enhanced data science will be discussed in Part III. Some of the experimental systems we have developed will be discussed in Part IV.

DOI: 10.1201/9781003081845-8

Part II

Data Science for Cyber Security

Introduction to Part II

Part II, consisting of four chapters, describes data science for cyber security. In particular, data science technologies such as data mining, stream analytics, and cloud computing are applied to cyber security applications such as malware analysis and insider threat detection.

Chapter 6 provides a discussion of data mining/data science techniques for detecting malicious executables. Chapter 7 describes stream analytics for malware detection and shows how novel malware classes can be detected with this approach. Chapter 8 discusses how the techniques such as those discussed in Chapters 5 and 6 could be enhanced with respect to performance with big data technologies such as cloud computing. Chapter 8 discusses how data science techniques can be applied for insider threat detection based on both supervised and unsupervised learning. Scalability with respect to big data technologies is also discussed.

DOI: 10.1201/9781003081845-10

6 Data Science for Malicious Executables

6.1 INTRODUCTION

Malicious code is a great threat to computers and computer society. Numerous kinds of malicious codes wander in the wild. Some of them are mobile, such as worms, and spread through Internet causing damage to millions of computers worldwide. Other kinds of malicious codes are static, such as viruses, but sometimes deadlier than their mobile counterparts. Malicious code writers usually exploit software vulnerabilities to attack host machines. A number of techniques have been devised by researchers to counter these attacks. Unfortunately, the more successful the researchers become in detecting and preventing the attacks, the more sophisticated malicious code appears in the wild. Thus, the battle between malicious code writers and researchers is virtually never-ending.

One popular technique followed by the antivirus community to detect malicious code is "signature detection." This technique matches the executables against a unique telltale string or byte pattern called *signature*, which is used as an identifier for a particular malicious code. Although signature detection techniques are being used widely, they are not effective against *zero-day* attacks (new malicious code), *polymorphic* attacks (different encryptions of the same binary), or *metamorphic* attacks (different code for the same functionality). So, there has been a growing need for fast, automated, and efficient detection techniques that are robust to these attacks. As a result, many automated systems [GOLB2004, KOLT2004, NEWM2002, NEWS2005] have been developed.

In this chapter, we describe our novel *hybrid feature retrieval* (HFR) model that can detect malicious executables efficiently [MASU2007a, MASU2007b]. Next, we describe our data mining tool for detecting malicious executables. It utilizes the feature extraction technique using *n*-gram analysis. We first discuss how we extract binary *n*-gram features from the executables, and then show how we select the best features using information gain. We also discuss the memory and scalability problem associated with the *n*-gram extraction and selection and how we solve it. Then we describe how the assembly features and dynamic link library (DLL) call features are extracted. Finally, we describe how we combine these three kinds of features and train a classifier using these features.

We also discuss the experiments and evaluation process in details. We use two different datasets with different number of instances and class distributions. We compare the features extracted with our approach, namely, the hybrid feature set (HFS) with two other baseline approaches, namely, only the binary feature set (BFS), and derived assembly feature (DAF) set. For classification, we compare the performance of three different classifiers on each of these feature sets, which are support vector machine (SVM), Naïve Bayes (NB), Bayes Net, decision tree, and boosted decision tree. We show the classification accuracy, false positive and false negative rates for our approach and each of the baseline techniques. We also compare the running times and performance/cost trade-off of our approach compared to the baselines.

The organization of this chapter is as follows. Aspects of malware executables are discussed in Section 6.2. In particular, our architecture, related work and our approach are given. Next, we discuss our data mining tools in Section 6.3. In particular, feature extracting using *n*-gram analysis, the hybrid feature retrieval models are discussed. Next, we discuss the experiments in Section 6.4. Datasets and experimental setup are discussed as well as results and example run are given. Finally, extensions for malware analysis with big data analytics are discussed in Section 6.5. Section 6.6 concludes this chapter. Figure 6.1 illustrates the concepts in this chapter.

DOI: 10.1201/9781003081845-11

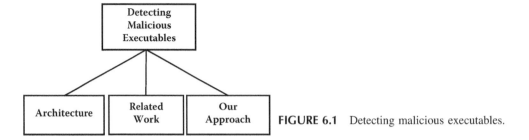

FIGURE 6.1 Detecting malicious executables.

6.2 MALICIOUS EXECUTABLES

6.2.1 Architecture

Figure 6.2 illustrates our architecture for detecting malicious executables. The training data consists of a collection of benign and malicious executables. We extract three different kinds of features (to be explained shortly) from each executable. These extracted features are then analyzed and only the best discriminative features are selected. Feature vectors are generated from each training instance, using the selected feature set. The feature vectors are used to train a classifier. When a new executable needs to be tested, at first the features selected during training are extracted from the executable, and a feature vector is generated. This feature vector is classified using the classifier to predict whether it is a benign or malicious executable.

In our approach, we extract three different kinds of features from the executables at different levels of abstraction and combine them into one feature set, called the *hybrid feature set* (HFS). These features are used to train a classifier (e.g., *support vector machine* (SVM), *decision tree,* etc.), which is applied to detect malicious executables. These features are: (i) binary *n*-gram features, (ii) derived assembly features (DAFs), and (iii) dynamic link library (DLL) call features. Each binary *n*-gram feature is actually a sequence of *n* consecutive bytes in a binary executable, extracted using a technique explained in Chapter 10. Binary *n*-grams reveal the distinguishing byte patterns between the benign and malicious executables. Each DAF is a sequence of assembly instructions in an executable, and corresponds to one binary *n*-gram feature. DAFs reveal the distinctive instruction usage patterns between the benign and malicious executables. They are extracted from the disassembled executables using our *assembly feature retrieval* (AFR) algorithm. Assembly *n*-gram features are not used in HFS because of our findings show that DAF performs better than them. Each DLL call feature actually corresponds to a DLL function call in an executable, extracted from the executable header. These features reveal the distinguishing DLL call patterns between the benign and malicious executables. We show empirically that the combination of these three features is always better than any single feature in terms of classification accuracy.

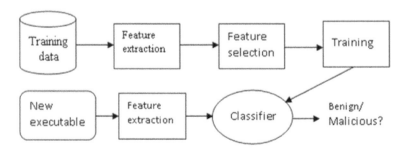

FIGURE 6.2 Architecture.

Our work focuses on expanding features at different levels of abstraction, rather than using more features at a single level of abstraction. There are two main reasons behind this. First, the number of features at a given level of abstraction (e.g., binary) is overwhelmingly large. For example, in our larger dataset, we obtain 200 million binary n-gram features. Training with this large number of features is way beyond the capabilities of any practical classifier. That is why we limit the number of features at a given level of abstraction to an applicable range. Second, we empirically observe the benefit of adding more levels of abstraction to the combined feature set (i.e., HFS). HFS combines features at three levels of abstraction, namely, binary executables, assembly programs, and system application programming interface (API) calls. We show that this combination has higher detection accuracy and lower false alarm rate than the features at any single level of abstraction.

Our technique is related to knowledge-management because of several reasons. First, we apply our knowledge of binary n-gram features to obtain DAFs. Second, we apply the knowledge obtained from the feature extraction process to select the best features. This is accomplished by extracting all possible binary n-grams from the training data, applying the statistical knowledge corresponding to each n-gram (i.e., its frequency in malicious and benign executables) to compute its *information gain* [MITC1997], and selecting the best S of them. Finally, we apply another statistical knowledge (presence/absence of a feature in an executable) obtained from the feature-extraction process to train classifiers.

Our research contributions are as follows. First, we propose and implement our HFR (hybrid feature retrieval) model, which combines three kinds of features mentioned above. Second, we apply a novel idea to extract assembly instruction features using binary n-gram features, implemented with the AFR algorithm. Third, we propose and implement a scalable solution to the n-gram feature extraction and selection problem in general. Our solution works well with limited memory, and significantly reduces running time by applying efficient and powerful data structures and algorithms. Thus, it is scalable to a large collection of executables (in the order of thousands), even with limited main memory and processor speed. Finally, we compare our results against the results of [KOLT2004], which use only binary n-gram feature and show that our method achieves better accuracy. We also report the performance/cost trade-off of our method against the method of [KOLT2004]. It should be pointed out here that our main contribution is an efficient feature extraction technique, not a classification technique. We empirically prove that the combined feature set (i.e., HFS) extracted using our algorithm performs better than other individual feature sets (such as binary n-grams) regardless of the classifier (e.g., SVM/decision tree) used.

6.2.2 RELATED WORK

There have been significant efforts in recent years to detect malicious executables. There are two mainstream techniques to automate the detection process: behavioral and content-based. The behavioral approach is primarily applied to detect mobile malicious code. This technique is applied to analyze network traffic characteristics such as source-destination ports/IP addresses, various packet level/flow level statistics, and application-level characteristics such as email attachment type, attachment size, etc. Examples of behavioral approaches include social network analysis [GOLB2004, NEWM2002] and statistical analysis [SCHU2001a]. A data mining-based behavioral approach for detecting email worms has been proposed by [MASU2007a]. [GARG2006] apply feature-extraction technique along with machine learning for *masquerade detection*. They extract features from user behavior in GUI-based systems, such as mouse speed, number of clicks per session, and so on. Then the problem is modeled as a binary classification problem, and trained and tested with SVM. Our approach is content-based, rather than behavioral.

The content-based approach analyzes the content of the executable. Some of them try to automatically generate signatures from network packet payloads. Examples are EarlyBird [SING2003], Autograph [KIM2004], and Polygraph [NEWS2005]. In contrast, our method does not require signature generation or signature matching. Some other content-based techniques extract features from the executables and apply machine learning to detect malicious executables. Examples are given in [SCHU2001b] and [KOLT2004]. The work in [SCHU2001a] and [SCHU2001b] extracts DLL call information using GNU Bin-Utils and character strings using GNU *strings*, from the header of Windows PE executables [CYGN1999, Windows P.E.]. Also, they use byte sequences as features. We use byte sequences and DLL call information, but we also apply disassembly and use assembly instructions as features. Besides, we extract byte patterns of various lengths (from 2 to 10 bytes), whereas they extract only 2-byte length patterns. A similar work is done by [KOLT2004]. They extract binary *n*-gram features from the binary executables and apply them to different classification methods, and report accuracy. Our model is different from [KOLT2004] in that we extract not only the binary *n*-grams but also assembly instruction sequences from the disassembled executables, and gather DLL call information from the program headers. We compare our model's performance only with [KOLT2004], since they report higher accuracy than that given in [SCHU2001a] and [SCHU2001b].

6.2.3 Hybrid Feature Retrieval Model

Our HFR model is a novel idea in malicious code detection. It extracts useful features from disassembled executables using the information obtained from binary executables. It then combines the assembly features with other features like DLL function calls and binary *n*-gram features. We have addressed a number of difficult implementation issues and provided efficient, scalable, and practical solutions. The difficulties that we face during implementation are related to memory limitations and long running times. By using efficient data structures, algorithms, and disk I/O, we are able to implement a fast, scalable, and robust system for malicious code detection. We run our experiments on two datasets with different class distribution, and show that a more realistic distribution improves the performance of our model.

Our model also has a few limitations. First, it does not directly handle obfuscated DLL calls or encrypted/packed binaries. There are techniques available for detecting obfuscated DLL calls in the binary [LAKH2005] and to unpack the packed binaries automatically. We may apply these tools for de-obfuscation/decryption and use their output to our model. Although this is not implemented yet, we look forward to integrating these tools with our model in our future versions. Second, the current implementation is an offline detection mechanism. Meaning, it cannot be directly deployed on a network to detect malicious code. However, it can detect malicious codes in near real time.

We address these issues in our future work, and vow to solve these problems. We also propose several modifications to our model. For example, we would like to combine our features with *run-time* characteristics of the executables. Besides, we propose building a feature database that would store all the features and be updated incrementally. This would save a large amount of training time and memory. Our approach is illustrated in Figure 6.3.

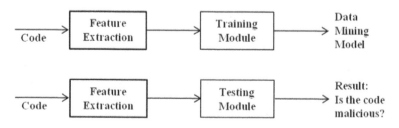

FIGURE 6.3 Our approach to detecting malicious executables.

6.3 DESIGN OF THE DATA MINING TOOL

6.3.1 FEATURE EXTRACTION USING n-GRAM ANALYSIS

Before going into the details of the process, we illustrate a code snippet in Figure 6.4 from the Email-Worm "Win32.Ainjo.e," and use it as a running example throughout this chapter.

Feature extraction using n-gram analysis involves extracting all possible n-grams from the given dataset (*training set*), and selecting the best n-grams among them. Each such n-gram is a feature. We extend the notion of n-gram from bytes to assembly instructions, and DLL function calls. That is, an n-gram may be either a sequence of n bytes, n assembly instructions, or n DLL function calls, depending on whether we are to extract features from binary executables, assembly programs, or DLL call sequences, respectively. Before extracting n-grams, we pre-process the binary executables by converting them to *hexdump* files and *assembly program* files, as explained shortly.

6.3.1.1 A Binary n-Gram Feature

Here the granularity level is a *byte*. We apply the UNIX "hexdump" utility to convert the binary executable files into text files, mentioned henceforth as "hexdump files," containing the hexadecimal numbers corresponding to each byte of the binary. This process is performed to ensure safe and easy portability of the binary executables. The feature extraction process consists of two phases: (i) feature collection, and (ii) feature selection, both of which are explained in the following subsections.

6.3.1.2 Feature Collection

We collect binary n-grams *from* the "hexdump" files. This is illustrated in example-I.

Example-I

The 4-grams corresponding to the first 6 bytes sequence (FF2108900027) from the executable in Figure 1 are the 4-byte sliding windows: FF210890, 21089000, and 08900027

The basic feature collection process runs as follows. At first, we initialize a list L of n-grams to empty. Then we scan each hexdump file by sliding an n-byte window. Each such n-byte sequence is an n-gram.

```
----------------------------------------------------------------
CODE SNIPPET:-

Program Entry Point = 00472E70
(Email-worm.win32.Ainjo.e File Offset:00000400)

   address   opcode                       assembly
   --------  ------                       -----------------------
   :00455000 FF21                         jmp dword[ecx]
   :00455002 089000270014                 or byte[eax+14002700], dl
   :00455008 00761E                       add byte[esi+1E], dh
   :0045500B 45                           inc ebp
   :0045500C 00DE                         add dh, bl
   :00455010 B4DE                         mov ah, -22

----------------------------------------------------------------
DLL FUNCTION CALL INFO FROM THE HEADER

     Module : KERNEL32.DLL

   Addr:00073CAE Name: LoadLibraryA
   Addr:00073CBC Name: GetProcAddress
   Addr:00073CCC Name: ExitProcess
----------------------------------------------------------------
```

FIGURE 6.4 Code snippet and DLL call info from the Email-Worm "Win32.Ainjo.e."

Each n-gram g is associated with two values: p_1 and n_1, denoting the total number of positive instances (i.e., malicious executables) and negative instances (i.e., benign executables), respectively, that contain g. If g is not found in L, then g is added to L, and p_1 and n_1 are updated as necessary. If g is already in L, then only p_1 and n_1 are updated. When all hexdump files have been scanned, L contains all the unique n-grams in the dataset along with their frequencies in the positive and negative instances. There are several implementation issues related to this basic approach. First, the total number of n-grams may be very large. For example, the total number of 10-grams in our second dataset is 200 million. It may not possible to store all of them in computer's main memory. To solve this problem, we store the n-grams in a disk file F. Second, if L is not sorted, then a linear search is required for each scanned n-gram to test whether it is already in L. If N is the total number of n-grams in the dataset, then the time for collecting all the n-grams would be $O(N^2)$, an impractical amount of time when $N = 200$ million.

In order to solve the second problem, we use a data structure called Adelson Velsky Landis (AVL) tree [GOOD2006] to store the n-grams in memory. An AVL tree is a height-balanced binary search tree. This tree has a property that the absolute difference between the heights of the left sub-tree and the right sub-tree of any node is at most one. If this property is violated during insertion or deletion, a balancing operation is performed, and the tree regains its height-balanced property. It is guaranteed that insertions and deletions are performed in logarithmic time. So, in order to insert an n-gram in memory, we now need only $O(\log_2 (N))$ searches. Thus, the total running time is reduced to $O(N\log_2 (N))$, making the overall running time about five million times faster for N as large as 200 million. Our feature collection algorithm *extract feature* implements these two solutions. It is illustrated in Algorithm 6.1.

Description of the algorithm: the *for* loop at line 3 runs for each hexdump file in the training set. The inner *while* loop at line 4 gathers all the n-grams of a file and adds it to the AVL tree if it is not already there. At line 8, a test is performed to see whether the tree size has exceeded the memory limit (a threshold value). If it exceeds and F is empty, then we save the contents of the tree in F (line 9). If F is not empty, then we merge the contents of the tree with F (line 10). Finally, we delete all the nodes from the tree (line 12).

Time Complexity: T = time (n-gram reading and inserting in tree) + time (merging with disk) = $O(B\log_2 K) + O(N)$, where B is the total size of the training data in *bytes*, K is the maximum number of nodes of the tree (i.e., threshold), and N is the total number of n-grams collected. Space Complexity: $O(K)$, where K is defined as above.

ALGORITHM 6.1   THE *N*-GRAM FEATURE COLLECTION ALGORITHM

Procedure Extract Feature (B)
   $B = \{B_1, B_2, ..., B_K\}$: all hexdump files
   1. $T \leftarrow$ empty tree // Initialize AVL-tree
   2. $F \leftarrow$ new file // Initialize disk file
   3. **for** each $B_i \in B$ **do**
   4. **while not** EOF(B_i) **do** // while not end of file
   5. $g \leftarrow$ next-gram (B_i) // read next n-gram
   6. T.insert(g) // insert into tree and/or update frequencies as necessary
   7. **end while**
   8. if T.size > *Threshold* **then** // save or merge
   9. **if** F is empty **then** $F \leftarrow T$.inorder() // save tree data in sorted order
   10. **else** $F \leftarrow$ merge(T.inorder(), F) // merge tree data with file data and save
   11. **end if**
   12. $T \leftarrow$ empty tree // release memory
   13. **end if**
   14. **end for**

6.3.1.3 Feature Selection

If the total number of extracted features is very large, it may not be possible to use all of them for training because of several reasons. First, the memory requirement may be impractical. Second, training may be too slow. Third, a classifier may become confused with a large number of features, because most of them would be noisy, redundant or irrelevant. So, we are to choose a small, relevant, and useful subset of features. We choose *information gain* (IG) as the selection criterion because it is one of the best criteria used in literature for selecting the best features.

IG can be defined as a measure of effectiveness of an attribute (i.e., feature) in classifying a training data [MITC1997]. If we split the training data based on the values of this attribute, then IG gives the measurement of the expected reduction in entropy after the split. The more an attribute can reduce entropy in the training data, the better the attribute is in classifying the data. IG of an attribute A on a collection of instances I is given by Equation (6.1):

$$Gain\,(I, A) \equiv Entropy\,(I) - \sum_{V \in values\,(A)} \frac{p_v + n_v}{p + n} Entropy\,(I_v) \tag{6.1}$$

where *values* (A) is the set of all possible values for attribute A; I_v is the subset of I where all instances have the value of $A = v$; p is the total number of positive instances in I; n is the total number of negative instances in I; p_v is the total number of positive instances in I_v; n_v is the total number of negative instances in I_v.

In our case, each attribute has only two possible values, that is, $v \in \{0, 1\}$. If an attribute A (i.e., an n-gram) is present in an instance X, then $X_A = 1$, otherwise it is 0. Entropy of I is computed using the following Equation (6.2):

$$Entropy\,(I) = -\frac{p}{p + n} \log_2\left(\frac{p}{p + n}\right) - \frac{n}{p + n} \log_2\left(\frac{n}{p + n}\right) \tag{6.2}$$

where I, p, and n are as defined above. Substituting (6.2) in (6.1) and letting $t = n + p$, we get

$$Gain\,(I, A) \equiv -\frac{p}{t} \log_2\left(\frac{p}{t}\right) - \frac{n}{t} \log_2\left(\frac{n}{t}\right) - \sum_{v \in \{0,1\}} \frac{t_v}{t}\left(-\frac{p_v}{t_v} \log_2\left(\frac{p_v}{t_v}\right) - \frac{n_v}{t_v} \log_2\left(\frac{n_v}{t_v}\right)\right) \tag{6.3}$$

Now, the next problem is to select the best S features (i.e., n-grams) according to IG. One naïve approach is to sort the n-grams in non-increasing order of IG and selecting the top S of them, which requires $O(N\log_2 N)$ time and $O(N)$ main memory. But this selection can be more efficiently accomplished using a *heap* that requires $O(N\log_2 S)$ time and $O(S)$ main memory. For $S = 500$ and $N = 200$ million, this approach is more than three times faster and requires 400,000 times less main memory. A heap is a balanced binary tree with the property that the root of any sub-tree contains the minimum (maximum) element in that sub-tree. We use a *min-heap* that always has the minimum value at its root. Algorithm 6.2 sketches the feature selection algorithm. At first, the heap is initialized to empty. Then the n-grams (along with their frequencies) are read from disk (line 2) and inserted into the heap (line 5) until the heap size becomes S. After the heap size becomes equal to S, we compare the IG of the next n-gram g against the IG of the root. If IG $(root) >=$ IG (g), then g is discarded (line 6) since *root* has the minimum IG. Otherwise, *root* is replaced with g (line 7). Finally, the heap property is *restored* (line 9). The process terminates when there are no more n-gramsin the disk. After termination, we have the S best n-grams in the heap.

ALGORITHM 6.2   THE *N*-GRAM FEATURE SELECTION ALGORITHM

Procedure Select_Feature (F, H, p, n)
    F: a disk file containing all *n*-grams
    H: empty heap
    p: total number of positive examples
    n: total number of negative examples
    1. **while** not EOF(*F*) **do**
    2. $<g, p_1, n_1> \leftarrow$ next_ngram(*F*) //read *n*-gram with frequency counts
    3. $p_0 = P - p_1, n_0 = N - n_1$ // #of positive and negative examples not containing *g*
    4. $IG \leftarrow$ Gain(p_0, n_0, p_1, n_1, p, n) // using Equation (6.3)
    5. **if** *H*.size() < *S***then***H*.insert(*g, IG*)
    6. **else if** *IG* <= *H.root.IG* **then continue** //discard lower gain *n*-grams
    7. **else** *H.root* $\leftarrow$ <*g, IG*> //replace root
    8. **end if**
    9. *H*.restore() //apply restore operation
    10. **end while**

The insertion and restoration takes only $O(\log_2(S))$ time. So, the total time required is $O(N\log_2 S)$, with only $O(S)$ main memory. We denote the best *S* binary features selected using IG criterion as the binary feature set (BFS).

6.3.1.4   Assembly *n*-Gram Feature

In this case, the level of granularity is an assembly instruction. First, we disassemble all the binary files using a disassembly tool called *PEDisassem* [Windows P.E.]. It is used to disassemble Windows Portable Executable (P.E.) files. Besides generating the assembly instructions with opcode and address information, PEDisassem provides useful information like list of resources (e.g., cursor) used, list of DLL functions called, list of exported functions, list of strings inside the code block, and so on. In order to extract assembly *n*-gram features, we follow a method similar to the binary *n*-gram feature extraction. First, we collect all possible *n*-grams, that is, sequences of *n* consecutive assembly instructions, and select the best *S* of them according to IG. We mention henceforth this selected set of features as assembly feature set (AFS). We face the same difficulties as in binary *n*-gram extraction, such as limited memory and slow running time, and solve them in the same way. Example-II illustrates the assembly *n*-gram features.

```
Example-II

The 2-grams corresponding to the first 4 assembly instructions
in Figure 1 are the two-instruction sliding windows:

jmp dword[ecx]                  ;   or byte[eax+14002700], dl
or byte[eax+14002700], dl       ;   add byte[esi+1E], dh
add byte[esi+1E], dh            ;   inc ebp
```

We adopt a standard representation of assembly instructions that has the following format: *name.param1.param2*. Name is the instruction name (e.g., *mov*), param1 is the first parameter, and param2 is the second parameter. Again, a parameter may be one of {*register, memory, constant*}. So, the second instruction above "*or byte [eax+14002700], dl*" becomes "*or.memory.register*" in our representation.

6.3.1.5   DLL Function Call Feature

Here the granularity level is a DLL function call. An *n*-gram of DLL function call is a sequence of *n* DLL function calls (possibly with other instructions in between two successive calls) in an executable. We extract the information about DLL function calls made by a program from the header of the disassembled file. This is illustrated in Figure 6.2. In our experiments, we use only 1 gram of DLL calls, since the higher grams have poorer performance. We enumerate all the DLL function names that have been used by each of the benign and malicious executables, and select the best *S* of them using information gain. We will mention this feature set as *DLL-call feature set* (DFS).

6.3.2   DETAILS OF THE HYBRID FEATURE RETRIEVAL MODEL

The HFR model extracts and combines three different kinds of features. HFR consists of different phases and components. The feature extraction components have already been discussed in details. Below is a brief description of the model.

6.3.2.1   Description of the Model

The HFR model consists of two phases: a training phase and a test phase. The training phase is shown in Figure 6.5(a), and the test phase is shown in Figure 6.5(b). In the training phase, we

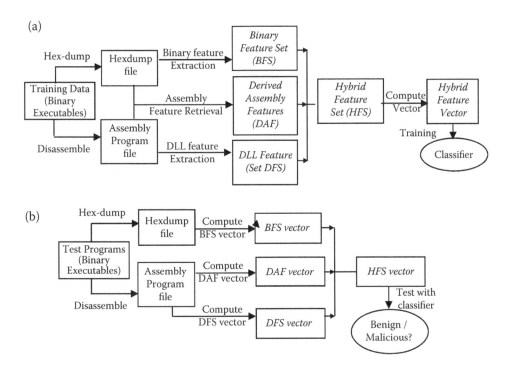

FIGURE 6.5   The hybrid feature retrieval model: (a) training phase, (b) test phase.

extract binary n-gram features (BFS) and DLL call features (DFS) using the approaches explained in this chapter. We then apply the AFR algorithm (to be explained shortly) to retrieve the derived assembly features (DAFs) that represent the selected binary n-gram features. These three kinds of features are combined into the HFS in short. Please note that DAF is different from assembly n-gram features (i.e., AFS).

AFS is not used in HFS because of our findings show that DAF performs better. We compute the binary feature vector corresponding to the HFS using the technique explained in this chapter and train a classifier using SVM, boosted decision tree, and other classification methods. In the test phase, we scan each test instance and compute the feature vector corresponding to the HFS. This vector is tested against the classifier. The classifier outputs the class prediction {benign, malicious} of the test file.

6.3.2.2   The Assembly Feature Retrieval (AFR) Algorithm

The AFR algorithm is used to extract assembly instruction sequences (i.e., DAFs) corresponding to the binary n-gram features. The main idea is to obtain the complete assembly instruction sequence of a given binary n-gram feature. The rationale behind using DAF is as follows. A binary n-gram may represent partial information, such as part(s) of one or more assembly instructions or a string inside the code block. We apply AFR algorithm to obtain the complete instruction or instruction sequence (i.e., a DAF) corresponding to the partial one. Thus, DAF represents more complete information, which should be more useful in distinguishing the malicious and benign executables. However, binary n-grams are still required because they also contain other information like string data, or important bytes at the program header. The AFR algorithm consists of several steps. In the first step, a *linear address matching* technique is applied as follows. The offset address of the n-gram in the hexdump file is used to find instructions at the same offset at the corresponding assembly program file. Based on the offset value, one of the three situations may occur:

   i. The offset is before program entry point, so there is no corresponding assembly code for the n-gram. We refer to this address as *address before entry point* (ABEP).
   ii. There is some data but no code at that offset. We refer to this address as DATA.
   iii. There is some code at that offset. We refer to this address as CODE. If this offset is in the middle of an instruction, then we take the whole instruction and consecutive instructions within n bytes from the instruction.

In the second step, the best CODE instance is selected among all CODE instances. We apply a heuristic to find the best sequence, called the *most distinguishing instruction sequence* (MDIS) heuristic. According to this heuristic, we choose the instruction sequence that has the highest IG. The AFR algorithm is shown in Algorithm 6.3.

Description of the algorithm: line 1 initializes the lists that would contain the assembly sequences. The *for* loop in line 2 runs for each hexdump file. Each hexdump file is scanned and n-grams are extracted (lines 4–5). If any of these n-grams are in the BFS (lines 6–7), then we read the instruction sequence from the corresponding assembly program file at the corresponding address (lines 8–10). This sequence is added to the appropriate list (line 12). In this way, we collect all the sequences corresponding to each n-gram in the BFS. In phase II, we select the best sequence in each n-gram list using IG (lines 18–21). Finally, we return the best sequences, that is, DAFs.

ALGORITHM 6.3   THE ASSEMBLY FEATURE RETRIEVAL ALGORITHM

Procedure Assembly_Feature_Retrieval (G, A, B)

$G = \{g_1, g_2, ..., g_M\}$: the selected n-gram features (BFS)

$A = \{A_1, A_2, ..., A_L\}$: all assembly files

$B = \{B_1, B_2, ..., B_L\}$: all hexdump files

S = size of BFS

L = #of training files

Q_i: a list containing the possible instruction sequences for g_i

//phase I: sequence collection

1. **for** $i = 1$ to S **do** $Q_i \leftarrow$ empty **end for** //initialize sequence lists
2. **for** each $B_i \in B$ **do** //phase I: sequence collection
3. *offset* $\leftarrow$ 0 //current offset in file
4. **while not** EOF(B_i) **do** //read the whole file
5. $g \leftarrow$ next_ngram(B_i) //read next n-gram
6. *<index, found>* $\leftarrow$ BinarySearch(G, g) // *seach g in G*
7. **if** *found* **then** // found
8. $q \leftarrow$ an empty sequence
9. **for** each instruction r in A_i with address(r)$\in$[*offset, offset + n*] **do**
10. $q \leftarrow q \cup r$
11. **end for**
12. $Q_{index} \leftarrow Q_{index} \cup q$ //add to the sequence
13. **end if**
14. *offset = offset + 1*
15. **end while**
16. **end for**
17. $V \leftarrow$ empty list //phase II: sequence selection
18. **for** $i = 1$ to S **do** //for each Q_i
19. $q \leftarrow t \in \{Q_i \mid \forall_{u \in Q_i}$ IG(t) >= IG(u) //the sequence with the highest IG
20. $V \leftarrow V \cup q$
21. **end for**
22. **return**V// DAF sequences

Time complexity of this algorithm is $O(nB\log_2 S)$, where B is the total size of training set in *bytes*, S is the total #of selected binary n-gram, and n is size of each n-gram in *bytes*. Space complexity is O (*SC*), where S is defined as above and C is the average #of assembly sequences found per binary n-gram. The running time and memory requirements of all three algorithms are given in Section 6.4.

6.3.2.3   Feature Vector Computation and Classification

Each feature in a feature set (e.g., HFS, BFS) is a binary feature, meaning, its value is either 1 or 0. If the feature is present in an instance (i.e., an executable), then its value is 1, otherwise its value is 0. For each training (or testing) instance, we compute a feature vector, which is a bit vector consisting of the feature-values of the corresponding feature set. For example, if we want to compute the feature vector V_{BFS} corresponding to BFS of a particular instance I, then for each feature $f \in$ BFS we search f in I. If f is found in I, then we set $V_{BFS}[f]$ (i.e., the bit corresponding to f) to 1, otherwise, we set it to 0. In this way, we set/reset each bit in the feature vector. These feature vectors are used by the classifiers for training/testing.

We apply SVM, Naïve Bayes (NB), boosted decision tree, and other classifiers for the classification task. SVM can perform either linear or non-linear classification. The linear classifier proposed by

Vladimir Vapnik creates a hyperplane that separates the data points into two classes with the maximum margin. A maximum-margin hyperplane is the one that splits the training examples into two subsets, such that the distance between the hyperplane and its closest data point(s) is maximized. A non-linear SVM [BOSE2003] is implemented by applying kernel trick to maximum-margin hyperplanes. The feature space is transformed into a higher dimensional space, where the maximum-margin hyperplane is found. A decision tree contains attribute tests at each internal node and a decision at each leaf node. It classifies an instance by performing attribute tests from root to a decision node. Decision tree is a rule-based classifier. Meaning, we can obtain human-readable classification rules from the tree. J48 is the implementation of C4.5 Decision Tree algorithm. C4.5 is an extension to the ID3 algorithm invented by Quinlan. A boosting technique called AdaBoost combines multiple classifiers by assigning weights to each of them according to their classification performance =. The algorithm starts by assigning equal weights to all training samples, and a model is obtained from this training data. Then each misclassified example's weight is increased, and another model is obtained from this new training data. This is iterated for a specified number of times. During classification, each of these models is applied on the test data, and a weighted voting is performed to determine the class of the test instance. We use the AdaBoost.M1 algorithm [FREU1996] on NB and J48. We only report SVM and Boosted J48 results because they have the best results. It should be noted that we do not have any preference of any of these two classifiers over the other. We discuss the experimental results in the next section.

6.4 EVALUATION AND RESULTS

6.4.1 EXPERIMENTS

We design our experiments to run on two different datasets. Each dataset has different sizes and distributions of benign and malicious executables. We generate all kinds of n-gram features (e.g., BFS, AFS, DFS) using the techniques explained in [MASU2011]. Notice that the BFS corresponds to the features extracted by the method of [KOLT2004]. We also generate the DAF and HFS using our model as explained in [MASU2011]. We test the accuracy of each of the feature sets applying a three-fold cross validation using classifiers such as SVM, decision tree, Naïve Bayes, Bayes Net, and boosted decision tree. Among these classifiers, we obtain the best results with SVM and boosted decision tree, reported in [MASU2011]. We do not report other classifier results due to space limitations. In addition to this, we compute the average accuracy, false positive and false negative rate, and receiver operating characteristic (ROC) graphs (using techniques in [FAWC2003]. We also compare the running time and performance/cost trade-off between HFS and BFS.

6.4.2 DATASET

We have two non-disjoint datasets. The first dataset (dataset1) contains a collection of 1,435 executables, 597 of which are benign and 838 are malicious. The second dataset (dataset2) contains 2,452 executables, having 1,370 benign and 1,082 malicious executables. So, the distribution of dataset1 is benign = 41.6%, malicious = 58.4%, and that of dataset2 is benign = 55.9%, malicious = 44.1%. This distribution was chosen intentionally to evaluate the performance of the feature sets in different scenarios. We collect the benign executables from different Windows XP and Windows 2000 machines, and collect the malicious executables from [VX-Heavens], which contains a large collection of malicious executables. The benign executables contain various applications found at the Windows installation folder (e.g., "C:\Windows"), as well as other executables in the default program installation directory (e.g., "C:\Program Files"). Malicious executables contain viruses, worms, Trojans, and backdoors. We select only the Win32 Portable Executables [Windows P.E.] in both the cases. We would like to experiment with the ELF executables in the future.

6.4.3 EXPERIMENTAL SETUP

Our implementation is developed in Java with JDK 1.5. We use the libSVM library [LIBSVM] for running SVM, and Weka ML toolbox [WEKA] for running Boosted decision tree and other classifiers. For SVM, we run C-SVC with a polynomial kernel; using gamma = 0.1, and epsilon = 1.0E-12. For boosted decision tree, we run ten iterations of the AdaBoost algorithm on the C4.5 decision tree algorithm, called J48.

We set the parameter S (#of selected features) to 500, since it is the best value found in our experiments. Most of our experiments are run on two machines: a Sun Solaris machine with 4GB main memory and 2GHz clock speed, and a LINUX machine with 2GB main memory and 1.8GHz clock speed. The reported running times are based on the latter machine. The disassembly and hexdump are done only once for all machine executables and the resulting files are stored. We then run our experiments on the stored files.

6.4.4 RESULTS

In this sub-section, we first report and analyze the results obtained by running SVM on the dataset. Later, we show the accuracies of Boosted J48. Since the results from Boosted J48 are almost the same as SVM, we do not report the analyses based on Boosted J48.

6.4.4.1 Accuracy
Table 6.1 shows the accuracy of SVM on different feature sets. The columns headed by HFS, BFS, and AFS represent the accuracies of the HFS (our method), BFS (Kolter & Maloof's feature set), and AFS, respectively. Note that the AFS is different from the DAF that has been used in the HFS. Table 6.1 reports that the classification accuracy of HFS is always better than other models, on both datasets. It is interesting to note that the accuracies for 1-gram BFS are very low in both datasets. This is because 1 gram is only a 1-byte long pattern, having only 256 different possibilities. Thus, this pattern is not useful at all in distinguishing the malicious executables from the normal, and may not be used in a practical application. So, we exclude the 1-gram accuracies while computing the average accuracies (i.e., the last row).

6.4.4.1.1 Dataset1
Here the best accuracy of the hybrid model is for $n = 6$, which is 97.4, and is the highest among all feature sets. On average, the accuracy of HFS is 1.68% higher than that of BFS, and 11.36% higher

TABLE 6.1

Classification accuracy (%) of SVM on different feature sets

n	Dataset1			Dataset2		
	HFS	BFS	AFS	HFS	BFS	AFS
1	93.4	63.0	88.4	92.1	59.4	88.6
2	96.8	94.1	88.1	96.3	92.1	87.9
4	96.3	95.6	90.9	**97.4**	92.8	89.4
6	**97.4**	95.5	87.2	96.9	93.0	86.7
8	96.9	95.1	87.7	97.2	93.4	85.1
10	97.0	95.7	73.7	97.3	92.8	75.8
Avg	96.30	89.83	86.00	96.20	87.25	85.58
Avg^1	96.88	95.20	85.52	97.02	92.82	84.98

than that of AFS. Accuracies of AFS are always the lowest. One possible reason behind this poor performance is that AFS considers only the CODE part of the executables. So, AFS misses any distinguishing pattern carried by the ABEP or DATA parts, and as a result, the extracted features have poorer performance. Moreover, the accuracy of AFS greatly deteriorates for $n >= 10$. This is because longer sequences of instructions are rarer in either class of executables (malicious/benign), so these sequences have less distinguishing power. On the other hand, BFS considers all parts of the executable, achieving higher accuracy. Finally, HFS considers DLL calls, as well as BFS and DAF. So, HFS has better performance than BFS.

6.4.4.1.2 Dataset2

Here the differences between the accuracies of HFS and BFS are greater than that of dataset1. The average accuracy of HFS is 4.2% higher than that of BFS. Accuracies of AFS are again the lowest. It is interesting to note that HFS has an improved performance over BFS (and AFS) in dataset2. Two important conclusions may be derived from this observation. First, dataset2 is much larger than dataset1, having a more diverse set of examples. Here HFS performs better than dataset1, whereas BFS performs worse than dataset1. This implies that HFS is more robust than BFS in a diverse and larger set of instances. Thus, HFS is more applicable than BFS in a large, diverse corpus of executables. Second, dataset2 has more benign executables than malicious, whereas dataset1 has less benign executables. This distribution of dataset2 is more likely in a real world, where benign executables outnumber malicious executables. This implies that HFS is likely to perform better than BFS in a real-world scenario, having a larger number of benign executables in the dataset.

6.4.4.1.3 Statistical significance test

We also perform a pair-wise two-tailed t-test on the HFS and BFS accuracies to test whether the differences between their accuracies are statistically significant. We exclude 1-gram accuracies from this test for the reason explained above. The result of the t-test is summarized in Table 6.2. The t-value shown in this table is the value of t obtained from the accuracies. There are $(5 + 5 - 2)$ *degrees of freedom*, since we have five observations in each group, and there are two groups (i.e., HFS and BFS). *Probability* denotes the probability of rejecting the NULL hypothesis (that there is no difference between HFS and BFS accuracies), while p-value denotes the probability of accepting the NULL hypothesis. For dataset1, the probability is 99.65%, and for dataset2, it is 100.0%. Thus, we conclude that the average accuracy of HFS is significantly higher than that of BFS.

6.4.4.1.4 DLL call feature

Here we report the accuracies of the DLL function call features (DFS). The 1-gram accuracies are: 92.8% for dataset1 and 91.9% for dataset2. The accuracies for higher grams are less than 75%, so

TABLE 6.2

Pair-wise two-tailed t-test results comparing HFS and BFS

	DataSet1	DataSet2
t-value	8.9	14.6
Degrees of freedom	8	8
Probability	0.9965	1.00
p-value	0.0035	0.0000

we do not report them. The reason behind this poor performance is possibly that there are no distinguishing call sequences that can identify the executables as malicious or benign.

6.4.4.2 ROC Curves

ROC curves plot the true positive rate against the false positive rates of a classifier. Figure 6.6 shows ROC curves of dataset1 for $n = 6$ and dataset2 for $n = 4$ based on SVM testing. ROC curves for other values of n have similar trends, except for $n = 1$, where AFS performs better than BFS. It is evident from the curves that HFS is always dominant (i.e., has larger area under the curve) over the other two, and it is more dominant in dataset2. Table 6.3 reports the area under the curve (AUC) for the ROC curves of each of the features sets. A higher value of AUC indicates a higher probability that a classifier will predict correctly. Table 6.3 shows that the AUC for HFS is the highest, and it improves (relative to other two) in dataset2. This also supports our hypothesis that our model will perform better in a more likely real-world scenario, where benign executables occur more frequently.

6.4.4.3 False Positive and False Negative

Table 6.4 reports the false positive and false negative rates (in percentage) for each feature set based on SVM output. The last row reports the average. Again, we exclude the 1-gram values from the average. Here we see that in dataset1, the average false positive rate of HFS is 4.9%, which is the lowest. In dataset2, this rate is even lower (3.2%). False positive rate is a measure of false alarm rate. Thus, our model has the lowest false alarm rate. We also observe that this rate decreases as we increase

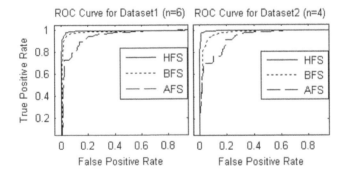

FIGURE 6.6 ROC curves for different feature sets in dataset1 (left), and dataset2 (right).

TABLE 6.3
Area under the ROC curve on different feature sets

n	Dataset1			Dataset2		
	HFS	**BFS**	**AFS**	**HFS**	**BFS**	**AFS**
1	0.9767	0.7023	0.9467	0.9666	0.7250	0.9489
2	0.9883	0.9782	0.9403	0.9919	0.9720	0.9373
4	0.9928	0.9825	0.9651	0.9948	0.9708	0.9515
6	0.9949	0.9831	0.9421	0.9951	0.9733	0.9358
8	0.9946	0.9766	0.9398	0.9956	0.9760	0.9254
10	0.9929	0.9777	0.8663	0.9967	0.9700	0.8736
Avg	**0.9900**	**0.9334**	**0.9334**	**0.9901**	**0.9312**	**0.9288**
Avg[1]	**0.9927**	**0.9796**	**0.9307**	**0.9948**	**0.9724**	**0.9247**

[1]Average value excluding 1-gram

TABLE 6.4

False positive and false negative rates on different feature sets

FEATURE

n	Dataset1			Dataset2		
	HFS	BFS	AFS	HFS	BFS	AFS
1	8.0/5.6	77.7/7.9	12.4/11.1	7.5/8.3	65.0/9.8	12.8/9.6
2	5.3/1.7	6.0/5.7	22.8/4.2	3.4/4.1	5.6/10.6	15.1/8.3
4	4.9/2.9	6.4/3.0	16.4/3.8	2.5/2.2	7.4/6.9	12.6/8.1
6	3.5/ 2.0	5.7/3.7	24.5/4.5	3.2/2.9	6.1/8.1	17.8/7.6
8	4.9/1.9	6.0/4.1	26.3/2.3	3.1/2.3	6.0/7.5	19.9/8.6
10	5.5/1.2	5.2/3.6	43.9/1.7	3.4/1.9	6.3/8.4	30.4/16.4
Avg	**5.4/2.6**	17.8/4.7	24.4/3.3	**3.9/3.6**	16.1/8.9	18.1/9.8
Avg[1]	**4.9/2.0**	5.8/4.1	26.8/1.7	**3.2/2.7**	6.3/8.1	19.2/17.8

[1]Average value excluding 1-gram

the number of benign examples. This is because the classifier gets more familiar with benign executables and misclassifies fewer of them as malicious. We believe that a large collection of training set with a larger portion of benign executables would eventually diminish false positive rate toward zero. The false negative rate is also the lowest for HFS as reported in Table 6.4.

6.4.4.4 Running Time

We compare in Table 6.5 the running times (feature extraction, training, testing) of different kind of features (HFS, BFS, AFS) for different values of n. Feature extraction time for HFS and AFS includes the disassembly time, which is 465 seconds (in total) for dataset1, and 865 seconds (in

TABLE 6.5

Running times (in seconds)

	n	Dataset1				Dataset2			
		HFS	BFS	AFS	Cost factor[1]	HFS	BFS	AFS	Cost factor[1]
Feature Extraction	1	498.41	135.94	553.2	3.67	841.67	166.87	908.42	5.04
	2	751.93	367.46	610.85	2.05	1157.5	443.99	949.7	2.61
	4	1582.2	1189.6	739.51	1.33	3820.7	3103.14	1194.4	1.23
	6	2267.9	1877.6	894.26	1.21	8010.2	7291.4	1519.5	1.1
	8	2971.9	2572.2	1035.0	1.16	11736.	11011.6	1189.0	1.07
	10	3618.3	3223.2	807.85	1.12	15594.	14858.6	2957	1.05
	Avg[2]	2610.0	2215.6	869.17	1.18	9790.6	9066.22	1714.9	1.08
Training	Avg[3]	2654.6	2258.8	910.68	**1.18**	9857.8	9134.36	1782.8	**1.08**
Testing	Avg[3]	195.25	40.09	194.9	**4.87**	377.89	83.91	348.35	**4.5**
Testing/MB		**1.74**	**0.36**	1.74	4.87	**1.57**	**0.35**	1.45	4.5
Throughput(MB/s)		**0.6**	**2.8**	0.6	---	**0.64**	**2.86**	0.69	---

[1]Ratio of time required for HFS to time required for BFS
[2]Average feature extraction times excluding 1-gram and 2-gram
[3]Average training/testing times excluding 1-gram and 2-gram

TABLE 6.6
Performance/cost trade-off between HFS and BFS

	Performance improvement (%) (HFS − BFS) /BFS	Training Cost Factor (HFS / BFS)	Testing Cost Factor (HFS / BFS)
Dataset1	1.73	1.17	4.87
Dataset2	4.52	1.08	4.5

total) for dataset2. Training time is the sum of feature extraction time, feature-vector computation time, and SVM training time. Testing time is the sum of disassembly time (except BFS) feature-vector computation time, and SVM classification time. Training and testing times based on Boosted J48 have almost similar characteristics, so we do not report them. Table 6.5 also reports the cost factor as a ratio of time required for HFS relative to BFS.

The column *cost factor* shows this comparison. The average feature-extraction times are computed by excluding the 1-gram and 2-grams, since these grams are unlikely to be used in practical applications. The boldface cells in the table are of particular interest to us. From the table we see that the running times for HFS training and testing on dataset1 are 1.17 and 4.87 times higher than those of BFS, respectively. For dataset2, these numbers are 1.08 and 4.5, respectively. The average throughput for HFS is found to be 0.6 MB/s (in both datasets), which may be considered as near real-time performance.

Finally, we summarize the cost/performance trade-off in Table 6.6. The column Performance Improvement reports the accuracy improvement of HFS over BFS. The cost factors are shown in the next two columns. If we drop the disassembly time from testing time (considering that disassembly is done offline), then the testing cost factor diminishes to 1.0 for both datasets. It is evident from Table 6.6 that the performance/cost trade-off is better for dataset2 than dataset1. Again, we may infer that our model is likely to perform better in a larger and more realistic dataset. The main bottleneck of our system is disassembly cost. The testing cost factor is higher because here a larger proportion of time is used up in disassembly. We believe that this factor may be greatly reduced by optimizing the disassembler, and considering that disassembly can be done offline.

6.4.4.5 Training and Testing with Boosted J48
We also train and test with this classifier and report the classification accuracies for different features and different values of n in Table 6.7. The second last row (*Avg*) of Table 6.7 is the average of 2-gram to x-gram accuracies. Again, for consistency, we exclude 1-gram from the average. We also include the average accuracies of SVM (from last row of Table 6.1) in the last row of Table 6.6 for ease of comparison. We would like to point out some important observations regarding this comparison. First, the average accuracies of SVM and Boosted J48 are almost the same, being within 0.4% of each other (for HFS). There is no clear winner between these two classifiers. So, we may use any of these classifiers for our model. Second, accuracies of HFS are again the best among all three. Besides, HFS has 1.84% and 3.6% better accuracies than BFS in dataset1 and dataset2, respectively. This result also justifies our claim that HFS is a better feature set than BFS, irrespective of the classifier used.

6.4.5 EXAMPLE RUN

Here we illustrate an example run of the AFR algorithm. The algorithm scans through each hexdump file, sliding a window of n bytes and checking the n-gram against the binary feature set

TABLE 6.7

Classification accuracy (%) of boosted J48 on different feature sets

N	Dataset1			Dataset2		
	HFS	BFS	AFS	HFS	BFS	AFS
1	93.9	64.1	91.3	93.5	58.8	90.2
2	96.4	93.2	89.4	97.1	92.7	85.1
4	96.3	95.4	92.1	97.2	93.6	87.5
6	96.3	95.3	87.8	97.6	93.6	85.4
8	96.7	94.1	89.1	97.6	94.3	83.7
10	96.6	95.1	77.1	97.8	95.1	82.6
Avg[1] (Boosted J48)	96.46	94.62	87.1	97.46	93.86	84.86
Avg[2](SVM)	96.88	95.20	85.52	97.02	92.82	84.98

[1]Average accuracy excluding 1-gram.

[2]Average accuracy for SVM

(BFS). If a match is found, then we collect the corresponding (same offset address) assembly instruction sequence in the assembly program file. In this way, we collect all possible instruction sequences of all the features in BFS. Later, we select the best sequence using information gain. Table 6.8 shows an example of the collection of assembly sequences and their IG values corresponding to the n-gram "00005068." Note that this n-gram has 90 occurrences (in all hexdump

TABLE 6.8

Assembly code sequence for binary 4-gram "00005068"

Sequence #	Op-code	Assembly code	Information Gain
1	E8B7020000 50 6828234000	call 00401818 push eax push 00402328	0.5
2	0FB6800D020000 50 68CC000000	movzx eax,byte[eax+20] push eax push 000000CC	0.1
3	8B805C040000 50 6801040000	mov eax, dword[eax+45] push eax push 00000401	0.2
29	8D8010010000 50 6807504000	lea eax, dword[eax+110] push eax push 00405007	0.7
50	25FFFF0000 50 68E8164100	and eax, 0000FFFF push eax push 004116E8	0.3
90	25FFFF0000 50 68600E4100	and eax, 0000FFFF push eax push 00410E60	0.4

TABLE 6.9
Time and space complexities of different algorithms

Algorithm	Time Complexity	Space complexity
Feature Collection	$O(Blog_2K) + O(N)$	$O(K)$
Feature Selection	$O(Nlog_2S)$	$O(S)$
Assembly Feature Retrieval	$O(nBlog_2S)$	$O(SC)$
Total (worst case)	$O(nBlog_2K)$	$O(SC)$

files). We have shown only 5 of them for brevity. The bolded portion of the op-code in Table 6.8 represents the *n*-gram. According to the *Most Distinguishing Instruction Sequence* (MDIS) heuristic, we find that sequence #29 attains the highest information gain, which is selected as the DAF of the *n*-gram. In this way, we select one DAF per binary *n*-gram, and return all DAFs.

Next, we summarize the time and space complexities of our algorithms in Table 6.9. B is the total size of training set in *bytes*, C is the average #of assembly sequences found per binary *n*-gram, K is the maximum #of nodes of the AVL tree (i.e., threshold), N is the total number of *n*-grams collected, *n* is size of each *n*-gram in *bytes,* and S is the total number of selected *n*-grams. The worst-case assumption: $B > N$ and $SC > K$

6.5   BIG DATA ANALYTICS

The previous sections discussed data mining techniques for malware detection. In particular we discussed data mining for malicious executables. In the real world the amount of cyber security data to be analyzed could be massive. That is, the amount of data to be analyzed could be in the Exabyte range. Therefore, traditional data mining techniques may not scale for very large datasets. We need big data analytics techniques to handle such massive amounts of data.

Figure 6.7 illustrates the use of big data analytics techniques for cyber security applications. We essentially describe a three-layer architecture. In particular, we use big data management systems such as HBase, Cassandra, and CouchDB for the middle layer to store the massive amounts of data. These data management systems are hosted on big data infrastructures such as Hadoop, MapReduce, and Spark. The analytics techniques such as SVM (support vector machines) and neural networks are implemented on the big data infrastructures. This way the analytics can scale to handle very large datasets.

In Chapter 8, we describe a data mining techniquea that is dedicated to the automated generation of signatures to defend against certain malware attacks. Due to the need for near real-time

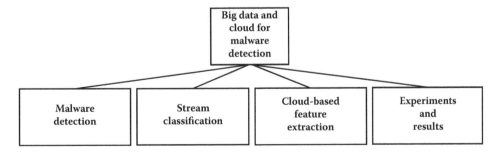

FIGURE 6.7   Big data analytics for malware detection.

performance of the malware detection tools, we have developed our data mining tool in the cloud. That is, the main objective is to show how the use of big data technologies such as the cloud would enhance performance and scalability of the malware detection techniques.

6.6 SUMMARY AND DIRECTIONS

In this work, we have designed and developed a data mining based model for malicious code detection. Our technique extracts three different levels of features from executables, namely, binary level, assembly level, and API function call level. These features then go through a feature selection phase for reducing noise and redundancy in the feature set and generate a manageable-sized set of features. These feature sets are then used to build feature vectors for each training data. Then a classification model is trained using the training data. This classification model classifies future instances (i.e., executables) to detect whether they are benign or malicious.

We have shown how to efficiently extract features from the training data. We also showed how scalability can be achieved using disk access. We have explained the algorithm for feature extraction and feature selection and analyzed their time complexity. Finally, we showed how to combine the feature sets, and build the feature vectors. We applied different machine learning techniques such as SVM, J48, and AdaBoost for building the classification model. In the next chapter, we will show how our approach performs on different datasets compared to several baseline techniques.

We have also described the experiments done on our approach and several other baseline techniques on two different datasets. We compared both the classification accuracy and running times of each baseline technique. We showed that our approach outperforms other baseline techniques in classification accuracy, without major performance degradation. We also analyzed the variation of results on different classification techniques and different datasets and explained these variations. Overall, our approach is superior over other baselines not only because of higher classification accuracy but also scalability and efficiency.

In the future, we would like to extend our work in multiple directions. First, we would like to extract and utilize behavioral features for malware detection. This is because obfuscation against binary patterns may be achieved by polymorphism, and metamorphism, but it will be difficult for the malware to obfuscate its behavioral pattern. We would like to add more features to the feature set, such as behavioral features of the executables. This is because binary features are susceptible to obfuscation by polymorphic and metamorphic malware. But it would be difficult to obfuscate behavioral patterns.

We would also like to enhance the scalability of our approach by applying cloud computing/big data framework for the feature extraction and selection task. This way feature extraction and classification would be more scalable. Cloud computing offers a cheap alternative to more CPU power and much larger disk space, which could be utilized for much faster feature extraction and selection process. Besides, we are also interested in extracting behavioral features from the executables to overcome the problem of binary obfuscation by polymorphic malware.

REFERENCES

[BOSE2003] B.E. Boser, I.M. Guyon, V.N. Vapnik, *A Training Algorithm for Optimal Margin Classifiers* (Editor: D. Haussler), 5th Annual ACM Workshop on COLT, ACM Press, 1992, pp. 144–152.

[CYGN1999] *GNU Binutils Cygwin*. http://sourceware.cygnus.com/cygwin.

[FREU1996] Y. Freund, R. Schapire, *Experiments with a New Boosting Algorithm*, Proceedings of the Thirteenth International Conference on Machine Learning, Morgan Kaufmann, San Francisco, CA, 1996, 148–156.

[GARG2006] A. Garg, R. Rahalkar, S. Upadhyaya, K. Kwiat, Profiling Users in GUI Based Systems for Masquerade Detection, *Proceedings of the 7th IEEE Information Assurance Workshop* (IAWorkshop 2006), West Point, NY, 2006, 48–54.

[GOLB2004] J. Golbeck, J. Hendler, *Reputation Network Analysis for Email Filtering*. CEAS, 2004.

[GOOD2006] M.T. Goodrich, R. Tamassia, *Data Structures and Algorithms in Java*, 4th ed., 2006, John Wiley & Sons, Inc.

[KIM2004] H.A. Kim, B. Karp, Autograph: Toward Automated, Distributed Worm Signature Detection, *Proceedings of the 13th Usenix Security Symposium* (Security 2004), San Diego, CA, 2004, 271–286.

[KOLT2004] J.Z. Kolter, M.A. Maloof, Learning to Detect Malicious Executables in the Wild, *Proceedings of the Tenth ACM SIGKDD International Conference on Knowledge Discovery and Data Mining*, 470–478.

[LAKH2005] A. Lakhotia, E.U. Kumar, M. Venable, A Method for Detecting Obfuscated Calls in Malicious Binaries, *IEEE Transactions on Software Engineering*, Volume 31, #11, 2005, 955–968.

[LIBSVM] (n.d.). *A Library for Support Vector Machine*. Retrieved June 1, 2006 from http://www. csie.ntu.edu.tw/~cjlin/libsvm/.

[MASU2007a] M.M. Masud, L. Khan, B. Thuraisingham, Feature-Based Techniques for Auto-Detection of Novel Email Worms, *Proceedings of the Eleventh Pacific-Asia Conference on Knowledge Discovery and Data Mining* (PAKDD'07), LNAI 4426, Nanjing, China, 2007, 205–216.

[MASU2007b] M.M. Masud, L. Khan, B. Thuraisingham, A Hybrid Model to Detect Malicious Executables, *Proceedings of the IEEE International Conference on Communication* (ICC'07), Glasglow, Sotland, 2007, 1443–1448.

[MASU2011] M.M. Masud, L. Khan, B. Thuraisingham, *Data Mining Tools for Malware Detection*, CRC Press, 2011.

[MITC1997] T. Mitchell, *Machine Learning*, McGraw Hill, 1997.

[NEWM2002] M.E.J. Newman, S. Forrest, J. Balthrop, Email Networks and the Spread of Computer Viruses, Physical Review, Volume 66, #3, 2002, 035101.

[NEWS2005] J. Newsome, B. Karp, D. Song, Polygraph: Automatically Generating Signatures for Polymorphic Worms, *Proceedings of the IEEE Symposium on Security and Privacy*, Oakland, CA, 2005, 226–241.

[SCHU2001a] M. Schultz, E. Eskin, E. Zadok, MEF Malicious Email Filter, a UNIX Mail Filter That Detects Malicious Mindows Executables, *Proceedings of the USENIX Annual Technical Conference – FREENIX Track*, Boston, MA, 2001, 245–252.

[SCHU2001b] M. Schultz, E. Eskin, E. Zadok, S. Stolfo, Data Mining Methods for Detection of New Malicious Executables, *Proceedings of the IEEE Symposium on Security and Privacy*, Oakland, CA, 2001, 178–184.

[SING2003] S. Singh, C. Estan, G. Varghese, S. Savage, *The EarlyBird System for Real-time Detection of Unknown Worms*. Technical report – cs2003-0761, UCSD.

[Windows P.E.] Windows P.E. Disassembler. (n.d.). Retrieved June 5, 2006 from http://www.geocities.com/ ~sangcho/inde6.html.

[VX-Heavens] (n.d.). Retrieved May 6, 2006 from http://vx.netlux.org/.

[WEKA] (n.d.). Retrieved August 1, 2006 from http://www.cs.waikato.ac.nz/ml/weka/.

7 Stream Analytics for Malware Detection

7.1 INTRODUCTION

It is a major challenge to the data mining/data science community to mine/analyze the ever-growing streaming data. There are three major problems related to stream data classification. First, it is impractical to store and use all the historical data for training since it would require infinite storage and running time. Second, there may be concept-drift in the data, meaning, the underlying concept of the data may change over time. Third, novel classes may evolve in the stream. There are many existing solutions in literature that solve the first two problems, such as single model incremental learning algorithms [CHEN2008, HULT2001, YANG2005] and ensemble classifiers [KOLT2005, MASU2008a, WANG2003]. However, most of the existing techniques are not capable of detecting novel classes in the stream. On the other hand, our approach can handle both concept-drift, and detect novel classes at the same time.

Traditional classifiers can only correctly classify instances of those classes with which they have been trained. When a new class appears in the stream, all instances belonging to that class will be misclassified until the new class has been manually identified by some experts and a new model is trained with the labeled instances of that class. Our approach provides a solution to this problem by incorporating a novel class detector within a traditional classifier so that the emergence of a novel class can be identified without any manual intervention. The proposed novel class detection technique can benefit many applications in various domains, such as network intrusion detection and credit card fraud detection. For example, in the problem of intrusion detection, when a new kind of intrusion occurs, we should not only be able to detect that it is an intrusion but also that it is a new kind of intrusion. With the intrusion type information, human experts would be able to analyze the intrusion more intensely, find a cure, set an alarm in advance, and make the system more secure.

In this chapter, we discuss what stream analytics (which we will also refer to as stream mining) is about and also discuss an approach for detecting novel classes. We describe algorithms for detecting novel classes and an architecture of the system. We provide the definition of novel class and existing classes. Then we state the assumptions based on which the novel class detection algorithm works. We illustrate the concept of *novel class* with an example and introduce several terms such as "used" space and "unused" spaces. We then discuss the three major parts in novel class detection process, which are: (i) saving the inventory of *used* spaces during training, (ii) outlier detection and filtering, and (iii) computing cohesion among outliers and separating the outliers from the training data. We also show how this technique can be made efficient by raw data reduction using clustering.

Finally, we evaluate our proposed method on a number of synthetic and real datasets, and we report results on four datasets. Two of the datasets for which we report the results are synthetic, and the other two are real benchmark datasets. The first synthetic dataset simulates only concept-drift. We use this dataset for evaluation to show that our approach can correctly distinguish between concept-drift and novel classes. The second synthetic dataset simulates both concept-drift and concept-evolution. The two benchmark datasets that we use are the KDD Cup 1999 intrusion detection dataset, and the Forest Cover type dataset, both of which have been widely used in data stream classification literature. Each of the synthetic and real datasets contain more than or equal to 250,000 data points.

DOI: 10.1201/9781003081845-12

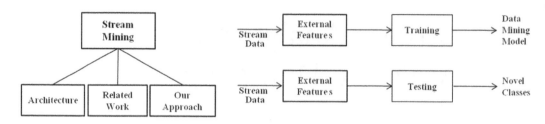

FIGURE 7.1   Stream analytics for novel class detection.

We compare our results with two baseline techniques. For each dataset and each baseline technique, we report the overall error rate, percentage of novel instances misclassified as existing class, and percentage of existing class instances misclassified as novel class. Besides, we also report the running times of each baseline technique on each dataset. On all datasets, our approach outperforms the baseline techniques in both classification accuracy, and false detection rates. Our approach also outperforms the baseline techniques in running time. The following sections discuss the results in detail.

The organization of this chapter is as follows. In Section 7.2, we describe our aspects of stream mining/analytics. In particular, we discuss our architecture, related work and our approach. Details of our algorithms are discussed in Section 7.3. In particular, some definitions and our novel class detection techniques are given. Experiments and evaluation are discussed in Section 7.4. In particular, our datasets, the experimental setup and performance results are given. Applications to malware detection are discussed in Section 7.5. Section 7.6 summarizes this chapter. Figure 7.1 illustrates the concepts in this chapter.

7.2   STREAM MINING

7.2.1   ARCHITECTURE

We propose an innovative approach to detect novel classes. It is different from traditional novelty (or anomaly/outlier) detection techniques in several ways. First, traditional novelty detection techniques [MARK2003, ROBE2000, YEUN2002] work by assuming or building a model of normal data and simply identifying data points as outliers/anomalies that deviate from the "normal" points. But our goal is not only to detect whether a single data point deviates from the normality but also to discover whether a group of outliers has any strong bond among themselves. Second, traditional novelty detectors can be considered as a "one-class" model, which simply distinguish between normal and anomalous data, but cannot distinguish between two different kinds of anomalies. But our model is a "multi-class" model, meaning, it can distinguish among different classes of data and at the same time can detect presence of a novel class data, which is a unique combination of a traditional classifier with a novelty detector.

Our technique handles concept-drift by adapting an ensemble classification approach, which maintains an ensemble of M classifiers for classifying unlabeled data. The data stream is divided into equal-sized chunks, so that each chunk can be accommodated in memory and processed online. We train a classification model from each chunk as soon as it is labeled. The newly trained model replaces one of the existing models in the ensemble, if necessary. Thus, the ensemble evolves, reflecting the most up-to-date concept in the stream.

The central concept of our novel class detection technique is that each class must have an important property: the data points belonging to the same class should be closer to each other (cohesion) and should be far apart from the data points belonging to other classes (separation). Every time a new data chunk appears, we first detect the test instances that are *well-separated* from the training data (i.e., outliers). Then filtering is applied to remove the outliers that possibly appear

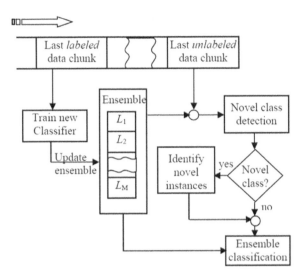

FIGURE 7.2   Architecture.

as a result of concept-drift. Finally, if we find strong cohesion among those filtered outliers, we declare a novel class. When the true labels of the novel class(es) arrive and a new model is trained with the labeled instances, the existing ensemble is updated with that model. Therefore, the ensemble of models is continuously enriched with new classes. Our architecture is illustrated in Figure 7.2.

We assume that the data stream is divided into equal-sized chunks. The heart of this system is an ensemble L of M classifiers: $\{L_1, ..., L_M\}$. When a new unlabeled data chunk arrives, the ensemble is used to detect novel class in that chunk. If a novel class is detected, then the instances belonging to the novel class are identified and tagged accordingly. All other instances in the chunk, that is, the instances that are not identified as novel class, are classified using majority voting. As soon as a data chunk is labeled, it is used to train a classifier, which replaces one of the existing classifiers in the ensemble. During training, we create an inventory of the *used* spaces.

We have several contributions. First, we provide a detailed understanding of the characteristic of a novel class, and propose a new technique that can detect novel classes in the presence of concept-drift in data streams. Second, we establish a framework for incorporating novel class detection mechanism into a traditional classifier. Finally, we apply our technique on both synthetic and real-world data and obtain much better results than state-of-the-art stream classification algorithms.

7.2.2 RELATED WORK

Our work is related to both stream classification and novelty detection. There have been many works in stream data classification. There are two main approaches: single-model classification and ensemble classification. Some single-model techniques have been proposed to accommodate concept drift [CHEN2008, HULT2001, YANG2005]. However, our technique follows the ensemble approach. Several ensemble techniques for stream data mining have been proposed [KOLT2005, MASU2008a, WANG2003]. These ensemble approaches require simple operations to update the current concept, and they are found to be robust in handling concept-drift. Although these techniques can efficiently handle concept-drift, none of them can detect novel classes in the data stream. On the other hand, our technique is not only capable of handling concept-drift but also is able to detect novel classes in data streams. In this light, our technique is also related to novelty detection techniques.

A comprehensive study on novelty detection has been discussed in [MARK2003]. The authors categorize novelty detection techniques into two categories: statistical and neural network-based. Our technique is related to the statistical approach. Statistical approaches are of two types: parametric and non-parametric. Parametric approaches assume that data distributions are known (e.g., Gaussian) and try to estimate the parameters (e.g., mean and variance) of the distribution. If any test data falls outside the normal parameters of the model, it is declared as novel [ROBE2000]. Our technique is a non-parametric approach. Non-parametric approaches like Parzen window method [YEUN2002] estimate the density of training data and reject patterns whose density is beyond a certain threshold. K-nearest neighbor (K-NN) based approaches for novelty detection are also non-parametric [YANG2002]. All of these techniques for novelty detection only consider whether a test instance is sufficiently close (or far) from the training data based on some appropriate metric (e.g., distance, density, etc.). Our approach is different from these approaches in that we not only consider separation from normal data but also consider cohesion among the outliers. Besides, our model assimilates a novel class into the existing model, which enables it to distinguish future instances of that class from other classes. On the other hand, novelty detection techniques just remember the "normal" trend, and do not care about the similarities or dissimilarities among the anomalous instances.

A recent work in the data stream mining domain [SPIN2007] describes a clustering approach that can detect both concept-drift and novel class. This approach assumes that there is only one "normal" class and all other classes are novel. Thus, it may not work well if more than one class is to be considered as "normal" or "non-novel." Our approach can handle any number of existing classes. This makes our approach more effective in detecting novel classes than [SPIN2007], which is justified by the experimental results.

7.2.3 OUR APPROACH

We have presented a novel technique to detect new classes in concept-drifting data streams. Most of the novelty detection techniques either assume that there is no concept-drift, or build a model for a single "normal" class and consider all other classes as novel. But our approach is capable of detecting novel classes in the presence of concept-drift, even when the model consists of multiple "existing" classes. Besides, our novel class detection technique is non-parametric, meaning, it does not assume any specific distribution of data. We also show empirically that our approach outperforms the state-of-the-art data stream-based novelty detection techniques in both classification accuracy and processing speed.

It might appear to readers that in order to detect novel classes, we are in fact examining whether new clusters are being formed, and therefore, the detection process could go on without supervision. But supervision is necessary for classification. Without external supervision, two separate clusters could be regarded as two different classes, although they are not. Conversely, if more than one novel class appears in a chunk, all of them could be regarded as a single novel class if the labels of those instances are never revealed. In future work, we would like to apply our technique in the domain of multiple-label instances. Our approach is illustrated in Figure 7.3.

7.2.4 OVERVIEW OF NOVEL CLASS DETECTION

Algorithm 7.1 outlines a summary of our technique. The data stream is divided into equal-sized chunks. The latest chunk, which is unlabeled, is provided to the algorithm as input. At first it detects if there is any novel class in the chunk (line 1). The term "novel class" will be defined shortly. If a novel class is found, we detect the instances that belong to the class(es) (line 2). Then we use the ensemble $L = \{L_1, ..., L_M\}$ to classify the instances that do not belong to the novel class(es). When the data chunk becomes labeled, a new classifier L' is trained using the chunk.

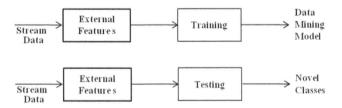

FIGURE 7.3   Our Approach to stream mining.

ALGORITHM 7.1   MINECLASS

Input: D_n: the latest data chunk
　　　L: Current ensemble of best M classifiers
　　　Output: Updated ensemble L
　　　1: found $\leftarrow$ *DetectNovelClass* (D_n, L) (Algorithm 7.2)
　　　2: **if** found **then** $Y \leftarrow$ Novel_instances (D_n), $X \leftarrow D_n$ - Y **else** $X \leftarrow D_n$
　　　3: **for** each instance $x \in X$ do *Classify* (L, x)
　　　4: /*Assuming that D_n is now labeled*/
　　　5: $L' \leftarrow$ *Train-and-create-inventory* (D_n) (Chapter 7.3)
　　　6: $L \leftarrow$ *Update*(L, L', D_n)

Then the existing ensemble is updated by choosing the best M classifiers from the $M + 1$ classifiers $L \cup \{L'\}$ based on their accuracies on the latest labeled data chunk.

Our algorithm will be mentioned henceforth as "MineClass," which stands for mining novel classes in data streams. MineClass should be applicable to any base learner. The only operation that is specific to a learning algorithm is *Train-and-create-inventory*. We will illustrate this operation for two base learners.

7.2.5   CLASSIFIERS USED

We apply our novelty detection technique on two different classifiers: decision tree and K-NN. We keep M classification models in the ensemble. For decision tree classifier, each model is a decision tree. For K-NN, each model is usually the set of training data itself. However, storing all the raw training data is memory-inefficient and using them to classify unlabeled data is time-inefficient. We reduce both the time and memory requirement by building K clusters with the training data, saving the cluster summaries as classification models, and discarding the raw data. This process is explained in detail in [MASU2008b]. The cluster summaries are mentioned henceforth as "pseudopoints." Since we store and use only K pseudopoints, both the time and memory requirements become functions of K (a constant number). The clustering approach followed here is a constraint-based K-means clustering, where the constraint is to minimize cluster impurity while minimizing the intra-cluster dispersion. A cluster is considered pure if it contains instances from only one class. The summary of each cluster consists of the centroid and the frequencies of data points of each class in the cluster. Classification is done by finding the nearest cluster centroid from the test point, and assigning the class that has the highest frequency to the test point.

7.3 DETAILS OF NOVEL CLASS DETECTION

7.3.1 DEFINITIONS

We begin with the definition of "novel" and "existing" class.

Definition 7.1: (existing class and novel class) Let L be the current ensemble of classification models. A class c is an existing class if at least one of the models $L_i \in L$ has been trained with the instances of class c. Otherwise, c is a novel class.

We assume that any class has the following essential property (Property 7.1):

Property 7.1: *A data point should be closer to the data points of its own class (cohesion) and farther apart from the data points of other classes (separation).*

Our main assumption is that the instances belonging to a class c are generated by an underlying generative model Θ_c, and the instances in each class are independently identically distributed. With this assumption, we can reasonably argue that the instances, which are close together, are supposed to be generated by the same model, that is, belong to the same class. We now show the basic idea of novel class detection using decision tree in Figure 7.4. We introduce the notion of *used space* to denote a feature space occupied by any instance, and *unused space* to denote a feature space unused by an instance.

According to Property 7.1 (separation), a novel class must arrive in the unused spaces. Besides, there must be strong cohesion (e.g., closeness) among the instances of the novel class. Thus, the two basic principles followed by our approach are as follows: keeping track of the used spaces of each leaf node in a decision tree and finding strong cohesion among the test instances that fall into the unused spaces.

7.3.2 NOVEL CLASS DETECTION

We follow two basic steps for novel class detection. First, the classifier is trained such that an inventory of the used spaces (described in Section 7.2) is created and saved. This is done by clustering and and saving the cluster summary as "pseudopoint." Secondly, these pseudopoints are

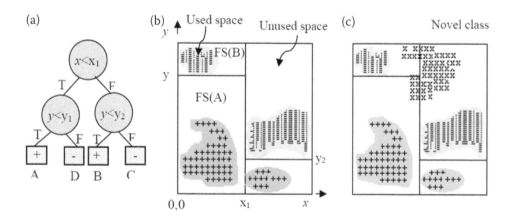

FIGURE 7.4 (a) A decision tree and (b) corresponding feature space partitioning. FS(X) denotes the feature space defined by a leaf node X. The shaded areas show the used spaces of each partition. (c) A novel class (denoted by x) arrives in the unused space.

used to detect outliers in the test data, and declare a novel class if there is strong cohesion among the outliers.

7.3.2.1 Saving the Inventory of Used Spaces during Training

The general idea of creating the inventory is to cluster the training data, and save the cluster centroids and other useful information as pseudopoints. These pseudopoints keep track of the used spaces. The way how this clustering is done may be specific to each base learner. For example, for decision tree, clustering is done at each leaf node of the tree, since we need to keep track of the used spaces for each leaf node separately. For the K-NN classifier discussed in Section 7.2, already existing pseudopoints are utilized to store the inventory.

It should be noted here that K-means clustering appears to be the best choice for saving the decision boundary and computing the outliers. Density-based clustering could also be used to detect outliers but it has several problems. First, we would have to save all the raw data points at the leaf nodes to apply the clustering. Second, the clustering process would take quadratic time, compared to linear time for K-means. Finally, we would have to run the clustering algorithm for every data chunk to be tested. However, the choice of parameter K in K-means algorithm has some impact on the overall outcome, which is discussed in the experimental results.

7.3.2.1.1 Clustering

We build total K clusters per chunk. For K-NN, we utilize the existing clusters that were created globally using the approach. For decision tree, clustering is done locally at each leaf node as follows. Suppose S is the chunk-size. During decision tree training, when we reach a leaf node l_i, we build $k_i = (t_i/S)*K$ clusters in that leaf, where t_i denotes the number of training instances that ended up in leaf node l_i.

7.3.2.1.2 Storing the cluster summary information

For each cluster, we store the following summary information in memory: (i) *Weight, w*: Defined as the total number of points in the cluster. (ii) *Centroid*, ζ. (iii) *Radius, R*: Defined as the maximum distance between the centroid and the data points belonging to the cluster. (iv) *Mean distance*, μ_d: The mean distance from each point to the cluster centroid. The cluster summary of a cluster H_i will be referred to henceforth as a "pseudopoint" ψ_i. So, $w(\psi_i)$ denotes the weight of pseudopoint ψ_i. After computing the cluster summaries, the raw data are discarded. Let ψ_j be the set of all pseudopoints stored in memory for a classifier L_j.

7.3.2.2 Outlier Detection and Filtering

Each pseudopoint ψ_i corresponds to a hypersphere in the feature space having center $\zeta(\psi_i)$ and radius $R(\psi i)$. Thus, the pseudopoints "memorize" the used spaces. Let us denote the portion of feature space covered by a pseudopoint ψ_i as the "region" of ψ_i or $RE(\psi_i)$. So, the union of the regions covered by all the pseudopoints is the union of all the used spaces, which forms a decision boundary $B(L_j) = \psi_{i \in \psi_j} RE(\psi_i)$, for a classifier L_j. Now, we are ready to define outliers.

Definition 7.2 : (Routlier) *Let x be a test point and ψ_{min} be the pseudopoint whose centroid is nearest to x. Then x is an Routlier (i.e., raw outlier) if it is outside $RE(\psi_{min})$, i.e., its distance from $\zeta(\psi_{min})$ is greater than $R(\psi_{min})$.*

In other words, any point x outside the decision boundary $B(L_j)$ is an *Routlier* for the classifier L_j. For K-NN, *Routlier*s are detected globally by testing x against all the pseudopoints. For decision tree, x is tested against only the pseudopoints stored at the leaf node where x belongs.

7.3.2.2.1 Filtering

According to Definition 7.3, a test instance may be erroneously considered as an *Routlier* because of one or more of the following reasons: (i) The test instance belongs to an existing class, but it is a noise. (ii) There has been a concept-drift and as a result, the decision boundary of an existing class has been shifted. (iii) The decision tree has been trained with insufficient data. So, the predicted decision boundary is not the same as the actual one.

Due to these reasons, the outliers are filtered to ensure that any outlier that belongs to the existing classes does not end up in being declared as a new class instance. The filtering is done as follows: if a test instance is a *Routlier* to *all* the classifiers in the ensemble, then it is considered as a filtered outlier. All other *Routlier*s are filtered out.

Definition 7.3 : (Foutlier) *A test instance is a Foutlier (i.e., filtered outlier) if it is a Routlier to all the classifiers. L_i*

Intuitively, being a *Foutlier* is a necessary condition for being in a new class. Because, suppose an instance x is not a *Routlier* to some classifier L_i in the ensemble. Then x must be inside the decision boundary $B(L_i)$. So, it violates Property 7.1 (separation), and therefore, it cannot belong to a new class. Although being a *Foutlier* is a necessary condition, it is not sufficient for being in a new class, since it does not guarantee the Property 7.1 (cohesion). So, we proceed to the next step to verify whether the *Foutliers* satisfy both cohesion and separation.

7.3.2.3   Detecting Novel Class

We perform several computations on the *Foutliers* to detect the arrival of a new class. First, we discuss the general concepts of these computations and later we describe how these computations are carried out efficiently. For every *Foutlier*, we define a λ_c-neighborhood as follows (Definition 7.4):

Definition 7.4 : (λ_c-neighborhood) *The λ_c-neighborhood of a Foutlier x is the set of N-nearest neighbors of x belonging to class c.*

Here N is a user defined parameter. For brevity, we denote the λ_c-neighborhood of a *Foutlier x* as $\lambda_c(x)$. Thus, $\lambda_+(x)$ of a *Foutlier x* is the set of N instances of class c_+, that are closest to the outlier x. Similarly, $\lambda_o(x)$ refers to the set of N *Foutliers* that are closest to x. This is illustrated in Figure 7.5, where the *Foutliers* are shown as black dots, and the instances of class c_+ and class c_- are shown with the corresponding symbols. $\lambda_+(x)$ of the *Foutlier x* is the set of $N (= 3)$ instances belonging to class c_+ that are nearest to x (inside the circle), and so on.

Next, we define the N-neighborhood silhouette coefficient (N-NSC) (Definition 7.5).

Definition 7.5 : (N-NSC) *Let $a(x)$ be the average distance from a Foutlier x to the instances in $\lambda_o(x)$, and be the average distance from x to the instances in $\lambda_c(x)$ (where c is an existing class). Let $b_{min}(x)$ be the minimum among all $b_c(x)$. Then N-NSC of x is given by:*

$$N - NSC(x) = \frac{b_{\min}(x) - a(x)}{\max(b_{\min}(x),\ a(x))} \qquad (7.1)$$

According to the definition, the value of N-NSC is between -1 and $+1$. It is actually a unified measure of cohesion and separation. A negative value indicates that x is closer to the other classes

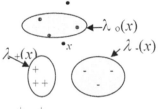

FIGURE 7.5 λ_c-neighborhood with $N = 3$.

(less separation) and farther away from its own class (less cohesion). We declare a *new class* if there are at least N' ($>N$) *Foutliers*, whose N-NSC is positive.

It should be noted that the larger the value of N, the greater the confidence with which we can decide whether a novel class has arrived. However, if N is too large, then we may also fail to detect a new class if the total number of instances belonging to the novel class in the corresponding data chunk is $\leq N$. We experimentally find an optimal value of N, which is explained in Section 7.4.

7.3.2.3.1 Computing the set of novel class instances

Once we detect the presence of a novel class, the next step is to find those instances, and separate them from the existing class data. According to the *necessary and sufficient condition*, a set of *Foutlier* instances belong to a novel class if the following three conditions satisfy: (i) all the *Foutliers* in the set have positive N-NSC, (ii) all the *Foutliers* in the set have within the set, and (iii) cardinality of the set $\geq N$. Let G be such a set. Note that finding the exact set G is computationally expensive, so we follow an approximation. Let G' be the set of all *Foutliers* that have positive N-NSC. If $|G'| \geq N$, then G' is an approximation of G. It is possible that some of the data points in G' may not actually be a novel class instance or vice versa. However, in our experiments, we found that this approximation works well.

7.3.2.3.2 Speeding up the computation

Computing N-NSC for every *Foutlier* instance x takes quadratic time in the number of *Foutliers*. In order to make the computation faster, we also create K_O pseudopoints from *Foutliers* using K-means clustering and perform the computations on the pseudopoints (referred to as *Fpseudopoints*), where $K_O = (N_O/S)*K$. Here S is the chunk size and N_O is the number of *Foutliers*. Thus, the time complexity to compute the N-NSC of all of the *Fpseudopoints* is $O(K_O*(K_O + K))$, which is constant, since both K_O and K are independent of the input size. Note that N-NSC of a *Fpseudopoint* is actually an approximate average of the N-NSC of each *Foutlier* in that *Fpseudopoint*. By using this approximation, although we gain speed, we also lose some precision. However, this drop in precision is negligible when we keep sufficient number of pseudopoints, as shown in the experimental results. The novel class detection process is summarized in Algorithm 7.2 (DetectNovelClass).

This algorithm can detect one or more novel classes concurrently (i.e., in the same chunk) as long as each novel class follows Property 7.1 and contains at least N instances. This is true even if the class distributions are skewed. However, if more than one such novel class appears concurrently, our algorithm will identify the instances belonging to those classes as novel, without imposing any distinction among dissimilar novel class instances (i.e., it will treat them simply as "novel"). But the distinction will be learned by our model as soon those instances are labeled, and a classifier is trained with them.

7.3.2.3.3 Time complexity

Lines 1–3 of Algorithm 7.1 require $O(KSL)$ time, where S is the chunk size. Line 4 (clustering) requires $O(KS)$ time, and the last for loop (5–10) requires time. Thus, the overall time complexity

---

ALGORITHM 7.2   *DETECTNOVELCLASS(D, L)*

Input: D: An unlabeled data chunk
   L: Current ensemble of best M classifiers
   Output: **true**, if novel class is found; **false**, otherwise
   1: **for** each instance $x \in D$ **do**
   2: **if** x is an *Routlier* to all classifiers $L_i \in L$
   then FList $\leftarrow$ FList $\cup$ $\{x\}$ /* x is a Foutlier*/
   3: **end for**
   4: Make $K_o = (K * |FList|/|D|)$ clusters with the instances in *FList* using K-means clustering, and create *Fpseudopoints*
   5: **for each** classifier $L_i \in L$ **do**
   6: Compute N-NSC(ψ_j) for each Fpseudopoint j
   7: $\psi_p \leftarrow$ the set of Fpseudopoints having positive N-NSC(.).
   8: $w(\text{p})$ sum of $w(.)$ of all Fpseudopoints in Ψ_p
   9: **if** $w(\text{p}) > N$ then NewClassVote++
   10: **end for**
   11: return NewClassVote $> M$ - NewClassVote /*Majority voting*/

---

of Algorithm 7.1 is = $O(K(S + SL + KL))$. Assuming that $S >> KL$, the complexity becomes $O(KS)$, which is linear in S. Thus, the overall time complexity (per chunk) of MineClass algorithm (Algorithm 7.1) is $O(KS + f_c(LS) + f_t(S))$, where $f_c(n)$ is the time required to classify n instances and $f_t(n)$ is the time required to train a classifier with n training instances.

7.3.2.3.4 Impact of evolving class labels on ensemble classification

As the reader might have realized already, arrival of novel classes in the stream causes the classifiers in the ensemble to have different sets of class labels. For example, suppose an older (earlier) classifier L_i in the ensemble has been trained with classes c_0 and c_1, and a newer (later) classifier L_j has been trained with classes c_1, and c_2, where c_2 is a new class that appeared after L_i had been trained. This puts a negative effect on voting decision, since the older classifier mis-classifies instances of c_2. So, rather than counting votes from each classifier, we selectively count their votes as follows: if a newer classifier L_j classifies a test instance x as class c, but an older classifier L_i does not have the class label c in its model, then the vote of L_i will be ignored if x is found to be an outlier for L_i. An opposite scenario occurs when the oldest classifier L_i is trained with some class c', but none of the later classifiers are trained with that class. This means class c' has been outdated, and, in that case, we remove L_i from the ensemble. In this way we ensure that older classifiers have less impact in the voting process. If class c' later re-appears in the stream, it will be automatically detected again as a novel class.

7.4   EVALUATION

7.4.1   DATASETS

7.4.1.1   Synthetic Data with Only Concept-Drift (SynC)

SynC simulates only concept-drift, with no novel classes. This is done to show that concept-drift does not erroneously trigger new-class detection in our approach. SynC data are generated with a moving hyperplane. The equation of a hyperplane is as follows: $\Sigma^d_{i=1} a_i x_i = a_0$. If $\Sigma^d_{i=1} a_i x_i <= a_0$, then an example is negative, otherwise it is positive. Each example is a randomly generated d-dimensional vector $\{x_1, ..., x_d\}$, where $x_i \in [0, 1]$. Weights $\{a_1, ..., a_d\}$ are also randomly initialized with a real number in the range [0, 1]. The value of a_0 is adjusted so that roughly the same number of positive and negative examples is generated. This can be done by choosing $a_0 = \Sigma^d_{i=1}a_i$. We also introduce noise randomly by switching the labels of $p\%$ of the examples, where $p = 5$ is set in our experiments. There are several parameters that simulate concept drift. Parameter m specifies the percent of total dimensions whose weights are involved in changing, and it is set to 20%. Parameter t specifies the magnitude of the change in every N example. In our experiments, t is set to 0.1, and N is set to 1,000. s_i, $i \in \{1, ..., d\}$ specifies the direction of change for each weight. Weights change continuously, that is, a_i is adjusted by $s_i.t/N$ after each example is generated. There is a possibility of 10% that the change would reverse direction after every N example is generated. We generate a total of 250,000 records.

7.4.1.2 Synthetic Data with Concept-Drift and Novel-Class (SynCN)

This synthetic data simulates both concept-drift and novel-class. Data points belonging to each class are generated using Gaussian distribution having different means (−5.0 to +5.0) and variances (0.5 to 6) for different classes. Besides, in order to simulate the evolving nature of data streams, the probability distributions of different classes are varied with time. This caused some classes to appear and some other classes to disappear at different times. In order to introduce concept-drift, the mean values of a certain percentage of attributes have been shifted at a constant rate. As done in the SynC dataset, this rate of change is also controlled by the parameters m, t, s, and N in a similar way.

The dataset is normalized so that all attribute values fall within the range [0, 1]. We generate the SynCN dataset with 20 classes, 40 real valued attributes, having a total of 400K data points.

7.4.1.3 Real Data – KDD Cup 99 Network Intrusion Detection

We have used the 10% version of the dataset, which is more concentrated, hence more challenging than the full version. It contains around 490,000 instances. Here different classes appear and disappear frequently, making the new class detection challenging. This dataset contains TCP connection records extracted from LAN network traffic at MIT Lincoln Labs over a period of two weeks. Each record refers to either to a normal connection or an attack. There are 22 types of attacks, such as buffer-overflow, portsweep, guess-passwd, neptune, rootkit, smurf, spy, etc. So, there are 23 different classes of data. Most of the data points belong to the normal class. Each record consists of 42 attributes, such as connection duration, the number bytes transmitted, number of root accesses, etc. We use only the 34 continuous attributes, and remove the categorical attributes. This dataset is also normalized to keep the attribute values within [0, 1].

7.4.1.4 Real Data – Forest Cover (UCI Repository)

The dataset contains geospatial descriptions of different types of forests. It contains 7 classes, 54 attributes, and around 581,000 instances. We normalize the dataset, and arrange the data so that in any chunk at most 3 and at least 2 classes co-occur, and new classes appear randomly.

7.4.2 EXPERIMENTAL SETUP

We implement our algorithm in Java. The code for decision tree has been adapted from the Weka machine learning open source repository (http://www.cs.waikato.ac.nz/ml/weka/). The experiments were run on an Intel P-IV machine with 2GB memory and 3GHz dual processor CPU. Our parameter settings are as follows, unless mentioned otherwise: (i) K (number of pseudopoints per chunk) = 50, (ii) N = 50, (iii) M (ensemble size) = 6, (iv) chunk-size = 1,000 for synthetic datasets, and 4,000 for real datasets. These values of parameters are tuned to achieve an overall satisfactory performance.

7.4.2.1 Baseline Method

To the best of our knowledge, there is no approach that can classify data streams *and* detect novel class. So, we compare MineClass with a combination of two baseline techniques: *OLINDDA* [SPIN2007] and Weighted Classifier Ensemble (*WCE*) [WANG2003], where the former works as novel class detector, and the latter performs classification. For each chunk, we first detect the novel class instances using Online Novelty and Drift Detection Algorithm *(OLINDDA)*. All other instances in the chunk are assumed to be in the existing classes, and they are classified using *WCE*. We use *OLINDDA* as the novelty detector, since it is a recently proposed algorithm that is shown to have outperformed other novelty detection techniques in data streams [SPIN2007].

However, *OLINDDA* assumes that there is only one "normal" class, and all other classes are "novel." So, it is not directly applicable to the multi-class novelty detection problem, where any combination of classes can be considered as the "existing" classes. We propose two alternative solutions. First, we build parallel *OLINDDA* models, one for each class, which evolve simultaneously. Whenever the instances of a novel class appear, we create a new *OLINDDA* model for that class. A test instance is declared as novel, if *all the existing class models* identify this instance as novel. We will refer to this baseline method as WCE-OLINDDA_PARALLEL. Second, we initially build an *OLINDDA* model with all the available classes. Whenever a novel class is found, the class is absorbed into the existing *OLINDDA* model. Thus, only one "normal" model is maintained throughout the stream. This will be referred to as WCE-OLINDDA_SINGLE. In all experiments, the ensemble size and chunk-size are kept the same for both these techniques. Besides, the same base learner is used for *WCE* and *MC*. The parameter settings for *OLINDDA* are: (i) number of data points per cluster (N_{excl}) = 15, (ii) least number of normal instances needed to update the existing model = 100, (iii) least number of instances needed to build the initial model = 30. These parameters are chosen either according to the default values used in [SPIN2007] or by trial and error to get an overall satisfactory performance. We will henceforth use the acronyms MC for MineClass, W-OP for WCE-OLINDDA_PARALLEL, and W-OS for WCE-OLINDDA_SINGLE.

7.4.3 Performance Study

7.4.3.1 Evaluation Approach

We use the following performance metrics for evaluation: M_{new} = % of novel class instances misclassified as existing class, F_{new} = % of existing class instances falsely identified as novel class, ERR = Total misclassification error (%)(including M_{new} and F_{new}). We build the initial models in each method with the first M chunks. From the M + 1st chunk onward, we first evaluate the performances of each method on that chunk, then use that chunk to update the existing model. The performance metrics for each chunk for each method are saved and averaged for producing the summary result.

7.4.3.2 Results

Figures 7.6(a)–(d) show the ERR for decision tree classifier of each approach up to a certain point in the stream in different datasets. K-NN classifier also has similar results. For example, at X axis = 100, the Y values show the average ERR of each approach from the beginning of the stream to chunk 100. At this point, the ERR of MC, W-OP, and W-OS are 1.7%, 11.6%, and 8.7%, respectively, for the KDD dataset (Figure 7.6(c)). The arrival of a novel class in each dataset is marked by a cross (x) on the top border in each graph at the corresponding chunk. For example, on the SynCN dataset (Figure 7.6(a)), W-OP and W-OS misses most of the novel class instances, which results in the spikes in their curves at the respective chunks (e.g., at chunks 12, 24, 37, etc.). W-OS misses almost 99% of the novel class instances. Similar spikes are observed for both W-OP and W-OS at the chunks, where novel classes appear for KDD and Forest Cover datasets. For example, many novel classes appear between chunks 9–14 in KDD, most of which are missed by

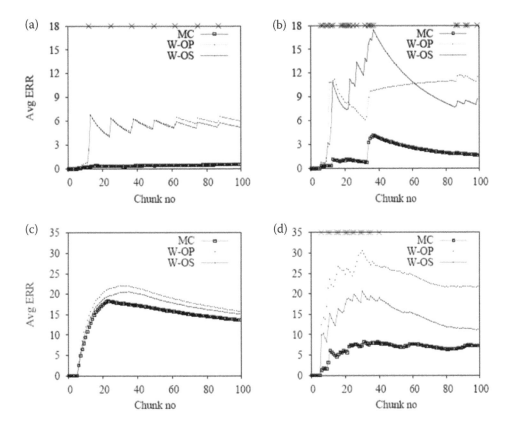

FIGURE 7.6 Error comparison on (a) SynCN, (b) SynC, (c) KDD, and (d) Forest Cover.

both W-OP and W-OS. Note that there is no novel class for SynC dataset. MC correctly detects most of these novel classes. Thus, MC outperforms both W-OP and W-OS in all datasets.

Table 7.1 summarizes the error metrics for each of the techniques in each dataset for decision tree, and K-NN. The columns headed by ERR, M_{new} and F_{new} report the average of the

TABLE 7.1

Performance comparison

Classifier	Dataset	ERR			M_{new}			F_{new}		
		MC	W-OP	W-OS	MC	W-OP	W-OS	MC	W-OP	W-OS
Decision tree	SynC	11.6	13.0	12.5	0.0	0.0	0.0	0.0	1.0	0.6
	SynCN	0.6	6.1	5.2	0.0	89.4	99.7	0.0	0.6	0.0
	KDD	1.7	11.6	8.7	0.7	26.7	99.4	1.5	7.0	0.0
	Forest Cover	7.3	21.8	8.7	9.8	18.5	99.4	1.7	15.0	0.0
K-NN	SynC	11.7	13.1	12.6	0.0	0.0	0.0	0.0	1.0	0.6
	SynCN	0.8	5.8	5.6	0	90.1	99.7	0.9	0.6	0.0
	KDD	2.3	10.0	7.0	2.7	29.0	99.4	2.2	7.1	0.0
	Forest Cover	5.4	19.2	8.9	1.0	18.5	94.0	4.5	15.0	0.3

corresponding metric on an entire dataset. For example, while using decision tree in the SynC dataset, MC, W-OP, and W-OS have almost the same ERR, which are 11.6%, 13.0%, and 12.5%, respectively. This is because SynC simulates only concept-drift, and both MC and WCE handle concept-drift in a similar manner. In SynCN dataset with decision tree, MC, W-OP, and W-OS have 0%, 89.4%, and 99.7% M_{new}, respectively. Thus, W-OS misses almost all of the novel class instances, whereas W-OP detects only 11% of them. MC correctly detects all of the novel class instances. It is interesting that all approaches have lower error rates in SynCN than SynC. This is because SynCN is generated using Gaussian distribution, which is naturally easier for the classifiers to learn. W-OS miss-predicts almost all of the novel class instances in all datasets. The comparatively better ERR rate for W-OS over W-OP can be attributed to the lower false positive rate of W-OS, which occurs since almost all instances are identified as "normal" by W-OS. Again, the overall error (ERR) of MC is much lower than other methods in all datasets and for all classifiers. K-NN also has similar results for all datasets.

Figures 7.7(a)–(d) illustrate how the error rates of MC change for different parameter settings on KDD dataset and decision tree classifier. These parameters have similar effects on other datasets, and K-NN classifier. Figure 7.7(a) shows the effect of chunk size on ERR, F_{new}, and M_{new} rates for default values of other parameters. M_{new} reduces when chunk size is increased. This is desirable, because larger chunks reduce the risk of missing a novel class. But F_{new} rate slightly increases since the risk of identifying an existing class instance as novel also rises a little. These changes stabilize from chunk size 4,000 (for Synthetic dataset, it is 1,000). That is why we use these values in our experiments. Figure 7.7(b) shows the effect of number of clusters (K) on error.

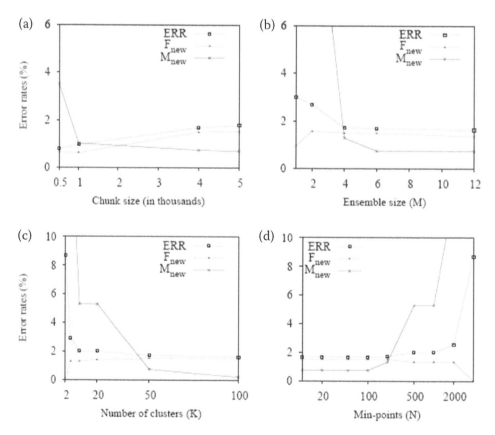

FIGURE 7.7 Sensitivity to different parameters. (a) Effect of Chunk Size on the Overall Error; (b) Effect of Ensemble Size on Error; (c) Effect of Number of Clusters on Error; (d) Effect of Min-Points on Error.

Increasing K generally reduces error rates, because outliers are more correctly detected, and as a result, M_{new} rate decreases. However, F_{new} rate also starts increasing slowly, since more test instances are becoming outliers (although they are not). The combined effect is that overall error keeps decreasing up to a certain value (e.g., $K = 50$), and then becomes almost flat. This is why we use $K = 50$ in our experiments. Figure 7.7(c) shows the effect of ensemble size (M) on error rates. We observe that the error rates decrease up to a certain size (= 6), and become stable since then. This is because when M is increased from a low value (e.g., 2), classification error naturally decreases up to a certain point because of the reduction of error variance [WANG2003]. Figure 7.7(d) shows the effect of N on error rates. The x-axis in this chart is drawn in a logarithmic scale. Naturally, increasing N up to a certain point (e.g., 20) helps reducing error, since we know that a higher value of N gives us a greater confidence in declaring a new class. But a too large value of N increases M_{new} and ERR rates, since a new class is missed by the algorithm if it has less than N instances in a data chunk. We have found that any value between 20 and 100 is the best choice for N.

7.4.3.3 Running Time

Table 7.2 compares the running times of MC, W-OP, and W-OS on each dataset for decision tree. K-NN also shows similar performances. The columns headed by "Time (sec)/chunk" show the average running times (train and test) in seconds per chunk, the columns headed by "Points/sec" show how many points have been processed (train and test) per second on average, and the columns headed by "speed gain" show the ratio of the speed of MC to that of W-OP and W-OS, respectively. For example, MC is 2,095, and 105 times faster than W-OP on KDD dataset, and Forest Cover dataset, respectively. Also, MC is 203 and 27 times faster than W-OP and W-OS, respectively, on the SynCN dataset. W-OP and W-OS are slower on SynCN than on SynC dataset because SynCN dataset has more attributes (20 vs. 10) and classes (10 vs. 2). W-OP is relatively slower than W-OS since W-OP maintains C parallel models, where C is the number of existing classes, whereas W-OS maintains only one model. Both W-OP and W-OS are relatively faster on Forest Cover than KDD since Forest Cover has less number of classes, and relatively less evolution than KDD. The main reason for this extremely slow processing of W-OP and W-OS is that the number of clusters for each OLINDDA model keeps increasing linearly with the size of the data stream, causing both the memory requirement and running time to increases linearly. But the running time and memory requirement of MC remain the same over the entire length of the stream.

7.5 SECURITY APPLICATIONS AND MALWARE DETECTION

The proposed novel class detection will be useful in several security applications. First, it can be used in detecting novel attacks in network traffic. If there is a completely new kind of attack in the

TABLE 7.2

Running time comparison in all datasets

Dataset	Time(sec)/chunk			Points/sec			Speed gain	
	MC	W-OP	W-OS	MC	W-OP	W-OS	MC over W-OP	MC over W-OS
SynC	0.18	0.81	0.19	5,446	1,227	5,102	4	1
SynCN	0.27	52.9	7.34	3,656	18	135	203	27
KDD	0.95	1369.5	222.8	4,190	2	17	2,095	246
Forest Cover	2.11	213.1	10.79	1,899	18	370	105	5

network traffic, existing intrusion detection techniques may fail to detect it. On the contrary, if a completely new kind of attack occurs in the network traffic, our approach should detect it as a "novel class" and would raise an alarm. This would invoke system analysts to quarantine and analyze the characteristics of these unknown kinds of events, and tag them accordingly. The classification models would also be updated with these new class instances. Should the same kind of intrusion occur in the future, the classification model would detect it as a known intrusion. Second, our approach can also be used for detecting a new kind of malware. Existing malware detection techniques may fail to detect a completely new kind of malware, but our approach should be able to detect the new malware as a novel class, quarantine it and raise an alarm. The quarantined binary would be later analyzed and characterized by human experts. In this way, the proposed novel class detection technique can be effectively applied to cyber security.

There are several potential security applications of the novel class detection technique, such as intrusion detection in network traffic or malware detection in a host machine. Consider the problem of malware detection. In order to apply our novel class detection technique, we first need to identify a set of features for each executable. This can be done using n-gram feature extraction and selection [MASU2008b]. As long as the feature set selected using the approach of [MASU2008b] also remains the best set of features for a new kind of malware, the new malware class should be detected as a novel class by our approach. The advantage of our approach with other classification approaches in this regard is two-fold. First, it will detect a new kind of malware as a novel class. This detection will lead to further analysis and characterization of the malware. On the contrary, if a new kind of malware emerges, traditional classification techniques would either detect as benign or simply a "malware." Thus, our approach will be able to provide more information about the new malware by identifying it as a novel type. The second advantage is, if an existing type of malware is tested using the novel class detection system, it will be identified as a malware, and also the "type" of the malware would be predicted.

7.6 SUMMARY AND DIRECTIONS

Data stream classification is a challenging task that has been addressed by different researchers in different ways. Most of these approaches ignore the fact that new classes may emerge in the stream. If this phenomenon is considered, the classification problem becomes more challenging. Our approach addresses this challenge in an efficient way.

In this chapter, we present the working details of the novel class detection algorithm. Our approach builds a decision boundary around the training data during training. During classification, if any instance falls outside the decision boundary, it is tagged as *outlier* and stored for further analysis. When enough outliers have been found, we compute the cohesion among the outliers and separation of the outliers from the training data. If both the cohesion and separation are significant, the outliers are identified as a novel class. In [THUR2017], we discussed the effectiveness of our approach on several synthetic and benchmark data streams. We also discussed the datasets, experimental setups, baseline techniques, and evaluation on the datasets. We used four different datasets, two of which are synthetic, and the two others are benchmark data streams. Our approach outperforms other baseline techniques in classification and novel class detection accuracies and running times on all datasets.

In the future, we would like to extend our approach in multiple directions. First, we would like to extend this technique to real time data stream classification. In order to achieve this goal, we will have to optimize the training, including the creation of decision boundary. Besides, the outlier detection and novel class detection should also be made more efficient. We believe a cloud computing framework can play an important role in increasing the efficiency of these processes. Second, we would like to address the real-time data stream classification problem. Real-time data stream mining is more challenging because of the overhead involved in data labeling and training classification models. Third, we would like to utilize the cloud computing framework for data stream mining. The cloud computing framework will be a cheaper alternative to more efficient and powerful computing that is necessary for real-time stream mining. Due to the streaming nature of the data, we expect massive amounts of data to be collected and analyzed. Therefore, in addition to a cloud computing framework, we expect to use big data technologies for storing and managing the data. This way larger and real world data streams can be analyzed and our approach can be extended to address the real-time classification and novel class detection problems in data streams. We discuss aspects of our work in this direction in the next two chapters.

REFERENCES

[CHEN2008] S. Chen, H. Wang, S. Zhou, P. Yu, Stop Chasing Trends: Discovering High Order Models in Evolving Data, *Proceedings of ICDE, Cancun, Mexico*, 2008, pp. 923–932.

[HULT2001] G. Hulten, L. Spencer, P. Domingos, Mining Time-Changing Data Streams, *Proceedings of ACM SIGKDD, San Francisco, CA*, 2001, pp. 97–106.

[KOLT2005] J. Kolter M. Maloof, Using Additive Expert Ensembles to Cope with Concept Drift, *Proceedings of ICML, Bonn, Germany*, 2005, pp. 449–456.

[MARK2003] M. Markou, S. Singh, Novelty Detection: A Review – Part 1: Statistical Approaches, Part 2: Neural Network-Based Approaches, *Signal Processing*, Volume 83, 2003, pp. 2499–2521.

[MASU2008a] M. Masud, Latifur Khan, Bhavani Thuraisingham, A Scalable Multi-level Feature Extraction Technique to Detect Malicious Executables, Information System Frontiers, Volume 10, #1, 2008, 33–45.

[MASU2008b] M. Masud, J. Gao, L. Khan, J. Han, B. Thuraisingham, A Practical Approach to Classify Evolving Data Streams: Training with Limited Amount of Labeled Data, *Proceedings of ICDM, Pisa, Italy*, 2008, pp. 929–934.

[ROBE2000] S.J. Roberts, Extreme Value Statistics for Novelty Detection in Biomedical Signal Processing, *Proceedings of International Conference on Advances in Medical Signal and Information Processing, Bristol, UK*, 2000, pp. 166–172.

[SPIN2007] E.J. Spinosa, A.P. de Leon, F. de Carvalho, J. Gama, Olindda: A Cluster-based Approach for Detecting Novelty and Concept Drift in Data Streams, *Proceedings 2007 ACM Symposium on Applied Computing, Seoul, Korea*, 2007, pp. 448–452.

[THUR2017] B. Thuraisingham, P. Pallabi, M.M. Masud, L. Khan, Big Data Analytics with Applications in Insider Threat Detection, Washington, DC: CRC Press, 2017.

[WANG2003] H. Wang, W. Fan, P. Yu, J. Han, Mining Concept-Drifting Data Streams Using Ensemble Classifiers, *Proceedings of ACM SIGKDD*, 2003, pp. 226–235.

[YANG2005] Y. Yang, X. Wu, X. Zhu, Combining Proactive and Reactive Predictions for Data Streams. *Proceedings of ACM SIGKDD, Chicago, IL*, pp. 710–715, 2005.

[YANG2002] Y. Yang, J. Zhang, J. Carbonell, C. Jin, Topic-Conditioned Novelty Detection, *Proceedings ACM SIGKDD, Edmonton, Alberta*, 2002, pp. 688–693.

[YEUN2002] D.Y. Yeung, C. Chow. Parzen-Window Network Intrusion Detectors, *Proceedings of International Conference on Pattern Recognition, Quebec City, QC, Canada*, 2002, pp. 385–388.

8 Cloud-Based Data Science for Malware Detection

8.1 INTRODUCTION

Malware is a potent vehicle for many successful cyber-attacks every year, including data and identity theft, system and data corruption, and denial of service; it therefore constitutes a significant security threat to many individuals and organizations. Malware includes viruses, worms, Trojan horses, time and logic bombs, botnets, and spyware. A number of techniques have been devised by researchers to counter these attacks; however, the more successful the researchers become in detecting and preventing the attacks, the more sophisticated malicious code appears in the wild. Thus, the arms race between malware authors and malware defenders continues to escalate. One popular technique applied by the antivirus community to detect malicious code is *signature detection*. This technique matches untrusted executables against a unique telltale string or byte pattern known as a *signature*, which is used as an identifier for a particular malicious code. Although signature detection techniques are widely used, they are not effective against zero-day attacks (new malicious code), polymorphic attacks (different encryptions of the same binary), or metamorphic attacks (different code for the same functionality) [CRAN2005]. There has therefore been a growing need for fast, automated, and efficient detection techniques that are robust to these attacks.

In Chapter 6, we discussed data mining tools for malware detection. This chapter describes a data mining technique that is dedicated to the automated generation of signatures to defend against certain malware attacks. Due to the need for near real-time performance of the malware detection tools, we have developed our data mining tool in the cloud. That is, the main objective of this chapter is to show how the use of big data technologies such as the cloud would enhance performance and scalability of the malware detection techniques. We describe the detailed design and implementation of this cloud-based tool in the remaining sections of this chapter.

This chapter is organized as follows: Section 8.2 discusses malware detection. Section 8.3 discusses related work. Section 8.4 discusses the classification algorithm and proves its effectiveness analytically. Section 8.5 then describes the feature extraction and selection technique using cloud computing for malware detection, and Section 8.6 discusses data collection, experimental setup, evaluation techniques, and results. Section 8.7 discusses several issues related to our approach, and finally, Section 8.8 summarizes our conclusions. Figure 8.1 illustrates the concepts of this chapter.

8.2 MALWARE DETECTION

8.2.1 MALWARE DETECTION AS A DATA STREAM CLASSIFICATION PROBLEM

The problem of detecting malware using data mining [KOLT2004, MASU2008a, SCHU2001] involves classifying each executable as either *benign* or *malicious*. Most past work has approached the problem as a static data classification problem, where the classification model is trained with fixed training data. However, the escalating rate of malware evolution and innovation is not well-suited to static training. Detection of continuously evolving malware is better treated as a *data stream* classification problem. In this paradigm, the data stream is a sequence of executables in which each data point is one executable. The stream is *infinite-length*. It also observes *concept-drift* as attackers relentlessly develop new techniques to avoid detection, changing the characteristics of

DOI: 10.1201/9781003081845-13

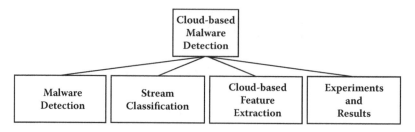

FIGURE 8.1 Big data and cloud for malware detection.

the malicious code. Similarly, the characteristics of benign executables change with the evolution of compilers and operating systems.

Data stream classification is a major area of active research in the data mining community, and requires surmounting at least three challenges: First, the storage and maintenance of potentially unbounded historical data in an infinite-length, concept-drifting stream for training purposes is infeasible [ZHAN2009]. Second, the classification model must be adapted continuously to cope with concept-drift. Third, if there is no predefined feature space for the data points in the stream, new features with high discriminating power must be selected and extracted as the stream evolves, which we call *feature evolution*.

Solutions to the first two problems are related. Concept-drift necessitates refinement of the hypothesis to accommodate the new concept; most of the old data must be discarded from the training set. Therefore, one of the main issues in mining concept-drifting data streams is the selection of training instances adequate to learn the evolving concept. Solving the third problem requires a feature selection process that is ongoing, since new and more powerful features are likely to emerge and old features are likely to become less dominant as the concept evolves. If the feature space is large, then the running time and memory requirements for feature extraction and selection become a bottleneck for the data stream classification system.

One approach to addressing concept-drift is to select and store the training data that are most consistent with the current concept [FAN2004]. Other approaches, such as Very Fast Decision Trees (VFDTs) [DOMI2000] update the existing classification model when new data appear. However, past work has shown that ensemble techniques are often more robust for handling un-expected changes and concept-drifts [KOLT2005, SCHO2005, WANG2003]. These maintain an ensemble of classifiers and update the ensemble when new data appear.

We design and develop a multi-partition, multi-chunk ensemble classification algorithm that generalizes existing ensemble methods. The generalization leads to significantly improved classification accuracy relative to existing single-partition, single-chunk ensemble approaches when tested on real-world data streams. The ensemble in our approach consists of Kv classifiers, where K is a constant and v is the number of partitions, to be explained shortly.

Our approach divides the data stream into equal sized chunks. The chunk size is chosen so that all data in each chunk fits into the main memory. Each chunk, when labeled, is used to train classifiers. Whenever a new data chunk is labeled, the ensemble is updated as follows. We take the r most recent labeled consecutive data chunks, divide these r chunks into v partitions and train a classifier with each partition. Therefore, v classifiers are trained using the r consecutive chunks. We then update the ensemble by choosing the best Kv classifiers (based on accuracy) among the newly trained v classifiers and the existing Kv classifiers. Thus, the total number of classifiers in the ensemble remains constant. Our approach is therefore parameterized by the number of partitions v, the number of chunks r, and the ensemble size K.

Our approach does not assume that new data points appearing in the stream are immediately labeled. Instead, it defers the ensemble updating process until labels for the data points in the latest data chunk become available. In the meantime, new unlabeled data continue to be classified using the current ensemble. Thus, the approach is well-suited to applications in which misclassifications solicit corrected labels from an expert user or other source. For example, consider the online credit card fraud detection problem. When a new credit card transaction takes place, its class (*fraud* or *authentic*) is predicted using the current ensemble. Suppose a fraudulent transaction is mis-classified as *authentic*. When the customer receives the bank statement, he identifies this error and reports it to the authority. In this way, the actual labels of the data points are obtained and the ensemble is updated accordingly.

8.2.2 Cloud Computing for Malware Detection

If the feature space of the data points is not fixed, a subproblem of the classification problem is the extraction and selection of features that describe each data point. As in prior work (e.g., [KOLT2004]), we use binary *n*-grams as features for malware detection. However, since the total number of possible *n*-grams is prohibitively large, we judiciously select *n*-grams that have the greatest discriminatory power. This selection process is ongoing; as the stream progresses, newer *n*-grams appear that dominate the older *n*-grams. These newer *n*-grams replace the old in our model in order to identify the best features for a particular period.

Naïve implementation of the feature extraction and selection process can be both time- and storage-intensive for large datasets. For example, our previous work [MASU2008a] extracted roughly a quarter billion *n*-grams from a corpus of only 3,500 executables. This feature extraction process required extensive virtual memory (with associated performance overhead), since not all of these features could be stored in main memory. Extraction and selection required about two hours of computation and many gigabytes of disk space for a machine with a quad-core processor and 12GB of memory. This is despite the use of a purely static dataset; when the dataset is a dynamic stream, extraction and selection must recur, resulting in a major bottleneck. In this chapter, we consider a much larger dataset of 105 thousand executables for which our previous approach is insufficient.

We therefore design and develop a scalable feature selection and extraction solution that leverages a cloud computing framework [DEAN2008]. We show that depending on the availability of cluster nodes, the running time for feature extraction and selection can be reduced by a factor of m, where m is the number of nodes in the cloud cluster. The nodes are machines with inexpensive commodity hardware. Therefore, the solution is also cost effective as high-end computing machines are not required.

8.2.3 Our Contributions

Our contributions can therefore be summarized as follows. We design and develop a generalized multi-partition, multi-chunk ensemble technique that significantly reduces the expected classifi-cation error over existing single-partition, single-chunk ensemble methods. A theoretical analysis justifies the effectiveness of the approach. We then formulate the malware detection problem as a data stream classification problem and identify drawbacks of traditional malicious code detection techniques relative to our data mining approach.

We design and develop a scalable and cost-effective solution to this problem using a cloud computing framework. Finally, we apply our technique to synthetically generated data as well as real botnet traffic and real malicious executables, achieving better detection accuracy than other stream data classification techniques. The results show that our ensemble technique constitutes a powerful tool for intrusion detection based on data stream classification.

8.3 RELATED WORK

Our work is related to both malware detection and stream mining. Both are discussed in this section. Traditional *signature-based* malware detectors identify malware by scanning untrusted binaries for distinguishing byte sequences or *features*. Features unique to malware are maintained in a *signature database*, which must be continually updated as new malware is discovered and analyzed. Traditionally, signature databases have been manually derived, updated, and disseminated by human experts as new malware appears and is analyzed. However, the escalating rate of new malware appearances and the advent of self-mutating, polymorphic malware over the past decade have made manual signature updating less practical. This has led to the development of automated data mining techniques for malware detection (e.g., [HAML2009, KOLT2004, MASU2008a, SCHU2001]) that are capable of automatically inferring signatures for previously unseen malware.

Data mining-based approaches analyze the content of an executable and classify it as malware if a certain combination of features are found (or not found) in the executable. These malware detectors are first trained so that they can generalize the distinction between malicious and benign executables, and thus detect future instances of malware. The training process involves feature extraction and model building using these features. Data mining-based malware detectors differ mainly on how the features are extracted and which machine learning technique is used to build the model. The performance of these techniques largely depends on the quality of the features that are extracted.

In the work reported in [SCHU2001], the authors extract DLL (Dynamic-Link Library) call information (using *GNU binutils*) and character strings (using *GNU strings*) from the headers of Windows PE executables, as well as 2-byte sequences from the executable content. The DLL calls, strings, and bytes are used as features to train models. Models are trained using two different machine learning techniques, RIPPER [COHE1996] and Naïve Bayes (NB) [MICH1994], to compare their relative performances. In [KOLT2004], the authors extract binary n-gram features from executables and apply them to different classification methods, such as k-Nearest Neighbor (KNN) [AHA1991], NB, Support Vector Machines (SVM) [BOSE1992], decision trees [QUIN2003], and boosting [FREU1996]. Boosting is applied in combination with various other learning algorithms to obtain improved models (e.g., boosted decision trees). Our previous work on data mining-based malware detection [MASU2008a] extracts binary n-grams from the executable, assembly instruction sequences from the disassembled executables, and DLL call information from the program headers. The classification models used in this work are SVM, decision tree, NB, boosted decision tree, and boosted NB.

Hamsa and Polygraph [LI2006, NEWS2005] apply a simple form of data mining to generate worm signatures automatically using binary n-grams as features. Both identify a collection of n-grams as a worm signature if they appear only in malicious binaries (i.e., positive samples) and never in benign binaries. This differs from the traditional data mining approaches already discussed (including ours) in two significant respects: First, Polygraph and Hamsa limit their attention to n-grams that appear only in the malicious pool, whereas traditional data mining techniques also consider n-grams that appear in the benign pool to improve the classification accuracy. Second, Polygraph and Hamsa define signature matches as simply the presence of a set of n-grams, whereas traditional data mining approaches build classification models that match samples based on both the presence and absence of features. Traditional data mining approaches therefore generalize the approaches of Polygraph and Hamsa, with corresponding increases in power.

Almost all past work has approached the malware detection problem as a static data classification problem in which the classification model is trained with fixed training data. However, the rapid emergence of new types of malware and new obfuscation strategies adopted by malware authors introduces a dynamic component to the problem that violates the static paradigm. We therefore argue that effective malware detection must be increasingly treated as a data stream classification problem in order to keep pace with attacks.

Many existing data stream classification techniques target infinite-length data streams that exhibit concept drift [AGGA2006, FAN2004, GAO2007, HASH2009, HULT2001, KOLT2005, WANG2003, YANG2005, ZHAO2009]. All of these techniques adopt a one-pass incremental update approach, but with differing approaches to the incremental updating mechanism. Most can be grouped into two main classes: single model incremental approaches and hybrid batch incremental approaches.

Single model incremental updating involves dynamically updating a single model with each new training instance. For example, decision tree models can be incrementally updated with incoming data [HULT2001]. In contrast, hybrid batch incremental approaches build each model from a batch of training data using a traditional batch learning technique. Older models are then periodically replaced by newer models as the concept drifts [BIFE2009, FAN2004, GAO2007, WANG2003, YANG2005]. Some of these hybrid approaches use a single model to classify the unlabeled data (e.g., [YANG2005] and [CHEN2008]) while others use an ensemble of models (e.g., [WANG2003] and [SCHO2005]). Hybrid approaches have the advantage that model updates are typically far simpler than in single model approaches; for example, classifiers in the ensemble can simply be removed or replaced. However, other techniques that combine the two approaches by incrementally updating the classifiers within the ensemble can be more complex [KOLT2005].

Accuracy-weighted classifier ensembles (AWEs) [SCHO2005, WANG2003] are an important category of hybrid incremental updating ensemble classifiers that use weighted majority voting for classification. These divide the stream into equal-sized chunks, and each chunk is used to train a classification model. An ensemble of K such models classifies the unlabeled data. Each time a new data chunk is labeled, a new classifier is trained from that chunk. This classifier replaces one of the existing classifiers in the ensemble. The replacement victim is chosen by evaluating the accuracy of each classifier on the latest training chunk. These ensemble approaches have the advantage that they can be built more efficiently than a continually updated single model and they observe higher accuracy than their single-model counterparts [TUME1996].

Our ensemble approach is most closely related to AWE, but with a number of significant differences. First, we apply multi-partitioning of the training data to build v classifiers from that training data. Second, the training data consists of r consecutive data chunks (i.e., a multi-chunk approach) rather than from a single chunk. We prove both analytically and empirically that both of these enhancements, that is, multi-partitioning and multi-chunk, significantly reduce ensemble classification error. Third, when we update the ensemble, v classifiers in the ensemble are replaced by v newly trained classifiers. The v classifiers that are replaced may come from different chunks; thus, although some classifiers from a chunk may have been removed, other classifiers from that chunk may still remain in the ensemble. This differs from AWE in which removal of a classifier means total removal of the knowledge obtained from one whole chunk. Our replacement strategy also contributes to error reduction. Finally, we use simple majority voting rather than weighted voting, which is more suitable for data streams, as shown in [GAO2007]. Thus, our multi-partition, multi-chunk ensemble approach is a more generalized and efficient form of that implemented by AWE.

Our work extends our previously published work [MASU2009]. Most existing data stream classification techniques, including our previous work, assume that the feature space of the data points in the stream is fixed. However, in some cases, such as text data, this assumption is not valid. For example, when features are words, the feature space cannot be fully determined at the start of the stream since new words appear frequently. In addition, it is likely that much of this large lexicon of words has low discriminatory power, and is therefore best omitted from the feature space. It is therefore more effective and efficient to select a subset of the candidate features for each data point. This feature selection must occur incrementally as newer, more discriminating candidate features arise and older features become outdated. Therefore, feature extraction and selection should be an integral part of data stream classification. In this chapter, we describe the design and implementation of an efficient and scalable feature extraction and selection technique using a cloud computing framework [DEAN2008, ZHAO2009]. This approach supersedes our previous work in that it considers the real challenges in data stream classification that occur when the feature space cannot be predetermined. This facilitates application of our technique to the detection of real malicious executables from a large, evolving dataset, showing that it can detect newer varieties of malware as malware instances evolve over time.

8.4 DESIGN AND IMPLEMENTATION OF THE SYSTEM

8.4.1 ENSEMBLE CONSTRUCTION AND UPDATING

Our *extended, multi-partition, multi-chunk* (EMPC) ensemble learning approach maintains an ensemble $A = \{A1, A2, ..., AKv\}$ of the most recent, best Kv classifiers. Each time a new data chunk Dn arrives, it tests the data chunk with the ensemble A. The ensemble is updated once chunk Dn is labeled. The classification process uses simple majority voting.

The ensemble construction updating process is illustrated in Figure 8.2 and summarized in Algorithm 8.1. Lines 1–3 of the algorithm compute the error of each classifier $Ai \in A$ on chunk Dn, where Dn is the most recent data chunk that has been labeled. Let D be the data of the most recently labeled r data chunks, including Dn. Line 5 randomly partitions D into v equal parts $\{d1, ...,\}$ such that all the parts have roughly the same class distributions. Lines 6–9 train a new batch of v classifiers, where each classifier An is trained with dataset $D - dj$. The error of each classifier $An \in An$ is computed by testing it on its corresponding test data. Finally, line 10 selects the best Kv classifiers from the $Kv + v$ classifiers in $An \cup A$ based on the errors of each classifier computed in lines 2 and 8. Note that any subset of the nth batch of v classifiers may be selected for inclusion in the new ensemble.

8.4.2 ERROR REDUCTION ANALYSIS

As explained in Algorithm 8.1, we build ensemble A of Kv classifiers. A test instance x is classified using a majority vote of the classifiers in the ensemble. We use simple majority voting rather than weighted majority voting (refer to [WANG2003]), since simple majority voting has been theoretically proven the optimal choice for data streams [GAO2007]. Weighted voting can be problematic in these contexts because it assumes that the distribution of training and test data are the same. However, in data streams, this assumption is violated because of concept-drift. Simple majority voting is therefore a better alternative. Our experiments confirm this in practice, obtaining better results with simple rather than weighted majority voting.

We have shown in [MASU2011] that EMPC can further reduce the expected error in classifying concept-drifting data streams compared to *single-partition, single-chunk* (SPC) approaches, which

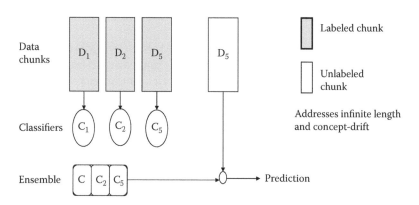

FIGURE 8.2 Ensemble construction.

ALGORITHM 8.1   UPDATING THE CLASSIFIER ENSEMBLE

Input: $\{D_{n-r+1}, \ldots, D_n\}$: the r most recently labeled data chunks
A: the current ensemble of best Kv classifiers
Output: an updated ensemble A
1: **for** each classifier $A_i \in A$ **do**
2:   $e(A_i) \leftarrow error\ of\ A_i\ on\ D_n$ // test and compute error
3: **end for**
4: $D \leftarrow \cup_{j=n-r+1}^{n} Dj$
5: Partition D into equal parts $\{d_1, d_2, \ldots, d_v\}$
6: **for** $j = 1$ to v **do**
7:   $A_j^n \leftarrow n$ newly trained classifier from data $D - d_j$
8:   $e\ (A_j) \leftarrow$ error of A_j on d_j// test and compute error
9: **end for**
10: $A \leftarrow$ best Kv from $A^n \cup A$ *based on computed error* $e\ (.)$

---

use only one data chunk for training a single classifier (i.e., $r = v = 1$). Intuitively, there are two main reasons for the error reduction. First, the training data per classifier is increased by introducing the multi-chunk concept. Larger training data naturally lead to a better trained model, reducing the error. Second, rather than training only one model from the training data, we partition the data into v partitions, and train one model from each partition. This further reduces error because the mean expected error of an ensemble of v classifiers is theoretically v times lower than that of a single classifier [TUME1996]. Therefore, both the multi-chunk and multi-partition strategies contribute to error reduction.

8.4.3 EMPIRICAL ERROR REDUCTION AND TIME COMPLEXITY

For a given partition size v, increasing the window size r only yields reduced error up to a certain point. After that, increasing r actually hurts the performance of our algorithm, because inequality (18) is violated. The upper bound of r depends on the magnitude of drift ρd. We have shown in [MASU2011] the relative error ER for $v = 2$, and different values of ρd, for increasing r. It is clear from the graph that for lower values of ρd, increasing r reduces the relative error by a greater margin. However, in all cases after r exceeds a certain threshold, ER becomes greater than one. Although it may not be possible to know the actual value of ρd from the data, we may determine the optimal value of r experimentally. In our experiments, we found that for smaller chunk sizes, higher values of r work better, and vice versa. However, the best performance-cost trade-off is found for $r = 2$ or $r = 3$. We have used $r = 2$ in our experiments. Similarly, the upper bound of v can be derived from inequality (18) for a fixed value of r. It should be noted that if v is increased, running time also increases. From our experiments, we obtained the best performance-cost trade-off for $v = 5$.

The time complexity of the algorithm is $O(vn(Ks + f\ (rs)))$, where n is the total number of data chunks, s is the size of each chunk, and $f\ (z)$ is the time required to build a classifier on a training data of size z. Since v is constant, the complexity becomes $O(n(Ks + f\ (rs)))$. This is at most a constant factor rv slower than the closest related work [WANG2003] but with the advantage of significantly reduced error.

ALGORITHM 8.2   *MAP(FILE_ID, BYTES)*

Input: file file id with content bytes
Output: list of pairs (g, l), where g is an n-gram and l is file id's label
1: $T \leftarrow \phi$
2: **for all** n-grams g in bytes **do**
3: $T \leftarrow T \cup \{g,\ label\ of\ (file,\ id)\}$ $\{(g,\ \text{labelof(fil\_id)})\}$
4: end for
5: for all $(g, l) \in T$ do
6: print (g, l)
7: end for

8.4.4   Hadoop/MapReduce Framework

We used the open-source Hadoop [APAC2010] MapReduce framework to implement our experiments. Here, we provide some of the algorithmic details of the Hadoop MapReduce feature extraction and selection algorithm. The *Map* function in a MapReduce framework takes a key-value pair as input and yields a list of intermediate key-value pairs for each.

$$Map: (MKey \times MVal) \to (RKey \times RVal)*$$

All the *Map* tasks are processed in parallel by each node in the cluster without sharing data with other nodes. Hadoop collates the output of the *Map* tasks by grouping each set of intermediate values $V \subseteq RVal$ that share a common intermediate key $k \in RKey$. The resulting collated pairs (k, V) are then streamed to *Reduce* nodes. Each reducer in a Hadoop MapReduce framework therefore receives a list of multiple (k, V) pairs, issued by Hadoop one at a time in an iterative fashion. *Reduce* can therefore be understood as a function having signature

$$Reduce: (RKey \times RVal*)* \to Val.$$

Codomain *Val* is the type of the final results of the MapReduce cycle.

In our framework, *Map* keys (*MKey*) are binary file identifiers (e.g., filenames), and *Map* values (*MVal*) are the file contents in bytes. *Reduce* keys (*RKey*) are n-gram features, and their corresponding values (*RVal*) are the class labels of the file instances whence they were found. Algorithm 8.2 shows the feature extraction procedure that *Map* nodes use to map the former to the latter. Lines 5–10 of Algorithm 8.3 tally the class labels reported by *Map* to obtain positive and negative instance counts for each n-gram. These form a basis for computing the information gain of each n-gram in line 11. Lines 12–16 use a min-heap data structure h to filter all but the best S features as evaluated by information gain. The final best S features encountered are returned by lines 18–20.

The q reducers in the Hadoop system therefore yield a total of qS candidate features and their information gains. These are streamed to a second reducer that simply implements the last half of Algorithm 8.3 to select the best S features.

ALGORITHM 8.3   *REDUCE$_{P,T}$(F)*

Input: list F of (g, L) pairs, where g is an n-gram and L is a list of class labels; total size t of original instance set; total number p of positive instances

Output: S pairs (g, i), where i is the information gain of n-gram g

1: **heap** h /* empty min-heap */
2: **for all** (g, L) in **F do**
3: $t' \leftarrow 0$
4: $p' \leftarrow 0$
5: **for all** l in L **do**
6: $t' \leftarrow t' + 1$
7: **if** $l = +$ **then**
8: $p \leftarrow p + 1$
9: **end if**
10: **end for**
11: $i \leftarrow \hat{H}(p', t', p't)$/*
12: **if** $h.size < S$ **then**
13: $h.\,insert(i_{(g)})$
14: **else if** $(h.root < i)$ **then**
15: $h.\,replace\,(h.root, i_{(g)})$
16: **end if**
17: **end for**
18: **for all** $i_{(g)}$ in h do
19: print $(g,)$
20: **end for**

8.5   MALICIOUS CODE DETECTION

8.5.1   OVERVIEW

Malware is a major source of cyber-attacks. Some malware varieties are purely static; each instance is an exact copy of the instance that propagated it. These are relatively easy to detect and filter once a single instance has been identified. However, a much more significant body of current day malware is polymorphic. Polymorphic malware self-modifies during propagation so that each instance has a unique syntax but carries a semantically identical malicious payload. The antivirus community invests significant effort and manpower toward devising, automating, and deploying algorithms that detect particular malware instances and polymorphic malware families that have been identified and analyzed by human experts. This has led to an escalating arms race between malware authors and antiviral defenders, in which each camp seeks to develop offenses and defenses that counter the recent advances of the other. With the increasing ease of malware development and the exponential growth of malware variants, many believe that this race will ultimately prove to be a losing battle for the defenders.

The malicious code detection problem can be modeled as a data mining problem for a stream having both infinite length and concept-drift. Concept-drift occurs as polymorphic malware mutates and as attackers and defenders introduce new technologies to the arms race. This conceptualization invites application of our stream classification technique to automate the detection of new malicious executables.

Feature extraction using n-gram analysis involves extracting all possible n-grams from the given dataset (training set), and selecting the best n-grams among them. Each such n-gram is a feature. That is, an n-gram is a sequence of n bytes. Before extracting n-grams, we pre-process the binary executables by converting them to hexdump files. Here, the granularity level is one byte. We apply the UNIX hexdump utility to convert the binary executable files into text files (*hexdump files*) containing the hexadecimal numbers corresponding to each byte of the binary. This process is performed to ensure safe and easy portability of the binary executables. In a non-distributed framework, the feature extraction process consists of two phases: feature extraction and feature selection, described shortly. Our cloud computing variant of this traditional technique is presented in this chapter.

8.5.2   Non-distributed Feature Extraction and Selection

In a non-distributed setting, feature extraction proceeds as follows. Each hexdump file is scanned by sliding an n-byte window over its content. Each n-byte sequence that appears in the window is an n-gram. For each n-gram g, we tally the total number tg of file instances in which g appears, as well as the total number $pg \leq tg$ of these that are positive (i.e., malicious executables).

This involves maintaining a hash table T of all n-grams encountered so far. If g is not found in T, then g is added to T with counts $tg = 1$ and $pg \in \{0, 1\}$ depending on whether the current file has a negative or positive class label. If g is already in T, then tg is incremented and pg is conditionally incremented depending on the file's label. When all hexdump files have been scanned, T contains all the unique n-grams in the dataset along with their frequencies in the positive instances and in total.

It is not always practical to use all n-gram features extracted from all the files corresponding to the current chunk. The exponential number of such n-grams may introduce unacceptable memory overhead, slow the training process, or confuse the classifier with large numbers of noisy, redundant, or irrelevant features. To avoid these pitfalls, candidate n-gram features must be sorted according to a selection criterion so that only the best ones are selected.

We choose *information gain* as the selection criterion, because it is one of the most effective criteria used in literature for selecting the best features. Information gain can be defined as a measure of the effectiveness of an attribute (i.e., feature) for classifying the training data. If we split the training data based on the values of this attribute, then information gain measures the expected reduction in entropy after the split. The more an attribute reduces entropy in the training data, the better that attribute is for classifying the data.

We have shown in [MASU2011] as new features are considered, their information gains are compared against the heap's root. If the gain of the new feature is greater than that of the root, the root is discarded and the new feature inserted into the heap. Otherwise the new feature is discarded and feature selection continues.

8.5.3   Distributed Feature Extraction and Selection

There are several drawbacks related to the non-distributed feature extraction and selection approach just described.

- The total number of extracted n-gram features might be very large. For example, the total number of 4 grams in one chunk is around 200 million. It might not be possible to store all of them in main memory. One obvious solution is to store the n-grams in a disk file, but this introduces unacceptable overhead due to the cost of disk read/write operations.
- If colliding features in hash table T are not sorted, then a linear search is required for each scanned n-gram during feature extraction to test whether it is already in T. If they are sorted, then the linear search is required during insertion. In either case, the time to extract all n-grams is worst case quadratic in the total number N of n-grams in each chunk, an impractical amount of time when $N \approx 10^8$. Similarly, the non-distributed feature selection process requires a sort of the n-grams in each chunk. In general, this requires $O(N \log N)$ time, which is impractical when N is large.

In order to efficiently and effectively tackle the drawbacks of the non-distributed feature extraction and selection approach, we leverage the power of cloud computing. This allows feature extraction, n-gram sorting, and feature selection to be performed in parallel, utilizing the Hadoop *MapReduce* framework.

MapReduce [DEAN2008] is an increasingly popular distributed programming paradigm used in cloud computing environments. The model processes large datasets in parallel, distributing the workload across many nodes (machines) in a share-nothing fashion. The main focus is to simplify the processing of large datasets using inexpensive cluster computers. Another objective is ease of usability with both load balancing and fault tolerance.

MapReduce is named for its two primary functions. The *Map* function breaks jobs down into subtasks to be distributed to available nodes, whereas its dual, *Reduce*, aggregates the results of completed subtasks. We will henceforth refer to nodes performing these functions as *mappers* and *reducers*, respectively. The details of the MapReduce process for n-gram feature extraction and selection are explained in [MASU2011]. In this section, we give a high-level overview of the approach.

Each training chunk containing N training files are used to extract the n-grams. These training files are first distributed among m nodes (machines) by the Hadoop Distributed File System (HDFS) (Figure 8.3, step 1). Quantity m is selected by HDFS depending on system availability. Each node then independently extracts n-grams from the subset of training files supplied to the node using the technique discussed in Section 4.1 (Figure 8.3, step 2). When all nodes finish their jobs, the n-grams extracted from each node are collated (Figure 8.3, step 3).

For example, suppose Node 1 observes n-gram *abc* in one positive instance (i.e., a malicious training file) while Node 2 observes it in a negative (i.e., benign) instance. This is denoted by pairs *abc*, + and *abc*, − under Nodes 1 and 2 (respectively) in Figure 8.3. When the n-grams are combined, the labels of instances containing identical n-grams are aggregated. Therefore, the aggregated pair for *abc* is *abc*, +−. The combined n-grams are distributed to q reducers (with q chosen by HDFS based on system availability). Each reducer first tallies the aggregated labels to obtain a positive count and a total count. In the case of n-gram *abc*, we obtain tallies of $pabc = 1$ and $tabc = 2$. The reducer uses these tallies to choose the best S n-grams from the subset of n-grams supplied to the node (Figure 8.3, step 5). This can be done efficiently using a min-heap of size S; the process requires $O(W \log S)$ time, where W is the total number of n-grams supplied to each reducer. In contrast, the non-distributed version requires $O(W \log W)$ time. Thus, from the q reducer nodes, we obtain qS n-grams. From these, we again select

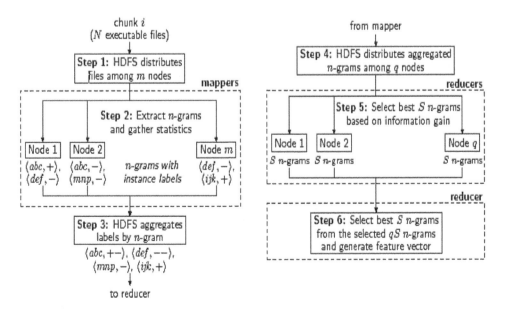

FIGURE 8.3 Distributed feature extraction and selection.

the best S by running another round of the MapReduce cycle in which the Map phase does nothing but the Reduce phase performs feature selection using only one node (Figure 8.3, step 6). Each feature in a feature set is binary; its value is 1 if it is present in a given instance (i.e., executable) and 0 otherwise. For each training or testing instance, we compute the feature vector whose bits consist of the feature values of the corresponding feature set. These feature vectors are used by the classifiers for training and testing.

8.6 EXPERIMENTS

We evaluated our approach on synthetic data, botnet traffic generated in a controlled environment and a malware dataset. The results of the experiments are compared with several baseline methods.

8.6.1 Datasets

8.6.1.1 Synthetic Dataset

To generate synthetic data with a drifting concept, we use a moving hyperplane, given by $\sum_{i=1}^{d} a_i x_i = a_0$ [WANG2003]. If $\sum_{i=1}^{d} a_i x_i \leq a_0$ then an example is negative; otherwise it is positive. Each example is a randomly generated d-dimensional vector $\{x_1, ..., x_d\}$, where $x_i \in [0, 1]$ weights $\{a_1, ..., a_d\}$ are also randomly initialized with a real number in the range $[0, 1]$. The value of a_0 is adjusted so that roughly the same number of positive and negative examples are generated. This can be done by choosing $a_0 = \frac{1}{2} \sum_{i=1}^{d} a_i$. We also introduce noise randomly by switching the labels of $p\%$ of the examples, where $p = 5$ in our experiments. There are several parameters that simulate concept-drift. We use parameters identical to those in [WANG2003]. In total, we generate 250,000 records and four different datasets having chunk sizes 250, 500, 750, and 1,000, respectively. Each dataset has 50% positive instances and 50% negative.

8.6.1.2 Botnet Dataset

Botnets are networks of compromised hosts known as *bots*, all under the control of a human attacker known as the *botmaster* [BARF2006]. The botmaster can issue commands to the bots to perform malicious actions, such as launching DDoS attacks, spamming, spying, and so on. Botnets are widely regarded as an enormous emerging threat to the internet community. Many cutting-edge botnets apply Peer-to-Peer (P2P) technology to reliably and covertly communicate as the botnet topology evolves. These botnets are distributed and small, making them more difficult to detect and destroy. Examples of P2P bots include Nugache [LEMO2006], Sinit [STEW2003], and Trojan.Peacomm [GRIZ2007].

Botnet traffic can be viewed as a data stream having both infinite length and concept-drift. Concept-drift occurs as the bot undertakes new malicious missions or adopts differing communication strategies in response to new botmaster instructions. We therefore consider our stream classification technique to be well-suited to detecting P2P botnet traffic.

We generate real P2P botnet traffic in a controlled environment using the Nugache P2P bot [LEMO2006]. The details of the feature extraction process are discussed in Masud et al. [MASU2008b]. There are 81 continuous attributes in total. The whole dataset consists of 30,000 records representing one week's worth of network traffic. We generate four different datasets having chunk sizes of 30 minutes, 60 minutes, 90 minutes, and 120 minutes, respectively. Each dataset has 25% positive (botnet traffic) instances and 75% negative (benign traffic).

8.6.1.3 Malware Dataset

We extract a total of 38,694 benign executables from different Windows machines, and a total of 66,694 malicious executables collected from an online malware repository VX Heavens [VX2010], which contains a large collection of malicious executables (viruses, worms, Trojans, and backdoors). The benign executables include various applications found at the Windows in-stallation folder, as well as other executables in the default program installation directory.

We select only the Win32 Portable Executables (PE) in both cases. Experiments with the ELF executables are a potential direction of future work. The collected 105,388 files (benign and malicious) form a data stream of 130 chunks, each consisting of 2,000 instances (executable files). The stream order was chosen by sorting the malware by version and discovery date, simulating the evolving nature of Internet malware. Each chunk has 1,500 benign executables (75% negative) and 500 malicious executables (25% positive). The feature extraction and selection process for this dataset is described in earlier sections.

Note that all these datasets are dynamic in nature. Their unbounded (potentially infinite-length) size puts them beyond the scope of purely static classification frameworks. The synthetic data also exhibits concept-drift. Although it is not possible to accurately determine whether the real datasets have concept-drift, theoretically the stream of executables should exhibit concept-drift when ob-served over a long period of time. The malware data exhibits feature evolution as evidenced by the differing set of distinguishing features identified for each chunk.

8.6.2 BASELINE METHODS

For classification, we use the Weka machine learning open-source package [HALL2009]. We apply two different classifiers: J48 decision tree and Ripper. We then compare each of the fol-lowing baseline techniques to our EMPC algorithm.

- *BestK:* This is a single-partition, single-chunk (SPC) ensemble approach, where an en-semble of the best K classifiers is used. The ensemble is created by storing all the clas-sifiers seen so far and selecting the best K based on expected error on the most recent training chunk. An instance is tested using simple majority voting.
- *Last:* In this case, we only keep the classifier trained on the most recent training chunk. This can be considered an SPC approach with $K = 1$.
- *AWE:* This is the SPC method implemented using accuracy-weighted classifier ensembles [WANG2003]. It builds an ensemble of K models, where each model is trained from one data chunk. The ensemble is updated as follows. Let Cn be the classifier built on the most recent training chunk. From the existing K models and the newest model Cn, the K best models are selected based on their error on the most recent training chunk. Selection is based on weighted voting where the weight of each model is inversely proportional to the error of the model on the most recent training chunk.
- *All:* This SPC uses an ensemble of all the classifiers seen so far. The new data chunk is tested with this ensemble by simple voting among the classifiers. Since this is an SPC approach, each classifier is trained from only one data chunk.

We obtain the optimal values of r and v to be between 2 and 3, and between 3 and 5, respectively, for most datasets. Unless mentioned otherwise, we use $r = 2$ and $v = 5$ in our experiments. To obtain a fair comparison, we use the same value for K (ensemble size) in EMPC and all baseline techniques.

8.6.3 HADOOP DISTRIBUTED SYSTEM SETUP

The distributed system on which we performed our experiments consists of a cluster of ten nodes. Each node has the same hardware configuration: an Intel Pentium IV 2.8 GHz processor, 4GB main memory, and 640GB hard disk space. The software environment consists of a Ubuntu 9.10 operating system, the Hadoop-0.20.1 distributed computing platform, the JDK 1.6 Java develop-ment platform, and a 100MB LAN network link.

8.7 DISCUSSION

Our work considers a feature space consisting of purely syntactic features: binary n-grams drawn from executable code segments, static data segments, headers, and all other content of untrusted files. Higher-level structural features such as call- and control-flow graphs, and dynamic features such as runtime traces, are beyond our current scope. Nevertheless, n-gram features have been observed to have very high discriminatory power for malware detection, as demonstrated by a large body of prior work as well as our experiments. This is in part because n-gram sets that span the entire binary file content, including headers and data tables, capture important low-level structural details that are often abstracted away by higher-level representations. For example, malware often contains handwritten assembly code that has been assembled and linked using non-standard tools. This allows attackers to implement binary obfuscations and low-level exploits not available from higher level source languages and standard compilers. As a result, malware often contains unusual instruction encodings, header structures, and link tables whose abnormalities can only be seen at the raw binary level, not in assembly code listings, control flow graphs, or system API call traces. Expanding the feature space to include these additional higher-level features requires an efficient and reliable method of harvesting them and assessing their relative discriminatory power during feature selection, and is reserved as a subject of future work.

The empirical results reported in [MASU2011] confirm our analysis that shows that multi-partition, multi-chunk approaches should perform better than single-chunk, single-partition approaches. Intuitively, a classifier trained on multiple chunks should have better prediction accuracy than a classifier trained on a single chunk because of the larger training data. Furthermore, if more than one classifier is trained by multi-partitioning the training data, the prediction accuracy of the resulting ensemble of classifiers should be higher than a single classifier trained from the same training data because of the error reduction power of an ensemble over single classifier. In addition, the accuracy advantages of EMPC can be traced to two important differences between our work and that of AWE. First, when a classifier is removed during ensemble updating in AWE, all information obtained from the corresponding chunk is forgotten; but in EMPC, one or more classifiers from an earlier chunk may survive. Thus, EMPC ensemble updating tends to retain more information than that of AWE, leading to a better ensemble. Second, AWE requires at least Kv data chunks, whereas EMPC requires at least $K + r - 1$ data chunks to obtain Kv classifiers. Thus, AWE tends to keep much older classifiers in the ensemble than EMPC, leading to some outdated classifiers that can have a negative effect on the classification accuracy.

However, the higher accuracy comes with an increased cost in running time. Theoretically, EMPC is at most rv times slower than AWE, its closest competitor in accuracy. This is also evident in the empirical evaluation which shows that the running time of EMPC is within five times that of AWE (for $r = 2$ and $v = 5$). However, some optimizations can be adopted to reduce the runtime cost. First, parallelization of training for each partition can be easily implemented, reducing the training time by a factor of v. Second, classification by each model in the ensemble can also be done in parallel, thereby reducing the classification time by a factor of Kv. Therefore, parallelization of training and classification should reduce the running time at least by a factor of v, making the runtime close to that of AWE. Alternatively, if parallelization is not available, parameters v and r can be lowered to sacrifice prediction accuracy for lower runtime cost. In this case, the desired balance between runtime and prediction accuracy can be obtained by evaluating the first few chunks of the stream with different values of v and r and choosing the most suitable values.

8.8 SUMMARY AND DIRECTIONS

Many intrusion detection problems can be formulated as classification problems for infinite-length, concept-drifting data streams. Concept-drift occurs in these streams as attackers react and adapt to defenses. We formulated both malicious code detection and botnet traffic detection as such problems, and introduced EMPC, a novel ensemble learning technique for automated classification of infinite-length, concept-drifting streams. Applying EMPC to real data streams obtained from polymorphic malware and botnet traffic samples yielded better detection accuracies than other stream data classification techniques. This shows that the approach is useful and effective for both intrusion detection and more general data stream classification.

EMPC uses generalized, multi-partition, multi-chunk ensemble learning. Both theoretical and empirical evaluation of the technique show that it significantly reduces the expected classification error over existing single-partition, single-chunk ensemble methods. Moreover, we show that EMPC can be elegantly implemented in a cloud computing framework based on MapReduce [DEAN2008]. The result is a low-cost, scalable stream classification framework with high classification accuracy and low runtime overhead.

At least two extensions to our technique offer promising directions of future work. First, our current feature selection procedure limits its attention to the best S features based on information gain as the selection criterion. The classification accuracy could potentially be improved by leveraging recent work on supervised dimensionality reduction techniques [RISH2008, SAJA2005] for improved feature selection. Second, the runtime performance of our approach could be improved by exploiting additional parallelism available in the cloud computing architecture. For example, the classifiers of an ensemble could be run in parallel as mappers in a MapReduce framework with reducers that aggregate the results for voting. Similarly, the candidate classifiers for the next ensemble could be trained and evaluated in parallel. Reformulating the ensemble components of the system in this way could lead to significantly shortened processing times, and hence opportunities to devote more processing time to classification for improved accuracy. Other big data platforms such as Storm and Spark also need to be explored to host our algorithms. Finally, while the amount of malware data collected for analysis could be massive, we need to explore the use of NoSQL database systems such as CouchDB to store, manage and query the data.

REFERENCES

[AGGA2006] C.C. Aggarwal, J. Han, J. Wang, P.S. Yu, A Framework for On-Demand Classification of Evolving Data Streams, *IEEE Transactions on Knowledge and Data Engineering*, Volume 18, #5, 2006, 577–589.

[AHA1991] D.W. Aha, D. Kibler, M.K. Albert, Instance-Based Learning Algorithms, *Machine Learning*, Volume 6, 1991, 37–66.

[APAC2010] Hadoop, 2010, hadoop.apache.org

[BARF2006] P. Barford, V. Yegneswaran, An Inside Look at Botnets, *Malware Detection*, Advances in Information Security, Springer (Editors: M. Christodorescu, S. Jha, D. Maughan, D. Song, C. Wang), 2006, 171–192.

[BIFE2009] A. Bifet, G. Holmes, B. Pfahringer, R. Kirkby, R. Gavalda`, New Ensemble Methods for Evolving Data Streams, *Proceedings of the 15th ACM International Conference on Knowledge Discovery and Data Mining (KDD)*, 2009, 139–148.

[BOSE1992] B.E. Boser, I.M. Guyon, V.N. Vapnik, A Training Algorithm for Optimal Margin Classifiers, *Proceedings of the 5th ACM Workshop on Computational Learning Theory*, ACM, Pittsburgh, PA, USA,1992, 144–152.

[CHEN2008] S. Chen, H. Wang, S. Zhou, P.S. Yu, Stop Chasing Trends: Discovering High Order Models in Evolving Data, *Proceedings of the 24th IEEE International Conference on Data Engineering (ICDE)*, Cancun, Mexico, 2008, 923–932.

[COHE1996] W.W. Cohen, Learning Rules That Classify E-mail, *Proceedings of the AAAI Spring Symposium on Machine Learning in Information Access* , AAAI, Stanford, CA, 1996, 18–27.

[CRAN2005] J.R. Crandall, Z. Su, S.F. Wu, F.T. Chong, On Deriving Unknown Vulnerabilities from Zero-Day Polymorphic and Metamorphic Worm Exploits, *Proceedings of the 12th ACM Conference on Computer and Communications Security (CCS'05)*, ACM, Alexandria, VA, 2005, 235–248.

[DEAN2008] J. Dean, S. Ghemawat, MapReduce: Simplified Data Processing on Large Clusters, *Communications of the ACM*, Volume 51, #1, 2008, 107–113.

[DOMI2000] P. Domingos, G. Hulten, Mining High-Speed Data Streams, *Proceedings of the 6th ACM International Conference on Knowledge Discovery and Data Mining (KDD)*, ACM, Boston, MA, 2000, 71–80.

[FAN2004] W. Fan, Systematic Data Selection to Mine Concept-Drifting Data Streams, *Proceedings of the 10th ACM International Conference on Knowledge Discovery and Data Mining (KDD)*, ACM, Seattle, WA, 2004, 128–137.

[FREU1996] Y. Freund, R.E. Schapire, Experiments with a New Boosting Algorithm, *Proceedings of the 13th International Conference on Machine Learning*, ACM, Bari, Italy, 1996, 148–156.

[GAO2007] J. Gao, W. Fan, J. Han, On Appropriate Assumptions to Mine Data Streams: Analysis and Practice, *Proceedings of the 7th IEEE International Conference on Data Mining (ICDM)*, IEEE, Omaha, NE, 2007, 143–152.

[GRIZ2007] J.B. Grizzard, V. Sharma, C. Nunnery, B.B. Kang, D. Dagon, Peer-to-Peer Botnets: Overview and Case Study, *Proceedings of the 1st Workshop on Hot Topics in Understanding Botnets (HotBots)*, USENIX, Cambridge, MA, 2007, 1–8.

[HALL2009] M. Hall, E. Frank, G. Holmes, B. Pfahringer, P. Reutemann, I.H. Witten, The WEKA Data Mining Software: An Update, *ACM SIGKDD Explorations*, Volume 11, #1, 2009, 10–18.

[HAML2009] K.W. Hamlen, V. Mohan, M.M. Masud, L. Khan, B.M. Thuraisingham, Exploiting an Antivirus Interface, *Computer Standards and Interfaces*, Volume 31, #6, 2009, 1182–1189.

[HASH2009] S. Hashemi, Y. Yang, Z. Mirzamomen, M.R. Kangavari, Adapted One-versus-All Decision Trees for Data Stream Classification, *IEEE Transactions on Knowledge and Data Engineering*, Volume 21, #5, 2009, 624–637.

[HULT2001] G. Hulten, L. Spencer, P. Domingos, Mining Time-Changing Data Streams, *Proceedings of the 7th ACM International Conference on Knowledge Discovery and Data Mining (KDD)*, ACM, San Francisco, CA, 2001, 97–106.

[KOLT2004] J. Kolter, M.A. Maloof, Learning to Detect Malicious Executables in the Wild, *Proceedings of the 10th ACM International Conference on Knowledge Discovery and Data Mining (KDD)*, ACM, San Francisco, CA, 2004, 470–478.

[KOLT2005] J.Z. Kolter, M.A. Maloof, Using Additive Expert Ensembles to Cope with Concept Drift, *Proceedings of the 22nd International Conference on Machine Learning (ICML)*, ACM Press, Bonn, Germany, 2005, 449–456.

[LEMO2006] R. Lemos, Bot Software Looks to Improve Peerage, *SecurityFocus*, 2006, www.securityfocus.com/news/11390

[LI2006] Z. Li, M. Sanghi, Y. Chen, M.-Y. Kao, B. Chavez, Hamsa: Fast Signature Generation for Zero-Day Polymorphic Worms with Provable Attack Resilience, *Proceedings of the*, IEEE, Berkeley, CA, 2006, 32–47.

[MASU2008a] M.M. Masud, J. Gao, L. Khan, J. Han, B. Thuraisingham, Mining Concept-Drifting Data Stream to Detect Peer to Peer Botnet Traffic, Technical report UTDCS-05-08, The University of Texas at Dallas, Richardson, Texas, 2008a, www.utdallas.edu/mmm058000/reports/UTDCS-05-08.pdf

[MASU2008b] M.M. Masud, L. Khan, B. Thuraisingham, A Scalable Multi-level Feature Extraction Technique to Detect Malicious Executables, Information System Frontiers, Volume 10, #1, 2008, 33–45.

[MASU2009] M.M. Masud, J. Gao, L. Khan, J. Han, B.M. Thuraisingham, A Multi-partition Multi-chunk Ensemble Technique to Classify Concept-Drifting Data Streams, *Proceedings of the 13th Pacific-Asia Conference on Advances in Knowledge Discovery and Data Mining*, Springer-Verlag, 2009, pp. 363–375.

[MASU2011] M.M. Masud, T. Al-Khateeb, K.W. Hamlen, J. Gao, L. Khan, J. Han, B.M. Thuraisingham, Cloud-Based Malware Detection for Evolving Data Streams, ACM Transactions on Management Information Systems, Volume 2, #3, 2011, 16.

[MICH1994] D. Michie, D.J., Spiegelhalter, C.C., Taylor, eds., *Machine Learning, Neural and Statistical Classification*. Ellis Horwood Series in Artificial Intelligence, Morgan Kaufmann, 1994, 50–83.

[NEWS2005] J. Newsome, B. Karp, D. Song, Polygraph: Automatically Generating Signatures for Polymorphic Worms, *Proceedings of the IEEE Symposium on Security and Privacy (S&P)*, IEEE, Oakland, CA, 2005, 226–241.

[QUIN2003] J.R. Quinlan, *C4.5: Programs for Machine Learning*, 5th ed., Morgan Kaufmann, 2003.

[RISH2008] I. Rish, G. Grabarnik, G.A. Cecchi, G.G. Pereira, Closed-Form Supervised Dimensionality Reduction with Generalized Linear Models, *Proceedings of International Conference on Machine Learning (ICML 2008)*, Helsinki, Finland, 2008, 832–839.

[SAJA2005] Sajama, A. Orlitsky, Supervised Dimensionality Reduction Using Mixture Models, *Proceedings of the 22nd ACM International Conference on Machine Learning (ICML)*, ACM, Bonn, Germany, 2005, 768–775.

[SCHO2005] M. Scholz, R. Klinkenberg, An Ensemble Classifier for Drifting Concepts, *Proceedings of the 2nd International Workshop on Knowledge Discovery in Data Streams (IWKDDS)*, Springer, Porto, Portugal, 2005, 53–64.

[SCHU2001] M.G. Schultz, E. Eskin, E. Zadok, S.J. Stolfo, Data Mining Methods for Detection of New Malicious Executables, *Proceedings of the IEEE Symposium on Security and Privacy (S&P)*, IEEE, Oakland, CA, 2001, 38–49.

[STEW2003] J. Stewart, Sinit P2P Trojan Analysis, 2003, www.secureworks.com/research/threats/sinit

[TUME1996] K. Tumer, J. Ghosh, Error Correlation and Error Reduction in Ensemble Classifiers, *Connection Science*, Volume 8, #3, 1996, 385–404.

[VX2010] Vx Heavens, VX Heavens, 2010, vx.netlux.org

[WANG2003] H. Wang, W. Fan, P.S. Yu, J. Han, Mining Concept-Drifting Data Streams Using Ensemble Classifiers, *Proceedings of the 9th ACM International Conference on Knowledge Discovery and Data Mining (KDD)*, ACM, Washington DC, 2003, 226–235.

[YANG2005] Y. Yang, X. Wu, X. Zhu, Combining Proactive and Reactive Predictions for Data Streams, *Proceedings of the 11th ACM International Conference on Knowledge Discovery and Data Mining (KDD)*ACM, Chicago, IL, 2005, 710–715.

[ZHAN2009] P. Zhang, X. Zhu, L. Guo, Mining Data Streams with Labeled and Unlabeled Training Examples, *Proceedings of the 9th IEEE International Conference on Data Mining (ICDM)*, ACM, Chicago, IL, 2009, 627–636.

[ZHAO2009] W. Zhao, H. Ma, Q. He, Parallel *K*-means Clustering Based on MapReduce, *Proceedings of the 1st International Conference on Cloud Computing (CloudCom)*, IEEE, Beijing, China, 2009, 674–679.

9 Stream Analytics for Insider Threat Detection

9.1 INTRODUCTION

Malicious insiders are perhaps the most potent threats to information assurance in many or most organizations [BRAC2004, HAMP1999, MATZ2004, SALE2011]. One traditional approach to the insider threat detection problem is supervised learning, which builds data classification models from training data. Unfortunately, the training process for supervised learning methods tends to be time-consuming and expensive, and generally requires large amounts of well-balanced training data to be effective. In our experiments we observe that less than 3% of the data in realistic datasets for this problem are associated with insider threats (the minority class); over 97% of the data is associated with non-threats (the majority class). Hence, traditional support vector machines (SVM) [CHAN2011, MANE2002] trained from such imbalanced data are likely to perform poorly on test datasets.

One-class SVMs (OCSVMs) [MANE2002] address the rare-class issue by building a model that considers only normal data (i.e., non-threat data). During the testing phase, test data is classified as normal or anomalous based on geometric deviations from the model. However, the approach is only applicable to bounded-length, static data streams. In contrast, insider threat-related data is typically continuous and threat patterns evolve over time. In other words, the data is a stream of unbounded length [CANG2006]. Hence, effective classification models must be adaptive (i.e., able to cope with evolving concepts) and highly efficient in order to build the model from large amounts of evolving data. Data that is associated with insider threat detection and classification is often continuous. In these systems, the patterns of average users and insider threats can gradually evolve. A novice programmer can develop his skills to become an expert programmer over time. An insider threat can change his actions to more closely mimic legitimate user processes. In either case, the patterns at either end of these developments can look drastically different when compared directly to each other. These natural changes will not be treated as anomalies in our approach. Instead, we classify them as natural concept-drift. The traditional static supervised and un-supervised methods raise unnecessary false alarms with these cases because they are unable to handle them when they arise in the system. These traditional methods encounter high false positive rates. Learning models must be adept in coping with evolving concepts and highly efficient at building models from large amounts of data to rapidly detecting real threats. For these reasons, the insider threat problem can be conceptualized as a stream mining problem that applies to continuous data streams. Whether using a supervised or unsupervised learning algorithm, the method chosen must be highly adaptive to correctly deal with concept-drifts under these conditions. Incremental learning and ensemble-based learning [ALKH2012a, ALKH2012b, KANG2011, MASU2008, MASU2009, MASU2010a, MASU2010b, MASU2011a, MASU2011b, MASU2011c, MASU2011d, MASU2013] are two adaptive approaches in order to overcome this hindrance. An ensemble of K models that collectively vote on the final classification can reduce the false negatives (FN) and false positives (FP) for a test set. As new models are created and old ones are updated to be more precise, the least accurate models are discarded to always maintain an ensemble of exactly K current models. An alternative approach to supervised learning is unsupervised learning, which can be effectively applied to purely unlabeled data – that is, data in which no points are explicitly identified as anomalous or non-anomalous. Graph-based anomaly detection (GBAD) is one important form of unsupervised learning [COOK2000, COOK2007, EBER2007] but has traditionally been limited to static, finite-length datasets. This limits its application to streams related to insider threats which tend to have unbounded length and threat patterns that evolve over time. Applying GBAD to the insider threat problem therefore requires that the models used be adaptive and efficient. Adding these qualities allows effective models to be built from vast amounts of evolving data.

We cast insider threat detection as a stream mining problem and propose two methods (supervised and unsupervised learning) for efficiently detecting anomalies in stream data [PARV2013]. To cope with concept-evolution, our supervised approach maintains an evolving ensemble of multiple OCSVM models [PARV2011a]. Our unsupervised approach combines multiple GBAD models in an ensemble of classifiers [PARV2006, PARV2011b]. The ensemble updating process is designed in both cases to keep the ensemble current as the stream evolves. This evolutionary capability improves the classifier's survival of concept-drift as the behavior of both legitimate and illegitimate agents varies over time. In experiments, we use test data that records system call data for a large, Unix-based, multi-user system [QUMR2013].

The above approach may not work well for sequence data [PARV2012a, PARV2012b]. For sequence data, our approach maintains an ensemble of multiple unsupervised stream-based sequence learning (USSL) [PARV2012a]. During the learning process, we store the repetitive sequence patterns from a user's actions or commands in a model called a quantized dictionary. In particular, longer patterns with higher weights due to frequent appearances in the stream are considered in the dictionary. An ensemble in this case is a collection of K models of type quantized dictionary. When new data arrives or is gathered, we generate a new quantized dictionary model from this new dataset. We will take the majority voting of all models to find the anomalous pattern sequences within this new dataset. We will update the ensemble if the new dictionary outperforms others in the ensemble and will discard the least accurate model from the ensemble. Therefore, the ensemble always keeps the models current as the stream evolves, preserving high detection accuracy as both legitimate and illegitimate behaviors evolve over time. Our test data consists of real-time recorded user command sequences for multiple users of varying experience levels and a concept-drift framework to further exhibit the practicality of this approach.

This chapter describes our approach to insider threat detection using stream data mining for both non-sequence and sequence data. In Section 9.2, we provide a survey of insider threat and stream mining. We also discuss scalability issues with big data/data science techniques. Insider threat for non-sequenced stream data are discussed in Section 9.3. Insider threat for sequence stream data is discussed in Section 9.4 (Figure 9.1). Section 9.5 summarizes this chapter. A more detailed discussion is given in [THUR2017].

9.2 SURVEY OF INSIDER THREAT AND STREAM MINING

9.2.1 INSIDER THREAT DETECTION

Insider threat detection work has applied ideas from both intrusion detection and external threat detection [MAXI2003, SCHO2001, SCHU2002, WANG2003]. Supervised learning approaches collect system call trace logs containing records of normal and anomalous behavior [FORR1996, GAO2004, HOFM1998, NGUY2003] extract n-gram features from the collected data, and use the extracted features to train classifiers. Text classification approaches treat each system call as a word in a bag-of-words model [LIAO2002]. Various attributes of system calls, including arguments, object path, return value, and error status, have been exploited as features in various supervised learning methods [KRUG2003, TAND2003].

Hybrid high-order Markov chain models detect anomalies by identifying a *signature behavior* for a particular user based on their command sequences [JU2001]. The Probabilistic Anomaly Detection (PAD) algorithm [STOL2005] is a general-purpose algorithm for anomaly detection (in the Windows environment) that assumes anomalies or noise is a rare event in the training data. Masquerade detection is argued over by some individuals. A number of detection methods were

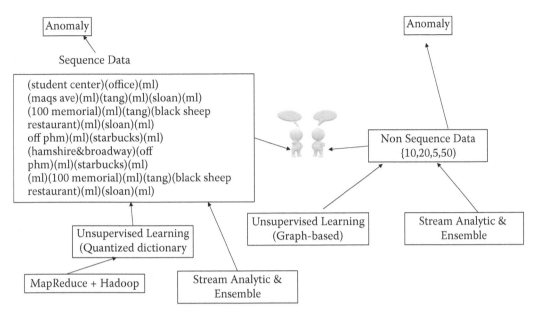

FIGURE 9.1   Stream analytics for insider threat detection.

applied to a dataset of "truncated" UNIX shell commands for 70 users [SCHO2001]. Commands were collected using the UNIX acct auditing mechanism. For each user, a number of commands were gathered over a period of time. The detection methods were supervised by a multi-step Markovian model and a combination of Bayes and Markov approaches. It was argued that the dataset was not appropriate for the masquerade detection task [MAXI2003]. It was pointed out that the period of data gathering varied greatly from user to user (from several days to several months). Furthermore, commands were not logged in the order in which they were typed. Instead, they were coalesced when the application terminated the audit mechanism. This leads to the unfortunate consequence of possible faulty analysis of strict sequence data. Therefore, in this proposed work we have not considered this dataset. These approaches differ from our supervised approach in that these learning approaches are static in nature and do not learn over evolving streams. In other words, stream characteristics of data are not explored further. Hence, static learning performance may degrade over time. On the other hand, our supervised approach will learn from evolving data streams. Our proposed work is based on supervised learning and it can handle dynamic data or stream data well by learning from evolving streams. In anomaly detection, a one class SVM algorithm is used [STOL2005]. OCSVM builds a model by training on normal data and then classifies test data as benign or anomalous based on geometric deviations from that normal training data. For masquerade detection, one class SVM training is as effective as two class training [STOL2005]. Investigations have been made into SVMs using binary features and frequency-based features. The one class SVM algorithm with binary features performed the best.

Recursive mining has been proposed to find frequent patterns [SZYM2004]. One class SVM classifiers were used for masquerade detection after the patterns were encoded with unique symbols and all sequences rewritten with this new coding. To the best of our knowledge there is no work that extends this OCSVM in a stream domain. Although our approach relies on OCSVM, it is extended to the stream domain so that it can cope with changes [PARV2011b, PARV2013]. Works have also explored unsupervised learning for insider threat detection, but only to static streams to our knowledge [ESKI2002, LIU2005]. Static graph-based anomaly detection (GBAD) approaches [COOK2000, COOK2007, EBER2007, YAN2002] represent threat and non-threat data as a graph and apply unsupervised learning to detect anomalies. The *minimum description length* (MDL) approach to GBAD has been applied to email, cell phone traffic, business processes, and cyber-crime datasets [KOWA2008, STAN1996]. Our work builds upon GBAD and MDL to support dynamic, evolving streams [PARV2011a, PARV2013].

Stream mining is a relatively new category of data mining research that applies to continuous data streams [FAN2004]. In such settings, both supervised and unsupervised learning must be adaptive in order to cope with data whose characteristics change over time. There are two main approaches to adaptation: *incremental learning* [DAVI1998, DOMI2001] and *ensemble-based learning* [FAN2004, MASU2010a, MASU2011a]. Past work has demonstrated that ensemble-based approaches are the more effective of the two, thus motivating our approach.

Ensembles have been used in the past to bolster the effectiveness of positive/negative classification [MASU2008, MASU2011a]. By maintaining an ensemble of K models that collectively vote on the final classification, the number of *false negatives* (FN) and *false positives* (FP) for a test set can be reduced. As better models are created, poorer models are discarded to maintain an ensemble of size exactly K. This helps the ensemble evolve with the changing characteristics of the stream and keeps the classification task tractable. A comparison of the above related works is summarized in Table 9.1. A more complete survey is available in [SALE2008].

Insider threat detection work has utilized ideas from intrusion detection or external threat detection areas [SCHO2001, WANG2003]. For example, supervised learning has been applied to detect insider threats. System call traces from normal activity and anomaly data are gathered [HOFM1998]; features are extracted from this data using n-gram and finally, trained with classifiers. Authors [LIAO2002] exploit the text classification idea in the insider threat domain, where each system call is treated as a word in a bag-of-words model. System call, related attributes, arguments, object path, return value, and error status of each system call are served as features in various supervised methods [KRUG2003, TAND2003]. A supervised model based on hybrid high-order Markov chain model was adopted by researchers [JU2001]. A *signature behavior* for a particular user based on the command sequences that the user executed is identified and then anomaly is detected (see also [ZLIO2011], [KOPP2009], [JAMA2012], and [SEKE2013]).

Schonlau et al. [SCHO2001] applied a number of detection methods to a dataset of "truncated" UNIX shell commands for 70 users. Commands were collected using the UNIX acct auditing mechanism. For each user a number of commands were gathered over a period of time. The detection methods are supervised based on multi-step Markovian model and combination of Bayes and Markov approach. Maxion et al. [MAXI2003] argued that the Schonlau dataset was not appropriate for the masquerade detection task and created a new dataset using the Calgary dataset and applied the static supervised model.

These approaches differ from our work in the following ways. These learning approaches are static in nature and do not learn over evolving stream. In other words, stream characteristics of data

TABLE 9.1
Capabilities and focuses of various approaches for non-sequence data

Approach	Learning	concept drift	insider threat	sequence based
(Ju and Vardi, 2001)	S	✗	✓	✓
(Maxion, 2003)	S	✗	✓	✗
(Liu et al., 2005)	U	✗	✓	✓
(Wang et al., 2003)	S	✗	✓	✗
(Masud et al., 2011a)	S	✓	✗	✗
(Parveen, Weger et al., 2011)	U	✓	✓	✗
(Parveen, McDaniel et al., 2012)	U	✓	✓	✓

are not explored further. Hence, static learner performance may degrade over time. On the other hand, our approach will learn from evolving data stream. We show that our approach is unsupervised and is as effective as a supervised model (incremental). Researchers have explored *unsupervised learning* [LIU2005] for insider threat detection. However, this learning algorithm is static in nature. Although our approach is unsupervised, it learns at the same time from evolving stream over time, and more data will be used for unsupervised learning. In anomaly detection, a one class support vector machine (SVM) algorithm (OCSVM) is used. OCSVM builds a model from training on normal data and then classifies a test data as benign or anomaly based on geometric deviations from normal training data. Wang et al. [WANG2003] showed for masquerade detection that one class SVM training is as effective as two class training. The authors have investigated SVMs using binary features and frequency-based features. The one-class SVM algorithm with binary features performed the best. To find frequent patterns, Szymanski et al. [SZYM2004] proposed recursive mining, encoded the patterns with unique symbols, and rewrote the sequence using this new coding. They used a one class SVM classifier for masquerade detection. These learning approaches are static in nature and do not learn over evolving stream.

9.2.2 STREAM MINING

Stream mining is a new data mining area where data is continuous [ALKH2012a, MASU2010b, MASU2011a, MASU2011b, MASU2011c, MASU2013]. In addition, characteristics of data may change over time (concept-drift). Here, supervised and unsupervised learning need to be adaptive to cope with changes. There are two ways adaptive learning can be developed. One is incremental learning and the other is ensemble-based learning. Incremental learning is used in user action prediction [DOMI2001] but not for anomaly detection. Davidson et al. [DAVI1998] introduced Incremental Probabilistic Action Modeling (IPAM), based on one-step command transition probabilities estimated from the training data. The probabilities were continuously updated with the arrival of a new command and modified with the usage of an exponential decay scheme. However, the algorithm is not designed for anomaly detection. Therefore, to the best of our knowledge, there is almost no work from other researchers that handles insider threat detection in the stream mining area. This is the first attempt to detect insider threat using stream mining [PARV2011a, PARV2011b, PARV2012b].

Recently unsupervised learning has been applied to detect insider threat in a data stream [PARV2011b, PARV2013]. This work does not consider sequence data for threat detection. Recall that sequence data is very common in an insider threat scenario. Instead, it considers data as graph/vector and finds normative patterns and applies an ensemble-based technique to cope with changes. On the other hand, in our proposed approach, we consider user command sequences for anomaly detection and construct quantized dictionary for normal patterns.

Users' repetitive daily or weekly activities may constitute user profiles. For example, a user's frequent command sequences may represent a normative pattern of that user. To find normative patterns over dynamic data streams of unbounded length is challenging due to the requirement of a one pass algorithm. For this, an unsupervised learning approach is used by exploiting a compressed/quantized dictionary to model common behavior sequences. This unsupervised approach needs to identify normal user behavior in a single pass [CHUA2011, PARV2012a, PARV2012b]. One major challenge with these repetitive sequences is their variability in length. To combat this problem, we generate a dictionary which will contain any combination of possible normative patterns existing in the gathered data stream. In addition, we have incorporated the power of stream mining to cope with gradual changes. We have done experiments and shown that our USSL approach works well in the context of concept-drift and anomaly detection.

Our work [PARV2012a, PARV2012b] differs from the work of [CHUA2011] in the following ways. First, the work in [CHUA2011] focuses on dictionary construction to generate normal profiles. In other words, their work does not address the insider threat issue which is our focus.

Second, [CHUA2011] does not consider ensemble-based techniques; our work exploits ensemble-based technique with the combination of unsupervised learning (i.e., dictionary for benign sequences). Finally, when a number of users will grow, dictionary construction will become a bottleneck. The work of [CHUA2011] does not consider the scalability issue; in our case, we address the scalability issue using a MapReduce framework.

In [PARV2012a], an incremental approach is used. Ensemble-based techniques are not incorporated, but the literature used shows that ensemble-based techniques are more effective than those of the incremental variety for stream mining [FAN2004, MASU2010a, MASU2011a]. Therefore, our approach focuses on ensemble-based techniques [PARV2012b]. We refer to Table 9.2 on which related approaches are unsupervised or supervised, and whether they focus on concept-drift, detecting insider threat and sequence data from stream mining. Some aspects of mining complex applications are given in [EAGL2006].

9.2.3 BIG DATA TECHNIQUES FOR SCALABILITY

Stream data are continuously coming with high velocity and large size [ALKH2012b]. This conforms to the characteristics of big data. "Big data" is data whose scale, diversity, and complexity require new architecture, techniques, algorithms, and analytics to manage it and extract value and hidden knowledge from it. Therefore, big data researchers are looking for tools to manage, analyze, summarize, visualize, and discover knowledge from the collected data in a timely manner and in a scalable fashion. Here, we will list some and discuss what problems we are solving in big data.

With regard to big data management, there are a number of techniques available that allow massively scalable data processing over grids of inexpensive commodity hardware such as the following. The Google File System [CHAN2006, DEAN2008] is a scalable distributed file system that utilizes clusters of commodity hardware to facilitate data intensive applications. The system is fault tolerant, where failure of machine is normal due to usage of commodity hardware. To cope with failure, data will replicate into multiple nodes. If one node is failing, the system will utilize the other node where replicated data exists.

MapReduce [CHAN2006, DEAN2008] is a programming model that supports data-intensive applications in a parallel manner. The MapReduce paradigm supports map and reduce functions. Map generates a set of intermediate key and value pairs and then the reduce function combines the results and deduces it. In fact, the map/reduce paradigm can solve many real-world problems as shown in [CHAN2006] and [DEAN2008].

Hadoop [ABOU2009, BU2010, XU2010] is an open source Apache project that supports Google File System and the MapReduce paradigm. Hadoop is widely used to address the scalability issue along with MapReduce. For example, with the huge amount of semantic web datasets,

TABLE 9.2

Capabilities and focuses of various approaches for sequence data

Approach	Learning	concept drift	insider threat	sequence based
(Ju and Vardi, 2001)	S	✗	✓	✓
(Maxion, 2003)	S	✗	✓	✗
(Liu et al., 2005)	U	✗	✓	✓
(Wang et al., 2003)	S	✗	✓	✗
(Masud et al., 2011a)	S	✓	✗	✗
(Parveen, Weger et al., 2011)	U	✓	✓	✗
(Parveen, McDaniel et al., 2012)	U	✓	✓	✓

Husain et al. [HUSA2009, HUSA2010, HUSA2011] showed that Hadoop can be used to provide scalable queries. In addition, MapReduce technology has been exploited by the BioMANTA project [DING2005] and SHARD (see also [BIOM] and [SHAR]).

Amazon developed Dynamo [DECA2007], a distributed key-value store. Dynamo does not support master-slave architecture, which is supported by Hadoop. Nodes in Dynamo communicate via a gossip network. To achieve high availability and performance, Dynamo supports a model called eventual consistency by sacrificing rigorous consistency. In eventual consistency, updates will be propagated to nodes in the cluster asynchronously and a new version of the data will be produced for each update.

Google developed BigTable [CHAN2006, CHAN2008], a column-oriented data storage system. BigTable utilizes the Google File System and Chubby [BURR2006], a distributed lock service. BigTable is a distributed multi-dimensional sparse map based on row keys, column names, and time stamps.

Researchers [ABOU2009] exploited the combined power of MapReduce and relational database technology. With regard to big data analytics, there are handfuls of works related to this topic. For example, on the one hand, some researchers focus on generic analytics tools to address the scalability issue. On the other hand, other researchers focus on specific analytics problems.

With regard to tools, Mahout is an open source big data analytics tool to support classification, clustering, and a recommendation system for big data [OWEN2011]. In [CHU2006], researchers customized well-known machine learning algorithms to take advantage of multicore machines and the MapReduce programming paradigm. MapReduce has been widely used for mining petabytes of data [MORE2008].

With regard to specific problems, Al-Khateeb et al. [ALKH2012b] and Haque et al. [HAQU2013a, HAQU2013b] proposed scalable classification over evolving stream by exploiting the MapReduce and Hadoop frameworks. There are some research works on parallel boosting with MapReduce. Palit et al. [PALI2012] proposed two parallel boosting algorithms: ADABOOST.PL and LOGITBOOST.PL.

For sequence data, quantized dictionary construction is time-consuming. Scalability is a bottleneck here. We exploit distributed computing to address this issue. There are two ways we can achieve this goal. The first one is parallel computing with a shared memory architecture that exploits expensive hardware. The latter approach is distributing computing with shared nothing architecture that exploits commodity hardware. For our case, we exploit the latter choice. Here, we use a MapReduce-based framework to facilitate quantization using Hadoop Distributed File System (HDFS). We propose a number of algorithms to quantize dictionary. For each of them, we discuss the pros and cons and report performance results on a large dataset.

9.3   ENSEMBLE-BASED INSIDER THREAT DETECTION

9.3.1   Ensemble Learning

The ensemble classification procedure is illustrated in Figure 9.2. We first build a model using OCSVM (supervised approach) or GBAD (unsupervised approach) from an individual chunk [PARV2011a, PARV2011b, PARV2013]. In the case of GBAD *normative substructures* are identified in the chunk, each represented as a subgraph. To identify an anomaly, a test substructure is compared against each model of the ensemble. A model will classify the test substructure as an anomaly based on how much the test differs from the model's normative substructure. Once all models cast their votes, weighted majority voting is applied to make a final classification decision. Ensemble evolution is arranged so as to maintain a set of exactly K models at all times. As each new chunk arrives, a $K + 1$st model is created from the new chunk and one victim model of these $K + 1$ models is discarded.

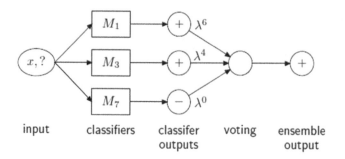

FIGURE 9.2 Ensemble classification.

The discard victim can be selected in a number of ways. One approach is to calculate the prediction error of each of the $K + 1$ models on the most recent chunk and discard the poorest predictor. This requires the *ground truth* to be immediately available for the most recent chunk so that prediction error can be accurately measured. If the ground truth is not available, we instead rely on majority voting; the model with least agreement with the majority decision is discarded. This results in an ensemble of the K models that best match the current concept.

9.3.2 ENSEMBLE FOR UNSUPERVISED LEARNING

Algorithm 9.1 summarizes the unsupervised classification and ensemble-based updating algorithm. Lines 3–4 build a new model from the most recent chunk and temporarily add it to the ensemble. Next, lines 5–13 apply each model in the ensemble to test graph t for possible anomalies. We use three varieties of GBAD for each model (P, MDL, and MPS), each discussed in this section. Finally, lines 14–30 update the ensemble by discarding the model with the most disagreements from the weighted majority opinion. If multiple models have the most disagreements, an arbitrary poorest-performing one is discarded. Note that no ground truth is used. However, majority voting of models serve so called "ground truth." Weighted majority opinions are computed in line 15 using the formula

$$WA\,(E,\,a) = \frac{\Sigma_{\{\,i|M_i \in E,\,a\,\in\,A_{M_i}\}}\,\lambda^{\ell-i}}{\Sigma_{\{i|M_i \in E\}}\,\lambda^{\ell-i}} \qquad (9.1)$$

where $M_i \in E$ is a model in ensemble E that was trained from chunk i, AM_i is the set of anomalies reported by model M_i, $\lambda \in [0, 1]$ is a constant *fading factor* [CHEN2009] and is the index of the most recent chunk. Model M_i's vote therefore receives weight λ_{-i}, with the most recently constructed model receiving weight $\lambda_0 = 1$, the model trained from the previous chunk receiving weight λ_1 (if it still exists in the ensemble), etc. This has the effect of weighting the votes of more recent models above those of potentially outdated ones when $\lambda < 1$. Weighted average $WA(E, a)$ is then rounded to the nearest integer (0 or 1) in line 15 to obtain the weighted majority vote. For example, in Figure 9.2, models M_1, M_3, and M_7 vote positive, positive, and negative, respectively, for input sample x. If $= 7$ is the most recent chunk, these votes are weighted λ_6, λ_4, and 1, respectively. The weighted average is therefore $WA(E, x) = (\lambda_6 + \lambda_4)/(\lambda_6 + \lambda_4 + 1)$. If $\lambda \le 0.86$, the negative majority opinion wins in this case; however, if $\lambda \ge 0.87$, the newer model's vote outweighs the two older dissenting opinions, and the result is a positive classification. Parameter λ can thus be tuned to balance the importance of large amounts of older information against smaller amounts of newer information. Our approach uses the results from previous iterations of GBAD to identify anomalies in subsequent data chunks. That is, normative substructures found in previous

---

ALGORITHM 9.1   UNSUPERVISED ENSEMBLE CLASSIFICATION AND UPDATING

1: Input: E (ensemble), t (test graph), and S (chunk)
2: Output: A (anomalies), and E (updated ensemble)
3: $M \leftarrow NewModel(S)$
4: $E \leftarrow E \cup \{M\}$
5: **for** each model M in ensemble E **do**
6:     $cM \leftarrow 0$
7:     **for** each q in model M **do**
8:             $A1 \leftarrow GBADP\ (t, q)$
9:             $A2 \leftarrow GBADMDL\ (t, q)$
10:            $A3 \leftarrow GBADMPS\ (t, q)$
11:            $AM \leftarrow ParseResults\ (A1, A2, A3)$
12:     **end for**
13:: **end for**
14: **for** each candidate a in $M \in E\ AM$ **do**
15:     **if** round(WeightedAverage(E', a)) = 1 then **then**
16:             $A \leftarrow A \cup \{a\}$
17:             **for** each model M in ensemble E **do**
18:             **if** $a \in AM$ then **then**
19:                     $cM \leftarrow cM + 1$
20:             **end if**
21:     **end for**
22: **else**
23:             **for** each model M in ensemble E **do**
24:                 **if** $a \in AM$ then **then**
25:                     $cM \leftarrow cM + 1$
26:                 **end if**
27:         **end for**
28:     **end if**
29: **end for**
30: $E \leftarrow E - \{choose(\arg \min M\ (cM))\}$

GBAD iterations may persist in each model. This allows each model to consider all data since the model's introduction to the ensemble, not just that of the current chunk. When streams observe concept-drift, this can be a significant advantage because the ensemble can identify patterns that are normative over the entire data stream or a significant number of chunks but not in the current chunk. Thus, insiders whose malicious behavior is infrequent can still be detected.

9.3.3 ENSEMBLE FOR SUPERVISED LEARNING

Algorithm 9.2 shows the basic building blocks of our supervised algorithm. Here, we first present how we update the model. Input for Algorithm 9.2 will be as follows: D_u is the most recently labeled data chunk (most recent training chunk) and A is the ensemble. Lines 3–4 calculate the prediction error of each model on D_u. Line 6 builds a new model using OCSVM on D_u. Line 7 produces $K + 1$ models. Line 8 discards the model with the maximum prediction error, keeping the K best models. Algorithm 9.3 focuses on ensemble testing. Ensemble A and the latest unlabeled

---

ALGORITHM 9.2   SUPERVISED ENSEMBLE CLASSIFICATION UPDATING

1: Input: D_u (most recently labeled chunk), and A (ensemble)
2: Output: A (updated ensemble)
3: **for** each model M in ensemble A **do**
4:      test(M, D_u)
5: **end for**
6: $Mn \leftarrow OCSV\ M\ (D_u)$
7: test(Mn, D_u)
8: $A \leftarrow \{K: M_n \cup A\}$

ALGORITHM 9.3   SUPERVISED TESTING ALGORITHM

1: Input: D_u (most recent unlabeled chunk), and A (ensemble)
2: Output: D_u (labeled/predicted D_u)
3: $F_u \leftarrow ExtractandSelectF\ eatures(D_u)$
4: **for** each feature $xj \in F_u$**do**
5:      $R \leftarrow N\ U\ LL$
6:      **for** each model M in ensemble A **do**
7:        $R \leftarrow R \cup$ predict(x_j, M)
8:      **end for**
9:      anomalies $\leftarrow$ MajorityVote(R)
10: **end for**

---

chunk of instance D_u will be the input. Line 3 performs feature extraction and selection using the latest chunk of unlabeled data. Lines 4–9 will take each extracted feature from D_u and do an anomaly prediction. Lines 6–7 use each model to predict the anomaly status for a particular feature. Finally, line 9 predicts anomalies based on majority voting of the results.

Our ensemble method uses the results from previous iterations of OCSVM executions to identify anomalies in subsequent data chunks. This allows the consideration of more than just the current data being analyzed. Models found in previous OCSVM iterations are also analyzed, not just the models of the current dataset chunk. The ensemble handles the execution in this manner because patterns identified in previous chunks may be normative over the entire data stream or a significant number of chunks but not in the current execution chunk. Thus insiders whose malicious behavior is infrequent will be detected. It is important to note that we always keep our ensemble size fixed. Hence, an outdated model which is performing the worst on the most recent chunks will be replaced by the new one.

It is important to note that the size of the ensemble remains fixed over time. Outdated models that are performing poorly are replaced by better-performing, newer models that are more suited to the current concept. This keeps each round of classification tractable even though the total amount of data in the stream is potentially unbounded.

In a chunk, a model is built using one class support vector machine (OCSVM) [MANE2002]. The OCSVM approach first maps training data into a high dimensional feature space (via a kernel). Next, the algorithm iteratively finds the maximal margin hyperplane which best separates the training data from the origin. The OCSVM may be considered as a regular two class SVM. Here the first class entails all the training data, and the second class is the origin. Thus, the hyperplane (or linear decision boundary) corresponds to the classification rule:

$$f(x) = w, \quad x + b \tag{9.2}$$

where w is the normal vector and b is a bias term. The OCSVM solves an optimization problem to find the rule with maximal geometric margin. This classification rule will be used to assign a label to a test example x. If $f(x) < 0$, we label x as an anomaly, otherwise it is labeled normal. In reality there is a trade-off between maximizing the distance of the hyperplane from the origin and the number of training data points contained in the region separated from the origin by the hyperplane.

9.3.4 UNSUPERVISED LEARNING

Algorithm 9.3 uses three varieties of graph-based anomaly detection (GBAD) [COOK2000, COOK2007, EBER2007, YAN2002] to infer potential anomalies using each model. GBAD is a graph-based approach to finding anomalies in data by searching for three factors: modifications, insertions, and deletions of vertices and edges. Each unique factor runs its own algorithm that finds a normative substructure and attempts to find the substructures that are similar but not completely identical to the discovered normative substructure. A normative substructure is a recurring subgraph of vertices and edges that, when coalesced into a single vertex, most compresses the overall graph. The rectangle in Figure 9.3 identifies an example of normative substructure for the depicted graph.

Our implementation uses SUBDUE [KETK2005] to find normative substructures. The best normative substructure can be characterized as the one with minimal description length (MDL):

$$L(S, G) = DL(G|S) + DL(S) \tag{9.3}$$

where G is the entire graph, S is the substructure being analyzed, $DL(G \square\square S)$ is the description length of G after being compressed by S, and $DL(S)$ is the description length of the substructure being analyzed. Description length $DL(G)$ is the minimum number of bits necessary to describe graph G [EBER2011].

Insider threats appear as small percentage differences from the normative substructures. This is because insider threats attempt to closely mimic legitimate system operations except for small variations embodied by illegitimate behavior. We apply three different approaches for identifying such anomalies, discussed below.

9.3.4.1 GBAD-MDL

Upon finding the best compressing normative substructure, GBAD-MDL searches for deviations from that normative substructure in subsequent substructures. By analyzing substructures of the same size as the normative one, differences in the edges and vertices' labels and in the direction or endpoints of edges are identified. The most anomalous of these are those substructures for which the fewest modifications is required to produce a substructure isomorphic to the normative one. In Figure 9.3, the shaded vertex labeled E is an anomaly discovered by GBAD-MDL.

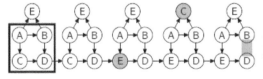

FIGURE 9.3 A graph with a normative substructure (boxed) and anomalies (shaded).

9.3.4.2   GBAD-P

In contrast, GBAD-P searches for insertions that, if deleted, yield the normative substructure. Insertions made to a graph are viewed as extensions of the normative substructure. GBAD-P calculates the probability of each extension based on edge and vertex labels, and therefore exploits label information to discover anomalies. The probability is given by:

$$P(A = v) = P(A = v|A)P(A) \qquad (9.4)$$

where A represents an edge or vertex attribute and v represents its value. Probability $P(A = v \mid A)$ can be generated by a Gaussian distribution:

$$\rho(x) = \frac{1}{\sigma\sqrt{2\pi}} \exp\left(-\frac{(x-\mu)^2}{2\sigma^2}\right) \qquad (9.5)$$

where μ is the mean and σ is the standard deviation. Higher values of $\rho(x)$ correspond to more anomalous substructures.

Using GBAD-P therefore ensures that malicious insider behavior that is reflected by the actual data in the graph (rather than merely its structure) can be reliably identified as anomalous by our algorithm. In Figure 9.3, the shaded vertex labeled C is an anomaly discovered by GBAD-P.

9.3.4.3   GBAD-MPS

Finally, GBAD-MPS considers deletions that, if re-inserted, yield the normative substructure. To discover these, GBAD-MPS examines the parent structure. Changes in size and orientation in the parent signify deletions amongst the subgraphs. The most anomalous substructures are those with the smallest transformation cost required to make the parent substructures identical. In Figure 9.3, the last substructure of A-B-C-D vertices is identified as anomalous by GBAD-MPS because of the missing edge between B and D marked by the shaded rectangle.

9.4   INSIDER THREAT DETECTION FOR SEQUENCE DATA

9.4.1   Classifying Sequence Data

As the length of the sequence is defined as the number of ordered elements, sequence data can be finite or infinite in length. Infinite sequences are known as stream sequence data. Insider threat detection-related sequence data is stream-based in nature. Sequence data may be gathered over time, maybe even years. In this case, we assume a data stream will be converted into a number of chunks. For example, each chunk may represent a week and contain the sequence data which arrived during that time period.

Figure 9.4 demonstrates how the classifier decision boundary changes over time (from one chunk to the next chunk). Data points are associated with two classes (normal and anomalous). In particular, a user command or a sub-sequence of commands may form a pattern/phrase, which will be called here as a data point. A non-repetitive pattern/phrase for a user may form an anomaly. There are three contiguous data chunks as shown in Figure 9.4. The dark straight line represents the decision boundary of its own chunk, whereas the dotted straight line represents the decision boundary of the previous chunk. If there were no concept-drift in the data stream, the decision boundary would be the same for both the current chunk and its previous chunk (the dotted and straight line). White dots represent the normal data (true negative), blue dots represent anomaly data (true positive), and striped dots represent the instances victim of concept-drift.

We show the two different cases in Figure 9.4 are as follows:

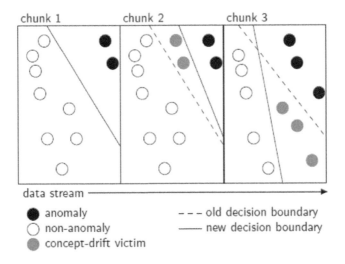

FIGURE 9.4 Concept-drift in stream data.

Case 1. The decision boundary of the second chunk moves upward compared to that of the first chunk. As a result, more normal data will be classified as anomalous by the decision boundary of the first chunk, thus FP will go up. Recall that a test point having true benign (normal) category classified as an anomalous by a classifier is known as a FP.

Case 2. The decision boundary of the third chunk moves downward compared to that of the first chunk. So, more anomalous data will be classified as normal data by the decision boundary of the first chunk, thus FN will go up. Recall that a test point having a true malicious category classified as benign by a classifier is known as a FN.

In the more general case, the decision boundary of the current chunk can vary which causes the decision boundary of the previous chunk to misclassify both normal and anomalous data. Therefore, both FP and FN may go up at the same time.

This suggests that a model built from a single chunk will not suffice. This motivates the adoption of adaptive learning. In particular, we will exploit two approaches:

9.4.1.1 Incremental Learning

A single dictionary is maintained [PARV2012a]. When a normative sequence pattern is learned from a chunk, it will be simply added to the dictionary. To find the normative pattern, we will exploit unsupervised stream-based sequence learning (USSL). The incremental learning classification procedure is illustrated in Figure 9.5. Here, first from a new chunk, patterns will be extracted and next these patterns will be merged with the old quantized dictionary from previous chunks. Finally, a new merged dictionary will be quantized (Figure 9.6).

9.4.1.2 Ensemble Learning

A number of dictionaries are maintained [PARV2012b]. In the ensemble, we maintain K models. For each model, we maintain a single dictionary. Our ensemble approach classifies data using an evolving set of K models. The ensemble classification procedure is illustrated in Figure 9.7. Recall that we use unsupervised stream-based sequence learning (USSL) to train models from an individual chunk. USSL identifies the normative patterns in the chunk and stores it in a quantized dictionary. In the literature [MASU2008, MASU2010a, MASU2011a], it shows that ensemble-based learning is more effective than incremental learning. Here, we will focus on ensemble-based

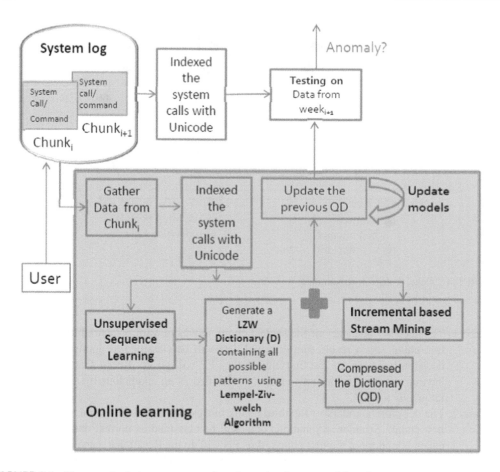

FIGURE 9.5   Unsupervised stream sequence learning using incremental learning.

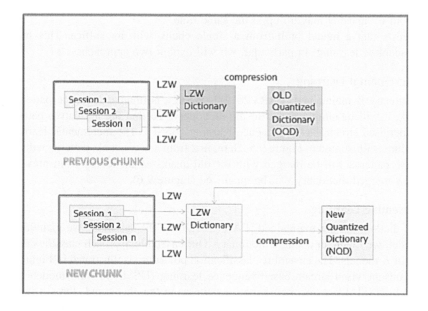

FIGURE 9.6   Block diagram of incremental learning.

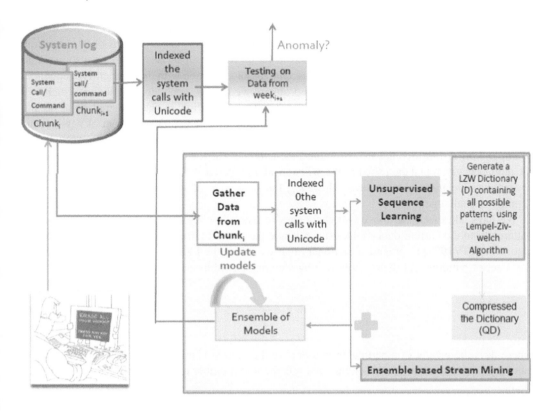

FIGURE 9.7 Ensemble-based unsupervised stream sequence learning.

learning. To identify an anomaly, a test point will be compared against each model of the ensemble.

Recall that a model will declare the test data as anomalous based on how much the test differs from the model's normative patterns. Once all models cast their vote, we will apply majority voting to make the final decision as to whether the test point is anomalous or not (as shown in Figure 9.7).

9.4.1.3 Model Update

We always keep an ensemble of fixed size models (K in that case). Hence, when a new chunk is processed, we already have K models in the ensemble and the $K + 1$st model will be created from the current chunk. We need to update the ensemble by replacing a victim model with this new model. Victim selection can be done in a number of ways. One approach is to calculate the prediction error of each model on the most recent chunk relative to the majority vote. Here, we assume *ground truth* on the most recent chunk is not available. If ground truth is available, we can exploit this knowledge for training. The new model will replace the existing model from the ensemble which gives the maximum prediction error.

9.4.2 Unsupervised Stream-Based Sequence Learning (USSL)

Normal user profiles are considered to be repetitive daily or weekly activities which are frequent sequences of commands, system calls, etc. These repetitive command sequences are called normative patterns. These patterns reveal the regular, or normal, behavior of a user. When a user suddenly demonstrates unusual activities that indicate a significant excursion from normal behavior, an alarm is raised for potential insider threat.

So, in order to identify an insider threat, first we need to find normal user behavior. For that we need to collect sequences of commands and find the potential normative patterns observed within these command sequences in an unsupervised fashion. This unsupervised approach also needs to identify normal user behavior in a single pass. One major challenge with these repetitive sequences is their variability in length. To combat this problem, we need to generate a dictionary which will contain any combination of possible normative patterns existing in the gathered data stream. Potential variations that could emerge within the data include the commencement of new events, the omission or modification of existing events, or the reordering of events in the sequence. For example, *liftliftliftliftliftcomcomecomecomecome-come,* is a sequence of commands represented by the alphabets given in a data stream. We will consider all patterns *li, if, ft, tl, lif, ift, ftl, lift, iftl,* etc., as our possible normative patterns. However, the huge size of the dictionary presents another significant challenge.

We have addressed the above two challenges in the following ways. First, we extract possible patterns from the current data chunk using a single pass algorithm (e.g., LZW, Lempel-Ziv Welch algorithm [ZIV1977] to prepare a dictionary that we called the LZW dictionary). LZW dictionary has a set of patterns and their corresponding weights according to

$$w_i = \frac{f_i}{\sum_{i=1}^{n} f_i} \tag{9.6}$$

where w_i is the weight of a particular pattern p_i in the current chunk, f_i is the number of times the pattern p_i appears in the current chunk, and n is the total number of distinct patterns found in that chunk.

Next, we compress the dictionary by keeping only the longest, frequent unique patterns according to their associated weight and length, while discarding other subsumed patterns. This technique is called compression method (CM) and the new dictionary is a quantized dictionary (QD). The quantized dictionary has a set of patterns and their corresponding weights. Here, we use edit distance to find the longest pattern. Edit distance is a measure of similarity between pairs of strings [BORG2011, VLAD1966]. It is the minimum number of actions required to transfer one string to another, where an action can be substitution, addition or deletion of a character into the string. As in case of the earlier example mentioned, the best normative pattern in the quantized dictionary would be lift, come, etc.

This process is a lossy compression but is sufficient enough to extract the meaningful normative patterns. The reason behind this is the patterns that we extract are the superset of the subsumed patterns. Moreover, as frequency is another control parameter in our experiment, the patterns which do not appear often cannot be regular user patterns.

Data relevant to insider threat is typically accumulated over many years of organization and system operations and is, therefore, best characterized as an unbounded data stream. As our data is a continuous stream of data, we use ensemble-based learning to continuously update our compressed dictionary. This continuous data stream is partitioned into a sequence of discrete chunks. For example, each chunk might be comprised of a day or weeks' worth of data and may contain several user sessions. We generate our quantized dictionary (QD) and their associated weight from each chunk. Weight is measured as the normalized frequency of a pattern within that chunk.

When a new chunk arrives, we generate a new quantized dictionary (QD) model and update the ensemble as mentioned earlier. Figure 9.8 shows the flow diagram of our *dynamic*, ensemble-based, unsupervised stream sequence learning method. Algorithm 9.4 shows the basic building block for updating the ensemble. It takes the most recent data chunk S, ensemble E and test chunk T. Lines 3–4 generate a new quantized dictionary model from the most recent chunk S and temporarily add it to the ensemble E. Lines 5–9 test chunk T for anomalies for each model in the

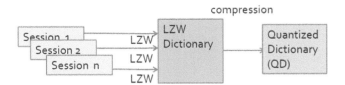

FIGURE 9.8 Unsupervised stream-based sequence learning (USSL) from a chunk in ensemble-based case.

ensemble. Lines 13–24 find and label the anomalous patterns in test chunk T according to the majority voting of the models in the ensemble. Finally, line 29 updates the ensemble by discarding the model with lowest accuracy. An arbitrary model is discarded in the case of multiple models having the same low performance.

ALGORITHM 9.4   UPDATE THE ENSEMBLE

1: Input: E (ensemble), T (test chunk), S (chunk)
2: Output: E (updated ensemble)
3: $M \leftarrow NewModel(S)$
4: $E \leftarrow E \cup \{M\}$
5: **for** each model M in ensemble E **do**
6:      $AM \leftarrow T$
7:      **for** each pattern p in M **do**
8:        **if** $EditDistance(x, p) \leq \alpha = \underline{1}$ of length **then** 3
9:            $AM = AM - x$
10:     **end if**
11:      **end for**
12: **end for**
13: **for** each candidate a in $M \in E$ AM **do**
14:      **if** $round(WeightedAverage(E, a)) = 1$ **then**
15:        $A \leftarrow A \cup \{a\}$
16:        **for** each model M in ensemble E **do**
17:              **if** $a \in AM$ **then**
18:                  $cM \leftarrow cM + 1$
19:              **end if**
20:        **end for**
21:      **else**
22:        **for** each model M in ensemble E **do**
23:              **if** $a \in AM$ **then**
24:                  $cM \leftarrow cM + 1$
25:              **end if**
26:        **end for**
27:      **end if**
28:**end for**
29: $E \leftarrow E - \{choose(\arg \min M (cM))\}$

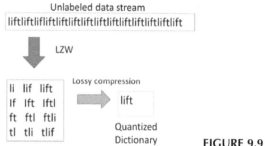

FIGURE 9.9 Quantization of dictionary.

9.4.2.1 Construct the LZW Dictionary by Selecting the Patterns in the Data Stream

At the beginning, we consider that our data is not annotated (i.e., unsupervised). In other words, we don't know the possible sequence of future operations by the user. So, we use LZW algorithm [ZIV1977] to extract the possible sequences that we can add to our dictionary. These can also be commands like *liftliftliftliftliftcomcomecomecomecomecome*, where each unique letter represents a unique system call or command. We have used Unicode to index each command. For example, ls, cp, find are indexed as *l*, *c*, and *f*. The possible patterns or sequences are added to our dictionary would be *li, if, ft, tl, lif, ift, ftl, lift, iftl, ftli, tc, co, om, mc,com, come,* and so on. When the sequence *li* is seen in the data stream for the second time, in order to avoid repetition, it will not be included in the LZW dictionary. Instead, we increase the frequency by 1 and extend the pattern by concatenating it with the next character in the data stream, thus turning up a new pattern *lif*. We will continue the process until we reach the end of the current chunk. Figure 9.9 demonstrates how we generate an LZW dictionary from the data stream.

9.4.2.2 Constructing the Quantized Dictionary

Once we have our LZW dictionary, we keep the longest and most frequent patterns and discard all their subsumed patterns. Algorithm 9.5 shows step-by-step how a quantized dictionary is

---

ALGORITHM 9.5   QUANTIZED DICTIONARY

1: Input: $D = \{Pattern, Weight\}$ (LZW Dictionary)
2: Output: QD (Quantized Dictionary
3: $Visited \leftarrow 0$
4: **while** $D = 0$ **do**
5:      $X \leftarrow D_j \mid j \in Visited, D_j \in D$
6:      $Visited \leftarrow Visited \cup j$
7:      **for** each pattern i in D **do**
8:          **if** $EditDistance(X, D_i) = 1$ **then**
9:              $P \leftarrow P \cup i$
10:          **end if**
11:      **end for**
12:      $D \leftarrow D - X$
13:      **if** $P = 0$ **then**
14:          $X \leftarrow choose(\arg \max_i(w_i \cdot l_i)) \mid l_i = Length(P_i), w_i = Weight(P_i), P_i \in$
15:          $QD \leftarrow QD \cup X$
16:          $D \leftarrow D - P$
17:      **end if**
18:      $X \leftarrow D_j \mid j \in Visited, D_j \in D$
19:      $Visited \leftarrow Visited \cup j$
20: **end while**

generated from the LZW dictionary. Inputs of this algorithm are as follows: LZW dictionary D which contains a set of patterns P and their associated weight W. Line 5 picks a pattern (e.g., li). Lines 7–9 find all the closest patterns that are 1 edit distance away. Lines 13–16 keep the pattern which has the highest weight multiplied by its length and discard the other patterns. We repeat the steps (line 5–16) until we find the longest, frequent pattern (*lift*). After that, we start with a totally different pattern (*co*) and repeat the steps until we have explored all the patterns in the dictionary. Finally, we end up with a more compact dictionary which will contain many meaningful and useful sequences. We call this dictionary our quantized dictionary. Figure 9.9 demonstrates how we generate a quantized dictionary from the LZW dictionary. Once, we identify different patterns *lift*, *come*, etc., any pattern with $X\%$ ($\geq \%30$ in our implementation) deviation from all these patterns would be considered as anomaly. Here, we will use edit distance to identify the deviation.

9.4.3 ANOMALY DETECTION

Given a quantized dictionary, we need to find out the sequences in the data stream which may raise a potential threat. To formulate the problem, given the data stream S and ensemble E where $E = QD1, QD2, QD3, \ldots,$ and $QD_i = qd_{i1}, qd_{i2}, \ldots,$ any pattern in the data stream is considered as an anomaly if it deviates from all the patterns qd_{ij} in E by more than $X\%$ (*say* >30%). In order to find the anomalies, we need to first find the matching patterns and delete those from the stream S. In particular, we find the pattern from the data stream S that is an exact match or α edit distance away from any pattern, qd_{ij} in E. This pattern will be considered as matching pattern. α can be half, one-third or one-fourth of the length of that particular pattern in qd_{ij}. Next, remaining patterns in the stream will be considered as anomalies.

In order to identify the non-matching patterns in the data stream S, we compute a distance matrix L which contains the edit distance between each pattern, qd_{ij} in E and the data stream S. If we have a perfect match, that is, edit distance 0 between a pattern qd_{ij} and S, we can move backward exactly the length of qd_{ij} in order to find the starting point of that pattern in S and then delete it from the data stream. On the other hand, if there is an error in the match which is greater than 0 but less than α, in order to find the starting point of that pattern in the data stream, we need to traverse either left, or diagonal or up within the matrix according to which one among the mentioned value ($L[i, j\text{-}1]$, $L[i\text{-}1, j\text{-}1]$, $L[i\text{-}1, j]$) gives the minimum, respectively. Finally, once we find the starting point, we can delete that pattern from the data stream. The remaining patterns in the data stream will be considered as anomalous.

9.5 SUMMARY AND DIRECTIONS

Our approach is to define the insider threat detection as a stream mining problem and we address both non-sequence and sequence data. For non-sequence we describe two methods (supervised and unsupervised learning) for efficiently detecting anomalies in stream data. In particular, we propose a supervised learning solution that copes with evolving concepts using one-class SVMs. We increase the accuracy of the supervised approach by weighting the cost of false negatives. We propose an unsupervised learning algorithm that copes with changes based on GBAD. We effectively address the challenge of limited labeled training data (rare instance issues). We exploit the power of stream mining and graph-based mining by effectively combining the two in a unified manner. This is the first work to our knowledge to harness these two approaches for insider threat detection.

In summary, to cope with concept-evolution, our supervised approach maintains an evolving ensemble of multiple OCSVM models. Our unsupervised approach combines multiple GBAD models in an ensemble of classifiers. The ensemble updating process is designed in both cases to keep the ensemble current as the stream evolves. This evolutionary capability improves the classifier's survival of concept-drift as the behavior of both legitimate and illegitimate agents varies over time.

Next we discuss insider threat for sequence data. Insider threat detection-related sequence data is stream based in nature. Sequence data may be gathered over time, maybe even years. In this case, we assume a continuous data stream will be converted into a number of chunks. For example, each chunk may represent a week and contain the sequence data which arrived during that time period. With regard to sequence data, we propose a framework that exploits an unsupervised learning (USSL) to find pattern sequences from successive user actions or commands using stream-based sequence learning. We effectively integrate multiple USSL models in an ensemble of classifiers to exploit the power of ensemble-based stream mining and sequence mining. With regard to scalability issues we utilize big data technologies. In particular, scalability is an issue for constructing benign pattern sequences for quantized dictionary. For this, we exploit the MapReduce-based framework and show effectiveness of our work.

We plan to extend the work, including in the following directions. For unsupervised learning, we assume that no ground truth is available. In fact, over time some ground truth may be available in terms of feedback. Once a model is created in an unsupervised manner, we would like to update the model based on user feedback. Right now, once the model is created, it remains unchanged. When ground truth is available over time, we will refine all our models based on this feedback immediately (see also [MASU2010a], [MASU2010b], and [MASU2010c]). Also, when we update models, collusion attack [WANG2009, ZHAO2005] may take place. In that case, a set of models among K models will not be replaced for a while. Each time, when a victim will be selected, these colluded models will survive. Recall that "collusion" is an agreement between two or more models so that they will always agree on the prediction. In particular, if we have $K = 3$ models, two models may maintain secretive agreement and their prediction will be the same and used as ground truth. Therefore, two colluded/secretive models will always survive and never be victim in model update case. Recall that the learning is unsupervised and majority voting will be taken as ground truth. Hence, we will not be able to catch an insider attack. Our goal is to identify a colluded attack. For this, during victim selection of models, we will take into account agreement of models over time. If agreement of models persists for a long time and survives, we will choose the victim from there.

REFERENCES

[ABOU2009] A. Abouzeid, K. Bajda-Pawlikowski, D.J. Abadi, A. Rasin, A. Silberschatz, HadoopDB: An Architectural Hybrid of Mapreduce and DBMS Technologies for Analytical Workloads, *PVLDB*, Volume 2, #1, 2009, 922–933.

[ALKH2012a] T. Al-Khateeb, M.M. Masud, L. Khan, C.C. Aggarwal, J. Han, B.M. Thuraisingham, Stream Classification with Recurring and Novel Class Detection Using Class-Based Ensemble, IEEE International Conference on Data Mining (ICDM), 2012, pp. 31–40.

[ALKH2012b] T. Al-Khateeb, M.M. Masud, L. Khan, B.M. Thuraisingham, Cloud Guided-Stream Classification Using Class-Based Ensemble, IEEE CLOUD, 2012, pp. 694–701.

[BARO2006] M. Baron, A. Tartakovsky, Asymptotic Optimality of Change-Point Detection Schemes in General Continuous-Time Models, *Sequential Analysis*, Volume 25, #3, 2006, 257–296.

[BIOM] http://www.itee.uq.edu.au/eresearch/projects/biomanta

[BORG2011] E.N. Borges, M.G. de Carvalho, R. Galante, M.A. Gon̦es, A.H.F. Laender, An Unsupervised Heuristic-Based Approach for Bibliographic Metadata Deduplication, *Informatiom Processing and Management*, Volume 47, #5, 2011, 706–718.

[BRAC2004] R.C. Brackney, R.H. Anderson, eds., *Understanding the Insider Threat*. RAND Corporation, March 2004.

[BU2010] Y. Bu, B. Howe, M. Balazinska, M. Ernst, Haloop: Efficient Iterative Data Processing on Large Clusters. *PVLDB*, Volume 3, #1, 2010, 285–296.

[BURR2006] M. Burrows, The Chubby Lock Service for Loosely-Coupled Distributed Systems, *OSDI'06: Proceedings of the 7th Symposium on Operating Systems Design and Implementation*, 2006, pp. 335–350.

[CANG2006] J.W. Cangussu, M. Baron, Automatic Identification of Change Points for the System Testing Process, *COMPSAC (1)*, 2006, pp. 377–384.

[CHAN2006] F. Chang, J. Dean, S. Ghemawat, W.C. Hsieh, D.A. Wallach, M. Burrows, T. Chandra, R. Fikes Gruber. Bigtable: A Distributed Storage System for Structured Data (awarded best paper), *OSDI*, 2006, pp. 205–218.

[CHAN2008] F. Chang, J. Dean, S. Ghemawat, W.C. Hsieh, D.A. Wallach, M. Burrows, T. Chandra, A. Fikes, R.E. Gruber, Bigtable: A Distributed Storage System for Structured Data, *ACM Transactions on Computer Systems*, Volume 26, #2, 2008.

[CHAN2011] C.-C. Chang, C.-J. Lin, LIBSVM: A Library for Support Vector Machines, *ACM Transactions on Intelligent Systems and Technology*, 2011, pp. 2:27:1–27:27. Software available at http://www.csie.ntu.edu.tw/cjlin/libsvm

[CHEN2009] L. Chen, S. Zhang, L. Tu, An Algorithm for Mining Frequent Items on Data Stream Using Fading Factor, *Proceedings under IEEE International Computer Software and Applications Conference (COMPSAC)*, 2009, pp. 172–177.

[CHU2006] C.T. Chu, S.K. Kim, Y.A. Lin, Y. Yu, G.R. Bradski, A.Y. Ng, K. Olukotun, Map-Reduce for Machine Learning on Multicore, *NIPS*, MIT Press (Editors: B. Schöpf, J.C. Platt, T. Hoffman), 2006, pp. 281–288.

[CHUA2011] S.-L. Chua, S. Marsland, H.W. Guesgen, Unsupervised Learning of Patterns in Data Streams Using Compression and Edit Distance. *IJCAI*, 2011, pp. 1231–1236.

[COOK2000] D.J. Cook, L.B. Holder, Graph-Based Data Mining. *IEEE Intelligent Systems*, Volume 15, #2, 2000, 32–41.

[COOK2007] D.J. Cook, L.B. Holder, eds., *Mining Graph Data*, John Wiley & Sons, Inc, 2007.

[DAVI1998] B.D. Davison, H. Hirsh, Predicting Sequences of User Actions in Working Notes of the Joint Workshop on Predicting the Future: AI Approches to Time Series Analysis, *15th National Conference on Artificial Intelligence and Machine*, AAAI Press, 1998, pp. 5–12.

[DEAN2008] J. Dean, S. Ghemawat, Mapreduce: Simplified Data Processing on Large Clusters, *Communications of ACM*, Volume 51, January 2008, 107–113.

[DECA2007] G. DeCandia, D. Hastorun, M. Jampani, G. Kakulapati, A. Lakshman, A. Pilchin, S. Sivasubramanian, P. Vosshall, W. Vogels, Dynamo: Amazon's Highly Available Key-Value Store, *SOSP*, ACM (Editors: T.C. Bressoud, M.F. Kaashoek), 2007, pp. 205–220.

[DING2005] L. Ding, T. Finin, Y. Peng, P.P. da Silva, D.L. Mcguinness, Tracking RDF Graph Provenance Using RDF Molecules, 2005.

[DOMI2001] P. Domingos, G. Hulten, Catching up with the Data: Research Issues in Mining Data Streams. *DMKD*, 2001.

[EAGL2006] N. Eagle, A. (Sandy) Pentland, Reality Mining: Sensing Complex Social Systems. *Personal Ubiquitous Computing*, Volume 10, #4, March 2006, 255–268.

[EBER2007] W. Eberle, L.B. Holder, Mining for Structural Anomalies in Graph-Based Data, *Procings of International Conference on Data Mining (DMIN)*, 2007, pp. 376–389.

[EBER2011] W. Eberle, J. Graves, L. Holder, Insider Threat Detection Using a Graph-Based Approach, *Journal of Applied Security Research*, Volume 6, #1, 2011, 32–81.

[ESKI2002] E. Eskin, A. Arnold, M. Prerau, L. Portnoy, S. Stolfo, A Geometric Framework for Unsupervised Anomaly Detection: Detecting Intrusions in Unlabeled Data, *Applications of Data Mining in Computer Security*, Springer (Editors: D. Barbar, S. Jajodia), 2002, Chapter 4.

[FAN2004] W. Fan, Systematic Data Selection to Mine Concept-Drifting Data Streams, *Proceedings of ACM SIGKDD*, Seattle, WA, USA, 2004, pp. 128–137.

[FORR1996] S. Forrest, S.A. Hofmeyr, A. Somayaji, T.A. Longstaf, A Sense of Self for Unix Processes, *Proceedings of IEEE Symposium on Computer Security and Privacy (S&P)*, 1996, pp. 120–128.

[GAO2004] D. Gao, M.K. Reiter, D. Song, On Gray-Box Program Tracking for Anomaly Detection, *Proceedings of USENIX Security Symposium*, 2004, pp. 103–118.

[HAMP1999] M.P. Hampton, M. Levi, Fast Spinning into Oblivion? Recent Developments in Money-Laundering Policies and Offshore Finance Centres, *Third World Quarterly*, Volume 20, #3, 1999, 645–656.

[HAQU2013a] A. Haque, B. Parker, L. Khan, Intelligent MapReduce Based Frameworks for Labeling Instances in Evolving Data Stream. *CloudCom*, 2013.

[HAQU2013b] A. Haque, B. Parker, L. Khan, Labeling Instances in Evolving Data Streams with Mapreduce, *BigData*, 2013.

[HOFM1998] S.A. Hofmeyr, S. Forrest, A. Somayaji, Intrusion Detection Using Sequences of System Calls, *Journal of Computer Security*, Volume 6, #3, 1998, 151–180.

[HUSA2009] M. Husain, P. Doshi, L. Khan, B. Thuraisingham, Storage and Retrieval of Large RDF Graph Using Hadoop and MapReduce, *Proceedings of the 1st International Conference on Cloud Computing*, CloudCom '09, Springer-Verlag, Berlin, Heidelberg, 2009, pp. 680–686.

[HUSA2010] M.F. Husain, L. Khan, M. Kantarcioglu, B. Thuraisingham, Data Intensive Query Processing for Large RDF Graphs Using Cloud Computing Tools, *Proceedings of the 2010 IEEE 3rd International Conference on Cloud Computing*, CLOUD '10, IEEE Computer Society, Washington, DC, USA, 2010, pp. 1–10.

[HUSA2011] M.F. Husain, J.P. McGlothlin, M.M. Masud, L.R. Khan, B.M. Thuraisingham, Heuristics-Based Query Processing for Large RDF Graphs Using Cloud Computing, *IEEE Transactions on Knowledge and Data Engineering*, Volume 23, #9, 2011, 1312–1327.

[JAMA2012] A. Jamak, A. Savatic, M. Can, Principal Component Analysis for Authorship Attribution, *Business Systems Research*, Volume 3, #2, 2012, 49–56.

[JU2001] W.-H. Ju, Y. Vardi, A Hybrid High-Order Markov Chain Model for Computer Intrusion Detection, *Journal of Computational and Graphical Statistics*, June 2001.

[KANG2011] U. Kang, C.E. Tsourakakis, C. Faloutsos, Pegasus: Mining Peta-Scale Graphs, *Knowledge and Information System*, Volume 27, #2, 2011, 303–325.

[KETK2005] N.S. Ketkar, L.B. Holder, D.J. Cook, Subdue: Compression-Based Frequent Pattern Discovery in Graph Data, *Proceedings of ACM KDD Workshop on Open-Source Data Mining*, 2005.

[KHAN2002] L. Khan, F. Luo, Ontology Construction for Information Selection, Proceedings of 14th IEEE International Conference on Tools with Artificial Intelligence (*ICTAI*), 2002, pp.122–127.

[KHAN2004] L. Khan, D. McLeod, E.H. Hovy, Retrieval Efectiveness of an Ontology-Based Model for Information Selection, *VLDB Journal*, Volume 13, #1, 2004, 71–85.

[KOPP2009] M. Koppe, J. Schler, S. Argamon, Computational Methods in Authorship Attribution, *JASIST*, Volume 60, #1, 2009, 9–26.

[KOWA2008] E. Kowalski, T. Conway, S. Keverline, M. Williams, D. Cappelli, B. Willke, A. Moore, Insider Threat Study: Illicit Cyber Activity in the Government Sector. Technical report, U.S. Department of Homeland Security, U.S. Secret Service, CERT, and the Software Engineering Institute (Carnegie Mellon University), January 2008.

[KRUG2003] C. Krugel, D. Mutz, F. Valeur, G. Vigna, On the Detection of Anomalous System Call Arguments, *Proceedings of 8th European Symposium on Research in Computer Security (ESORICS)*, 2003, pp. 326–343.

[LIAO2002] Y. Liao, V.R. Vemuri, Using Text Categorization Techniques for Intrusion Detection, *Proceedings of 11th USENIX Security Symposium*, 2002, pp. 51–59.

[LIU2005] A. Liu, C. Martin, T. Hetherington, S. Matzner, A Comparison of System Call Feature Representations for Insider Threat Detection, *Proceedings of IEEE Information Assurance Workshop (IAW)*, 2005, pp. 340–347.

[MANE2002] L.M. Manevitz, M. Yousef, One-Class SVMS for Document Classification, *The Journal of Machine Learning Research*, March 2002, 2.

[MASU2008] M.M. Masud, J. Gao, L. Khan, J. Han, B. Thuraisingham, A Practical Approach to Classify Evolving Data Streams: Training with Limited Amount of Labeled Data, *Proceedings of IEEE International Conference on Data Mining (ICDM)*, 2008, pp. 929–934.

[MASU2009] M. Masud, J. Gao, L. Khan, J. Han, B. Thuraisingham, A Multi-partition Multi-chunk Ensemble Technique to Classify Concept-Drifting Data Streams, Advances in Knowledge Discovery and Data Mining, Springer Berlin/Heidelberg, 2009, pp. 363–375.

[MASU2010a] M.M. Masud, Q. Chen, J. Gao, L. Khan, C. Aggarwal, J. Han, B. Thuraisingham, Addressing Concept-Evolution in Concept-Drifting Data Streams, *Proceedings of IEEE International Conference on Data Mining (ICDM)*, 2010, pp. 929–934.

[MASU2010b] M.M. Masud, Q. Chen, J. Gao, L. Khan, J. Han, B.M. Thuraisingham, Classification and Novel Class Detection of Data Streams in a Dynamic Feature Space, *CML/PKDD (2)*, 2010, pp. 337–352.

[MASU2010c] M.M. Masud, J. Gao, L. Khan, J. Han, B.M. Thuraisingham, Classification and Novel Class Detection in Data Streams with Active Mining, *PAKDD (2)*, 2010, pp. 311–324.

[MASU2011a] M.M. Masud, J. Gao, L. Khan, J. Han, B.M. Thuraisingham, Classification and Novel Class Detection in Concept-Drifting Data Streams under Time Constraints, *IEEE Transactions on Knowledge and Data Engineering (TKDE)*, Volume 23, #6, 2011, 859–874.

[MASU2011b] M.M. Masud, J. Gao, L. Khan, J. Han, B.M. Thuraisingham, Classification and Novel Class Detection in Concept-Drifting Data Streams under Time Constraints, *IEEE Transactions on Knowledge and Data Engineering*, Volume 23, #6, 2011, 859–874.

[MASU2011c] M.M. Masud, C. Woolam, J. Gao, L. Khan, J. Han, K.W. Hamlen, N.C. Oza, Facing the Reality of Data Stream Classification: Coping with Scarcity of Labeled Data, *Knowledge and Information Systems*, Volume 33, #1, 2011, 213–244.

[MASU2011d] M.M. Masud, T. Al-Khateeb, L. Khan, C.C. Aggarwal, J. Gao, J. Han, B.M. Thuraisingham, Detecting Recurring and Novel Classes in Concept-Drifting Data Streams, *ICDM*, 2011, pp. 1176–1181.

[MASU2013] M.M. Masud, Q. Chen, L. Khan, C.C. Aggarwal, J. Gao, J. Han, A. N. Srivastava, N.C. Oza, Classification and Adaptive Novel Class Detection of Feature-Evolving Data Streams, *IEEE Transactions on Knowledge and Data Engineering*, Volume 25, #7, 2013, 1484–1497.

[MATZ2004] S. Matzner, T. Hetherington, Detecting Early Indications of a Malicious Insider, *IA Newsletter*, Volume 7, #2, 2004, 42–45.

[MAXI2003] R.A. Maxion, Masquerade Detection Using Enriched Command Lines, *Proceedings of IEEE International Conference on Dependable Systems & Networks (DSN)*, 2003, pp. 5–14.

[MORE2008] C. Moretti, K. Steinhaeuser, D. Thain, N.V. Chawla, Scaling up Classifiers to Cloud Computers, *Proceedings of the 2008 Eighth IEEE International Conference on Data Mining*, IEEE Computer Society, Washington, DC, USA, 2008, pp. 472–481.

[NGUY2003] N. Nguyen, P. Reiher, G.H. Kuenning, Detecting Insider Threats by Monitoring System Call Activity, *Proceedings IEEE Information Assurance Workshop (IAW)*, 2003, pp. 45–52.

[OWEN2011] S. Owen, R. Anil, T. Dunning, E. Friedman, *Mahout in Action*, 2011.

[PALI2012] I. Palit, C.K. Reddy, Scalable and Parallel Boosting with Mapreduce, *IEEE Transactions on Knowledge and Data Engineering*, Volume 24, #10, 2012, 1904–1916.

[PARV2006] P. Parveen, B.M. Thuraisingham, Face Recognition Using Multiple Classifiers, *ICTAI '06: Proceedings of the 18th IEEE International Conference on Tools with Artificial Intelligence*, 2006, pp. 179–186.

[PARV2011a] P. Parveen, J. Evans, B. Thuraisingham, K.W. Hamlen, L. Khan, Insider Threat Detection Using Stream Mining and Graph Mining, *Proceedings of the 3rd IEEE Conference on Privacy, Security, Risk and Trust (PASSAT) MIT, Boston, USA. (acceptance rate 8%) (Nominated for Best Paper Award)*, October 2011.

[PARV2011b] P. Parveen, Z.R. Weger, B. Thuraisingham, K.W. Hamlen, L. Khan, Supervised Learning for Insider Threat Detection Using Stream Mining, *Proceedings of the 23rd IEEE International Conference on Tools with Artificial Intelligence, November 7–9, 2011, Boca Raton, Florida, USA (acceptance rate 30%) (Best Paper Award)*, November 2011.

[PARV2012a] P. Parveen, B. Thuraisingham, Unsupervised Incremental Sequence Learning for Insider Threat Detection, *Proceedings IEEE International Conference on Intelligence and Security (ISI)*, Washington DC, June 2012.

[PARV2012b] P. Parveen, N. McDaniel, B. Thuraisingham, L. Khan, Unsupervised Ensemble Based Learning for Insider Threat Detection, *Proceedings of 4th IEEE International Conference on Information Privacy, Security, Risk and Trust (PASSAT)*, Amsterdam, Netherlands, September 2012.

[PARV2013] P. Parveen, N. McDaniel, J. Evans, B. Thuraisingham, K.W. Hamlen, L. Khan, Evolving Insider Threat Detection Stream Mining Perspective, *International Journal on Artificial Intelligence Tools (World Scientific Publishing)*, Volume 22, #5, October 2013, 1360013-1–1360013-24.

[QUMR2013] S.M. Qumruzzaman, L. Khan, B.M. Thuraisingham, Behavioral Sequence Prediction for Evolving Data Stream, *IRI*, 2013, pp. 482–488.

[SALE2008] M.B. Salem, S. Herkshkop, S.J. Stolfo, A Survey of Insider Attack Detection Research, *Insider Attack and Cyber Security*, Volume 39, 2008, 69–90.

[SALE2011] M.B. Salem, S.J. Stolfo, Modeling User Search Behavior for Masquerade Detection, *Proceedings of Recent Advances in Intrusion Detection (RAID)*, 2011.

[SCHO2001] M. Schonlau, W. DuMouchel, W.-H. Ju, A. F. Karr, M. Theus, Y. Vardi, Computer Intrusion: Detecting Masquerades, *Statistical Science*, Volume 16, #1, 2001, 1–17.

[SCHU2002] E.E. Schultz, A Framework for Understanding and Predicting Insider Attacks, *Computers and Security*, Volume 21, #6, 2002, 526–531.

[SEKE2013] S.E. Seker, K. Al-Naami, L. Khan, Author Attribution on Streaming Data, *2013 IEEE 14th International Conference on Information Reuse and Integration (IRI)*, 2013, pp. 497–503.

[SHAR]   http://www.cloudera.com/blog/2010/03/how-raytheon-esearchers-are-using-hadoop-to-build-a-scalable-distributed-triple-store

[STAN1996] S. Staniford-Chen, S. Cheung, R. Crawford, M. Dilger, J. Frank, J. Hoagland, K. Levitt, C. Wee, R. Yip, D. Zerkle, GrIDS – A Graph Based Intrusion Detection System for Large Networks, *Proceedings of 19th National Information Systems Security Conference*, 1996, pp. 361–370.

[STOL2005] S.J. Stolfo, F. Apap, E. Eskin, K. Heller, S. Hershkop, A. Honig, K. Svore, A Comparative Evaluation of Two Algorithms for Windows Registry Anomaly Detection, *Journal of Computer Security*, Volume 13, #4 (issn 0926-227), July 2005, 659–693.

[SZYM2004] B.K. Szymanski, Y. Zhang, Recursive Data Mining for Masquerade Detection and Author Identification, *13th Annual IEEE Information Assurance Workshop.* IEEE Computer Society Press, 2004.

[TAND2003] G. Tandon, P. Chan, Learning Rules from System Call Arguments and Sequences for Anomaly Detection, *Proceedings of ICDM Workshop on Data Mining for Computer Security (DMSEC)*, 2003, pp. 20–29.

[THUR2017] B. Thuraisingham, et al., Big Data Analytics with Applications in Insider Threat Detection, CRC Press, 2017.

[VLAD1966] L. Vladimir, Binary Codes Capable of Correcting Deletions, Insertions and Reversals. *Soviet Physics Doklady*, Volume 10, #8, 1966, 707–710.

[WANG2003] H. Wang, W. Fan, P.S. Yu, J. Han, Mining Concept-Drifting Data Streams Using Ensemble Classifiers, *Proceedings of SIGKDD*, Washington, DC, USA, 2003, pp. 226–235.

[WANG2009] X. Wang, L. Qian, H. Jiang, Tolerant Majority-Colluding Attacks for Secure Localization in Wireless Sensor Networks, *5th International Conference on Wireless Communications, Networking and Mobile Computing, 2009. WiCom '09*, 2009, pp. 1–5.

[XU2010] Y. Xu, P. Kostamaa, L. Gao, Integrating Hadoop and Parallel DBMs, *Proceedings of the 2010 International Conference on Management of Data*, SIGMOD '10, ACM, New York, NY, USA, 2010, pp. 969–974.

[YAN2002] X. Yan, J. Han, gSpan: Graph-based Substructure Pattern Mining, *Proceedings of International Conference on Data Mining (ICDM)*, 2002, pp. 721–724.

[ZHAO2005] H. Zhao, M. Wu, J. Wang, K. Liu, Forensic Analysis of Nonlinear Collusion Attacks for Multimedia Fingerprinting , *IEEE Transactions on Image Processing*, Volume 14, #5, 2005, 646–661.

[ZIV1977] J. Ziv, A. Lempel, A Universal Algorithm for Sequential Data Compression, *IEEE Transactions on Information Theory*, Volume 23, #3, 1977, 337–343.

[ZLIO2011] I. Zliobaite, A. Bifet, G. Holmes, B. Pfahringer, Moa Concept Drift Active Learning Strategies for Streaming Data, *Journal of Machine Learning Research - Proceedings Track*, Volume 17, 2011, 48–55.

Conclusion to Part II

Part II, consisting of four chapters, described data science technologies for cyber security applications. In particular, stream data analytics techniques with emphasis on big data for malware analysis as well as insider threat detection are discussed.

We discussed data mining for malware detection in Chapter 6. In particular, our architecture, related work, and our approach were given. We also discussed our data mining tools for malware detection. In particular, feature extraction using *n*-gram analysis and the hybrid feature retrieval model were discussed. We also discussed our experiments and datasets.

In Chapter 7, we discussed what stream analytics (which we also referred to as stream mining) is about and also discussed an approach for detecting malware detection. We described algorithms for detecting novel classes (of malware) and an architecture of the system. We discussed three major parts in novel class detection process, which are: (i) saving the inventory of *used* spaces during training, (ii) outlier detection and filtering, and (iii) computing cohesion among outliers and separating the outliers from the training data. We also showed how this technique can be made efficient by raw data reduction using clustering. Finally, we evaluate our proposed method on a number of synthetic and real datasets, and we report results on four datasets.

In Chapter 8, we discussed how cloud computing could be used to provide scalability for malware detection. In particular, we described the feature extraction and selection technique using cloud computing for malware detection. We also discussed data collection, experimental setup, evaluation techniques, and the results obtained.

In Chapter 9, we described our approach to insider threat detection using stream data mining for both nonsequenced and sequenced data. We provided a survey of insider threat and stream mining. We also discussed scalability issues with big data/data science techniques.

Now that we have discussed the various aspects of data science technologies for cyber security applications, in Part III we will describe various security and privacy-enhanced techniques for data science. In particular, we will discuss how malicious attacks to the data science techniques could be handled. In addition, we also discuss how privacy could be enhanced with the data science techniques.

DOI: 10.1201/9781003081845-15

Part III

Security and Privacy-enhanced
Data Science

Introduction to Part III

Part III, consisting of five chapters, will discuss security and privacy-enhanced data science. In particular, attacks to the data science techniques as well as the privacy violations that could occur due to the data science techniques are discussed.

Chapter 10 discusses attacks to data science systems and describes our approach to adversarial machine learning in general and support vector machine learning in particular. Chapter 11 describes adversarial relevant vector machine learning. Privacy-enhanced data science with decision trees as an example is discussed in Chapter 12. Our work on a privacy-aware policy-based data management framework for the quantified self-applications is discussed in Chapter 13. Finally in Chapter 14 we discuss how our work can be applied to a specific application and that is the COVID-19 pandemic.

DOI: 10.1201/9781003081845-17

10 Adversarial Support Vector Machine Learning

10.1 INTRODUCTION

In this chapter, we begin the discussion of security-enhanced data science. In particular, we discuss how the data science techniques may be adapted to handle cyber-attacks. The specific data science technique we will focus on is SVM (support vector machine).

As stated in Chapter 3, learning tasks, such as intrusion detection and spam filtering, face adversarial attacks. Adversarial exploits create additional challenges to existing learning paradigms. Generalization of a learning model over future data cannot be achieved under the assumption that current and future data share identical properties which is essential to the traditional approaches. In the presence of active adversaries, data used for training in a learning system is unlikely to represent future data the system would observe. The difference is not just simple random noise which most learning algorithms have already taken into consideration when they are designed. What typically fail these learning algorithms are targeted attacks that aim to make the learning system dysfunctional by disguising malicious data that otherwise would be detected. Existing learning algorithms cannot be easily tailored to counter this kind of attack because there is a great deal of uncertainty in terms of how much the attacks would affect the structure of the sample space. Despite the sample size and distribution of malicious data given at training time, we would need to make an educated guess about how much the malicious data would change, as sophisticated attackers adapt quickly to evade detection. Attack models that foretell how far an adversary would go in order to breach the system need to be incorporated into learning algorithms to build a robust decision surface. In this chapter, we present two attack models that cover a *wide range of attacks* tailored to match the adversary's motives. Each attack model makes a simple and realistic assumption on what is known to the adversary. Optimal SVM learning strategies are then derived against the attack models. For more details we refer to [ZHOU2012].

Some earlier work lays important theoretical foundations for problems in adversarial learning [DALVI2004, KEAR1993, LOWD2005b]. However, earlier work often makes strong assumptions such as unlimited computing resources and both sides having a complete knowledge of their opponents. Some propose attack models that may not permit changes made to arbitrary sets of features [LOWD2005b]. In security applications, some existing research mainly explores practical means of defeating learning algorithms used in a given application domain [LOWD2005a, PERD2006, WITT2004]. Meanwhile, various learning strategies are proposed to fix application-specific weaknesses in learning algorithms [LI2006, NEWS2005, WANG2006], but only to find new doors open for future attacks [FOGL2006, PERD2006]. A recent survey of adversarial machine learning for malware attacks can be found in [MAIO2019]. The main challenge remains as attackers continually exploit unknown weaknesses of a learning system. Regardless of how well designed a learning system appears to be, there are always "blind" spots it fails to detect, leading to escalating threats as the technical strengths on both sides develop. Threats are often divided into two groups, with one group aiming to smuggle malicious content past learning based detection mechanism, while the other is trying to undermine the credibility of a learning system by raising both false positive and false negative rates [BARR2006]. The grey area in between is scarcely researched. In this work, we set ourselves free from handling application-specific attacks and addressing specific weaknesses of a learning algorithm.

DOI: 10.1201/9781003081845-18

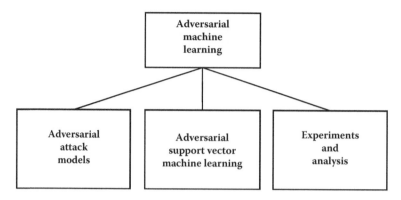

FIGURE 10.1   Adversarial support vector machine learning.

Our main contributions lie in the following three aspects:

- We develop a learning strategy that solves a general convex optimization problem where the strength of the constraints is tied to the strength of attacks.
- We derive optimal support vector machine learning models against an adversary whose attack strategy is defined under a general and reasonable assumption.
- We investigate how the performance of the resulting optimal solutions changes with different parameter values in two different attack models. The empirical results suggest our proposed adversarial SVM learning algorithms are quite robust against various degrees of attacks.

The rest of the chapter is organized as follows. Section 10.2 presents the related work in the area of adversarial learning. Section 10.3 describes our approach. Section 10.4 defined the problem and Section 10.5 describes the adversarial SVM models. Section 10.6 presents experimental results on both artificial and real datasets. Section 10.7 concludes our work and presents future directions. Figure 10.1 illustrates the concepts in this chapter.

10.2   RELATED WORK

Kearns and Li [KEAR1993] provide theoretical upper bounds on tolerable malicious error rates for learning in the presence of malicious errors. They assume the adversary has unbounded computational resources. In addition, they assume the adversary has the knowledge of the target concept, target distributions, and internal states of the learning algorithm. They demonstrate that error tolerance needs not come at the expense of efficiency or simplicity, and there are strong ties between learning with malicious errors and standard optimization problems.

Dalvi et al. [DALVI2004] propose a game theoretic framework for learning problems where there is an optimal opponent. They define the problem as a game between two cost-sensitive opponents: a Naive Bayes classifier and an adversary playing optimal strategies. They assume all parameters of both players are known to each other and the adversary knows the exact form of the classifier. Their adversary-aware algorithm makes predictions according to the class that maximizes the conditional utility. Finding optimal solutions remains to be computational intensive which is typical in game theory.

Lowed and Meek [LOWD2005b] point out that assuming the adversary has perfect knowledge of the classifier is unrealistic. Instead they suggest the adversary can confirm the membership of an arbitrary instance by sending queries to the classifier. They also assume the adversary has available an adversarial cost function over the sample space that maps samples to cost values. This assumption essentially means the adversary needs to know the entire feature space to issue optimal attacks. They propose an adversarial classifier reverse engineering (ACRE) algorithm to learn vulnerabilities of given learning algorithms.

Adversarial learning problems are often modeled as games played between two opponents. Brückner and Scheffer model adversarial prediction problems as Stackelberg games [BRUC2011]. To guarantee optimality, the model assumes adversaries behave rationally. However, it does not require a unique equilibrium. Kantarcioglu et al. [KANT2011] treat the problem as a sequential Stackelberg game. They assume the two players know each other's payoff functions. They use simulated annealing and genetic algorithm to search for Nash equilibrium. Later on such equilibrium is used to choose the optimal set of attributes that give good equilibrium performance. Improved models in which Nash strategies are played have also been proposed [BRUC2009, LIU2010].

Other game theoretic models play zero-sum minimax strategies. Globerson and Roweis [GLOB2006] consider a problem where some features may be missing at testing time. This is related to adversarial learning in that the adversary may simply delete highly weighted features in malicious data to increase its chance to evade detection. They develop a game theoretic framework in which classifiers are constructed to be optimal in the worst case scenario. Their idea is to prevent assigning too much weight on any single feature. They use the support vector machine model which optimally minimizes the hinge loss when at most K features can be deleted. El Ghaoui et al. [GHAO2003] apply a minimax model to training data bounded by hyper-rectangles. Their model minimizes the worst-case loss over data in given intervals. Other robust learning algorithms for handling classification-time noise are also proposed [DEKE2008, DEKE2010, LANC2002, TEO2007].

Our work differs from the existing ones in several respects. First of all, we do not make strong assumptions on what is known to either side of the players. Second, both wide-range attacks and targeted attacks are considered and incorporated into the SVM learning framework. Finally, the robustness of the minimax solutions against attacks over a wide range of parameters is investigated.

10.3 OUR APPROACH

While the details of our approach are discussed later in this chapter, in this section we will provide an overview of our approach. The idea being our approach is that the adversary is trying to learn as much as possible about the data we are using as well as the models we are using. Based on what the adversary has learned, it will try to thwart our models so that it does not get caught. So with the SVM approach, the adversary is trying to push as many instances as possible in the "good" category. This way some of the bad instances will be considered to be good by our model. So what we do to combat the adversary's behavior is to try and move the SVM boundary line. We do that after considering many factors as well discuss in Sections 10.3 and 10.4. Also, the way we move the line depends on the attack models we are considering. When we move the boundary line then some of the bad instances which pretended to be good instances will show as bad instances.

Figure 10.2 illustrates our approach. In Figure 10.2, we show the original boundary line (dashed line) and the good instances as well as the bad instances. The bad instances are shown as crosses and the good instances are shown as circles. We can see that some of the bad instances are moved as good instances by the adversary. In Figure 10.2(b), we have moved the boundary line. We can see that some of the bad instances that would have shown up as good instances are now showing as bad instances. One can ask the question as to how far do we move the boundary line. We can move the line far enough in such a way that all the bad instances will show up as bad instances. But this also means some of the good instances will show up as bad instances. That is, there will be many false positives if we move the line by a large amount. So our challenge is to move the boundary line in such a way that we catch as many bad instances as possible without having many false positives. Our goal us to increase

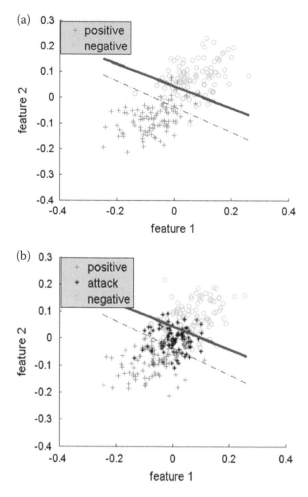

FIGURE 10.2 (a) Bad instances pretending to be good instances. (b) By moving the boundary line, more bad instances are caught.

the accuracy and at the same time reduce the false negatives and false positives. In the end it becomes a game between us and the adversary.

In the ensuing sections we present the key points in our attack models as well as SVM-based learning models. More details can be found in [ZHOU2012]. We discuss two types of attack model: the free-range attack model and the restricted attack model. In the free-range attack model, the adversary can move malicious data anywhere in the domain. In the restrained attack model, the adversary can move malicious data closer to a target point.

10.4 THE PROBLEM AND THE ATTACKS

10.4.1 PROBLEM DEFINITION

Denote a sample set by

$$\{(x_i, y_i) \in (X, Y)\}_{i=1}^n, \text{ where } x_i \text{ is the } i^{th} \text{ sample and } y_i \in \{-1, 1\} \text{ is its label, } X \subseteq \mathbb{R}^d$$

is a d-dimensional feature space, n is the total number of samples. We consider an adversarial learning problem where the adversary modified malicious data to avoid detection and hence achieves his planned goals. The adversary has the freedom to move only the malicious data ($y_i = 1$) in any direction by adding a non-zero displacement vector δi to

$$x_i | y_i = 1.$$

That is, the goal is to learn a hypothesis H robust against adversarial attacks that modify malicious data by adding a non-zero displacement vector δ. For example, in spam-filtering the adversary may add good words to spam email to defeat spam filters. On the other hand, adversary will not be able to modify legitimate email.

We make no specific assumptions on the adversary's knowledge of the learning system. Instead, we simply assume there is a trade-off or cost of changing malicious data. For example, a practical strategy often employed by an adversary is to move the malicious data in the feature space as close as possible to where the innocuous data is frequently observed. However, the adversary can only alter a malicious data point so much that its malicious utility is not completely lost. If the adversary moves a data point too far away from its own class in the feature space, the adversary may have to sacrifice much of the malicious utility of the original data point. For example, in the problem of credit card fraud detection, an attacker may choose the "right" amount to spend with a stolen credit card to mimic a legitimate purchase. By doing so, the attacker will lose some potential profit.

10.4.2 Adversarial Attack Models

We present two attack models: *free-range* and *restrained*, each of which makes a simple and realistic assumption about how much is known to the adversary. The models differ in their implications for (i) the adversary's knowledge of the innocuous data, and (ii) the loss of utility as a result of changing the malicious data. The *free-range* attack model assumes the adversary has the freedom to move data anywhere in the feature space. The *restrained* attack model is a more conservative attack model. The model is built under the intuition that the adversary would be reluctant to let a data point move far away from its original position in the feature space. The reason is that greater displacement often entails loss of malicious utility.

10.4.2.1 Free-range Attack

In this model, the adversary can move malicious data anywhere in the domain. The only knowledge the adversary needs is the valid range of each feature.

Let x_j^{max} and x_j^{min} be the largest and the smallest values that the jth feature of a data point x_i—x_{ij}—can take. For all practical purposes, we assume both x_j^{max} and x_j^{min} are bounded. For example, for a Gaussian distribution, they can be set to the 0.01 and 0.99 quantiles. The resulting range would cover most of the data points and discard a few extreme values. An attack is then bounded in the following form:

$$C_f(x_j^{min} - x_{ij}) \le \delta_{ij} \le C_f(x_j^{max} - x_{ij}), \forall j \in [1, d],$$

where $C_f \in [0, 1]$ controls the aggressiveness of attacks. $C_f = 0$ means no attacks, while $C_f = 1$ corresponds to the most aggressive attacks involving the widest range of permitted data movement. More formally, the free-range attack model can be defined as follows:

$$\arg\min_{w,b,\xi_i,t_i,u_i,v_i} \frac{1}{2}\|w\|^2 + C\Sigma_i\,\xi_i$$

$$s.t. \quad \xi_i \geq 0$$

$$\xi_i \geq 1 - y_i\cdot(w\cdot x_i + b) + t_i$$

$$t_i \geq \Sigma_j\, C_f\left(v_{ij}(x_j^{\max} - x_{ij}) - u_{ij}(x_j^{\min} - x_{ij})\right)$$

$$u_i - v_i = \frac{1}{2}(1 + y_i)w$$

$$u_i \geq 0$$

$$v_i \geq 0$$

The great advantage of this attack model is that it is sufficiently general to cover all possible attack scenarios as far as data modification is concerned. When paired with a learning model, the combination would produce good performance against the most severe attacks. However, when there are mild attacks, the learning model becomes too "paranoid" and its performance suffers accordingly. Next, we present a more realistic model for attacks where significant data alteration is penalized.

10.4.2.2   Restrained Attack

In this model, adversary can move malicious data closer to a target point. Let x_i be a malicious data point the adversary aims to alter. Let x_i^t, a d-dimensional vector, be a potential target to which the adversary would like to push x_i. The adversary chooses x_i^t according to his estimate of the innocuous data distribution. Ideally, the adversary would optimize x_i^t for each x_i to minimize the cost of changing it and maximize the goal it can achieve. Optimally choosing x_i^t is desired, but often requires a great deal of knowledge about the feature space and sometimes the inner working of a learning algorithm [DALV2004]. More realistically, the adversary can set x_i^t to be the estimated centroid of innocuous data, a data point sampled from the observed innocuous data, or an artificial data point generated from the estimated innocuous data distribution. Note that x^t could be a rough guess if the adversary has a very limited knowledge of the innocuous data, or a very accurate one if the adversary knows the exact make-up of the training data.

In most cases, the adversary cannot change x_i to x_i^t as desired since x_i may lose too much of its malicious utility. Therefore, for each attribute j in the d-dimensional feature space, we assume the adversary adds

$$\delta_{ij} \ \text{ to } \ x_{ij}$$

where

$$|\delta_{ij}| \leq |x_{ij}^t - x_{ij}|, \quad \forall \ j \ \in \ d.$$

Furthermore, we place an upper bound on the amount of displacement for attribute j as follows:

$$0 \leq (x_{ij}^t - x_{ij})\delta_{ij} \leq \left(1 - C_\delta \frac{|x_{ij}^t - x_{ij}|}{|x_{ij}| + |x_{ij}^t|}\right)(x_{ij}^t - x_{ij})^2,$$

where $C_\delta \in [0, 1]$ is a constant modeling the loss of malicious utility as a result of the movement δ_{ij}. This attack model specifies how much the adversary can push x_{ij} toward x_{ij}^t based on how far apart they are from each other.

The term is

$$1 - C_\delta \frac{|x_{ij}^t - x_{ij}|}{|x_{ij}| + |x_{ij}^t|}$$

the percentage of $x_{ij}^t - x_{ij}$ that δ_{ij} is allowed to be at most. When C_δ is fixed the closer x_{ij} is to x_{ij}^t, the more x_{ij} is allowed to move toward x_{ij}^t is to x_{ij}^t, the more x_{ij} is allowed to move toward x_{ij}^t percentage wise. The opposite is also true. The farther apart x_{ij} is to x_{ij}^t, the smaller $|\delta_{ij}|$ will be. For example, when x_{ij} and x_{ij}^t reside on different sides of the origin, that is, one is positive and the other is negative, then no movement is permitted (that is, $\delta_{ij} = 0$) when $C_\delta = 1$. This model balances between the needs of disguising maliciousness of data and retaining its malicious utility in the mean time. $(x_{ij}^t - x_{ij})$, $\delta_{ij} \geq 0$ ensures δ_{ij} moves in the same direction as $x_{ij}^t - x_{ij}$. C_δ is related to the loss of malicious utility after the data has been modified. C_δ sets how much malicious utility the adversary is willing to sacrifice for breaking through the decision boundary. A larger C_δ means smaller loss of malicious utility, while a smaller C_δ models greater loss of malicious utility. Hence a larger C_δ leads to less aggressive attacks while a smaller C_δ leads to more aggressive attacks.

The attack model works great for well-separated data as shown in Figure 10.3(a). When data from both classes are near the separation boundary as shown in Figure 10.3(b), slightly changing attribute values would be sufficient to push the data across the boundary. Note that the X and Y axis in both figures are features (as in Figure 10.2). Also, the X and Y axis in Figure 10.3(a) range from −0.2 to 0.2 while the X axis in Figure 10.3(a) ranges from −0.25 to 0.25 while the Y axis from −0.3 to 0.3 (details are given in [ZHOU2012]). In this case, even if C_δ is set to 1, the attack from the above model would still be too aggressive compared with what is needed. We could allow $C_\delta > 1$ to further reduce the aggressiveness of attacks, however, for simplicity and more straightforward control, we instead apply a discount factor C_ξ to $|x_{ij}^t - x_{ij}|$ directly to model the severeness of attacks:

$$0 \leq (x_{ij}^t - x_{ij})\delta_{ij} \leq C_\xi \left(1 - \frac{|x_{ij}^t - x_{ij}|}{|x_{ij}| + |x_{ij}^t|} \right)(x_{ij}^t - x_{ij})^2,$$

where $C_\xi \in [0, 1]$. A large C_ξ gives rise to a greater amount of data movement, and a small C_ξ sets a narrower limit on data movement. Combining these two cases, the *restrained-attack* model is given as follows:

$$0 \leq (x_{ij}^t - x_{ij})\delta_{ij} \leq C_\xi \left(1 - C_\delta \frac{|x_{ij}^t - x_{ij}|}{|x_{ij}| + |x_{ij}^t|} \right)(x_{ij}^t - x_{ij})^2.$$

More formally stated, the restrained attack model can be defined as follows:

$$\arg\min_{w,b,\xi_i,t_i,u_i,v_i} \frac{1}{2}\|w\|^2 + C\sum_i \xi_i$$

$$s.t. \quad \xi_i \geq 0$$

$$\xi_i \geq 1 - y_i \cdot (w \cdot x_i + b) + t_i$$

$$t_i \geq \sum_j u_{ij} C_\xi \left(1 - C_\delta \frac{|x_{ij}^t - x_{ij}|}{|x_{ij}| + |x_{ij}^t|} \right)(x_{ij}^t - x_{ij})^2$$

$$(-u_i - v_i) \circ (x_i^t - x_i) = \frac{1}{2}(1 + y_i)w$$

$$u_i \geq 0$$

$$v_i \geq 0$$

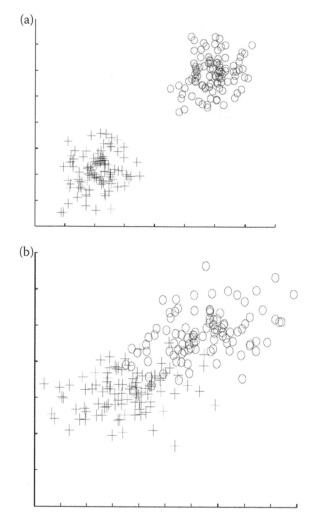

FIGURE 10.3 (a) Data well separated. (b) Data cluttered near separating boundary. Data well separated and data cluttered near separating boundary.

10.5   ADVERSARIAL SVM LEARNING

We now present an adversarial support vector machine model (AD-SVM) against each of the two attack models discussed in the previous section. We assume the adversary cannot modify the innocuous data. Note that this assumption can be relaxed to model cases where the innocuous data may also be altered.

10.5.1   AD-SVM AGAINST FREE-RANGE ATTACK MODEL

We first consider the free-range attack model. The hinge loss model is given as follows:

$$h(w, b, x_i) = \begin{cases} \max_{\delta_i} \lfloor 1 - (w \cdot (x_i + \delta_i) + b) \rfloor + & \text{if } y_i = 1 \\ \lfloor 1 + (w \cdot x_i + b) \rfloor + & \text{if } y_i = -1 \end{cases}$$

$$s.t. \quad \delta_i \le C_f (x^{max} - x_i)$$

$$\delta_i \ge C_f (x^{min} - x_i)$$

where δ_i is the displacement vector for x_i, and denote component wise inequality.

Following the standard SVM risk formulation, we have

$$\underset{w,b}{\arg\min} \quad \sum_{\{i|y_i=1\}} \max_{\delta_i} \lfloor 1 - (w{\cdot}(x_i + \delta_i) + b) \rfloor +$$
$$+ \sum_{\{i|y_i=-1\}} \lfloor 1 + (w{\cdot}x_i + b) \rfloor$$
$$+ \mu\|w\|^2$$

Combining cases for positive and negative instances, this is equivalent to:

$$\underset{w,b}{\arg\min} \quad \sum_i \max_{\delta_i} \lfloor 1 - y_i(w{\cdot}x_i + b) - \frac{1}{2}(1 + y_i)w{\cdot}\delta_i \rfloor +$$
$$+ \mu\|w\|^2$$

Note that the worst-case hinge loss of x_i is obtained when δ_i is chosen to minimize its contribution to the margin, that is,

$$f_i \quad = \quad \min_{\delta_i} \frac{1}{2}(1 + y_i)w{\cdot}\delta_i$$
$$s.t. \quad \delta_i \leq C_f(x^{max} - x_i)$$
$$\delta_i \geq C_f(x^{min} - x_i)$$

$$h(w, b, x_i) \quad = \quad \begin{cases} \max_{\delta_i} \lfloor 1 - (w{\cdot}(x_i + \delta_i) + b) \rfloor + & \text{if } y_i = 1 \\ \lfloor 1 + (w{\cdot}x_i + b) \rfloor + & \text{if } y_i = -1 \end{cases}$$
$$s.t. \quad \delta_i \leq C_f(x^{max} - x_i)$$
$$\delta_i \geq C_f(x^{min} - x_i)$$

where δ_i is the displacement vector for x_i, and denote component wise inequality.

This is a disjoint bilinear problem with respect to w and δ_i. Here, we are interested in discovering optimal assignment to δ_i with a given w. We can reduce the bilinear problem to the following asymmetric dual problem over

$$u_i \in \mathbb{R}^d, \quad v_i \in \mathbb{R}^d$$

where d is the dimension of the feature space:

$$g_i \quad = \quad \max - \sum_j C_f(v_{ij}(x_j^{max} - x_{ij}) - u_{ij}(x_j^{min} - x_{ij}))$$
$$\text{or}$$
$$g_i \quad = \quad \min \sum_j C_f(v_{ij}(x_j^{max} - x_{ij}) - u_{ij}(x_j^{min} - x_{ij}))$$
$$s.t. \quad (u_i - v_i) = \frac{1}{2}(1 + y_i)w$$
$$u_i \geq 0$$
$$v_i \geq 0$$
$$s.t. \quad (u_i - v_i) = 1(1 + y_i)w$$

The SVM risk minimization problem can be rewritten as follows:

$$\arg\min_{w,b,t_i,u_i,v_i} \quad \frac{1}{2}\|w\|^2 + C \sum_i \lfloor 1 - y_i \cdot (w \cdot x_i + b) + t_i \rfloor +$$

$$s.t. \quad t_i \geq \sum_j C_f (v_{ij}(x_j^{max} - x_{ij}) - u_{ij}(x_j^{min} - x_{ij}))$$

$$u_i - v_i = \frac{1}{2}(1 + y_i)w$$

$$u_i \geq 0$$

$$v_i \geq 0$$

Adding a slack variable and linear constraints to remove the non-differentiality of the hinge loss, we can rewrite the problem as follows:

$$\arg\min_{w,b,\xi_i,t_i,u_i,v_i} \quad \frac{1}{2}\|w\|^2 + C \sum_i \xi_i$$

$$s.t. \quad \xi_i \geq 0$$

$$\xi_i \geq 1 - y_i \cdot (w \cdot x_i + b) + t_i$$

$$t_i \geq \sum_j Cf (v_{ij}(x_j^{max} - x_{ij}) - u_{ij}(x_j^{min} - x_{ij}))$$

$$u_i - v_i = \frac{1}{2}(1 + y_i)w$$

$$u_i \geq 0$$

$$v_i \geq 0$$

10.5.2 AD-SVM against Restrained Attack Model

With the restrained attack model, we modify the hinge loss model and solve the problem following the same steps:

$$h(w, b, x_i) = \begin{cases} \max_{\delta_i} \lfloor 1 - (w \cdot (x_i + \delta_i) + b) \rfloor + & \text{if } y_i = 1 \\ \lfloor 1 + (w \cdot x_i + b) \rfloor + & \text{if } y_i = -1 \end{cases}$$

$$s.t.$$

$$(x_i^t - x_i) \circ \delta_i \leq C_\xi \left(1 - C_\delta \frac{|x_i^t - x_i|}{|x_i| + x_i^t}\right) \circ (x_i^t - x_i)^{\circ 2}$$

$$(x_i^t - x_i) \circ \delta_i \geq 0$$

where δ_i denotes the modification to x_i, $\leq$ is component-wise inequality, and $\circ$ denotes component-wise operations.

The worst case hinge loss is obtained by solving the following minimization problem:

$$f_i = \min_{\delta_i} \frac{1}{2}(1 + y_i)w \cdot \delta_i$$

$$s.t. \quad (x_i^t - x_i) \circ \delta_i \leq C_\xi \left(1 - C_\delta \frac{|x_i^t - x_i|}{|x_i| + |x_i^t|}\right) \circ (x_i^t - x_i)^{\circ 2}$$

$$(x_i^t - x_i) \circ \delta_i \geq 0$$

We reduce the bilinear problem to the following asymmetric dual problem over $u_i \in \mathbb{R}^d$, $v_i \in \mathbb{R}^d$, where d is the dimension of the feature space

$$g_i = \max - \textstyle\sum_j e_{ij} u_{ij}, \quad \text{or}$$

$$g_i = \min \textstyle\sum_j e_{ij} u_{ij}$$

$$s.t. \quad (-u_i + v_i) \circ (x_i^t - x_i) = \frac{1}{2}(1 + y_i)w$$

$$u_i \geq 0$$

$$v_i \geq 0$$

The SVM risk minimization problem can be rewritten as follows:

$$\operatorname*{arg\,min}_{w,b,t_i,u_i,v_i} \frac{1}{2}\|w\|^2 + C\textstyle\sum_i \left\lfloor 1 - y_i \cdot (w \cdot x_i + b) + t_i \right\rfloor +$$

$$s.t. \quad t_i \geq \textstyle\sum_j e_{ij} u_{ij}$$

$$(-u_i + v_i) \circ (x_i^t - x_i) = \frac{1}{2}(1 + y_i)w$$

$$u_i \geq 0$$

$$v_i \geq 0$$

After removing the non-differentiality of the hinge loss, we can rewrite the problem as follows:

$$\operatorname*{arg\,min}_{w,b,\xi_i,t_i,u_i,v_i} \frac{1}{2}\|w\|^2 + C\textstyle\sum_i \xi_i$$

$$s.t. \quad \xi_i \geq 0$$

$$\xi_i \geq 1 - y_i \cdot (w \cdot x_i + b) + t_i$$

$$t_i \geq \textstyle\sum_j e_{ij} u_{ij}$$

$$(-u_i + v_i) \circ (x_i^t - x_i) = \frac{1}{2}(1 + y_i)w$$

$$u_i \geq 0$$

$$v_i \geq 0$$

10.6   EXPERIMENTS

10.6.1   OUR APPROACH

We test the AD-SVM models on both artificial and real datasets. In our experiments, we investigate the robustness of the AD-SVM models as we increase the severeness of the attacks. We let x_i^t be the centroid of the innocuous data in our AD-SVM model against restrained attacks. We also tried setting x_i^t to a random innocuous data point in the training or test set, and the results are similar. Due to space limitations, we do not report the results in the latter cases.

Attacks on the test data used in the experiments are simulated using the following model:

$$\delta_{ij} = f_{attack}(x_{ij}^- - x_{ij})$$

where x_i^- is an innocuous data point randomly chosen from the test set, and $f_{attack} > 0$ sets a limit for the adversary to move the test data toward the target innocuous data points. By controlling the value of f_{attack}, we can dictate the severity of attacks in the simulation. The actual attacks on the test data are intentionally designed not to match the attack models in AD-SVM so that the results are not biased. For each parameter C_f, C_δ, and C_ξ in the attack models considered in AD-SVM, we tried different values as f_{attack} increases. This allows us to test the robustness of our AD-SVM model in all cases where there are no attacks and attacks that are much more severe than the model has anticipated. We compare our AD-SVM model to the standard SVM and one-class SVM models. We implemented our AD-SVM algorithms in CVX – a package for specifying and solving convex programs [GRAN2011]. Experiments using SVM and one-class SVM are implemented using Weka [HALL2000].

10.6.2   Experiments on Artificial Dataset

We generate two artificial datasets from bivariate normal distributions with specified means and covariance matrices. Data in the first dataset is well separated. The second dataset consists of data more cluttered near the separating boundary. All results are averaged over 100 random runs.

10.6.2.1   Data Points Well Separated

Figure 10.4 illustrates the data distributions when different levels of distortion are applied to the malicious data by setting f_{attack} to 0 (original distribution), 0.3, 0.5, 0.7, and 1.0. As can be observed, as f_{attack} increases, the malicious data points are moved more aggressively toward innocuous data.

Here is the axis information in Figure 10.4. Figure 10.4(a) X and Y axis both range from −0.2 to 0.15. Figure 10.4(b)–(e) X axis ranges from −0.2 to 0.15 while the Y axis ranges from −0.15 to 0.2. Figure 10.4(d) X axis ranges from −0.15 to 0.2 while the Y axis ranges from −0.2 to 0.15 (details are given in [ZHOU2012].

Table 10.1 lists the predictive accuracy of our AD-SVM algorithm with the free-range attack model, the standard SVM algorithm, and the one-class SVM algorithm. AD-SVM clearly outperforms both SVM and one-class SVM when it assumes reasonable adversity ($C_f \in [0.1, 0.5]$). When there is mild attack or no attack at all, AD-SVM with more aggressive free-range assumptions ($C_f \in [0.5, 0.9]$) suffers great performance loss as we expect from such pessimistic model.

Compared to the free-range attack model, the restrained attack model works much more consistently across the entire spectrum of the learning and attack parameters. Here C_δ reflects the aggressiveness of attacks in our AD-SVM learning algorithm. Table 10.2 shows the classification results as C_δ decreases, from less aggressive ($C_\delta = 0.9$) to very aggressive ($C_\delta = 0.1$). Clearly, the most impressive results are lined up along the diagonal when the assumptions on the attacks made in the learning model match the real attacks. The results of our AD-SVM in the rest of the experiments are mostly superior to both SVM and one-class SVM too. This relaxes the requirement of finding the best C_δ. Regardless of what C_δ value is chosen, our model delivers solid performance.

10.6.2.2   Data Cluttered Near Separating Boundary

Figure 10.5 illustrates the distributions of our second artificial dataset under different levels of attacks. Malicious data points can be pushed across the boundary with little modification. We again consider both the free-range and the restrained attack models. Similar conclusions can be drawn: restrained AD-SVM is more robust than free-range AD-SVM; AD-SVMs in general cope much better with mild adversarial attacks than standard SVM and one-class SVM models.

Here is the axis information in Figure 10.5. Figure 10.5(a) X axis ranges from −0.2 to 0.3 while Y axis from and −0.25 to 0.25. Figure 10.5(b) X axis ranges from −0.4 to 0.3 while Y axis from and −0.2 to 0.25. Figure 10.5(c) X axis ranges from −0.4 to 0.3 while Y axis from and −0.25 to 0.2.

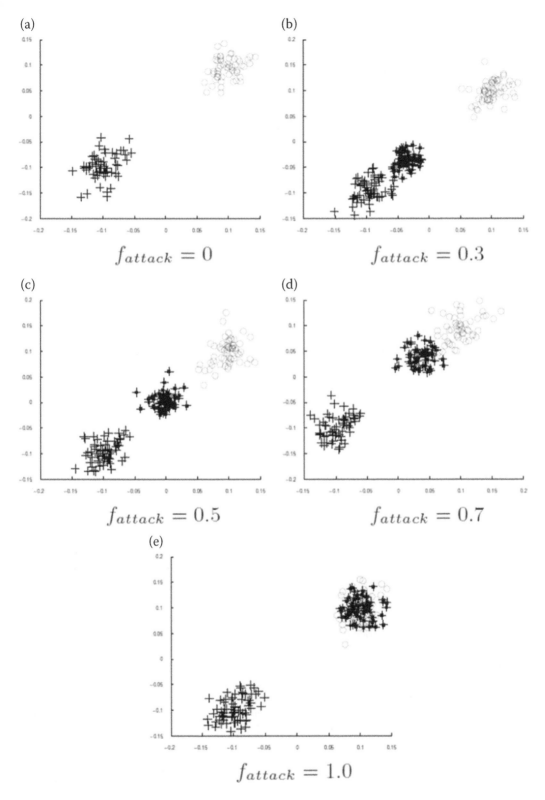

FIGURE 10.4 (a) f_{attack} is 0. (b) f_{attack} is 0.3. (c) f_{attack} is 0.5. (d) f_{attack} is 0.7. (e) f_{attack} is 1.0. Data distributions of the *first* dataset after attacks. f_{attack} varies from 0 (no attack) to 1.0 (most aggressive). Plain "+" marks the original positive data points, "+" with a central black square marks positive data points after alteration, and "∘" represents negative data.

TABLE 10.1

Accuracy of *free-range* AD-SVM, SVM, and one-class SVM under data distributions, shown in Figure 10.4(a)–(e). C_f increases as the learning model assumes more aggressive attacks

		$f_{attack} = 0$	$f_{attack} = 0.3$	$f_{attack} = 0.5$	$f_{attack} = 0.7$	$f_{attack} = 1.0$
	$C_f = 0.1$	1.000	**1.000**	**0.887**	**0.512**	0.500
	$C_f = 0.3$	1.000	**1.000**	**0.997**	**0.641**	0.500
AD-SVM	$C_f = 0.5$	0.996	0.996	**0.996**	**0.930**	0.500
	$C_f = 0.7$	0.882	0.886	**0.890**	**0.891**	0.500
	$C_f = 0.9$	0.500	0.500	0.500	0.500	0.500
SVM		1.000	0.999	0.751	0.502	0.500
One-class SVM		1.000	0.873	0.500	0.500	0.500

TABLE 10.2

Accuracy of *restrained* AD-SVM, SVM, and one-class SVM under data distributions, shown in Figure 10.4(a)–(e). C_δ decreases as the learning model assumes more aggressive attacks

		$f_{attack} = 0$	$f_{attack} = 0.3$	$f_{attack} = 0.5$	$f_{attack} = 0.7$	$f_{attack} = 1.0$
	$C_\delta = 0.9$	1.000	**1.000**	**0.856**	**0.505**	0.500
AD-SVM	$C_\delta = 0.7$	1.000	**1.000**	**0.975**	**0.567**	0.500
$(C_\xi = 1)$	$C_\delta = 0.5$	1.000	**1.000**	**0.999**	**0.758**	0.500
	$C_\delta = 0.3$	0.994	0.994	**0.994**	**0.954**	0.500
	$C_\delta = 0.1$	0.878	0.876	**0.878**	**0.878**	0.500
SVM		1.000	0.998	0.748	0.501	0.500
One-class SVM		1.000	0.873	0.500	0.500	0.500

Figure 10.5(d) X axis ranges from −0.4 to 0.3 while Y axis from and −0.25 to 0.25. Figure 10.5(e) both X and Y axis range from −0.4 to 0.3 (details are given in [ZHOU2012].

Table 10.3 lists the predictive accuracy of our AD-SVM algorithm with the free-range attack model on the second dataset. The results of the standard SVM algorithm and the one-class SVM algorithm are also listed. The free-range model is overly pessimistic in many cases, which overshadows its resilience against the most severe attacks. For the restrained attack model, since the two classes are not well separated originally, C_ξ is used (not combined with C_δ) to reflect the aggressiveness of attacks in AD-SVM. A larger C_ξ is more aggressive while a smaller C_ξ assumes mild attacks. Table 10.4 shows the classification results as C_ξ increases, from less aggressive ($C_\xi = 0.1$) to very aggressive ($C_\xi = 0.9$).

The restrained AD-SVM model still manages to improve the predictive accuracy compared to SVM and one-class SVM, although the improvement is much less impressive. This is understandable since the dataset is generated to make it harder to differentiate between malicious and innocuous data, with or without attacks. The model suffers no performance loss when there are no attacks.

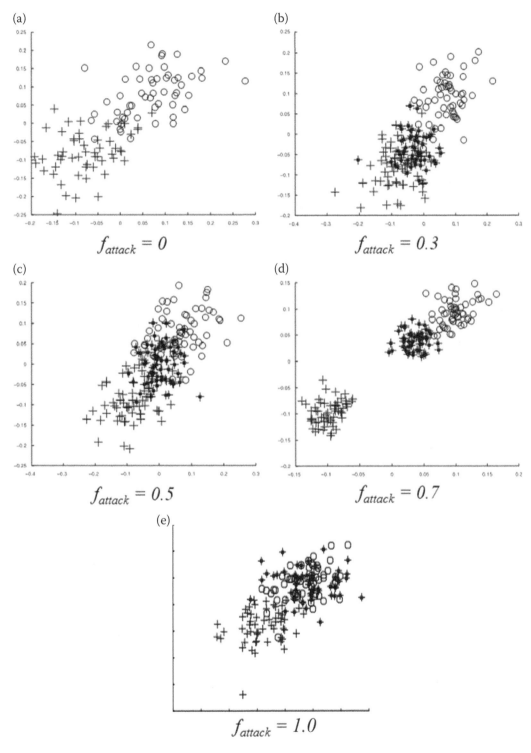

FIGURE 10.5 (a) f_{attack} is 0. (b) f_{attack} is 0.3. (c) f_{attack} is 0.5. (d) f_{attack} is 0.7. (e) f_{attack} is 1.0. Data distributions of the *second* dataset after attacks. f_{attack} varies from 0 (none) to 1.0 (most aggressive). Plain "+" marks the original positive data points, "+" with a central black square is for positive data points after alteration, and "∘" represents negative data.

TABLE 10.3

Accuracy of *free-range* AD-SVM, SVM, and one-class SVM under data distributions, shown in Figure 10.5(a)–(e). C_f increases as the learning model assumes more aggressive attacks

		$f_{attack} = 0$	$f_{attack} = 0.3$	$f_{attack} = 0.5$	$f_{attack} = 0.7$	$f_{attack} = 1.0$
	$C_f = 0.1$	0.928	**0.884**	**0.771**	**0.609**	0.500
	$C_f = 0.3$	0.859	0.848	**0.807**	**0.687**	0.500
AD-SVM	$C_f = 0.5$	0.654	0.649	0.658	**0.638**	0.500
	$C_f = 0.7$	0.500	0.500	0.500	0.500	0.500
	$C_f = 0.9$	0.500	0.500	0.500	0.500	0.500
SVM		0.932	0.859	0.715	0.575	0.500
One-class SVM		0.936	0.758	0.611	0.527	0.500

TABLE 10.4

Accuracy of *restrained* AD-SVM, SVM, and one-class SVM under data distributions, shown in Figure 10.5(a)–(e). C_ξ increases as the learning model assumes more aggressive attacks

		$f_{attack} = 0$	$f_{attack} = 0.3$	$f_{attack} = 0.5$	$f_{attack} = 0.7$	$f_{attack} = 1.0$
	$C_\xi = 0.9$	0.932	**0.860**	**0.719**	**0.575**	0.500
AD-SVM	$C_\xi = 0.7$	0.930	**0.858**	**0.717**	**0.576**	0.500
$(C_\delta = 1)$	$C_\xi = 0.5$	**0.935**	**0.860**	**0.721**	**0.578**	0.500
	$C_\xi = 0.3$	0.931	**0.855**	**0.718**	**0.577**	0.500
	$C_\xi = 0.1$	0.933	**0.858**	**0.718**	**0.575**	0.500
SVM		0.930	0.856	0.714	0.574	0.500
One-class SVM		0.933	0.772	0.605	0.525	0.500

10.6.3 EXPERIMENTS ON REAL DATASETS

We also test our AD-SVM model on two real datasets: *spam base* taken from the UCI data repository [UCI2012], and *web spam* taken from the LibSVM website [LIBS2012].

In the *spam base* dataset, the spam concept includes advertisements, make money fast scams, chain letters, etc. The spam collection came from the postmaster and individuals who had filed spam. The non-spam email collection came from filed work and personal emails [UCI2012]. The dataset consists of 4,601 total number of instances, among which 39.4% is spam. There are 57 attributes and one class label. We divide the datasets into equal halves, with one half Tr for training and the other half Ts for test only. Learning models are built from 10% of random samples selected from Tr. The results are averaged over 10 random runs.

We took the second dataset from the LibSVM website [LIBS2012]. According to the website, the *web spam* data is the subset used in the Pascal Large-Scale Learning Challenge. All positive examples were kept in the dataset while the negative examples were created by randomly traversing the Internet starting at well-known websites. They treat continuous n bytes as a word and use word count as the feature value and normalize each instance to unit length. We use their unigram dataset in which the number of features is 254. The total number of instances is 350,000.

We again divide the dataset into equal halves for training and test. We use 2% of the samples in the training set to build the learning models and report the results averaged over 10 random runs.

Tables 10.5 and 10.6 show the results on the *spam base* dataset. AD-SVM, with both the free-range and the restrained attack models, achieved solid improvement on this dataset. C_δ alone is used in the restrained learning model. Except for the most pessimistic cases, AD-SVM suffers no performance loss when there are no attacks. On the other hand, it achieved much more superior classification accuracy than SVM and one-class SVM when there are attacks.

Tables 10.7 and 10.8 illustrate the results on the *web spam* dataset. Unlike the *spam base* dataset where data is well separated, *web spam* data is more like the second artificial dataset. The AD-SVM model exhibits similar classification performance as on the second artificial dataset. The free-range model is too pessimistic when there are no attacks, while the restrained model performs consistently better than SVM and one-class SVM and, more importantly, suffers no loss when there are no attacks. We use C_ξ alone in our learning model. Which parameter, C_ξ or C_δ, to use in the restrained attack model can be determined through cross validation on the initial data. The next subsection has a more detailed discussion on model parameters.

TABLE 10.5

Accuracy of AD-SVM, SVM, and one-class SVM on the *spam base* dataset as attacks intensify. The *free-range* attack is used in the learning model. C_f increases as attacks become more aggressive

		$f_{attack} = 0$	$f_{attack} = 0.3$	$f_{attack} = 0.5$	$f_{attack} = 0.7$	$f_{attack} = 1.0$
	$C_\xi = 0.9$	0.932	**0.860**	**0.719**	**0.575**	0.500
AD-SVM	$C_\xi = 0.7$	0.930	**0.858**	**0.717**	**0.576**	0.500
$(C_\delta = 1)$	$C_\xi = 0.5$	**0.935**	**0.860**	**0.721**	**0.578**	0.500
	$C_\xi = 0.3$	0.931	0.855	**0.718**	**0.577**	0.500
	$C_\xi = 0.1$	0.933	**0.858**	**0.718**	0.575	0.500
SVM		0.930	0.856	0.714	0.574	0.500
One-class SVM		0.933	0.772	0.605	0.525	0.500

TABLE 10.6

Accuracy of AD-SVM and SVM on *spam base* dataset as attacks intensify. The *restrained* attack model is used in the learning model. C_δ decreases as attacks become more aggressive

		$f_{attack} = 0$	$f_{attack} = 0.3$	$f_{attack} = 0.5$	$f_{attack} = 0.7$	$f_{attack} = 1.0$
	$C_\delta = 0.9$	0.874	**0.821**	**0.766**	**0.720**	0.579
AD-SVM	$C_\delta = 0.7$	**0.888**	**0.860**	**0.821**	**0.776**	0.581
$(C_\xi = 1)$	$C_\delta = 0.5$	0.874	**0.860**	**0.849**	**0.804**	0.586
	$C_\delta = 0.3$	0.867	**0.855**	**0.845**	**0.809**	0.590
	$C_\delta = 0.1$	0.836	**0.840**	**0.839**	**0.815**	**0.597**
SVM		0.884	0.812	0.761	0.686	0.591
One-class SVM		0.695	0.687	0.676	0.653	0.574

TABLE 10.7

Accuracy of AD-SVM, SVM, and one-class SVM on *web spam* dataset as attacks intensify. The *free-range* attack model is used in the learning model. C_f increases as attacks become more aggressive

		$f_{attack} = 0$	$f_{attack} = 0.3$	$f_{attack} = 0.5$	$f_{attack} = 0.7$	$f_{attack} = 1.0$
	$C_f = 0.1$	0.814	**0.790**	**0.727**	**0.591**	**0.463**
	$C_f = 0.3$	0.760	0.746	**0.732**	**0.643**	**0.436**
AD-SVM	$C_f = 0.5$	0.684	0.649	0.617	**0.658**	**0.572**
	$C_f = 0.7$	0.606	0.606	0.606	**0.606**	**0.606**
	$C_f = 0.9$	0.606	0.606	0.606	**0.606**	**0.606**
SVM		0.874	0.769	0.644	0.534	0.427
One-class SVM		0.685	0.438	0.405	0.399	0.399

TABLE 10.8

Accuracy of AD-SVM, SVM, and one-class SVM on *web spam* dataset as attacks intensify. The *restrained* attack model is used in the learning model. C_ξ increases as attacks become more aggressive

		$f_{attack} = 0$	$f_{attack} = 0.3$	$f_{attack} = 0.5$	$f_{attack} = 0.7$	$f_{attack} = 1.0$
	$C_\xi = 0.1$	**0.873**	**0.822**	**0.699**	0.552	0.435
AD-SVM	$C_\xi = 0.3$	0.870	**0.837**	**0.748**	0.597	0.444
$(C_\delta = 1)$	$C_\xi = 0.5$	0.855	**0.833**	**0.772**	0.641	0.454
	$C_\xi = 0.7$	0.841	**0.820**	**0.773**	0.663	0.467
	$C_\xi = 0.9$	0.822	**0.803**	**0.749**	0.671	0.478
SVM		0.871	0.769	0.659	0.512	0.428
One-class SVM		0.684	0.436	0.406	0.399	0.400

10.6.4 SETTING C_F, C_Ξ, AND C_Δ

The remaining question is how to set the parameters in the attack models. The AD-SVM algorithms proposed in this chapter assume either a free-range attack model or a restrained attack model. In reality we might not know the exact attack model or the true utility function of the attackers. However, as Tables 10.1 to 10.8 demonstrate, although the actual attacks may not match what we have anticipated, our AD-SVM algorithm using the restrained attack model exhibits overall robust performance by setting C_δ or C_ξ values for more aggressive attacks. If we use the restrained attack model, choosing C_δ 0.5 (C_ξ 0.5) consistently returns robust results against all f_{attack} values. If we use the free-range attack model in AD-SVM, we will have to set parameter values to avoid the very pessimistic results for mild attacks. Hence choosing C_f 0.3 in general returns good classification results against all f_{attack} values.

As a general guideline, the baseline of C_f, C_δ, or C_ξ has to be chosen to work well against attack parameters suggested by domain experts. This can be done through cross-validation for various attack scenarios. From there, we gradually increase C_f or C_ξ, or decrease in the case of C_δ. The best value of C_f, C_δ, or C_ξ is reached right before performance deteriorates. Also note that it is sufficient to set only one of C_ξ and C_δ while fixing the other to 1. Furthermore, C_f, C_δ, and C_ξ do not have to be a scalar parameter. In many applications, it is clear some attributes can be changed while others cannot. A C_f, C_δ/C_ξ parameter vector would help enforce these additional rules.

10.7   SUMMARY AND DIRECTIONS

As stated earlier, many learning tasks such as spam filtering and credit card fraud detection face an active adversary that tries to avoid detection. For learning problems that deal with an active adversary, it is important to model the adversary's attack strategy and develop robust learning models to mitigate the attack. These are the two objectives of this chapter. We consider two attack models: a *free-range* attack model that permits arbitrary data corruption and a *restrained* attack model that anticipates more realistic attacks that a reasonable adversary would devise under penalties. We then develop optimal SVM learning strategies against the two attack models. The learning algorithms minimize the hinge loss while assuming the adversary is modifying data to maximize the loss. Experiments are performed on both artificial and real datasets. We demonstrate that optimal solutions may be overly pessimistic when the actual attacks are much weaker than expected. More important, we demonstrate that it is possible to develop a much more resilient SVM learning model while making loose assumptions on the data corruption models. When derived under the *restrained* attack model, our optimal SVM learning strategy provides more robust overall performance under a wide range of attack parameters.

Adversarial attacks can lead to severe misrepresentation of real data distributions in the feature space. Learning algorithms lacking the flexibility of handling the structural change in the samples would not cope well with attacks that modify data to change the make-up of the sample space. We present two attack models and an adversarial SVM learning model against each attack model. We demonstrate that our adversarial SVM model is much more resilient to adversarial attacks than standard SVM and one-class SVM models. We also show that optimal learning strategies derived to counter overly pessimistic attack models can produce unsatisfactory results when the real attacks are much weaker. On the other hand, learning models built on restrained attack models perform more consistently as attack parameters vary. One future direction for this work is to add cost-sensitive metrics into the learning models. Another direction is to extend the single learning model to an ensemble in which each base learner handles a different set of attacks.

REFERENCES

[BARR2006] M. Barreno, B. Nelson, R. Sears, A.D. Joseph, J.D. Tygar, Can Machine Learning Be Secure?, *Proceedings of the 2006 ACM Symposium on Information, Computer and Communications Security*, ACM, New York, NY, USA, 2006, pp. 16–25.

[BRUC2009] M. Bruckner, T. Scheffer, Nash Equilibria of Static Prediction Games. *Advances in Neural Information Processing Systems*. MIT Press, 2009.

[BRUC2011] M. Bruckner, T. Scheffer, Stackelberg Games for Adversarial Prediction Problems, *Proceedings of the 17th ACM SIGKDD International Conference on Knowledge Discovery and Data Mining* , San *Diego, CA*, 2011, pp. 547–555.

[DALVI2004] N. Dalvi, P. Domingos, Mausam, S. Sanghai, D. Verma, Adversarial classification, *Proceedings of the Tenth ACM SIGKDD International Conference on Knowledge Discovery and Data Mining*, KDD '04, ACM, New York, NY, USA, 2004, pp. 99–108.

[DEKE2008] O. Dekel, O. Shamir, Learning to Classify with Missing and Corrupted Features, *Proceedings of the International Conference on Machine Learning*, ACM, 2008, pp. 216–223.

[DEKE2010] O. Dekel, O. Shamir, L. Xiao, Learning to Classify with Missing and Corrupted Features, *Machine Learning*, Volume 81, #2, 2010, 149–178.

[FOGL2006] P. Fogla, W. Lee, Evading Network Anomaly Detection Systems: Formal Reasoning and Practical Techniques, *Proceedings of the 13th ACM Conference on Computer and Communications Security*, CCS '06, ACM, New York, NY, USA, 2006, pp. 59–68.

[GHAO2003] L. El Ghaoui, G.R.G. Lanckriet, G. Natsoulis, Robust Classification with Interval Data, Technical Report UCB/CSD-03-1279, EECS Department, University of California, Berkeley, October 2003.

[GLOB2006] A. Globerson, S. Roweis, Nightmare at Test Time: Robust Learning by Feature Deletion, *Proceedings of the 23rd International Conference on Machine Learning*, ICML '06, ACM, 2006, 353–360.

[GRAN2011] M. Grant, S. Boyd, CVX: Matlab Software for Disciplined Convex Programming, version 1.21, April 2011, http://cvxr.com/cvx/

[HALL2000] M. Hall, E. Frank, G. Holmes, B. Pfahringer, P. Reutemann, I.H. Witten, The Weka Data Mining Software: An Update, *SIGKDD Explorations Newsletter*, Volume 11, November 2009, 10–18.

[KANT2011] M. Kantarcioglu, B. Xi, C. Clifton, Classifier Evaluation and Attribute Selection against Active Adversaries, *Data Mininig and Knowledge Discovery*, Volume 22, January 2011, 291–335.

[KEAR1993] M. Kearns, M. Li, Learning in the Presence of Malicious Errors, *SIAM Journal on Computing*, Volume 22, 1993, 807–837.

[LANC2002] G.R.G. Lanckriet, L.E. Ghaoui, C. Bhattacharyya, M.I. Jordan, A Robust Minimax Approach to Classification, *Journal of Machine Learning Research*, Volume 3, 2002, 555–582.

[LI2006] Z. Li, M. Sanghi, Y. Chen, M.-Y. Kao, B. Chavez, Hamsa: Fast Signature Generation for Zero-day Polymorphic Worms with Provable Attack Resilience, *Proceedings of the 2006 IEEE Symposium on Security and Privacy*, IEEE Computer Society, 2006.

[LIBS2012] LIBSVM Data: Classification, Regression, and Multi-label, 2012. https://www.csie.ntu.edu.tw/~cjlin/libsvmtools/datasets/

[LIU2010] W. Liu, S. Chawla, Mining Adversarial Patterns via Regularized Loss Minimization, *Machine Learning*, Volume 81, October 2010, 69–83.

[LOWD2005a] D. Lowd, Good Word Attacks on Statistical Spam Filters, *Eleventh Conference on Email and Anti-spam (CEAS), Stanford University, Palo Alto, CA*, 2005.

[LOWD2005b] D. Lowd, C. Meek, Adversarial Learning, *Proceedings of the Eleventh ACM SIGKDD International Conference on Knowledge Discovery in Data Mining, KDD '05, Chicago, IL*, 2005, 641–647.

[MAIO2019] D. Maiorca, B. Biggio, G. Giacinto, Towards Adversarial Malware Detection: Lessons Learned from PDF-based Attacks, ACM Computing Surveys, Volume 52, #4, 2019, 78:1–78:36.

[NEWS2005] J. Newsome, B. Karp, D.X. Song, Polygraph: Automatically Generating Signatures for Polymorphic Worms. *2005 IEEE Symposium on Security and Privacy*, IEEE Computer SocietyOakland, CA, USA, May 8–11, 2005, pp. 226–241.

[PERD2006] R. Perdisci, D. Dagon, W. Lee, P. Fogla, M. Sharif, Misleading Worm Signature Generators Using Deliberate Noise Injection, *Proceedings of the 2006 IEEE Symposium on Security and Privacy, Oakland, CA*, 2006, pp. 17–31.

[TEO2007] C.H. Teo, A. Globerson, S.T. Roweis, A.J. Smola, Convex Learning with Invariances, *Proceedings of the 20th International Conference on Neural Information Processing Systems (NIPS), Vancouver, Canada*, 2007, pp. 1489–1496.

[UCI2012] UCI Machine Learning Repository, 2012. https://archive.ics.uci.edu/ml/index.php

[WANG2006] K. Wang, J.J. Parekh, S.J. Stolfo, Anagram: A Content Anomaly Detector Resistant to Mimicry Attack, *Recent Advances in Intrusion Detection, 9th International Symposium, Hamburg, Germany*, 2006, pp. 226–248.

[WITT2004] G.L. Wittel, S.F. Wu, On Attacking Statistical Spam Filters, *Proceedings of the First Conference on Email and Anti-spam (CEAS), Mountain View, California, USA,*2004.

[ZHOU2012] Y. Zhou, M. Kantarcioglu, B.M. Thuraisingham, B. Xi, Adversarial Support Vector Machine Learning, KDD, 2012, 1059–1067.

11 Adversarial Learning Using Relevance Vector Machine Ensembles

11.1 INTRODUCTION

As stated in Chapter 10, many learning tasks such as spam filtering and credit card fraud detection face an active adversary that tries to avoid detection. For learning problems that deal with an active adversary, it is important to model the adversary's attack strategy and develop robust learning models to mitigate the attack. Much of the research in adversarial learning varies in the types of constraints considered in the problem definition. The assumption of unconstrained adversaries is impractical since arbitrary modification to data and its class membership can result in a worst-case error rate of 100% [AUER1998, KEAR1993]. Therefore, the majority of the recent research focuses on constrained adversaries.

Under the constrained-adversary assumption, major research results can be further divided between game-theoretic solutions and non-game theoretic solutions. For practitioners, the difficulty lies in choosing the most appropriate method for problems at hand. Solutions developed in the game-theoretic framework almost always assume a rational game. In addition, each player is assumed to have a certain amount of knowledge about the opponent. Similarly, non-game theoretic methods often make assumptions on the opponent's knowledge, the distribution of corrupted data, and available computing resources. In practice, adversaries are seldom optimal and the knowledge and the resources they possess are hard to assess. For classification problems, the common assumption is that data are independently and identically distributed. This assumption is easily violated when there is an active adversary who modifies data to influence the prediction. When data is constantly modified in an unpredictable way, training data would never be sufficient to induce an accurate classifier. On the positive side, at training time we can explore the feature space and find the most effective direction for the adversary to move data in the feature space to influence the classifier. Once we find such a direction, we can improve the classifier by countering these potential moves.

While in Chapter 10 we discuss adversarial support vector machine learning, the learning model we discuss in this chapter is the *relevance vector machine* (RVM). Similar to the support vector machine method, the RVM [TIPP2001] is a sparse linearly parameterized model. It is built on a Bayesian framework of the sparse model. Unlike the support vector machine in which a penalty term is introduced to avoid over-fitting the model parameters, the relevance vector machine model introduces a prior over the weights in the form of a set of hyperparameters, one associated independently with each weight. Very large values of the hyperparameters (corresponding to zero-weights) imply irrelevant inputs. Training data points associated with the remaining non-zero weights are referred to as *relevance vectors*. The relevance vector machine typically use much fewer kernel functions compared to the SVM.

In this chapter, we propose a sparse relevance vector machine ensemble for adversarial learning. The basic idea of this approach is to learn an individual kernel parameter η_i for each dimension d_i in the input space. The parameters are iteratively estimated from the data along with the weights and the hyperparameters associated with the weights. The kernel parameters are updated in each iteration so that the likelihood of the positive (malicious) data points are minimized. This

DOI: 10.1201/9781003081845-19

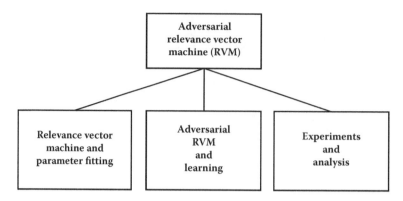

FIGURE 11.1 Adversarial learning using relevance vector machine ensembles.

essentially models adversarial attack as if the adversary were granted access to the internal states of the learning algorithm. Instead of using fixed kernel parameters, we search for kernel parameters that simulate worst-case attacks while the learning algorithm is updating the weights and the weight priors of a relevance vector machine. We learn M such models and combine them to form the final hypothesis.

Our main contributions are:

- Extending the sparse Bayesian relevance vector machine model to counter adversarial attacks;
- Developing a kernel parameter fitting technique to model adversarial attacks within the RVM framework.

The use of individualized kernel parameters has been shown beneficial to kernel-based learning [TIPP2001]; however, this is the first time it is applied to adversarial learning.

The rest of the chapter is organized as follows. Section 11.2 presents the related work in adversarial learning. Section 11.3 discusses the relevance vector machine model. Section 11.4 presents the gradient-based method for modeling adversarial attacks and Section 11.5 presents experimental results on both artificial and real datasets. Section 11.6 concludes our work and discusses future directions. For more details we refer to [ZHOU2012b]. Figure 11.1 illustrates the concepts discussed in this chapter.

11.2 RELATED WORK

There are several theoretical conclusions regarding bounds on malicious noise rate and learning accuracy. Kearns and Li [KEAR1993] prove theoretical upper bounds on tolerable malicious error rates in the sample. They assume the adversary can generate malicious errors with an unknown and unpredictable nature. Bshouty et al. [BSHO1999] introduce a variant of the PAC learning model for learning in the presence of nasty noise. They prove that when the sample noise rate is η no learning algorithm can learn non-trivial concept classes with accuracy less than 2η. Auer and Cesa-Bianchi [AUER1998] present an online learning model for learning with corrupted data. They extend the "Closure Algorithm" and prove a worst case mistake bound for learning an arbitrary intersection-closed concept class. Lowed and Meek [LOWD2005] present an algorithm that finds the instance with minimal adversarial cost. They refer to this algorithm as an adversarial classifier reverse engineering (ACRE) algorithm. Adversarial learning problems have been extensively studied in the framework of game theory. Dalvi et al. [DALVI2004] consider the learning problem as a game between two cost-sensitive opponents. The adversary always plays optimal strategies.

Given a cost function, their algorithm predicts the class that maximizes the conditional utility. Kantarcioglu et al. [KANT2011] present a simulated annealing and genetic algorithm to search for a Nash equilibrium for choosing an optimal set of attributes. They assume the two players know each other's payoff function. Similar work with improvement on how Nash strategies are played has also been proposed [BRÜC2009, LIU2010]. Brückner and Scheffer [BRÜC2011] present an optimal game by assuming the adversaries always behave rationally. Their algorithm does not require a unique equilibrium.

In a slightly different research avenue, robust learning techniques have been proposed for handling classification-time noise [DEKE2008, DEKE2010, LANC2002, TEO2007]. Globerson and Roweis [GLOB2006] consider classification-time feature deletion. They present an SVM algorithm that constructs an optimal classifier under a pre-defined constraint. El Ghaoui et al. [GHAO2003] present a minimax strategy for training data bounded by hyper-rectangles. They minimize the worst-case loss over data in given intervals.

Zhou et al. [ZHOU2012a] present two attack models for which optimal learning strategies are derived. They formulate a convex optimization problem in which the constraint is defined over the sample space based on the proposed attack models. They demonstrate that their adversarial SVM model is more resilient to adversarial attacks compared to the standard SVM and one-class SVM models.

11.3 RELEVANCE VECTOR MACHINE

Given a set of N training data (x_i, y_i), $i = 1, ..., N$, where $x_i \in \mathbb{R}^d$ re d-dimensional data points, and $y_i \{0, 1\}$ are the labels, a function $h(x)$ over the input space is inferred in the following linearly weighted form:

$$h(x; w) = w^T \varphi(x)$$

where $\varphi(x)$ represents basis functions, and

$$\varphi(x) = [1, K(x, x_1), K(x, x_2), ..., K(x, x_N)]$$

where $K(x, x_i)$ is a kernel function. For a binary classification problem, the posterior probability of the class membership given x as the input is:

$$p(y|w) = \prod_{i=1}^{N} g(h(x_i; w))^{y_i} [1 - g(h(x_i; w))]^{1-y_i} \qquad (11.1)$$

where $g(t)$ is the sigmoid function $g(t) = 1/(1 + e^{-t})$ applied to t.

Since there are as many weight parameters as the training examples, the model would suffer over-fitting. To avoid over-fitting, a zero-mean Gaussian prior is defined over the weights, with each prior controlled by its own hyperparameter α. Therefore,

$$p(w|\alpha) = \prod_{0}^{N} N(w_i|0, \alpha_i^{-1})$$

where α_i is the hyperparameter of w_i. The assignment of an individual hyperparameter to each weight gives an equivalent regularization penalty term. When a hyperparameter has a very large value (often approaching infinity), the regularizing effect becomes so large that the corresponding weight parameter rapidly converges to zero and thus the corresponding basis function can be pruned. When a hyperparameter has a small value, the prior has very little effect on the weight parameter it moderates, and therefore the corresponding basis function $\varphi_k(x)$ is a relevant feature, and the example x_k it centers is selected as a relevant vector.

Since the weight posterior $p(w|y, \alpha)$ and the marginal likelihood $p(y|\alpha)$ cannot be computed analytically, Tipping [TIPP2001] adopted a Laplacian approximation method to iteratively estimate the posterior covariance for a Gaussian approximation to $p(w|y, \alpha)$ centered at the mean $\bar{w}$. The mean and the covariance are then used to optimize the hyperparameter α. Details can be found in his work [TIPP2001].

Within the Bayesian framework of the relevance vector machine, we introduce another set of parameters that directly weigh the difference between two vectors in each dimension in the input space. In the next section, we discuss the use of individual kernel parameters to model adversarial attacks.

11.4   KERNEL PARAMETER FITTING

11.4.1   OUR APPROACH

The RVM training process iteratively updates the weight vector w and the hyperparameter vector α. Imagine in each iteration the adversary has an opportunity to modify the training data, particularly the positive (malicious) training data, so that it could cross the decision boundary inferred in the current iteration. What would be the best strategy for the adversary to modify the data? If the adversary has the freedom to move each data point in his own favor, he would follow the directions that increase the likelihood of misclassifying a positive instance the greatest. Before we discuss the technique to search for this direction, we first discuss the kernel and its input scale parameters.

11.4.2   KERNEL PARAMETER VECTOR

Consider the RBF kernel

$$K(x_i, x_j) = \exp(-\eta \| (x_i - x_j) \|^2)$$

where $\eta = (\eta_1, ..., \eta_d)$ is a vector of d parameters, and η_k is its kth parameter preceding the squared distance $(x_{ik} - x_{jk})^2$ in the kth input dimension. Normally, there is only one kernel parameter and its value is typically determined through cross-validations. We use individual kernel parameters so that we can model adversarial data modification in each dimension. For example, when the adversary modifies the kth dimension such that $x_{ik} \approx x_{jk}$, the same effect can be achieved by having $\eta_k \approx 0$. Therefore, by adjusting the kernel parameter of the kth dimension of the input, we could model adversarial attacks in both the input space and the feature space. We can then update the weight parameter and the corresponding hyperparameters to counter the attacks.

Below we illustrate the typical RBF Kernel and the RBF Kernel that we use.

Typical RBF kernel

$$K(x_i, x_j) = \exp(-\eta \| (x_i - x_j) \|^2)$$

Instead, we use RBF with,

$$\eta = (\eta_1, \ldots, \eta_d)$$
$$K(x_i, x_j) = \exp(-\|\eta \cdot (x_i - x_j)\|^2)$$

That is,

$$K(x_i, x_j) = \exp\left(-\sum_{k=1}^{d} \eta_k \cdot (x_{ik} - x_{jk})^2\right)$$

11.4.3 ATTACKS MINIMIZING THE LOG-LIKELIHOOD

Our motivation is to determine the adversary's behavior and shift the boundary line of the RVM appropriately. Figure 11.2 illustrates our motivation.

We model adversarial data corruption by introducing individual kernel parameters. Learning is with respect to the worst case attacks via kernel parameter fitting. Assuming the adversary is only interested in disguising positive data during RVM training we search for a kernel parameter vector η that renders the most effective attacks on positive training instances. (This is a reasonable assumption since it is typically harder for adversaries to influence negative (legitimate) data.)

With a given w and α, we update η in the direction that decrease $\mathcal{L}_+$, the log-likelihood of the posterior distribution $p(y|)$ given in Equation (11.1) for all positive instances. Taking the logarithm of both sides of Equation (11.1), we have:

$$log(p(t|w)) = \sum_{i=1}^{N}\left[y_i log(\sigma_i) + (1 - y_i)(1 - log(\sigma_i))\right] \qquad (11.2)$$

where $\sigma_i = g(h(x_i; w))$ is the output of the sigmoid function. Let $\mathcal{L} = log(p(t|w)) = \mathcal{L}_+ + \mathcal{L}_-$, where

$$\mathcal{L}_+ = \sum_{i=1}^{N} y_i log(\sigma_i) \text{ and } \mathcal{L}_- \sum_{i=1}^{N} (1 - y_i)(1 - log(\sigma_i)).$$

The gradient of $\mathcal{L}$ given in (11.2) with respect to the η_k is:

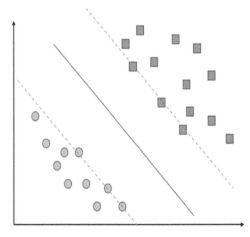

FIGURE 11.2 Boundary line separates the good instances (circles) from the bad instances (squares).

$$\frac{\partial \mathcal{L}}{\partial \eta k} = \sum_{i=1}^{N} \sum_{j=1}^{N} \frac{\partial \mathcal{L}}{\partial K_{ij}} \frac{\partial K_{ij}}{\partial \eta k}$$

$$= \sum_{i=1}^{N} \sum_{j=1}^{N} \left(\frac{\partial \mathcal{L}_+}{\partial K_{ij}} + \frac{\partial \mathcal{L}_-}{\partial K_{ij}} \right) \frac{\partial K_{ij}}{\partial \eta k}$$

where K_{ij} is the kernel function K applied to the ith and jth input x_i and x_j. To model attacks on the positive instances, we negate

$$\frac{\partial \mathcal{L}_+}{\partial K_{ij}}$$

and use the following for a gradient-based local optimization over η:

$$\mathcal{G} = \sum_{i=1}^{N} \sum_{j=1}^{N} \left(-\frac{\partial \mathcal{L}_+}{\partial K_{ij}} + \frac{\partial \mathcal{L}_-}{\partial K_{ij}} \right) \frac{\partial K_{ij}}{\partial \eta k}. \qquad (11.3)$$

Working out each term, we have:

$$\frac{\partial \mathcal{L}_+}{\partial K_{ij}} = y_i \cdot \frac{1}{\sigma_i} \cdot \frac{\partial \sigma_i}{\partial h} \cdot \frac{\partial h}{\partial K_{ij}}$$

$$= y_i \cdot (1 - \sigma_i) \cdot w_j$$

$$\frac{\partial \mathcal{L}_-}{\partial K_{ij}} = (1 - y_i) \cdot \frac{-1}{1 - \sigma_i} \cdot \frac{\partial \sigma_i}{\partial h} \cdot \frac{\partial h}{\partial K_{ij}}$$

$$= -(1 - y_i) \cdot \sigma_i \cdot w_j$$

$$\frac{\partial K_{ij}}{\partial \eta k} = -K_{ij} \cdot (x_{ik} - x_{jk})^2$$

Therefore,

$$\mathcal{G} = \sum_{i=1}^{N} \sum_{j=1}^{N} -(y_i - \sigma_i) \cdot w_j \cdot K_{ij} \cdot (x_{ik} - x_{jk})^2$$

which will be the basis for updating η in each iteration of training a relevance vector machine.

In summary, RVM adversarial learning can be described as follows: We assume the adversary only corrupts positive (malicious) data to evade detection. During RVM training, we search for an η that renders most effective attacks on positive data.

Log-likelihood of the posterior is as follows:

$$L = \log(p(t|w)) = L_+ + L_-$$

$$\frac{\partial L}{\partial \eta_k} = -\frac{\partial L_+}{\partial \eta_k} + \frac{\partial L_-}{\partial \eta_k}$$

$$-\frac{\partial L_+}{\partial \eta_k} = -\frac{\partial L_+}{\partial K_{ij}} \cdot \frac{\partial K_{ij}}{\partial \eta_k}$$

11.4.4 TRAINING ISSUES

During training, we need to iteratively update three parameters: the weight w, the hyperparameter α, and the kernel parameter vector η. One way to update these parameters is to optimize over $w|\alpha$

and η simultaneously. This allows us to find the optimal solution, but will be computationally intensive. Another way to do it is to interleave the update of w/α and η. For each $(w,)$, we search a few steps for $\Delta\eta$ based on the gradient of the log-likelihood, and update η by adding $\tau \cdot \Delta\eta$ to it, where $\tau > 0$ is the momentum. This approach may not lead to the desired solution, but is more efficient. In this chapter, we follow the local update approach. We train multiple adversarial RVM models, and select M models that satisfy $u_+ < \cdot u_-$, where u_+ denotes the uncertainty of predicting a positive training instance, and u_- the uncertainty of predicting a negative training instance, and $\rho \in (0, 1]$ is a positive constant. The smaller the ratio

$$\rho = \frac{u_+}{u_-},$$

the farther away the decision boundary from the positive training examples. That is, while the number of classifiers in the ensemble is less than M, train an adversarial RVM classifier h_i by learning w/α and η; then add h_i to the ensemble if

$$u_+ < \rho \cdot u_-$$

The uncertainties u_+ and u_- are estimated on the positive and negative training data as follows:

$$u_+ = \frac{\sum_{i=1}^{N} y_i \cdot (1 - h(x_i; w))}{\sum_{i=1}^{N} y_i} \tag{11.4}$$

$$u_- = \frac{\sum_{i=1}^{N} (1 - y_i) \cdot h(x_i; w)}{\sum_{i=1}^{N} (1 - y_i)} \tag{11.5}$$

where

$$\sum_{i=1}^{N} y_i$$

is the total number of positive training instances, and

$$\sum_{i=1}^{N} (1 - y_i)$$

is the number of negative training instances. We select M such models and combine them to make the final predications through majority vote.

11.4.5   ADVERSARIAL RVM LEARNING ALGORITHM

We now present the algorithm of adversarial RVM learning, namely *AD-RVM*. Given a set of training data, we first initialize the value of α and use it to update the weight vector w; next, we update the kernel parameter vector η with the given w and α; finally we update the hyperparameter α. The process iterates for a pre-defined maximum number of rounds. We train multiple such classifiers and select M classifiers that satisfy $\rho u_+ < u_-$ to form an ensemble. The detailed algorithm is given in Algorithm 11.1.

ALGORITHM 11.1   THE *AD-RVM* ALGORITHM

Input: L, T – training and test data
    w, α – weight and hyperparameter
    η – kernel parameter
    M – number of classifiers in the ensemble
    τ – momentum of updating η in each iteration
    I_w – number of iterations updating w and α
    I_η – number of inner cycles updating η
Output: ensemble $\{h_1, h_2, ..., h_M\}$
   1: Initialize α
   2: **repeat**
   3:    **for** $i = 1$ **to** I_w **do**
   4:       Update w with current α values
   5:       **for** $i = 1$ **to** I_η **do**
   6:          Compute $\Delta\eta$ using Equation (11.3)
   7:          $\eta = \eta + \tau\,\Delta\eta$
   8:          Update feature space with new kernel parameters // *end for*
   9:       Solve for α with w and η
  10:    Compute u_+ and u_- using Equations (11.4) and (11.5) // *end for*
  11:    **if** $\rho \cdot u_+ < u_-$ **then**
  12:       add $h(w, \alpha, \eta)$ to the ensemble
  13: **until** M RVMs are added to the ensemble
  14: **return** $\{h_1, h_2, ..., h_M\}$

11.5   EXPERIMENTAL RESULTS

11.5.1   DATASETS

We used one artificial dataset and two real datasets in our experiments. We model the attacks at classification time by moving positive test instances closer to randomly selected negative instances plus local random noise. Attacks on the test data are designed to challenge all the learning models at increasingly more difficult levels. The difficulty is controlled using the attack factor f_{attack}. More specifically,

$$x_{ij}^+ = x_{ij}^+ + f_{attack} \cdot (x_{ij}^- - x_{ij}^+) + \epsilon \qquad (11.6)$$

where ϵ is local random noise. Notice $f_{attack} = 1$ models the worst case attacks where a positive data point is arbitrarily close to a negative one within the range of the random local noise. Figure 11.3 illustrates the attack with $f_{attack} = 0.3$.

We compare four learning models: AD-RVM, RVM, SVM, and One-class SVM on the three datasets. All results reported are averaged over 10 random runs.

11.5.2   EXPERIMENTS ON THE ARTIFICIAL DATASET

The synthetic dataset is generated from a bivariate normal distribution with specified means $(-5.0, -6.0)$ and $(5.0, 6.0)$, and covariance matrix

2–class synthetic data with attacks

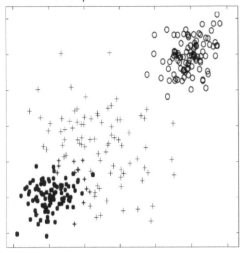

FIGURE 11.3 Attack factor = 0.3. White dots: negative data, black dots: positive data before attacks, black "+": positive data after attacks.

$$\begin{pmatrix} 1.0 & 0.5 \\ 0.5 & 2.0 \end{pmatrix}.$$

We first consider the cases where the training data is clean and only the test data has been corrupted. Attacks on the test data are created using Equation (11.6). Table 11.1 shows the classification performance on this set of data in terms of error rates. The ρ value which controls the uncertainty of predicting positive and negative data is chosen as 0.67. We discuss the impact of ρ later.

From Table 11.1, we can see that adversarial RVM algorithm has much lower error rates compared to its non-adversarial self, SVM, and one-class SVM. The improvement is attributed to its adjustment to the decision boundary to counter adversarial attacks. The adjustment includes shifting and curving toward the negative data points, as shown in Figure 11.4.

In forming the ensemble, we use the positive and negative uncertainty ratio to determine which hypothesis is included in the ensemble. The higher the ratio, the more confident the classifier is when predicting an instance as a positive example. Note that this is necessary because we took the non-simultaneous updating approach in searching for the kernel parameters. This approach is less reliable than the more expensive simultaneous updating technique. However, we gain speed and, with little additional effort, accuracy as well. We now illustrate the impact of the ρ value used in the uncertainty test. Smaller ρ values imply more bias against the negative prediction, while larger values have less bias.

Figure 11.5 illustrates the impact of the ρ values on the classification errors using AD-RVM. The y-axis shows the improvement of error rates of AD-RVM compared to RVM without adversarial treatment. As can be observed, the lower the ρ value, the more improvement achieved. However, if the ρ value is set too small, eventually false positives will start increasing and defeating the purpose of adversarial learning. The lower bound of the ρ value needs to be carefully set, especially when there are dense positive and negative data points distributed near the decision boundary.

We also tested cases where the training data is not clean. Again, AD-RVM is clearly more robust against adversarial attacks although its superiority becomes less marked. Due to space limitations, we do not report the results here.

Figure 11.6 illustrates the decision boundary learned from corrupted training datasets. Figure 11.6(a) shows how the decision boundary can be forced to move drastically closer to the

TABLE 11.1

Classification errors of AD-RVM, RVM, SVM, and 1-CLASS SVM on synthetic data. Best results are bolded

	f_{attack}				
	0.1	**0.3**	**0.5**	**0.7**	**0.9**
AD-RVM	**0.0025**	**0.0175**	**0.1435**	**0.3205**	**0.4500**
RVM	0.0100	0.0810	0.2542	0.4305	0.5000
SVM	0.0105	0.0705	0.2500	0.4355	0.4910
1-class SVM	0.0059	0.1310	0.5000	0.5000	0.5000

(a)

RVM Classification: the decision boundary of the synthetic data

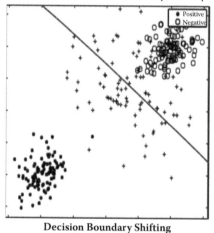

Decision Boundary Shifting

(b)

RVM Classification: the decision boundary of the synthetic data

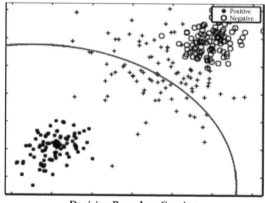

Decision Boundary Curving

FIGURE 11.4   Adjustment to decision boundary to take into account potential adversarial attacks. Solid lines in the plots illustrate the decision boundary. (a) Decision Boundary Shifting; (b) Decision Boundary Curving.

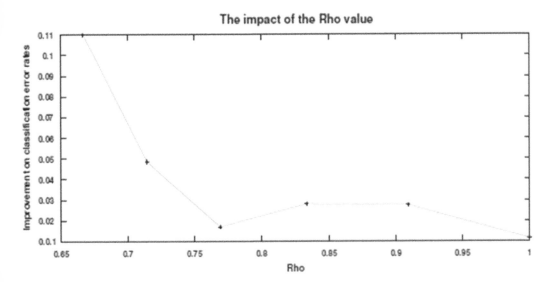

FIGURE 11.5   The impact of the ρ (rho) values. Smaller ρ values has higher inherent bias against negative class membership.

negative side with $f_{attack} = 0.1$ on the test data. The ρ value is set to 0.67. A slightly better decision boundary is learned with $\rho = 0.76$ as shown in Figure 11.6(b). This experiment reminds us of the importance of setting the lower bound of the ρ value. When the ρ value is too small, false positives become more likely in the output. In practice, we suggest the ρ value not be greater than 0.5. However, in any domain where adversarial attacks could be very aggressive, a smaller ρ value is preferred.

Like any other kernel-based approaches, it is important to select the initial η value. Small η values may cause the learning model over-sensitive to the training samples. Large η vales may lead to serious over-fitting. On the negative side, this may require cross-validation, adding additional computational cost. On the positive side, inappropriate initial η values often quickly lead to deterioration to non-positive definite feature vector, which causes the solver to terminate prematurely. If this happens, it often means a larger η value is required.

11.5.3   EXPERIMENTS ON REAL DATASETS

The two real datasets used in our experiments are: *spam base* from the UCI data repository (http://archive.ics.uci.edu/ml), and *web spam* from the LibSVM website (http://www.csie.ntu.edu.tw/~cjlin/libsvmtools/datasets/).

Both datasets are collected from applications typically running in an adversarial environment.

In the *spam base* dataset, there are 4,601 e-mail examples in total, among which 39.4% is spam. Each example is represented with 57 attributes and one class label. In our experiment, the dataset was divided into two equal halves, one for training and the other for testing. Five percent of the training data is randomly sampled to build the four learning models in each run. The results are averaged over 10 random runs. Table 11.2 shows the classification error rates of the four learning algorithms. The one-class SVM output the best results when f_{attack} 0.5 while our adversarial RVM algorithm ranked second and had a better performance than RVM and SVM. Our AD-RVM outperformed all the other algorithms when $f_{attack} > 0.5$.

The *web spam* dataset is the unigram version from the LibSVM website. There are 254 features in each example. We further reduce the number of features to 50. The total number of instances is 350,000. We used one-half for training and the other half for testing. We randomly selected 2% of

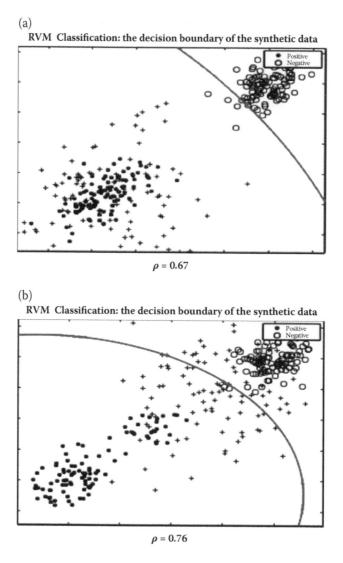

(a)
RVM Classification: the decision boundary of the synthetic data

$\rho = 0.67$

(b)
RVM Classification: the decision boundary of the synthetic data

$\rho = 0.76$

FIGURE 11.6 Adjustment to decision boundary to take into account potential adversarial attacks. Sold lines in the plots illustrate the decision boundary. (a) Rho value = 0.67; (b) Rho value = 0.76.

the samples in the training set to build the learning models. The results are averaged over 10 random runs and are shown in Table 11.3. As can be observed, adversarial-RVM is clearly superior to the other three models.

11.6   SUMMARY AND DIRECTIONS

Data mining tasks are made more complicated when adversaries attack by modifying malicious data to evade detection. The main challenge lies in finding a robust learning model that is insensitive to unpredictable malicious data distribution. In this chapter, we present a sparse relevance vector machine ensemble for adversarial learning. The novelty of our work is the use of individualized kernel parameters to model potential adversarial attacks during model training. We allow the kernel parameters to drift in the direction that minimizes the likelihood of the positive data. This step is interleaved with learning the weights and the weight priors of a relevance vector

TABLE 11.2

Classification errors of AD-RVM, RVM, SVM, and 1-CLASS SVM on the spam base dataset. Best results are bolded

| | f_{attack} | | | | |
	0.1	0.3	0.5	0.7	0.9
AD-RVM	0.3158	0.3270	0.3368	**0.3438**	**0.3809**
RVM	0.3875	0.3753	0.3775	0.3899	0.3902
SVM	0.3641	0.3751	0.3793	0.4149	0.4079
1-class SVM	**0.3127**	**0.3147**	**0.3248**	0.3555	0.4011

TABLE 11.3

Classification errors of AD-RVM, RVM, SVM, and 1-CLASS SVM on the web spam dataset. Best results are bolded

| | f_{attack} | | | | |
	0.1	0.3	0.5	0.7	0.9
AD-RVM	0.2426	**0.2926**	**0.3373**	**0.4945**	**0.5866**
RVM	**0.2355**	0.3169	0.4541	0.5560	0.5876
SVM	0.2725	0.4725	0.5604	0.6061	0.6061
One-class SVM	0.3155	0.5625	0.5945	0.6009	0.5997

machine. Our empirical results demonstrate that an ensemble of such relevance vector machine models is more robust to adversarial attacks.

We present a sparse Bayesian adversarial learning model. The algorithm sets individual kernel parameters to model adversarial attacks in the feature space by minimizing the log-likelihood of the positive instances in the training set. The learning models trained under this setup are more robust against attacks including the very aggressive ones. The open problem is to discover an efficient approach to simultaneously update the kernel and the learning parameters. The solution would help find the optimal learning model against the worst case attacks in the sample space.

REFERENCES

[AUER1998] P. Auer, N. Cesa-Bianchi, On-Line Learning with Malicious Noise and the Closure Algorithm, *Annals of Mathematics and Artificial Intelligence*, Volume 23, #1–2, 1998, 83–99.

[BRÜC2009] M. Bruckner, T. Scheffer, Nash Equilibria of Static Prediction Games, *Advances in Neural Information Processing Systems*, MIT Press, 2009.

[BRÜC2011] M. Bruckner, T. Scheffer, Stackelberg Games for Adversarial Prediction Problems, *Proceedings of the 17th ACM SIGKDD*, ACM, 2011.

[BSHO1999] N.H. Bshouty, N. Eiron, E. Kushilevitz, PAC Learning with Nasty Noise, *Theoretical Computer Science*, Volume 288, 1999, 2002.

[DALVI2004] N. Dalvi, P. Domingos, Mausam, S. Sanghai, D. Verma, Adversarial Classification, *Proceedings of the Tenth ACM SIGKDD*, ACM, 2004, pp. 99–108.

[DEKE2008] O. Dekel, O. Shamir, Learning to Classify with Missing and Corrupted Features, *Proceedings of the International Conference on Machine Learning*, ACM, 2008, pp. 216–223.

[DEKE2010] O. Dekel, O. Shamir, L. Xiao, Learning to Classify with Missing and Corrupted Features, *Machine Learning*, Volume 81, #2, 2010, 149–178.

[GHAO2003] L. El Ghaoui, G.R.G. Lanckriet, G. Natsoulis, Robust Classification with Interval Data, EECS Department, Tech. Rep. UCB/CSD-03-1279, UC Berkeley, October 2003.

[GLOB2006] A. Globerson, S. Roweis, Nightmare at Test Time: Robust Learning by Feature Deletion, *Proceedings of the 23rd ICML*, ACM, 2006, pp. 353–360.

[KANT2011] M. Kantarcioglu, B. Xi, C. Clifton, Classifier Evaluation and Attribute Selection against Active Adversaries, *Data Mining and Knowledge Discovery*, Volume 22, January 2011, 291–335.

[KEAR1993] M. Kearns, M. Li, Learning in the Presence of Malicious Errors, *SIAM Journal of Computing*, Volume 22, 1993, 807–837.

[LANC2002] G.R.G. Lanckriet, L.E. Ghaoui, C. Bhattacharyya, M.I. Jordan, A Robust Minimax Approach to Classification, *Journal of Machine Learning Research*, Volume 3, 2002, 555–582.

[LIU2010] W. Liu, S. Chawla, Mining Adversarial Patterns via Regularized Loss Minimization, *Machine Learning*, Volume 81, October 2010, 69–83.

[LOWD2005] D. Lowd, C. Meek, Adversarial Learning, *Proceedings of the Eleventh ACM SIGKDD International Conference on Knowledge Discovery in Data Mining, Chicago, IL*, August 2005, pp. 641–647.

[TEO2007] C.H. Teo, A. Globerson, S.T. Roweis, A.J. Smola, Convex Learning with Invariances, Proceedings of the 20th International Conference on Neural Information Processing Systems (NIPS), *Vancouver, Canada* , December 2007, pp. 1489–1496.

[TIPP2001] M.E. Tipping, Sparse Bayesian Learning and the Relevance Vector Machine, *Journal of Machine Learning Research*, Volume 1, September 2001, 211–244.

[ZHOU2012a] Y. Zhou, M. Kantarcioglu, B. Thuraisingham, B. Xi, Adversarial Support Vector Machine Learning, *Proceedings of the 18th ACM SIGKDD*, ACM, 2012, pp. 1059–1067.

[ZHOU2012b] Y. Zhou, M. Kantarcioglu, B.M. Thuraisingham, Sparse Bayesian Adversarial Learning Using Relevance Vector Machine Ensembles, ICDM 2012, pp. 1206–1211.

12 Privacy Preserving Decision Trees

12.1 INTRODUCTION

While Chapters 10 and 11 focused on security-aware data science, in this chapter we discuss privacy-aware data science. In particular, we discuss privacy preserving data mining with decision trees as an example. Data mining techniques (which have now evolved into machine learning and data science techniques) are used to derive patterns from massive amounts of data [THUR1998]. However, such techniques could extract nuggets that are previously known. These nuggets could violate individual privacy [THUR2002]. Due to increasing concerns related to privacy, various privacy-preserving data mining techniques have been developed to address different privacy issues [THUR2005]. These include privacy preserving association rule mining techniques and privacy preserving decision trees [AGRA2000, AGGA2004, LIU2009]. The idea behind privacy preserving data mining is to randomize and/or perturb the data and then carry out data mining. This way the sensitive data could be kept private. Figure 12.1 illustrates the idea behind privacy preserving data mining.

As stated in Chapter 3, privacy preserving data mining techniques usually operate under various assumptions and employ different methods. The previous works mainly fall into two categories: (1) perturbation- and randomization-based approaches and (2) secure multiparty computation-based approaches. In the case of perturbation-based approaches, the data are perturbed so that the sensitive data could be kept private. In the case of the randomized approach, random values are introduced to the data. In the case of secure multiparty computation-based approaches, the idea is for each party to encrypt its secret. Privacy preserving data mining is carried out on the encrypted secrets. The final results are divulged to the parties. However, each party's secret is only known to that party.

The earlier perturbation and randomization approaches have a step to reconstruct the original data distribution. More recent research in this area adopts different data distortion methods or modifies the data mining techniques to make it more suitable to the perturbation scenario. Secure multiparty computation approaches which employ cryptographic tools to build data mining models face high communication and computation costs, especially when the number of parties participating in the computation is large.

In this chapter, we focus on the perturbation method that is extensively used in privacy preserving data mining. It differs from several of the previous techniques in that we build data mining models directly from the perturbed data without trying to solve the general data distribution reconstruction as an intermediate step. In our solution, we modify the data mining algorithms so that they can be directly used on the perturbed data. In other words, we directly build a classifier for the original data set from the perturbed training data set.

More precisely, we describe a modified C4.5 [QUIN1993] decision tree classifier that can deal with perturbed numeric continuous attributes. Our privacy preserving decision tree C4.5 (PPDTC4.5) classifier uses perturbed training data, and builds a decision tree model which could be used to classify the original or perturbed data sets. Our experiments have shown that our PPDTC4.5 classifier can obtain a high degree of accuracy when used to classify the original data set. We chose the decision trees for this study due to the fact that many of the prior approaches have focused on privacy preserving association rule mining. Also, our effort on privacy preserving decision trees is part of a larger effort on developing privacy aware approaches for decision trees [LIU2009].

This chapter is organized as follows: Section 12.2 describes related work. Section 12.3 introduces a privacy metric system used to measure privacy in our work. Section 12.4 shows the

DOI: 10.1201/9781003081845-20

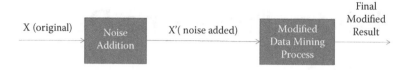

FIGURE 12.1   Privacy Preserving Data Mining.

construction of the decision tree. Section 12.5 describes how to build Naive Bayesian models from the perturbed data sets. In Section 12.6, we explain our PPDTC4.5 in detail. Section 12.7 presents our experimental results. In Section 12.8, we conclude with a discussion of future work.

12.2   RELATED WORK AND MOTIVATION

Previous work in privacy-preserving data mining has addressed two issues. In one, the aim is to preserve customer privacy by perturbing the data values [AGRA2000]. In this scheme random noise data is introduced to distort sensitive values, and the distribution of the random data is used to generate a new data distribution which is close to the original data distribution without revealing the original data values. The estimated original data distribution is used to reconstruct the data, and data mining techniques, such as classifiers and association rules are applied to the reconstructed data set. Later refinement of this approach has tightened estimation of original values based on the distorted data [AGRA2000]. The data distortion approach has also been applied to Boolean values in research work [DU2003, EVFI2002, RIZV2002]. Perturbation methods and their privacy protection have been criticized because some methods may derive private information from the reconstruction step [KARG2003].

Different to the original noise additive method in [AGRA2000], many distinctive perturbation methods have been proposed. One important category is multiplicative perturbation method. In the view of geometric property of the data, multiplying the original data values with a random noise matrix is to rotate the original data matrix, so it is also called rotated based perturbation. In [CHEN2005], authors have given a sound proof of "Rotationinvariant Classifiers" to show some data mining tools can be directly applied to the rotation based perturbed data. In the later work [LIU2006], Liu et al. have proposed multiplicative random projection which provided more enhanced privacy protection. There are some other interesting techniques, such as condensation based approach [AGRA2000], matrix decomposition [XU2006] and so on. As pointed out in [LIU2007], these recently research works on perturbation-based approaches apply the data mining techniques directly on the perturbed data skipping the reconstruction step. Choosing the suitable data mining techniques is determined by the method which noise has been introduced. To our knowledge, only a few efforts focus on mapping or modifying the data mining techniques to meet the perturbation data needs.

The other approach uses cryptographic tools to build data mining models. For example, in [LIND2000], the goal is to securely build an ID3 decision tree where the training set is distributed between two parties. Different solutions were given to address different data mining problems using cryptographic techniques (e.g., [CLIF2002, KANT2004, and VAID2003]). This approach treats privacy-preserving data mining as a special case of secure multi-party computation and not only aims for preserving individual privacy but also tries to preserve leakage of any information other than the final result. But when the numbers of parties become bigger, the communication and computation cost grow exponentially.

Our approach is a modified C4.5 decision tree algorithm [QUIN1993] and adopts noise additive method. Our approach is suitable for the scenarios where many parties want to perform data mining, but each of them only has a small portion of the data. To get the global data mining patterns, the various parties must share their data, but each party has its privacy and security concerns. Our approach is the solution for such a situation. In our approach, each party perturbs its data according to the distribution of a pre-set random noise, and sends its perturbed data to the data miner. The data miner collects the perturbed data sets from each party, and also knows the distribution used to perturb the data. Based on this information, the data miner builds a classifier, and returns the classifier to every participating party. Then each party can use this classifier to classify its data. In this case, each party only knows its own data and the classifier, and it does not have any knowledge about the data of others. The data miner only has access to the perturbed data and the distribution of the noise data. This way, privacy is preserved, and the communication and computation costs for each party are minimized.

12.3 PRIVACY METRICS

In the work [AGRA2001], Agrawal and Aggarwal have proposed a privacy measure based on differential entropy. We briefly repeat the ideas here. The differential entropy h(A) of a random variable A is defined as follows:

$$h(A) = - \int_{\Omega_A} f_A(a) log_2 f_A(a) da \qquad (12.1)$$

where ΩA is the domain of A.

Actually $h(A)$ is a measure of uncertainty inherent in the value of A in the statistics. Agrawal and Aggarwal [AGRA2001] based on this, proposed that the privacy measure inherent in the random variable A as $\Pi(A)$.

$$\prod (A) = 2^{h(A)} \qquad (12.2)$$

For example, a random variable U distributed uniformly between 0 and a has privacy

$$\prod (U) = 2^{log_2(a)} = a.$$

Thus, if $\Pi(A) = 1$, then A has as much privacy as a random variable distributed uniformly in an interval of length 1. Furthermore, if,

$$f_B(x) = 2f_A(2x),$$

then, B offers half as much privacy as A. This can be easily illustrated as a random variable uniformly distributed over [0, 1] has half as much privacy as a random variable uniformly distributed over [0, 2]. In [AGRA2001], Agrawal and Aggarwal have also defined conditional privacy and information loss. For more detail please refer the original work [AGRA2001]. We choose this privacy measure in our work to quantify the privacy in our experiments.

12.4 OVERVIEW OF DECISION TREE CONSTRUCTION

We propose a modified C4.5 decision tree classifier which builds the decision tree from perturbed data and can be used to classify both the original and the perturbed data. The idea behind this approach is the following: when we consider the splitting point of the attribute, we consider the bias of the noise data set as well. We calculate the bias whenever we try to find the best attribute, the best split point and partition the training data. The C4.5 algorithm is an extension of the ID3 algorithm, and proposed by Quinlan in [QUIN1993]. After years of improvement, C4.5 algorithm is one of the best algorithms in handling numeric continuous attributes [QUIN1996]. It finds the best splitting attribute and the best splitting point of the numeric continuous attributes.

12.4.1 SPLITTING CRITERION

Splitting criterion is very important in building a decision tree. It decides which attribute to use for the splitting, and for the numeric continuous attribute, and also determines which value is used for this splitting. It determines whether a decision tree is efficient. It dramatically affects the classification accuracy. ID3 uses information gain as splitting criterion. C4.5 algorithm uses information gain ratio which takes the number of branches into account when examining an attribute. The formulas of information gain and gain ratio are given as follows:

$$Info(S) = - \sum_{j=1}^{k} \frac{freq(C_j, S)}{|S|} \times log_2 \left(\frac{freq(C_j, S)}{|S|} \right) \tag{12.3}$$

$$Info_{Test_A}(S) = \sum_{i=1}^{n} \frac{|S_i|}{|S|} \times Info(S_i) \tag{12.4}$$

$$gain(Test_A) = Info(S) - Info_{Test_A}(S) \tag{12.5}$$

$$splitInfo(Test_A) = - \sum_{i=1}^{n} \frac{|S_i|}{|S|} \times log_2 \left(\frac{|S_i|}{S} \right) \tag{12.6}$$

$$gainRatio(Test_A) = \frac{gain(Test_A)}{splitInfo(Test_A)} \tag{12.7}$$

Let S be the training set, $|S|$ is the number of instance in S, and $freq(C_i, S)$ is the number of instance that belongs to class i where i from 1, to n. $|S_I|$ is the number of instance in the category S_i. $Test_A$ is the attribute chosen.

12.4.2 DISCRETIZING CONTINUOUS ATTRIBUTES

Binary Split Approach C4.5 algorithm is also designed to handle numeric attributes. Instead of using the fix range, C4.5 algorithm searches among possible split points to find the best split point. Let us assume that a numeric attribute A_i has the values $\{x_1, x_2, ..., x_m\}$ in increasing order. C4.5 partitions the instances into two groups S_1 and S_2 where S_1consists of the values up to and including x_j, and S_2 consists those that have values greater than x_j. For each of these partitions, C4.5 computes the gain ratio and chooses the partition that maximizes the gain ratio.

12.4.3 STOPPING CRITERIA

The stopping criteria decides when to stop growing a decision tree. In C4.5 algorithm, the tree stops growing when one of the two criteria is met. One is that all the instances at the node have the same class label C_i; we say this node is pure. Another is when the number of instances at the node is less than or equal to a pre-set threshold number; we say this number is minimum instance number of the node. We use the same stopping criteria in our privacy preserving decision tree C4.5 (PPDTC4.5) too.

12.5 NAIVE BAYES CLASSIFIER CONSTRUCTION OVER PERTURBED DATA

As stated in [LIU2007], Naive Bayes classifier can be applied directly on the perturbed data. For the completeness, we briefly describe here.

12.5.1 NAIVE BAYES CLASSIFIER

The Naive Bayes classifier labels a new instance by assigning the most probable class value. Besides, it assumes that attribute values are conditionally independent given the class value to simplify the estimation of the required probabilities. Using the above assumptions, Naive Bayes classifier selects the most likely classification C_{nb}

$$C_{nb} = argmax_{C_j \in C} P(C_j) \prod_i P(X_i|C_j) \tag{12.8}$$

where $X = X_1, X_2, ..., X_n$ denotes the set of attributes, $C = C_1, C_2, .., C_d$ denotes the finite set of possible class labels, and C_{nb} denotes the class label output by the Naive Bayes classifier [MITC1997].

Clearly, we need to calculate the probabilities $P(X_i = x|C_j)$ used in the Equation 12.8 based on the training data. In practice, for numeric attributes, $P(X_i = x|C_j)$ is estimated by using Gaussian distribution $N(\mu_{ij}, \sigma_{ij}^2)$. The required parameters, $\mu_{ij} = E(X_i|c_j)$ and $\sigma_{ij}^2 = Var(X_i|C_j)$, are estimated by using the training data. Next, we show how to estimate the parameters, μ_{ij} and σ_{ij}^2, using the perturbed training data.

12.5.2 OVER PERTURBED NUMERIC DATA

We need to estimate μ_{ij} and, σ_{ij}^2 for each attribute X_i and for each class label C_j using the perturbed numeric data to construct a Naive Bayes classifier. In the perturbed data case, instead of the original attribute value X_i, we only see the $W_i = X_i + R$ values. Let w_{ij}^t be the ith attribute value of the tth training data instance with class label C_j. In addition, we assume that there are n instances with class label C_j.

We also know that $w_{ij}^t = x_{ij}^t + r_{ij}^t$, where r_{ij}^t is the randomly generated noise with mean zero and known variance σ_R^2. Using the above facts, we can show that the expected value of

$$\bar{w}_{ij} = \frac{1}{n} \cdot \sum_{t=1}^n (w_{ij}^t)$$

is equal to μ_{ij}.

As the sample variance

$$S^2 = \frac{1}{n-1} \cdot \sum_{t=1}^n (w_{ij}^t - \bar{w}_i j)^2$$

has an expected value $\sigma_{ij}^2 + \sigma_R^2$, we can use S^2 and the known σ_R^2 to estimate the σ_{ij}^2 (i.e., use $S^2 - \sigma_R^2$ to estimate σ_{ij}^2).

As a result, as long as we do not change the class labels, we can directly construct Naive Bayes classifier from the perturbed data. Even more, since the parameter estimations done by using the perturbed data and the original data have the same expected values, we should be able to get similar classification accuracy in both cases. To verify the above intuition, we have performed some experiments using the Naive Bayes classifier from the WEKA machine learning toolkit [WITT2005].

Using the same data set with all six numeric continuous attributes, we construct the Naive Bayes classifier from the original data set, and we get 79.7% classification accuracy. Similarly, if we directly construct the Naive Bayes classifier from the perturbed training data set and test it on the perturbed test set, we get 78% classification accuracy. As expected, the two classification accuracy values are very close.

12.6 PRIVACY PRESERVING DECISION TREE C4.5 (PPDTC4.5)

12.6.1 MOTIVATION

In this section, we will describe how to build a decision tree classifier from the perturbed training data set. We will show threshold and random path selection two different ways to build classifiers. The threshold algorithm gives reasonably good accuracy for classifying the original data set. The random path selection algorithm uses the probability as weight and finds good splitting points for the attributes. However, as we will see that randomly selecting the path to partition the training data set does not build a good decision tree classifier.

We include the random path selection algorithms mainly for comparison purposes as well as to provide some directions for future work to building decision tree classifiers to classify perturbed data set. We believe that with proper improvement on tight bounds of random variables R, the performance of random path selection algorithm can be improved.

The goal is to build a decision tree model from perturbed data which can classify the original data set or perturbed data set accurately. In our case, we do not know the original x_j values due to added noise. Instead, we observe $w_j = x_j + R$ where R is random noise which we know its distribution. Clearly, for a split point t for attribute A_i, if we know the x_j values, we use the following rule to split instances into S_1 and S_2:

$$split(x_j, t) = \begin{cases} S_1, & x_j \le t \\ S_2, & x_j > t \end{cases} \tag{12.9}$$

As we do not know the x_j values, therefore, we can only calculate the probability of w_j belongs to S_1 that for given split point t and w_j. Note that $P\,r\{w_j \in S_1\} = P\,r\{w_j - R \le t\} = P\,r\{w_j - t \le R\}$. As we know the cumulative distribution function of R, we can calculate the probability easily. Let p_{S1} $(w_j|t)$ is the probability that w_j belongs to S_1 given the split point t and w_j. Similarly, define p_{S2} $(w_j|t) = 1 - p_{S1}(w_j|t)$. In general, let us define $p_{S2}(w_j|t)$ is the probability that w_j belongs to set S. Now instead of splitting according to equation (12.9), we can use the $p_S(w_j|t)$ values to estimate the best split point and partition the w_j just as the original data x_j would have been partitioned.

12.6.2 SPLITTING CRITERION USING THRESHOLD

We can calculate the probability $p_{S1}(w_j|t)$, for given split point t for each w_j value. This $p_{S1}(w_j|t)$ value indicates the likelihood $w_j \in S_1$. We can set a threshold, and count the number of w_j having a class label C_j and $p_{S1}(w_j)$ value greater than the threshold. This can be expressed in the form of equation as follows:

$$freq'(C_j, S_i) = \sum_{w_j \in S_i} \left(I_{w_j \in C_j}, p_{Si}(w_j) > threshold \right) \tag{12.10}$$

In the above equation, we calculate the frequency of a class value by using the $p_{S1}(w_j)$. $I_{w_j \in C_j}$ is an indicator function and returns 1, if w_j has a class label C_j. The equation (12.3) is changed to as follows:

$$Info(S) = -\sum_{j=1}^{k} \frac{freq'(C_j, S)}{|S|} \times log_2\left(\frac{freq'(C_j, S)}{|S|}\right) \tag{12.11}$$

Using above equation (12.11), plus equations (12.4), (12.5), (12.6), and (12.7) we can find the best splitting attribute and the best splitting point for the numeric continuous attribute by maximizing the *gainRatio*.

12.6.3   SPLITTING TRAINING DATA BY THRESHOLD

The splitting criteria for the training data is straightforward.

$$splitThreshold(w_j, t) = \begin{cases} S_1, & p_{S_1}(w_j|t) > threshold \\ S_2, & p_{S_1}(w_j|t) \leq threshold \end{cases} \tag{12.12}$$

Notice that the condition $p_{S1}(w_j|t) >$ threshold is equivalent to the condition $p_{S2}(w_j|t) \leq (1 - threshold)$, vice versa. For example, condition pS1 (wj |t) > 0.2 is equivalent to the condition pS2 (wj |t) ≤ 0.8. Pseudo-code is shown in the Algorithm 12.1.

Using the threshold approach seems like a simple method, but setting the appropriate threshold that will lead to a successful classifier is not trivial. By definition, $p_{S1}(w_j|t)$ is the probability that w_j belongs to S_1 given the split point t and w_j. When the split point t and

---

ALGORITHM 12.1   PARTITION TRAINING INSTANCES USING THRESHOLD

1 *Partition (Node N)* ;
2 **if** *Stopping Criteria is Met* **then**
3 return;
4 **else**
5 Using *ThresholdSplittingCriterion* Compute the Best Attribute $Best_A$ and the Best Splitting Point t ;
6 **for** *each Instance $w_j$in Node N* **do**
7 Calculate the $p_{S1}(w_j|t) = p_1$
8 Based on the best splitting attribute $Best_A$
9 and the best splitting point t;
10 **if** $p_1 >$ *threshold* **then**
11 *addChild(N.leftChild, w_j)*;
12 **else**
13 *addChild(N.rightChild, w_j)*;
14 **end**
15 **end**
16 **end**
17 *Partition (N.leftChild)*;
18 *Partition (N.rightChild)*;

perturbed instance w_j are given, the only uncertainty is the random noise R. In another words, the choice of threshold is related to the distribution of the random noise. In our experiments, we have used both the Uniform and Gaussian distributions for random noise. The thresholds are different for these two kinds of distributions. For Gaussian distribution, when the threshold is set to 0.30, the classifier gives higher accuracy; for Uniform distribution, when the threshold is set to 0.50, the classifier gives higher accuracy. The experimental results are discussed in the next section.

Another good way to decide the threshold is to keep it flexible, just like what the C4.5 algorithm does to find the best splitting point t for the numeric continuous attribute. This would lead to good results, but the computation costs are increased.

12.6.4 CLASSIFYING THE ORIGINAL INSTANCE

Using the algorithm described in the previous two subsections, we choose the splitting attributes and splitting points that actually belong to the original data. We also partition the perturbed training data as decided by our estimation of its original values. This way we can build a decision tree classifier for the original data. Then, when we use it to classify the original data, we just classify the data based on whether an attribute value is less than or greater than the certain attribute splitting point. The pseudo-code of classifying the original data is shown in Algorithm 12.2.

12.6.5 SPLITTING CRITERION

Using probability as weight, we use the $p_{S1}(w_j|t)$ and $p_{S2}(w_j|t)$ values as weight to rewrite all the equations as follows:

$$freq''(C_j, S_i, S) = \sum_{w_j \in S} \left(I_{w_j \in C_j} \times p_{S_i}(w_j) \right) \tag{12.13}$$

ALGORITHM 12.2   CLASSIFY ORIGINAL INSTANCES

1 for *each Instance x_j in X from the root node* **do**
2 Classify(Node N, Instance x_j);
3 if *N is a leaf node* **then**
4 use the rule given at the leaf
5 return class value;
6 else
7 Based on the attribute A_i used in *N*
8 and the split point t;
9 if $x_j(A_i) \leq t$ **then**
10 return Classify(*N.leftChild*, x_j);
11 else
12 return Classify(*N.rightChild*, x_j);
13 end
14 end
15 end

In the above equation, we calculate the frequency of a class value by using the $p_{S1}(w_j)$ as weights. $I_{w_j \in C_j}$ is an indicator function and returns 1 if w_j has a class label C_j. To normalize, we need to calculate the sum of the total weights (i.e., sum of the all $p_{S1}(w_j)$ values)

$$w(S_i, S) = \sum_{w_j \in S} (p_{S_i}(w_j)) \tag{12.14}$$

Now using the above two definitions, we are ready to redefine the conditional entropy using the $p_{S1}(w_j)$ values.

$$Prob(S_i, S) = \frac{freq''(C_j, S_i, S)}{|w(S_i, S)|} \tag{12.15}$$

$$Info'(S_i, S) = - \sum_{j=1}^{k} Prob(S_i, S) \times log_2(Prob(S_i, S)) \tag{12.16}$$

$$Prob(S_i, S) = \frac{freq''(C_j, S_i, S)}{|w(S_i, S)|} \tag{12.17}$$

$$Info'(S_i, S) = - \sum_{j=1}^{k} Prob(S_i, S) \times log_2(Prob(S_i, S)) \tag{12.18}$$

Similarly, we need to update information gain of choosing an attribute A with split point t.

$$Info'_{Test_A}(S) = \sum_{i=1}^{2} \frac{|w(S_i, S)|}{|S|} \times Info'(S_i, S) \tag{12.19}$$

Also, in calculating the *splitInfo*, we need to use $w(S_i, S)$.

$$splitInfo'(Test_A) = - \sum_{i=1}^{n} \frac{|w(S_i, S)|}{|S|} \times log_2 \left(\frac{|w(S_i, S)|}{|S|} \right) \tag{12.20}$$

Now, we can plug the above modified definitions to original tests to choose the split point and attribute.

$$gain'(Test_A) = Info(S) - Info'_{Test_A}(S) \tag{12.21}$$

$$gainRatio'(Test_A) = \frac{gain'(Test_A)}{splitInfo'(Test_A)} \tag{12.22}$$

Now, we can use the (12.22) to choose a split point and an attribute. Please note that the main difference between the original equations used in C4.5 and ours is that we use the probability of being in a certain partition as a weight in the formulas. The rationale behind this modification is the following: If we write the original formulas, in clear form, we can see that there exists an implicit indicator function that assigns 0 or 1 based on the membership instances to set S_1 and set S_2. As we cannot be sure whether a certain instance is in S_1 or in S_2, we use the probability of being in S_1 or in S_2 as a weight.

12.6.6 SPLITTING TRAINING DATA SET USING RANDOM PATH SELECTION

This method is an alternative way to split the training data into two after finding a split point and an attribute. Again, in our implementation, we use a random split based on the $p_{S1}(w_j)$ and $p_{S2}(w_j)$ values.

$$splitRandom(w_j, t) = \begin{cases} S_1, & \text{with prob.} \quad p_{S_1}(w_j) \\ S_2, & \text{with prob.} \quad p_{S_2}(w_j) \end{cases} \qquad (12.23)$$

Pseudo-code is shown in Algorithm 12.3.

12.6.7 CLASSIFYING THE PERTURBED INSTANCE USING RANDOM PATH SELECTION

For each test instance, w_j in the perturbed data set W and for each chosen split point in the constructed tree, we calculate $p_{S1}(w_j) |t) = p_1$. Next, we place the instance to the left child of the node with prob p1 and to the right child with prob $1 - p_1$. We continue with this until we reach a leaf node. The Pseudo-code is shown in Algorithm 12.4.

12.7   EXPERIMENTAL RESULTS

12.7.1   OUR APPROACH

In our experiments, we use the data extracted from the census database 1994 ("Census Income" or "Income"), which can be downloaded from University of California, Irvine (UCI), machine

---

ALGORITHM 12.3   PARTITION TRAINING INSTANCES USING RANDOM CRITERIA

1 *Partition (Node N)*;
2 if *Stopping Criteria is Met* **then**
3 return;
4 else
5 Using *RandomSplittingCriterion* Compute the Best Attribute $Best_A$ and the Best Splitting Point t ;
6 for *each Instance $w_j$in Node N* **do**
7 Calculate the $p_{S1}(w_j|t) = p_1$
8 Based on attribute $Best_A$ and splitting point t;
9 Let R be a uniform random value between [0, 1];
10 if $R \le p_1$ **then**
11 *addChild(N.lef tChild, w_j)*;
12 else
13 *addChild(N.rightChild, w_j)*;
14 end
15 end
16 end
17 *Partition (N.leftChild)*;
18 *Partition (N.rightChild)*;

ALGORITHM 12.4   CLASSIFY NOISY INSTANCES

1 for *each Instance w_j in W from the root node* **do**
2 Classify(Node N, Instance w_j);
3 if *N is a leaf node* **then**
4 use the rule given at the leaf
5 return class value;
6 else
7 Calculate the $p_{S1}(w_j|t) = p_1$
8 Based on the attribute A_i used in N
9 and the split point t;
10 Let R be a uniform random value between [0, 1];
11 if $R \leq p_1$ **then**
12 return Classify(*N.leftChild*, w_j);
13 else
14 return Classify(*N.rightChild*, w_j);
15 end
16 end
17 end

---

learning database repository 1. This data set has 14 attributes, 6 continuous, and 8 nominal. It altogether has 48,842 instances, separate as training data 32,561 instances and testing data 16,281 instances. The data are used to predict whether the income exceeds 50K annually. We choose this data set to have fair comparison with reconstruction-based techniques that require relatively large data sets. Since, in this chapter, we focus on the numeric continuous attributes, we only keep the six numeric continuous attributes in our data set. Also, for efficiency purposes, we randomly choose 10,000 instances from the training data set, and keep all the instances in the testing data set.

We use the noise addition framework proposed in [AGRA2000], and add both Gaussian and Uniform random noise to each attribute. When using Gaussian random noise, we know that the variance σ^2 can dramatically affect the results. We use four different Gaussian distribution noise data with different variance values. To quantify the relative amount of noise added to actual data, we used the Signal-to-Noise Ratio (SNR), that is the ratio of variance .3 of actual data to variance σ^2 of noise data [KARG2003]. We also use the privacy measure mentioned in Section 12.2 to quantify the privacy loss. The Table 12.1 shows the five perturbed data sets with their SNR values and privacy measures. In our experiments, we only use one data set which perturbed by uniform noise, shown as data 5. We can see from Table 12.1, when the SNR value is higher, the variance σ^2 of noise data is lower, thus the perturbed data preserves less privacy. The uniform distributed noise is generated by a given data range. We can calculate the SNR for each attribute for uniform noise

---

TABLE 12.1
Privacy measure of different data sets

	Data 1	Data 2	Data 3	Data 4	Data 5
Noise Distribution	Gaussian	Gaussian	Gaussian	Gaussian	Uniform
SNR	1.7	1.3	1.0	0.5	N/A
Privacy loss	0.2183	0.1909	0.1619	0.1026	0.2604

data, in our experimental data set, the SNR values for six attributes are 1.3, 2.7, 1.2, 53.6, 1.9, and 1.1, respectively.

12.7.2 LOCAL VS. GLOBAL DATA MINING

First note that by local data mining, each participant mines its own data. By global data mining, we mean that the participants share the data and mine to obtain global patterns. As we have mentioned before, our approach is suitable for the scenarios where many parties are participating to perform global data mining without compromising their privacy. The data sets distributed among each party can be horizontally or vertically partitioned. Horizontally partitioned data means the instances are split across the parties, and vertically partitioned data means the attributes are split across the parties. Experimental results show that for both types of partitioning local data mining results are less accurate compared with those obtained from global data mining. This supports the fact that extracting information from globally shared data is better.

We use the data set described in the previous subsection with six attributes. We randomly choose instances to form small data sets with different sizes, denoted as group 1, group 2 to group 10. We apply standard C4.5 classifier on these data sets, and the accuracy numbers are shown in Table 12.2. It is clear that when the number of instances are increased, the C4.5 decision tree algorithm has better performance.

Similarly, we have removed some attributes from the "Income" data set, and then applied standard C4.5 decision tree classifier on the new data sets, and the accuracy of the classification results are shown in Table 12.3. We can see that when the attribute number is increased the C4.5 decision tree algorithm performs better.

12.7.3 RECONSTRUCTION-BASED APPROACHES RESULTS

For comparison purposes, we report the data mining results obtained by using original data distribution reconstruction methods. We apply two notable reconstruction techniques to the perturbed

TABLE 12.2
C4.5 decision tree classifier accuracy over horizontally partitioned data

Accuracy(%)	Data 1	Data 2	Data 3	Data 4	Data 5
50 Instances	73.47	74.23	73.13	73.23	73.63
100 Instances	78.54	73.33	77.43	78.13	75.63
Accuracy(%)	Data 6	Data 7	Data 8	Data 9	Data 10
50 Instances	74.63	72.37	74.23	76.27	77.73
100 Instances	78.77	75.4	78.13	76.2	77.77

TABLE 12.3
C4.5 decision tree classifier accuracy over vertically partitioned data

Accuracy(%)	2 Attributes	3 Attributes	4 Attributes
5k Instances	77.54	77.84	78.9
32k Instances	78.06	78.51	79.05

data set. The first technique is Bayesian inference estimation (BE)-based approach proposed by Agrawal et al [AGRA2000]. The second technique is the principal component analysis (PCA)-based approach proposed by Kargupta et al. [KARG2003]. Please refer to the original work for the algorithms' details. We apply the two techniques on the five data sets. We first reconstruct the original distribution, and then use this estimated distribution to build the data mining models. We perform three different tests to compare data mining accuracy. In the first case, we test the classifier on the reconstructed test data; in the second case, we test the classifier on the original test data; and in the third case, we test the classifier on the perturbed test data. The data mining models' prediction accuracy is shown in the Tables 12.5 and 12.6. As comparison Table 12.4 shows the data mining accuracy obtained directly from the perturbed data sets.

Our results indicate that both reconstruction techniques fail to produce good data mining models. This result is not surprising since, in general, estimating data distributions on finite data is a very hard problem. If we use this original data distribution reconstruction phase as a intermediate step to do privacy preserving data mining, we may not always get good performance results. In the work [LIU2007], the authors have investigated three different real world data sets, and the reconstruction-based approaches have failed on all those data sets. These results support our motivation of finding direct ways to perform privacy preserving data mining from perturbed data.

12.7.4 PPDTC4.5 CLASSIFIER ACCURACY

Using the data sets described earlier, we perform different experiments. Applying WEKA [WITT2005] C4.5 algorithm on the original training data set to build the decision tree, and classify the original testing data set, we get 83.40% accuracy. Table 12.4 shows the data mining accuracy when apply data mining tools directly on the perturbed data sets. Table 12.7 shows data mining accuracy of our proposed PPDTC4.5 algorithms. We can see, when we use our proposed PPDTC4.5 Threshold Method on these five data sets to build the decision tree, and classify on the original data set. We get higher accuracy than which classify on the perturbed data for data 1 and data 2; equivalent accuracy for data 5; lower accuracy on data 3 and data 4. The reason is SNR value plays an important role here. Table 12.1 shows different perturbed data sets with different SNR values. When SNR less than 1.0 means the variance σ^2 of noise data greater than the variance σ^2 of actual data. In other words data 3 and data 4 are introduced more noise. Our algorithm gets good results when the SNR value is greater than 1.0. When the threshold method builds a decision tree classifier which is not suitable to classify the perturbed data set, because our algorithm estimates the splitting point and partition the training data as the original data would have.

TABLE 12.4

Data Mining accuracy of applying data mining techniques directly on 10k perturbed training data set

Data mining on perturbed data set

Data Set	Data 1	Data 2	Data 3	Data 4	Data 5
Decision Tree C4.5 Classifier Accuracy (%)					
Test on Original	79.61	79.04	77.73	77.32	80.29
Test on Perturbed	78.56	78.14	77.45	77.05	80.47
Naive Bayes Classifier Accuracy (%)					
Test on Original	78.45	78.21	78.17	77.99	80.45
Test on Perturbed	78.08	77.78	77.46	76.47	80.29

TABLE 12.5

Data Mining accuracy with BE-based reconstruction technique

BE-based reconstruction technique

Data Set	Data 1	Data 2	Data 3	Data 4	Data 5
Decision Tree C4.5 Classifier Accuracy (%)					
Test on BE-recon	91.91	90.50	86.26	93.97	86.35
Test on Original	24.45	25.17	69.32	35.96	78.72
Test on Perturbed	38.29	36.47	58.45	43.63	74.06
Original Data Mining Accuracy (%)				83.40	
Naive Bayes Classifier Accuracy (%)					
Test on BE-recon	88.68	87.09	84.32	94.59	77.53
Test on Original	26.30	21.66	23.01	23.08	76.46
Test on Perturbed	37.19	39.91	33.09	37.30	49.66
Original Data Mining Accuracy (%)				79.87	

TABLE 12.6

BE-based reconstruction technique data mining accuracy

PCA-based reconstruction technique

Data Set	Data 1	Data 2	Data 3	Data 4	Data 5
Decision Tree C4.5 Classifier Accuracy (%)					
Test on PCA-recon	99.23	98.16	98.34	95.10	99.61
Test on Original	70.31	71.71	72.35	68.42	76.86
Test on Perturbed	54.76	63.49	59.17	61.08	61.49
Original Data Mining Accuracy (%)				83.40	
Naive Bayes Classifier Accuracy (%)					
Test on PCA-recon	97.83	98.10	97.42	94.33	98.63
Test on Original	66.12	64.29	63.21	59.84	64.81
Test on Perturbed	46.08	41.71	39.07	28.05	51.08
Original Data Mining Accuracy (%)				79.87	

To build a classifier to classify the perturbed data, we use the probability as weight to find the best splitting point, and use random path selection to partition the training data, so far the classifier accuracy has not been improved much compared with directly applying WEKA C4.5 algorithm. The reason is when partitioning the training data set, and classifying the test data set, the random path selection method does not bound the random noise R well. In the future, we would like to find a better way to bound the R value, to build a better classifier for classifying the perturbed data.

As we have seen in our experimental results, our proposed PPDTC4.5 classifiers may not get very excited high accuracy comparing with those obtained from directly applying data mining techniques to the perturbed data sets. But comparing with reconstructed based approaches, our methods obtain very good results. We try to represent the message here is, avoiding to solving the hard distribution problem,

TABLE 12.7

Proposed PPDTC4.5 data mining accuracy

Our proposed PPDTC4.5 classifier accuracy (%)

Data set	Data 1	Data 2	Data 3	Data 4	Data 5
PPDTC4.5 threshold method					
Test on original	80.74	79.69	76.63	77.02	80.29
Test on perturbed	76.09	76.14	74.41	76.03	80.52
PPDTC4.5 random path selection method					
Test on Original	78.72	77.21	77.67	78.01	80.31
Test on Perturbed	78.40	77.77	77.30	77.06	80.32

instead, mapping the data mining functions to construct privacy preserving data mining methods. This is a promising direction. Furthermore, our experimental results have also indicated that when huge data set is available, white noise is no longer can prevent data mining tools to abstract patterns. So, directly mining the perturbed data set is also a good approach when the data set is big enough.

In the PPDTC4.5 threshold method, we know that choosing different threshold values affect the data mining accuracy. Choosing the threshold to get good data mining results is related to the distribution of the random noise added to the data and the data itself. In our experiments, when using Uniform distribution random noise to distort the data, 0.5 is a good threshold to get a classifier with high accuracy; when using Gaussian distribution random noise to distort the data, 0.3 is a good threshold to get a classifier with high accuracy. The relationship between data mining accuracy and threshold values are shown in Figures 12.2 and 12.3. The best threshold should change from data to data. In other words, this is dependent on the data property.

12.7.5 ALGORITHM COMPLEXITY

Given n instances, m attributes, and p label values, the number of potential splitting points t of numeric continuous attribute at most is $n - 1$. The complexity C4.5 algorithm on training phase is

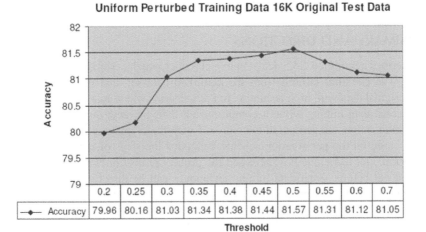

FIGURE 12.2 Threshold method of PPDTC4.5 classifier accuracy on 10k uniform perturbed training data 16k original test data.

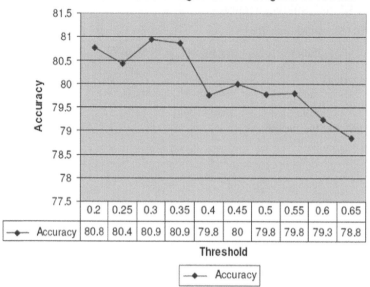

FIGURE 12.3   Threshold method of PPDTC4.5 classifier accuracy on 32K Gaussian Perturbed training data 16k original test data.

O(nlgn + tmp). Our algorithm evaluates the probability, for instance w_j for every given potential splitting point *t*, which increases the complexity of algorithm in the worst-case scenario to *O(ntmp)*. Since our algorithm skips the steps of reconstruction the original distribution for each attribute, the running time is very reasonable comparing with the BE reconstruction algorithm given in [AGRA2000]. In BE reconstruction algorithm, there is a stop parameter to determine when to stop the calculation of the estimated distribution. However, when there is more loop calculations, the running time is higher and we get better accuracy of the estimated distribution. In our experiments, based on different choice of the stop parameter, the running time of the BE reconstruction algorithm is ranged from three to five times longer than our proposed algorithm running on the same configuration computers.

12.8   SUMMARY AND DIRECTIONS

We have described a modified C4.5 decision tree classifier which is suitable for privacy-preserving data mining. The classifier is built from the perturbed data set, and the model can be used to classify the original data with high accuracy. In the scenarios where many parties are participating to perform global data mining without compromising their privacy, our algorithm decreases the costs of communication and computation compared with the cryptography-based approaches. Our algorithm is based on the perturbation scheme, but skips the steps of reconstructing the original data distribution. Out technique has increased the privacy protection with less computation time.

As pointed out before, some data mining techniques can be directly applied to the perturbed data due to the perturbation process and still preserve some nature of the data. Naive Bayes classifier can be directly applied to the additive perturbation data, and Euclidean-based data mining tools, for example, k-Nearest Neighbor Classifier, Support Vector Machines, and Perceptrons Neural Network can be applied to the multiplicative perturbation data. But, the data mining accuracy is reduced due to the information loss in the process and some data mining methods themselves may not have good performance. As we know k-Nearest Neighbor is a simple but poor performance classifier. In this chapter, we discuss an approach which modifies the data mining functions to suit the perturbed data. Our method skips the reconstructing the original data distribution from the perturbed data. In this way, the method performs privacy preserving data mining without solving the hard distribution problem. One thing to note is that when data set is big enough, performing data mining techniques directly on the perturbed data sets could obtain good data mining accuracy. For example, applying decision tree classifier to additive perturbation data could obtain good data mining accuracy. This can be observed in our experimental results.

A future direction is to build the classifiers, which can be used to classify the perturbed data set. As we have mentioned before, with a better bound of the random noise data R, using the probability as weighting is an approach that needs further investigation. Also, as novel machine learning techniques are being developed such as deep learning-based approaches, we need to explore privacy preserving machine learning for these approaches.

REFERENCES

[AGGA2004] C.C. Aggarwal, P.S. Yu, A Condensation Approach to Privacy Preserving Data Mining, EDBT, Crete, Greece, 2004.

[AGRA2000] R. Agrawal, R. Srikant, Privacy-Preserving Data Mining, SIGMOD Conference, 2000, pp. 439–450.

[AGRA2001] D. Agrawal, C.C. Aggarwal, On the Design and Quantification of Privacy Preserving Data Mining Algorithms, *PODS*, ACM, 2001.

[CHEN2005] K. Chen, L. Liu, Privacy Preserving Data Classification with Rotation Perturbation, *ICDM*, 2005, pp. 589–592.

[CLIF2002] C. Clifton, M. Kantarcioglu, J. Vaidya, X. Lin, M.Y. Zhu, Tools for Privacy Preserving Data Mining, *SIGKDD Explorations*, Volume 4, #2, 2002, 28–34.

[DU2003] W. Du, Z. Zhan, Using Randomized Response Techniques for Privacy-Preserving Data Mining, *KDD*, 2003, pp. 505–510.

[EVFI2002] A.V. Evfimievski, R. Srikant, R. Agrawal, J. Gehrke, Privacy Preserving Mining of Association Rules. *Proceedings of the Eighth ACM SIGKDD International Conference on Knowledge Discovery and Data Mining*, 2002, pp. 217–228.

[KANT2004] M. Kantarcioglu, C. Clifton, Privately Computing a Distributed k-nn Classifier, In J.-F. Boulicaut, F. Esposito, F. Giannotti, D. Pedreschi, editors, *PKDD*, Volume 3202 of *Lecture Notes in Computer Science*, Springer, 2004, pp. 279–290.

[KARG2003] H. Kargupta, S. Datta, Q. Wang, K. Sivakumar. On the Privacy Preserving Properties of Random Data Perturbation Techniques. *ICDM*, IEEE Computer Society, 2003, pp. 99–106.

[LIND2000] Y. Lindell, B. Pinkas. Privacy Preserving Data Mining In M. Bellare, editor, *CRYPTO*, volume 1880 of *Lecture Notes in Computer Science*, Springer, 2000, pp. 36–54.

[LIU2006] K. Liu, H. Kargupta, J. Ryan. Random Projection-Based Multiplicative Data Perturbation for Privacy Preserving Distributed Data Mining. *IEEE Transactions on Knowledge and Data Engineering (TKDE)*, Volume 18, #1, 2006, 92–106.

[LIU2007] L. Liu, M. Kantarcioglu, B. Thuraisingham, The Applicability of the Perturbation Based Privacy Preserving Data Mining for Real-world Data. *Data and Knowledge Engineering Journal*, Volume 65, #1, 2008, pp. 5–21.

[LIU2009] Li Liu, M. Kantarcioglu, B.M. Thuraisingham, *Privacy Preserving Decision Tree Mining from Perturbed Data*, HICSS, 2009, pp. 1–10

[MITC1997] T.M. Mitchell, *Machine Learning*, Mcgraw-Hill, 1997.

[QUIN1993] J.R. Quinlan, *C4.5: Programs for Machine Learning*, Morgan Kaufmann, 1993.

[QUIN1996] J.R. Quinlan. Improved Use of Continuous Attributes in c4.5. *Journal of Artificial Intelligence Research (JAIR)*, Volume 4, 1996, 77–90.

[RIZV2002] S. Rizvi, J.R. Haritsa. Maintaining Data Privacy in Association Rule Mining. *Proceedings of Very Large Data Bases (VLDB) Conference*, Morgan Kaufmann, 2002, pp. 682–693.

[THUR1998] B. Thuraisingham, Data Mining: Technologies, Techniques, Tools and Trends, CRC Press, 1998.

[THUR2002] B. Thuraisingham, Data Mining, National Security, Privacy and Civil Liberties, SIGKDD Explorations, Volume 4, #2, December 2002.

[THUR2005] B.M. Thuraisingham, Privacy Constraint Processing in a Privacy-enhanced Database Management System, Data Knowledge in Engineering, Volume 55, #2, 2005, 159–188.

[VAID2003] J. Vaidya, C. Clifton, Privacy-Preserving K-Means Clustering over Vertically Partitioned Data, *KDD'03: Proceedings of the Ninth ACM SIGKDD International Conference on Knowledge Discovery and Data Mining*, 2003, pp. 206–215.

[WITT2005] I.H. Witten, E. Frank, *Data Mining: Practical Machine Learning Tools and Techniques*, Morgan Kaufmann, 2nd edition, 2005.

[XU2006] S. Xu, J. Zhang, D. Han, J. Wang, Singular value decomposition based data distortion strategy for privacy protection, *Knowledge and Information Systems*, Volume 10, #3, 2006, 383–397.

13 Towards a Privacy Aware Quantified Self Data Management Framework

13.1 INTRODUCTION

While Part I discussed the foundational technologies for secure data science and Part II discussed Data Science for Cyber Security, Part III focuses on Secure and Privacy-aware Data Science. In particular, while Chapters 10 and 11 discussed attacks to the Data Science techniques, Chapter 12 focused on Privacy Preserving Data Science. In this chapter (i.e., Chapter 13), we discuss how policies may be enforced to envelop a privacy-aware framework for quantified self-applications. This work resulted directly from the Big Data Security and Privacy workshop recommendations on privacy-enhanced Big Data Management and Analytics. In particular, we focus on privacy for the massive amounts of information collected on mobile devices.

Mobile devices such as smartphones have become a prevalent computing platform with billions of users. Smartphone app downloads have seen a steady rise including a multitude of apps for monitoring personal data such as health, food intake, exercise, and sleep patterns, among others. With the recent emergence of the *Quantified Self* (*QS*) movement, personal data collected by wearable devices and smartphone apps are being analyzed to give guidance to users in improving their health or personal life habits. These data are also being shared with other service providers (e.g., retailers) using cloud-based services, bringing potential benefits to users (e.g., information about health products). But such data collection and sharing are often being carried out without the user's knowledge, bringing grave danger that personal data may be used for improper purposes. For example, data collected by a device monitoring blood glucose levels might be used by an insurance company to deny coverage to a user or even a user's blood relatives. Such privacy violations could easily get out of control if data collectors could aggregate financial and health-related data with tweets, Facebook activity, and purchase patterns. This could result in lawsuits against data collectors and psychological and physical distress in individuals. To address these growing challenges, we urgently need tools and techniques for privacy protection in QS applications.

Our work is motivated by examples and scenarios such as the ones discussed in Section 13.2 to solve the problem. Specifically, our objective is to develop novel mobile and cloud-based data storage architectures combined with innovative cryptographic protocols, access control techniques, privacy enhancing techniques, information leakage analysis, and usability analysis to securely store, process and share privacy sensitive QS data without violating individual privacy. In particular, our goal is to develop a privacy-aware QS data management framework that controls the entire lifecycle of QS data and consists of the components (i) privacy-aware data collection, (ii) privacy-aware data storage and access, and (iii) privacy-aware data analytics/mining and sharing. The organization of this chapter is as follows: Section 13.2 describes our approach. Section 13.3 describes the high-level design of the framework; Section 13.4 discusses novel directions such as the behavioral aspects of information sharing as well as aspects of developing a formal framework as well as our work on applying such a framework for other applications such as the Internet of Transportation systems. Section 13.5 concludes the chapter. Figure 13.1 illustrates this concepts discussed in this chapter. More details can be found in [THUR2018].

DOI: 10.1201/9781003081845-21

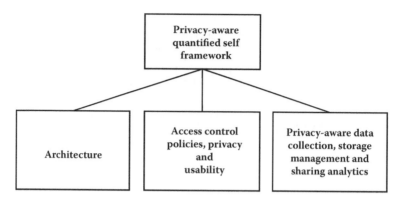

FIGURE 13.1   Concepts discussed in this chapter.

13.2   PRIVACY-AWARE QUANTIFIED SELF-DATA MANAGEMENT FRAMEWORK

13.2.1   MOTIVATIONAL SCENARIO

Massive amounts of data are being collected, stored, and analyzed for various business and marketing purposes. While such data analysis is critical for many applications, it could also violate the privacy of individuals. This chapter describes the issues involved in designing a privacy-aware data management framework for collecting, storing, and analyzing the data. We also discuss behavioral aspects of data sharing as well as aspects of a formal framework based on rewriting rules that encompasses the privacy-aware data management framework.

To understand the impact of environmental (e.g., air pollution) and lifestyle (e.g., sleep quality) factors on childhood asthma attacks, the U.S. National Institutes of Health (NIH) recently started a "Pediatric Research using Integrated Sensor Monitoring Systems (PRISMS)" program. The goal of this program is "to address significant data science and tool development challenges associated with integrated monitoring systems datasets to enable important advances in our understanding of environmental determinants of pediatric asthma" [NIH2015]. As a part of this study, it is expected that monitoring devices will be attached to children to collect data about their lifestyles (e.g., physical activity, blood oxygen levels) and these lifestyle datasets will be combined with environmental (e.g., air pollution near the child's home) and medical (e.g., number of hospitalizations due to asthma attacks) datasets to better understand and predict asthma attacks. This NIH program requires researchers to have "demonstrated expertise to enable data security and maintain confidentiality of personally identifiable information" since parents need strong assurances about their children's privacy before participating in such a study. Similarly, QS data gathered about employees (e.g., sleep quality, activity data) could be used to predict employee stress levels and to improve employee well-being provided that adequate measures for protecting privacy are adopted. According to a recent survey by PwC (Price Waterhouse Coopers) only "more than half of employees would consider wearing a smartwatch from their employer if their data was used to improve things such as working hours, stress levels and where they can work from." The good news is that according to the survey, "people are also more open to the idea if the data is anonymized and shared at an aggregate level, rather than being personalized." These examples show the potential of collecting and sharing QS data to improve healthcare outcomes and employee productivity, provided, however, that individual privacy is protected. Therefore, we need a framework to enforce appropriate privacy-aware policies guided by users' privacy needs to determine which data are to be collected, stored, and shared by whom, when, where, why and how, as well as tools and techniques to efficiently enforce the policies while getting as much utility as possible from the QS data.

13.2.2 ARCHITECTURE OVERVIEW

We need to develop a privacy-aware QS data management framework that controls the entire lifecycle of the QS data (Figure 13.2). We envision that different data sources and devices will be providing sensitive information to our *Data Collection Layer* (Section 13.2.3) running on the mobile device based on the privacy-aware data collection policies. These policies will specify when, where, and what can be collected and stored by the device. For example, a device that automatically captures all of the images (e.g., Narrative Clip [NARR2014]) may not be used in certain locations such as the immigration status check area at an international airport. Such data collection restrictions will be automatically managed by the privacy-aware data collection manager running on the device.

In our platform, we assume that only the mobile device is trusted, for example, that it adopts state-of-the art techniques for smartphone security such as containerization [OLUW2015, ASOK2013], and is allowed to access all the incoming data in plaintext form; the mobile device plays the role of "gatekeeper" in controlling what information is released. However, cloud-based services and apps running on the device are not trusted. Later on, the collected data will be indexed and certain statistics (e.g., average sleep per day for the last 12 months) and basic data analytics functions (e.g., correlation coefficients between two data streams) will be computed locally on the incoming QS data. As more data are collected, the storage on the device will not be sufficient to store all of the data. We envision an encrypted cloud storage component where older data and/or less frequently accessed data are pushed to cloud. For example, pictures captured from a prior event may be stored in encrypted form in the cloud. Appropriate local indexes will be maintained to efficiently retrieve the encrypted data stored in the cloud as needed. In addition, based on the access control policies, local apps running on the device will be given access to some of the collected data. When needed, these apps will be allowed to access some of the encrypted data stored in the cloud via a simple query interface. We emphasize that our architecture does not require change to any existing application or device. For example, if a user is happy to use the Fitbit app, the user can continue using it as it is. On the other hand, using the application

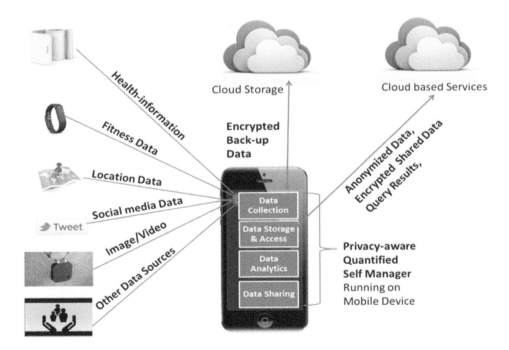

FIGURE 13.2 Privacy-aware quantified self-architecture.

programming interface (API) provided by Fitbit, our agent running on the mobile device can collect the necessary activity data and combine it with location data collected from the mobile device to enforce some policies or enable other applications. We need to develop a proof-of-concept architecture integrating different types of data using the APIs provided by device manufacturers.

The *Data Storage and Access Layer* will also deal with managing the lifecycle of the data. In some cases, the data may not be needed in fine-grained form any longer. For example, storing 20-year-old daily weight data may not be necessary; instead storing and mining monthly average weight data could be sufficient for supporting various medical applications. In other cases, the data may have to be deleted to preserve privacy (e.g., delete and/or generate fake location data to hide the fact that the user participated in a protest). Such data deletion policies will be automatically managed by the storage layer and the potential privacy impact of such deletions would be analyzed using quantitative information flow analysis (e.g., only deleting sensitive information may create some inference side channels). Since people change or lose their mobile devices frequently, we envision that the information stored on the mobile device will be continuously backed up using another cloud service provider. Thus, in the event that the mobile device is lost, a new mobile device could be set up using the encrypted back-up copy. Of course, cloud service providers need to make sure that the stored encrypted data are reliably accessible [KIRK2010].

Another key component of the architecture is a set of secure and privacy-aware mechanisms to mine and share the collected data (i.e., the Data Analytics/Mining and Sharing Layer). We envision that such data sharing and mining will be carried out using the services running in the cloud. Based on different scenarios some of the data could be sent without any modification (e.g., heart rate data for medical diagnosis), some will be sent after sanitization (e.g., randomized response-based techniques [ERLI2014] to hide user's true response) and some will be sent in an encrypted format that will enable the distributed computation of exact data mining results as needed. To provide such capabilities, we need to develop novel approaches that combine cloud-based distributed data mining, and secure multiparty computation techniques with mobile device-based data sanitization, randomized response, efficient stream pre-processing, and local data caching. Our main assumption in the framework is that the mobile device is trusted. Other than that, our architecture could be easily modified if the research carried out shows us different needs. One major contribution of this project would be to understand the best ways to integrate different components running on the device and the cloud while preserving privacy.

13.2.3 Related Work

Our work touches on many different topics ranging from personal data stores to access control policy issues. In this section, we discuss some prior research in the context of quantified self-data lifecycle (i.e., capturing, storage and sharing of QS data).

13.2.3.1 Access Control Policies, Privacy, and Usability

Previous work on access control policies has not addressed the problem of the continuous collection of personal data. The only previous work focusing on personal data collected by mobile devices is the FENCE system (short for "Continuous Access Control Enforcement in Dynamic Data Stream Environments") [NEHM2013] by the project PI and collaborators. However, FENCE does not associate context information with policies, and, thus, it is unable to automatically select the policy to be associated with specific data. Previous work on security for mobile operating systems focuses on restricting applications from accessing sensitive data and resources, but lacks efficient techniques for enforcing those restrictions according to fine-grained contexts that differentiate between closely located subareas [CONT2011]. Moreover, much of this work focuses on developing policy systems that do not restrict privileges per application and are only effective system-wide [KUSH2011]. Also, existing policy systems do not cover all of the possible ways in which applications access user data and device resources. Finally, existing location-based policy systems only provide a single mechanism, such as special hardware or location devices, for detecting the location [CONT2011, KIRK2010, KUMA2009]. In most cases, such systems assume the context as given without providing or evaluating the context detection methods of mobile devices [CONT2011, GUPT2012].

Setting of policy rules relating to privacy and access is a topic that has been investigated in several domains of computer science and human–computer interaction, including system access control, privacy policies of organizations [ANTO2007], and policy management for online social networks [CHEE2012]. Research in these domains has examined users' comprehension of policies and how to present the privacy information in a manner that is easy for users to comprehend. In general, users do not comprehend policies of any type very well [STRA2008,VU2007], and they will seldom engage in the time and effort needed to try to comprehend them. Whether a user will purchase a product from an Internet vendor is influenced by the perceived security of their personal data provided by the vendor [FLAV2006]. Similarly, it can be expected that allowing one's personal data to be shared more widely will depend on trust that this sharing will be done as intended and that unauthorized access to the data will be prevented. Sociological and theoretical literature has emphasized the significance of perceptions about context to the appropriateness of data flows such as those envisioned in our design [NISS2009].

Effort has been devoted by researchers to develop alternative mechanisms for privacy and security that reduce the cognitive demands on the users, while at the same time enabling them to make informed decisions. For the authoring of policies, evidence for the effectiveness of a template-based approach has been provided [JOHN2010a, JOHN2010b]. Such an approach reduces the cognitive demands on the policy author by providing templates (developed by policy experts and domain experts) that decompose the overall task into subtasks composed of relevant policy elements. Reduction of cognitive demands was also the idea behind the tool Privacy Bird developed to provide a signal (red, yellow, or green bird) to indicate whether a website's policy is consistent with the user's specified preferences prior to the user entering information into the site [CRAN2006]. Laboratory and crowd-sourcing studies have shown that users tend to make less risky app-selection decisions when a summary risk score is provided, particularly when that information is conveyed as the amount of safety associated with the app [CHEN2014, GATE2014].

13.2.3.2 Personal Data Stores

There have been recent efforts to manage personal data collected by smartphones. One of the most notable efforts is the OpenPDS project that provides an open-source implementation of Personal Data stores for mobile platforms [MONT2014]. Similarly, companies such as Mydex [MYDE2014] provide cloud-based personal data stores. Recently, Apple released an app called Health [APPL2014] to enable the storage of health and fitness data on mobile devices. To our knowledge, such systems do not integrate mobile devices with cloud storage in a secure manner to enable a wide range of data access and/or querying functionalities, and work under the assumption that the cloud-based service provider is trusted. One way to securely process QS data stored in the cloud is to encrypt the data prior to moving it to the cloud and to perform secure analysis over encrypted QS data. Although the research community has made significant progress in developing cryptographic approaches that allow some computation over encrypted data such as searchable encryption techniques (e.g., [CURM2011, GOH2003, STEF2014]), order preserving encryption (e.g., [BOLD2009]), fully homomorphic encryption (e.g., [GENT2009]), and practical Oblivious RAM techniques (e.g., [STEF2012, STEF2013])—no generic and cost-efficient solution for the QS data storage setting has yet emerged. In this project, we will leverage existing cryptographic advances as much as possible in the context of QS data back-up in the cloud. Especially, we will focus on how best to use the mobile device storage and potential processing of the data on the device to enable efficient privacy-preserving QS data processing.

13.2.3.3   Mining Quantified Self-Data

We need to leverage existing research and significantly improve and enhance the state-of-the-art in several important directions. Recent studies have reported on mining QS data to provide useful results. For example, "collaborative recommendation" is an evidence-based recommendation technique in which information such as ratings from many training users is leveraged to make recommendations for a specific test user [RESN1997], [HERL2004], [ADOM2005]. However, such previous work has not addressed the problem of (i) assessing the quality of recommender systems obtained when data used for training such systems is anonymized and (ii) whether and how such systems could be personalized for specific users using nonanonymized data in the context of mobile QS data collection. In addition, there are many projects that try to mine user data collected by mobile phones. For example, the Reality mining project [EAGL2006] tries to infer individuals' habits from data collected by the mobile device. MoodSense [LIKA2011] leverages the collected mobile data to infer the mood of the user. BeWell [LANE2011] tries to infer metrics such as user's sociality by mining various mobile phone sensors. Eigenbehaviors [EAGL2009] uses principal component analysis techniques to predict daily activity. Recently, the Lifestreams project [HSIE2013] tries to provide a platform where other data mining tasks can be built by leveraging the analytics building blocks provided by the system. To our knowledge, none of the existing work and platforms tries to integrate privacy-aware technologies with a wide range of QS data mining tasks.

13.2.3.4   Differential Privacy and Privacy-Preserving Data Mining

Recently, many differentially private data mining tools have been developed, ranging from generic differential private statistical estimation framework (e.g., [DWOR09]) to machine learning algorithms such as differentially private support vector machines (e.g., [CHAU11]). Although these developments are quite interesting, they are not directly applicable to our case since they assume that the data are already collected in a database controlled by the curator. On the other hand, recent randomized response-based differential private data collection techniques [ERLI2014] are relevant but it is not clear how such randomized response ideas could be leveraged for mining QS data. As a part of this project, we will extend noise addition techniques combined with distributed cryptographic protocols (e.g., [DWOR2006]) to produce differentially private data mining results and leverage cloud infrastructure to scale to millions of individuals by delegating some work to cloud-based services. Our work on privacy-preserving distributed data mining has explored how to leverage cryptographic techniques to mine data from different parties (e.g., [KANT04]). Many of the existing privacy-preserving distributed data mining protocols implicitly assume that the number of parties participating is small. Scaling these protocols to potentially millions of mobile devices remains an important challenge. We need to tackle these challenges by combining peer-to-peer cryptographic protocols with secure outsourcing of some computation to the cloud using secret sharing-based techniques.

13.3   HIGH LEVEL DESIGN OF THE FRAMEWORK

13.3.1   Privacy-Aware Data Collection

Users typically carry and use their smartphones and other personal devices in public and private places and in a variety of different contexts, some of which are privacy sensitive. For example, a user is likely to consider being in a hospital or doctor's office as personally sensitive information. Therefore, we must allow users to specify policies restricting which data can be collected in which contexts. These policies allow an individual to specify his/her own personal privacy policies with respect to the collection of his/her own personal data. Policies must be tightly coupled with the data because the policies may change over time and, for accountability reasons, it is important to keep track of the policies under which data were collected. Also, in many contexts, a user is not alone;

therefore, use of certain devices may have to be prevented or controlled as these devices may record information about other users, thus violating their privacy. Moreover, corporations and other organizations may forbid their employees and visitors to bring, or use, camera-enabled devices to the workplace, including smartphones, even though employees might need to have their devices with them at all times (e.g., an employee who uses his/her device to store information relevant to his/her health). Furthermore, default privacy policies are needed for aggregated and individual data that reveals the location and even layout of sensitive facilities, such as fitness data within military bases outside of the United States [SLY2018]. We thus need fine-grained context-based access control policies by which certain devices or resources within devices can be blocked from acquiring data. We refer to these policies as *context-based device resource usage policies*. An essential requirement for supporting the enforcement of both types of policies is the support for context information acquisition. In addition, such collection decisions need to be analyzed to address potential privacy implications (e.g., not collecting images may disclose that the user is in a sensitive location). To address the above challenges, we need to design a privacy aware data collection system. Our high level design consists of the following four components:

1. *A policy language for specifying context-based data collection policies and context-based device resource usage policies:* A key element in such a language is the constructs for specifying contexts. As discussed by Nissembaum [NISS09], the appropriateness of information handling is best judged by the situational context of a disclosure. Even though her work did not address the specific case of personal data, advanced by our notion of QS data, we believe that her idea nicely maps onto it. Our notion of a context-based policy language, and a corresponding enforcement engine, is our approach to introducing such an idea into our system. We need to support three different types of contexts: location, time, and situation. Situation refers to application-specific context, such as a task that the user is currently engaged in. For all the context types, we will allow users to associate symbolic names with specific contexts. For example, consider a hospital located in a certain street in a given city. The hospital can be denoted in many ways, for example, by using geographical coordinates or by using a postal address. However, it will be easier for the user to associate his/her shorthand name to the hospital. Our policy language will support different constructs for the specification of contexts and also the specification of complex contexts by which one can combine different types of contexts, and will incorporate social constraints where the absence and/or presence of other users nearby impact the data collection process [KIRK2011]; an example would be a policy specifying that images can be acquired in a given location only if no one else is present.

2. *A policy authoring tool for the specification of policies according to our policy language:* The tool will provide an easy-to-use interface for the specification of policies as well as a mechanism to import policies (e.g., the corporate policies that have to be enforced on user devices). We need to leverage existing work on policy-by-example [CHEE2012]; however, this approach has been developed for social networks and mainly deals with grouping friends in order to assign them permissions. We need to borrow the notion of "policy-by-example" and tailor it to our context. The authoring tool will also support graphical location-based interfaces for the specification of location information.

3. *A flexible location and presence detection mechanism:* We need to develop a suite of mechanisms for detecting the location of the user so that the most convenient mechanism can be used depending on the type of location (such as closed/open location), and networks and sensing devices available. Our location detection system will leverage Wi-Fi-based positioning techniques to retrieve the location of the device. In addition to these techniques, our system will also collect location data retrieved from GPS and cellular networks for situations where there is no Wi-Fi coverage in the areas of interest. As part of the system, we will develop a user-specific database of Wi-Fi access points, recording

the areas that the user has visited and thus allowing the user to associate names with these areas and refer to them in policies. Concerning presence detection, we will develop mechanisms based on the use of near field communication (NFC) techniques [KIRK2011], physical access control, motion sensors, surveillance devices, and other approaches [GUPT2012].

4. *A policy enforcement engine:* The engine, located in the devices, will be in charge of enforcing the policies. A major challenge is the enforcement of policies requiring that certain resources on a device not be used in a particular context. Our initial approach will address this problem on Android and leverage our previous work in the IdentiDroid anonymity system [SHEB2014, MIDI2014] on dynamically revoking Android permissions. In our system, a main challenge is that permissions must be dynamically revoked or reinstated based on the context, whereas in IdentiDroid the switch is executed when the user requires to enter or exit the anonymous mode.

A detailed analysis needs to be carried out to identify privacy issues that are specific to our target environment consisting of continuous/pervasive personal data collection by each individual about himself/herself. In addition, we need to explore ways of designing the following:

1. *Policy languages for privacy-aware data collections:* We need to develop a policy language as an extension of the well-known XACML standard [XACM2005].
2. *Policy authoring tool:* We need to adapt or develop a user-friendly tool supporting the specification of policies expressed in our language. One possibility is using conversational agent with a high-level representation of information [PARI2012]. The tool needs to support the analysis and evolution of policies, based on user feedback and policy overrides. The tool also needs to support policy integration supporting the merging of different policies (for example, a corporate policy on what data can be captured while working in the office and the personal policy defined by the user) and include simple mechanisms and defaults for policy conflict resolution.
3. *Location and presence detection mechanism:* We need to design location detection mechanisms for devices such as the smartphones.
4. *Policy enforcement engine:* We need to design the engine to apply the policies. An important challenge in the design of the engine is to ensure that the policies are not bypassed by (possibly) malicious users, in the case of corporate policies by users who do not want to comply with the policies, or by malicious software whose goal is to gather private data about users. To address such challenges we need to integrate and extend Trusted Platform Management TPM technology, containerization techniques, and application profiling techniques originally developed for protecting data from insider threats [HUSS2015].

13.3.2 PRIVACY-AWARE DATA STORAGE AND ACCESS

After collecting QS data from different sensors (e.g., health monitors), devices (e.g., Narrative clip), and mobile sources (e.g., tweets and text messages sent by the mobile device user), we need to store these data for mining and analysis to extract interesting patterns. In some cases (e.g., correlating location data with air quality data to understand long-term asthma trends), there may be long-term value in storing all of the data captured based on the policies. Storage of such collected data creates interesting research challenges. First, the smartphones that are currently becoming the hub for all the captured data may not be able to store all the data on the device. To address the storage limitations of smartphones, one can leverage cloud storage. Many mobile devices support automatic cloud back-up and storage mechanisms. For example, iPhone comes with a default iCloud-based data back-up support. Unfortunately, as recent events show [DUKE2014], privacy-sensitive data stored in the cloud in plaintext format could be vulnerable to attacks. Encrypting such data before moving them to the cloud prevents some of these attacks, but straightforward data encryption results in many query execution and data retrieval challenges. There are recent advances in querying encrypted data that could be leveraged to enable secure cloud data storage while allowing selective retrieval of the data, but important challenges remain that need to be addressed to satisfy the requirements of various QS applications. Existing techniques such as range queries (e.g., [SHI2007]), key-word search (e.g., [CURM2011, GOH2003, STEF2014]), and attribute-based encryption (e.g., [WANG2010]), and fully homomorphic encryption (e.g., [GENT2009]), do not directly support queries such as "find the pictures taken in New York City that have Jim in the picture." Adapting and improving existing encrypted data querying techniques while leveraging the capabilities of the smartphones remains an important research direction. As we discuss later, we plan to address these challenges by extracting important features from the QS data and then modifying existing searchable encryption techniques to work with these extracted features.

Another important requirement is to support mobile apps that provide valuable services to users. Consider an app that accesses movement data to automatically extract sleep patterns and correlate it with weight information to understand the impact of someone's weight on sleep patterns. To support such an app, we may want to provide motion sensor data only in the evening, hiding the activity pattern during the day. Providing fine-grained access to collected QS data would be the first step in allowing useful QS applications while protecting privacy. Given the large number of potential apps that may combine different types of QS data to provide value-added services, enabling users to define access control policies for each app becomes a challenge. Understanding users' needs for easy-to-use mechanisms is critical; otherwise users will end up not making use of fine-grained access control policies.

Finally, keeping all the collected data forever creates significant privacy challenges. For instance, remembering all location data forever might allow a malicious app or malicious party to infer important information about user movement patterns going back many years. To enhance privacy, we envision certain scenarios where users may want to delete some information based on pre-defined conditions. For example, a user may want to delete some information captured (e.g., photos taken) during a visit to a particular location (e.g., Las Vegas) after a certain period (e.g., 10 years). Of course, facilitating such secure deletion of data would require us to track where the data are stored. To support automatic QS data deletion policies, efficient techniques are needed to track and delete sensitive data.

To address the above challenges, we need to design a Privacy-Aware Data Storage and Access System. Our high-level design is illustrated in Figure 13.3 where all the data coming from different sources will first be processed and stored on the mobile device. The local storage will keep different types of indexes locally (i.e., on the smartphone) to help in querying the stored data. In addition, the framework will manage the data access policies for different mobile apps. We need to make the framework compatible with existing efforts such as OpenPDS [MONT2014] so that multiple different apps can be used on top of the framework by using basic mechanisms to access the stored data. Later on, as the mobile device storage space fills up, some of the stored QS data will be pushed to the cloud using different heuristics. For example, heart rate data from the previous month may be pushed to the cloud in an encrypted format. Before such an action, appropriate local indexes will be updated to enable easy retrieval later. Furthermore, locally built models will be kept to enable certain tasks. For example, a time series model that is built to find anomalies in the heart rate could be updated locally even if the underlying data is shifted to the cloud using stream processing techniques. In addition, the framework will keep track of which apps accessed which data (i.e., keep basic provenance information) to facilitate data deletion in the future. Clearly, enabling such a framework will require us to address many research challenges. Below, we summarize the activities that need to be explored.

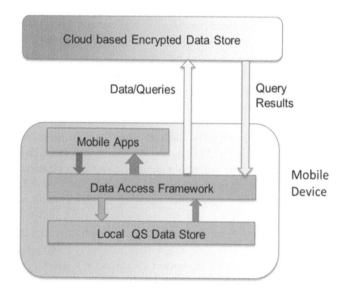

FIGURE 13.3 Storage architecture.

1. *Secure long-term storage of QS data:* We envision that a typical user may generate terabytes of data during his/her life. Based on current smartphone capabilities, clearly it is not possible to store all the data locally. At the same time, as discussed earlier, we must push data in encrypted format to the cloud to protect individual privacy. We need to explore how existing searchable encryption techniques could be applied seamlessly to query local and (encrypted) cloud data. Because most of the QS data will be indexed, queried, and accessed based on time and location, we will start by building encrypted indexes on these two dimensions for different types of QS data. To be able to leverage existing keyword search techniques, we need to discretize each dimension (e.g., discretize time based on day, month and year) and convert a given search into a keyword search and/ or simple one-dimensional range-query search. This simple approach will provide us with basic capabilities for data querying based on location and time. Such encrypted querying may form the basis for building data mining models from QS data. Furthermore, we need to explore ways of pre-computing certain interesting functions on the data before the QS data are pushed to the cloud. For example, a face detection algorithm can be used to automatically detect faces in a given image. Later on, such information related to a detected face may be inserted into an appropriate index for fast image retrieval. We need to explore pre-computation of various interesting features from the data (e.g., faces in a given image, moving averages of sensor information) to build indexes to enable fast retrieval of encrypted data from the cloud using existing range and keyword search techniques.

2. *Secure and privacy-aware query interfaces for QS Apps:* To enable a wide range of applications, we need to provide interfaces for apps to access the stored data. Some of the data that are used by an app may need to be retrieved from the cloud as well as from the local mobile storage. During this data access, we want to make sure that apps only access data at a granularity that does not violate individual privacy. Providing a full-fledged query language support, such as SQL, in a secure and privacy preserving manner to QS apps may be too costly. We need to explore simple interfaces (e.g., a limited subset of SQL) to enable apps to provide value-added services while simplifying the access control and privacy policy enforcement requirements. We also need to explore aggregation (i.e.,

disclose results aggregated to hide sensitive data) and noise addition techniques (i.e., local differentially privacy techniques).

3. *Usability/Human Factors:* Because end users must interact through the interfaces to define policies, set the data management options, and use the data for their own purposes, interfaces must be designed consistent with human capabilities. Of critical importance, users need to understand recommendations and suggestions given by the applications/recommenders. We need to exploit our knowledge and experience dealing with comprehension of organizations' privacy policies and specification of users' privacy preferences [PROC2007], as well as comprehension of the permissions requested by Android app's [GATE2014], to design and evaluate interfaces that are easy and intuitive to use for the different types of users who will be involved in the different phases of the QS data lifecycle.

4. *QS Data Deletion/Sanitization Support:* As we discussed earlier, we may want to delete or sanitize some of the data for privacy and efficiency reasons. Assessing the efficiency implications of data deletion or sanitization is straightforward, but it is more challenging to assess the implications for privacy. A striking example was given by the *William Weld re-identification* [SWEE2002] which was not prevented by sanitizing records down to just (Date of birth, Sex, Zip Code). One fruitful approach is to study the effectiveness of particular sanitizations against particular adversaries [HEAT2013]. But we believe that stronger privacy guarantees could be achieved through quantitative information flow analysis. The idea is to view a deletion/sanitization mechanism as an information-theoretic channel that takes the original data to a sanitized output. The amount of leakage of this channel quantifies the effectiveness of the sanitization against arbitrary adversaries. As discussed in Section 13.2.2, a challenge is that there are *many* leakage measures that might be most appropriate, depending on the operational scenario. For this reason, it is attractive to focus on *min-capacity* which by the Miracle Theorem of [ALVI2012] is an upper bound on leakage in all scenarios. Min-capacity is also relatively easy to compute; in the case of a deterministic channel, for instance, it just requires calculating the number of feasible channel outputs. For the (Date of birth, Sex, Zip Code) channel, for example, the number of feasible outputs can be crudely estimated to be about 240 million. (There are around 40,000 Zip Codes, each with an average population of around 8000, or about 4000 of each sex. Since there are 36,500 possible dates of birth, we can presume that the 4000 people of each sex in a given Zip Code have mostly distinct dates of birth, giving $40,000 \times 2 \times 3000 = 240$ million feasible outputs.) Hence, if the secret is a uniformly-distributed American, the channel increases its vulnerability to being guessed correctly by a factor of 240 million, giving a posterior vulnerability of $240/320 = 0.75$, showing that this sanitization is completely inadequate. We need to then develop sanitization mechanisms with small min-capacity, allowing precise statements about the privacy protection that they provide. One challenge is the possibility of *correlations* among secrets. Some leakage bounds in the presence of arbitrary correlations are shown in [ALVI2014], but we need to explore this further. Some details on data sanitization are provided in [RACH2013, RACH2014a, RACH2014b].

13.3.3 PRIVACY-AWARE DATA ANALYTICS AND SHARING

We believe that to create more value from the QS data, we need to support more functionality on top of the storage and querying framework. Personal data collected by each individual can be used in different ways to the benefit of the individual, others, and to society in general. For example, running a large-scale medical research project on understanding the impact of regular exercise on high blood pressure could easily be carried out by collecting and aggregating sport activity data with blood pressure data from millions of individuals. However, even though individuals may have incentives to share data, privacy concerns may impede such sharing. Thus, it is critical that privacy-aware sharing be supported. Consequently, we need techniques allowing one to specify and evolve access control policies to support selective sharing of personal data with other individuals.

In certain scenarios, directly allowing apps to access even a subset of the data may disclose sensitive information, so, instead we may want to share results that are mined locally. For example, incoming QS data can be mined locally to find interesting association rules (e.g., a fitness app that is used to enter food intake information may be combined with blood pressure data measurements to find associations). This way we can limit the app's access to a few data mining or query results (e.g., local association rule results). Furthermore, the user's data can be mined locally by an app developed by a third party, but the results may be shared only when a user explicitly approves sharing the result.

Also, data coming from different individuals may need to be integrated to create aggregated/sample-level/population-level models. One way to facilitate such data sharing would be to send data using techniques such as Onion routing (e.g., using Tor [DING2004]) to avoid data being linked to the individual who is donating the data. However, previous research on identifiability [SWEE2002] clearly indicates that even if data contains no identifiers and are sent using Onion routing, it can still be used to identify individuals. Another option could be to add noise to the data so that the shared data become less accurate (e.g., randomized response type application [ERLI2014]) and therefore, less likely to cause negative outcomes for individuals. We believe the right combination of techniques for QS data that can support a large number of applications needs to be explored. Especially important is that suitable privacy-aware techniques are in place and tools and guidelines be available for individuals to be able to trade off privacy risks with personal benefits.

Finally, as indicated by this chapter's previous sections, for the data sharing scheme to accomplish its goal of enforcing personalized privacy policies for individual users, the interface will need to be designed to fulfill users' needs and to be "user friendly." For users to allow data sharing, they must trust their data will be protected in the manner that they intend and will not be vulnerable to leakage and attacks. Also, users must be able to comprehend the policy management options so they understand their choices and the possible consequences of their selections. Because these options involve the data that can be collected and the contexts in which they can be collected, as well as who will be allowed access to their data, policy specification by the user will necessarily be a complex process. Consequently, the interactions with the interface necessary for a user to define his/her policies and set the data management options need to be as straightforward as possible and allow for personalization. Not all users may desire to have detailed control over their personal information, so the interface needs to support decisions at different levels of granularity and smart default settings that would be acceptable to the majority of users. Smart default settings are critical because the majority of users do not change privacy/security settings (e.g., >90% of Google accounts do not have two factor authentication enabled [SULL18]).

Our high-level design for data sharing consists of multiple components. The first component comprises a personal access control system supporting the specification and enforcement of access control policies for personal data as well as the evolution and merging of different policies ranging from event-based sharing to data donations by the individual for research. The access control system will also include an authoring tool. The second component is a data mining system able to work on sanitized data. An important issue is to assess the quality of data mining models derived from sets of anonymized data. More importantly, it is crucial to determine whether and how a data mining model built from a large population can then be refined by using nonanonymized personal data of each user or if the predictions obtained by such a public data mining system can be combined with recommendations obtained by a local data mining system (i.e., a local data mining system based on the data of the specific users). The goal would be to create global data mining models based on the sanitized data of multiple users and then personalize these models for each a specific user.

We need to build a framework where the QS streams coming from different sources will be analyzed locally. Using the computational power of the mobile device, important statistics as well as the data mining models for the individual will be computed. In addition, as needed, the encrypted querying mechanisms discussed earlier will be used to retrieve data archived in the cloud to improve the local models and statistics. Later on, these models and statistics will be shared based on the policies and events registered by the user. We also need to develop cloud-based secure distributed data mining techniques to allow individuals to securely donate and/or sell data to the various data mining needs. Based on the data sharing policies, the data that will be submitted to data mining models will be automatically extracted. In certain scenarios, the data also will be aggregated using the information coming from the peers (i.e., information coming from nearby friends). In some cases, the information will be sanitized by adding noise before sharing with the cloud-based services (e.g., by leveraging randomized response-based differential-privacy techniques [ERLI2014]). This locally computed information will be shared using secret sharing-based techniques [CRAM2000, CRAM2003] with multiple servers located on the public cloud using service such as Tor [DING2004] so that linking back the data to a particular individual will be harder. Once the data are sent to multiple servers using secret sharing mechanisms, secret sharing-based secure protocols will be executed among the servers to build the population-level data mining models. To scale to a large number of users, we plan to combine effective sampling and randomized response techniques in conjunction with secret sharing-based, secure multiparty ideas. For example, we may want to combine user data from a certain subpopulation (e.g., people above age 65 with hypertension) to build a linear regression model. If user i is participating in the system with their data vectors x_i where $1 \leq i \leq n$, we can write the data mining process as secure multiparty evaluation of linear regression function f as $f\left(I_{C(x_1)} \cdot x_1, \ I_{C(x_2)} \cdot x_2, \ldots, I_{C(x_n)} \cdot x_n\right)$, where $I_{C(x_i)}$ is the indicator function that describe the selection condition for the user data. First of all, as this is a data mining model, to be statistically significant, we may not need to get all the samples. Given the selection condition C, we may estimate the number of users t that can satisfy the condition C, if $t \gg s$ where s is the number of samples required for statistical significance, than we can subsample from the user population that matches the condition with probability $\frac{s}{t}$ to reduce the amount of data that is secretly shared for SMC phase. Of course, while doing sampling, we may disclose which users match condition C. To prevent this, we may want to sample from the users for whom condition C is not satisfied as well. The sampling rates could be adjusted to balance individual privacy protection versus efficiency. Once user data are selected after this sampling step, noise addition techniques or secret sharing techniques with multiple servers could be used to send the data to a cloud-based secret sharing-based SMC framework. In some cases, these built models will be sent back to the users to locally customize to improve their utility for the user.

Finally, to investigate data sharing from a human factors point of view, we need to take a multimethod approach in which a variety of methods, including interviews, surveys, laboratory experiments, and crowd-sourcing experiments, are used to obtain qualitative and quantitative data in naturalistic and controlled settings [PROC2007]. This information will be used to determine smart defaults. We need to leverage our access to various user populations at Purdue University and through its Center for Education and Research in Information Assurance and Security (CERIAS) partners to develop and test our interface design concepts on groups that are most relevant to the particular issue in QS data storage. For research requiring large samples of experienced computer users, we will conduct studies on Amazon Mechanical Turk (MTurk) for which we obtain performance measures as well as survey and demographic information, as we have done in our app-selection research [CHEN2014, GATE2014]. As a first stage of our approach, we will identify human factors issues related to personal data sharing by determining the risks and benefits associated with QS data storage, including consideration of legal rules under which those risks can be created (e.g., search warrants) or avoided (e.g., bans on certain data-handling practices in statutes such as the Health Insurance Portability and Accountability Act [HIPAA]). As a next stage, we will establish whether typical users are aware of these risks and benefits, and perceive them to be substantial. A third stage will be to evaluate usability issues involved in specifying personal privacy policies. A central focus of this stage will be to focus on ways to present the policy information in a comprehensible manner during the specification process. We need to evaluate not only the usability of alternative interfaces but also whether the users have an accurate understanding of what their policy specifications allow and do not allow. The following six items outline the activities that need to be explored.

1. *A risk-aware access control system for personal data:* The system will include a policy language for the specification of policies, based on extensions/customizations of the XACML standard, a policy authoring tool able to merge and evolve access control policies, and a policy enforcement engine. In addition, we will also explore quantitative methods to analyze and quantify risks in sharing QS data and automatically adjust policies in the light of existing risks. In our past work [BENS2014], we explored risk-based data sharing issues in the context of sharing large datasets. We need to integrate the risk acceptance behaviors captured during human subject experiments into quantitative models to better account for human behavior in real life. We need to explore how event-based sharing policies can be built on top of XACML extensions. In addition, the data also have to be trusted [LIM2012].

2. *A local data analytics framework to build models and local statistics based on streaming data and encrypted data stored in the cloud:* We need to explore how existing stream mining techniques [MAS2008, MAS2013] could be used to maintain local statistics and data sketches for different data mining tasks. However, current stream learning algorithms [MASU2010] may not be readily used in the context of privacy-aware or encrypted data. A small change in the training set may affect the quality and performance of the learned model. For this, we will explore ways of maintaining basic statistics such as correlations among multiple streams. As needed, some of the older models and statistics will be back-up encrypted in the cloud. In some cases, such learned models and statistics will be combined to answer important questions based on approximation. Such approximations generally utilize a sliding window or sampling approach. For example, to answer a question as to how an individual's sleep quality is affected by his/her weight, previous models about sleep patterns and weight data (stored in the cloud) will be selectively utilized to compute such correlations.

3. *A global recommender system able to work on sanitized data:* We need to develop a recommender system able to work on data value ranges, rather than precise values. Furthermore, noise addition techniques such as randomized response will be explored to add noise to the data before sharing it. We need to test the relative effectiveness of the recommender systems built using sanitized data following the same testing approach we used to test the quality of classifiers learned on anonymized data.

4. *Cloud-based privacy-aware distributed data mining protocols to build population-level data mining models:* In addition to noise addition/sanitization techniques discussed earlier, we need to build distributed data mining techniques that do not disclose any information about the individuals other than the final data mining model. Initially, we will explore whether each user can push his/her data to a few non-colluding, semi-honest servers sitting in the cloud. For example, to facilitate a scientific study that tries to find the impact of regular exercise, the location of the user, and air pollution on asthma attacks, a local data mining model can automatically create statistics about weekly exercise numbers combined with the user's demographic information and asthma attacks (assuming the user keeps an electronic journal) and location information. These statistics will be divided into secret shares [DESM1992, CRAM2003] and will be sent to different servers. Later on, existing data about local pollution information will be securely linked to user's location data by using secret sharing-based distributed data mining techniques. Building such an application

will have unique challenges on how best to summarize local data so that the secret sharing-based protocols in the cloud could be best leveraged and scaled to a large number of users. In addition, we may need to explore how additional external sources of data can be used locally to improve the efficiency of the global distributed data mining protocols. For example, each mobile device may download the local pollution data from the internet and do the linkage locally (again using a system like TOR to prevent linkage to an individual). This will reduce the amount of cryptographic protocol execution needed in the public cloud.

5. *A customization system able to refine the global recommender system for specific users:* We need to investigate an approach based on the multiple mixture model [LEE2013] by which we will combine the recommendations obtained by a local recommender, built on the nonsanitized data of a single user, with the recommendations obtained by the global recommender system, to obtain customized recommendations for the specific user. It is important to note the local recommender system will be obtained based on a very small set of data, and very precise because it is not sanitized. Whereas the global recommender system will be based on a very large set of data, which is less precise because of the potential data sanitization. Extensive experimental analysis will be carried out to assess the accuracy of such a two-step approach.

6. *A human-factors analysis to determine the risks and benefits associated with QS data sharing perceived by both expert and typical users:* One-on-one interviews and online survey methods will be used for such an analysis. Policy experts will be invited for one-on-one, semi-structured interviews and asked about their thoughts concerning the possible risks and benefits associated with QS data storage. Different categories of risks and benefits, and their perceived importance, will be identified from the interview data. Typical users will be recruited through MTurk to answer a questionnaire that will allow us to determine whether they distinguish the same categories as the policy experts and perceive their relative importance similarly. In both studies, users will be asked about the degree to which they have trust in the QS data storage, and the categories of risks and benefits will be analyzed as a function of different levels of trust. If the typical users' perceived risks and benefits differ from those identified by the expert users, ways of educating users about these risks and benefits will be devised and tested by comparing users' responses before and after the education. We need to also compare findings concerning user preferences to legal doctrine defining adequate consent to data collection or processing and identify ways to ensure that user decisions constitute legally effective limitations. To enable personalization of privacy policies for QS data sharing, the different options for setting the privacy policies should be identified. We need to query the policy experts and typical users with regard to the choices that they would like a privacy specification interface to accommodate. From this information, we will evaluate the identified design features in controlled experiments conducted in the lab with a population of college-student computer users or on MTurk with a broader range of computer users. Many users will not want to engage in detailed specifications because of the high information-processing demands, so we will develop smart default settings that are acceptable to the majority users, and also evaluate ways of presenting pre-set options that allow relatively simple setting of policies, but at a more aggregate level than specifying each factor separately. We need to incorporate the results of the experiments in the design of one or more possible interfaces, for which we will perform usability evaluations.

13.4 NOVEL DIRECTIONS

Section 13.3 described our high-level design of the privacy-aware data management framework for data collection, data storage, data sharing and data analysis. To develop a useful framework, we need to take into consideration some additional aspects such as (i) the security of user devices, (ii) formalizing the framework, (iii) behavioral aspects, and (iv) novel applications such as the Internet of Things (IoT) so that we can prove properties such as consistency and completeness. We discuss these additional aspects in this section.

13.4.1 SECURITY OF USER DEVICES

In order privacy to be maintained, user devices must remain secure over time. Privacy risks throughout the data lifecycle (collect, store, and analyze) can be mitigated by informing users about device vulnerabilities that are found over time. More importantly, the framework can help users update their smartphones and especially IoT devices. Almost half of all users never update IoT devices [ROUF2016]. In addition, users can be notified if they are using (vulnerable) devices that are no longer receiving updates.

While security and privacy have to be a major consideration in designing data management systems for the IoT devices, usability is also important. For example, what happens if the user has forgotten his or her password and is unable to access the smart home or smart hospital records. Therefore, it is important to consider multifactor authentication for the user and also we need appropriate standards to be developed. For example, standards such as SAML and XACML have to be considered for authentication and authorization. Therefore, the user interface framework has to be integrated with the data management framework so that we can ensure security, privacy and usability of the IoT devices.

13.5 BEHAVIORAL ASPECTS

Users' behavioral patterns can be analyzed from the data collected (see also [SULL2018]). For example, user habits such as smoking, consuming alcohol and drugs as well as depression and possibly mood swings could be detected by analyzing the massive amounts of data collected. While such data collection could benefit the users by sending them information about potential treatments and advice, it could also result in the violation of user privacy. Therefore, we need policy aware data collection so that the user could benefit from the advice without violating his/her privacy.

We are now living during one of the worst pandemics in over a century. While the physical well-being of the people is of utmost importance, we also need to gather information about the peoples' moods to prevent them from committing suicide. Therefore, analyzing the data collected would hugely benefit the prevention of suicides. However, this could also violate an individual's privacy. In Chapter 14, we discuss privacy issues related to COVID-19.

13.6 TOWARD A FORMAL FRAMEWORK

To be able to accommodate any solutions, we need to develop a formal framework. In a recent chapter, we discussed some aspects of a formal framework based on rewriting rules [FERN2016]. In particular, we described a general framework, whereby users cannot only specify how their data are managed, but also restrict data collection from their connected devices as well as the storage and analysis of this data. More precisely, we discussed the use of data collection policies to govern the transmission of data from various devices (e.g., IoT devices), coupled with policies to ensure that once the data have been transmitted, it is stored and shared in a secure and privacy-preserving way. In other words, we discussed a framework for secure data collection, storage and management, with logical foundations that enable verification of policy properties. Our main focus however was on the aspect of specifying and reasoning about the policies for data collection.

While the work discussed in [FERN2016] is the first step toward designing such a formal framework for specifying and reasoning about security and privacy policies, we need to explore the use of such a framework for the privacy-aware data management framework we have discussed in Section 13.3. This is a research direction we are pursuing while we continue to carry out a more

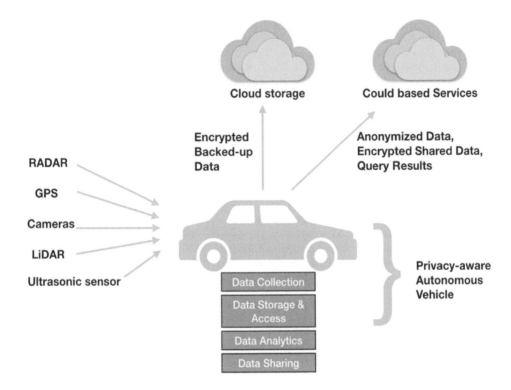

FIGURE 13.4 Privacy-aware Internet of Transportation.

detailed design of the data management framework. In addition we are also applying the result to Internet of Transportation Systems as illustrated in Figure 13.4.

13.7 SUMMARY AND DIRECTIONS

This chapter has discussed the problem of securing, collecting, storing, and analyzing the data with a motivational example. Then, we discussed the challenges involved in designing a privacy-aware data management framework for data collection, management, and analysis. We also discussed the behavioral aspects of information sharing as well as some aspects of a formal framework for privacy-aware policy management. Finally, we discussed briefly the need for formalizing the framework so that one can specify and reason about the security and privacy policies regardless of the implementation solutions.

This chapter mainly raises the awareness of the need for incorporating security and privacy policies at all levels of data management. The next step is to carry out a detailed design and implementation of the framework. We also have to design the formal framework so we can specify and reason about the policies regardless of the solutions implemented. Finally, we need to adapt the framework for applications such as the Internet of Transportation Systems.

REFERENCES

[ADOM2005] G. Adomavicius, A. Tuzhilin, Toward the Next Generation of Recommender Systems: A Survey of the State-of-the-Art and Possible Extensions, IEEE Transactions on Knowledge and Data Engineering, Volume 17, # 6, 2005, 734–749.

[ALVI2012] M.S. Alvim, K. Chatzikokolakis, C. Palamidessi, G. Smith, Measuring Information Leakage using Generalized Gain Functions, *Proceedings of CSF 2012: 25th IEEE Computer Security Foundations Symposium*, Cambridge, MA, June 2012, pp. 265–279.

[ALVI2014] M.S. Alvim, K. Chatzikokolakis, A. McIver, C. Morgan, C. Palamidessi, G. Smith. Additive and Multiplicative Notions of Leakage, and their Capacities, *Proceedings of CSF 2014: 27th IEEE Computer Security Foundations Symposium*, Vienna, Austria, July 2014, pp. 308–322.

[ANTO2007] A.I. Anton, E. Bertino, N. Li, T. Yu, A Roadmap for Comprehensive Online Privacy Policy Management, Communications of the ACM, Volume 50, #7, 2007, 109–116.

[APPL2014] Apple Health Web Site, https://www.apple.com/ios/whats-new/health/. Accessed on 2014 November.

[ASOK2013] N. Asokan, L.V. Davi, A. Dmitrienko, S. Heuser, K. Kostiainen, E. Reshetova, A.R. Sadeghi, Mobile Platform Security. Synthesis Lectures on Information Security, Privacy, and Trust, Morgan & Claypool Publishers, 2013

[BENS2014] A. Bensoussan, M. Kantarcioglu, S. Hoe. A Trust-Score-Based Access Control in Assured Information Sharing Systems: An Application of Financial Credit Risk Score Model. Risk and Decision Analysis, IOS Press, 2014.

[BOLD2009] A.Boldyreva, N. Chenette , Y. Lee , A. O'Neil , Order-Preserving Symmetric Encryption, EUROCRYPT, Cologne, Germany, 2009, pp. 224–241.

[CHAU2011] K. Chaudhuri, C. Monteleoni, A.D. Sarwate, Differentially Private Empirical Risk Minimization, Journal of Machine Learning and Research Volume 12 , 2011, 1069–1109.

[CHEE2012] G.P. Cheek, M. Shehab, Policy-by-Example for Online Social Networks. *Proceedings of 17th ACM Symposium on Access Control Models and Technologies, SACMAT '12,* Newark, NJ, USA. June 20–22, 2012, pp. 23–32.

[CHEN2014] J. Chen, C.S. Gates, R.W. Proctor, N. Li, Framing of Summary Risk/Safety Information and App Selection. *Proceedings of the 2014 Annual Meeting of the Human Factors and Ergonomics Society*, Santa Monica, CA, HFES, 2014.

[CONT2011] M. Conti, V.T.N. Nguyen, B. Crispo, Crepe: Context-Related Policy Enforcement for Android, *Proceedings of the 13th International Conference on Information Security, ISC '10*, Berlin, Heidelberg, Springer-Verlag, 2011, pp. 331–345.

[CRAM2000] R. Cramer, I. Damgård, U. Maurer, General Secure Multi-Party Computation from Any Linear Secret-Sharing Scheme. *Proceedings of the 19th international Conference on Theory and Application of Cryptographic Techniques (EUROCRYPT'00)*, B. Preneel (Ed.). Springer-Verlag, Berlin, Heidelberg, 2000, pp. 316–334.

[CRAM2003] R. Cramer, S. Fehr, Y. Ishai, E. Kushilevitz, Efficient Multi-party Computation Over Rings. *Advances in Cryptology—EUROCRYPT 2003*, Springer Berlin Heidelberg, 2003, pp. 596–613.

[CRAN2006] L.F. Cranor, P. Guduru, M. Arjula, User Interfaces for Privacy Agents, ACM Transactions on Computer-Human Interaction, Volume 13, 2006, 135–178.

[CURM2011] R. Curtmola, J. Garay, S. Kamara, R. Ostrovsky, Searchable Symmetric Encryption: Improved Definitions and Efficient Constructions, Journal of Computer Security, Volume 19, #5, 2011, 895–934.

[DESM1992] Y. Desmedt, Y. Frankel, Perfect Homomorphic Zero-Knowledge Threshold Schemes over any Finite Abelian Group, SIAM Journal of Discrete Math, Volume 7, #4, 1994, 667–679.

[DING2004] R. Dingledine, N. Mathewson, P. Syverson. Tor: The second-Generation Onion Router, *13th USENIX Security Symposium*, San Diego, CA, 2004, pp. 303–320.

[DUKE2014] A. Duke, Five Things to Know about the Celebrity Nude Photo Hacking Scandal, CNN, October 2014.

[DWOR2006] C. Dwork, K. Kenthapadi, F. McSherry, I. Mironov, M. Naor, Our Data, Ourselves: Privacy via Distributed Noise Generation, *Proceedings of the 24th Annual International Conference on The Theory and Applications of Cryptographic Techniques (EUROCRYPT'06)*, S. Vaudenay (Ed.), Springer-Verlag, Berlin, Heidelberg, 2006, pp. 486–503, DOI=10.1007/11761679_29 http://dx.doi.org/10.1007/11761679_29

[DWOR2009] C. Dwork, J. Lei, Differential Privacy and Robust Statistics, *Proceedings of the Forty-First Annual ACM symposium on Theory of Computing (STOC '09)*, ACM, New York, NY, USA, 2009, pp. 371–380.

[EAGL2006] N. Eagle, A. Pentland, Reality Mining: Sensing Complex Social Systems, Personal and Ubiquitous Computing, Volume 10, #4, 2006, 255–268.

[EAGL2009] N. Eagle, A.S. Pentland, Eigenbehaviors: Identifying Structure in Routine, Behavioral Ecology and Sociobiology, Volume 63, #7, 2009.

[ERLI2014] Ú. Erlingsson, V. Pihur, A. Korolova, RAPPOR: Randomized Aggregatable Privacy-Preserving Ordinal Response, *CCS*, 2014, pp. 1054–1067.

[FERN2016] M. Fernandez, M. Kantarcioglu, B. Thuraisingham, A Framework for Secure Data Collection and Management for Internet of Things, *Proceedings ACSAC Conference Workshop (ICSS)*, Los Angeles, CA, December 2016.

[FLAV2006] C. Flavián, M. Guinalíu, Consumer Trust, Perceived Security and Privacy Policy, Industrial Management & Data Systems, Volume 106, #5, 2006, 601–620.

[GATE2014] C.S. Gates, N. Li, H. Peng, B.P. Sarma, Y. Qi, R. Potharaju, C. Nita-Rotaru, I. Molloy, Generating Summary Risk Scores for Mobile Applications, IEEE Transactions on Dependable Secure Computing, Volume 11, #3, 2014, 238–251.

[GENT2009] C. Gentry, A Fully Homomorphic Encryption Scheme, PhD thesis, Stanford University, 2009, crypto.stanford.edu/craig

[GOH2003] E.J. Goh, Secure Indexes, Cryptology ePrint Archive, Report 2003/216, 2003.

[GUPT2012] A. Gupta, M. Miettinen, N. Asokan, M. Nagy, Intuitive Security Policy Configuration in Mobile Devices using Context Profiling, *IEEE International Conference on Social Computing, SOCIALCOM-PASSAT '12*, Washington, DC, USA, IEEE, pp. 471–480.

[HEAT2013] R. Heatherly, M. Kantarcioglu, B.M. Thuraisingham, *Preventing Private Information Inference Attacks on Social Networks*, IEEE Transactions of Knowledge of Data Engineering, Volume 25, 2013, 1849.

[HERL2004] J.L. Herlocker, J.A. Konstan, L.G. Terveen, J.T. Riedl, Evaluating Collaborative Filtering Recommender Systems, ACM Transactions on Information Systems (TOIS), Volume 22, #1, 2004, 5–53.

[HSIE2013] C.K. Hsieh, H. Tangmunarunkit, F. Alquaddoomi, J. Jenkins, J. Kang, C. Ketcham, B. Longstaff, J. Selsky, B. Dawson, D. Swendeman, D. Estrin, N. Ramanathan, Lifestreams: A Modular Sense-making Toolset for Identifying Important Patterns from Everyday Life, *Proceedings of the 11th ACM Conference on Embedded Networked Sensor Systems (SenSys '13)*, ACM, New York, NY, USA.

[HUSS2015] S.R. Hussain, A. Sallam, E. Bertino, DetAnomDetecting Anomalous Database Transactions by Insiders, CODASPY , San Antonio, TX, 2015, pp. 25–35.

[JOHN2010a] M. Johnson, J. Karat, C.M. Karat, J. Grueneberg, Optimizing a Policy Authoring Framework for Security and Privacy Policies, *Symposium on Usable Privacy and Security (SOUPS)*, , Redmond, WA , 2010.

[JOHN2010b] M. Johnson, J. Karat, C.M. Karat, J. Grueneberg, An Empirical Study of Policy Template Authoring, ACITA, Redmond, WA, 10, 2010, pp. 1–9.

[KANT2004] M. Kantarcioglu, C. Clifton, Privacy-preserving Distributed Mining of Association Rules on Horizontally Partitioned Data, IEEE TKDE, Volume 16, #9, 2004, 1026–1037 .

M. S. Kirkpatrick, E. Bertino, Enforcing Spatial Constraints for mobile RBAC systems, *Proceedings of the 15th ACM Symposium on Access Control Models and Technologies, ser. SACMAT '10*, New York, NY, USA: ACM, 2010, pp. 99–108.

[KIRK2011] M.S. Kirkpatrick, M.L. Damiani, E. Bertino, Prox-RBAC: A Proximity-based Spatially Aware RBAC, *Proceedings of 19th ACM SIGSPATIAL International Symposium on Advances in Geographic Information Systems, ACM-GIS 2011*, November 1–4, 2011, Chicago, IL, USA, pp. 339–348.

[KUMA2009] S. Kumar, M.A. Qadeer, A. Gupta, Location Based Services Using Android, *Proceedings of the 3rd IEEE International Conference on Internet Multimedia Services Architecture and Applications, ser. IMSAA '09*, 2009, pp. 335–339.

[KUSH2011] A. Kushwaha, V. Kushwaha, Location Based Services using Android Mobile Operating System. International Journal of Advances in Engineering & Technology, 2011, pp. 11–20.

[LANE2011] N. D. Lane, M. Mohammod, M. Lin, X. Yang, H. Lu, S. Ali, A. Doryab, E. Berke, T. Choudhury, A.T. Campbell, Bewell: A Smartphone Application to Monitor, Model and Promote Wellbeing, 5th International ICST Conf. Pervasive Computing Technologies for Healthcare, Dublin, Ireland, 2011.

[LEE2013] J. D. Lee, R. Gilad-Bachrach, R. Caruana, Using Multiple Samples to Learn Mixture Models, NIPS, 2013, 324–332.

[LIKA2011] R. LiKamWa, Y. Liu, N.D. Lane, L. Zhong, Can Your Smartphone Infer Your Mood. PhoneSense Workshop, Seattle, WA, November 2011.

[LIM2012] H.-S. Lim, G. Ghinita, E. Bertino, M. Kantarcioglu, A Game-theoretic Approach for High-assurance of Data Trustworthiness in Sensor Networks, *IEEE ICDE*, Washington DC, 2012, pp. 1192–1203.

[MASU2008] M. Masud, J. Gao, L. Khan, J. Han, B. Thuraisingham, A Practical Approach to Classify Evolving Data Streams: Training with Limited Amount of Labeled Data, *IEEE ICDM,* Pisa, Italy, 2008, pp. 929–934.

[MASU2010] M. Masud, Q. Chen, L. Khan, C. Aggarwal, J. Gao, J. Han, B. Thuraisingham. Addressing concept-evolution in concept-drifting data streams, IEEE ICDM, 2010, pp. 929–934.

[MASU2013] M. Masud, Q. Chen, L. Khan, C. Aggarwal, J. Gao, H. Han, A. Srivastava, N.C. Oza. Classification and Adaptive Novel Class Detection of Feature-Evolving Data Streams, IEEE Transactions on Knowledge and Data Engineering, Volume 25, 2013.

[MIDI2014] D. Midi, O. Oluwatimi, B. Shebaro, E. Bertino. Demo Overview: Privacy-Enhancing Features of IdentiDroid. *ACM Conference on Computer and Communications Security,* 2014, pp.1481–1483.

[MONT2014] Y. A. de Montjoye, E. Shmueli, S.S. Wang, A.S. Pentland, openPDS: Protecting the Privacy of Metadata through SafeAnswers, PLoS ONE, Volume 9, #7,e98790.

[MYDE2014] Mydex website. URL http://mydex.org/. Accessed 2014 October.

[NARR2014] Narrative Clip, 2014, http://getnarrative.com/

[NEHM2013] R.V. Nehme, H.S. Lim, E. Bertino, FENCE: Continuous Access Control Enforcement in Dynamic Data Stream Environments, *Proceedings of Third ACM Conference on Data and Application Security and Privacy, CODASPY '13,* San Antonio, TX, USA, February 18–20, 2013, pp. 243–254.

[NIH2015] NIH. Pediatric Research Using Integrated Sensor Monitoring Systems (PROSMS): Informatics Platform Technologies for Asthma (U54).

[NISS2009] H. Nissembaum. Privacy in Context: Technology, Policy, and the Integrity of Social Life (Stanford Law Books) – November 24, 2009.

[OLUW2015] O. Oluwatimi, D. Midi, E. Bertino, Mobile Device Containerization: Survey and Open Research Directions. Submitted for publication, July 2015.

[PARI2012] C. Parizas, D. Pizzocaro, A. Preece, P. Zerfos, Managing ISR Sharing Policies at the Network Edge Using Controlled English, Ground/Air Multisensor Interoperability, Integration, and Networking for Persistent ISR, SPIE, Volume 8742, 2013.

[PROC2007] R. W. Proctor, K.-P. L. Vu, A Multimethod Approach to Examining Usability of Web Privacy Policies and User Agents for Specifying Privacy Preferences. Behavior Research Methods, Volume 39, 2007, 205-221.

[RACH2013] J. Rachapalli, V. Khadilkar, M. Kantarcioglu, B. Thuraisingham, REDACT: A Framework for Sanitizing RDF Data, to appear, WWW 2013.

[RACH2014a] J. Rachapalli, V. Khadilkar, M. Kantarcioglu, B.M. Thuraisingham, Towards Fine Grained RDF Access Control, SACMAT, 2014, 165–176.

[RACH2014b] J. Rachapalli, V. Khadilkar, M. Kantarcioglu, B. M. Thuraisingham, Redaction Based RDF Access Control Language, SACMAT, 2014, 177–180.

[RESN1997] P. Resnick, H.R. Varian, Recommender Systems. Communications of the ACM, Volume 40, #3, 1997, 56–58.

[ROUF2016] T. Rouffineau, Research: Consumers Are Terrible at Updating Their Connected Devices, Ubuntu Insights Blog: https://insights.ubuntu.com/2016/12/15/research-consumers-are-terrible-at-updating-their-connected-devices/

[SHEB2014] B. Shebaro, O. Oluwatimi, D. Midi, E. Bertino, IdentiDroid: Android Can Finally Wear its Anonymous Suit, Transactions on Data Privacy, Volume 7, #1, 2014, 27–50.

[SHI2007] E. Shi, J. Bethencourt, T.-H. Hubert Chan, D. Song, A. Perrig, Multidimensional Range Query over Encrypted Data, *SP '07: Proceedings of the 2007 IEEE Symposium on Security and Privacy,* Washington, DC, USA, 2007, IEEE Computer Society, pp. 350–364.

[SLY2018] L. Sly, U.S. Soldiers Are Revealing Sensitive and Dangerous Information by Jogging, The Washington Post, 2018: https://www.washingtonpost.com/world/a-map-showing-the-users-of-fitness-devices-lets-the-world-see-where-us-soldiers-are-and-what-they-are-

[STEF2012] E. Stefanov, E. Shi, D. Song. Towards Practical Oblivious RAM, *NDSS,* San Diego, CA, 2012.

[STEF2013] E. Stefanov, E. Shi, Oblivistore: High Performance Oblivious Cloud Data Store, NDSS, San Diego, CA, 2013.

[STEF2014] E. Stefanov, C. Papamanthou, E. Shi. Practical dynamic searchable encryption with small leakage, NDSS '14, San Diego, CA, 2014.

[STRA2008] K. Strater, H.R. Lipford, Strategies and Struggles with Privacy in an Online Social Networking Community, *Proceedings of the 22nd British HCI Group Annual Conference on People and Computers: Culture, Creativity, Interaction* - Volume 1, BCS-HCI '08, pp. 111–119, Swinton, UK,British Computer Society, 2008.

[SULL2018] A. Sulleyman, GMAIL Two-Step Verification: Less than 10% of Google Users Have Its Most Important Security Feature Enabled, The Independent, 2018: http://www.independent.co.uk/life-style/gadgets-and-tech/news/gmail-two-step-verification-2fa-google-account-users-security-feature-cyber-crime-a8172391.htmldoing/2018/01/28/86915662-0441-11e8-aa61-f3391373867e_story.html?utm_term=.f83cd627a229

[SWEE2002] L. Sweeney. K-Anonymity: A Model for Protecting Privacy. International Journal of Uncertainty, Fuzziness and Knowledge-Based Systems, Volume 10, 2002, 557–570.

[THUR2018] B.M. Thuraisingham, M. Kantarcioglu, E. Bertino, J.Z. Bakdash, M. Fernández. Towards a Privacy-Aware Quantified Self Data Management Framework, SACMAT 2018, 173–184.

[VU2007] K.-P. L. Vu, V. Chambers, F.P. Garcia, B. Creekmur, J. Sulaitis, D. Nelson, R. Pierce, R.W. Proctor, How Users Read and Comprehend Privacy Policies, In M.J. Smith, G. Salvendy (Eds.), Human Interface. Part II. HCII 2007, Lecture Notes in Computer Science 4558, Springer-Verlag, Berlin, 2007, pp. 802–811.

[WANG2010] G. Wang, Q. Liu, J. Wu, Hierarchical Attribute-based Encryption for Fine Grained Access Control in Cloud Storage Services, *Proceedings of the*, New York, NY, USA, ACM, 2010, pp. 735–737.

[XACM2005] OASIS https://www.oasis-open.org/committees/tc_home.php?wg_abbrev=xacml

14 Data Science, COVID-19 Pandemic, Privacy, and Civil Liberties

14.1 INTRODUCTION

While the previous two chapters discussed security and privacy issues for more generic applications, this chapter focuses on one specific application and that is in healthcare in general and the COVID-19 pandemic in particular. In many ways we have drawn parallels between the COVID-19 security and privacy issues related to the COVID-19 pandemic and 9/11 terrorist attacks and counter-terrorism. In the early 2000s, our work focuses on applying data mining for counter-terrorism and the privacy violations that could occur [THUR2002a, THUR2003]. In this chapter, we explore such issues for the COVID-19 pandemic. One of the main reasons is because while terrorism was one of the most important public safety concerns back in the early 2000s, the COVID-19 pandemic is the most important public safety concerns in the early 2020s.

The COVID-19 pandemic is the worst we have seen in a century since the Spanish Flu (which is supposed to have originated in Kansas). Since then, the world has seen many wars including World War II among others, other pandemics such as SARS and the Swine Flu, the terrorist attacks such as the 9/11 in the United States and 7/7 in the United Kingdom, and hurricanes like Katrina and Maria. But never before has the entire world been gripped with fear like we are now due to COVID-19. It is a nightmare that dwarfs everything else that has happened to us in a century. We dread going out in case we catch the virus and could die as a result of it and yet staying home night and day makes us restless, depressed, and/or anxious.

The one bright spot we have in this case is technology. Due to technology, we have been able to work from home. Video conferencing technologies such as ZOOM, WebEx, Blue Jean, and Teams are helping us immensely not only to attend project meetings but also to participate in conferences and panels as well as socialize with family and friends. It is technology that is keeping us sane. At the same time technology, especially Data Science and Artificial Intelligence (DS/AI), are helping to detect and possibly prevent the spread of COVID-19. Furthermore, DS/AI is also helping with the development of the vaccines that is the ultimate solution to the pandemic. While DS/AI is helping humans to survive during the pandemic, it also has its problems. This is because data collection, data storage, data analytics, and data sharing are at the heart of the solution to the pandemic. But such data-intensive activities can also cause serious privacy violations. That is, if the data about the individuals goes into the wrong hands, then it could cause the violation of the privacy of individuals and subsequently cause great harm such as being blacklisted by insurance companies or blackmailed by adversaries. While privacy is of the utmost importance to an individual, healthcare professionals have to gather as much information as possible to treat the individual for COVID-19. Therefore, we need a balance between safety and privacy.

This chapter discusses the use of DS/AI for detecting and preventing COVID-19 and at the same time explores how the privacy of the individuals may be preserved. It draws parallels between 9/11 attacks and the COVID-11 pandemic. Back in 2002, we wrote a paper titled "Data Mining, National Security, Privacy and Civil Liberties" where we argued the need for data mining for counter-terrorism and yet discussed the violations due to data privacy [THUR2002a]. We are faced with a similar situation today with the COVID-19 pandemic.

DOI: 10.1201/9781003081845-22

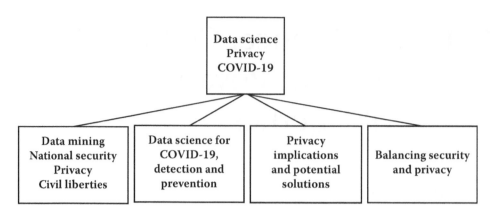

FIGURE 14.1 Data science, COVID-19 pandemic, privacy, and civil liberties.

The organization of this chapter is as follows. We set the stage first by discussing our previous work on data mining and counter-terrorism and its implications for privacy in Section 14.2. DS/AI for COVID-19 is discussed in Section 14.3. Privacy violations are discussed in Section 14.4. Section 14.5 revisits the multi-objective framework for data privacy. Achieving a balance between DS/AI for COVID-19 and data privacy is discussed in Section 14.6. A note about Civil Liberties is provided in Section 14.7. Section 14.8 discusses balancing safety and security vs. privacy and civil liberties. This chapter concludes with Section 14.8. This chapter is an extended version of the keynote address presented at the IEEE BigData Conference Workshop on BigCyber [THUR2020a]. Figure 14.1 illustrates the various concepts discussed in this chapter.

14.2 DATA MINING, NATIONAL SECURITY, PRIVACY, AND CIVIL LIBERTIES

We have conducted research on applying data mining for counter-terrorism problems [THUR2003]. At the same time, we have also investigated the privacy implications of data mining [THUR2005]. To understand the similarities between national security and the pandemic, we will review some of the discussions in [THUR2002a]. While there are many similarities from a technology point of view, there are also some differences from a societal point of view.

Data mining is the process of posing queries against large quantities of data and extracting nuggets often previously unknown [THUR1998]. Data mining has evolved into Data Science, with the emergence of big data technologies, and now with the prominence of machine learning, it is considered part of AI. Nevertheless, data mining gained a lot of prominence after 9/11 when there was great interest to gather data about various individuals and apply data mining techniques to determine whether they were engaged in terrorist acts. For example, the system would examine all the associations of an individual together with his/her behavior patterns to determine whether the person was suspicious.

This resulted in a lot of concern among privacy advocates and the ACLU (American Civil Liberties Union). The privacy advocates were extremely concerned about false positives that could result from data mining and as a result innocent individuals could be branded as terrorists. There was also a concern about a false sense of security due to data mining and whether it was worth sacrificing one's civil liberties in the name of national security.

Subsequently, there was active research on combining data mining and privacy and the first paper on an area called privacy-preserving data mining was published [AGRA2000]. The ideas are to introduce perturbation and randomization into the data and then carry out data mining while ensuring that the end results would be the same. This way, the individual data values can be hidden from the adversaries who want to obtain personal data. The initial work was on privacy-preserving association rule mining and then evolved into addressing various types of data mining techniques including decision trees [LIU2009].

There were many debates and panels on data mining, national security, and privacy [THUR2002b, THUR2002c, THUR2002d, THUR2002e]. We need tradeoffs between data mining, national security, and privacy and policies should guide the data mining process. More details on this will be given in a later section as well as in [THUR2015].

14.3   DATA SCIENCE FOR COVID-19 DETECTION AND PREDICTION

Data mining combined with statistics and big data have evolved into Data Science over the past ten years. At the same time, machine learning has exploded as a field resulting in AI gaining a lot of prominence. We will use the terms Data Science and Machine Learning interchangeably while AI goes beyond machine learning to include planning and reasoning, among other things.

Data are the heart of Epidemiology and in the study of infectious diseases. Data are used not only to detect and prevent the spread of infectious diseases but also to find treatments and vaccines to treat and possibly prevent them. Data are being collected on those infected with COVID-19, including information about the individuals' personal, work, and travel details, their contacts and associations with others as well as their social activities. The data being collected can be analyzed using various data science techniques to extract nuggets to detect the spread of the disease as well as to prevent it. For example, the graphs built for contact tracing purposes are analyzed using say link analysis techniques to determine the persons likely to get COVID-19 from the current infections. Clustering techniques can be used to determine the clusters of potential COVID-19 cases from the data gathered. Decision trees can be used for the classification of the individuals such as those from a certain ethnic origin in a certain county are more susceptible to COVID-19 infections. What we are hoping is that such data science techniques can be used to determine those who are asymptomatic and could be potential spreaders of the virus. For example, if those who are asymptomatic test positive for the virus then one can study the behavior patterns and the genetic markup of these people to understand the reasons as to why they may be asymptomatic. From this information, other asymptomatic people could be tested for the virus and their contacts warned.

While detecting the virus in patients is of the utmost importance, prevention is even more critical. Due to the impact on one's life even if a person survives the disease, it is better to prevent it than to get the virus. Therefore, one could gather data from countries that have very few cases of COVID-19 and learn the trends. Then the information gleaned can be used to prevent the disease in other parts of the world.

Data Science can also be used in developing treatments and vaccines. Data driven science and medicine has been widely accepted by scientists and medical doctors. Information about the DNA of the virus, the genetic makeup of the individuals susceptible to the virus, and all information pertaining to the disease as well as information in various databases can be integrated and analyzed to determine the treatments that could be useful to COVID-19 patients. Also, data from diseases such as the Spanish Flu and other infectious diseases such as SARS and the treatments and vaccines generated for these diseases can be used to develop new treatments and vaccines for COVID-19. In other words, every piece of data including data about the patients, the prior related infections diseases, treatment and vaccines that exists for the various infectious diseases as well as historical trends in the populations of humans and non-humans has to be gathered, stored and analyzed to provide solutions to the pandemic we are faced with today.

Data collection, data storage, data sharing (between different agencies and countries and data analysis (e.g., applying data science techniques) are activities that are critical for developing solutions to handle the pandemic. These solutions could be medical solutions or behavioral and social solutions such as wearing a mask covering the nose and mouth, eye goggles, face shield, gloves, hair coverings and other protective equipment. For example, experiments could be conducted with one group of people wearing masks only and another group of people wearing masks and face shields to determine of the former group has a higher probability of getting COVID-19. Similarly, the number of people in social gatherings could be increased gradually and the outcomes studied. It is critical that such investigations need accurate and sound data if we are to analyze the data to produce useful results. In addition, it is also important that we carry out a thorough risk analysis under various scenarios and keep the public informed of the potential dangers.

14.4 PRIVACY IMPLICATIONS AND POTENTIAL SOLUTIONS

Whenever data are collected about individuals and these data are stored, managed, shared, and analyzed, there is a high probability that the individual's privacy is violated. The simple fact that a person may test positive for COVID-19 could result in the person having a huge stigma and being shunned by everyone even if the person has recovered. On the other hand, we need to inform various individuals that they may have come into contact with a person who has COVID-19. One could do that without identifying the name of the person.

Another problem with collecting and analyzing data is contact tracing. One could examine the data stored in the smart phone of the person and from that data find out about all the contacts of the person. It is crucial that we inform the person's contacts. However, this means having to go through the data in his/her phone or finding out all the activities the person carried out over the past two weeks or so. This means the person's privacy would be violated when data are collected about him/her without his/her knowledge. The data collected may not just be about the person's symptoms or who he/she has contacted. It could also pertain to his/her genetic profile.

The privacy dilemma poses a huge challenge to those working in healthcare analytics. Denying access to the data means potentially millions of deaths. Having access to the data means violating the privacy of individuals that could result in serious consequences to the person such as being denied health coverage for a preexisting condition or using the data to determine the behavioral patterns of the person and subsequently blackmailing the person. Furthermore, to treat the person, the healthcare providers may need access to his/her genetic profile. From this information they may learn about potential diseases the person could get. The insurance companies may deny coverage for diseases the person may not have yet. Therefore, what should we do to ensure that we provide the best care to the COVID-19 patients but at the same time ensure their privacy? The solution may lie in privacy-aware and policy-based data collection, storage, management, sharing, and analysis.

We have conducted research on privacy-aware and policy-based data collection, storage, management, sharing, and analysis [THUR2018]. That is, policies guide the activities for the entire data life cycle. For example, what are the policies for collecting the data, storing the data, managing the data, sharing the data, and analyzing the data? The various privacy-preserving data science techniques look at privacy for analysis purposes. Policies should guide this process. Similarly, policies should guide the other processes also such as with whom do I share the data I have collected about patients? What are the data sharing policies? Even with data deletion, we need policies as we need to ensure that the data are deleted properly.

The next step is to examine various aspects of data science activities including the privacy-aware policy-based data life cycle process and explore how blockchain technologies can be securely applied for various distributed transactions involved in these activities. In addition, smart contracts in supply chains including data supply chain as well as executing financial transactions need to be explored. Finally, blockchain applications in cyber security need to be explored further including areas such as ransom-ware and adversarial machine learning. We believe that blockchain is the glue that integrates data science with cyber security.

14.5 REVISITING THE MULTI-OBJECTIVE FRAMEWORK FOR DATA PRIVACY

In this section, we revisit the multi-objective framework discussed at the NSF workshop and presented in Chapter 5 for privacy aspects of COVID-19. As stated earlier, although there are attempts at coming up with a privacy solution/definition that can address many different scenarios, we believe that there is no one size fits all solution for data privacy. Instead, multiple dimensions need to be tailored for different application domains to achieve practical solutions. First of all, different domains require different definitions of data utility. Second, we need to understand the right definitions of privacy risk. For example, in data sharing scenarios, the probability of re-identification given certain background knowledge could be considered the right measure of privacy risk. Finally, the computation, storage, and communication costs of given protocols need to be considered. These costs could be especially significant for privacy-preserving protocols that involve cryptography. Therefore, the first step is to come up with the definitions of data utlity, determining the acceptable risks, and computing the costs say for storage for COVID-19 applications. Given these three dimensions, one can envisage the multi-objective framework where different dimensions were emphasized as follows:

- *Maximize utility, given the risk and costs constraints:* This would be suited for scenarios where limiting certain privacy risks are paramount.
- *Minimize privacy risks, given the utility and cost constraints:* In some scenarios (e.g., medical care such as COVID-19 care), significant degradation of the utility may not be allowed. In this setting, the parameter values of the protocol (e.g., ε in differential privacy) are chosen in such a way that we try to do our best in terms of privacy given our utility constraints. Please note that in some scenarios, there may not be any parameter settings that can satisfy all the constraints.
- *Minimize cost, given the utility and risk constraints:* In some cases (e.g., cryptographic protocols), you may want to find the protocol parameter settings that may allow for the least expensive protocol that can satisfy all the utility and cost constraints.

To better illustrate these dimensions, consider the privacy-preserving record matching problem addressed in [INAN2012]. Existing solutions to this problem generally follow two approaches: sanitization techniques and cryptographic techniques. In [INAN2012], a hybrid technique that combines these two approaches is presented. This approach enables users to make trade-offs between privacy, accuracy, and cost. This is similar to the multi-objective optimization framework discussed in this chapter. These multi-objective optimizations are achieved by using a blocking phase that operates over sanitized data to filter out pairs of records, in a privacy-preserving manner that do not satisfy the matching condition. By disclosing more information (e.g., differentially private data statistics), the proposed method incurs considerably lower costs than those for cryptographic techniques. On the other hand, it yields matching results that are significantly more accurate when compared to the sanitization techniques, even when privacy requirements are high. The use of different privacy-parameter values allows for different cost, risk, and utility outcomes.

To enable the multi-objective optimization framework for data privacy, we believe that more research needs to be done to identify appropriate utility, risk and cost definitions for different application domains. Especially defining correct and realistic privacy risks is paramount. Many human actions ranging from oil extraction to airline travel, involve risks and benefits. In many cases, such as trying to develop an aircraft that may never malfunction, avoiding all risks are either too costly or impossible. Similarly, we believe that avoiding all privacy risks for all individuals would be too costly. In addition, assuming that an attacker may know everything is too pessimistic. Therefore, coming up with privacy risk definitions under realistic attacker scenarios is needed.

As we have discussed in some of the chapters in Part III, a major issue arising from big data is that in correlating many (big) datasets, one can extract unanticipated information. That is, we need privacy-preserving data correlation techniques. We revisit the relevant issues and research directions discussed in Chapter 5 specific to COVID-19 applications:

- *Techniques to control what is extracted and to check that what is extracted can be used and/or shared.*
- *Support for both personal privacy and population privacy:* In the case of population privacy, it is important to understand what is extracted from the data as this may lead to discrimination. Also, when dealing with security with privacy, it is important to understand the trade-off of personal privacy and collective security.
- *Efficient and scalable privacy-enhancing techniques:* Several such techniques have been developed over the years, including oblivious RAM, security multi-party computation, multi-input encryption, and homomorphic encryption. However, they are not yet practically applicable to large datasets. We need to engineer these techniques, using for example parallelization, to fine tune their implementation and perhaps combine them with other techniques, such as differential privacy (like in the case of the record linkage protocols described in [SCAN2007]). A possible further approach in this respect is to first use anonymized/sanitized data, and then depending on the specific situation to get specific non-anonymized data.
- *Usability of data privacy policies:* Policies must be easily understood by users. We need tools for the average users and we need to understand user expectations in terms of privacy.
- *Approaches for data services monetization:* Instead of selling data, organizations owning datasets can sell privacy-preserving data analytic services based on these datasets. The question to be addressed then is: how would the business model around data change if privacy-preserving data analytic tools were available? Also, if data are considered as a good to be sold, are there regulations concerning contracts for buying/selling data? Can these contracts include privacy clauses be incorporated requiring, for example, that users to whom these data pertain to have been notified?
- *Data publication:* Perhaps, we should abandon the idea of publishing data, given the privacy implications, and rather require the user of the data to utilize a controlled environment (perhaps located in a cloud) for using the data. In this way, it would be much easier to control the proper use of data. An issue would be the case of research data used in universities and the repeatability of data-based research.
- *Privacy implication on data quality:* Recent studies have shown that people lie especially in social networks because they are not sure that their privacy is preserved. This results in a decrease in data quality that then affects decisions and strategies based on these data. Furthermore, A lot of fake news was published with respect to COVID-19 in 2020 and 2021. Therefore, we need techniques to separate the actual useful data from the fake data.
- *Risk models:* Different types of relationship of risks with big data can be identified: (a) big data can increase privacy risks; (b) big data can reduce risks in many domains (e.g., national security). The development of models for these two types of risk is critical to identify suitable trade-off and privacy-enhancing techniques to be used.
- *Data ownership:* The question about who is the owner of a piece of data (e.g., hospital data about COVID-19 patients) is often a difficult question. It is perhaps better to replace this concept with the concept of stakeholder. Multiple stakeholders can be associated with each data item. The concept of stakeholder ties well with risks. Each stakeholder would have different (possibly conflicting) objectives and this can be modeled according to multi-objective optimization. In some cases, a stakeholder may not be aware of the others. For example, a user about whom the data pertains to (and thus a stakeholder for the data) may not be aware that a law enforcement agency is using this data. Technology solutions need to be investigated to eliminate conflicts.
- *Human factors:* All solutions proposed for privacy (as well as confidentiality to be discussed in a later chapter) need to be investigated to determine human involvement, for

example, how would the user interact with the data and his/her specific tasks concerning the use and/or protection of the data, to enhance usability?

- *Data lifecycle framework:* A comprehensive approach to privacy for big data needs to be based on a systematic data lifecycle approach (as discussed in Chapter 13). Phases in the lifecycle need to be identified and their privacy requirements and implications need to be identified. Relevant phases include:
  - *Data acquisition:* We need mechanisms and tools to prevent devices from acquiring data about other individuals (relevant when devices like Google glasses are used); for example, can we come up with mechanisms that automatically block devices from recording/acquiring data at certain locations (or notify a user that recording devices are around). We also need techniques by which each recorded subject may have a say about the use of the data.
  - *Data sharing:* User need to be informed about data sharing/transferred to other parties. In some situations regarding COVID-19, users may have to grant permissions to share data about them.

Addressing the above challenges requires multi-disciplinary research drawing from many different areas including computer science and engineering, information systems, statistics, risk models, economics, social sciences, political sciences, human factors, and psychology. We believe that all these perspectives are needed to develop effective solutions to the problem of privacy in the era of big data as well as to reconcile security with privacy.

14.6   ROLE OF CONFIDENTIALITY AND ACCESS CONTROL

While maintaining the privacy of the patients is of utmost importance while at the same time ensuring that the data have utility, controlling access to the data is also critical to maintaining confidentiality. We will therefore revisit the access control challenges discussed at the NSF Big Data Security and Privacy workshop and listed in Chapter 5 of this book. In particular, we will discuss the access control policies for big data as related to COVID-19 applications. Several data confidentiality techniques and mechanisms exist, the most notable being access control systems and encryptions. Both techniques have been widely investigated. However, for access control systems for big data, which includes the massive amounts of data collected for COVID-19, we need approaches for the following:

- *Merging large numbers of access control policies:* In many cases, big data entails integrating data originating from multiple sources (e.g., patient data related to COVID-19, history of the patient, data about the vaccines). These data may be associated with their own access control policies (referred to as "sticky policies") and these policies must be enforced even when the data are integrated with other data. Therefore, policies need to be integrated and conflicts solved.
- *Automatically administering authorizations for big data and in particular for granting permissions:* If fine-grained access control is required, manual administration on large datasets is not feasible. We need techniques by which authorization can be automatically granted, possibly based on the users' digital identity, profile, and context, and on the data contents and metadata.
- *Enforcing access control policies on heterogeneous multi-media data and geospatial data:* Content-based access control is an important type of access control by which authorizations are granted or denied based on the content of data. Content-based access control is critical when dealing with video surveillance applications which are important for security. As for privacy, such videos have to be protected. Supporting content-based access control requires understanding the contents of protected data and this is very challenging when dealing with multimedia large data sources. Finally, in some cases the

geospatial information about the patients (e.g., location) and vaccines (where the vaccines are stored) have to be protected.

- *Enforcing access control policies in big data stores:* Some of the recent big data systems allow its users to submit arbitrary jobs using programming languages such as Java. For example, in Hadoop, users can submit arbitrary MapReduce jobs written in Java. This creates significant challenges to enforce fine-grained access control efficiently for different users. Although there is some existing work [KHAN2014,ULUS2014] that tries to inject access control policies into submitted jobs, more research needs to be done on how to efficiently enforce such policies in recently developed big data stores.

- *Automatically designing, evolving, and managing access control policies:* When dealing with dynamic environments where sources, users, and applications as well as the data usage are continuously changing, the ability to automatically design and evolve policies is critical to make sure that data are readily available for use while at the same time assuring data confidentiality. Environments and tools for managing policies are also crucial.

14.7   WHAT ABOUT CIVIL LIBERTIES?

The ACLU (American Civil Liberties Union) has published excellent articles on balancing contact tracing vs. privacy [COVID, APPL]. These articles discuss the proposals put forward by smartphone companies such as Apple and Google on contact tracing using Bluetooth technology. ACLU also strongly support policy-based data collection and analysis. For example, the article states the following:

> Technology principles that embed privacy by design are one important type of protection. There still need to be strict policies (https://www.justsecurity.org/69444/how-to-think-about-the-right-to-privacy-and-using-location-data-to-fight-covid-19/) to mitigate against overreach and abuse. These policies, at a minimum, should include the following:
>
> - *Voluntariness:* Whenever possible, a person testing positive must consent to any data sharing by the app. The decision to use a tracking app should be voluntary and uncoerced. Installation, use, or reporting must not be a precondition for returning to work or school, for example.
> - *Use Limitations:* The data should not be used for purposes other than public health – not for advertising and especially not for any punitive or law enforcement purposes.
> - *Minimization:* Policies must be in place to ensure that only necessary information is collected and to prohibit any data sharing with anyone outside of the public health effort.
> - *Data Destruction:* Both the technology and related policies and procedures should ensure deletion of data when there is no longer a need to hold it.
> - *Transparency:* If the government obtains any data, it must be fully transparent about what data it is acquiring, from where, and how it is using that data.
> - *No Mission Creep:* Policies must be in place to ensure tracking does not outlive the effort against COVID-19.
>
> These policies, at a minimum, must be in place to ensure that any tracking app will be effective and will accord with civil liberties and human rights.

While privacy advocates are still concerned about the privacy violations, they also understand the need for data collection and analysis that would save lives. However, when we compare the ACLU's position with their position back in 2002, we see a change. This is partly due to the fact that we know more now about policy-aware data collection and analysis. The concern back then was that we do not want to have a false sense of security at the expense of privacy. Furthermore, at that time certain individuals were detained by the government even when they had no connection to terrorism. However, the pandemic is quite different. Even if a person seems perfectly healthy it may be necessary to test the person as he/she may be asymptomatic. Therefore, there seems to be more tolerance toward testing and contact tracing with COVID-19 then there was in investigating people with respect to counter-terrorism.

Apart from privacy advocates, there are also people who refuse to wear masks and stop going to bars as they claim that their civil liberties are being violated. Although back in 2002, the general public did not raise as much concern when they were pulled from lines at airports for more extensive examination. This may be due to the reasons that we were able to see the gruesome terrorist attacks on television. With respect to COVID-19, we see what happens in hospitals and for some reason people do not seem as concerned about it because they may think that this would not happen to them. I believe that constant education is key to this problem. People have to be warned daily that by not taking precautions not only could they die, they could also infect others including their elderly relatives who have a much higher probability of dying. Wearing a mask or face shield causes some inconvenience, but it is worth making small sacrifices (or even big sacrifices) to save the human race. Politics should not interfere with human lives not in 2001 and 2002 and certainly not today.

14.8   BALANCING SAFETY AND SECURITY VS. PRIVACY AND CIVIL LIBERTIES

The discussions in the previous sections show that regardless of whether we are discussing national security or the pandemic, it is all about balancing safety and security (e.g., saving people's lives and protecting the individuals from terrorist attacks with privacy and civil liberties). Would it not be wonderful if we can have all: safety, security, privacy, and civil liberties? But we know it is not possible. To be safe, we need to sacrifice some aspects of our civil liberties. The question is how much? That is our challenge.

Some would argue that if we do not have all the data to analyze and give advice to epidemiologists and physicians so that the COVID-19 patients get the proper medical care, we are in grave danger of having mass casualties. Those who believe that civil liberties come first would argue we are not a civilized society if the data are used for bad purposes to blackmail individuals and deny them health coverage. Furthermore, they argue that data getting into the wrong hands could also cause hostile acts like murder and rape. That is, knowing the whereabouts of individuals would give ideal opportunities for murders and rapists. In the end, we need tradeoffs. During certain times, we must focus on safety (e.g., pandemic worsening) and during some other times, privacy should be given greater consideration (e.g., when the number of cases is few and far between).

There is now a global initiative called "AI for Good" [UN] and the United Nations is also promoting this initiative. This initiative focuses on all the benefits of AI to help humans. But recently, we wrote an article "Can AI be for Good in the Midst of Cyber Security Attacks and Privacy Violations" [THUR2020b]. For example, we argued that what happens if the AI techniques are attacked? We also discussed the privacy implications of AI. The focus in that article was on children's rights and preventing child abuse. We need to examine this initiative with respect to COVID-19. We need organizations such as ACLU and the United Nations to work together to handle the challenge we are faced with and that is how do we balance safety and security with privacy and civil liberties?

14.9   SUMMARY AND DIRECTIONS

The world has seen pandemics, terrorism, hurricanes, and other natural and man-made disasters. Each time such an event occurs, we discuss technologies that can solve the problem and their impact on our privacy and civil liberties. Such discussions occurred after the 9/11 terrorist attacks and are happening now during the COVID-19 pandemic, the worst human crisis we have faced in a century. This chapter discusses the applications of data science to detect and possibly prevent such pandemics and its impact on our privacy and civil liberties.

This chapter has discussed the applications of data science to the COVID-19 pandemic and then described the serious side effects such as violations of data privacy and civil liberties. It also provides an analogy to the dilemma we were faced with soon after 9/11 on the conflicts between national security and privacy. We argued that we need a privacy aware and policy-based framework for data collection, storage, management, sharing, analytics, and even detection. We also mentioned that we should make small sacrifices such as wearing masks to save the human race from this global pandemic.

We have only discussed the problem and solutions at a very high level. We need to develop a conceptual framework and subsequently the detailed design to develop an architecture and a system that would carry out policy-aware activities for COVID-19. We need to take into consideration the guidance provided by organizations such as the ACLU and the activities of UN to develop such a framework. Our framework has to be flexible in the sense that during certain times, such as a massive increase in the number of COVID-19 cases, we must focus on data collection and analysis and during other times such as less cases we can give more attention to privacy and civil liberties. But we have to be careful as we cannot afford to be complacent. This is because if we relax sometimes even a little, then the infections could continue to explode. Therefore, we need an ideal balance between the two and that will be our challenge as we go forward to achieve a new normal that we are all comfortable with.

REFERENCES

[AGRA2000] R. Agrawal, R. Srikant, Privacy-Preserving Data Mining, *Proceedings of the ACM SIGMOD Conference*, Dallas, TX, May 2000.

[APPL] Apple and Google Announced a Coronavirus Tracking System. How Worried Should We Be? https://www.aclu.org/news/privacy-technology/apple-and-google-announced-a-coronavirus-tracking-system-how-worried-should-we-be/

[COVID] A COVID-19 Balancing Act: Public Health and Privacy (EP. 97), https://www.aclu.org/podcast/covid-19-balancing-act-public-health-and-privacy-ep-97

[INAN2012] A. Inan, M. Kantarcioglu, G. Ghinita, E. Bertino, A Hybrid Approach to Private Record Matching, IEEE Transactions on Dependable Secure Computing (TDSC), Volume 9, #5, 2012, 684–698.

[KHAN2014] L. Khan, K. Hamlen, M. Kantarcioglu, Silver Lining: Enforcing Secure Information Flow at the Cloud Edge, IC2E, 2014, 37–46.

[LIU2009] L. Liu, M. Kantarcioglu, B.M. Thuraisingham, Privacy Preserving Decision Tree Mining from Perturbed Data, HICSS, 2009: 1–10.

[SCAN2007] M. Scannapieco, I. Figotin, E. Bertino, A. Elmagarmid, "Privacy Preserving Schema and Data Matching, *Proceedings of 2007 ACM SIGMOD International Conference on Management of Data, Beijing China*, 653–664.

[THUR1998] B. Thuraisingham, Data Mining: Technologies, Techniques, Tools and Trends, CRC Press, 1998.

[THUR2002a] B. Thuraisingham, Data Mining, National Security, Privacy and Civil Liberties, SIGKDD Explorations, Volume 4, #2, 2002, 1–5.

[THUR2002b] B. Thuraisingham, Data Mining for Counter-Terrorism, Presented at the White House Office of Science and Technology Policy, Washington DC, February 2002.

[THUR2002c] B. Thuraisingham, Data Mining for Counter-Terrorism, Presented at the Database Program panel at Stanford University, Palo Alto, March 2002.

[THUR2002d] B. Thuraisingham, Data Mining for Counter-Terrorism, Panel at the IFIP 113 Conference on Data and Applications Security, University of Cambridge, England, July 2002.

[THUR2002e] B. Thuraisingham, Data Mining for Counter-Terrorism, Presented at the United Nations, September 2002 (also at the White House Office of Technology and Policy, 2002).

[THUR2003] B. Thuraisingham, Web Data Mining with Applications to Counter-terrorism and Business Intelligence, CRC Press, 2003.

[THUR2005] B. Thuraisingham, Privacy-Preserving Data Mining: Development and Directions, Journal of Database Management, Volume 16, #1, 2005, 75–87.

[THUR2015] B. Thuraisingham, Keeping Better Tabs on Suspicious Persons (NY Times Opinion Column), January 13, 2015. https://www.nytimes.com/roomfordebate/2015/01/12/when-known-jihadists-come-home/keeping-better-tabs-on-suspicious-persons

[THUR2018] B. M. Thuraisingham, M. Kantarcioglu, E. Bertino, J. Z. Bakdash, M. Fernández, Towards a Privacy-Aware Quantified Self Data Management Framework, SACMAT, Indianapolis, Indiana, 2018, 173–184.

[THUR2020a] B. Thuraisingham, Data Science, COVID-19, Privacy and Civil Liberties, *Proceedings IEEE BigCyber,* December 2020.

[THUR2020b] B. Thuraisingham, Can AI be for Good in the Midst of Cyber Attacks and Privacy Violations? A Position Paper, ACM CODASPY, 2020, 1–4.

[ULUS2014] H.Ulusoy, M. Kantarcioglu, E. Pattuk, K. W. Hamlen, Vigiles: Fine-Grained Access Control for MapReduce Systems, 2014 *IEEE International Congress on Big Data (BigData Congress)*, Anchorage, Alaska, pp. 40–47

[UN] United Nations, AI for Good, https://aiforgood.itu.int/

Conclusion to Part III

In Part III, we discussed security and privacy aware data science. Some of the directions include the following. In the case of adversarial support vector machine learning (Chapter 10), a future direction for this work is to add cost-sensitive metrics into the learning models. Another direction is to extend the single learning model to an ensemble in which each base learner handles a different set of attacks. We would also like to include an investigation of other adversarial machine learning techniques as well as different types of attacks. Also, we would like to consider additional game theoretic models. In the case of adversarial relevant vector machine learning (Chapter 11), the open problem is to discover an efficient approach to simultaneously update the kernel and the learning parameters. The solution would help to find the optimal learning model against the worst-case attacks in the sample space. As in the case of adversarial support vector machine learning, another direction is to consider different types of attacks.

In the case of privacy preserving data mining (Chapter 12), a future direction is to build the classifiers which can be used to classify the perturbed data set. As we have mentioned before, with a better bound of the random noise data R, using the probability as weighting is an approach that needs further investigation. Also, as novel machine learning techniques are being developed such as deep learning-based approaches, we need to explore privacy preserving machine learning for these approaches. In the case of privacy-aware policy-based data management framework (Chapter 13), the next step is to carry out a detailed design and implementation of the framework. We also have to design the formal framework so we can specify and reason about the policies regardless of the solutions implemented. We also need to take the behavioral aspects of the users into consideration. We need to adapt the framework for applications such as the Internet of Transportation Systems.

Finally, in Chapter 14, we discussed the application of data science for COVID-19 related applications and discussed the privacy violations that could occur. We also discussed the various frameworks being proposed by organizations such as the American Civil Liberties Union.

DOI: 10.1201/9781003081845-23

Part IV

Access Control and Data Science

Introduction to Part IV

Part IV, consisting of five chapters, describes access control and data science. In particular, some of the experimental systems that we have developed will be discussed.

Chapter 15 describes a secure cloud query processing system based on access control for big data. Chapter 16 describes a policy-based information sharing system we have developed that operates in a cloud. Our information sharing policies are rooted in access control policies. An access control framework based on semantic web for social media data which we consider to be a form of big data is discussed in Chapter 17. We describe the inference controller we have developed based on access control for semantic web-based big data in Chapter 18. Finally, we discuss how some of our work could be applied to an application such as the Internet of Transportation system in Chapter 19.

DOI: 10.1201/9781003081845-25

15 Secure Cloud Query Processing Based on Access Control for Big Data Systems

15.1 INTRODUCTION

As stated in Chapter 4, cloud computing is an emerging paradigm in the information technology and data processing communities. Enterprises utilize cloud computing services to outsource data maintenance, which can result in significant financial benefits. Businesses store and access data at remote locations in the "cloud." As the popularity of cloud computing grows, the service providers face ever increasing challenges. They have to maintain huge quantities of heterogeneous data while providing efficient information retrieval. Thus, the key emphasis for cloud computing solutions is scalability and query efficiency. In other words, cloud computing is a critical technology for big data management and analytics.

Also, as stated in Chapter 4, semantic web technologies are being developed to present data in a standardized way such that data can be retrieved and understood by both humans and machines. Historically, webpages are published in plain HTML (Hypertext Markup Language) files that are not suitable for reasoning. Instead, the machine treats these HTML files as a bag of keywords. Researchers are developing semantic web technologies that have been standardized to address such inadequacies. The most prominent standards are Resource Description Framework (RDF) [W3b], SPARQL Protocol and RDF Query Language [W3c] (SPARQL). RDF is the standard for storing and representing data, and SPARQL is a query language to retrieve data from an RDF store. RDF is being used extensively to represent social networks. Cloud computing systems can utilize the power of these semantic web technologies to represent and manage the social networks so that the users of these networks have the capability to efficiently store and retrieve data for data-intensive applications.

Semantic web technologies could be especially useful for maintaining data in the cloud. Semantic web-based social networks provide the ability to specify and query heterogeneous data in a standardized manner. Moreover, using the Web Ontology Language (OWL), ontologies, different schemas, classes, data types, and relationships can be specified without sacrificing the standard RDF/SPARQL interface. Conversely, cloud computing solutions could be of great benefit to the semantic web-based big data community, such as the social network community. Semantic web datasets are growing exponentially. In the web domain, scalability is paramount. Yet, high speed response time is also vital in the web community. We believe that the cloud computing paradigm offers a solution that can achieve both of these goals.

Existing commercial tools and technologies do not scale well in cloud computing settings. Researchers have started to focus on these problems recently. They are proposing systems built from scratch. In [WANG2010], researchers propose an indexing scheme for a new distributed database [COMP] which can be used as a cloud system. When it comes to semantic web data such as RDF, we are faced with similar challenges. With storage becoming cheaper and the need to store and retrieve large amounts of data, developing systems to handle billions of RDF triples requiring terabytes of disk space is no longer a distant prospect. Researchers are already working on billions of triples [NEWM2008, ROHL2007]. Competitions are being organized to encourage researchers to build efficient repositories [CHAL]. At present, there are just a few frameworks (e.g., RDF-3X

DOI: 10.1201/9781003081845-26

[NEUM2008], Jena [CARR2004], Sesame [OPEN], and BigOWLIM [KIRY2005]) for semantic web technologies, and these frameworks have limitations for large RDF graphs. Therefore, storing a large number of RDF triples and efficiently querying them is a challenging and important problem.

In this chapter, we discuss a secure query processing system based on access control that functions in the cloud and manages a large number of RDF triples. These RDF triples can be used to represent big data applications such as social networks as discussed in our previous book [THUR2015]. We have developed a SPARQL query optimizer on top of JENA for the query processing engine. We have developed two access control models on top of the SPARQL query optimizer to control the access to the data. One is based on a token-based access control mechanism and the other is based on the XACML (eXtensive Access Control Markup Language) access control framework [XACM]. That is, we essentially discuss access control models for big data systems.

The organization of this chapter is as follows. Our approach is discussed in Section 15.2. In Section 15.3, we discuss related work. In Section 15.4, we discuss our system and operational architectures. In Section 15.5, we discuss how we answer a SPARQL query. In Section 15.6, we present the results of our experiments. In Section 15.7, we discuss our work on security policy enforcement mechanisms that we have built on top of our prototype system. Finally, in Section 15.8, we draw some conclusions and discuss the areas that we have identified for improvement in the future. Key concepts discussed in this chapter are illustrated in Figure 15.1. A more detailed discussion of the concepts, architectures, and experiments are provided in [HUSA2011a] and [HUSA2011b]. Since semantic web technologies can be used to model big data systems such as social network systems, our query processing system can be utilized to query social networks and related big data systems.

15.2 OUR APPROACH

A distributed system can be built to overcome the scalability and performance problems of current semantic web frameworks. Databases are being distributed to provide such scalable solutions. However, to date, there is no distributed repository for storing and managing RDF data. Researchers have only recently begun to explore the problems and technical solutions which must be addressed to build such a distributed system. One promising line of investigation involves making use of readily available distributed database systems or relational databases. Such database systems can use relational schema for the storage of RDF data. SPARQL queries can be answered by converting them to SQL first [CHEB2007, CHON2005, CYGA2005]. Optimal relational

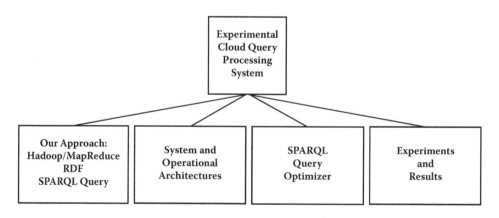

FIGURE 15.1 Experimental cloud query processing system.

schemas are being probed for this purpose [ABAD2007]. The main disadvantage with such systems is that they are optimized for relational data. They may not perform well for RDF data, especially because RDF data are sets of triples [W3a] (an ordered tuple of three components called subject, predicate, and object, respectively) which form large directed graphs. In a SPARQL query, any number of triple patterns (TPs) [W3e] can join on a single variable [W3d] which makes a relational database query plan complex. Performance and scalability will remain a challenging issue due to the fact that these systems are optimized for relational data schemata and transactional database usage.

Yet, another approach is to build a distributed system for RDF from scratch. Here, there will be an opportunity to design and optimize a system with specific application to RDF data. In this approach, the researchers would be reinventing the wheel. Instead of starting with a blank slate, we built a solution with a generic distributed storage system which utilizes a cloud computing platform. We then tailored the system and schema specifically to meet the needs of semantic web data. Finally, we built a semantic web repository using such a storage facility.

Hadoop [HADOa] is a distributed file system where files can be saved with replication. It is an ideal candidate for building a storage system. Hadoop features high fault tolerance and great reliability. In addition, it also contains an implementation of the MapReduce [DEAN2004] programming model, a functional programming model which is suitable for the parallel processing of large amounts of data. Through partitioning data into a number of independent chunks, MapReduce processes run against these chunks, making parallelization simpler. Moreover, the MapReduce programming model facilitates and simplifies the task of joining multiple triple patterns.

In this chapter, we describe a schema to store RDF data in Hadoop, and we will detail a solution to process queries against these data. In the preprocessing stage, we process RDF data and populate files in the distributed file system. This process includes partitioning and organizing the data files and executing dictionary encoding. We will then detail a query engine for information retrieval. We will specify exactly how SPARQL queries will be satisfied using MapReduce programming. Specifically, we must determine the Hadoop "jobs" that will be executed to solve the query. We present a greedy algorithm that produces a query plan with the minimal number of Hadoop jobs. This is an approximation algorithm using heuristics, but we prove that the worst case has a reasonable upper bound. Finally, we utilize two standard benchmark datasets to run experiments. We present results for the dataset ranging from 0.1 to over 6.6 billion triples. We show that our solution is exceptionally scalable. We also show that our solution outperforms leading state-of-the-art semantic web repositories using standard benchmark queries on very large datasets.

We have also designed and developed two types of access control models for big data. One is a token-based mechanism and the other is based on XACML. Both systems are built on top of our SPARQL query optimizer and the JENA data management system for semantic web data. Our contributions are listed below and illustrated in Figure 15.2. More details are given in [HUSA2011a].

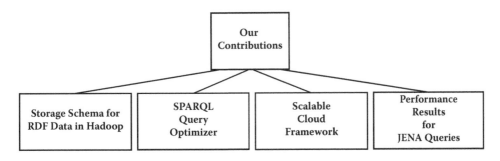

FIGURE 15.2   Our contributions.

1. We designed a storage scheme to store RDF data in Hadoop distributed file system (HDFS) [HADOb].
2. We developed an algorithm that is guaranteed to provide a query plan whose cost is bounded by the log of the total number of variables in the given SPARQL query. It uses summary statistics for estimating join selectivity to break ties.
3. We built a framework which is highly scalable and fault-tolerant and supports data-intensive query processing.
4. We demonstrated that our approach performs better than Jena for all queries and BigOWLIM and RDF-3X for complex queries having large result sets.
5. We developed two access control systems on top of the RDF data system.

15.3 RELATED WORK

MapReduce, though a programming paradigm, is rapidly being adopted by researchers. This technology is becoming increasingly popular in the community which handles large amounts of data. It is the most promising technology to solve the performance issues researchers are facing in cloud computing. In [ABAD09a], the author discusses how MapReduce can satisfy most of the requirements to build an ideal Cloud DBMS. Researchers and enterprises are using MapReduce technology for web indexing, searches, and data mining. In this section, we first investigate research related to MapReduce. Next, we discuss works related to the semantic web.

Google uses MapReduce for web indexing, data storage, and social networking [CHAN2006]. Yahoo! uses MapReduce extensively in its data analysis tasks [OLST2008]. IBM has successfully experimented with a scale-up scale-out search framework using MapReduce technology [MORE07]. In [SISM2010], they have reported how they integrated Hadoop and System R. Teradata did a similar work by integrating Hadoop with a parallel DBMS [XU2010].

Researchers have used MapReduce to scale up classifiers for mining petabytes of data [MORE2008]. They have worked on data distribution and partitioning for data mining, and have applied three data mining algorithms to test the performance. Data mining algorithms are being rewritten in different forms to take advantage of MapReduce technology. In [CHU2006], researchers rewrite well-known machine learning algorithms to take advantage of multicore machines by leveraging the MapReduce programming paradigm. Another area where this technology is successfully being used is simulation [MCNA2007]. In [ABOU09], researchers reported an interesting idea of combining MapReduce with existing relational database techniques. These works differ from our research in that we use MapReduce for semantic web technologies. Our focus is on developing a scalable solution for storing RDF data and retrieving them by SPARQL queries.

In the semantic web arena, there has not been much work done with MapReduce technology. We have found two related projects: BioMANTA [ITEE] project and Scalable, High-Performance, Robust and Distributed (SHARD) [CLOU]. BioMANTA proposes extensions to RDF molecules [DING2005] and implements a MapReduce-based molecule store [NEWM2008]. They use MapReduce to answer the queries. They have queried a maximum of four million triples. Our work differs in the following ways: first, we have queried one billion triples. Second, we have devised a storage schema which is tailored to improve query execution performance for RDF data. We store RDF triples in files based on the predicate of the triple and the type of the object. Finally, we also have an algorithm to determine a query processing plan whose cost is bounded by the log of the total number of variables in the given SPARQL query. By using this, we can determine the input files of a job and the order in which they should be run. To the best of our knowledge, we are the first ones to come up with a storage schema for RDF data using flat files in HDFS and a MapReduce job determination algorithm to answer a SPARQL query.

SHARD is an RDF triple store using the Hadoop Cloudera distribution. This project shows initial results demonstrating Hadoop's ability to improve scalability for RDF datasets. However, SHARD stores its data only in a triple store schema. It currently does no query planning or reordering, and its query processor will not minimize the number of Hadoop jobs. There has been significant research into semantic web repositories with particular emphasis on query efficiency and scalability. In fact, there are too many such repositories to fairly evaluate and discuss each. Therefore, we pay attention to semantic web repositories which are open source or available for download and which have received favorable recognition in the semantic web and database communities.

In [ABAD2009b] and [ABAD2007], researchers reported a vertically partitioned DBMS for storage and retrieval of RDF data. Their solution is a schema with a two-column table for each predicate. Their schema is then implemented on top of a column-store relational database such as CStore [STON2005] or MonetDB [BONC06]. They observed performance improvement with their scheme over traditional relational database schemes. We have leveraged this technology in our predicate-based partitioning within the MapReduce framework. However, in the vertical partitioning research, only small databases (<100 million) were used. Several papers [SIDI2008, MCGL2009, WEIS2008] have shown that vertical partitioning's performance is drastically reduced as the dataset size is increased.

Jena [CARR2004] is a semantic web framework for Jena. True to its framework design, it allows integration of multiple solutions for persistence. It also supports inference through the development of reasoners. However, Jena is limited to a triple store schema. In other words, all data are stored in a single three column table. Jena has very poor query performance for large datasets. Furthermore, any change to the dataset requires complete recalculation of the inferred triples.

BigOWLIM [KIRY2005] is among the fastest and most scalable semantic web frameworks available. However, it is not as scalable as our framework and requires very high-end and costly machines. It requires expensive hardware (a lot of main memory) to load large datasets and it has a long loading time. As our experiments show, it does not perform well when there is no bound object in a query. However, the performance of our framework is not affected in such a case.

RDF-3X [NEUM2008] is considered the fastest existing semantic web repository. In other words, it has the fastest query times. RDF-3X uses histograms, summary statistics, and query optimization to enable high-performance semantic web queries. As a result, RDF-3X is generally able to outperform any other solution for queries with bound objects and aggregate queries. However, RDF-3X's performance degrades exponentially for unbound queries, and queries with even simple joins if the selectivity factor is low. This becomes increasingly relevant for inference queries which generally require unions of subqueries with unbound objects. Our experiments show that RDF-3X is not only slower for such queries, it often aborts and cannot complete the query. For example, consider the simple query "Select all students." This query in LUBM requires us to select all graduate students, select all undergraduate students, and union the results together. However, there are a very large number of results in this union. While both subqueries complete easily, the union will abort in RDF-3X for LUBM (30,000) with 3.3 billion triples.

RDF Knowledge Base (RDFKB) [MCGL2010] is a semantic web repository using a relational database schema built on bit vectors. RDFKB achieves better query performance than RDF-3X or vertical partitioning. However, RDFKB aims to provide knowledge base functions such as inference forward chaining, uncertainty reasoning, and ontology alignment. RDFKB prioritizes these goals ahead of scalability. RDFKB is not able to load LUBM (30,000) with three billion triples, so it cannot compete with our solution for scalability.

Hexastore [WEIS08] and BitMat [ATRE2008] are main memory data structures optimized for RDF indexing. These solutions may achieve exceptional performance on hot runs, but they are not optimized for cold runs from persistent storage. Furthermore, their scalability is directly associated with the quantity of main memory RAM available. These products are not available for testing and evaluation.

In our previous work [HUSA2009, HUSA2010], we proposed a greedy and an exhaustive search algorithm to generate a query processing plan. However, the exhaustive search algorithm was expensive and the greedy one was not bounded and its theoretical complexity was not defined. In this chapter, we present a new greedy algorithm with an upper bound. Also, we did observe scenarios in which our old greedy algorithm failed to generate the optimal plan. The new algorithm is able to obtain the optimal plan in each of these cases. The Join Executer component runs the jobs using MapReduce framework. It then relays the query answer from Hadoop to the user.

15.4 ARCHITECTURE

Our system architecture is illustrated in Figure 15.3. It essentially consists of a SPARQL query optimizer and an RDF data manager implemented in the cloud. The operational architecture is illustrated in Figure 15.4. It consists of two components. The upper part of Figure 15.4 depicts the

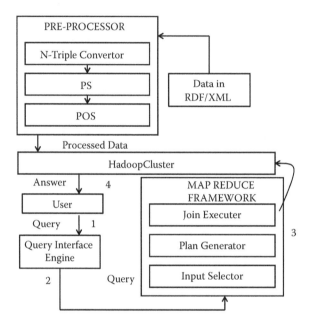

FIGURE 15.3   System architecture.

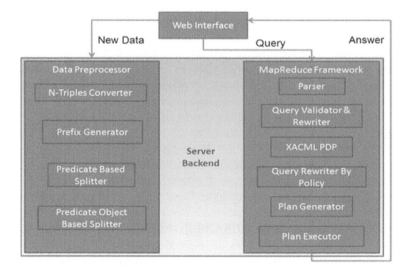

FIGURE 15.4   Operational architecture.

data preprocessing component and the lower part shows the query answering one. We have three subcomponents for data generation and preprocessing. We convert RDF/XML [W3f] to N-Triples [W3a] serialization format using our N-triples converter component. The predicate split (PS) component takes the N-triples data and splits it into predicate files. The predicate files are then fed into the Predicate Object Split (POS) component which splits the predicate files into smaller files based on the type of objects. These steps are described in the following figures.

15.4.1 DATA GENERATION AND STORAGE

For our experiments, we use the LUBM [GUO2005] dataset. It is a benchmark dataset designed to enable researchers to evaluate a semantic web repository's performance [GUO2004]. The LUBM data generator generates data in RDF/XML serialization format. This format is not suitable for our purpose because we store data in HDFS as flat files and so to retrieve even a single triple, we would need to parse the entire file. Therefore, we convert the data to N-triples to store the data, because with that format, we have a complete RDF triple (Subject, Predicate, and Object) in one line of a file which is very convenient to use with MapReduce jobs. The processing steps to go through to get the data into our intended format are described in the following sections.

15.4.2 FILE ORGANIZATION

We do not store the data in a single file because, in a Hadoop and MapReduce framework, a file is the smallest unit of input to a MapReduce job and in the absence of caching, a file is always read from the disk. If we have all the data in one file, the whole file will be input to jobs for each query. Instead, we divide the data into multiple smaller files. The splitting is done in two steps which we discuss in the following sections.

15.4.3 PREDICATE SPLIT

In the first step, we divide the data according to the predicates. This division immediately enables us to cut down the search space for any SPARQL query which does not have a variable predicate. For such a query, we can just pick a file for each predicate and run the query on those files only. For simplicity, we name the files with predicates, e.g., all the triples containing a predicate p1:pred go into a file named p1-pred. However, in case we have a variable predicate in a triple pattern [W3e] and if we cannot determine the type of the object, we have to consider all files. If we can determine the type of the object, then we consider all files having that type of object. We discuss more on this in Section 15.5. In real-world RDF datasets, the number of distinct predicates is in general not a large number [STOC2008]. However, there are datasets having many predicates. Our system performance does not vary in such a case because we just select files related to the predicates specified in a SPARQL query.

15.4.4 SPLIT USING EXPLICIT TYPE INFORMATION OF OBJECT

In the next step, we work with the explicit type information in the rdf_type file. The predicate rdf:type is used in RDF to denote that a resource is an instance of a class. The rdf_type file is first divided into as many files as the number of distinct objects the rdf:type predicate has. For example, if in the ontology, the leaves of the class hierarchy are c_1, c_2, ...,c_n, then we will create files for each of these leaves and the file names will be like type_c_1, type_c_2; ..., type_c_n. Please note that the object values c_1, c_2, ...,c_n are no longer needed to be stored within the file as they can be easily retrieved from the file name. This further reduces the amount of space needed to store the data. We generate such a file for each distinct object value of the predicate rdf:type.

15.4.5 Split Using Implicit Type Information of Object

We divide the remaining predicate files according to the type of the objects. Not all the objects are URIs (Uniform Resource Identifier); some are literals. The literals remain in the file named by the predicate; no further processing is required for them. The type information of a URI object is not mentioned in these files but they can be retrieved from the type_*files. The URI objects move into their respective file named as predicate type. For example, if a triple has the predicate p and the type of the URI object is c_i, then the subject and object appear in one line in the file p_c_i. To do this split, we need to join a predicate file with the type_*files to retrieve the type information.

Our MapReduce framework, described in Section 15.5, has three subcomponents in it. It takes the SPARQL query from the user and passes it to the Input and Plan Generator. This component selects the input files by using our algorithm described in Section 15.5, decides how many MapReduce jobs are needed, and passes the information to the Join Executer component which runs the jobs using MapReduce framework. It then relays the query answer from Hadoop to the user.

15.4.6 Access Control Models

We have developed a token-based access control mechanism as well as an XACML-based access control model on top of the RDF data system. The right-hand side of the operational architecture shows how the XACML policies are implemented. That is, as the data arrive from the optimization component (in the left-hand side), the policies are enforced on the data according to the XACML model. That is, the request is submitted to the PEP (Policy Enforcement Point). The PEP then carries out some checks and then gives it to the PDP (Policy Decision Point) to make a decision. The PDP then checks with the PAP (Policy Access Point) and PIP (Policy Information Pont) and then makes a decision as to how the policy should be enforced. The PEP then enforces the decision. It should be noted that the XACML-based framework can be replaced by any access control model and therefore we have also implemented a token-based access control model. These security models will be discussed in Section 15.7.

15.5   MAPREDUCE FRAMEWORK

15.5.1   Overview

The MapReduce framework is at the heart of our cloud computing efforts. In this section, we discuss how we answer SPARQL queries in our MapReduce framework component.

Section 15.5.2 discusses our algorithm to select input files for answering the query. Section 15.5.3 describes the cost estimation needed to generate a plan to answer a SPARQL query. It introduces a few terms which we use in the following discussions. We also describe the ideal model we should follow to estimate the cost of a plan, and introduce the heuristics-based model we use in practice. Section 15.5.4 presents our heuristics-based greedy algorithm to generate a query plan which uses the cost model introduced in Section 15.5.3. We face tie situations in order to generate a plan in some cases. In Section 15.5.5 we discuss how we handle these special cases. Section 15.5.6 shows how we implement a join in a Hadoop MapReduce job by working through an example query.

15.5.2   Input Files Selection

Before determining the jobs, we select the files that need to be input to the jobs. We have some query rewriting capability which we apply at this step of query processing. We take the query submitted by the user and iterate over the triple patterns. We may encounter the following cases:

1. In a triple pattern, if the predicate is variable, we select all the files as input to the jobs and terminate the iteration.
2. If the predicate is rdf:type and the object is concrete, we select the type file having that particular type. For example, for LUBM query 9 (Listing 1), we could select file type_Student as part of the input set. However, this brings up an interesting scenario. In our dataset, there is actually no file named type_Student because Student class is not a leaf in the ontology tree. In this case, we consult the LUBM ontology [LEHI] to determine the correct set of input files. We add the files type_GraduateStudent, type_UndergraduateStudent, and type_ResearchAssistant as GraduateStudent; UndergraduateStudent, and ResearchAssistant are the leaves of the subtree rooted at node Student.
3. If the predicate is rdf:type and the object is variable, then if the type of the variable is defined by another triple pattern, we select the type file having that particular type. Otherwise, we select all type files.
4. If the predicate is not rdf:type and the object is variable, then we need to determine if the type of the object is specified by another triple pattern in the query. In this case, we can rewrite the query and eliminate some joins. For example, in LUBM Query 9 (Listing 1), the type of Y is specified as Faculty and Z as Course and these variables are used as objects in the last three triple patterns. If we choose files advisor_Lecturer, advisor_PostDoc, advisor_FullProfessor, advisor_AssociateProfessor, advisor_AssistantProfessor, and advisor_ VisitingProfessor as part of the input set, then the triple pattern in line 2 becomes unnecessary. Similarly, triple pattern in line 3 becomes unnecessary if files takesCourse_Course and takesCourse_GraduateCourse are chosen. Hence, we get the rewritten query shown in Listing 2. However, if the type of the object is not specified, then we select all files for that predicate.
5. If the predicate is not rdf:type and the object is concrete, then we select all files for that predicate.

Listing 1: LUBM Query 9

```
SELECT?X?Y?Z WHERE {
?X rdf:type ub:Student.
?Y rdf:type ub:Faculty.
?Z rdf:type ub:Course.
?X ub:advisor?Y.
?Y ub:teacherOf?Z.
?X ub:takesCourse?Z}
```

Listing 2: Rewritten LUBM Query 9

```
SELECT?X?Y?Z WHERE {
?X rdf:type ub:Student.
?X ub:advisor?Y.
?Y ub:teacherOf?Z.
?X ub:takesCourse?Z}
```

15.5.3 COST ESTIMATION FOR QUERY PROCESSING

We run Hadoop jobs to answer a SPARQL query. In this section, we discuss how we estimate the cost of a job. However, before doing that, we introduce some definitions which we will use later:

Definition 15.1: *Triple Pattern, TP:* A triple pattern is an ordered set of subject, predicate, and object which appears in a SPARQL query WHERE clause. The subject, predicate, and object can be either a variable (unbounded) or a concrete value (bounded).

Definition 15.2: *Triple Pattern Join, TPJ:* A triple pattern join is a join between two TPs on a variable.

Definition 15.3: *MapReduceJoin, MRJ:* A MapReduceJoin is a join between two or more triple patterns on a variable.

Definition 15.4: *Job, JB:* A job JB is a Hadoop job where one or more MRJs are done. JB has a set of input files and a set of output files.

Definition 15.5: *Conflicting MapReduceJoins, CMRJ:* Conflicting MapReduceJoins is a pair of MRJs on different variables sharing a triple pattern.

Definition 15.6: *Nonconflicting MapReduceJoins, NCMRJ:* Nonconflicting MapReduceJoins is a pair of MRJs either not sharing any triple pattern or sharing a triple pattern and the MRJs are on same variable.

An example will illustrate these terms better. In Listing 3, we show LUBM Query 12. Lines 2, 3, 4, and 5 each have a triple pattern. The join between TPs in lines 2 and 4 on variable?X is an MRJ. If we do two MRJs, one between TPs in lines 2 and 4 on variable?X and the other between TPs in lines 4 and 5 on variable?Y, there will be a CMRJ as TP in line 4 (?X ub:worksFor?Y) takes part in two MRJs on two different variables ?X and ?Y. This type of join is called CMRJ because in a Hadoop job, more than one variable of a TP cannot be a key at the same time and MRJs are performed on keys. An NCMRJ, shown would be one MRJ between triple patterns in lines 2 and 4 on variable ?X and another MRJ between triple patterns in lines 3 and 5 on variable?Y. These two MRJs can make up a JB.

Listing 3: LUBM Query 12

```
SELECT?X WHERE {
?X rdf:type ub:Chair.
?Y rdf:type ub:Department.
?X ub:worksFor?Y.
?Y ub:subOrganizationOf http://www.U0.edu}
```

15.5.3.1   Ideal Model

To answer a SPARQL query, we may need more than one job. Therefore, in an ideal scenario, the cost estimation for processing a query requires individual cost estimation of each job that is needed to answer that query. A job contains three main tasks which are reading, sorting, and writing. We estimate the cost of a job based on these three tasks. For each task, a unit cost is assigned to each triple pattern it deals with. In the current model, we assume that costs for reading and writing are the same.

$$\text{Cost} = \left(\sum_{i=1}^{n-1} MI_i + MO_i + RI_i + RO_i \right) + MI_n + MO_n + RI_n \tag{15.1}$$

$$= \left(\sum_{i=1}^{n-1} Job_i \right) + MI_n + MO_n + RI_n \tag{15.2}$$

$$Job_i = +MI_i + MO_i + RO_i + RI_i (\text{if } i < n) \tag{15.3}$$

where

$$MI_i = \text{Map Input phase for job } i$$

$$MO_i = \text{Map Output phase for job } i$$

$$RI_i = \text{Reduce Input phase for job } i$$

$$RO_i = \text{Map Output phase for job } i$$

Equation (15.1) is the total cost of processing a query. It is the summation of the individual costs of each job and only the map phase of the final job. We do not consider the cost of the reduce output of the final job because it would be same for any query plan as this output is the final result which is fixed for a query and a given dataset. A job essentially performs a MapReduce task on the file data. Equation (15.2) shows the division of the MapReduce task into subtasks. Hence, to estimate the cost of each job, we will combine the estimated cost of each subtask.

15.5.3.1.1 Map input (MI) phase

This phase reads the triple patterns from the selected input files stored in the HDFS. Therefore, we can estimate the cost for the MI phase to be equal to the total number of triples in each of the selected files.

15.5.3.1.2 Map output (MO) phase

The estimation of the MO phase depends on the type of query being processed. If the query has no bound variable (e.g., [?X ub:worksFor?Y]), then the output of the Map phase is equal to the input. All of the triple patterns are transformed into key-value pairs and given as output. Therefore, for such a query the MO cost will be the same as MI cost. However, if the query involves a bound variable, (e.g., [?Y ub:subOrganizationOf <http://www.U0.edu>]), then before making the key-value pairs, a bound component selectivity estimation can be applied. The resulting estimate for the triple patterns will account for the cost of Map Output phase. The selected triples are written to a local disk.

15.5.3.1.3 Reduce input (RI) phase

In this phase, the triples from the Map Output phase are read via HTTP and then sorted based on their key values. After sorting, the triples with identical keys are grouped together. Therefore, the cost estimation for the RI phase is equal to the MO phase. The number of key-value pairs that are sorted in RI is equal to the number of key-value pairs generated in the MO phase.

15.5.3.1.4 Reduce output (RO) phase

The RO phase deals with performing the joins. Therefore, it is in this phase we can use the join triple pattern selectivity summary statistics to estimate the size of its output. Later, we talk in detail about the join triple pattern selectivity summary statistics needed for our framework.

However, in practice, the earlier discussion is applicable for the first job only. For the subsequent jobs, we lack both the precise knowledge and estimate of the number of triple patterns selected after applying the join in the first job. Therefore, for these jobs, we can take the size of the RO phase of the first job as an upper bound on the different phases of the subsequent jobs.

Equation (15.3) shows a very important postulation. It illustrates the total cost of an intermediate job, when $i < n$ includes the cost of the RO phase in calculating the total cost of the job.

15.5.3.2 Heuristic Model

In this section, we show that the ideal model is not practical or cost effective. There are several issues that make the ideal model less attractive in practice. First, the ideal model considers simple abstract costs, namely, the number of triples read and written by the different phases, ignoring the actual cost of copying, sorting, etc., these triples and the overhead for running jobs in Hadoop. But accurately incorporating those costs in the model is a difficult task. Even making a reasonably good estimation may be nontrivial. Second, to estimate intermediate join outputs, we need to maintain comprehensive summary statistics. In a MapReduce job in Hadoop, all the joins on a variable are joined together. For example, in the rewritten LUBM Query 9 (Listing 2), there are three joins on variable X. When a job is run to do the join on X, all the joins on X between triple patterns 1, 2, and 4 are done. If there were more than three joins on X, all will still be handled in one job. This shows that to gather summary statistics to estimate join selectivity, we face an exponential number of join cases. For example, between triple patterns having p_1, p_2, and p_3, there may be multiple types of joins because in each triple pattern, a variable can occur either as a subject or an object. In the case of the rewritten Query 9, it is a subject–subject–subject join between 1, 2, and 4. There can be more types of join between these three, for example, subject–object–subject and object–subject–object. That means, between P predicates, there can be 2^P types of joins on a single variable (ignoring the possibility that a variable may appear both as a subject and object in a triple pattern). If there are P predicates in the dataset, a total number of cases for which we need to collect summary statistics can be calculated by the formula:

$$2^2 \times C_2^P + 2^3 \times C_3^P + \ldots + 2^P \times C_P^P$$

In the LUBM dataset, there are 17 predicates. So, in total, there are 129,140,128 cases which is a large number. Gathering summary statistics for such a large number of cases would be very time- and space-consuming. Hence, we took an alternate approach.

We observe that there is significant overhead for running a job in Hadoop. Therefore, if we minimize the number of jobs to answer a query, we get the fastest plan. The overhead is incurred by several disk I/O and network transfers that are integral part of any Hadoop job. When a job is submitted to a Hadoop cluster, at least the following set of actions takes place:

1. The Executable file is transferred from client machine to Hadoop JobTracker [WIKIa].
2. The JobTracker decides which TaskTrackers [WIKIb] will execute the job.
3. The Executable file is distributed to the TaskTrackers over the network.
4. Map processes start by reading data from HDFS.
5. Map outputs are written to discs.
6. Map outputs are read from discs, shuffled (transferred over the network to TaskTrackers which would run Reduce processes), sorted and written to discs.
7. Reduce processes start by reading the input from the discs.
8. Reduce outputs are written to discs.

These disk operations and network transfers are expensive operations even for a small amount of data. For example, in our experiments, we observed that the overhead incurred by one job is almost equivalent to reading a billion triples. The reason is that in every job, the output of the map process is always sorted before feeding the reduce processes. This sorting is unavoidable even if it is not needed by the user. Therefore, it would be less costly to process several hundred million more triples in n jobs, rather than processing several hundred million less triples in $n + 1$ jobs.

To further investigate, we did an experiment where we used the query shown in Listing 4. Here, the join selectivity between TPs 2 and 3 on ?Z is the highest. Hence, a query plan generation algorithm which uses selectivity factors to pick joins would select this join for the first job. As the other TPs 1 and 4 share variables with either TP 2 or 3, they cannot take part in any other join, moreover, they do not share any variables so the only possible join that can be executed in this job is the join between TPs 2 and 3 on ?X. Once this join is done, the two joins left are between TP 1 and the join output of first job on variable ?X and between TP 4 and the join output of first job on variable ?Y. We found that the selectivity of the first join is greater than the latter one. Hence, the second job will do this join and TP 4 will again not participate. In the third and last job, the join output of the second job will be joined with TP 4 on ?Y. This is the plan generated using join selectivity estimation. But the minimum job plan is a two job plan where the first job joins TPs 1 and 2 on?X and TPs 3 and 4 on ?Y. The second and final job joins the two join outputs of the first job on ?Z. The query runtimes we found are given in [HUSA2011a].

Listing 4: Experiment Query

?S1 ub:advisor?X.
?X ub:headOf?Z.
?Z ub:subOrganizationOf?Y.
?S2 ub:mastersDegreeFrom?Y

For each dataset, we found that the two job plan is faster than the three job plan even though the three job plan produced less intermediate data because of the join selectivity order. We can explain this by an observation we made in another small experiment. We generated files of sizes 5 and 10 MB containing random integers. We put the files in HDFS. For each file, we first read the file by a program and recorded the time needed to do it. While reading, our program reads from one of the three available replicas of the file. Then, we ran a MapReduce job which rewrites the file with the numbers sorted. We utilized MapReduce sorting to have the sorted output. Please also note than when it writes the file, it writes three replications of it. We found that the MapReduce job, which does reading, sorting, and writing, takes 24.47 times longer to finish for 5 MB. For 10 MB, it is 42.79 times. This clearly shows how the write and data transfer operations of a MapReduce job are more expensive than a simple read from only one replica. Because of the number of jobs, the three job plan is doing much more disk read and write operations as well as network data transfers and as a result is slower than the two job plan even if it is reading less input data.

Because of these reasons, we do not pursue the ideal model. We follow the practical model which is to generate a query plan having a minimum of possible jobs. However, while generating a minimum job plan, whenever we need to choose a join to be considered in a job among more than one joins, instead of choosing randomly, we use the summary join statistics. This is described in Section 15.5.6. More details of our experimental results with the charts are provided in [HUSA2011a].

15.5.4   QUERY PLAN GENERATION

In this section, first we define the query plan generation problem and show that generating the best (i.e., least cost) query plan for the ideal model as well as for the practical model is computationally expensive. Then, we will present a heuristic and a greedy approach to generate an approximate solution to generate the best plan.

Running example. We will use the following query as a running example in this section:

Listing 5: Running Example

SELECT?V,?X,?Y,?Z WHERE{
?X rdf:type ub:GraduateStudent
?Y rdf:type ub:University

?Z?V ub:Department
?X ub:memberOf?Z
?X ub:undergraduateDegreeFrom?Y}

To simplify the notations, we will only refer to the TPs by the variable in that pattern. For example, the first TP (?X rdf:type ub:GraduateStudent) will be represented as simply X. Also, in the simplified version, the whole query would be represented as follows: {X,Y,Z,XZ,XY}.

We will use the notation join (XY,X) to denote a join operation between the two TPs XY and X on the common variable X.

Definition 15.7: *The Minimum Cost Plan Generation Problem (Bestplan Problem):* For a given query, the Bestplan problem is to generate a job plan so that the total cost of the jobs is minimized. Note that Bestplan considers the more general case where each job has some cost associated with it (i.e., the ideal model).

Example. Given the query in our running example, two possible job plans are as follows:

Plan 1. $job_1 = \{X, XY, XZ\}$,
resultant TPs $= \{YZ, YZ\}$. $job_2 = \{Y, YZ\}$,
resultant TPs $= \{Z, Z\}$,. $job_3 = \{Z, Z\}$. Total cost $= cost(job_1) + cost(job_2)$.
Plan 2. $job_1 = \{XZ, Z\}$ and $join(XY, Y)$
resultant TPs $= \{X, X, X\}$. $job_2 = join(X, X, X)$.
Total cost $= cost(job_1) + cost(job_2)$.

The Bestplan problem is to find the least cost job plan among all possible job plans.

Definition 15.8: *Joining Variable:* A variable that is common in two or more triple patterns. For example, in the running example query, X,Y, Z are joining variables, but is not.
Definition 15.9: *Complete Elimination:* A join operation that eliminates a joining variable. For example, in the example query, Y can be completely eliminated if we join (XY,Y).
Definition 15.10: *Partial Elimination:* A join operation that partially eliminates a joining variable. For example, in the example query, if we perform join (XY,Y) and join (X,ZX) in the same job, the resultant triple patterns would be {X,Z,X}. Therefore, Y will be completely eliminated, but X will be partially eliminated. So, the join(X,ZX) performs a partial elimination.
Definition 15.11: *E-Count(v)* E-count(v) is the number of joining variables in the resultant triple pattern after a complete elimination of variable v. In the running example, join(X,XY, XZ) completely eliminates X and the resultant triple pattern (YZ) has two joining variablesand Z. So, E-count(X) = 2. Similarly, E-count(Y) = 1 and E-count(Z) = 1.

15.5.4.1 Computational Complexity of Bestplan
It can be shown that generating the least cost query plan is computationally expensive, since the search space is exponentially large. At first, we formulate the problem, and then show its complexity.

15.5.4.2 Problem Formulation
We formulate Bestplan as a search problem. Let $G = (V, E)$be a weighted directed graph, where each vertex $v_i \in V$ represents a state of the triple patterns, and each edge $e_i \in (v_{i_1}, v_{i_2}) \in E$ represents a job that makes a transition from state v_{i_1} to state v_{i_2}. v_0 is the initial state, where no joins have been performed, i.e., the given query. Also, v_{goal} is the goal state, which represents a state of

the triple pattern where all joins have been performed. The problem is to find the shortest weighted path from v_0 to v_{goal}.

For example, in our running example query, the initial state $v_0 = \{X, Y, Z, XY, XZ\}$, and the goal state, $v_{goal} = \varnothing$, that is, no more triple patterns left. Suppose the first job (job1) performs $join\,(X, XY, XZ)$. Then, the resultant triple patterns (new state) would be $v_1 = \{Y, Z, YZ\}$, and job1 would be represented by the edge (v_0, v_1). The weight of edge (v_0, v_1) is the cost of $job_1 = cost\,(job_1)$, where cost is the given cost function. Figure 15.4 shows the partial graph for the example query.

15.5.4.3   Search Space Size

Given a graph $G = (V, E)$, Dijkstra's shortest path algorithm can find the shortest path from a source to all other nodes in $O\,(|V|log|V| + |E|)$ time. However, for Bestplan, it can be shown that in the worst case, $|V| \geq 2^K$, where K is the total number of joining variables in the given query. Therefore, the number of vertices in the graph is exponential, leading to an exponential search problem. In [HUSA11a], we have shown that the worst case complexity of the Bestplan problem is exponential in K, the number of joining variables in the given query.

15.5.4.4   Relaxed Bestplan Problem and Approximate Solution

In the Relaxed Bestplan problem, we assume uniform cost for all jobs. Although this relaxation does not reduce the search space, the problem is reduced to finding a job plan having the minimum number of jobs. Note that this is the problem for the practical version of the model.

Definition 15.12: *Relaxed Bestplan Problem:* The Relaxed Bestplan problem is to find the job plan that has the minimum number of jobs.

Next, we show that if joins are reasonably chosen, and no eligible join operation is left undone in a job, then we may set an upper bound on the maximum number of jobs required for any given query. However, it is still computationally expensive to generate all possible job plans. Therefore, we resort to a greedy algorithm (Algorithm 15.1), that finds an approximate solution to the Relaxed Bestplan problem, but is guaranteed to find a job plan within the upper bound.

Definition 15.13: *Early Elimination Heuristic:* The early elimination heuristic makes as many complete eliminations as possible in each job.

This heuristic leaves the fewest number of variables for join in the next job. To apply the heuristic, we must first choose the variable in each job with the least E-count. This heuristic is applied in Algorithm 15.1.

Description of Algorithm 15.1

The algorithm starts by removing all the non-joining variables from the query Q. In our running example, $Q = \{X, Y, VZ, XY, XZ\}$, and removing the non-joining variable V makes $Q = \{X, Y, Z, XY, XZ\}$. In the while loop, the job plan is generated, starting from Job_1. In line 4, we sort the variables according to their E-count. The sorted variables are: $U = \{Y, Z, X\}$, since Y, and Z have E-count $=1$, and X has E-count $= 2$. For each job, the list of join operations is stored in the variable Job_j, where J is the ID of the current job. Also, a temporary variable tmp is used to store the resultant triples of the joins to be performed in the current job (line 6). In the for loop, each variable is checked to see if the variable can be completely or partially eliminated (line 8). If yes, we store the join result in the temporary variable (line 9), update Q (line 10), and add this join to the current job (line 11). In our

---

ALGORITHM 15.1   RELAXED BESTPLAN (QUERY Q)

1: $Q \leftarrow$ Remove non $-$ joining variables(Q)
2: **while** $Q \neq$ Empty **do**
3:    $J \leftarrow 1$ //Total number of jobs
4:    $U = \{u_1, \ldots, u_K\} \leftarrow$ All variables sorted in non-decreasing order of their E-counts
5:    $Job_J \leftarrow$ Empty // List of join operations in the // current job
6:    $tmp \leftarrow$ Empty // Temporarily stores resultant // triple patterns
7:    **for** $i = 1$ to K **do**
8:        **if** $Can - Eliminate\,(Q, u_i) = true$ **then** //complete or partial elimination possible
9:            $tmp \leftarrow tmp \cup Join - result\,(TP\,(Q, u_i))$
10:           $Q \leftarrow Q - TP\,(Q, u_i)$
11:           $Job_J \leftarrow Job_J \cup join\,(TP\,(Q, u_i))$
12:       **end if**
13:   **end for**
14:   $Q \leftarrow Q \cup tmp$
15:   $J \leftarrow J + 1$
16: **end while**
17: $return$ $\{Job_1, \ldots, Job_{J-1}\}$

---

running example, this results in the following operations: Iteration 1 of the for loop: $u_1 = (Y)$ can be completely eliminated. Here, $TP\,(Q, Y)$ the triple patterns in Q containing Iteration 3 of the for loop: $u_3 = (X)$ cannot be completely or partially eliminated, since there is no other TP left to join with it. Therefore, when the for loop terminates, we have $job_1 = \{join\,(Y, XY), join\,(Z, XZ)\}$, and $Q = \{X, X, X\}$. In the second iteration of the while loop, we will have $\{job_2 = \{X, X, X\}$. Since after this join, Q becomes Empty, the while loop is exited. Finally, $\{job_1, job_2\}$ are returned from the algorithm.

In [HUSA2011a], we have proved that for any given query Q, containing K joining variables and N triple patterns, Algorithm Relaxed Bestplan (Q) generates a job plan containing at most J jobs, where

$$
J = \begin{cases}
0 & N = 0 \\
1 & N = 1 \ or \ K = 1 \\
\min(\lceil 1.71 \ \log_2 N \rceil, \ K) & N, K > 1
\end{cases}
\tag{4}
$$

15.5.5   Breaking Ties by Summary Statistics

We frequently face situations where we need to choose a join for multiple join options. These choices can occur when both query plans (i.e., join orderings) require the minimum number of jobs. For example, the query shown in Listing 6 poses such a situation.

Listing 6: Query Having Tie Situation

```
?X rdf:type ub:FullProfessor.
?X ub:advisorOf?Y.
?Y rdf:type ub:ResearchAssistant.
```

The second triple pattern in the query makes it impossible to answer and solve the query with only one job. There are only two possible plans: we can join the first two triple patterns on X first and then join its output with the last triple pattern on Y or we can join the last two patterns first on Y and then join its output with the first pattern on X. In such a situation, instead of randomly choosing a join variable for the first job, we use join summary statistics for a pair of predicates. We select the join for the first job which is more selective to break the tie. The join summary statistics we use are described in [STOC2008].

15.5.6 MapReduce Join Execution

In this section, we discuss how we implement the joins needed to answer SPARQL queries using the MapReduce framework of Hadoop. Algorithm 15.1 determines the number of jobs required to answer a query. It returns an ordered set of jobs. Each job has associated input information. The Job Handler component of our MapReduce framework runs the jobs in the sequence they appear in the ordered set. The output file of one job is the input of the next. The output file of the last job has the answer to the query.

Listing 7: LUBM Query 2

```
SELECT ?X, ?Y, ?Z WHERE {
?X rdf:type ub:GraduateStudent.
?Y rdf:type ub:University.
?Z rdf:type ub:Department.
?X ub:memberOf ?Z.
?Z ub:subOrganizationOf ?Y.
?X ub:undergraduateDegreeFrom ?Y }
```

Listing 7 shows LUBM Query 2, which we will use to illustrate the way we do a join using map and reduce methods. The query has six triple patterns and nine joins between them on the variable X, Y, and Z.

Our input selection algorithm selects files *type_GraduateStudent*, type_University, *type_Department*, all files having the prefix *memberOf*, all files having the prefix *subOrganizationOf*, and all files having the prefix *underGraduateDegreeFrom* as the input to the jobs needed to answer the query.

The query plan has two jobs. In job 1, triple patterns of lines 2, 5, and 7 are joined on X and triple patterns of lines 3 and 6 are joined on Y. In job 2, triple pattern of line 4 is joined with the outputs of previous two joins on Z and also the join outputs of job 1 are joined on Y.

The input files of job 1 are type_GraduateStudent, type_University, all files having the prefix memberOf, all files having the prefix subOrganizationOf, and all files having the prefix underGraduateDegreeFrom. In the map phase, we first tokenize the input value which is actually a line of the input file. Then, we check the input file name and, if input is from type_GraduateStudent, we output a key-value pair having the subject URI prefixed with X# the key and a flag string GS# as the value. The value serves as a flag to indicate that the key is of type GraduateStudent. The subject URI is the first token returned by the tokenizer. Similarly, for input from file type_University output a key-value pair having the subject URI prefixed with Y# the key and a flag string U# as the value. If the input from any file has the prefix memberOf, we retrieve the subject and object from the input line by the tokenizer and output a key-value pair having the subject URI prefixed with X# the key and the object value prefixed with MO# as the value. For input from files having the prefix subOrganizationOf, we output key-value pairs making the object prefixed with Y# the key and the subject prefixed with SO# the value. For input from files having the prefix underGraduateDegreeFrom, we output key-value pairs making the subject URI prefixed with X# the key and the object value prefixed with UDF# the value. Hence, we make either the subject or the object a map output key based on which we are joining. This is the reason why the object is made the key for the triples from files having the prefix subOrganizationOf because the joining variable *Y* is an object in the triple pattern in line 6. For all other inputs, the subject is made the key because the joining variables *X* and are subjects in the triple patterns in lines 2, 3, 5, and 7.

In the reduce phase, Hadoop groups all the values for a single key and for each key provides the key and an iterator to the values collection. Looking at the prefix, we can immediately tell if it is a value for *X* or *Y* because of the prefixes we used. In either case, we output a key-value pair using the same key and concatenating all the values to make a string value. So after this reduce phase, join on *X* is complete and on *Y* is partially complete.

The input files of job 2 are type_Department file and the output file of job 1, job1.out. Like the map phase of job 1, in the map phase of job 2, we also tokenize the input value which is actually a line of the input file. Then, we check the input file name and if input is from type_Department, we output a key-value pair having the subject URI prefixed with Z# the key and a flag string D# as the value. If the input is from job1.out, we find the value having the prefix Z#. We make this value the output key and concatenate the rest of the values to make a string and make it the output value. Basically, we make the Z# values the keys to join on *Z*.

In the reduce phase, we know that the key is the value for *Z*. The values collection has two types of strings. One has *X* values, which are URIs for graduate students and also *Y* values from which they got their undergraduate degree. The *Z* value, that is, the key, may or may not be a subOrganizationOf the *Y* value. The other types of strings have only *Y* values which are universities and of which the *Z* value is a suborganization. We iterate over the values collection and then join the two types of tuples on *Y* values. From the join output, we find the result tuples which have values for *X*, *Y*, and *Z*.

15.6 RESULTS

15.6.1 EXPERIMENTAL SETUP

In this section, we first present the benchmark datasets with which we experimented. Next, we present the alternative repositories we evaluated for comparison. Then, we detail our experimental setup. Finally, we present our evaluation results.

15.6.1.1 Datasets

In our experiments with SPARQL query processing, we use two synthetic datasets: LUBM [GUO2005] and SP2B [SCHM2009]. The LUBM dataset generates data about universities by using an ontology [LEHI]. It has 14 standard queries. Some of the queries require inference to answer. The LUBM dataset is very good for both inference and scalability testing. For all LUBM datasets, we used the default seed. The SP2B dataset is good for scalability testing with complex queries and data access patterns. It has 16 queries most of which have complex structures.

15.6.1.2 Baseline Frameworks

We compared our framework with RDF-3X [NEUM08], Jena [JENA], and BigOWLIM [ONTO]. RDF-3X is considered the fastest semantic web framework with persistent storage. Jena is an open-source framework for semantic web data. It has several models which can be used to store and retrieve RDF data. We chose Jena's in-memory and SDB models to compare our framework with. As the name suggests, the in-memory model stores the data in main memory and does not persist data. The SDB model is a persistent model and can use many off-the-shelf database management systems. We used MySQL database as SDB's back-end in our experiments. BigOWLIM is a proprietary framework which is the state-of-the-art significantly fast framework for semantic web data. It can act both as a persistent and nonpersistent storage. All of these frameworks run in a single machine setup.

15.6.1.3 Hardware

We have a 10-node Hadoop cluster which we use for our framework. Each of the nodes has the following configuration: Pentium IV 2.80 GHz processor, 4 GB main memory, and 640 GB disk space. We ran Jena, RDF-3X, and BigOWLIM frameworks on a powerful single machine having 2.80 GHz quad core processor, 8 GB main memory, and 1 TB disk space.

15.6.1.4 Software

We used Hadoop-0.20.1 for our framework. We compared our framework with Jena-2.5.7, which used MySQL 15.12 for its SDB model. We used BigOWLIM version 3.2.6. For RDF-3X, we utilized version 0.3.5 of the source code.

15.6.2 Evaluation

We present performance comparison between our framework, RDF-3X, Jena In-Memory and SDB models, and BigOWLIM. More details are found in [HUSA2011a]. We used three LUBM datasets: 10,000, 20,000, and 30,000 which have more than 1.1, 2.2, and 3.3 billion triples, respectively. Initial population time for RDF-3X took 655, 1,756, and 3,353 minutes to load the datasets, respectively. This shows that the RDF-3X load time is increasing exponentially. LUBM (30,000) has three times as many triples as LUBM (10,000) yet it requires more than five times as long to load.

For evaluation purposes, we chose LUBM Queries 1, 2, 4, 9, 12, and 13 to be reported in this work. These queries provide a good mixture and include simple and complex structures, inference, and multiple types of joins. They are representatives of other queries of the benchmark and so reporting only these covers all types of variations found in the queries we left out and also saves space. Query 1 is a simple selective query. RDF-3X is much faster than HadoopRDF for this query. RDF-3X utilizes six indexes [NEUM2008] and those six indexes actually make up the dataset. The indexes provide RDF-3X a very fast way to look up triples, similar to a hash table. Hence, a highly selective query is efficiently answered by RDF-3X. Query 2 is a query with complex structures, low selectivity, and no bound objects. The result set is quite large. For this query, HadoopRDF outperforms RDF-3X for all three dataset sizes. RDF-3X fails to answer the query at all when the dataset size is 3.3 billion triples. RDF-3X returns memory segmentation fault error messages and does not produce any query results. Query 4 is also a highly selective query, that is, the result set size is small because of a bound object in the second triple pattern but it needs inferencing to answer it. The first triple pattern uses the class Person which is a superclass of many classes. No resource in LUBM dataset is of type Person, rather there are many resources which are its subtypes. RDF-3X does not support inferencing so we had to convert the query to an equivalent query having some union operations. RDF-3X outperforms HadoopRDF for this query. Query 9 is similar in structure to Query 2 but it requires significant inferencing. The first three triple patterns of this query use classes which are not explicitly instantiated in the dataset. However, the dataset includes many instances of the corresponding subclasses. This is also the query which requires the largest dataset join and returns the largest result set out of the queries we evaluated. RDF-3X is faster than HadoopRDF for 1.1 billion triples dataset but it fails to answer the query at all for the other two datasets. Query 12 is similar to Query 4 because it is both selective and has inferencing in one triple pattern. RDF-3X beats HadoopRDF for this query. Query 13 has only two triple patterns. Both of them involve inferencing. There is a bound subject in the second triple pattern. It returns the second largest result set. HadoopRDF beats RDF-3X for this query for all datasets. RDF-3X's performance is slow because the first triple pattern has very low selectivity and requires low selectivity joins to perform inference via backward chaining.

These results lead us to some simple conclusions. RDF-3X achieves the best performance for queries with high selectivity and bound objects. However, HadoopRDF outperforms RDF-3X for queries with unbound objects, low selectivity, or large dataset joins. RDF-3X cannot execute the two queries with unbound objects (Queries 2 and 9) for a 3.3 billion triples dataset. This demonstrates that HadoopRDF is more scalable and handles low selectivity queries more efficiently than RDF-3X.

We also compared our implementation with the Jena In-Memory, the SDB and BigOWLIM models. Due to space and time limitations, we performed these tests only for LUBM Queries 2 and 9 from the LUBM dataset. We chose these queries because they have complex structures and require inference. It is to be noted that BigOWLIM needed 7 GB of Java heap space to successfully load the billion triples dataset. We ran BigOWLIM only for the largest three datasets as we are interested in its performance with large datasets. For each set we obtained the results for the Jena In-Memory model, Jena SDB model, our Hadoop implementation and BigOWLIM, respectively. At times the query could not complete or it ran out of memory. In most of the cases, our approach was the fastest. For Query 2, Jena In-Memory and Jena SDB models were faster than our approach, giving results in 3.9 and 0.4 seconds, respectively. However, as the size of the dataset grew, the Jena In-Memory model ran out of memory space. Our implementation was much faster than the Jena SDB model for large datasets. For example, for 110 million triples, our approach took 143.5 seconds as compared to about 5,000 seconds for Jena SDB model. We found that the Jena SDB model could not finish answering Query 9. Jena In-Memory model worked well for small datasets but became slower than our implementation as the dataset size grew and eventually ran out of memory.

For Query 2, BigOWLIM was slower than ours for the 110 and 550 million datasets. For the 550 million dataset, it took 22693.4 seconds, which is abruptly high compared to its other timings. For the billion triple dataset, BigOWLIM was faster. It should be noted that our framework does not have any indexing or triple cache whereas BigOWLIM exploits indexing which it loads into main memory when it starts. It may also prefetch triples into main memory. For Query 9, our implementation is faster than BigOWLIM in all experiments.

It should also be noted that our RDF-3X and HadoopRDF queries were tested using cold runs. What we mean by this is that main memory and file system cache were cleared prior to execution. However, for BigOWLIM, we were forced to execute hot runs. This is because it takes a significant amount of time to load a database into BigOWLIM. Therefore, we will always easily outperform BigOWLIM for cold runs. So, we actually tested BigOWLIM for hot runs against HadoopRDF for cold runs. This gives a tremendous advantage to BigOWLIM, yet for large datasets, HadoopRDF still produced much better results. This shows that HadoopRDF is much more scalable than BigOWLIM, and provides more efficient queries for large datasets.

The final tests we have performed are an in-depth scalability test. For this, we repeated the same queries for eight different dataset sizes, all the way up to 6.6 billion.

In our experiments we found that Query 1 is simple and requires only one join, thus it took the least amount of time among all the queries. Query 2 is one of the two queries having the greatest number of triple patterns. Even though it has three times more triple patterns, it does not take thrice the time of Query 1 answering time because of our storage schema. Query 4 has one less triple pattern than Query 2, but it requires inferencing. As we determine inferred relations on the fly, queries requiring inference take longer times in our framework. Queries 9 and 12 also require inferencing. Details are given in [HUSA2011a].

As the size of the dataset grows, the increase in time to answer a query does not grow proportionately. The increase in time is always less. For example, there are 10 times as many triples in the dataset of 10,000 universities than 1,000 universities, but for Query 1, the time only increases by 3.76 times and for query 9 by 7.49 times. The latter is the highest increase in time, yet it is still less than the increase in the size of the datasets. Due to space limitations, we do not report query runtimes with PS schema here. We found that PS schema is much slower than POS schema.

15.7 SECURITY EXTENSIONS

We have implemented security models based on (i) a token-based access control model on top of the JENA framework as well as (ii) XACML-based security model on top of the SPARQL Query Optimizer. This section describes our security models. More details of the system can be found at [KHAL2010]. It should be noted that we have also designed and developed a third secure query processing system using XACML access control for relational data. This system uses the HIVE relational database system and also operates in the cloud. The design and implementation of the HIVE-based system is discussed in [THUR2010] as well as in Chapter 16.

15.7.1 TOKEN-BASED ACCESS CONTROL MODEL

DEFINITION 15.15: *Access Tokens (AT)* permit access to security-relevant data. An agent in possession of an AT may view the data permitted by that AT. We denote AT's by positive integers.

Definition 15.15: *Access Token Tuples* (ATT) have the form ⟨*AccessToken, Element, ElementType, ElementName*⟩, where *Element* can be *Subject, Object,* or Predicate, and *ElementType* can be described as *URI,* DataType, *Literal, Model,* or *BlankNode.* Model is used to access subject models, and will be explained later in the section.

For example, in the ontology/knowledge base in Figure 15.5, *David* is a subject and ⟨1, *Subject, URI, David*⟩ is an ATT. Any agent having AT 1 may retrieve *David*'s information over all files (subject to any other security restrictions governing access to URI's, literals, etc., associated with *David*'s objects). While describing ATT's for, we leave the *ElementName* blank (–).

Based on the record organization, we support six access levels along with a few subtypes described later. Agents may be assigned one or more of the following access levels. Access levels with a common AT combine conjunctively, while those with different AT's combine disjunctively.

1. *Predicate data access:* If an object type is defined for one particular predicate in an access level, then an agent having that access level may read the whole predicate file (subject to any other policy restrictions). For example, ⟨1, *Predicate, isPaid, _*⟩ is an ATT that permits its possessor to read the entire predicate file *isPaid.*
2. *Predicate and subject data access:* Agents possessing a subject ATT may access data associated with a particular subject, where the subject can be either a *URI* or a *DataType.*

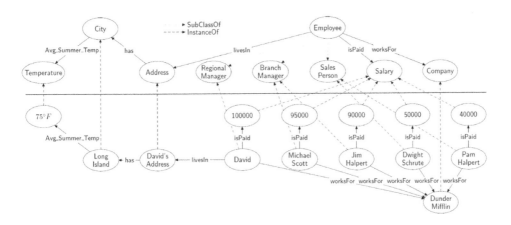

FIGURE 15.5 Knowledge base.

Combining one of these subject ATT's with a predicate data access ATT having the same AT, grants the agent access to a specific subject of a specific predicate. For example:

a. *Predicate and subject as URIs:* Combining ATT's ⟨1, *Predicate, isPaid* ⟩, and ⟨1, *Subject, URI, MichaelScott* ⟩ (drawn from the ontology in Figure 15.5) permits an agent with AT 1 to access a subject with URI *MichaelScott* of predicate *isPaid*.

b. *Predicate and subject as DataTypes:* Similarly, Predicate and DataType ATT's can be combined to permit access to subjects of a specific data type over a specific predicate file.

For brevity, we omit descriptions of the different subject and object variations of each of the remaining access levels.

3. *Predicate and object:* This access level permits a principal to extract the names of subjects satisfying a particular predicate and object. For example, with ATT's ⟨1, *Predicate, hasVitamins, _*⟩, and ⟨1, *Object, URI, E*⟩, an agent possessing AT 1 may view the names of subjects (e.g., foods) that have vitamin *E*. More generally, if X_1 and X_2 are the set of triples generated by Predicate and Object triples (respectively) describing an AT, then agents possessing the AT may view set $X1 \cap X2$ of triples. An illustration of this example is displayed in Figure 15.6.

4. *Subject access:* With this access level an agent may read the subject's information over all the files. This is one of the less restrictive access levels. The subject can be a *DataType* or *BlankNode*.

5. *Object access:* With this access level, an agent may read the object's subjects over all the files. Like the previous level, this is one of the less restrictive access levels The object can be a *URI, DataType,Literal*, or *BlankNode*.

6. *Subject model level access:* Model level access permits an agent to read all necessary predicate files to obtain all objects of a given subject. Of these objects, the ones that are URIs are next treated as subjects to extract their respective predicates and objects. This process continues iteratively until all objects finally become literals or blank nodes. In this manner, agents possessing model level access may generate models on a given subject.

The following example drawn from Figure 15.5 illustrates *David* lives in *LongIsland*. *LongIsland* is a subject with an *Avg_Summer_ Temp* predicate having object 75°F. An agent with model level access of *David* read the average summer temperature of.

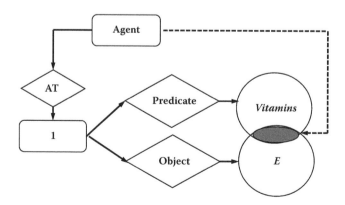

FIGURE 15.6   Conjunctive combination of ATT's with a common AT.

15.7.2 Access Token Assignment

Definition 15.16: An *Access Token List* (AT-list) is an array of one or more ATs granted to a given agent, along with a time stamp identifying the time at which each was granted. A separate AT list is maintained for each agent.

When a system administrator decides to add an AT to an agent's AT list, the AT and time stamp are first stored in a temporary variable. Before committing the change, the system must first detect potential conflicts in the new AT list.

15.7.2.1 Final output of an Agent's ATs

Each AT permits access to a set of triples. We refer to this set as the AT's *result set*. The set of triples accessible by an agent is the union of the result sets of the ATs in the agent's AT list. Formally, if Y_1, Y_2, ..., Y_n are the result sets of ATs AT_1, AT_2, ..., AT_n (respectively) in an agent's AT list, then the agent may access the triples in set $Y_1 \cup Y_2 \cup ... \cup Y_n$.

15.7.2.2 Security Level Defaults

An administrator's AT assignment burden can be considerably simplified by conservatively choosing default security levels for data in the system. In our implementation, all items in the data store have default security levels. Personal information of individuals is kept private by denying access to any URI of data type *Person* by default. This prevents agents from making inferences about any individual to whom they have not been granted explicit permission. However, if an agent is granted explicit access to a particular type or property, the agent is also granted default access to the subtypes or subproperties of that type or property.

As an example, consider a predicate file *Likes* that lists elements that an individual likes. Assume further that *Jim* is a person who likes *Flying*, *SemanticWeb*, and *Jenny*, which are URIs of type *Hobby*, *ResearchInterest*, and *Person*, respectively, and 1 is an AT with ATTs $\langle 1,$ *Subject*, *URI*, *Jim*$\rangle$ and $\langle 1,$ *Likes*, *Predicate*, _$\rangle$. By default, agent *Ben*, having only AT 1, cannot learn that *Jenny* is in *Jim*'s *Likes* list since *Jenny*'s data type is *Person*. However, if *Ben* also has AT 2 described by ATT $\langle 2,$ *Object*, *URI*, *Jenny*$\rangle$, then *Ben* will be able to see *Jenny* in *Jim*'s *Likes* list.

15.7.3 Conflicts

A conflict arises when the following three conditions occur: (1) an agent possesses two ATs 1 and 2, (2) the result set of AT 2 is a proper subset of AT 1, and (3) the time stamp of AT 1 is earlier than the time stamp of AT 2. In this case the latter, more specific AT supersedes the former, so AT 1 is discarded from the AT list to resolve the conflict. Such conflicts arise in two varieties, which we term *subset conflicts* and *subtype conflicts* .

A subset conflict occurs when AT 2 is a conjunction of ATTs that refines those of AT 1. For example, suppose AT 1 is defined by ATT $\langle 1,$ *Subject*, *URI*, *Sam*$\rangle$ and AT 2 is defined by ATTs $\langle 2,$ *Subject*, *URI*, *Sam*$\rangle$ and $\langle 2,$ *Predicate*, *Has Accounts*, _$\rangle$. In this case, the result set of AT 2 is a subset of the result set of AT 1. A conflict will therefore occur if an agent possessing AT 1 is later assigned AT 2. When this occurs, AT 1 is discarded from the agent's AT list to resolve the conflict.

Subtype conflicts occur when the ATTs in AT 2 involve data types that are subtypes of those in AT 1. The data types can be those of subjects, objects or both.

Conflict resolution is summarized by Algorithm 15.2. Here, Subset(AT_1, AT_2) is a function that returns true if the result set of AT_1 is a proper subset of the result set of AT_2, and SubjectSubType (AT_1, AT_2) returns true if the subject of AT_1 is a subtype of the subject of AT_2. Similarly, ObjectSubType(AT_1, AT_2), decides subtyping relations for objects instead of subjects.

ALGORITHM 15.2   CONFLICT DETECTION AND RESOLUTION

Input: AT *newAT* with time stamp TS_{newAT}
Result: Detect conflict and, if none exists, add
              $(newAT, T\ S_{newAT})$ to the agent's AT-list
1 *currentAT* []← the AT's and their time stamps;
2 if (!Subset(newAT, tempATTS) AND
   !Subset(tempATTS, newAT) AND
   !SubjectSubType(newAT, tempATTS)) AND
   !SubjectSubType(tempATTS, newAT) AND
   !ObjectSubType(newAT, tempATTS)) AND
   !ObjectSubType(tempATTS, newAT)) then
3   *currentAT* [$length_{currentAT}$]. $AT ← newAT$;
4   *currentAT* [$length_{currentAT}$]. $TS ← TS$ newAT;
5   else
6   *count* ← 0;
7   **while** *count* < $length_{currentAT}$ **do**
8   *AT   tempATTS* ← *currentAT* [*count*]. AT;
9   *tempTS* ← *currentAT* [*count*]. TS;
10   /* the timestamp during the AT assignment */
11   **if** $(Subset\,(newAT, tempATTS)\,AND\,(TS_{newAT} ≥ tempTS))$ **then**
12   /* a conflict occurs */
13   *currentAT* [*count*]. $AT ← newAT$;
14   *currentAT* [*count*]. $TS ← TS$ newAT;
15   **else if** $((Subset\,(tempATTS, \ newAT))\ AND\ (tempTS < TS_{newAT}))$ **then**
16   *currentAT* [*count*]. $AT ← newAT$;
17   *currentAT* [*count*]. $TS ← TS\ newAT$;
18   **else if** $((SubjectSubType\,(newAT, \ tempATTS)\,OR$
                    $ObjectSubType\ (newAT, \ tempATTS))\ AND\ TS_{newAT} ≥ tempTS)$ **then**
19   /* a conflict occurs */
20   *currentAT* [*count*]. $AT ← newAT$;
21   *currentAT* [*count*]. $TS ← TS$ newAT;
22 **else if** $((SubjectSubType\,(tempATTS, \ newAT)\ OR\ ObjectSubType\ (tempATTS, newAT))$
    $AND\,(tempATTS < TS_{newAT}))$ **then**
23   *currentAT* [*count*]. $AT ← newAT$;
24   *currentAT* [*count*]. $TS ← TS\ newAT$;
25   end
26   *count* ← *count* + 1;
27   end
28   end

15.7.4   XACML-BASED ACCESS CONTROL

XACML based access control is based on the ABAC (Attribute-Based Access Control Model. XACML consists of four major modules. The PEP (Policy Enforcement Point), PDP (Policy Decision Point), PIP (Policy Information Point), and PAP (Policy Access Point).

In the ABAC model, the user presents his/her credentials and makes a request to the resource. XACML's PEP takes the request and the credentials and asks the PDP to make a decision as to whether the user should be given access. PDP works with PAP to get the policies and the PIP to get the information about the resources as well as the user's credentials. Based on the policies, the user is granted or denied access to the resource. The decisions are made by the PDP and give the result to the PEP. The PEP then carried out the request or denied the request. More details are given in [THUR2013].

15.8 SUMMARY AND DIRECTIONS

We have presented a framework capable of handling enormous amounts of RDF data that can be used to represent big data systems such as social networks. Since our framework is based on Hadoop, which is a distributed and highly fault-tolerant system, it inherits these two properties automatically. The framework is highly scalable. To increase capacity of our system, all that needs to be done is to add new nodes to the Hadoop cluster. We have proposed a schema to store RDF data, an algorithm to determine a query processing plan, whose worst case is bounded, to answer a SPARQL query and a simplified cost model to be used by the algorithm. Our experiments demonstrate that our system is highly scalable. If we increase the data volume, the delay introduced to answer a query does not increase proportionally. The results indicate that for very large datasets (over one billion triples), Hadoop RDF is preferable and more efficient if the query includes low selectivity joins or significant inference. Other solutions may be more efficient if the query includes bound objects which produce high selectivity. We also provided an overview of our security model that we built on top of the query processing system.

In the future, we would like to extend the work in multiple directions. First, we will investigate a more sophisticated query model. We will cache statistics for the most frequent queries and use dynamic programming to exploit the statistics. Second, we will evaluate the impact of the number of reducers, the only parameter of a Hadoop job specifiable by user, on the query runtimes. Third, we will investigate indexing opportunities and further usage of binary formats. Fourth, we will handle more complex SPARQL patterns, for example, queries having OPTIONAL blocks. Fifth, we will demonstrate our system with realistic big data applications such as social networking systems. Finally, we will incorporate security at all levels of the system. That is, security should not be just an add-on to the query processing prototype. It has to be built into the SPARQL query optimizer

REFERENCES

[ABAD2007] D.J. Abadi, A. Marcus, S. R. Madden, K. Hollenbach, Scalable Semantic Web Data Management Using Vertical Partitioning, *Proceedings of 33rd Interntional Conference on Very Large Data Bases*, Vienna, Austria, 2007.

[ABAD2009a] D.J. Abadi, Data Management in the Cloud: Limitations and Opportunities, *IEEE Data Engineering Bulletin*, Volume 32, #1, 2009, 3–12.

[ABAD2009b] D.J. Abadi, A. Marcus, S.R. Madden, K. Hollenbach, SW- Store: A Vertically Partitioned DBMS for Semantic Web Data Management, *VLDB Journal*, Volume 18, #2, 2009, 385–406.

[ABOU2009] A. Abouzeid, K. Bajda-Pawlikowski, D.J. Abadi, A. Silberschatz, A. Rasin, HadoopDB: An Architectural Hybrid of MapReduce and DBMS Technologies for Analytical Workloads, *Proceedings of VLDB Endowment*, Volume 2, 2009, 922–933.

[ATRE2008] M. Atre, J. Srinivasan, J. A. Hendler, BitMat: A Main-Memory Bit Matrix of RDF Triples for Conjunctive Triple Pattern Queries, *Proceedings of International Semantic Web Conference*, Karlsruhe, Germany, 2008.

[BONC2006] P. Boncz, T. Grust, M. van Keulen, S. Manegold, J. Rittinger, J. Teubner, MonetDB/XQuery: A Fast XQuery Processor Powered by a Relational Engine, *Proceedings of ACM SIGMOD International Conference on Management of Data*, Chicago, IL, 2006, pp. 479–490.

[CARR2004] J.J. Carroll, I. Dickinson, C. Dollin, D. Reynolds, A. Seaborne, K. Wilkinson, Jena: Implementing the Semantic Web Recommendations, *Proceedings of 13th International World Wide Web Conference on Alternate Track Papers and Posters*, New York, NY, 2004, pp. 74–83.

[CHAL] Semantic Web Challenge, http://challenge.semanticweb.org.

[CHAN2006] F. Chang, J. Dean, S. Ghemawat, W.C. Hsieh, D.A. Wallach, M. Burrows, T. Chandra, A. Fikes, R.E. Gruber, Bigtable: A Distributed Storage System for Structured Data, *Proceedings of Seventh USENIX Symposium on Operating System Design and Implementation*, Seattle, WA, November 2006, pp. 205 – 218.

[CHEB2007] A. Chebotko, S. Lu, F. Fotouhi, Semantics Preserving SPARQL- to-SQL Translation, Technical Report TR-DB-112007-CLF, 2007.

[CHON2005] E.I. Chong, S. Das, G. Eadon, J. Srinivasan, An Efficient SQL- Based RDF Querying Scheme, *Proceedings of International Conference on Very Large Data Bases (VLDB '05)*, Trondheim, Norway, 2005, pp. 1216–1227.

[CHU2006] C.T. Chu, S.K. Kim, Y.A. Lin, Y. Yu, G. Bradski, A.Y. Ng, and K. Olukotun, Map-Reduce for Machine Learning on Multicore, *Proceedings of Neural Information Processing Systems (NIPS)*, Vancouver, BC, Canada, 2006.

[CLOU] Cloudera University, http://www.cloudera. com/b l og /20 10/ 03/h o w - raytheon-researchers-are-using-hadoop-to-build-a-scalable-distributed-triple-store.

[COMP] National University of Singapore School of Computing, http://www.comp.nus.edu.sg/~epic/.

[CYGA2005] R. Cyganiak, A Relational Algebra for SPARQL, Technical Report HPL-2005-170, 2005.

[DEAN2004] J. Dean, S. Ghemawat, MapReduce: Simplified Data Processing on Large Clusters, *Proceedings of Sixth Conference on Symposium on Operating Systems Design and Implementation*, San Francisco, CA, 2004, pp. 137–150.

[DING2005] L. Ding, T. Finin, Y. Peng, P.P. da Silva, D.L. Mcguinness, Tracking RDF Graph Provenance Using RDF Molecules, *Proceedings of Fourth International Semantic Web Conference*, Galway, Ireland, 2005

[GUO2004] Y. Guo, Z. Pan, J. Heflin, An Evaluation of Knowledge Base Systems for Large OWL Datasets, *Proceedings of International Semantic Web Conference,* Hiroshima, Japan, 2004.

[GUO2005] Y. Guo, Z. Pan, and J. Heflin, LUBM: A Benchmark for OWL Knowledge Base Systems, *Web Semantics: Science, Services and Agents on the World Wide Web*, Volume 3, 2005, 158–182.

[HADOa] Apache Software Foundation, http://hadoop.apache.org.

[HADOb] Apache Software Foundation, http://hadoop.apache.org/core/docs/r0.18.3/hdfs_design.html.

[HUSA2009] M.F. Husain, P. Doshi, L. Khan, B. Thuraisingham, Storage and Retrieval of Large RDF Graph Using Hadoop and MapReduce, *Proceedings of First International Conference on Cloud Computing*, Bejing, China, 2009. http://www.utdal- las.edu/mfh062000/techreport1.pdf

[HUSA2010] M.F. Husain, L. Khan, M. Kantarcioglu, B. Thuraisingham, Data Intensive Query Processing for Large RDF Graphs Using Cloud Computing Tools, *Proceedings of IEEE International Conference on Cloud Computing*, Miami, FL, July 2010, pp. 1–10.

[HUSA2011a] M.F. Husain, J.P. McGlothlin, M.M. Masud, L.R. Khan, B.M. Thuraisingham,Heuristics-Based Query Processing for Large RDF Graphs Using Cloud Computing. *IEEE Transactions on Knowledge and Data Engineering*, Volume 23, #9, 2011, 1312–1327.

[HUSA2011b] M.F. Husain, Data Intensive Query Processing for Semantic Web Data Using Hadoop and MapReduce, PhD Thesis, The University of Texas at Dallas, May 2011.

[ITEE] The University of Queensland Australia, School of Information Technology and Electrical Engineering, http://www.itee.uq.edu.au/eresearch/projects/biomanta.

[JENA] Apache Software Foundation, http://jena.sourceforge.net.

[KHAL2010] A. Khaled, M.F. Husain, L. Khan, K.W. Hamlen, B.M. Thuraisingham, A Token-Based Access Control System for RDF Data in the Clouds, *Proceedings of CloudCom, Indianapolis*, 2010, 104–111.

[KIRY2005] A. Kiryakov, D. Ognyanov, D. Manov, OWLIM: A Pragmatic Semantic Repository for OWL, *Proceedings of International Workshop on Scalable Semantic Web Knowledge Base Systems (SSWS)*, New York, NY, 2005.

[LEHI] Lehigh University, http://www.lehigh.edu/~zhp2/2004/0401/univ-bench.owl.

[MCGL2009] J.P. McGlothlin, L.R. Khan, RDFKB: Efficient Support for RDF Inference Queries and Knowledge Management, *Proceedings of International Database Engineering and Applications Symposium, (IDEAS)*, Cetraro, Italy, 2009.

[MCGL2010] J.P. McGlothlin, L. Khan, Materializing and Persisting Inferred and Uncertain Knowledge in RDF Datasets, *Proceedings of AAAI Conference on Artificial Intelligence*, Atlanta, GA, 2010.

[MCNA2007] A.W. Mcnabb, C.K. Monson, K.D. Seppi, MRPSO: MapReduce Particle Swarm Optimization, *Proceedings of Annual Conference on Genetic and Evolutionary Computation (GECCO)*, London, England, UK, 2007.

[MORE2007] J.E. Moreira, M.M. Michael, D. Da Silva, D. Shiloach, P. Dube, L. Zhang, Scalability of the Nutch Search Engine, *Proceedings of 21st Annual International Conference on Supercomputing (ICS '07)*, Rotterdam, The Netherlands, June 2007, pp. 3–12.

[MORE2008] C. Moretti, K. Steinhaeuser, D. Thain, N. Chawla, Scaling Up Classifiers to Cloud Computers, *Proceedings of IEEE International Conference on Data Mining (ICDM '08)*, Pisa, Italy, 2008

[NEUM2008] T. Neumann, G. Weikum, RDF-3X: A RISC-Style Engine for RDF, *Proceedings of VLDB Endowment*, Volume 1, #1, 2008, 647–659.

[NEWM2008] A. Newman, J. Hunter, Y.F. Li, C. Bouton, M. Davis, A Scale- Out RDF Molecule Store for Distributed Processing of Biomedical Data, *Proceedings of Semantic Web for Health Care and Life Sciences Workshop*, Karlsruhe, Germany, 2008.

[OLST2008] C. Olston, B. Reed, U. Srivastava, R. Kumar, A. Tomkins, Pig Latin: A Not-So-Foreign Language for Data Processing, *Proceedings of ACM SIGMOD International Conference on Management of Data*, Vancouver, BC, Canada, 2008.

[ONTO] Ontotext AD, http://www.ontotext.com/owlim/big/index.html.

[OPEN] Open RDF, http://www.openrdf.org.

[ROHL2007] K. Rohloff, M. Dean, I. Emmons, D. Ryder, J. Sumner, An Evaluation of Triple-Store Technologies for Large Data Stores, *Proceedings of OTM Confederated International Conference on the Move to Meaningful Internet Systems*, Vilamoura, Portugal, 2007.

[SCHM2009] M. Schmidt, T. Hornung, G. Lausen, C. Pinkel, SP2Bench: A SPARQL Performance Benchmark, *Proceedings of 25th International Conference on Data Engineering. (ICDE '09)*, Shanghai, China, 2009.

[SIDI2008] L. Sidirourgos, R. Goncalves, M. Kersten, N. Nes, S. Manegold, Column-Store Support for RDF Data Management: Not All Swans Are White, *Proceedings of VLDB Endowment*, Volume 1, # 2, 2008, 1553–1563.

[SISM2010] Y. Sismanis, S. Das, R. Gemulla, P. Haas, K. Beyer, J. McPherson, Ricardo: Integrating R and Hadoop, *Proceedings of ACM SIGMOD International Conference Management of Data (SIGMOD)*, Indianapolis, IN, 2010.

[STOC2008] M. Stocker, A. Seaborne, A. Bernstein, C. Kiefer, D. Reynolds, SPARQL Basic Graph Pattern Optimization Using Selectivity Estimation, *WWW '08: Proceedings of 17th International Conference World Wide Web*, Beijing, China, 2008.

[STON2005] M. Stonebraker, D.J. Abadi, A. Batkin, X. Chen, M. Cherniack, M. Ferreira, E. Lau, A. Lin, S. Madden, E. O'Neil, P. O'Neil, A. Rasin, N. Tran, S. Zdonik, C-Store: A Column-Oriented DBMS, *VLDB '05: Proceedings of 31st International Conference on Very Large Data Bases*, Trondheim, Norway, 2005, pp. 553–564.

[THUR2010] B.M. Thuraisingham, V. Khadilkar, A. Gupta, M. Kantarcioglu, L. Khan, Secure Data Storage and Retrieval in the Cloud. *Proceedings CollaborateCom, Chicago, IL*, 2010, 1–8.

[THUR2013] B. Thuraisingham, *Developing and Securing the Cloud*, CRC Press, 2013.

[THUR2015] B. Thuraisingham, S. Abrol, R. Heatherly, M. Kantarcioglu, V. Khadilkar, L. Khan, *Analyzing and Securing Social Networks*, CRC Press, 2016.

[W3a] World Wide Web Consortium, http://www.w3.org/2001/sw/RDFCore/ntriples.

[W3b] World Wide Web Consortium, http://www.w3.org/TR/rdf-concepts/#dfn-rdf-triple.

[W3c] World Wide Web Consortium, http://www.w3.org/TR/rdf-primer.

[W3d] World Wide Web Consortium, http://www.w3.org/TR/rdf-sparql-query/#defn_QueryVariable.

[W3e] World Wide Web Consortium, http://www.w3.org/TR/rdf-sparql-query/#defn_TriplePattern.

[W3f] World Wide Web Consortium, http://www.w3.org/TR/rdf-syntax-grammar.

[WANG2010] J. Wang, S. Wu, H. Gao, J. Li, B.C. Ooi, Indexing Multi-Dimensional Data in a Cloud System, *Proceedings of ACM SIGMOD International Conference on Management of Data (SIGMOD)*, Indianapolis, IN, 2010.

[WEIS2008] C. Weiss, P. Karras, A. Bernstein, Hexastore: Sextuple Indexing for Semantic Web Data Management, *Proceedings of VLDB Endowment*, Volume 1, #1, 2008, 1008–1019.

[WIKIa] http://wiki.apache.org/hadoop/JobTracker.

[WIKIb] http://wiki.apache.org/hadoop/TaskTracker.

[XACM] XACML: eXtensible Access Control Markup Language, https://www.oasis-open.org/committees/tc_home.php?wg_abbrev=xacml

[XU2010] Y. Xu, P. Kostamaa, L. Gao, Integrating Hadoop and Parallel DBMs, *Proceedings of ACM SIGMOD International Conference on Management of Data (SIGMOD)*, Indianapolis, IN, 2010.

16 Access Control-Based Assured Information Sharing in the Cloud

16.1 INTRODUCTION

The advent of cloud computing and the continuing movement toward software as a service (SaaS) paradigms have posed an increasing need for assured information sharing (AIS) as a service in the cloud. The urgency of this need was voiced in April 2011 by NSA (National Security Agency) CIO (Chief Information Officer), Lonny Anderson, while describing the agency's focus on a "cloud-centric" approach to information sharing with other agencies [NSA2011]. Likewise, the DoD has been embracing cloud computing paradigms to more efficiently, economically, flexibly, and scalably meet its vision of "delivering the power of information to ensure mission success through an agile enterprise with freedom of maneuverability across the information environment" [DoD, DoD2007]. Furthermore, there is also an urgent need for most industries such as healthcare and finance to share information in the cloud securely and in a timely manner.

The cloud computing paradigm enables the sharing of large amounts of data securely and efficiently. Furthermore, the advent of *cloud computing* and the continuing movement toward SaaS paradigms has posed an increasing need for AIS as a service in the cloud. To satisfy the cloud-centric AIS needs of coalition organization, there is a critical need to develop an AIS framework that operates in the cloud.

Although a number of AIS tools have been developed in recent years for policy-based information sharing [AWAD2010, FINI2009, THUR2008, RAO2008], which is based on controlling access to the data, to our knowledge none of these tools operate in the cloud and big data and hence do not provide the scalability needed to support large numbers of users such as social media users involving massive amounts of data that include text, images, and video. The prototype systems we developed for supporting cloud-based AIS have applied cloud-centric query engines (e.g., the SPARQL query optimizer discussed in Chapter 15) that query large amounts of data in relational and semantic web databases by utilizing policy engines that are token-based or that enforce policies expressed in XACML [THUR2010, THUR2011]. While this is a significant improvement over prior efforts (and has given us insights into implementing cloud-based solutions), it nevertheless has some limitations. First, XACML-based policy specifications are not expressive enough to support many of the complex policies needed for AIS applications such as healthcare and defense. Second, to meet the scalability and efficiency requirements of mission-critical tasks, the policy engine needs to operate in the cloud. For example, while our policy engines discussed in Chapter 15 are hosted on the cloud, they do not take advantage of all the features offered by the cloud.

To share the large amounts of data securely and efficiently, there clearly needs to be a seamless integration of the policy and data managers for social media in the cloud. Therefore, to satisfy the cloud-centric AIS needs, we need (i) a cloud-resident policy manager that enforces information sharing policies expressed in a semantically rich language, and (ii) a cloud-resident data manager that securely stores and retrieves data and seamlessly integrates with the policy manager. To our knowledge, no such system currently exists. Therefore, our project has designed and developed such cloud-based AIS systems for social media users. Our policy engine as well as a data are represented using semantic web technologies and therefore can represent and reason about social

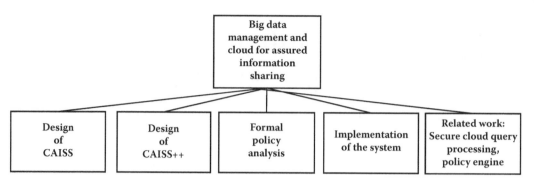

FIGURE 16.1   Big data management and cloud for assured information sharing.

media data. That is, we have developed a cloud-centric policy manager that enforces policies specified in RDF and a cloud-centric data manager that will store and manage data, such as social graphs and associated data, also specified in RDF. This RDF data manager is essentially a query engine for SPARQL, a language widely used by the semantic web community to query RDF data. Furthermore, our policy manager and data manager will have seamless integration as they both manage RDF data.

We have designed and developed a series of cloud-based AIS systems that handle massive amounts of data. That is, we have essentially used big data management techniques for AIS. This chapter provides an overview of our design and proof of implementation efforts. In particular, we describe the detailed design and implementation of AIS in a semantic cloud. That is, we have used semantic web technologies for providing cloud-based semantic web services. These semantic web services enable information sharing. Our framework consists of a three-layer architecture that includes a user interface layer, a policy engine layer and a data connection layer that integrates multiple data sources in the cloud. It should be noted that to store critical data in the cloud, we need to encrypt the data and carry out the information sharing operation on encrypted data. This is especially important for a public cloud. However, our prior work for AIS does not encrypt the data in the cloud. This aspect will be part of our future research.

The organization of this chapter is as follows. The overall system design is discussed in Section 16.2. Our design philosophy is discussed in Section 16.2.1. In particular, we will discuss the design of two AIS systems: CAISS (Cloud-based AIS System) and CAISS++ (a more advanced CAISS). Our implementation details are discussed in Section 16.3. Related efforts are discussed in Section 16.4. Section 16.5 concludes this chapter. Figure 16.1 illustrates the contents of this chapter. Details of our work can also be found in [THUR2012].

16.2   SYSTEM DESIGN

16.2.1   Design Philosophy

Our design has proceeded in two phases. During Phase 1, we have designed and implemented a proof-of-concept prototype of a Cloud-centric Assured Information Sharing System (CAISS) that utilizes the technology components we have designed in-house as well as open source tools. CAISS consists of two components: a cloud-centric policy manager that enforces policies specified in RDF (resource description framework), and a cloud-centric data manager that will store and manage data also specified in RDF. This RDF data manager is essentially a query engine for SPARQL (SPARQL protocol and RDF query language), a language widely used by the semantic web community to query RDF data. RDF is a semantic web language that is considerably more expressive than XACML for specifying and reasoning about policies. Furthermore, our policy manager and data manager will have seamless integration as they both manage RDF data. We have chosen this RDF-based approach for cloud-centric AIS during Phase 1 because it satisfies the two necessary conditions stated in the previous paragraph, and we have already developed an RDF-based noncloud-centric policy manager [CADE2011a] and an RDF-based cloud-centric data manager for AFOSR [HUSA2011]. Having parts of the two critical components needed to build a useful cloud-centric AIS system puts us in an excellent position to build a useful proof-of-concept demonstration system CAISS. Specifically, we are enhancing our RDF-based policy engine to operate on a cloud, extend our cloud-centric RDF data manager to integrate with the policy manager, and build an integrated framework for CAISS. Our goal is to extend CAISS for a social media environment.

While our initial CAISS design and implementation will be the first system-supporting cloud-centric AIS, it will operate only on a single trusted cloud and will therefore not support information sharing across multiple clouds. Furthermore, while CAISS's RDF-based, formal semantics approach to policy specification will be significantly more expressive than XACML-based approaches, it will not support an enhanced machine interpretability of content as RDF does not provide a sufficiently rich vocabulary (e.g., support for classes and properties). Phase 2 will therefore develop a fully functional and robust AIS system called CAISS++ that addresses these deficiencies. The preliminary design for CAISS++ is completed and will be discussed later in this chapter. CAISS is an important stepping-stone toward CAISS++ because CAISS can be used as a baseline framework against which CAISS++ can be compared along several performance dimensions, such as storage model efficiency and OWL-based policy expressiveness. Furthermore, as CAISS and CAISS++ share the same core components (policy engine and query processor), the lessons learned from the implementation and integration of these components in CAISS will be invaluable during the development of CAISS++. Finally, the evaluation and testing of CAISS will provide us with important insights into the shortcomings of CAISS which can then be systematically addressed in the implementation of CAISS++.

We will also conduct a formal analysis of policy specifications and the software-level protection mechanisms that enforce them to provide exceptionally high-assurance security guarantees for the resulting system. We envisage CAISS++ to be used in highly mission-critical applications. Therefore, it becomes imperative to provide guarantees that the policies are enforced in a provably correct manner. We have extensive expertise in formal policy analysis [JONE2010, JONE2011] and their enforcement via machine-certified, in-line reference monitors [HAML2006a, HAML2006b, SRID2010]. Such analyses will be leveraged to model and certify security properties enforced by core software components in the trusted computing base of CAISS++.

CAISS++ will be a breakthrough technology for information sharing due to the fact that it uses a novel combination of cloud-centric policy specification and enforcement along with a cloud-centric data storage and efficient query evaluation. CAISS++ will make use of ontologies, a sublanguage of the web ontology language (OWL), to build policies. A mixture of such ontologies with a semantic web-based rule language (e.g., SWRL) facilitates distributed reasoning on the policies to enforce security. Additionally, CAISS++ will include an RDF processing engine that provides cost-based optimization for evaluating SPARQL queries based on information sharing policies.

16.2.2 DESIGN OF CAISS

We are enhancing our tools developed for AFOSR on (i) secure cloud query processing with semantic web data, and (ii) semantic web-based policy engine to develop CAISS. Details of our tools are given in Section 16.4 (under related work). In this section, we discuss the enhancements to be made to our tools to develop CAISS.

First, our RDF-based policy engine enforces access control, redaction, and inference control policies on data represented as RDF graphs. Second, our cloud SPARQL query engine for RDF data uses the Hadoop/MapReduce framework. Note that Hadoop is the Apache distributed file system and MapReduce sits on top of Hadoop and carries out job scheduling. As in the case of our cloud-based relational query processor prototype [THUR2010], our SPARQL query engine also handles policies specified in XACML and the policy engine implements the XACML protocol. The use of XACML as a policy language requires extensive knowledge about the general concepts used in the design of XACML. Thus, policy authoring in XACML requires a steep learning curve, and is therefore a task that is left to an experienced administrator. A second disadvantage of using XACML is related to performance. Current implementations of XACML require an access request to be evaluated against every policy in the system until a policy applies to the incoming request. This strategy is sufficient for systems with relatively few users and policies. However, for systems with a large number of users and a substantial number of access requests, the aforementioned strategy becomes a performance bottleneck. Finally, XACML is not sufficiently expressive to capture the semantics of information sharing policies. Prior research has shown that semantic web-based policies are far more expressive. This is because semantic web technologies are based on description logic and have the power to represent knowledge as well as reason about knowledge. Therefore, our first step is to replace the XACML-based policy engine with a semantic web-based policy engine. As we already have our RDF-based policy engine for the Phase 1 prototype, we will enhance this engine and integrate it with our SPARQL query processor. As our policy engine is based on RDF and our query processor also manages large RDF graphs, there will be no impedance mismatch between the data and the policies.

16.2.2.1 Enhanced Policy Engine

Our current policy engine has a limitation in that it does not operate in a cloud. Therefore, we will port our RDF policy engine to the cloud environment and integrate it with the SPARQL query engine for federated query processing in the cloud. Our policy engine will benefit from the scalability and the distributed platform offered by Hadoop's MapReduce framework to answer SPARQL queries over large distributed RDF triple stores (billions of RDF triples). The reasons for using RDF as our data model are as follows: (1) RDF allows us to achieve data interoperability between the seemingly disparate sources of information that are catalogued by each agency/organization separately. (2) The use of RDF allows participating agencies to create data-centric applications that make use of the integrated data that is now available to them. (3) As RDF does not require the use of an explicit schema for data generation, it can be easily adapted to ever-changing user requirements. The policy engine's flexibility is based on its accepting high-level policies and executing them as query rules over a directed RDF graph representation of the data. While our prior work focuses on provenance data and access control policies, our CAISS prototype will be flexible enough to handle data represented in RDF and will include information sharing policies. The strength of our policy engine is that it can handle any type of policy that could be represented using RDF and horn logic rules.

The second limitation of our policy engine is that it currently addresses certain types of policies such as confidentiality, privacy, and redaction policies. We need to incorporate information sharing policies into our policy engine. We have however conducted simulation studies for incentive-based AIS as well as AIS prototypes in the cloud. We have defined a number of information sharing policies such as "US gives information to UK provided UK does not share it with India." We specify such policies in RDF and incorporate them to be processed by our enhanced policy engine.

16.2.2.2 Enhanced SPARQL Query Processor

While we have a tool that will execute SPARQL queries over large RDF graphs on Hadoop, there is still the need for supporting path queries (i.e., SPARQL queries that provide answers to a request for paths in an RDF graph). An RDF triple can be viewed as an arc from the subject to object with the predicate used to label the arc. The answers to the SPARQL query are based on reachability (i.e., the paths between a source node and a target node). The concatenation of the labels on the arcs along a path can be thought of as a word belonging to the answer set of the path query. Each term of a word is contributed by some predicate label of a triple in the RDF graph. We have designed an algorithm to determine the candidate triples as an answer set in a distributed RDF graph. First, the RDF document is converted to an N-triple file that is split based on predicate labels. A term in a word could correspond to some predicate file. Second, we form the word by tracing an appropriate path in the distributed RDF graph. We use MapReduce jobs to build the word and to get the candidate RDF triples as an order set. Finally, we return all of the set of ordered RDF triples as the answers to the corresponding SPARQL query.

16.2.2.3   Integration Framework

Figure 16.2 provides an overview of the CAISS architecture. The integration of the cloud-centric RDF policy engine with the enhanced SPARQL query processor must address the following. First, we need to make sure that RDF-based policies can be stored in the existing storage schema used by the query processor. Second, we need to ensure that the enhanced query processor is able to efficiently evaluate policies (i.e., path queries) over the underlying RDF storage. Finally, we need to conduct a performance evaluation of CAISS to verify that it meets the performance requirements of various participating agencies. Figure 16.3 illustrates the concept of operation of CAISS. Here,

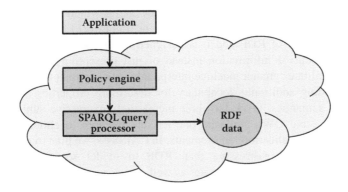

FIGURE 16.2   CAISS prototype overview.

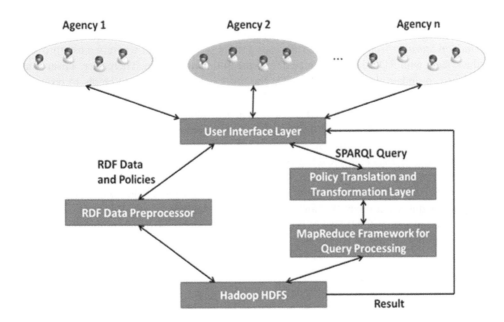

FIGURE 16.3   Operation of CAISS.

multiple agencies will share data in a single cloud. The enhanced policy engine and the cloud-centric SPARQL query processor will enforce the information sharing policies. This proof-of-concept system will drive the detailed design and implementation of CAISS++.

There are several benefits in developing a proof-of-concept prototype such as CAISS before we embark on CAISS++. First CAISS itself is useful to share data within a single cloud. Second, we will have a baseline system that we can compare against with respect to efficiency and ease-of-use when we implement CAISS++. Third, this will give us valuable lessons with respect to the integration of the different pieces required for AIS in the cloud. Finally, by running different scenarios on CAISS, we can identify potential performance bottlenecks that need to be addressed in CAISS++.

16.2.3   LIMITATIONS OF CAISS

We have examined alternatives and carried out a preliminary design of CAISS++. Based on the lessons learned from the CAISS prototype and the preliminary design of CAISS++, we will carry out a detailed design of CAISS++ and subsequently implement an operational prototype of CAISS++ during phase 2. In this section we will discuss the limitations of CAISS.

1. *Policy Engine:* CAISS uses an RDF-based policy engine which has limited expressivity. The purpose of RDF is to provide a structure (or framework) for describing resources. OWL is built on top of RDF and it is designed for use by applications that need to process the content of information instead of just presenting information to human users. OWL facilitates greater machine interpretability of content than that supported by RDF by providing additional vocabulary for describing properties and classes along with a formal semantics. OWL has three increasingly expressive sublanguages: OWL Lite, OWL DL, and OWL Full and one has the freedom to choose a suitable sub-language based on application requirements. In CAISS++, we plan to make use of OWL which is much more expressive than RDF to model security policies through organization-specific domain ontologies as well as a system-wide upper ontology. (Note that CAISS++ will reuse an organization's existing domain ontology or facilitate the creation of a new domain ontology if it does not exist. Additionally, we have to engineer the upper ontology that will be used by the centralized component of CAISS++.) Additionally, CAISS++ will make use of a distributed reasoning algorithm which will leverage ontologies to enforce security policies.

2. *Hadoop Storage Architecture:* CAISS uses a static storage model wherein a user provides the system with RDF data only once during the initialization step. Thereafter, a user is not allowed to update the existing data. On the other hand, CAISS++ attempts to provide a flexible storage model to users. In CAISS++, a user is allowed to append new data to the existing RDF data stored in HDFS. Note that only allowing a user to append new data rather than deleting/modifying existing data comes from the append-only restriction for files that is enforced by HDFS.

3. *SPARQL Query Processor:* CAISS only supports simple SPARQL queries that make use of basic graph patterns (BGP). In CAISS++, support for other SPARQL query operators such as FILTER, GROUP BY, and ORDER BY, will be added. Additionally, CAISS uses a heuristic query optimizer that aims to minimize the number of MapReduce jobs required to answer a query. CAISS++ will incorporate a cost-based query optimizer that will minimize the number of triples that are accessed during the process of query execution.

16.2.4   DESIGN OF CAISS++

CAISS++ overcomes the limitations of CAISS. The detailed design of CAISS++ and its implementation will be carried out during phase 2. The lessons learned from CAISS will also drive the detailed design of CAISS++. We assume that the data are encrypted with appropriate DoD encryption technologies and therefore will not conduct research on encryption in this project. The concept of operation for CAISS++ is shown in interaction with several participating agencies in Figure 16.4 where multiple organizations share data in a single cloud.

The design of CAISS++ is based on a novel combination of an OWL-based policy engine with an RDF processing engine. Therefore, this design is composed of several tasks, each of which is solved separately after which all tasks are integrated into a single framework. (1) *OWL-based policy engine:* the policy engine uses a set of agency-specific domain ontologies as well as an upper ontology to construct policies for the task of AIS. The task of enforcing policies may require the use of a distributed reasoner; therefore, we will evaluate existing distributed reasoners. (2) *RDF processing engine:* the processing engine requires the construction of sophisticated storage architectures as well as an efficient query processor. (3) *Integration Framework:* the final task is to combine the policy engine with the processing engine into an integrated framework. The initial design of CAISS++ will be based on a trade-off between simplicity of design vs. its scalability and efficiency. The first design alternative is known as centralized CAISS++ and it chooses simplicity as the trade-off whereas the second design alternative (known as decentralized CAISS++) chooses scalability and efficiency as the trade-off. Finally, we also provide a hybrid CAISS++ architecture that tries to combine the benefits of both, centralized and decentralized CAISS++. As CAISS++ follows a requirements-driven design, the division of tasks that we outlined earlier to achieve AIS are present in each of the approaches that we present next.

16.2.4.1 Centralized CAISS++

Figure 16.5 illustrates two agencies interacting through Centralized CAISS++. Centralized CAISS++ consists of shared cloud storage to store the shared data. All the participating agencies store their respective knowledge bases consisting of domain ontology with corresponding instance data. Centralized CAISS++ also consists of an upper ontology, a query engine (QE) and a distributed reasoner (DR). The upper ontology is used to capture the domain knowledge that is common across the domains of participating agencies, whereas domain ontology captures the knowledge specific to a given agency or a domain. Note that the domain ontology for a given agency will be protected from the domain ontologies of other participating agencies. Policies can either be captured in the upper ontology or in any of the domain ontologies depending on their scope of applicability. Note that the domain ontology for a given agency will be protected from domain ontologies of other participating agencies.

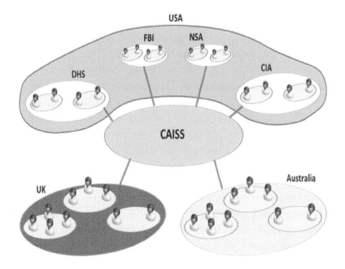

FIGURE 16.4 CAISS++ Scenario.

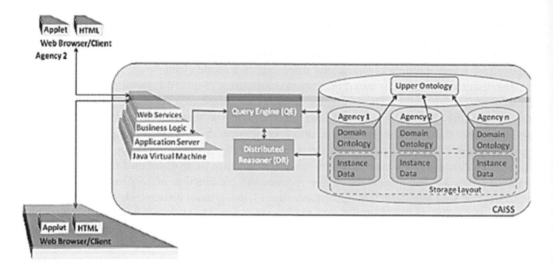

FIGURE 16.5 Centralized CAISS++.

The design of an upper ontology as well as domain ontologies that capture the requirements of the participating agencies is a significant research area and is the focus of the ontology engineering problem. Ontologies will be created using suitable dialects of OWL which are based on *description logics*. Description logics are usually decidable fragments of First Order Logic and will be the basis for providing sound formal semantics. Having represented knowledge in terms of ontologies, reasoning will be done using existing optimized reasoning algorithms. Query answering will leverage reasoning algorithms to formulate and answer intelligent queries. The encoding of policies in OWL will ensure that they are enforced in a provably correct manner. Later we present an ongoing research project at The University of Texas at Dallas that focuses on providing a general framework for enforcing policies in a provably correct manner using the same underlying technologies. This work can be leveraged toward modeling and enforcement of security policies in CAISS++. The instance data can choose between several available data storage formats. The QE receives queries from the participating agencies, parses the query and determines whether the computation requires the use of a DR. If the query is simple and does not require the use of a reasoner, the query engine executes the query directly over the shared knowledge base. Once the query result has been computed, the result is returned to the querying agency. If however, the query is complex and requires inferences over the given data, the query engine uses the distributed reasoner to compute the inferences and then returns the result to the querying agency. A distributed DL reasoner differs from a traditional DL reasoner in its ability to perform reasoning over cloud data storage using the MapReduce framework. During the preliminary design of CAISS++ in Phase 1, we will conduct a thorough investigation of the available distributed reasoners using existing benchmarks such as LUBM [GUO2005]. The goal of this investigation is to determine whether we can use one of the existing reasoners or whether we need to build our own distributed reasoner. In Figure 16.5, an agency is illustrated as a stack consisting of a web browser, an applet and HTML. An agency uses the web browser to send the queries to CAISS++ which are handled by the query processor.

The main differences between centralized CAISS++ and CAISS are as follows: (1) CAISS will use RDF to encode security policies whereas centralized CAISS++ will use a suitable sublanguage of OWL which is more expressive than RDF and can therefore capture the security policies better. (2) The SPARQL query processor in CAISS will support a limited subset of SPARQL expressivity, that is, it will provide support only for Basic Graph Patterns (BGP), whereas the SPARQL query processor in centralized CAISS++ will be designed to support maximum expressivity of SPARQL. (3) The Hadoop storage architecture used in CAISS only supports data insertion during an initialization step. However, when data need to be updated, the entire RDF graph is deleted and a new dataset is inserted in its place. On the other hand, centralized CAISS++, in addition to supporting the previous feature, also opens up Hadoop HDFS's append-only feature to users. This feature allows users to append new information to the data that they have previously uploaded to the system.

16.2.4.2 Decentralized CAISS++

Figure 16.6 illustrates two agencies in interaction with decentralized CAISS++. Decentralized CAISS++ consists of two parts, namely global CAISS++ and local CAISS++. Global CAISS++ consists of a shared cloud storage which is used by the participating agencies to store only their respective domain ontologies and not the instance data unlike centralized CAISS++. Note that domain ontologies for various organizations will be sensitive, therefore, CAISS++ will make use of its own domain ontology to protect a participating agency from accessing other domain ontologies. When a user from an agency queries the CAISS++ data store, global CAISS++ processes the query in two steps. In the first step, it performs a check to verify whether the user is authorized to perform the action specified in the query. If the result of step 1 verifies the user as an authorized user, then it proceeds to step 2 of query processing. In the second step, global CAISS++ federates the actual query to the participating agencies. The query is then processed by the local CAISS++ of a participating agency. The result of computation is then returned to the global CAISS++ which aggregates the final result and returns it to the user. The step 2 of query processing may involve query splitting if the data required to answer a query spans multiple domains. In this case, the results of subqueries from several agencies (their local CAISS++) will need to be combined for further query processing. Once the results are merged and the final result is computed, the result is returned to the user of the querying agency. The figure illustrates agencies with a set of two stacks, one of which corresponds to the local CAISS++ and the other consisting of a web browser, an applet and HTML, which is used by an agency to query global CAISS++. Table 16.1 shows the pros and cons of the centralized CAISS++ approach, whereas Table 16.2 shows the pros and cons of the decentralized CAISS++ approach.

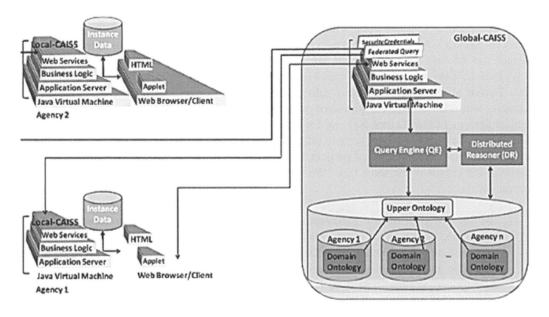

FIGURE 16.6 Decentralized CAISS++.

TABLE 16.1

The pros and cons of centralized CAISS++

PROS	CONS
Simple approach	Difficult to update data
Simple approach	Expensive approach as data needs to be migrated to central storage on each update or a set of updates
Ease of implementation	Leads to data duplication
Easier to query	If data are available in different formats, it needs to be homogenized by translating it to RDF

TABLE 16.2

The pros and cons of decentralized CAISS++

Advantages	Disadvantages
No duplication of data	Complex query processing
Scalable and Flexible	Difficult to implement
Efficient	May require query rewriting and query splitting

16.2.4.3   Hybrid CAISS++

Figure 16.7 illustrates an overview of hybrid CAISS++, which leverages the benefits of centralized CAISS++ as well as decentralized CAISS++. Hybrid CAISS++ architecture is illustrated in Figure 16.8. It is a flexible design alternative as the users of the participating agencies have the freedom to choose between centralized CAISS++ or decentralized CAISS++. Hybrid CAISS++ is made up of global CAISS++ and a set of local CAISS++'s located at each of the participating agencies. Global CAISS++ consists of a shared cloud storage which is used by the participating agencies to store the data they would like to share with other agencies.

A local CAISS++ of an agency is used to receive and process a federated query on the instance data located at the agency. A participating group is a group comprised of users from several agencies who want to share information with each other. The members of a group arrive at a mutual agreement on whether they opt for the centralized or decentralized approach. Additional users can join a group at a later point in time if the need arises. Hybrid CAISS++ will be designed to simultaneously support a set of participating groups. Additionally, a user can belong to several participating groups at the same time. We describe a few use-case scenarios which illustrate the operation.

1. The first case corresponds to the scenario where a set of users who want to securely share information with each other opt for a centralized approach. Suppose users from Agency 1 want to share information with users of Agency 2 and vice versa, then both the agencies store their knowledge bases comprising of domain ontology and instance data on the shared cloud storage located at global CAISS++. The centralized CAISS++ approach works by having the participating agencies arrive at mutual trust on using the central cloud storage. Subsequently, information sharing proceeds as in centralized CAISS++.

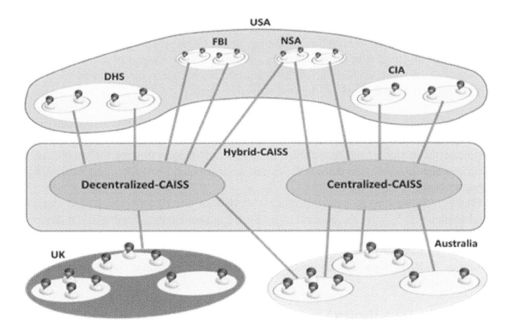

FIGURE 16.7 Hybrid CAISS++ overview.

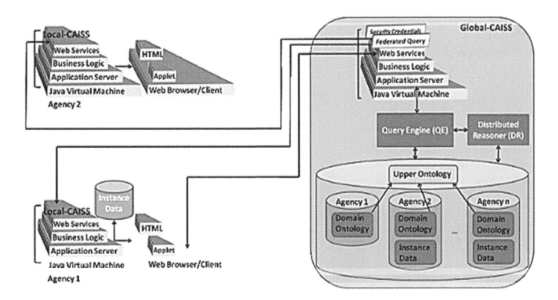

FIGURE 16.8 Hybrid CAISS++ architecture.

2. The second corresponds to the scenario where a set of users opts for a decentralized approach. For example, Agencies 3, 4, and 5 wish to share information with each other and mutually opt for the decentralized approach. All the three agencies store their respective domain ontologies at the central cloud storage and this information is only accessible to members of this group. The subsequent information sharing process proceeds in the manner described earlier for the decentralized CAISS++ approach.

3. The third corresponds to the scenario where a user of an agency belongs to multiple participating groups, some of which opt for the centralized approach and others for the

decentralized approach. As the user is a part of a group using the centralized approach to sharing, he/she needs to make his/her data available to the group by shipping his/her data to the central cloud storage. Additionally, as the user is also a part of a group using the decentralized approach for sharing, he/she needs to respond to the federated query with the help of the local CAISS++ located at his/her agency.

Table 16.3 shows the trade-offs between the different approaches and this will enable users to choose a suitable approach of AIS based on their application requirements. Next, we describe details of the cloud storage mechanism that makes use of Hadoop to store the knowledge bases from various agencies and then discuss the details of distributed SPARQL query processing over the cloud storage.

In Figure 16.9, we present an architectural overview of our Hadoop-based RDF storage and retrieval framework. We use the concept of a "Store" to provide data loading and querying capabilities on RDF graphs that are stored in the underlying HDFS. A store represents a single RDF dataset and can therefore contain several RDF graphs, each with its own separate layout. All operations on an RDF graph are then implicitly converted into operations on the underlying layout including the following:

- *Layout Formatter:* This block performs the function of formatting a layout, which is the process of deleting all triples in an RDF graph while preserving the directory structure used to store that graph.

TABLE 16.3

A comparison of the three approaches based on functionality Hadoop Storage Architecture

Functionality	Centralized CAISS++	Decentralized CAISS++	Hybrid CAISS++
No data duplication	X	✓	✓
Flexibility	X	X	✓
Scalability	X	✓	✓
Efficiency	✓	✓	✓
Simplicity – no query rewriting	✓	X	X
Trusted centralized cloud data storage	✓	X	X

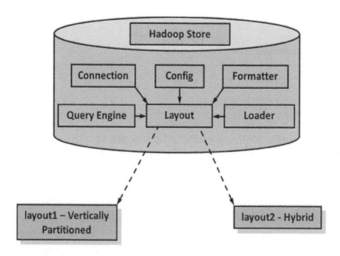

FIGURE 16.9   Hadoop storage architecture used by CAISS++.

- *Loader:* This block performs loading of triples into a layout.
- *Query Engine:* This block allows a user to query a layout using a SPARQL query. As our framework operates on the underlying HDFS, the querying mechanism on a layout involves translating a SPARQL query into a possible pipeline of MapReduce jobs and then executing this pipeline on a layout.
- *Connection:* This block maintains the necessary connections and configurations with the underlying HDFS.
- *Config:* This block maintains configuration information such as graph names for each of the RDF graphs that make up a store.

As RDF data will be stored under different HDFS folders in separate files as a part of our storage schema, we need to adopt certain naming conventions for such folders and files.

16.2.4.4 Naming Conventions

A Hadoop store can be composed of several distinct RDF graphs in our framework. Therefore, a separate folder will be created in HDFS for each such Hadoop Store. The name of this folder will correspond to the name that has been selected for the given store. Furthermore, an RDF graph is divided into several files in our framework depending on the storage layout that is selected. Therefore, a separate folder will be created in HDFS for each distinct RDF graph. The name of this folder is defined to be "default" for the default RDF graph while for a named RDF graph, the Uniform Resource Identifier (URI) of the graph is used as the folder name. We use the abstraction of a store in our framework for the reason that this will simplify the management of data belonging to various agencies. Two of the layouts to be supported by our framework are discussed later. These layouts use a varying number of HDFS files to store RDF data.

16.2.4.5 Vertically Partitioned Layout

Figure 16.10 presents the storage schema for the vertically partitioned layout. For every unique predicate contained in an RDF graph, this layout creates a separate file using the name of the predicate as the file name, in the underlying HDFS. Note that only the local name part of a predicate URI (Universal Resource Identifier) is used in a file name and a separate mapping exists between a file name and the predicate URI. A file for a given predicate contains a separate line for every triple that contains that predicate. This line stores the subject and object values that make up the triple. This schema will lead to significant storage space savings because moving the predicate name to the name of a file completely eliminates the storage of this predicate value. However, multiple occurrences of the same resource URI or literal value will be stored multiple times across all files as well as within a file. Additionally, a SPARQL query may need to lookup multiple files to

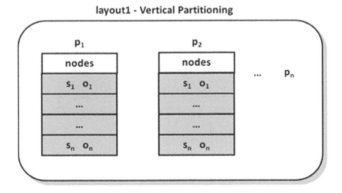

FIGURE 16.10   Vertically partitioned layout.

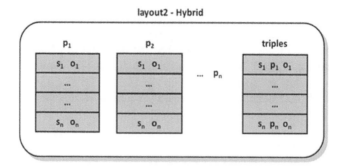

FIGURE 16.11   Hybrid layout.

ensure that a complete result is returned to a user, for example, a query to find all triples that belong to a specific subject or object.

16.2.4.6   Hybrid Layout

Figure 16.11 presents the storage schema for the hybrid layout. This layout is an extension of the vertically partitioned layout, as in addition to the separate files that are created for every unique predicate in an RDF graph, it also creates a separate triples file containing all the triples in the SPO (Subject, Predicate, Object) format. The advantage of having such a file is that it directly gives us all triples belonging to a certain subject or object. Recall that such a search operation required scanning through multiple files in the vertically partitioned layout. The storage space efficiency of this layout is not as good as the vertically partitioned layout due to the addition of the triples file. However, a SPARQL query to find all triples belonging to a certain subject or object could be performed more efficiently using this layout.

16.2.4.7   Distributed processing of SPARQL

Query processing in CAISS++ comprises of several steps (Figure 16.12). The first step is query parsing and translation where a given SPARQL query is first parsed to verify syntactic correctness and then a parse tree corresponding to the input query is built. The parse tree is then translated into a SPARQL algebra expression. As a given SPARQL query can have multiple equivalent SPARQL

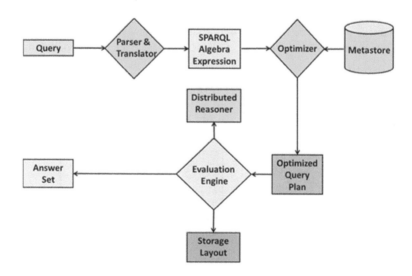

FIGURE 16.12   Distributed processing of SPARQL in CAISS++.

algebra expressions, we annotate each such expression with instructions on how to evaluate each operation in this expression. Such annotated SPARQL algebra expressions correspond to query-evaluation plans which serve as the input to the optimizer. The optimizer selects a query plan that minimizes the cost of query evaluation. To optimize a query, an optimizer must know the cost of each operation. To compute the cost of each operation, the optimizer uses a metastore that stores statistics associated with the RDF data. The cost of a given query-evaluation plan is alternatively measured in terms of the number of MapReduce jobs or the number of triples that will be accessed as a part of query execution. Once the query plan is chosen, the query is evaluated with that plan and the result of the query is output. As we use a cloud-centric framework to store RDF data, an evaluation engine needs to convert SPARQL algebra operators into equivalent MapReduce jobs on the underlying storage layouts (described earlier). Therefore, in CAISS++ we will implement a MapReduce job for each of the SPARQL algebra operators. Additionally, the evaluation engine uses a distributed reasoner to compute inferences required for query evaluation.

16.2.4.8 Framework Integration

The components that we have outlined that are a part of CAISS++ need to be integrated to work with one another. Furthermore, this process of integration depends on a user's selection of one of the three possible design choices provided with CAISS++, namely, centralized CAISS++, decentralized CAISS++, or hybrid CAISS++. The integration of the various pieces of CAISS++ that have been presented so far needs to take into account several issues. First, we need to make sure that our ontology engineering process has been successful in capturing an agency's requirements and additionally, the ontologies can be stored in the storage schema used by the Hadoop storage architecture. Second, we need to ensure that the distributed SPARQL query processor is able to efficiently evaluate queries (i.e., user-generated SPARQL queries as well as SPARQL queries that evaluate policies) over the underlying RDF storage. Finally, we need to conduct a performance evaluation of CAISS++ to verify that it meets the performance requirements of various participating agencies as well as leads to significant performance advantages when compared with CAISS.

16.2.4.9 Policy Specification and Enforcement

The users of CAISS++ can use a language of their choice (e.g., XACML, RDF, and Rei) to specify their information sharing policies. These policies will be translated into a suitable sublanguage of OWL using existing or custom-built translators. We will extend our policy engine for CAISS to handle policies specified in OWL. In addition to RDF policies, our current policy engine can handle policies in OWL for implementing role-based access control, inference control, and social network analysis.

16.2.5 Extensions to the Design

16.2.5.1 Formal Policy Analysis

Our framework is applicable to a variety of mission-critical, high-assurance applications that span multiple possibly mutually distrusting organizations. To provide maximal security assurance in such settings, it is important to establish strong formal guarantees regarding the correctness of the system and the policies it enforces. To that end, we examined the development of an infrastructure for constructing formal, machine-checkable proofs of important system properties and policy analyses for our system. While machine-checkable proofs can be very difficult and time-consuming to construct for many large software systems, our choice of SPARQL, RDF, and OWL as query, ontology and policy languages, opens unique opportunities to elegantly formulate such proofs in a logic programming environment. We will encode policies, policy-rewriting algorithms, and security properties as a rule-based, logical derivation system in Prolog, and will apply model-checking and theorem-proving systems such as ACL2 to produce machine-checkable proofs that these properties are obeyed by the system. Properties that we intend to consider in our model include soundness, transparency, consistency, and completeness. The results of our formal policy analysis will drive our detailed design and implementation of CAISS++. To our knowledge, none of the prior work has focused on such formal policy analysis for SPARQL, RDF, and OWL. Our extensive research on formal policy analysis with in-line reference monitors is discussed under related work.

By reducing high-level security policy specifications and system models to the level of the denotational and operational semantics of their binary-level implementations, our past work has developed formally machine-certifiable security enforcement mechanisms of a variety of complex software systems, including those implemented in.NET [HAML2006b], ActionScript [SRID2010], Java [JONE2010], and native code [HAML2010b]. Working at the binary level provides extremely high formal guarantees because it permits the tool chain that produces mission-critical software components to remain untrusted; the binary code produced by the chain can be certified directly. This strategy is an excellent match for CAISS++ because data security specification languages such as XACML and OWL can be elegantly reflected down to the binary level of bytecode languages with XML-aware system application program interfaces (API), such as Java bytecode. Our past work has applied binary-instrumentation (e.g., in-lined reference monitoring) and a combination of binary type-checking [HAML2006b], model-checking [SRID2010], and automated theorem proving (e.g., via ACL2) to achieve fully automated machine certification of binary software in such domains.

16.2.5.2 Extensions for Big Data-based Applications

In Chapter 17, we will discuss an access control framework for social media data. We can combine that work with the work discussed in this chapter (i.e., Chapter 16) and develop approaches for AIS for social media based on big data. There are several variations of the designs discussed in this chapter that we can adapt for social media applications utilizing big data management and analytics. First, members of a network may want to share data. Therefore, they could implement the information sharing policies with each member having his/her own data store. In the second design, the members could use a shared space or a cloud to store the data and the policies and share the data securely.

The member could also belong to multiple social networks. That is, one person could belong to more than one network or a person could belong to just one network. In this case, a member could share more data with the members of his/her network while sharing limited data with members of another network. Also, different networks may use heterogeneous technologies for representation. Therefore, the heterogeneous representations have to be resolved. One could also develop a logical representation of the multiple networks and have mappings to the individual networks. Over time, the number of users in the multiple social networks could grow rapidly and the amount of data they store and share in the networks could be massive. Therefore, several of the big data technologies we have discussed in Chapter 5 as well as in other chapters in Parts I and II have to be explored for use in AIS between multiple social networks.

16.3   IMPLEMENTATION DETAILS

We have implemented a series of systems for CAISS and CAISS++. We provide an overview of these implementations.

16.3.1   PROTOTYPE IMPLEMENTATIONS

16.3.1.1   Secure Data Storage and Retrieval in the Cloud

We have built a web-based application that combines existing cloud computing technologies such as Hadoop, an open source distributed file system and Hive data warehouse infrastructure built on

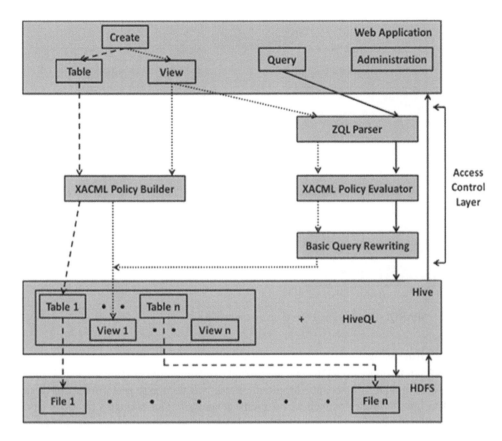

FIGURE 16.13   Hive-based assured cloud query processing.

top of Hadoop with a XACML policy-based security mechanism to allow collaborating organizations to securely store and retrieve large amounts of data [HUSA2011, THUR2010, UTD1]. Figure 16.13 presents the architecture of our system. We use the services provided by the Hive layer and Hadoop including the Hadoop Distributed File System (HDFS) layer that makes up the storage layer of Hadoop and allows the storage of data blocks across a cluster of nodes. The layers we have implemented include the web application layer, the ZQL parser layer, the XACML policy layer, and the query rewriting layer. The web application layer is the only interface provided by our system to the user to access the cloud infrastructure. The ZQL parser [ZQL] layer takes as input any query submitted by a user and either proceeds to the XACML policy evaluator if the query is successfully parsed or returns an error message to the user. The XACML policy layer is used to build (XACML policy builder) and evaluate (XACML policy evaluation) XACML policies. The basic query rewriting layer rewrites SQL queries entered by the user. The Hive layer is used to manage relational data that is stored in the underlying Hadoop HDFS [THUS2009]. In addition, we have also designed and implemented secure storage and query processing in a hybrid cloud [KHAD2011].

16.3.1.2   Secure SPARQL Query Processing on the Cloud

We have developed a framework to query RDF data stored over Hadoop as shown in Figure 16.14. We used the Pellet reasoner to reason at various stages. We carried out real-time query reasoning using the pellet libraries coupled with Hadoop's MapReduce functionalities. Our RDF query processing is composed of two main steps: (i) the pre-processing and (ii) the query optimization and execution.

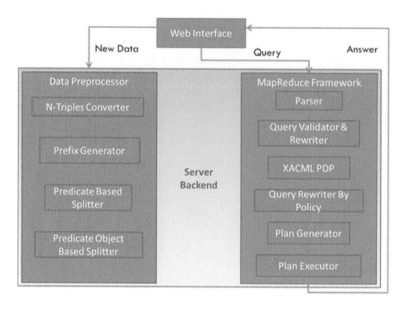

FIGURE 16.14   SPARQL-based assured cloud query processing.

16.3.1.3   Pre-processing

To execute a SPARQL query on RDF data, we carried out data pre-processing steps and stored the pre-processed data in HDFS. A separate MapReduce task was written to perform the conversion of RDF/XML data into N-Triples as well as for prefix generation. Our storage strategy is based on predicate splits [HUSA2011].

16.3.1.4   Query Execution and Optimization

We have developed a SPARQL query execution and optimization module for Hadoop. As our storage strategy is based on predicate splits, first, we examine the predicates present in the query. Second, we examine a subset of the input files that are matched with predicates. Third, SPARQL queries generally have many joins in them and all of these joins may not be possible to perform in a single MapReduce job. Therefore, we have developed an algorithm that decides the number of jobs required for each kind of query. As part of optimization, we applied a greedy strategy and cost-based optimization to reduce query processing time. We have also developed a XACML-based centralized policy engine that will carry out federated RDF query processing on the cloud. Details of the enforcement strategy are given in [HAML2010a, HUSA2011, KHAL2010].

16.3.1.5   RDF Policy Engine

In our prior work [CADE2011a], we have developed a policy engine to process RDF-based access control policies for RDF data. The policy engine is designed with the following features in mind: scalability, efficiency, and interoperability. This framework (Figure 16.15) can be used to execute various policies, including access control policies and redaction policies. It can also be used as a testbed for evaluating different policy sets over RDF data and to view the outcomes graphically. Our framework presents an interface that accepts a high-level policy which is then translated into the required format. It takes a user's input query and returns a response which has been pruned using a set of user-defined policy constraints. The architecture is built using a modular approach, therefore it is very flexible in that most of the modules can be extended or replaced by another application module. For example, a policy module implementing a discretionary access control (DAC) could be replaced entirely by an RBAC module or we may decide to enforce all our

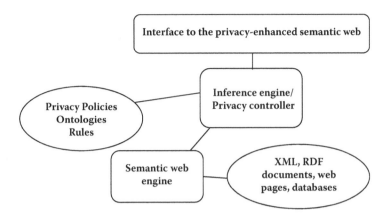

FIGURE 16.15 RDF policy engine.

constraints based on a generalized redaction model. It should be noted that our policy engine also handles role-based access control policies specified in OWL and SWRL [CADE2010]. In addition, it handles certain policies specified in OWL for inference control such as association-based policies where access to collections of entities is denied and logical policies where A implies B and if access to B is denied then access to A should also be denied [CADE2010, CADE2011b, CARM2009]. This capability of our policy engine will be useful in our design and implementation of CAISS++ where information is shared across multiple clouds.

16.3.1.6 Assured Information Sharing Prototypes

We have developed multiple systems for AIS. Under an AFOSR funded project (between 2005 and 2008), we developed an XACML-based policy engine to function on top of relational databases and demonstrated the sharing of (simulated) medical data [THUR2008]. In this implementation, we specified the policies in XACML and stored the data in multiple Oracle databases. When one organization requests data from another organization, the policies are examined and authorized data are released. In addition, we also conducted simulation studies on the amount of data that would be lost by enforcing the policies while information sharing. Under our MURI project, also funded by AFOSR, we conducted simulation studies for incentive-based information sharing [KANT2010]. We have also examined risk-based access control in an information sharing scenario [CELI2007]. In addition to access control policies, we have specified different types of policies including need-to-share policies and trust policies (e.g., A shared data with B provided B does not share the data with C). Note that the 9/11 commission report calls for the migration from the more restrictive need-to-know to the less restrictive need-to-share policies. These policies are key to support the specification of the directive concerning AIS obligations.

16.3.2 OTHER IMPLEMENTATIONS

For example, one of the implementations of CAISS was carried out in Java and is based on a flexible design where we can plug and play multiple components. A service provider and/or user will have the flexibility to use the SPARQL query processor as well as the RDF-based policy engine as separate components or combine them. The open-source component used for CAISS will include the Pellet reasoner as well as our in-house tools such as the SPARQL query processor on the Hadoop/MapReduce framework and the cloud-centric RDF policy engine. CAISS will allow us to demonstrate basic AIS scenarios on our cloud-based framework.

We have also completed a preliminary implementation of CAISS+. In the implementation of CAISS++, we have used Java as the programming language. We have used Protégé as our ontology editor during the process of ontology engineering which includes designing domain ontologies as well as the upper ontology. In the future, we will evaluate several existing distributed reasoning algorithms such as WebPIE and QueryPIE to determine the best algorithm that matches an agency's requirements. The selected algorithm will then be used to perform reasoning over OWL-based security policies. Additionally, the design of the Hadoop storage architecture is based on Jena's SPARQL database (SDB) architecture and features some of the functionalities that are available with Jena SDB. The SPARQL query engine also features code written in Java. This code consists of several modules including query parsing and translation, query optimization and query execution. The query execution module will consist of MapReduce jobs for the various operators of the SPARQL language. Finally, our web-based user interface makes use of several components such as JBoss, EJB, JSF, among others. We are also exploring the use of other big data technologies such as Storm and Spark for our cloud platform. In addition, NoSQL database systems such as Hbase and CouchDB are also being explored for integration into our AIS platform.

16.3.3 IMPLEMENTATION OF THE DEMONSTRATION SYSTEMS

16.3.3.1 Architecture

This section describes the details of the architecture and systems we implemented for thee demonstration, the modules and other details. Our policy engine framework is driven by RDF configuration documents which encode the logic of the policy engines and their usage, the user interface layouts and customizable parameters and the mappings of dereferenceable URIs to the data stores using the available data connections. Our policy engine framework can be used as a key enabler in augmenting security for RDBMS (Relational Database Management Systems) as well as cloud-based systems. RDBMS are developed with atomicity, concurrency and durability in mind, but are normally shipped with limited support for access control. A cloud storage layer allows the agencies to store and scale policies with finer levels of control over RDF resources. The cloud was developed with scalability and availability in mind, but security considerations were neglected. Our policy engine can be configured to complement policies in an RDBMS with an entry point for supporting security policies over cloud-based back-ends. We first present an overview of the configuration of the framework. Then we define the layers in our architecture, and finally, we provide a description of the novel features of our implementation. Figure 16.16 illustrates our architecture and Figure 16.17 illustrates our configuration framework.

A loosely coupled system provides easy configuration and flexibility to our RDF policy engine framework. Each component is abstracted from the others by employing RDF documents consisting of an agency's preferences for a policy or data connection to a data store. Furthermore, a loosely coupled web front-end promotes easier maintenance and reusability of the policy framework, because an adapter pattern abstracts the mapping of the web interfaces (and communications) to the other layers. An abstraction hides the actual implementation and intricacies of the policy engine manager and data managers from the agencies. This therefore allows agencies to specify their policies in any representation languages, such as XML, RDF, or Rei [KAGA2002]; an adapter hides the translation of high-level policy specification to policy implementation.

Our system architecture consists of three layers. At the front-end, we have a user interface; the middle layer consists of our policy engine logic; and at the backend, we have our data stores. We provide a discussion of these modules next. It should be noted that in this implementation our focus is on sharing the provenance of the data. This implementation was motivated by the prototypes discusses earlier in this chapter we well as the provenance-based inference controller discussed in Chapter 17.

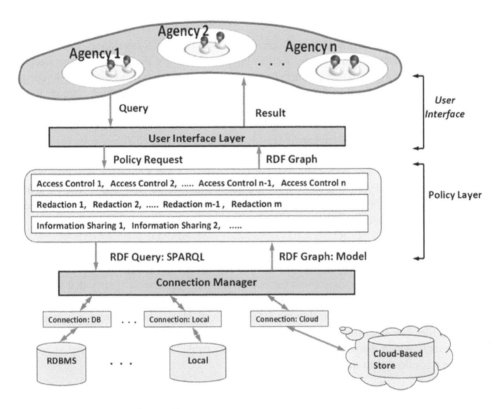

FIGURE 16.16   Implementation architecture.

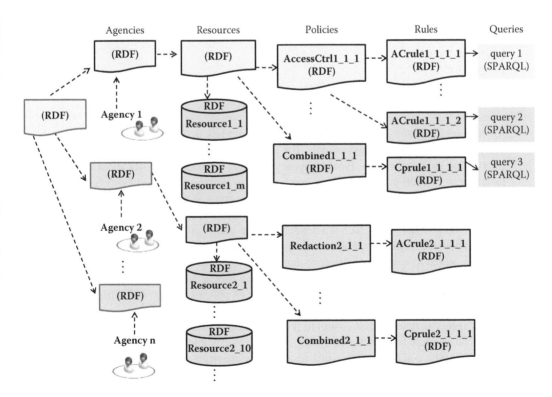

FIGURE 16.17   Configuration overview.

16.3.3.1.1 User interface layer

To enable a one-to-one interaction with our framework, a web-based user interface is built on top of the policy layer. Rich client and open-source web technologies simplify the interactions between users, web pages and the underlying policy and data layers. This integration has many advantages. The policy framework operates in a distributed environment and has a greater geographical spread; therefore, agencies and users have mobility. The web interface requires users to create an account (also a registration) and choose unique credentials which will then be used by the users to identify them to the policy framework. A form-based authentication pattern, as well as a challenge-response test distinguishes legitimate users from robots (which may pose as normal users). The legitimate users are presented with a querying screen that allows them to compose SPARQL queries once they have been authenticated. Note that SPARQL [PRUD2006] is a query language for RDF and is used for retrieving data from triple stores. The SPARQL queries are validated and then sent to our policy engine layer which in turn returns a resultant RDF graph that is then displayed on a web page.

- *User registration:* The User Registration presents the user the opportunity to register with the system using a web registration form. The registration form captures the user's name, password, and other metadata about the user. Metadata could be an agency that the user is a part of, or data that is used for mapping the user's credentials to a role which is to be performed by the user. The following RDF graph displays contents from a user configuration file. The final triple in the RDF graph contains a dereferenceable URI to another RDF graph, which then contains a list of dereferenceable URIs of the actual resources that the user is allowed to query.

  <http://policy.org/agency/pol#users>
  pol:user <http://policy.org/agency/pol#user1>.

  # resources
  <http://policy.org/agency/pol#user1>
  pol:name "user1" ;
  pol:passwd "_:b1" ;
  pol:organization <http://policy.org/agency/pol#Agency1> ;
  pol:resourcelist <http://example/users/resources/user1> .

- *Agency registration:* The Agency Registration comprises a sequence of web pages, each being a child page of the previous one. The process commences with an agency registering information to describe itself. First, an agency registers important metadata about itself. This metadata is an RDF document which can be used to introduce one agency to another, and therefore, should be self-describing. Some example triples in this metadata could assert an agency's name, address, industry, affiliations, etc. Second, an agency records its resources. A resource has a unique URI which is a dereferenceable URI to an agency's RDF document that contains both the sensitive and nonsensitive data for the agency; this is the information that is normally stored in a relational database, but is now migrated to the cloud. Third, an agency defines the policies for its resources. An agency may choose among the various policies that are supported at the policy engine layer. Examples of policies are access control, redaction, information sharing, etc. Fourth, an agency describes various policy rules for a policy. Note that an agency may use access control to protect its resources; however, the agency may need more than one rule for a particular policy choice. For example, one access control rule may specify a positive authorization, while another may specify a negative authorization on the same resource. Finally, an agency specifies queries. It is a very popular technique to write policy rules as views (i.e., SPARQL queries) over a data store. An agency may specify in its policy rule configuration document that queries are be materialized or that they be non-materialized. A materialized query may speed up the policy execution, while a non-materialized query refreshes the result set in real-time.

16.3.3.1.2   Policy engines

The *Policy Engine Layer* first evaluates the user queries against the stored data resources (which can be traditional data, or provenance metadata). A data resource is characterized by a uniform resource identifier (URI), which connects to an actual RDF graph in the data storage layer. The policy layer uses a factory object to create the underlying policies. The factory exposes a policy through a consistent interface, and thus making it easy to extend our policy engine to support other types of policies in the future. We currently support access control, redaction, and information sharing policies. To support traditional policies, we use SPARQL queries to define views over resources, where a view can be associated with positive and negative authorizations or a target in a subgraph replacement procedure. An important metadata is provenance, which records the history of a piece of data item. However, provenance takes on a directed acyclic graph (DAG) structure, and as such requires its own policies ([BRAU2008], [DING2005]). Therefore, we support the use of regular expression SPARQL queries for access control policies [CADE2011a], as well as redaction policies [CADE2011b]. We have also implemented information sharing policies over data and provenance that allow cooperating agencies to share information based on mutual agreements [CADE2012b].

An agile environment pushes policy designers to constantly fine-tune or extend their policies to rapidly adapt to ever-changing conditions, thus ensuring that data integrating and combinations does not violate data confidentiality, especially when quick actions are critical (e.g., in intelligence). To meet this demand, our policy engine layer supports many policy engines, while the cloud supports many policy configuration documents.

A policy engine takes as input a user's credential and a dereferenceable URI; it then evaluates the underlying logic of a policy before returning a new RDF graph (or model) to the user interface layer. The dereferenceable URI points to a configuration document which itself contains other dereferenceable URIs to the policies about an agency's resource and to the agency's resource at the data layer. An agency's resource is an RDF document with triples at one or more classification levels; for example, an entire RDF document would be classified as sensitive in case it contains intelligence information or some subset of triples may have actual intelligence information. An agency therefore requires more than one type of policy to achieve fine grain control over its resources. A policy is therefore defined by an interface, which allows the implementation of the logic of each policy. The policy engine evaluates the underlying logic of a policy before returning a new RDF graph (or model) to the user interface layer. By migrating its policies to the cloud, an agency overcomes the restriction on the number of policy definitions previously possible. The following subsections summarize various policy types. In the following subsections, we discuss the details of the policy engine layer. This layer comprises many policy types, for example, access control, redaction, and information sharing, to name a few. We will also motivate the need for a flexible policy engine by discussing each of these policy types in turn.

- *Access control policy engine:* An access control policy authorizes a set of *users* to perform a set of *actions* on a set of *resources* within an *environment*. Unless authorized through one or more access control policies, users have no access to any resource of the system. There are different kinds of access control policies which can be grouped into three main classes [SAMA2001]. These policies differ by the constraints they place on the sets of *users, actions,* and *objects* (access control models often refer to *resources* as *objects*). These classes are (1) RBAC, which restricts access based on roles; (2) discretionary access control (DAC), which controls access based on the identity of the user; and (3) mandatory access control (MAC), which controls access based on mandated regulations determined by a central authority.

Policies based on RBAC are often used to simplify the management of policy mappings which is a common feature in the three classes of access control policies. Policy creation and manageability are important in getting finer levels of access control over the shared resources. We use the convention that a permission is a unique pair of (*action, resource*). Given n resources, m users and a set of only two actions (read, write), we have a maximum of $2 \times n$ possible permissions. This gives $m \times (2 \times n) = c_1 n$ mappings. A further improvement of RBAC is the case where there is at least one role with two or more users assigned to it, from a possible set of r roles. Therefore, we have $r \times (2 \times n) = c_2 n$ mappings and we also assume that $c_2 \leq c_1$. However, even with this simplification, the number of policies needed to achieve finer levels of access control in a dynamic and agile community may be intractable. Our cloud-centric policy framework addresses this by providing the agencies the ability to support and scale their access control policies to meet their ever growing security needs.

- *Redaction policy engine:* A redaction policy identifies and removes sensitive information from a document before releasing it to a user. Unlike access control policies, which restrict access, redaction policies encourage sharing of information by ensuring that sensitive or proprietary information is removed (or obscured) before providing the final RDF graph (referred to as a redacted graph) to a user's query. Redaction policies rely on a transformation operation to circumvent any identifying or sensitive information. The redaction policy engines currently supported rely on a graph transformation technique that is based on a graph grammar approach (which is presented in [EHRI2006], [ROZE2007]. Basically, there are two steps to applying a redaction policy over a directed labeled RDF graph: (i) identify a resource (or subgraph) in the original RDF graph that we want to protect. This can be done with a graph query (*i.e.*, a query equipped with regular expressions). (ii) Apply a redaction policy to this identified resource in the form of a graph transformation rule. An implementation of this graph transformation is used in [CADE2011b] for redacting provenance graphs.

- *Information sharing policy engine:* An information sharing policy allows agencies to determine the context in which their resources are shared or combined with resources from other agencies. An information sharing policy engine has logic for processing a query requesting information on two or more RDF graphs simultaneously. We illustrate this using the following SPARQL query.

$$\text{SELECT} \vec{B} \text{ FROM NAMED uri1 FROM NAMED uri2 WHERE P,}$$

where P is a graph pattern, $\vec{B}$ is a tuple of variables appearing in P and uri1 and uri2 are dereferenceable URIs for two resources, R1 and R2. Resources R1 and R2 may be from the same agency, in case an agency strictly requires a partitioning of its resources based on confidentiality concerns or they could belong to two agencies, Agency 1 and Agency 2, respectively. Therefore, each of these resources may define individual information sharing policy rules. We define an operator $\odot$, so that an information sharing policy is now evaluated over uri1 $\odot$ uri2. The operator $\odot$ can be implemented as a graph operation over an RDF graph. Note that, $\odot$, could be one of the following operators: $\cap$, $\cup$, or $-$ and can also be applied to an original RDF graph or to previous one, which resulted from the operator, $\odot$. To execute the operator, $\odot$, we define a graph recursively as follows.

- ε is a graph.
- The set of graphs are closed under intersection, union and set difference. Let G_1 and G_1 be two graphs, then $G_1 \cup G_2$, $G_1 \cap G_2$ and $G_1 - G_2$ are graphs, such that if $t \in G_1 \cup G_2$ then $t \in G_1$ or $t \in G_2$; if $t \in G_1 \cup G_2$ then $t \in G_1$ and $t \in G_2$; or if $t \in G_1 - G_2$ then $t \in G_1$ and $t \notin G_2$.

The following RDF graph lists the triples of a combined policy configuration document containing policies with embedded logic for sharing two resources, R1 and R2, which belong to two agencies, Agency 1 and Agency 2, respectively.

```
# entity

<http://policy.org/entity/pol#Combined1_1_1>
   pol:owner <http://policy.org/entity/pol#Agency1>;
     pol:rule <http://policy.org/entity/pol#Cprule1_1_1_1>.


# mappings

<http://policy.org/entity/pol#Cprule1_1_1_1>
   pol:agency<http://policy.org/entity/pol#Agency2>;
     pol:operator     "UNION";
     pol:type     "combined1".
```

This policy works at the level of the agencies. For example, agency 1 shares all its resources as a union with all of agency 2 resources. The policy type allows an agency to have modes of sharing. For example, a type *combined1* provides sharing at the agency level, while another policy type, *combined2*, could offer a finer level of control in determining how Agency 1 shares each of its resources with a classification of a resource for Agency 2. In other words, information sharing policies can incorporate contextual information about an agency and metadata about each of its resources at the resource level. The following shows two policy types for our information sharing policies:

1. *combined1:* $\forall r1 \in Agency1, \forall r2 \in Agency2$, use $r1 \cup r2$. This policy states that Agency 1 shares all its resources with Agency 2 as a union of the resources.
2. *combined2:* let $rl_1, rl_2, \ldots, rl_n \in$ Agency1 use $rl_1 \cup r2, rl_2 \cap r2, \forall r2 \in Agency2$. This policy offers a finer level of control.

- *Provenance policy engines:* Sometimes the relationships among the triples in an RDF graph need be taken into consideration when defining policies. The three policy types discussed so far fail to address the cases where sensitive information is implicit in the various paths within an RDF graph. We will explore other policy engines in this section. The focus will be on the definition of policy engines tailored to the execution of access control and redaction policies over a provenance graph. We will base the logic of these policy engines on [CADE2011a] which discusses an access control policy language for provenance and [CADE2012b], which discusses how to perform redaction over provenance. We will first give an example of a provenance graph and the type of provenance information which may exist in the example provenance graph. Then, we will present brief definitions of some of the theory behind executing policies over a provenance graph.

Figure 16.18 shows an intelligence example as a provenance graph using an RDF representation that outlines a flow of a document through a server located in some unfriendly territory (or at another agency posing a potential threat). This document was given to a journalist. The contents of this provenance graph could serve to evaluate the trustworthiness of the servers (i.e., processes in the example graph) from which the document originated. This example provenance graph also shows the base skeleton of the actual provenance, which is usually annotated with RDF triples indicating contextual information, for example, time and location. Note that the predicates (i.e., arcs) are labeled with the OPM abstract predicate [MORE2010] labels and that the final report can be traced back to a CIA agent.

The information embedded in the graph in Figure 16.18 represents a directed RDF graph. A provenance path in Figure 16.18 is defined as follows:

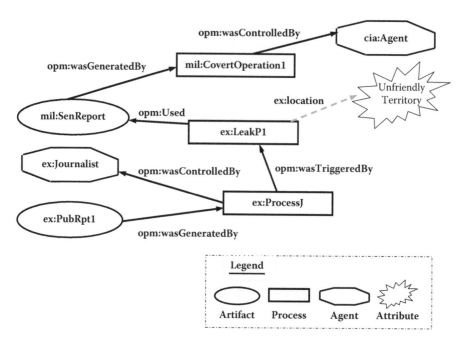

FIGURE 16.18 Provenance Graph.

Definition 3: *(Provenance Path) Given a provenance graph, a provenance path (s p o) is a paths $\xrightarrow{p}$ o that is defined over the provenance vocabulary V using regular expressions.*
Definition 4: *(Regular Expressions) Let Σ be an alphabet of terms in V, then the set RE(Σ) of regular expressions is inductively defined by:*

- $\forall x \in \Sigma, x \in RE(\Sigma)$;
- $\Sigma \in RE(\Sigma)$;
- $\varepsilon \in RE(\Sigma)$;
- *If $A \in RE(\Sigma)$ and $B \in RE(\Sigma)$ then:*

$$A|B, \quad A/B*, \quad A^+, \quad A? \in RE(\textstyle\sum)$$

The symbols I and / are interpreted as logical OR and composition, respectively.

Our intention is to define paths between two nodes by edges equipped with * for paths of arbitrary length, including length 0 or + for paths that have at least length 1. Therefore, for two nodes *x*, *y*, and predicate name *p*, $x(\xrightarrow{p})*y$ and $x(\xrightarrow{p})^+y$ are paths in *G*.

A SPARQL query extended with regular expressions [HARR2010] can define a resource (or subgraph) of the provenance graph in Figure 16.18 as follows:

Example 16.1: *(Provenance Path Query)*

Select ?x
{ex:PubRpt1 arq:OnPath("([opm:WasGeneratedBy]/
[opm:WasTriggeredBy]/[ex:location])" ?x). }

This query would return the location as a binding to the variable x and could be used to pinpoint the origin of a compromise (and leakage) of the original report. This could also serve to alert policy designers to add appropriate policies for reports and servers in their respective agencies.

- *Policy sequence:* The execution of the policies over an agency's resource results in a policy sequence. In particular, a protected resource could employ the services of multiple policy engines and policy types. Each policy type produces a new subgraph of its input RDF graph. It is important to note that the effect of a policy is directly dependent on the RDF graph it receives as input, and furthermore, the effect may be different from the original effect the policy was intended to achieve. A sequence takes the original input graph through a series of transformations until a final RDF graph is returned to the user. Note that the success of a policy rule (which is implemented as a SPARQL query) returning a particular set of RDF triples is dependent on the transformation step at which the rule was applied in a policy sequence. We illustrate this using the following SPARQL query:

CONSTRUCT G WHERE P,

G is a newly constructed graph, which contains a set of triples that satisfy condition P in the input graph. A policy protecting the following RDF triples,

<http://cs.utdallas.edu/semanticweb/Prov-AC/agency#agent_1>
  foaf:name "John brown";
  foaf:projectHomepage <http://www.agency1.gov/>

will fail if either the name or project home page triple was earlier removed or altered by a previous policy rule.

A policy precedence feature in the framework helps an agency determine the ordering of its policies. In the user interface layer, an agency configures the ordering of its policies. The policy sequence is then stored in an RDF sequence file (using the "rdf:seq" feature of the RDF specification). When a query is evaluated, the policy framework will in turn invoke each policy in the intended order.

- *Rule sequence:* In a similar way, a policy may be implemented using a set of rules. For example, to fully redact a shared resource, an agency may need a separate rule to redact each sensitive triple in an RDF graph. Each rule is triggered when a triple (or set of triples) meet some specified criteria in the input graph. Note that each rule transforms the current state of a shared resource. Therefore, each sequencing of the rules will impact the final graph (also called the redacted graph).

16.3.3.1.3 Data layer

At the Data Layer is a connection factory which acts as a facade for creating connection objects. These connection objects expose the same properties (functionally) as public methods to the policy designer. This makes it easier for the policy designer to concentrate on the policy engine design. The policy designer makes a call to an RDF Policy Factory which returns an RDF model object. This RDF model object is backed by a connection store which can be a local connection, a relational database connection or a cloud connection. During the registration process, an agency is given an opportunity to decide where it wants to store its resources and configuration documents. It is recommended that the smaller configuration documents be stored locally on disk (or in a local database) to enable quick access to them. Local connections also consume lower bandwidth, offers real-time access and enable development before deployment. However, an agency may decide to store them in a private cloud (or on a remote database server) to take advantage of the added protection there.

The connection factory also enables agencies to store their resources in any cloud infrastructure. For example, an agency's resources could reside on a private cloud, a community cloud or a public cloud. A private cloud deployment provides more control in that agencies could house their own cloud. A community cloud is provisioned for exclusive access by a specific community thus serving the common interest of cooperating agencies. A public cloud is open to the public and thus susceptible to more vulnerabilities due to the loss of control over the data uploaded onto the public cloud. Agencies may choose to use a mixture of connections and also employ more than one deployment simultaneously (e.g., a hybrid cloud model).

16.3.3.2 Features of Our Policy Engine Framework

In the following subsections below, we present some novel features of our policy engine framework.

16.3.3.2.1 Policy reciprocity

Policy reciprocity enables agencies to specify policies when knowledge of the other agencies, their resources or policy specification are available. This is made possible via the registration process, where agencies make metadata available about themselves, their recourses and associated policies. The following discussion provides scenarios for policy reciprocity.

*Agency*1 wishes to share its resources if *Agency*2 also shares its resources with it. Current access control and redaction policies do not provide for this reciprocity. Our framework provides information sharing policies which allow agents to define policies based on reciprocity and mutual interest amongst cooperating agencies.

We present the following two sample information sharing policies:

1. $\forall r1 \in Agency1, \forall r2 \in Agency2$, use r1∪r2.
   This policy states that *Agency*1 shares all its resources with any resource of *Agency*2 as a union of the resources (i.e., $\odot \in \{\cup\}$).
2. let $r1_1, r1_2, \ldots, r1_n \in$ Agency1. Agency1 can use $r1_1 \cup r2, r1_1 \cap r2, \forall r2 \in Agency2$.
   This policy offers a finer level of control and defines the combined operator, $\odot \in \{\cap, \cup\}$.

- *Conditional policies:* A consequence of policy reciprocity is allowing the use of conditional sharing policies. For example, *Agency*1 shares its resources with *Agency*2 if *Agency*2 does not share *Agency*1's resources with *Agency*3. We present the following sample information sharing policy:

1. $\forall r1 \in Agency1$, $\forall r2 \in Agency2$, *Agency*1 defines r1∩r2. If $\forall r3 \in Agency3$, then
   - *Agency*2 does not define any sharing policy of the form r1∩r3,
   - or *Agency*2 does not define any sharing policy of the form r1 $\subseteq$ r2 $\odot$ r3, where $\odot \in \{\cup, \cap\}$.

- *Policy symmetry:* Another consequence of policy reciprocity is to have symmetry in the sharing of policies. For example, *Agency*1 shares its resources with *Agency*2 with a combined operator, $\odot$, if *Agency*2 also shares its resources with *Agency*1 using the same combined operator, $\odot$. We present the following sample information sharing policy:

1. $\forall r1 \in Agency1, \forall r2 \in Agency2$, *Agency*1 uses r1∪ r2 if *Agency*2 also uses r2 ∪ r1.

16.3.3.2.2 Develop and scale policies

To enable freedom of maneuverability across the information environment and to deliver the power of information to ensure mission success, an agency should be able to rapidly develop policies and deploy them as needed. We next discuss the features that are available to an agency during and after development of its policies.

- *Policy development: Agency1* wishes to simulate a live environment and create test scenarios to visualize the results of each policy configuration. Our policy framework provides three configurations: (i) a stand-alone version for development and testing; (ii) a version backed by a relational database; and (iii) a cloud-based version that achieves high availability and scalability while maintaining low set-up and operation costs.

- *Sequencing effects: Agency1* wishes to vary the result set to a user's query based on the user's credentials. The policy sequence feature can be used to configure different outcomes by permuting the policies and their respective rules.

- *Rapid elasticity: Agency1* identifies recent security vulnerabilities in its existing policy configurations and wishes to extend (or grow) its existing policy set with support for policies at a finer granularity. Our policy engine provides a policy interface that should be implemented by all policies; therefore, we can add newer types of policies as needed. In addition, our policy engine gives an agency rapid elasticity, whereby the capabilities available by our policy framework appear unlimited.

- *Location independence: Agency1* wishes to store its resources closer to where it is consumed, but with little or no change at the policy layer. Our policy engine provides location independence whereby the policy engine has no control or knowledge over the exact location of the resources, but may be able access the resources through a specified location using the connection manager. Note that an agency's resources can be in any cloud, geographically. The ability to locate any resource by a dereferenceable URE provides much flexibility.

- *Deployment models: Agency1* can take advantage of different deployment models. For example, a private cloud, a hybrid cloud, a community or a public cloud. The connection manager allows an agency to choose among a list of connection types based on different risk factors and objectives to protect data confidentiality.

16.3.3.2.3 Justification of resources

Provenance makes available an explanation about why information was manipulated and a trace to the source of the information manipulation. This establishes trust among agencies, thus facilitating partnerships for common goals.

Agency1 asks *Agency2* for a justification of resource R2. The current commercial access control policies are mainly designed to protect single data items, while current redaction policies are designed for redacting text and images. Our policy engine allows agents to define policies over provenance; therefore, *Agency2* can provide the provenance to *Agency1*, but protect it by using access control or redaction policies.

16.3.3.2.4 Policy specification and enforcement

Our architectural design supports a high-level specification of policies, thus separating the business layer from a specific policy implementation.

Agency1 wishes to express its policies in a high-level language (e.g., XACML), and would prefer not learning RDF or any of its variations. The framework exposes a web interface layer between the users and the policy engine layer, whereby the users can specify their policies independent of the actual implementation of the policy. A suitable adapter, also known as a data translator, will translate each high-level policy specification into the appropriate RDF representation used by the appropriate policy which protects an agency's resources.

Policies may be specified using more expressive languages than RDF by extending RDF with a formal vocabulary, in particular a sublanguage of OWL. OWL has a formal semantics that is based on description logics, a decidable fragment of first order logic. Thus, by supporting this adapter pattern, our framework is extended to handle semantic policies specified in OWL and high-level policies can be translated into a suitable sublanguage of OWL using existing or custom-built translators.

16.4   RELATED WORK

16.4.1   Research Efforts

While there are some related efforts, none of the efforts have provided a solution to AIS in the cloud, or have they conducted such a formal policy analysis.

16.4.1.1   Secure Data Storage and Retrieval in the Cloud

Security for cloud has received recent attention [TALB09]. Some efforts on implementing at the infrastructure level have been reported [OMAL09]. Such development efforts are an important step toward securing cloud infrastructures but are only in their inception stages. The goal of our system is to add another layer of security above the security offered by Hadoop [UTD1]. Once the security offered by Hadoop becomes robust, it will only strengthen the effectiveness of our system. Similar efforts have been undertaken by Amazon and Microsoft for their cloud computing offerings [AMAZ2016, MARS2010]. However, this work falls in the public domain whereas our system is designed for a private cloud infrastructure. This distinguishing factor makes our infrastructure "trusted" over public infrastructures where the data must be stored in an encrypted format.

16.4.1.2   SPARQL Query Processor

Only a handful of efforts have been reported on SPARQL query processing. These include BioMANTA [BIOM] and SHARD [SHAR2011]. BioMANTA proposes extensions to RDF Molecules [DING05] and implements a MapReduce-based Molecule store [NEWM2008]. They use MapReduce to answer the queries. They have queried a maximum of 4 million triples. Our work differs in the following ways: first, we have queried 1 billion triples. Second, we have devised a storage schema which is tailored to improve query execution performance for RDF data. To our knowledge, we are the first to come up with a storage schema for RDF data using flat files in HDFS, and a MapReduce job determination algorithm to answer a SPARQL query. SHARD (Scalable, High-Performance, Robust and Distributed) is an RDF triple store using the Hadoop Cloudera distribution. This project shows initial results demonstrating Hadoop's ability to improve scalability for RDF datasets. However, SHARD stores its data only in a triple store schema. It does no query planning or reordering, and its query processor will not minimize the number of Hadoop jobs. None of the efforts have incorporated security policies.

16.4.1.3   RDF-based Policy Engine

There exists prior research devoted to the study of enforcing policies over RDF stores. These include the work in [CARM2004] which uses RDF for policy specification and enforcement. In addition, the policies are generally written in RDF. In [JAIN2006], the authors propose an access control model for RDF. Their model is based on RDF data semantics and incorporates RDF and RDF Schema (RDFS) entailments. Here, protection is provided at the resource level, which adds granularity to their framework. Other frameworks enforcing policies over RDF\OWL include [KAGA2002, USZO2004]. [USZO2004] describes KAoS, a policy and domain services framework that uses OWL, both to represent policies and domains. [KAGA2002] introduces Rei, a policy framework that is flexible and allows different kinds of policies to be stated. Extensions to Rei have been proposed recently [KHAN2010]. The policy specification language allows users to develop declarative policies over domain specific ontologies in RDF, DAML+OIL, and OWL. The authors in [REDD2005] also introduced a prototype, RAP, for implementation of an RDF store with integrated maintenance capabilities and access control. These frameworks, however, do not address cases where the RDF store can become very large or the case where the policies do not scale with the data. Under an IARPA-funded project, we have developed techniques for very large RDF graph processing [UTD2].

16.4.1.4   Hadoop Storage Architecture

There has been significant interest in large-scale distributed storage and retrieval techniques for RDF data. The theoretical designs of a parallel processing framework for RDF data are presented in the work done by Castagna et al. [CAST2009]. This work advocates the use of a data distribution model with varying levels of granularity such as triple level, graph level and dataset level. A query over such a distributed model is then divided into a set of subqueries over machines containing the distributed data. The results of all subqueries will then be merged to return a complete result to a user application. Several implementations of this theoretical concept exist in the research community. These efforts include the work done by Choi et al. [CHOI2009] and Abraham et al. [ABRA2010]. A separate technique that has been used to store and retrieve RDF data makes use of peer-to-peer systems [ABER2004, CAI2004, HART2007, VALL2006]. However, there are some drawbacks with such systems as peer-to-peer systems need to have super peers that store information about the distribution of RDF data among the peers. Another disadvantage is a need to federate a SPARQL query to every peer in the network.

16.4.1.5   Distributed Reasoning

InteGrail system uses distributed reasoning, whose vision is to shape the European railway organization of the future [INTE2009]. In [URBA2009], authors have shown a scalable implementation of RDFS reasoning based on MapReduce which can infer 30 billion triples from a real-world dataset in less than two hours, yielding an input and output throughput of 123.000 triples/second and 3.27 million triples/second, respectively. They have presented some non-trivial optimizations for encoding the RDFS ruleset in MapReduce and have evaluated the scalability of their implementation on a cluster of 64 compute nodes using several real-world datasets.

16.4.1.6   Access Control and Policy Ontology Modeling

There have been some attempts to model access control and policy models using semantic web technologies. In [CIRI2007], authors have shown how OWL and Description Logic can be used to build an access control system. They have developed a high-level OWL-DL ontology that expresses the elements of a role-based access control system and have built a domain-specific ontology that captures the features of a sample scenario. Finally, they have joined these two artifacts to take into account attributes in the dentition of the policies and in the access control decision. In [REUL2010], authors first presented a security policy ontology based on the DOGMA which is a formal ontology engineering framework. This ontology covers the core elements of security policies (i.e., Condition, Action, Resource) and can easily be extended to represent specific security policies, such as access control policies. In [ANDE2009], authors present an ontologically motivated approach to multi-level access control and provenance for information systems.

16.4.2   Commercial Developments

16.4.2.1   RDF Processing Engines

Research and commercial RDF processing engines include Jena by HP Labs, BigOWLIM and RDF-3X. Although the storage schemas and query processing mechanisms for some of these tools are proprietary, they are all based on some type of indexing strategy for RDF data. However, only a few tools exist that use a cloud-centric architecture for processing RDF data and moreover, these tools are not scalable to a very large number of triples. In contrast, our query processor in CAISS++ will be built as a planet-scale RDF processing engine that supports all SPARQL operators and will provide optimized execution strategies for SPARQL queries and can scale to billions of triples.

16.4.2.2   Semantic Web-based Security Policy Engines

As stated in Section 16.2, the current work on semantic web-based policy specification and enforcement does not address the issues of policy generation and enforcement for massive amounts of data and support large number of users. **Cloud:** To the best of our knowledge, there is no significant commercial competition for cloud-centric AIS. As we have taken a modular approach to the creation of our tools, we can iteratively refine each component (policy engine, storage architecture, and query processor) separately. Due to the component-based approach we have taken, we will be able to adapt to changes in the platforms we use (e.g., Hadoop, RDF, OWL, and SPARQL) without having to depend on the particular features of a given platform.

16.5   SUMMARY AND DIRECTIONS

This chapter has described our design and implementation of a cloud-based information sharing system called CAISS. CAISS utilizes several of the technologies we have developed as well as open-source tools. We also described the design of an ideal cloud-based AIS system called CAISS++. We discussed a series of implementations of CAISS, CAISS+ and a demonstration system.

We have developed a proof-of-concept prototype of both CAISS and CAISS++. In the implementation of CAISS, we utilized our SPARQL query processor in the cloud with the policies specified in both XACML and RDF. Our policies include both access control policies as well as information sharing policies. In the implementation of CAISS++, we specified policies in OWL, developed the policy engine in the cloud and integrated it with the SPARQL data engine. These systems are discussed in [CADE2012a] and [CADE2012b].

CAISS++ is the first of its kind AIS framework that operates in the cloud. As stated earlier, the idea is for each organization to store their data and the information sharing policies in a cloud. The information is shared according to the policies. We described a cloud-based information sharing framework that utilized semantic web technologies. Our framework consists of a policy engine that reasons about the policies for information sharing purposes and a secure data engine that stores and queries data in the cloud. We also described the operation of our system with example policies. Our framework is flexible so that additional data sources and cloud can be added. Furthermore, by using RDF for a policy engine, we can add more sophisticated policies for information sharing. This is one of the major strengths of our system. Future directions include specifying and reasoning about more sophisticated policies as well as testing our system in a real-world environment.

In the future, we will continue to enhance our prototypes by implementing more complex policies as well as implementing the distributed version CAISS++. We will also carry out a formal analysis of the execution of the policies. Finally, we will examine AIS between users of multiple social networks and explore the use of technologies such as Spark, Storm, and CouchDB in the implementation.

REFERENCES

[ABER2004] K. Aberer, P. Cudr´e-Mauroux, M. Hauswirth , T. Van Pelt, GridVine: Building Internet-Scale Semantic Overlay Networks, *Proceedings of International Semantic Web Conference*, Hiroshima, Japan, 2004.

[ABRA2010] J. Abraham, P. Brazier, A. Chebotko, J. Navarro, A. Piazza, Distributed Storage and Querying Techniques for a Semantic Web of Scientific Workflow Provenance, *Proceedings IEEE International Conference on Services Computing (SCC)*, Miami, FL, 2010.

[AMAZ2016] Overview of Security Processes, 2016, https://aws.amazon.com/whitepapers/overview-of-security-processes/

[Ande2009] B. Andersen, F. Neuhaus, An Ontological Approach to Information Access Control and Provenance, *Proceedings of Ontology for the Intelligence Community*, Fairfax, VA, October 2009.

[AWAD2010] A. Khan, B.M. Thuraisingham, Policy Enforcement System for Inter-Organizational Data Sharing, Journal of Information Security and Privacy, Volume 4, #3, 2010, 22–39.

[BIOM] Biomanta http://www.itee.uq.edu.au/eresearch/projects/biomanta

[BRAU2008] U. Braun, A. Shinnar, M. Seltzer, Securing Provenance, *Proceedings of the 3rd Conference on Hot Topics in Security*,2008, USENIX Association, pp. 4.

[CARM2009] B. Carminati, E. Ferrari, R. Heatherly, M. Kantarcioglu, B. M. Thuraisingham, A Semantic Web Based Framework for Social Network Access Control, *SACMAT 2009, 14th ACM Symposium on Access Control Models and Technologies, Stresa, Italy*, 2009, pp. 177–186.

[CADE2010] T. Cadenhead, M. Kantarcioglu, B. Thuraisingham, Scalable and Efficient Reasoning for Enforcing Role-Based Access Control, *Proceedings of Data and Applications Security and Privacy XXIV, 24th Annual IFIP Working Group 11.3 Working Conference*, Rome, Italy, 2010, pp. 209–224.

[CADE2011a] K. Cadenhead, M. Kantarcioglu, B. Thuraisingham, Transforming Provenance Using Redaction, *Proceedings of ACM Symposium on Access Control Models and Technologies (SACMAT)*, Innsbruck, Austria, 2011, pp. 93–102.

[CADE2011b] T. Cadenhead, V. Khadilkar, M. Kantarcioglu, B. Thuraisingham, A Language for Provenance Access Control, *Proceedings of ACM Conference on Data Application Security and Privacy (CODASPY)*, San Antonio, TX, 2011, pp. 125–144.

[CADE2012a] T. Cadenhead, V. Khadilkar, M. Kantarcioglu, B. M. Thuraisingham, A Cloud-based RDF Policy Engine for Assured Information Sharing, *Proceedings of ACM Symposium on Access Control Models and Technologies* (SACMAT 2012*)*, Newark, NJ, 2012, pp. 113–116.

[CADE2012b] T. Cadenhead, M. Kantarcioglu, V. Khadilkar, B. M. Thuraisingham, Design and Implementation of a Cloud-Based Assured Information Sharing System, *Proceedings of International Conference on Mathematical Methods, Models and Architectures for Computer Network Security*, St. Petersburg, Russia, 2012, pp. 36–50.

[CAI2004] M. Cai, M. Frank, RDFPeers: A Scalable Distributed RDF Repository Based on a Structured Peer-to-Peer Network, *Proceedings ACM World Wide Web Conference (WWW)*, New York, NY, 2004.

[CARM2004] B. Carminati, E. Ferrari, B.M. Thuraisingham, Using RDF for Policy Specification and Enforcement, *Proceedings of International Workshop on Database and Expert Systems Applications*, Zaragoza, Spain, 2004, pp. 163–167.

[CARM2004] B. Carminati, E. Ferrari, R. Heatherly, M. Kantarcioglu, B.M. Thuraisingham, Design and Implementation of a Cloud-based Assured Information Sharing System, *Proceedings of ACM Symposium on Access Control Models and Technologies*, Stresa, Italy, 2009, pp. 177–186.

[CAST2009] P. Castagna, A. Seaborne, C. Dollin, A Parallel Processing Framework for RDF Design and Issues, Technical report, HP Laboratories, HPL-2009-346, 2009.

[CELI2007] E. Celikel, M. Kantarcioglu, B. Thuraisingham, E. Bertino, Managing Risks in RBAC Employed Distributed Environments, *On the Move to More Meaningful Internet Systems 2007: CoopIS, DOA, ODBASE, GADA, and IS.* Volume 4804 of Lecture Notes in Computer Science, Spring, New York, 2007, pp. 1548–1566.

[CHOI2009] H. Choi, J. Son, Y. Cho, M. Sung, Y. Chung, SPIDER: A System for Scalable, Parallel/Distributed Evaluation of Large-scale RDF Data, *Proceedings of ACM Conference on Information and Knowledge Management (CIKM)*, Hong Kong, China, 2009, pp. 2087–2088.

[CIRI2007] L. Cirio, I. Cruz, R. Tamassia, A Role and Attribute Based Access Control System Using Semantic Web Technologies, *IFIP Workshop on Semantic Web and Web Semantics*, Vilamoura, Algarve, Portugal, 2007.

[DING2005] L. Ding, T. Finin, Y. Peng, P. da Silva, D. McGuinness, Tracking RDF Graph Provenance using RDF Molecules, *Proceedings of International Semantic Web Conference*, Galway, Ireland, 2005.

[DoD] Department of Defense Information Enterprise Strategic Plan, 2010–2012, http://dodcio.defense.gov/Portals/0/Documents/DodIESP-r16.pdf

[DoD2007] Department of Defense Information Sharing Strategy, 2007, http://www.defense.gov/releases/release.aspx?releaseid=10831

[EHRI2006] H. Ehrig, *Fundamentals of algebraic graph transformation*, Springer-Verlag New York Inc, 2006.

[FINI2009] T. Finin, J. Joshi, H. Kargupta, Y. Yesha, J. Sachs, E. Bertino, Li et al, Assured Information Sharing Life Cycle, *Proceedings of Intelligence and Security Informatics*, Dallas, TX, 2009, 307–309.

[GUO2005] Y. Guo, Z. Pan, J. Hefflin, LUBM: A Benchmark for OWL Knowledge Base Systems, Web Semantics, Volume 3(2,5), 2005, 158–182.

[Haml2006a] K. Hamlen, G. Morrisett, F. Schneider, Computability Classes for Enforcement Mechanisms, ACM Transactions on Programming Languages and Systems, Volume 28, #1, 2006, 175–205.

[Haml06b] K. Hamlen, G. Morrisett, F. Schneider, Certified In-Lined Reference Monitoring on.NET, *Proceedings of ACM Workshop on Programming Language and Analysis for Security*, Ottawa, Canada, 2006, pp. 7–16.

[Haml2010a] K. Hamlen, M. Kantarcioglu, L. Khan, B. Thuraisingham, Security Issues for Cloud Computing, Journal of Information Security and Privacy, Volume 4, #2, 2010, 36–48.

[Haml2010b] K.V. Hamlen Mohan, R. Wartell, Reining in Windows API Abuses with In-lined Reference Monitors, Tech. Rep. UTDCS-18-10, Computer Science Dept., The University of Texas at Dallas, 2010.

[HARR2010] S. Harris, A. Seaborne, SPARQL 1.1 Query Language, W3C Working Draft, 2010.

[HART2007] A. Harth, J. Umbrich, A. Hogan, S. Decker, YARS2: A Federated Repository for Searching and Querying Graph Structured Data, *Proceedings of International Semantic Web Conference*, Busan, Korea, 2007.

[HUSA2011] M. Husain, J. McGlothlin, M. Masud, L. Khan, B. Thuraisingham, Heuristics-Based Query Processing for Large RDF Graphs Using Cloud Computing, IEEE Transansactions on Knowledge and Data Engineering, Volume 23, 2011, 1312–1327.

[INTE2009] Distributed Reasoning: Seamless integration and processing of distributed knowledge. http://www.integrail.eu/documents/fs04.pdf.

[JAIN2006] A. Jain, C. Farkas, Secure Resource Description Framework: An Access Control Model, *Proceedings of ACM Symposium on Access Control Models and Technologies (SACMAT)*, Lake Tahoe, CA, 2006.

[JONE2010] M. Jones, K. Hamlen, Disambiguating Aspect-Oriented Security Policies, *Proceedings of 9th International Conference on Aspect-Oriented Software Development*, Rennes and St. Malo, France, 2010, pp. 193–204.

[JONE2011] M. Jones, K. Hamlen, A Service-Oriented Approach to Mobile Code Security. *Proceedings of 8th International Conference on Mobile Web Information Systems (MobiWIS)*, Niagara Falls, Ontario, Canada, 2011.

[KAGA2002] L. Kagal, Rei: A Policy Language for the ME-Centric Project. HPL-2002-270, 2002, http://www.hpl.hp.com/techreports/2002/HPL-2002-270.html

[KANT10] M. Kantarcioglu, Incentive-based Assured Information Sharing, AFOSR MURI Review, October 2010.

[KHAD2011] V. Khadilkar, M. Kantarcioglu, B. Thuraisingham, S. Mehrotra, Secure Data Processing in a Hybrid Cloud, *Proceedings of Computering Research Repository (CoRR)* abs/1105.1982, 2011.

[KHAL2010] A. Khaled, M. Husain, L. Khan, K. Hamlen, B. Thuraisingham, A Token-Based Access Control System for RDF Data in the Clouds,, Indianapolis, IN, 2010.

[KHAN2010] A. Khandelwal, J. Bao, L. Kagal, I. Jacobi, L. Ding, J. Hendler, Analyzing the AIR Language: A Semantic Web (Production) Rule Language. *Proceedings of International Web Reasoning and Rule Systems*, Bressanone, Brixen, Italy, 2010, pp. 58–72.

[MARS2010] A. Marshall, M. Howard, G. Bugher, B. Harden, Security Best Practices in Developing Windows Azure Applications, Microsoft Corp., Redmond, WA, 2010.

[MORE2010] L. Moreau, B. Clifford, J. Freire et al., The Open Provenance Model Core Specification (v1.1), Future Generation Computer Systems, 2010.

[NEWM2008] A. Newman, J. Hunter, Y. Li, C. Bouton, M. Davis, A Scale-Out RDF Molecule Store for Distributed Processing of Biomedical Data, Semantic Web for Health Care and Life Sciences Workshop, *World Wide Web Conference (WWW)*, Beijing, China, 2008.

[NSA2011] http://www.informationweek.com/news/government/cloud-saas/229401646, 2011.

[OMAL2009] D. O'Malley, K. Zhang, S. Radia, R. Marti, C. Harrell, Hadoop Security Design, https://issues.apache.org/jira/secure/attachment/12428537/security-design.pdf.

[RAO2008] P., Rao, D. Lin, E. Bertino, N. Li, J. Lobo, EXAM: An Environment for Access Control Policy Analysis and Management, *Proceedings of IEEE Workshop on Policies for Distributed Systems and Networks (POLICY)*, Palisades, NY, 2008.

[PRUD2006] E. Prud'hommeaux, A. Seaborne, SPARQL Query Language for RDF. *W3C working draft*, 4 (2006).

[REDD2005] P. Reddivari, T. Finin, J. Joshi, A. Policy-Based Access Control for an RDF Store, Policy Management for the Web, *Proceedings of International Joint Conference on Artificial Intelligence Workshop (IJCAI)*, Edinburgh, Scotland, UK, 2005.

[REUL2010] Q. Reul, G. Zhao, R. Meersman, Ontology-Based Access Control Policy Interoperability, *Proceedings of 1st Conference on Mobility, Individualisation, Socialisation and Connectivity (MISC)*, London, UK, 2010.

[ROZE1997] G. Rozenberg, H. Ehrig, *Handbook of Graph Grammars and Computing by Graph Transformation*, World Scientific, 1997.

[SAMA2001] P. Samarati, S. de. Vimercati, Access Control: Policies, Models, and Mechanisms, *Foundations of Security Analysis and Design,* 2001, 137–196.

[SHAR2011] SHARD, http://blog.cloudera.com/blog/2010/03/how-raytheon-researchers-are-using-hadoop-to-build-a-scalable-distributed-triple-store/.

[SRID2010] M. Sridhar, K. Hamlen, Model-Checking In-lined Reference Monitors, *Proceedings of 11th International Conference on Verification, Model Checking, and Abstract Interpretation*, Madrid, Spain, 2010, pp. 312–327.

[TALB2009] D. Talbot, How Secure is Cloud Computing? http://www.technologyreview.com/computing/23951/

[THUR2008] H.K. Thuraisingham, L. Khan, Design and Implementation of a Framework for Assured Information Sharing Across Organizational Boundaries, Journal of Information Security and Privacy, Volume 2, #4, 2008, 67–90.

[THUR2010] B. Thuraisingham, V. Khadilkar, A. Gupta, M. Kantarcioglu, L. Khan, Secure Data Storage and Retrieval in the Cloud, CollaborateCom, Chicago, IL, 2010.

[THUR2011] B. Thuraisingham, V. Khadilkar, Assured Information Sharing in the Cloud, UTD Tech. Report. September 2011.

[THUS2009] A. Thusoo, J. Sharma, N. Jain, Z. Shao, P. Chakka, S. Anthony, H. Liu, P. Wyckoff, R. Murthy, Hive – A Warehousing Solution Over a Map-Reduce Framework, *Proceedings of VLDB Endowment*, Lyon, France, 2009.

[THUR2012] B.M. Thuraisingham, V. Khadilkar, J. Rachapalli, T. Cadenhead, M. Kantarcioglu, K.W. Hamlen, L. Khan, M.F. Husain, Cloud-Centric Assured Information Sharing, *Proceedings of the Pacific Asia Workshop on Intelligence and Security Informatics (PAISI)*, Kuala Lumpur, Malaysia , 2012, pp. 1–26.

[URBA2009] J. Urbani, S. Kotoulas, E. Oren, F. van Harmelen, Scalable Distributed Reasoning using MapReduce, *Proceedings of the International Semantic Web Conference* 2009, Lecture Notes in Computer Science, Vol. 5823, Springer Berlin Heidelberg, (eds: A., Bernstein, D.R., Karger, T., Heath, et al.).

[USZO2004] A. Uszok, J. Bradshaw, M. Johnson, R. Jeffers, A. Tate, J. Dalton, S. Aitken, KAoS Policy Management for Semantic Web Services, IEEE Intelligent Systems, 2004, 32–41.

[UTD1] UTD Secure Cloud Repository, http://cs.utdallas.edu/secure-cloud-repository/.

[UTD2] UTD Semantic Web Repository, http://cs.utdallas.edu/semanticweb/.

[VALL2006] E. Valle, A. Turati, A. Ghioni, AGE: A Distributed Infrastructure for Fostering RDF-Based Interoperability. *Proceedings of Distributed Applications and Inter-Operable Systems (DAIS)*, Bologna, Italy, 2006.

[ZQL] Zql: A Java SQL parser. http://zql.sourceforge.net/.

17 Access Control for Social Network Data Management

17.1 INTRODUCTION

In the chapters of Part IV, we have shown methods of using data within the social network to improve local and relational classification methods. While the fields of epidemiology and counter-terrorism are generally agreed to be important areas for these tasks, a major emergent field is using this data in marketing by partnering with social network providers. This usage has prompted privacy concerns with many users of these social networks. Here, we provide a framework for giving users far greater control over access to their information within the social network. By utilizing semantic web technologies, we are able to propose very granular controls for managing everything from user photos to who is able to send messages or videos to underage children.

Online Social Networks (OSNs) are platforms that allow people to publish details about themselves and to connect to other members of the network through links. Recently, the popularity of OSNs is increasing significantly. For example, Facebook now claims to have close to three billion active users (https://www.businessofapps.com/data/facebook-statistics/). The existence of OSNs that include person-specific information creates both interesting opportunities and challenges. For example, social network data could be used for marketing products to the right customers. At the same time, security and privacy concerns can prevent such efforts in practice [BERT2007]. Improving the OSN access control systems appears as the first step toward addressing the existing security and privacy concerns related to online social networks. However, most of current OSNs implement very basic access control systems, by simply making a user able to decide which personal information is accessible by other members by marking a given item as public, private, or accessible by their direct contacts. To give more flexibility, some online social networks enforce variants of these settings, but the principle is the same. For instance, besides the basic settings, Bebo (http://bebo.com), Facebook (http://facebook.com), and Multiply (http://multiply.com) support the option "selected friends"; Last.fm (http://last.fm) the option "neighbors" (i.e., the set of users having musical preferences and tastes similar to mine); Facebook, Friendster, and Orkut (http://www.orkut.com) the option "friends of friends"; Xing (http://xing.com) the options "contacts of my contacts" (2nd degree contacts), and "3rd" and "4th degree contacts." It is important to note that all these approaches have the advantage of being easy to be implemented, but they lack flexibility. In fact, the available protection settings do not allow users to easily specify their access control requirements, in that they are either too restrictive or too loose. Furthermore, existing solutions are platform-specific and they are hard to be implemented for various different online social networks.

To address some of these limitations, we propose an extensible, fine-grained OSN access control model based on semantic web technologies. Our main idea is to encode social network-related information by means of an ontology. In particular, we suggest to model the following five important aspects of OSNs using semantic web ontologies: (1) user's profiles, (2) relationships among users (e.g., Bob is Alice's close friend), (3) resources (e.g., online photo albums), (4) relationships between users and resources (e.g., Bob is the owner of the photo album), and (5) actions (e.g., post a message on someone's wall). By constructing such an ontology, we model the Social Network Knowledge Base (SNKB). The main advantage for using an ontology for modeling OSN data is that relationships among many different social network concepts can be naturally represented using OWL. Furthermore, by using reasoning, many inferences about such relationships could be done

DOI: 10.1201/9781003081845-28

automatically. Our access control enforcement mechanism is then implemented by exploiting this knowledge. In particular, the idea is to define security policies as rules (see Section 17.4), whose antecedents state conditions on SNKB, and consequents specify the authorized actions. In particular, we propose to encode the authorizations implied by security policies by means of an ontology, obtaining the SAKB. Thus, security policies have to be translated as rules whose antecedents and consequents are expressed on the ontology. To achieve this goal, we use the Semantic Web Rule Language (SWRL) [HORR2004]. As a consequence, the access control policies can be enforced by simply querying the authorizations, that is, the SAKB. The query can be easily directly implemented by the ontology reasoner by means of instance checking operations, or can be performed by a SPARQL query, if the ontology is serialized in RDF. In this chapter, we focus on how to model such a fine-grained social network access control system using semantic web technologies. We also assume that a centralized reference monitor hosted by the social network manager will enforce the required policies. As our proposed approach depends on extensible ontologies, it could be easily adapted to various online social networks by modifying the ontologies in our SNKB. Furthermore, as we discuss in details later in this chapter, semantic web tools allow us to define more fine-grained access control policies than the ones provided by current OSNs.

This chapter is organized as follows. In Section 17.2, we provide a brief discussion of current security and privacy research related to online social networks. In Section 17.3, we discuss how to model social networks using semantic web technologies. In Section 17.4, we introduce a high level overview of the security policies we support in our framework. In addition to access control policies, we state filtering policies that allow a user (or one of her supervisors) to customize the content she accesses. We also introduce admin policies, stating who is authorized to specify access control and filtering policies. In Section 17.5, we introduce the authorization ontology and the SWRL rule encoding of security policies. In Section 17.6, we discuss how security policies could be enforced. Implementation issues for our design are discussed in Section 17.7. In Section 17.8, we describe our architecture, which we also refer to as our framework. In Section 17.9, we discuss the experiments we have carried out with our implementation of semantic web-based access control for social networks. Scalability with big data and cloud technologies is discussed in Section 17.10. Section 17.11 concludes this chapter. Figure 17.1 illustrates the concepts of this chapter. Our research has been influenced by the work reported in [FINI2008].

17.2   RELATED WORK

Past research on OSN security has mainly focused on privacy-preserving techniques to allow statistical analysis on social network data without compromising OSN members' privacy (see

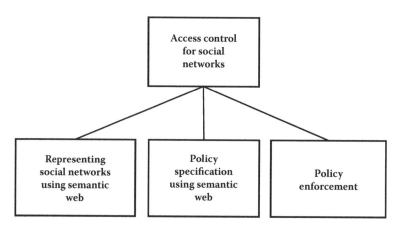

FIGURE 17.1   Access control for social networks.

[CARM2008, CARM2009a, CARM2009b, CARM2011] for discussion on this topic). In contrast, access control for OSNs is a relatively new research area. As far as we are aware, the only other proposals of an access control mechanism for online social networks are [KRUK2006], [ALI2007], and [CARM2009b]. The D-FOAF system [KRUK2006] is primarily a Friend of a Friend (FOAF) ontology-based distributed identity management system for social networks, where access rights and trust delegation management are provided as additional services. In D-FOAF, relationships are associated with a trust level, which denotes the level of *friendship* existing between the users participating in a given relationship. Although [KRUK2006] discusses only generic relationships, corresponding to the ones modeled by the foaf:knows RDF property in the FOAF vocabulary [BRIC2007], another D-FOAF-related paper [CHOI20I0] considers also the case of multiple relationship types. As far as access rights are concerned, they denote authorized users in terms of the minimum trust level and maximum length of the paths connecting the requester to the resource owner. In [ALI2007], authors adopt a multi-level security approach, where trust is the only parameter used to determine the security level of both users and resources. In [CARM2009a], a semi-decentralized discretionary access control model and a related enforcement mechanism for controlled sharing of information in OSNs is presented. The model allows the specification of access rules for online resources, where authorized users are denoted in terms of the relationship type, depth, and trust level existing between nodes in the network.

Compared with existing approaches, we use semantic web technologies to represent much richer forms of relationships among users, resources and actions. For example, we are able to represent access control rules that leverage relationship hierarchies and by using OWL reasoning tools, we can infer a "close friend" is also a "friend" and anything that is accessible by friend could be also accessible by a "close friend." In addition, our proposed solution could be easily adapted for very different online social networks by modifying the underlying SNKB. A further discussion on the differences between the proposed framework and the access control mechanism in [CARM2009b] is provided in Section 17.4.

Semantic web technologies have been recently used for developing various policy and access control languages for domains different from OSNs. For example, in [TONT2003], authors compare various policy languages for distributed agent-based systems that define authorization and obligation policies. In [FINI2008], OWL is used to express role-based access control policies. In [YAGU2005], authors propose a semantic access control model that separates the authorization and access control management responsibilities to provide solutions for distributed and dynamic systems with heterogeneous security requirements. None of this previous work deals with the access control issues related to online social networks. Among the existing work, [ELAH2008] is the most similar to our proposal. Compared to [ELAH2008], we provide a much richer OWL ontology for modeling various aspects of online social networks. In addition, we propose authorization, admin and filtering policies that depend on trust relationships among various users.

17.3 MODELING SOCIAL NETWORKS USING SEMANTIC WEB TECHNOLOGIES

17.3.1 TYPE OF RELATIONSHIPS

Recently, semantic web technologies such as Resource Description Framework (RDF) and the Web Ontology Language (OWL) have been used for modeling social network data [MIKA2007]. Although our goal in this chapter is not to propose new semantic approaches for modeling online social network data, we would like to give a brief overview of current approaches for the sake of completeness by pointing out also other social network information that could be modeled by semantic technologies. In our discussion, we will use Facebook as a running example. At the same time, we would like to stress that our discussion could be easily extended to other social networking frameworks.

In general, we identify five categories of social network data that could be modeled by semantic technologies. These are as follows: (1) personal information; (2) personal relationships; (3) social network resources; (4) relationships between users and resources; and (5) actions that can be performed in a social network. In the following, we discuss how these social network data can be represented. In the ensuing subsections, we will discuss aspects of modeling of each of the above four relationships.

17.3.2 MODELING PERSONAL INFORMATION

Some of the personal information provided on OSNs such as Facebook can be modeled by using the Friend-of-a-Friend (FOAF) ontology [BRIC2007]. FOAF is an OWL-based format for representing personal information and an individual's social network. FOAF provides various classes and properties to describe social network data such as basic personal information, online account, projects, groups, documents, and images. However, these basic mechanisms are not enough to capture all the available information. For example, there is no FOAF construct to capture the meaning for *lookingFor* (e.g., John Smith is looking for friendship). Thanks to the extensibility of the RDF/OWL language, this is easily solvable. For example, consider the following case where we capture the information related to an individual with Facebook Profile Id 999999 using a new Facebook ontology written in the RDF/OWL language. In this example, we assume that "fb" ontology has a property name *lookingFor* to capture the required information.

```
@prefix rdf: <http://www.w3.org/1599/02/22-rdf-syntax-ns>.
@prefix foaf: <http://xmlns.com/foaf/0.1/>.
@prefix fb: <http://example.org/facebook>.
<http://www.facebook.com/profile.php?id=999999999>
foaf:name "John Smith" .
<http://www.facebook.com/profile.php?id=999999999>
fb:lookingFor "Friendship".
```

As the example suggests, existing ontologies such as FOAF could be easily extended to capture personal information available on online social networks.

17.3.3 MODELING PERSONAL RELATIONSHIPS

Currently, online social networks do not support fine-grained definitions of relationships. For instance, Facebook allows you to specify whether you attended school or work with a friend, but offers no way to express what that truly means, that is, the strength of the relationship. It is this fine-grained structure that we wish to capture. Mika [MIKA2007] proposes a reification-based model for capturing relationship strength. Instead, to comply with W3C specifications [WWW1999], we adopt the use of the n-ary relation pattern rather than use simple statement reification, which is a violation of the specification [WWW2006]. If we were to violate the specification, then relationships would be modeled using a series of four RDF statements to create an identifier for the relationship. Unfortunately, as a result of that, SWRL would be unable to understand these relationships. We believe that using a specification-recommended pattern and retaining the ability to use SWRL to do inference on relationships is the best solution.

For the reasons stated earlier, we choose to model personal relationships using n-ary relation pattern. To comply with n-ary relation specification [WWW2006], we define a *FriendshipRelation* class which has subclasses that denote a general strength of friendship. The root *FriendshipRelation* class implies an unspecific friendship while the three subclasses, *Family*, *CloseFriend*, and *DistantFriend*, give an indicator of the closeness between people. The *CloseFriend* subclass has a further extension: *BestFriend*.

This basic structure allows us to easily mimic the existing structure of Facebook relationship types. However, as mentioned previously, these relationship types have no predefined meanings. To begin to quantify the meaning of relationship assignments, each instance of *FriendshipRelation* has a data property *TrustValue*. This represents the level of trust that the initiator has with the friend.

As an example suppose that an individual (e.g., John Smith) defines a relationship with a colleague (e.g., Jane Doe). This creates an instance of the *FriendshipRelation* class with the *TrustValue* data property, which represents the level of trust between the initiator and his friend. The instance also has an object property that links it to the instance of the friend. This instance of the *FriendshipRelation* class is then tied back to John Smith through the use of the *Friendship* object property.

It is important to note that any (uni-directional) relationship in the social network is a single instance of the *FriendshipRelation* class. Thus, to model the standard bi-directional nature of social network relations, we need two instances of this class. However, the simple logical inference that if B is a friend of A, then A is a friend of B can not be implemented by SWRL, in that this would imply to create a new instance of the Friendship class. Unfortunately, this is outside the realm of SWRL's capability. So, this must be taken care of outside of the SWRL framework by an external application. It is also important to note that the *TrustValue* property of relationships is a value that is computed automatically outside the OWL/SWRL component of the social network. This value is used to do various inference tasks further in the network. At the most basic level, where the *TrustValue* is a static number based on the friendship type, this is a trivial component. We assume that there will be a more complicated formula used in calculating the *TrustValue* that may be beyond the bounds of the built-in mathematical operators of SWRL.

We experience a similar difficulty with indirect relationships. To define an inferred relationship, we would once again need to create a new instance of *FriendshipRelation*. We can, however, create these indirect relationships similar to how we maintain symmetry of relationships, detailed earlier. The only difference in the indirect relationship is that instead of creating an instance of the class *FriendshipRelation*, we create an instance of a separate class, *InferredRelation*, which has no detailed subclasses, yet is otherwise identical to the FriendshipRelation base class.

17.3.4 MODELING RESOURCES

A typical OSN provides some resources such as "albums" or "walls" to share information among individuals. Clearly, RDF/OWL could be used to capture the fact that albums are composed of pictures and each picture may have multiple people in it. In our framework, we model resources as a class, beginning with a generic *Resource* class. As subclasses to this, we can have, for example, *PhotoAlbum*, *Photo*, and *Message*. Each of these has specific, unique properties and relationships. For instance, *PhotoAlbum* has a name and a description as data properties and has an object property called *containsPhoto* that links it to instances of *Photo*. These have a name, a caption, and a path to the stored location of the file. Messages have a sender, a receiver, a subject, a message, and a time stamp. We can also create a subclass of messages called *WallMessage* which is similar to messages in that it has the same data properties, but it has additional restrictions such as that a *WallMessage* may only be sent to a single individual.

17.3.5 MODELING USER/RESOURCE RELATIONSHIPS

Current applications such as Facebook assume that the only relationship between users and resources is the ownership. However, from an access control point of view this is not enough. Let us consider, for example, a photograph that contains both John Smith and Jane Doe. Jane took the picture and posted it on the social network. Traditionally, Jane would be the sole administrator of that resource. As the photo contains the image of John (we say that John is tagged to the photo), in our model John may have some determination as to which individuals can see the photo.

To model something like a photo album, we can use two classes. The first is a simple *Photo* class that simply has an optional name and caption of the photo and a required path to the location of the file. A photo is then linked to each person that is listed as being in the photo. A *PhotoAlbum* has a name and a description. *PhotoAlbum* and *Photo* are linked using the *containsPhoto* relationship. The individual owner – the person who uploaded the photos – is indicated by the *ownsAlbum* relationship. Similarly, we can represent other relationships between users and resources.

17.3.6 MODELING ACTIONS

In a social network, actions are the basis of user participation. According to the proposed representation, an action is defined as object property that relates users, resources, and actions. Moreover, we model hierarchies for actions by means of subproperty. Take, for instance, three generic actions: *Read, Write, Delete*. We define a hierarchy in which *Delete* is a subtype of *Write* which is, itself, a subtype of *Read*. In a nonhierarchical model, if John Smith was able to read, write, and delete a photo, then we would need three authorizations to represent this property. However, as we have defined the hierarchy, with only the authorizations of <"John Smith," Delete, Photo1>, John Smith has all three properties allowed.

We can also extend traditional access restrictions to take advantage of social networking extensions. For instance, the action *Post* can be defined as a subtype of Write. So, let us say that we define the actions *Write* to mean that an individual can send a private message to another individual, and that the action *Post* means that an individual can post a message to another's Wall so that any of their friends can see it. Then, allowing a user the *Post* action would allow them to see the friends wall, send them a private message, and write on their wall, but she could not delete anything.

17.4 SECURITY POLICIES FOR OSNS

17.4.1 RUNNING EXAMPLE

In the remainder of this chapter, we will use the small network shown in Figure 17.2 to illustrate our access control mechanism. Our running example has four individuals: Alice, Bob, Charlie, and David. Alice, Bob, and Charlie form a clique with different strengths of friendship connecting them. David is a friend only of Bob via the default Friendship type. There is also a *PhotoAlbum* that was uploaded by Alice that contains a single photo that is a picture of Charlie.

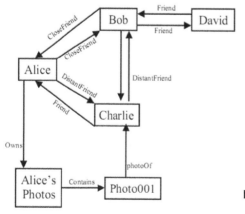

FIGURE 17.2 A portion of an OSN.

As evidenced by recent work on social network security, protecting resources in social networks requires us to revise traditional access control models and mechanisms. However, the approaches proposed so far have focused only on access control policies, that is, on the problem of regulating the access to OSN resources. We think that this is not enough, in that the complexity of the social network scenario requires the definition of further security policies, besides standard access control policies. In this section, we outline the security policies our framework supports.

17.4.2 ACCESS CONTROL POLICIES

The framework supports access control policies to regulate how resources can be accessed by OSN participants. In particular, the supported access control policies are defined on the basis of our previous work [CARM2009b]. Here, authorized users are denoted in terms of the type, depth, and trust level of the relationships existing between nodes in the network. For instance, an access control policy can state that the only OSN participants authorized to access a given resource are those with a direct or indirect friendship relationship with the resource owner, provided that this relationship has a given trust value. However, the access control policies supported by the proposed framework have some notable improvements with regard to those presented in [CARM2009b]. These improvements are mainly due to the fact that our access control policies are defined according to the SNKB described in Section 17.3. This means that the object, subject, and privilege of an access control policy are defined exploiting the semantic modeling of resources, users and actions. In particular, as it will be explained in Section 17.5, access control policies are defined as rules over ontologies representing the concepts introduced in Section 17.3. Thus, rather than access control policies specified over each single participant and resource of a OSN, we are able to specify access control policies directly on the OSN semantic concepts. Indeed, it is possible to specify a generic access control policy stating that the photos can be accessed only by friends, by simply specifying the *Photo* class as a protected object. As such, the access control policy will be applied to all instances of the *Photo* class, that is, to all photos, thus greatly simplifying policy administration. Specifying access control policies over semantic concepts has another benefit in that it is possible to exploit the hierarchy defined over the concepts to automatically propagate access control policies. For example, with respect to resources, if *Photo* has been defined with some subclasses, say *PrivatePhoto* and *HolidaysPhoto*, the previous access control policy can be automatically applied to all the instances belonging to any subclass of *Photo*. Access control policies can be also propagated along other dimensions, that is, according to hierarchies specified in the ontologies of other OSN concepts (e.g., ontologies for relationship types and actions). For example, in case the supported relationship ontology defines a hierarchy for the friendship relationship, the previous access control policy is propagated to all OSN participants with which the resource owner has any kind of friendship relationship. A similar propagation arises if the action ontology defines an hierarchy of actions. Note that also in [CARM2009b], authorized subjects are defined in terms of user relationships rather than by listing specific instances (i.e., person ids). However, in that work policy propagation is not possible, because no hierarchies are defined over resources, relationships, and actions. Moreover, the semantic modeling we propose in this chapter makes us able to specify authorized users not only in terms of the relationships they should have with the resource owner (as in [CARM2009b]), but also in terms of the relationships they should have with the resource. Thus, for example it is possible to specify an access control policy stating that all OSN participants that are tagged to a photo are authorized to access that photo. The only way to specify this access control policy in [CARM2009b] as well as in all the other existing models for OSNs is to explicitly specify a different access control policy for each OSN participant tagged to the photo.

17.4.3 FILTERING POLICIES

In an OSN, users can publish information of very heterogeneous content, ranging from family photos to adult-oriented contents. In this sense, the access control issues arising in OSNs are similar to those we have in the web, where the availability of inappropriate information could be harmful for some users (e.g., young people). To protect users from inappropriate or unwanted contents, we introduce *filtering policies*, by which it is possible to specify which data has to be filtered out when a given user browses the social network pages. By means of a filtering policy, it is, for example, possible to state that from OSN pages fetched by user Alice, all videos that have not been published by Alice's direct friends have to be removed. Similar to access control policies, filtering policies are defined as rules over ontologies representing the concepts introduced in Section 17.3 (see Section 17.5). This implies that policy propagation is possible also in case of filtering policies. Another relevant aspect of filtering policies is related to the user that specifies the policy (i.e., the grantor). Indeed, in our framework, a filtering policy can be specified in two different ways. According to the first one, a filtering policy is specified by a user to state which information she prefers not to access, that is, which data has to be filtered out from OSN pages fetched by her. Thus, in this case the grantor and the user to which the policy applies, that is, the target user, are the same. These policies state user preferences with regard to the contents one wants to access and for that reason are called *filtering preferences*. However, we also support the specification of filtering policies where the target user and the grantor are different. This kind of filtering policies makes the grantor able to specify how the SN pages fetched by target users have to be filtered. By means of these filtering policies, a grantor can *supervise* the content a target user can access. In this case, we refer to the filtering policy as *supervised filtering policy*. This represents an extremely useful feature in open environments like OSNs. For example, a parent can specify a supervised filtering policy stating that her children do not have to access those videos published by users that are not trusted by the parent herself. As it will be more clear later on, semantic technologies greatly facilitate the specification of this kind of policies.

It is worth noticing that both filtering preferences and supervised filtering policies can not be enforced by simply supporting negative access control policies, that is, policies avoiding access to resources. This is due to the fact that access control policies and filtering policies have totally different semantics. Indeed, an access control policy is specified by the resource owner to state who is authorized or denied to access her resources. Rather, a filtering policy is specified by a supervisor for a target user or by the target user herself, to specify how resources have to be filtered out when she fetches an OSN page. Note that, according to the proposed semantics, this filtering takes place even in the case the target user is authorized to access the resource, that is, even if she satisfies the access control policies specified by the resource owner.

17.4.4 ADMIN POLICIES

Introducing access control and filtering policies in a multi-user environment like OSNs requires determining who is authorized to specify policies and for which target users and objects. To address this issue, we introduce *admin policies*, that make the Security Administrator (SA) of the social network able to state who is authorized to specify access control and filtering policies. Admin policies have to be flexible enough to model some obvious admin strategies that are common to traditional scenarios (e.g., the resource owner is authorized to specify access control policies for her resources) as well as more complex strategies, according to the security and privacy guidelines adopted by the OSN. For instance, the SA could specify an admin policy stating that users tagged to a given resource are authorized to specify access control policies for that resource. Note that, as previously pointed out, the ontology modeling the relationships between users and resources described in Section 17.3 is extremely useful in the specification of such admin policies. Other kinds of admin policies are those related to filtering policies. For instance, by means of an admin policy, an SA could authorize parents to define supervised filtering policies for their young children. This admin policy can be defined by stating that if a user U1 has a relationship of type ParentOf with a user U2, which has age less than 17 (i.e., with the property age less than 17), then U1 can state supervised filtering policies where the target user is U1. The SA could further refine this admin policy to specify that the parents can state supervised filtering policies for their young children only for video resources. This would modify the previous admin policy by limiting the scope of the supervised filtering policy the parents are authorized to specify.

17.5   SECURITY POLICY SPECIFICATION

17.5.1   POLICY LANGUAGE

A policy language defines security policies according to three main components: a *subject specification* aiming to specify the entity to which a security policy applies (e.g., users, processes), an *object specification* to identify the resources to which the policy refers to (e.g., files, HW resources, relational tables), and an *action specification*, specifying the action (e.g., read, write execute, admin) that subjects can exercise on objects. Moreover, to make easier the task of policy evaluation, policies are enforced through a set of *authorizations*, stating for each subject the rights she has on the protected resources. We encode security policies by means of rules. In general, a rule consists of two formulae and an implication operator, with the obvious meaning that if the first formula, called the antecedent, holds then the second formula, called the consequent, must also hold. Thus, we encode each security policy as a *security rule*, that is, a rule whose antecedent represents the conditions stated in the policy subject and object specifications, and the consequent represents the entailed authorizations. Note that since the framework supports different types of security policies, the security rules could entail different types of authorizations. In particular, if the antecedent of a security rule encodes an access control or admin policy, the consequent denotes the entailed access control or admin authorizations. In contrast, if the rule's antecedent encodes a filtering policy (either a filtering preference or a supervised filtering policy), the consequent entails *prohibitions* rather than authorizations, because this policy limits access to resources.

We adopt SWRL to encode security rules. SWRL has been introduced to extend the axioms provided by OWL to also support rules. In SWRL, the antecedent, called the body, and the consequent, called the head, are defined in terms of OWL classes, properties and individuals. More precisely, they are modeled as positive conjunctions of *atoms*. Atoms can be of the form: (1) $C(x)$, where C is an OWL description or data range; (2) $P(x, y)$, where P is an OWL property and x and y could be variables, OWL individuals or OWL data values; (3) sameAs(x, y); (4) differentFrom(x, y); (5) builtIn$(r, x, ...)$, where r is a built-in predicate that takes one or more arguments and evaluates to true if the arguments satisfy the predicate. More precisely, an atom $C(x)$ holds if x is an instance of the class description or data range C, an atom $P(x, y)$ holds if x is related to y by property P, an atom sameAs(x, y) holds if x is interpreted as the same object as y, an atom differentFrom(x, y) holds if x and y are interpreted as different objects, and builtIn$(r, x,...)$ holds if the built-in relation r holds on the interpretations of the arguments.

Exploiting SWRL to specify security rules implies that authorizations and prohibitions must be represented in some ontology, thus to be encoded as a SWRL head. For this reason, before presenting the encoding of a security policy, we first introduce an ontology to model authorizations and prohibitions. We refer to the knowledge base derived by this ontology as Security Authorization Knowledge Base (SAKB).

17.5.2   AUTHORIZATIONS AND PROHIBITIONS

As the framework supports three different types of security policies, it has to manage three different types of authorizations, namely access control authorizations, admin authorizations, and prohibitions. In the following, we introduce the proposed ontology for their representations. However, it is relevant to notice that this ontology is strictly related to the ontologies supported by the OSN (see Section 17.3), in that it defines authorizations/prohibitions on the basis of the supported actions and resources. As such, the following does not intend to be the standard ontology for SAKBs, rather it is the one that we adopt in our framework, based on the semantic modeling presented in Section 17.3. Thus, the discussion presented here must be read as a guideline for the definition of an ontology of a SAKB.

17.5.2.1 Access Control Authorizations

The first kind of authorizations are those entailed by access control policies. In general, an access control authorization can be modeled as a triple (u,p,o) stating that subject u has the right to execute privilege p on object o. Thus, in some way, an access control authorization represents a relationship p between u and o, meaning that u can exercise p on o. Therefore, we decide to encode an access control authorization for privilege p as an instance of an OWL object property, named p, defined between the authorized person and the authorized resource. To model all possible access control authorizations, we have to introduce a different object property for each action supported in the OSN (see Section 17.3). It is interesting to note that by properly defining the object property encoding access control authorizations we can automatically propagate the authorizations on the basis of the classification defined among actions.

Let us consider, for example, the action Post and assume it has been defined as subclass of action Write. In terms of access control, if the post privilege is authorized to a user, then the write privilege is also authorized. In the proposed framework, the access control authorizations can be automatically inferred provided that object property *Post* has been defined as subproperty of the object property *Write*. We do note that this hierarchy may be different than in traditional access control systems. When we use SWRL, anything that is defined for a superclass will also be defined for its subclasses. However, the reverse is not true. So, when we allow an individual to *Write*, it does not automatically confer the *Post* authority.

17.5.2.2 Prohibitions

Filtering policies state whether the target user is not authorized to access a certain object, in the case of supervised filtering policies, or the target user prefers not to access, in the case of filtering preferences. Similarly to access control authorizations, a prohibition specifies a relationship between a user and the resource the user is not authorized prefers not to access. For this reason, also prohibitions can be expressed as an object property between *Person* and *Resource* classes. More precisely, a prohibition for the Read privilege is defined as the OWL object property *PRead*. An instance of this object property <John, URI1>:*PRead* states that Bob has not to read resource URI1. Similarly, to access control authorizations, it is possible to specify how prohibitions have to be propagated by simply defining subproperty.

Let us again consider the three basic actions: *Read, Write, Delete*, and their prohibited versions: *PRead, PWrite, PDelete*. We again wish to form a hierarchy of actions in a logical order. That is, if an individual is prohibited from *reading* a resource, then she should also be prohibited from *writing* and *deleting* that resource. To do this, we can simply define *PRead* to be a subtype of *PWrite*, which is a subtype of *PDelete*.

17.5.2.3 Admin Authorizations

Admin authorizations are those authorizations implied by admin policies, which, we recall, have the aim to authorize users to specify access control or filtering policies. Therefore, admin policies entail two types of authorizations: authorizations to specify access control policies, to which we simply refer as *admin authorizations*, and authorizations to specify filtering policies, that is, *admin prohibitions*. In general, an admin authorization can be represented as a triple (u,p,o) stating that user u is authorized to specify access control policies for privilege p on object o. Thus, similarly to authorizations and prohibitions also admin authorizations can be expressed as an object property between *Person* and *Resource* classes. According to this modeling, we can define the Object property *AdminRead*, whose instances state that a given user is authorized to express access control policies granting the read privilege on a given object. Consider the instance <Bob,URI1>:*AdminRead*, which states that Bob is authorized to specify access control policies granting the read privilege on the URI1 object.

Similarly, to access control authorizations, it is possible to specify how admin authorizations have to be propagated by simply defining subproperty. Let us declare the previously mentioned property *AdminRead* and further create the properties AdminWrite and AdminAll. We declare *AdminAll* to be a subproperty of both *AdminWrite* and *AdminRead*. Consider our running example where Alice owned a photo. Let us assume that this grants her the *AdminAll* authorization on the photo. If Alice attempts to allow Bob to Read the photo, an action which is restricted to individuals with the *AdminRead* property, then this is allowed via the *AdminAll* property.

In contrast, an admin prohibition can be represented as a tuple (s, t, o, p), which implies that user s (supervisor) is authorized to specify filtering policies for the privilege p applying to the target user t and to object o. Differently from previous authorizations, admin prohibitions cannot be represented as properties in that they do not represent a binary relationship. For that reason, we decide to model admin prohibitions as an OWL class *Prohibition*. This makes us able to specify all the components of the prohibition as class properties. More precisely, given an admin prohibition (s, t, o, p), we can model the authorized supervisor has an object property *Supervisor* between the *Prohibition* and *Person* classes. Similarly, the target user can be represented as an object property *TargetUser* between the *Prohibition* and *Person* classes, and the target object as an object property *TargetObject* between the *Prohibition* and the *Resource* classes. In contrast, the privilege over which the supervisor is authorized to state filtering policies is not represented as an object property. Indeed, to automatically propagate admin prohibitions we prefer to specify the privilege directly as the class name. Thus, as an example, instances of the *ProhibitionRead* class state admin prohibitions authorizing the specification of filtering policies for the read privilege. By properly defining subclasses, it is possible to automatically infer new admin prohibitions.

Suppose, we have a generic *Prohibition* class with the subclasses *PRead* and *PView*. We then create another subclass of each of these as *PAll*. Suppose, we have two individuals, John and Jane, and John is Jane's father. In this scenario, John should be allowed to filter what videos his daughter is able to see. That is, we have a prohibition ("John," "Jane," Video, *PAll*). Now, for any video and any permission, John can disallow those that he wishes.

17.5.3 SECURITY RULES

The proposed framework translates each security policy as a SWRL security rule where the antecedent encodes the conditions specified in the policy (e.g., conditions denoting the subject and object specifications), whereas the consequent encodes the implied authorizations or prohibitions. In particular, since we model security rules as SWRL rules, the SWRL body states policy conditions over the SNKB, that is, conditions on ontologies introduced in Section 17.3, whereas the SWRL head entails new instances of the SAKB, that is, instances of the ontology introduced in Section 17.3. As a consequence, the specification of SWRL security rules is strictly bound to the ontologies supported by the OSN to model SN and SA knowledge bases. This implies that it is not possible to provide a formalization of generic SWRL rules, because these can vary based on the considered ontologies. In contrast, in this section, we aim to present some meaningful examples of possible SWRL security rules defined on top of ontologies adopted in our framework.

We start by considering the admin policy stating that the owner of an object is authorized to specify access control policies for that object. The corresponding SWRL rule defined according to the ontologies presented in the previous sections is the following:

$$Owns(?grantor, \ ? targetObject) \Rightarrow AdminAll(?grantor, \ ? targetObject)$$

The evaluation of the aforementioned rule has the result of generating a different instance of the object property *AdminAll* for each pairs of user and corresponding owned resource. It is relevant to note that this authorization is propagated according to the ontology modeling the SAKB. Thus, since the framework exploits the one introduced in Section 17.5.1, the above authorization is propagated also to *AdminRead* and *AdminWrite*.

Another meaningful admin policy for a social network is the one stating that if a user is tagged to a photo then she is authorized to specify access control policies for the read privilege on that photo. This can be encoded by means of the following SWRL security rule:

$$\text{Photo}(?\text{targetObject}) \land \text{photoOf}(?\text{grantor},\ ?\ \text{targetObject})$$

$$\Rightarrow \text{AdminRead}(?\text{grantor},\ ?\ \text{targetObject})$$

The aforementioned rules are interesting examples stressing how in the proposed framework, it is possible to easily specify admin policies whose implementation in a non semantic-based access control mechanism would require complex policy management. Indeed, providing the OSN with ontologies modeling the relationships between users and resources (e.g., modeling ownership or tagging relationships) makes the SA able to specify admin policies by simply posing conditions on the type of the required relationship. In contrast, enforcing these admin policies in a traditional access control mechanism would require implementing complex policy management functionalities, in that it would be required to first determine all possible relationships between users and resources then to specify admin authorizations for all of them. Rather in the proposed framework this task is performed by the reasoner.

Table 17.1 presents some examples of SWRL security rules. The first security rule encodes a filtering policy stating that Bob's children can not access videos. Once this rule is evaluated, an instance of prohibition for each of Bob's children and video resource is created. In contrast, the second security rule corresponds to an access control policy stated by Bob to limit the read access to his photos only to his direct friend, whereas the third encodes an access control policy specifying that photos where Alice is tagged can be accessed by her direct friends. Finally, the fourth rule specifies that if a person has a photo, then friends of their friends (an indirect relationship) can view that photo.

17.6   SECURITY RULE ENFORCEMENT

17.6.1   OUR APPROACH

Our framework acts like a traditional access control mechanism, where a *reference monitor* evaluates a request by looking for an authorization granting or denying the request. Exploiting this principle in the proposed framework implies retrieving the authorizations/prohibitions by querying the SAKB ontology. Thus, for example, to verify whether a user u is authorized to specify access control policies for the read privilege on object o, it is necessary to verify if the instance *AdminRead(u,o)* is in the ontology, that is, to perform an instance checking. This implies that before any possible requests evaluation all the SWRL rules encoding security policies have to be evaluated, thus to infer all access control/admin authorizations as well as all prohibitions. For this reason, before policy enforcement it is required to execute a preliminary phase, called *policy refinement*. This phase aims to populate the SAKB with the inferred authorizations/prohibitions, by executing all the SWRL rules encoding security policies.

Once authorizations/prohibitions are inferred, security policy enforcement can be carried out. In particular, access control and filtering policies are evaluated upon an *access request* is submitted, whereas admin policies are evaluated when an *admin request* is submitted. In the following, we present both the request evaluation by showing how the corresponding policies are enforced.

TABLE 17.1
Examples of SWRL security rules

SWRL rule

(1)   Video(?targetObject,) ∧ ParentOf(Bob,?controlled) ⇒
PRead(?controlled,?targetObject)

(2)   Owner(Bob,?targetObject) ∧ Photo(?targetObject) ∧
Friend(Bob,?targetSubject) ⇒ Read(?targetSubject,?targetObject)

(3)   Photo(?targetObject) ∧ photoOf(Alice,?targetObject) ∧
Friend(Alice,?targetSubject) ⇒ Read(?targetSubject,?targetObject)

(4)   Photo(?targetObject) ∧ Owns(?owner, ?targetObject) ∧
Friend(?owner, ?targetSubject1) ∧ Friend(?targetSubject1,
?targetSubject2) ⇒
Read(?targetSubject2, ?targetObject)

17.6.2 ADMIN REQUEST EVALUATION

An admin request consists of two pieces of information: the name of the *grantor*, that is, the user that has submitted the admin request, and the access control or filtering policy the grantor would like to specify, encoded as SWRL rule, that is, the *submitted SWRL*. The submitted SWRL has to be inserted in the system only if there exists an admin authorization in the SAKB for the grantor. For example, if the submitted rule requires to specify an access control policy for the read privilege on targetObject, then there must exist an instance of <grantor, targetObject>:*Read*. Note that information about the privilege and the targetObject can be retrieved directly from the submitted SWRL. Thus, to decide whether the request above can be authorized or not, a possible way is to query the SAKB to retrieve the corresponding admin authorization, if any. If there exists an instance, then the submitted SWRL can be evaluated, otherwise the framework denies to the grantor the admin request. An alternative way is to rewrite the submitted SWRL by adding in its body also condition to verify whether there exists an admin authorization in the SAKB authorizing the specification of the rule. The following example will clarify the underlying idea.

Let us assume that the system receives the following admin request: {Bob, SWRL$_1$}, where SWRL$_1$ is the following:

```
SWRL₁: Owns(Bob,?targetObject) ^ Photo(?targetObject)
```
   ^ Friend(Bob,?targetSubject) ⇒ Read(?targetSubject,?targetObject)

To determine the result of the admin request, the framework has to verify the existence of <Bob,targetObject>: *AdminRead* instance in the SAKB. This check can be incorporated in the body of SWRL$_1$ by simply modifying it as follows:

   New_SWRL$_1$: AdminRead(Bob,?targetObject)^
   Owns(Bob,?targetObject) ^ Photo(?targetObject) ^
```
Friend(Bob,?targetSubject)
```
   ⇒Read(?targetSubject, ?targetObject)

Then New_SWRL$_1$ is evaluated with the consequence that Read access control authorizations will be inserted in SAKB only if Bob is authorized to specify them by an admin policy.

In case of an admin request submitting a filtering policy, to decide whether the grantor is authorized to specify that policy, a search is required in the *Prohibitions* class (i.e., the subclass corresponding to the action the filtering policy requires to prohibit) for an instance having the property *Grantor* equal to the grantor and the properties *Controlled* and *TargetObject* equal to the controlled and *TargetObject* specified in the head of the submitted SWRL rule, respectively. Also in this case, we can adopt an approach based on SWRL rewriting.

Let us assume that the framework receives the following admin request: {Bob, SWRL$_2$}, where SWRL$_2$ is the following:

```
SWRL₂ : Video(?targetObject) ^ ParentOf(Bob,?controlled) ⇒
PRead(?controlled,?targetObject)
Then, the system can modify the submitted SWRL as:
    New_SWRL₂: PRead(?p) ^ Grantor(?p,Bob) ^ Controlled(?p,?controlled) ^
TargetObject(?p,?targetObject)       ^       Video(?targetObject)       ^       ParentOf
(Bob,?controlled) ⇒ PRead(?controlled,?targetObject)
whose evaluation has the effect to insert instances of PRead property (i.e.,
read prohibitions) only if there exists an Admin Prohibition (Bob,c,o,Read),
where c is Bob's children, and o is a video resource. Note that this is valid also
if the submitted SWRL explicitly specifies the name of the controlled user (e.g.,
….⇒ PRead(Alice,?targetObject)).
```

17.6.3 ACCESS REQUEST EVALUATION

In general, an access request can be modeled as a triple (*u*, *p*, *URI*), which means that a user *u* requests to execute the privilege *p* on the resource located at *URI*. To evaluate this request the framework has to verify whether there exists an access control authorization granting *p* on *URI* to requester *r*. However, since the proposed system also supports filtering policies, the presence of such an authorization does not necessarily imply that *r* is authorized to access *URI* because there could be a prohibition denying access to the resource to the user. Thus, to evaluate whether an access request has to be granted or denied, it is necessary to perform two queries to the SAKB. The first to retrieve authorizations and the second to retrieve prohibitions. More precisely, if *u* requires the read privilege *Read*, the system has to query the instances of object property *Read* and *PRead*. In particular, both the queries look for instance *<u,URI>* (i.e.,*<u,URI>:Read* and *<u,URI>:PRead*). Then, the access is granted if the first query returns an instance and the second returns the empty set. It is denied otherwise.

Consider again the examples in Sections 17.3 and 17.4 with the addition of a person named "Susan." Susan is a friend of Jane and has posted a video which she allows to be seen by all of her friends. However, Jane's father prohibits her from viewing videos. When a request is made by Jane to see Susan's video, the authorization and the prohibition queries are performed. The authorization query returns a Read permission, but the prohibition query returns a PRead. This means that Jane will be unable to view the video.

17.7 IMPLEMENTATION OF AN ACCESS CONTROL FRAMEWORK

In the previous sections, we provided a framework for social network access control using semantic web technologies. Here, we show the results of an initial implementation of our framework on synthetic data. As stated earlier, we have designed an extensible, fine-grained OSN access control model based on semantic web technologies. Our main idea is to encode social network-related information by means of an ontology. In particular, we suggest to model the following five important aspects of OSNs using semantic web ontologies: (1) user's profiles, (2) relationships among users (e.g., Bob is Alice's close friend), (3) resources (e.g., online photo albums), (4) relationships between users and resources (e.g., Bob is the owner of the photo album), (5) actions (e.g., post a message on someone's wall). By constructing such an ontology, we model the Social

Network Knowledge Base (SNKB). Our access control enforcement mechanism is then implemented by exploiting this knowledge. In particular, the idea is to define security policies as rules, whose antecedents state conditions on SNKB, and consequents specify the authorized actions. We assume that a centralized reference monitor hosted by the social network manager will enforce the required policies. Our architecture is extensible in that we can add modules to carry out funtions such as inference control. Furthermore, we can also extend our policies to include information sharing policies in addition to access control policies. For a detailed discussion of the use of semantic technologies in online social networks, please refer to our work in [CARM2009a]. Here, we will constrain our discussions to those specific topics which impact our implementation of an access control mechanism for resources in an online social network.

In the recent past, Facebook has made significant changes to its method of defining the relationships between friends on the network. Previously, if we had two Facebook users who were friends, John and Jane for instance, either John or Jane could select one of the pre-chosen friendship types that Facebook allowed, where the other friend would be required to confirm or reject this label of their friendship. Following this, any friend of either John or Jane could see the definition that was applied to this friendship. Now, however, instead of defining link types that are visible to others, each individual has the ability to create meaningful lists. Friends can then be added into as many lists as a user chooses. These lists can then be used to control visibility to status updates, wall posts, etc. However, there is no way to define a hierarchy of these lists. For instance, if one was to create a "High School Classmates" and then a "College Classmates" list, there is no way to create a "Classmates" list, without individually adding each individual person to that third list.

We represent a friendship using the n-ary relation pattern, as specified by the W3C [WWW1999]. This means that each friendship is an instance of a class, which we call *FriendshipRelation*. This allows us to maintain separate information about each friendship. Specifically, we maintain a *TrustValue* for each friendship. This allows us to determine a specific strength of a friendship, even when compared to those in the same class. Our implementation supports access control policies to regulate how resources can be accessed by the members of an online social network. In particular, the supported access control policies are defined on the basis of our previous work [CARM2009b]. Here, authorized users are denoted in terms of the type and/ or trust level of the relationships between nodes in the network. For instance, an access control policy can state that the only OSN participants authorized to access a given resource are those with a direct friendship relationship with the resource owner, as long as the relationship also has a certain trust level.

Note, however, that using semantic reasoning can give some improvements over the capabilities discussed in [CARM2009b]. This benefit comes from our ability to specify access control policies over semantic concepts in the OSN. For example, as a default, Facebook may specify that photos can only be viewed by direct friends. In the absence of policies defined by individual users, reasoning will default to this general policy. The design of our approach to providing security in OSNs is discussed in Chapter 19. The major aspects include filtering policies, security rule enforcement, administration policy evaluation, and the access request evaluation. In the next section, we will describe our implementation framework.

17.8   FRAMEWORK ARCHITECTURE

In our proposed framework, we plan to build several layers on top of the existing online social network application. We plan to implement our prototype using Java based open source semantic web application development framework called JENA (http://jena.sourceforge.net/), because it offers an easy to use programmatic environment for implementing the ideas discussed in this chapter. Here, we describe each of these layers independently, as well as the motivation behind choosing specific technologies in our framework. While we use specific instances of Facebook as

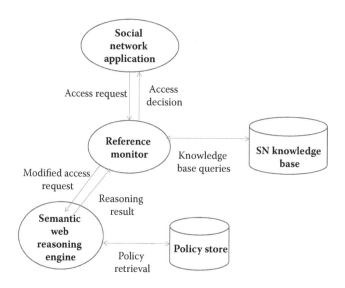

FIGURE 17.3 Framework for social network access control.

the over-arching application utilizing the lower level semantic layers, any social network appli-cation could be modified to use the design we describe here. Figure 17.3 describes our framework. The policies and data are stored as RDF triples. The reference monitor controls access to the data. It will carry out functions such as query rewriting. Some key points in the framework are discussed in the ensuing paragraphs. Next, we will discuss the components of the framework.

RDF Datastore : We assume the use of a general RDF triple-store to hold the un-derlying data. In this representation, all facts about an entity are recorded as a triple of the form <Subject, Predicate, Object>. So, suppose we have an in-dividual named John Smith, who is assigned a unique identifier 999999, would give us the tuple <999999, *foaf:Name*, "John Smith">.

We plan to use a similar format in a separate table to store a list of authorizations so that we do not have to re-infer them each time an authorization is requested. For the data storage system, we plan to use MySQL because of its availability and because of its ease of interface with JENA.

We note here that an RDF datastore differs from a relational database in that there is no da-tabase method of ensuring that constraints are maintained on the ontology as a whole, such as making sure that a defined *Person* has a name. The database representation of this fact is no different than the nonessential statement that the person lives in Albuquerque. However, we plan to use OWL-DL statements to define these constraints, and then allow the RDF/OWL engine to enforce the constraints as described later.

- *Reasoner:* Any reasoner that supports SWRL rules can be used to perform the inferences described in this chapter. However, we chose SweetRules (https://ebiquity.umbc.edu/project/ html/id/60/SweetRules) because it interfaces with JENA and has a rule-based inference engine. This means that we can use both forward- and backward-chaining to improve the efficiency of reasoning for enforcing our access control policies. Forward chaining is an inference method where the engine will begin with the data provided and look at the established inference rules in an attempt to derive further information. This can be used when the system needs to infer permissions on a large scale, such as when a resource is added for the first time.

  At this point, there will be a large one-time addition of authorizations to the allowed list of users. However, later, after other friends are added, checking to see if a user has access to a limited number of resources can be done through backward chaining. Basically, in backward-chaining, we begin with the desired goal (e.g., goal is to infer whether "John has permission to see the photo album A"), and check whether it is explicitly stated or whether it could be inferred by some other rules in a recursive fashion. Obviously, this will allow a result to be inferred about an individual (e.g., John) without re-checking all other individuals. In [MIKA2007], Mika proposes a basic general social network, called Flink, based on a semantic datastore using a similar framework to that we have proposed, but using several different specific semantic technologies. However, he does specify that their implementation, using backward- and forward-chaining is efficiently scalable to millions of tuples, which provides an evidence of the viability of our proposed scheme.

- *RDF/OWL engine:* For the RDF/OWL interface, we chose to use the JENA API. We use this to translate the data between the application and the underlying data store. JENA has several important features that were considered in its use. First, it is compatible with SweetRules. Second, it supports OWL-DL reasoning which we could use to verify that the data is consistent with the OWL restrictions on the ontology. The OWL restrictions are simple cardinality and domain/range constraints such as every person has to have a name and must belong to at least one network. To enforce these constraints, we plan to have the application layer pass the statements to be entered about an individual until all have been collected. We then have JENA insert these statements into the database and then check the new model for consistency. If there are any constraints that have been violated, then we pass this information back to the social network application and have it gather the required information from the user.

In our system, we built several layers on top of a reduced online social network application. We considered the actions of a social network (messages, wall posts, viewing profiles, viewing images, etc.) and examined those that involved the most access requests. For example, if a user, John, was to go to Jane's profile, then in the best case, there is a single check (are John and Jane friends of an appropriate level) on permissions. However, when you consider an image, which can easily have a dozen people tagged in it, and each of those individuals may specify their own additional constraints to the viewership of that image, then it is easy to see that this will be the more complicated example of permissions inference in a system. In effect, we built our system to test a consistent series of worst-case scenarios to test its ability to handle a testing load.

We implement our prototype using the Java-based open source semantic web application development framework called JENA (http://jena.sourceforge.net/), because it offers an easy-to-use programmatic environment for implementing the ideas discussed in this chapter, as well as generally being a framework that is supported by most semantic products currently available. While we use specific instances of Facebook as the over-arching application utilizing the lower level semantic layers, any social network application could potentially be modified to use the design we describe here. As discussed earlier, the major components of our system are the RDF Datastore, the Reasoner and the RDF/OWL Engine.

17.9 EXPERIMENTS

17.9.1 DATA GENERATION

As we began our implementation, it was apparent we would need to be able to measure the performance of our implementation on large datasets. Because the size of Facebook (at the time we started the implementation) was approximately 300 million users, we established 350 million as the required number of nodes in our dataset, to ensure that our implementation could scale to match the numbers Facebook would reach (close to three billion at present (https://www.businessofapps.com/data/facebook-statistics/). Unfortunately, there are no publicly available data sets of this size that we could use. Instead, we generated our own dataset.

That is, we created a data generator that generates n nodes. We began with creating a group of 50 nodes, and generated 50 edges that were distributed randomly across the 50 nodes in the graph. We then chose a random node, n_i with at least one friend and performed Dijkstra's Algorithm to determine whether the subgraph was connected. If the subgraph was not connected, then there were j nodes which were not reachable from n_i. We then chose $0 < r_i \leq j$ to be a number of new edges to create. For each edge, we randomly chose a node from the connected subgraph containing n_i and chose a destination node in the disconnected portion of the subgraph. As long as there was a disconnected portion of the subgraph, we continued generating edges. By performing subgraph-joins in this manner, we are able to generate a social network-like graph while still maintaining randomness and not hand-picking which edges would have links between them.

It is important to note at this point that our datastore records each linked twice. Even though the graph is undirected, there is a link type (used in inference) that is directed. For instance, while the generic 'Friend' link type is bi-directional, the specific 'BestFriend' link type is not necessarily. To maintain this, we recorded each direction of the link with its associated link type. Once the initial subgraph was complete, we iterated through the nodes to assign each edge a link type. We established three generic link types: Friend, Family, and Co-Worker, and recorded them for each direction of the edge. That is, $(n_i, n_j) \in \mathcal{E}$, if assigned the Friend link type, would have generated the tuples $\{n_i, n_j, \text{Friend}\}$, and $\{n_j, n_i, \text{Friend}\}$.

We uniformly chose a generic type for each edge that a node is a member of. After this, we then assigned specific subtypes. For 10% of Friend generic link types, we assigned the specific (uni-directional) link type of bestFriend. That is, in the above example, if n_i declared n_j to be a bestFriend, then the tuple $\{n_i, n_j, \text{Friend}\}$ would have become $\{n_i, n_j, \text{bestFriend}\}$. Note that the second tuple would have remained unchanged at this time.

Next, we used a Pareto distribution over the number of defined Family Members to determine how many relationships would be defined as "ParentOf." We use a Pareto distribution because while having one or two parents listed is what we may generally think of as reasonable for a child, in today's mixed families, it would not be outside the realm of the believable to have more parents listed for a child. It is also important to note that when a link was defined as ParentOf, its partner tuple was automatically assigned the inverse relationship of ChildOf. That is, suppose that our earlier example was instead, $\{n_i, n_j, \text{Family}\}$ and $\{n_j, n_i, \text{Family}\}$. If n_i was determined to be the parent, in a single step, we would have the amended tuples $\{n_i, n_j, \text{ParentOf}\}$ and $\{n_j, n_i, \text{ChildOf}\}$.

For the Co-worker generic link type, we did not further define a specific link type.

For each node, we also defined a security policy. For clarity, we defined three security policies, which are chosen uniformly at random:

1. *Strict:* Only BestFriends and Family can view photos of self and any children; their children may not view any videos.
2. *Casual:* Anyone can see photos; no restriction on children.
3. *ParentStrict:* Anyone can see photos of the parent, only family can see photos of their children; child cannot see any videos.

We then generated m resources, where m is a random number less than 4.5 million and more than 750,000, which should allow us to model both more active and more passive social networks. A resource could be either a photo or a video. We weighted the probability of a resource being a photo to 75%. We then drew from a uniform distribution between 1 and 25, inclusive, to represent the number of people to "tag" in a photo. This "tag" indicated a person appearing in the photo, and we viewed this as having a "stake" in the individuals in the network who could see the photo.

It is important here to note several things. The first is that while our uniform distribution may not reflect a true probabilistic model of the realities of photos on a social networking site such as Facebook, the inclusion of larger groups having a stake in photos represents a more difficult inference problem for such a site. The second is that we do not restrict the individuals being tagged in a photo to only those friends of the photo owner. Because this functionality exists in current online social networks, we needed to support this type of tagging. This ability can support photos of events such as weddings where a person taking a photo may only know a subset of individuals in the photo, but people who view the photo can supply more details as to other individuals who were photographed. We also note at this point that our method generates a graph where the average number of friends that a person has is 102 users (average number of friends on Facebook is 338 https://www.onaverage.co.uk/other-averages/average-number-of-facebook-friends).

- *Event Generation:* We next generated a series of events that will be processed to examine the effect of using a semantic web-based reasoner for social network access control. We condensed the full set of actions that can be performed in a social network (such as games, posting on walls, changing one's status, etc.) to those that would most strongly affect the ability of a reasoner: Adding friends, accessing existing resources, creating new resources, and changing permissions. When creating users, adding friends, or creating new resources we performed the task as described previously. However, when we accessed an existing resource, a randomly chosen user attempted to access a randomly selected resource.
- *Experiments:* We performed two independent implementations of reasoners. Our first implementation relied on the SweetRules inference engine. We attempted to perform inference on the entire dataset. Performing inference in this way took 17 hours to load the initial model into memory, and then several seconds to perform each specific reasoning request. However, we noticed that when our model needed to be updated (through new resources, friends, or a change in security policy) these changes were not reflected in our in-memory model. This caused inference done later to become more and more incorrect.

Because of this, we implemented a reasoning solution using Pellet which has become a very popular reasoner. Initially, we simply changed the reasoner that we used to Pellet. However, in the initial loading step with Pellet, we received out of memory errors and were unable to proceed to the reasoning segment. We then decided that we needed to implement some type of partitioning scheme for the social network. A naive approach of partitioning would have resulted in some friendship links that spanned partitions. These cross-partition edges would have resulted in one of two things:

1. *Reconstructing partitions:* Suppose that a partition, P_i, has an user u_a with n friends, $u_1, \ldots, u_n$ who are stored in partitions $P_1, \ldots P_n$, respectively. Remember that we can determine who the friends of u_a are from our *Friends* datastore. This ability, however, does not assist us in determining which specific partition their friends are in without an additional index. We must then devote considerable resources to recombining specific partitions to be able to effectively infer access permissions.
2. *Ignoring links:* The other option is that we can simply ignore any friendship links that lead to another partition. This is clearly not a viable option, because it will obviously result in far too many invalid access requests.

We then realized that for any individual access request, there are only groups of users whose security policies and friends are important to determining the success or failure of the request: (1) the resource owner, (2) the person making the access request, and (3) those individuals tagged in the resource. So, we adopt an amended partitioning scheme. For any access request, we generate a temporary table that contains only the members of the three groups mentioned earlier, all links involving those individuals, the requestor, and the security policies of all these people.

We then use three methods of measuring trust values and perform experiments to determine how each type affects the time required to perform inference:

TABLE 17.2
Time to conduct inference (in seconds)

	Average	Low	High
LTO	0.585	0.562	0.611
TVO	0.612	0.534	0.598
VTH	0.731	0.643	0.811

- Link Type Only (LTO) is the method described earlier, where there is only a link type for each edge.
- Trust Value Only (TVO) is a method in which we use only a trust value in place of most link types. Note, however, that because of the unique constraints held by a "ParentOf"/ "ChildOf" relationship, we do still maintain only this link type. We do not maintain other generic or specific link types here, however. We assume that the trust value (which would be assigned by a user) are more specific measures than a defined link type.
- Value/Trust Hybrid (VTH) is an approach where we retain all generic link type declarations, the "ParentOf" specific type, and add on top of this a Trust Value. This provides for a finer granularity in a security policy. For instance, instead of just being a BestFriend, a specific user can define various security policies, such as only accessible to Friend's with a trust value greater than 7, where they may declare a BestFriend to be a trust value of 6 or higher. This allows the user to restrict even among best friends or family.

The results of our experiments are provided in Table 17.2. This table shows the average amount of time that it takes to perform inference tasks, as well as the longest time taken and the shortest time taken. Note that this includes the time required to generate the temporary table that is required for the request to be evaluated. Additionally, we ran other series of tests to determine the effect of the number of friends in a graph, as shown in Figure 17.4. For these tests, we generated a subgraph where each person had a specific number of friends, ranging between 50 and 150. We repeated tests using our three types of trust measurement (LTO, TVO, and VTH) and report the average time taken for inference. Again, we see that LTO clearly takes the least time for inference. However, additionally, we can see that there is only a slight increase in the time taken for inference at each additional group of friends. Further, there is only a slight decrease at the point where all members have 50 friends which indicates that most of the time for our inference operation is consumed by the overhead of the inference engine, including our dynamic partitioning method.

17.10   SCALABILITY WITH BIG DATA AND CLOUD TECHNOLOGIES

We have used semantic web for representing and reasoning about social media data for access control, Our policies and data are specified using semantic web technologies. Social media databases are massive supporting billions of users. Therefore, we need scalable techniques for representing and reasoning about the data with respect to security and privacy. We now have big data management technologies that include systems such as MongoDB, Google's Big Query and Apache HIVE. The big data solutions are being developed by cloud providers including Amazon, IBM, Google, and Microsoft. In addition, infrastructures/platforms based on products such as Apache's Hadoop, Spark, and Storm are being developed. There are infrastructure management tools as well as big data management tools.

Infrastructure management tools include the following: Apache Hadoop: Hadoop is an open source distributed framework for processing large amounts of data. It uses the MapReduce programming model. Its storage system is called the Hadoop Distributed File System (HDFS). It is

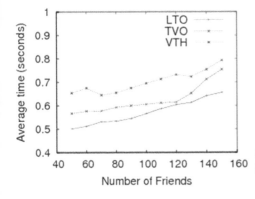

FIGURE 17.4 Average time for inference by number of friends.

hosted on clusters of machines. MapReduce: MapReduce is a programming model and an associated implementation that takes the client requests and transforms them into MapReduce jobs. These jobs are then executed by Hadoop. The main feature of the programming model is the generation of the jobs. Apache Spark: Apache Spark is an open source distributed computing framework for processing massive amounts of data. The application programmers use Spark through an interface that consists of a data structure called the Resilient Distributed Dataset (RDD). Spark was developed to overcome the limitations in the MapReduce programming model Apache Storm: Apache Storm is an open source distributed real-time computation system for processing massive amounts of data. Storm is essentially a real-time framework for processing streaming data and real-time analytics. It can be integrated with the HDFS.

Big Data Management Tools include the following: Apache Hive: Apache Hive is an open source SQL-like database/data warehouse that is implemented on top of the Hadoop/MapReduce platform. It was initially developed by Facebook to store the information related to Facebook data. However, later it became an open source project and a trademark of Apache. Google Big Query: Big Query is essentially a data warehouse that manages petabyte scale data. It runs on Google's infrastructure and can process SQL queries or carry out analytics extremely fast. NoSQL Database: NoSQL database is a generic term for essentially a nonrelational database design or scalability for the web. It is known as a nonrelational high-performance database. The data models for NoSQL databases may include graphs, document structures, and key-value pairs. Some of the popular NoSQL databases include MongoDB and HBase.

Figure 17.5 illustrates our architecture for the scalable secure social media systems. Here, the big data management tools are hosted on the infrastructure tools. The Big data management tools are augmented with inference engines. These inference engines essentially implement various machine learning algorithms including deep learning algorithms as well as clustering algorithms. These algorithms will examine the policies, learn about the data and then extract patterns and make predictions. If the patterns and predictions are not what the users are authorized to see, then they are not given to the users. More details are given in [THUR2020].

17.11   SUMMARY AND DIRECTIONS

In this chapter, we have proposed an extensible fine-grained online social network access control model based on semantic web tools. In addition, we propose authorization, admin and filtering policies that are modeled using OWL and SWRL. The architecture of a framework in support of this model has also been presented. We also described the implementation of an extensible fine-grained online social network access control model based on semantic web tools. In particular we discussed the implementation of the authorization, administration, and filtering policies that are modeled using OWL and SWRL. That is, we discussed the implementation of a version of the framework described in Chapter 19 and presented experimental results for the length of time access control can be evaluated using this scheme. Further work could be conducted in the area of

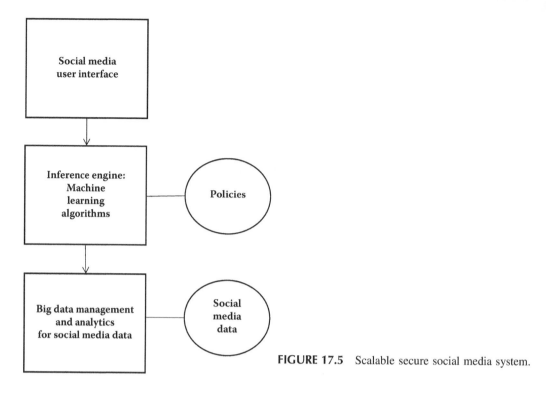

FIGURE 17.5   Scalable secure social media system.

determining a minimal set of access policies that could be used in evaluating access requests in a further attempt to increase the efficiency of these requests.

We intend to extend this work toward several directions. A first direction arises by the fact that supporting flexible admin policies could bring the system to a scenario where several access control policies specified by distinct users can be applied to the same resource. Indeed, in our framework social network's resources could be related to different users according to the supported ontology. For example, a given photo could be connected to the owner, say Bob, as well as to all users with which is tagged with, say Alice and Carl. According to the semantics of admin policies, it could be the case that some of these tagged users are authorized to specify access control policies for that resource, say only Alice. For example, Alice could have specified that the photos tagged to her can be accessed only by her direct friends, whereas Bob could have specified that his photos have to be accessed by his direct friend and colleagues. To enforce access control, the framework has to decide how the specified access control policies have to be combined together. As such, a first important extension of the proposed framework will be the support of a variety of policy integration strategies. As a further important future work, we plan to implement our framework using the ideas discussed in this chapter and test the efficiency of various ways of combining forward- and backward-chaining based reasoning for different scenarios.

Additionally, we have shown that existing social networks need some form of reasonable data partitioning in order for semantic inference of their access control to be reasonable in its speed and memory requirements, due to constraints on the memory available to perform inference. Additionally, further work can be used in determining the best method of representing the individual information of a person in a social network to determine whether a hybrid semantic/relational approach or a pure approach offers the best overall system.

REFERENCES

[ALI2007] B. Ali, W. Villegas, M. Maheswaran, A Trust Based Approach for Protecting User Data in Social Networks, *2007 Conference of the Center for Advanced Studies on Collaborative research (CASCON'07)*, 2007, pp. 288–293.

[BERT2007] S. Berteau, Facebook's misrepresentation of Beacon's Threat to Privacy: Tracking Users Who Opt Out or Are Not Logged. CA Security Advisor Research Blog, March 2007. Available at: http://community.ca.com/blogs/securityadvisor/archive/2007/11/29/facebook-s-misrepresentation-of-beacon-s-threat-to-privacy-tracking-users-who-opt-out-or-are-not-logged-in.aspx.

[BRIC2007] D. Brickley, L. Miller, FOAF Vocabulary Specification 0.91, RDF Vocabulary Specification, November 2007. Available at http://xmlns.com/foaf/0.1.

[CARM2008] B. Carminati, E. Ferrari, A. Perego, *Security and Privacy in Social Networks*, volume VII of *Encyclopedia of Information Science and Technology*,IGI Publishing, 2nd edition, 2008, pp. 3369–3376.

[CARM2009a] B. Carminati, E. Ferrari, R. Heatherly, M. Kantarcioglu, B.M. Thuraisingham, A Semantic Web Based Framework for Social Network Access Control, In B. Carminati and J. Joshi, editors, *SACMAT*, ACM, 2009, pp. 177–186.

[CARM2009b] B. Carminati, E. Ferrari, A. Perego, Enforcing Access Control in Web-based Social Networks, *ACM Transactions on Information Systems Security*, Volume 13, #1, 2009, pp. 1–38.

[CHOI2006] H. Choi, S. R. Kruk, S. Grzonkowski, K.Stankiewicz, B. Davis, J. G. Breslin, Trust Models for Community Aware Identity Management, The Identity, Reference and Web Workshop (IRW2006) at the 15th International World Wide Web Conference (WWW2006), 2006.

[CARM2011] B. Carminati, E. Ferrari, R. Heatherly, M. Kantarcioglu, B. Thuraisingham, Semantic Web-based Social Network Access Control, *Computers & Security*, Volume 30, #2-3, 2011, pp. 108–115.

[ELAH2008] N. Elahi, M.M.R. Chowdhury, J. Noll, Semantic Access Control in Web Based Communities, *Computing in the Global Information Technology, 2008. ICCGI'08. The Third International Multi-Conference, Washington, DC, USA*, 2008, pp. 131–136.

[FINI2008] T. W. Finin, A. Joshi, L. Kagal, J. Niu, R.S. Sandhu, W.H. Winsborough, B.M. Thuraisingham, R. OWL BAC: Representing Role based Access Control in OWL, In I. Ray and N. Li, editors, *SACMAT*, ACM, 2008, pp. 73–82.

[HORR2004] I. Horrocks, P.F. Patel-Schneider, H. Boley, S. Tabet, B. Grosof, M. Dean, SWRL: A Semantic Web Rule Language Combining OWL and RuleML. W3C Member Submission, World Wide Web Consortium, May 2004. Available at: http://www.w3.org/Submission/SWRL.

[KRUK2006] S.R. Kruk, S. Grzonkowski, A. Gzella, T. Woroniecki, H. Choi, D-FOAF: Distributed Identity Management with Access Rights Delegation, In R. Mizoguchi, Z. Shi, and F. Giunchiglia, editors, *ASWC*, volume 4185 of *Lecture Notes in Computer Science*, Springer, 2006, pp. 140–154.

[MIKA2007] P. Mika, Social Networks and the Semantic Web, Springer, 2007.

[THUR2020] B. Thuraisingham, Multigenerational Database Inference Controllers, *IEEE Big Data Security Conference*, May 2020.

[TONT2003] G. Tonti, J.M. Bradshaw, R. Jeffers, R. Montanari, N. Suri, A. Uszok, Semantic Web Languages for Policy Representation and Reasoning: A Comparison of KAoS, rei, and ponder, In D. Fensel, K.P. Sycara, and J. Mylopoulos, editors, *International Semantic Web Conference*, volume 2870 of *Lecture Notes in Computer Science*, Springer, 2003, pp. 419–437.

[WWW2006] World Wide Web Consortium, Defining n-ary Relations on the Semantic Web, 2006, http://www.w3.org/TR/swbp-n-aryRelations/

[WWW1999] World Wide Web Consortium, Status for Resource Description Framework (rdf) Model and Syntax Specification, 1999, http://www.w3.org/1999/.status/PR-rdf-syntax-19990105/status

[YAGU2005] M.L. Yague, M.-del-M. Gallardo, A. Mana, Semantic Access Control Model: A Formal Specification, ESORICS: European Symposium on Research in Computer Security, LNCS, Springer-Verlag, 2005.

REFERENCES

18 Inference and Access Control for Big Data

18.1 INTRODUCTION

Inference is the process of forming conclusions from premises. This process is harmful if the user draws unauthorized conclusions from the legitimate responses he/she receives. This problem has come to be known as the inference problem. An inference controller is the device that prevents a user from drawing unauthorized conclusions. We have studied the inference problem extensively in the past. Specifically, we have defined various types of inference strategies and developed inference controllers that handle certain types of inference strategies [THUR1993].

Previous work to build an inference controller to protect data confidentiality was described in the late 1980s and early 1990s [THUR1987, THUR1993]; however, this work was mainly in the area of multi-level secure databases and supported limited reasoning capabilities. Our current work is a substantial improvement over prior efforts with more sophisticated reasoning and policy representation techniques through the use of semantic web technologies [THUR2014]. We use as our data model the Resource Description Framework (RDF), which supports the interoperability of multiple databases having disparate data schemas. In addition, we express policies and rules in terms of semantic web rules and constraints, and we classify data items and relationships between them using semantic web software tools, such as Pellet, Jena, and Protégé [SIRI2007, CARR2004, KNUB2004].

Our work has focused on classifying and protecting provenance data which is a kind of metadata that captures the origins of single data items of interest, as well as other relevant information such as data manipulation operations and temporal information [THUR2014]. Though it is acceptable to represent provenance in any data format, it is sometimes easier to visualize its structure using a directed graph layout. Therefore, we will refer to the provenance data as a directed graph, because a directed graph structure, besides being popular, has many advantages with respect to data modeling in a semantic web environment. The semantic web extends the RDF graph data model to have reasoning capabilities through the use of formal semantics. In our work, we used the reasoning capabilities of the semantic web to support the inference strategies of the inference controller. Furthermore, we presented several new query modification (i.e., rewriting) techniques that can be used to enforce security policies over a provenance graph.

In this chapter, we discuss inference control that employs inference strategies and techniques built around semantic web technologies which can be utilized for inference control in social media. Our work has focused on inference control for provenance data that is represented as RDF graphs. Our methods can be adapted for social network data since such data can also be modeled as RDF graphs. We have also provided the detailed implementation of the inference controller. It should be noted that access control is at the heart of our work on inference control. That is, not only do we prevent access to unauthorized data directly, but we also prevent access to unauthorized data indirectly via inference.

The organization of this chapter is as follows. Our design is discussed in Section 18.2. Query modification is discussed in Section 18.3. Our approach to the implementation is discussed in Section 18.4. Provenance aspects will be discussed in Section 18.5. Implementation details are given in Section 18.6. Concepts in generators are discussed in Section 18.7. A medical example is given in Section 18.8. Constraints are discussed in Section 18.9. Next-generation inference

DOI: 10.1201/9781003081845-29

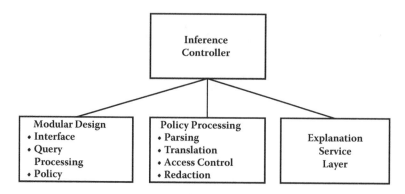

FIGURE 18.1 Architecture for an inference controller.

controllers are discussed in Section 18.10. Section 18.11 summarizes this chapter. Figure 18.1 describes an architecture for an inference controller.

18.2 DESIGN OF AN INFERENCE CONTROLLER

18.2.1 ARCHITECTURE

The unsolvability of the inference problem was proved in [THUR1990]. Its complexity is an open problem. While there is a need to analyze the complexity classes of the inference problem, still a lot of research has been pivoted around the implementations based on traditional databases. However, since provenance has a logical graph structure, it can also be represented and stored in a graph data model, therefore, it is not limited to any particular data format. Although our focus in this design is on building an inference controller over the graph representation of provenance, our inference controller could be used to protect the case with the traditional database as well. Also, the use of an RDF data model does not overburden our implementation with restrictions, because other data formats are well served by an RDF data model. Furthermore, tools such as the one discussed in [BIZE2003] convert relational data to RDF data.

Our architecture takes a user's input query and returns a response which has been pruned using a set of user-defined policy constraints. We assume that a user could interact with our system to obtain both traditional and provenance data. However, as our focus will be on protecting provenance, we will focus more on the design of the inference controller and the provenance data layers.

In our design, we assume that the available information is divided into two parts: the actual data and provenance. Both the data and provenance are represented as RDF graphs. The reader should note that we do not make any assumptions about how the actual information is stored. A user may have stored data and provenance in two different triple stores or in the same store. A user application can submit a query for access to the data and its associated provenance or vice versa. Figure 18.2 shows our design and some modules in our prototype implementation of an inference controller over provenance data. We now present a description of the modules in Figure 18.2.

18.2.1.1 User Interface Manager

The user interface manager is responsible for processing the user's requests, authenticating the user and providing suitable responses back to the user. The interface manager also provides an abstraction layer that allows a user to interact with the system. A user can therefore pose either a data query or a provenance query to this layer. The user interface manager also determines whether the query should be evaluated against the traditional data or provenance.

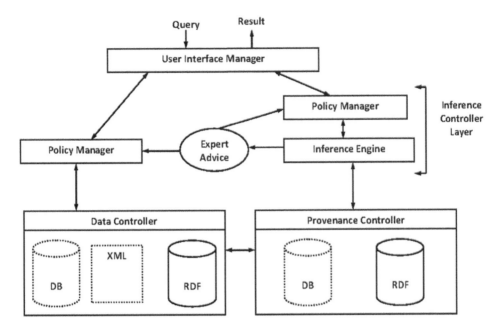

FIGURE 18.2 System modules.

18.2.1.2   Policy Manager

The policy manager is responsible for ensuring that the querying user is authorized to use the system. It evaluates the policies against a user's query and associated query results to ensure that no confidential information is released to unauthorized users. The policy manager may enforce the policies against the traditional data or against the provenance data. Each data type may have its own policy manager, for example, the traditional data may be stored in a different format from the provenance data. Hence, we may require different implementations of each policy manager.

18.2.1.3   Inference Engine

The inference engine is the heart of the inference controller. The engine is equipped to use a variety of inference strategies that are supported by a particular reasoner. Since there are many implementations of reasoners available, our inference controller offers an added feature of flexibility, whereby we can select from among any reasoning tool for each reasoning task. We can improve the efficiency of the inference controller because each inference strategy (or a combination of strategies) could be executed on a separate processor. An inference engine typically uses software programs that have the capability of reasoning over some data representation, for example a relational data model or an RDF graph model representation.

18.2.1.4   Data controller

The data controller is a suite of software programs that stores and manages access to data. The data could be stored in any format such as in a relational database, in XML files or in an RDF store. The controller accepts requests for information from the policy manager (or the inference engine layer) if a policy allows the requesting user access to the data item. This layer then executes the request over the stored data and returns results back to the policy layer (or inference engine layer) where it is re-evaluated based on a set of policies.

18.2.1.5   Provenance Controller

The provenance controller is used to store and manage provenance information that is associated with data items that are present in the data controller. In the case when we select a graph representation of provenance, the provenance controller stores information in the form of logical graph structures in any appropriate data representation format. This controller also records the on-going activities associated with the data items stored in the data controller. This controller takes as input a graph query and evaluates it over the provenance information. This query evaluation returns a sub-graph back to the inference controller layer where it is re-examined using a set of policies.

18.3   INFERENCE CONTROL THROUGH QUERY MODIFICATION

18.3.1   QUERY MODIFICATION

Query modification technique has been used in the past to handle discretionary security and views [STON1975]. This technique has been extended to include mandatory security in [DWYE1987]. In our design of the query processor, this technique is used by the inference engine to modify the query depending on the security constraints, the previous responses released, and real world information. When the modified query is posed, the response generated will not violate security.

Consider the architecture for the inference controller discussed in Section 18.2. The inference engine has access to the knowledge base which includes security constraints, previously released responses, and real world information. Conceptually, one can think of the database as part of the knowledge base. We illustrate the query modification technique with examples. The actual implementation of this technique could adapt any of the proposals given in [GALL1978] for deductive query processing.

We have conducted extensive investigation on applying query modification for processing security policies (also known as constraints) to determine whether any unauthorized inferences can be deduced by the user [THUR1993]. Our inference controller will then sanitize the data and give the results to the user. Much of our prior work has built inference controllers on top of relational databases. In our current work, we have developed inference controllers for semantic web data.

18.3.2   QUERY MODIFICATION WITH RELATIONAL DATA

Security policies are rules (or constraints) which assign confidential values (or scores) to data items. In implementing these rules in a semantic web environment, we have several options available to help us implement these rules. A policy can be handled by TBox at design time, by a query modification module at run time and by a release knowledge base, which tracks the release of provenance.

In this section, we discuss query modification with relational data. We have obtained this information from our prior work. Figure 18.3 illustrates inference control through query modification.

18.3.2.1   Query Modification

We could modify the query according to the access control rules, for example, Retrieve all employee information where salary < 30K and Dept is not Security.

Example 18.1: *rules: John does not have access to Salary in EMP and Budget in DEPT.*

Query: *join the EMP and DEPT relations on Dept #.*
Modify Query: *Join EMP and DEPT on Dept # and project on all attributes except Salary and Budget*
Output *is the resulting query*

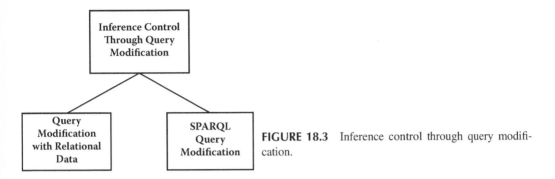

FIGURE 18.3   Inference control through query modification.

- Security Constraints/Access Control Rules/Security Policies
  - *Simple constraint:* John cannot access the attribute Salary of relation EMP
  - *Content-based constraint:* If relation MISS contains information about missions in the Middle East, then John cannot access MISS
  - *Association-based constraint:* Ship's location and mission taken together cannot be accessed by John; individually each attribute can be accessed by John
  - *Release constraint:* After X is released, Y cannot be accessed by John
  - *Aggregate constraint:* Ten or more tuples taken together cannot be accessed by John
  - *Dynamic constraint:* After the mission, information about the mission can be accessed by John

- Security Constraints for Healthcare
  - *Simple constraint:* Only doctors can access medical records
  - *Content-based constraint:* If the patient has AIDS, then this information is private
  - *Association-based constraint:* Names and medical records taken together are private
  - *Release constraint:* After medical records are released, names cannot be released
  - *Aggregate constraint:* The collection of patients is private, individually public
  - *Dynamic constraint:* After the patient dies, information about him becomes public

- Query Modification Algorithm
  - *Inputs:* Query, Access Control Rules
  - *Output:* Modified Query
  - *Algorithm:*
    - Given a query Q, examine all the access control rules relevant to the query
    - Introduce a Where Clause to the query that negates access to the relevant attributes in the access control rules

18.3.3 SPARQL QUERY MODIFICATION

RDF is increasingly used to store information as assertions about a domain. This includes both confidential and public information. SPARQL has been selected as a query language that extracts data from RDF graphs. As confidential data are accessed during the querying process, we need to filter SPARQL queries so that only authorized information is released with respect to some confidentiality policy. Our aim is to rewrite the SPARQL queries so that the results returned are compliant with the confidential policies.

A considerable amount of work has been carried out in the area of databases that apply query modification techniques over the SQL querying language. These traditional approaches use rewrite procedures to modify the WHERE clause so that additional restrictions are added according to some constraints in the set of policies. More recently, the work in [OULM2012] describes a query modification technique based on RDF/SPARQL. However, their techniques deal with privacy and do not take inference control into consideration. Our focus will be on applying similar query modification techniques to SPARQL queries.

We design security mechanisms that control the evaluation of SPARQL queries to prevent the disclosure of confidential provenance information. Our approach is to modify the graph patterns in the SPARQL query by adding filters and/or property functions that evaluate over a triple pattern. These approaches may return answers different from the user's initial query intent. It may be necessary to decide on appropriate actions in these cases. We propose two approaches which may be followed. The first approach checks the query validity against that of the initial query and notifies the user that the query validity is not guaranteed. The second approach takes into consideration that a feedback about the validity of a query result may lead the user to draw undesirable inferences.

In some cases it may be possible to return only the answers that we know comply with the policy constraints. In other cases, it may be necessary to replace a restricted subgraph satisfying a query according to some transformation rules that leaves the released knowledge base consistent with the policy constraints. Yet another approach may be to lie; this is similar to polyinstantiation in multi-level secure databases where users at different clearance levels see different versions of reality.

18.3.4 QUERY MODIFICATION FOR ENFORCING CONSTRAINTS

Approaches for modifying the graph patterns in a SPARQL query make use of different techniques, for example, SPARQL filters and property functions, graph transformations and match/apply pattern. To determine the type of triple with respect to a security classification, the inference engine would use a domain ontology to determine the concept each data item belongs as well as a query modification based on a SPARQL BGP (Basic Graph Pattern Matching) transformation.

18.3.4.1 SPARQL Query Filter

The SPARQL specification provides another technique for modifying a graph pattern [PRUD2006]. SPARQL FILTERs restrict solutions to those for which the filter expression evaluates to TRUE. We briefly discuss how to rewrite a SPARQL query by applying SPARQL filters. The following is a SPARQL query requesting the age of a patient.

http://cs.utdallas.edu/semanticweb/Prov-AC/medical#

```
PREFIX med:
SELECT?patient
WHERE {?patient med:age?age }
After query modification, we restrict the query to only patients with age greater
than 18.
```

http://cs.utdallas.edu/semanticweb/Prov-AC/medical#

```
PREFIX med:
SELECT ?patient
WHERE { ?patient med:age ?age
    FILTER (?age> 18)
}
```

TABLE 18.1
Regular Path Expression

Uri	A URI or a prefixed name. A path of length one.
^*elt*	Reverse path (object to subject).
(elt)	A group path elt, brackets control precedence.
*elt*1/*elt*2	A sequence path of *elt*1, followed by *elt*2
*elt*1 ^ *elt*2	Shorthand for *elt*1 ^ *elt*2, that is elt1 followed by reverse elt2.
*elt*1 | *elt*2	A alternative path of *elt*1, or *elt*2 (all possibilities are tried)
*elt**	A path of zero or more occurrences of *elt*.
elt+	A path of one or more occurrences of *elt*.
elt?	A path of zero or one *elt*.
elt{*n,m*}	A path between n and m occurrences of *elt*.
elt{*n*}	Exactly n occurrences of elt. A fixed length path.
elt{*n,*}	n or more occurrences of *elt*.
elt{,*n*}	Between 0 and n occurrences of *elt*.
!*uri*	A path matching a property which isn't uri (negated property set)
!(*uri*1 |...|*uri*$_N$)	A path matching a property that isn't any of uri1...*uri*$_N$ (negated property set)

18.3.4.2 Property Paths

A property path is a possible route through a graph between two graph nodes. A trivial case is a property path of length exactly 1, which is a triple pattern. A property path expression (or just "path") is similar to a regular expression string but over properties, not characters. Table 18.1 describes regular path expressions as well as their descriptions.

18.3.4.3 Property Path Queries

These queries allow us to modify the property of a triple pattern (note that the property can be a directed label edge or a directed path between a subject and an object). One important application is supporting regular expressions. We intend to build constraints over the paths in a graph pattern as a way of reducing leakages which cause the inference problem. We write code that can execute in accordance to the content of a user query. The code can examine various aspects of a user query, such as the literal text of a triple or triple patterns and take immediate actions to ensure the appropriate policy constraints are intact. The following is an example of using regular expressions as part of the BGP of a SELECT query over a provenance graph, which uses the OPM vocabulary.

```
{
med:Doc_n_4 gleen:Subgraph("([opm:WasDerivedFrom]*/
   [opm:WasGeneratedBy]/
   [opm:WasControlledBy])" ?x).
}
```

This query pattern would give access to the artifacts, processes and agents on the path to John's record. This query is written using the Gleen regular expression library [DETW2008]. The Gleen library [DETW2008] provides two useful functions, OnPath and Subgraph. The OnPath function can be used to locate all of the resources in a graph that stand in a particular relationship pattern to a query resource by returning the set of reachable resources. The Subgraph function returns the set of resources and properties traversed on paths to these results.

Secure Data Science

18.3.4.4   Overview of Query Modification

An overview of a query modification for SPARQL could be as follows:

1. Iterate over the graph patterns.
2. Identify the $sub(t)$, $obj(t)$, $pred(t)$ for each triple t in a graph pattern.
3. If a $sub(t)$, $obj(t)$ or $pred(t)$ is confidential then isolate t or transform it.
4. Create a new query with modified graph patterns.

18.3.4.5   Graph transformation of a SPARQL Query BGP

SPARQL is based around graph pattern matching and a SPARQL query BGP is a graph pattern (i.e., a set of triples) [PRUD2006].

Definition 18.1: *(Graph pattern) A SPARQL graph pattern expression is defined recursively as follows:*

1. A triple pattern is a graph pattern.
2. If P1 and P2 are graph patterns, then expressions (P1 AND P2), (P1 OPT P2), and (P1 UNION P2) are graph patterns.
3. If P is a graph pattern and R is a built-in SPARQL condition, then the expression (PFILTER R) is a graph pattern.
4. If P is a graph pattern, V is a set of variables and X ∈ U ∪V then (X GRAPH P)is a graph pattern.

In a SPARQL query rewriting process, a BGP is replaced with an updated graph pattern. A graph transformation rule takes the original BGP as its LHS (left hand side) and specifies another pattern as the RHS (right hand side).

Example 18.2: *Hide the surgery of a patient.*

```
{
med:Doc_n_4 gleen:OnPath("([opm:WasDerivedFrom]*/
[opm:WasGeneratedBy])"?x).
}
```

This pattern matches a path where an entry in the patient's record, which is optionally derived from other versions of the patient's record, is created as a result of some process. That process is the surgery. This pattern, when it is the LHS of a graph transformation rule, could be replaced by another pattern, the RHS of the rule, so that the surgery is not disclosed. A possible RHS pattern would be the following:

```
{
med:Doc_n_4 gleen:OnPath("([opm:WasDerivedFrom])"?x).
}
```

This pattern would only return the previous version of the patient's record without any entry that some version of the record had a path to the surgery.

18.3.4.6   Match Pattern/ApplyPattern

In [ORAC12], a data access constraint is described using two graph patterns: a match pattern and an apply pattern. A match pattern determines the type of access restriction to enforce and binds one or more variables to the corresponding data instances accessed in the user query.

Example 18.3: *A data access constraint using match and apply patterns.*

```
Match: {?contract pred:hasContractValue?cvalue }
Apply: {?contract pred:hasManageremp:Andy }
```

This example ensures that the *hasContractValue* of a contract can be accessed only if *Andy* is the manager of the contract being accessed. The important feature in Example 18.3 is that a variable defined in the match pattern is used in the corresponding apply pattern to enforce the access restrictions on the identified resources.

18.3.4.6.1 Processing Rules

There is a difference between a query engine that simply queries an RDF graph, but does not handle rules and an inference engine that also handles rules. In the literature, this difference is not always clear. The complexity of an inference engine is a lot higher than a query engine. The reason is that rules permit us to make sequential deductions. In the execution of a query, these deductions are to be constructed. This is not necessary in the case of a query engine. Note that there are other examples of query engines that rely on a formal model for directed labeled graphs such as DQL and RQL [FIKE2002, KARV2002].

Rules also support a logic base that is inherently more complex than the logic in the situation without rules. For an RDF query engine, only the simple principles of entailment on graphs are necessary. RuleML is an important effort to define rules that are usable for the World Wide Web. The inference web is a recent realization that defines a system for handling different inference engines on the semantic web [MCGU2004].

18.3.4.6.2 Enforcing Constraints by Graph Rewriting

Graph rewriting, also called graph transformation, is a technique for creating a new graph out of an original graph by using some automatic machine. This is usually a compilation abstraction, where the basic idea is that the state of a computation can be represented as a graph, and further steps in the computation are then represented as transformation rules on the graph [EHRI2006, ROZE1997].

Graph rewriting came out of logic and database theory where graphs are treated as database instances, and rewriting operations as a mechanism for defining queries and views. Popular graph rewriting approaches include double-pushout approach, single-pushout approach and algebraic approach [EHRI1991]. The approach we describe is similar to the one for single-pushout approach. A graph rewriting system consists of a set of rewrite rules of the form $p: L \rightarrow R$, with L being a graph pattern (or left hand side) and R being the replacement graph (or right hand side of the rule). A graph rewrite rule is applied to the original graph by searching for an occurrence of the pattern graph and replacing the found occurrence by the existence of the replacement graph.

18.4 OUR APPROACH TO THE IMPLEMENTATION OF THE INFERENCE CONTROLLER

Our approach to implementing the Inference Controller is illustrated in Figure 18.4. Traditionally, we protect data using policies such as access control policies and sanitization-based policies. However, current mechanisms for enforcing these policies do not operate over data which takes the form of a directed graph [BRAU2008]. Additionally, users can infer sensitive information from the results returned by performing frequent queries over a provenance graph. We are particularly interested in any conclusion formed from premises where the conclusion is formed without any expressed or prior approval from anyone or any organization that controls or processes the premises or information from which the conclusion is formed. We also refer to the process of forming these conclusions from the premises as inference. When the information inferred is something unauthorized for the user to see, we say we have an instance of the inference problem. This problem is always present in systems which contain both public and private information. The inferred knowledge could depend on data obtained from a knowledge base, or it could depend on some prior knowledge possessed by the user in addition to the information obtained from the knowledge base [THUR1993].

The inferred knowledge obtained from a knowledge base alone could be used to reveal what is and what is not in a knowledge base. For example, if a user asks for information relating to a patient's X-ray procedure, any response could indicate whether the patient had an X-ray or not. In general, a positive answer to a query discloses what is in a knowledge base, while a negative answer could have more than one interpretation. For example, a user could interpret a negative answer to mean that the answer is not in the knowledge base, or the user could interpret that it is in the knowledge base, but the knowledge base chooses not to reveal the correct answer to the query. These two interpretations could also depend on whether the knowledge base uses a closed-world or an open-world assumption [REIT1977]. Normally, an open-world assumption indicates that data are incomplete or it could be somewhere else in the system and are not restricted to a particular file or location. In a closed-world assumption, data are complete and a negative answer to a query usually indicates that the data are not present in the knowledge base. We assume an open-world assumption; in particular, a user should not be able to distinguish, with accuracy, between the presence of facts hidden by the inference controller and the absence of facts that are available elsewhere.

Our main focus is on classifying and protecting social media data presented as RDF graphs. However, our initial implementation of the inference controller was for provenance data which is present in numerous domains including for social media data. Our inference controller can be adapted for social media data because our social networks as represented as RDF graphs. The semantic web extends the RDF graph model to have inferencing capabilities by using formal semantics. It is this inferencing service that we use to support the inference strategies of the inference controller. Furthermore, we have shown how to perform new query modification techniques to enforce the security policies over a provenance graph which can be extended for social media graphs discussed in Chapters 19 and 20.

A semantic reasoner enables us to infer logical consequences from a set of axioms. It provides a richer set of mechanisms that enables us to draw inferences from a provenance graph encoded using OWL vocabulary. We can specify the inference rules by means of an ontology language. Reasoners often use first-order predicate logic to perform reasoning. The inference proceeds by forward chaining and backward chaining. (Figure 18.4).

18.5   INFERENCE AND PROVENANCE

The organization of this section of this chapter is as follows. In Section 18.5.1, we provide examples to motivate the reader. In Section 18.5.2, we discuss approaches to the inference problem. Inferences in provenance are discussed in Section 18.5.4. We provide use cases in Section 18.5.4. Rule processing is discussed in Section 18.5.5

18.5.1   EXAMPLES

Rules of inference can be used to infer a conclusion from a premise to create an argument. It is important to point out that a set of rules can be used to infer any valid conclusion if it is complete. A set of rules is sound if no invalid conclusion is drawn. Some rules may be redundant and thus a sound and complete set of rules need not include every rule when arriving at a conclusion. As stated earlier, when the conclusion is not something authorized to be seen by a user, we have a security leak and a case of the inference problem.

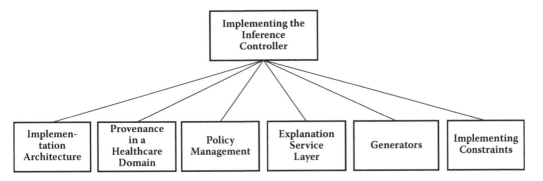

FIGURE 18.4 Implementing an inference controller.

A rule can be invoked in forward-chaining or backward-chaining:

- If a forward-chaining mode, we are given some set of statements and we use the rules to deduce new statements. In principle, repeated application of forward-chaining will find all facts that can be deduced by the inference rule from some initial set of facts from a knowledge base.

Example 18.4:

Consider the following two rules:

1. (med: HeartSurgery opm:wasControlledBy?X) → (X rdf:type med:Surgeon)
2. (med:Results_n_1 opm:Used med:Doc_n_6) ^ (med:Results_n_1 opm:wasControlledBy?X) → (X rdf:type med:Surgeon)

If our knowledge base contains the following triples:

```
<med:HeartSurgery_n_1 ><opm:Used ><med:Doc_n_5 >
<med:Doc_n_6 ><opm:WasGeneratedBy>< med:HeartSurgery_n_1 >
<med:Doc_n_6 ><opm:wasDerivedFrom ><med:Doc_n_5 >
<med:Results_n_1 ><opm:Used >< med:Doc_n_6 >
<med:Results_n_1 ><opm:WasControlledBy><med:Surgeon_n_1 >
<med:HeartSurgery_n_1 ><opm:WasControlledBy><med:Surgeon_n_1 >
```

We can conclude that ?X is a Surgeon, by using the last triple in the above knowledge base. The triple (med:Surgeon_n_1 rdf:type med:Surgeon) would then be added to the knowledge base. Note that the execution of rule 2 would also add this triple to the knowledge base.

In backward-chaining, we are given some expression and we determine all of the antecedents that must be satisfied in order for the given consequent expression to be true.

Example 18.5:

Consider the following rules:

1. (med: HeartSurgery opm:wasControlledBy?X) → (X rdf:type med:Surgeon)
2. (med:Results_n_1 opm:Used med:Doc_n_6) ∧ (med:Results_n_1 opm:wasControlledBy?X) → (X rdf:type med:Surgeon)

If we want to satisfy rule 1, the reasoner woud conclude that med: HeartSurgery opm:wasControlledBy?X. Given the statement:
`<med:HeartSurgery_n_1 ><opm:WasControlledBy><med:Surgeon_n_1 >`
`This derivation will cause the reasoner to produce med:Surgeon_n_1 as the answer`
`to the question (X rdf:type med:Surgeon).`

18.5.2 Approaches to the Inference Problem

Different approaches can be employed for building an inference controller. For example, we can use state-of-the-art machine learning techniques to build a learner that automatically learns to recognize complex patterns and make intelligent decisions based on some explicit data. We can also build an inference controller which uses semantic web technologies equipped with reasoners, which perform inferences over the data in the knowledge base. In this section, we illustrate some approaches of our inference controller which are based on the use of semantic web technologies.

Aggregation problem is a special case of the inference problem – collections of data elements is secret but the individual elements are Unclassified.

$$A \sqcup B \sqcup C \sqsubseteq Secret$$

We could enforce this rule by checking if there are any sensitive concepts in the provenance KB or the Released KB.

$$A \sqcap B \sqcap C \sqsubseteq Secret$$

$$\geq 10R. \, (A \sqcap B \sqcap C)$$

If we know that at least ten person have a property, then classify KB.

Association problem: attributes A and B taken together are Secret, but individually they are Unclassified.

Example 18.3: *AandBandC → Secret*.

We could encode this as a SWRL rule, then check the priovenance KB or the Released KB if there is anything secret.

$$(med: Doc\_n\_6 \; opm: wasDerivedFrom \; med: Doc\_n\_5)$$
$$\wedge (med: Doc\_n\_6 \; opm: WasGeneratedBy \; med: HeartSurgery\_n\_1)$$
$$\wedge (med: HeartSurgery\_n\_1 \; opm: WasControlledBy \; med: Surgeon\_n\_1)$$
$$\rightarrow$$
$$(med: HeartSurgery\_n\_1 \; med: Classification \; Secret)$$

If we consider the surgery operation to be sensitive, we can classify it as Secret. Similary, the resulting version of the patient's record that was generated by the this operation should be considered secret as well.

(med: Doc_n_6 opm: wasDerivedFrom med: Doc_n_5)

$\land$(med: Doc_n_6 opm: WasGeneratedBy med: HeartSurgery_n_1)

$\land$(med: HeartSurgery_n_1 opm: WasControlledBy med: Surgeon_n_1)

$\rightarrow$

(med: Doc_n_6 med: Classification Secret)

Example 18.4: *Something that is all three classes is private*:

$$A \sqcap B \sqcap C \sqsubseteq Secret$$

Example 18.5: *If at most one individual in all three classes, then classify KB*:

$$\leq 1R. (A \sqcap B \sqcap C)$$

18.5.2.1 Domain Restriction

We can put a range restriction on a qualified value for a property as secret. For example, a property whose value is something with 9 digits is Sensitive. Note that a SSN contains 9 digits, therefore if something with 9 digits is released, then we need to classify the KB. Similarly, we could specify that something with 16 digits is a credit card number.

18.5.2.2 Statistical Reasoning

In statistical reasoning we are given the summary data; the object is to learn macro properties about a population.

Example 18.6: *If at most one heart surgeon on duty during a patient's visit and we reveal the following triple to a user*:

```
<med:HeartSurgery_n_1 ><opm:WasControlledBy><_:b>
```

Then, the user can conclude that the surgeon on duty performed the surgery operation on the patient.

18.5.2.2.1 Machine Learning Techniques

In [CHAN1998], the authors approach the inference problem with a parsimonious downgrading framework using decision trees. The assumption is that when Low needs information for purposes such as performance and functionality, High must decide whether to give (i.e., downgrade) information to Low. In other words, when High wishes to downgrade a set of data to Low, it may be necessary, because of inference channels, to trim the set. Basically, decision trees are used to form rules from the downgraded data High makes available to Low. Remember that we can use the nonsensitive attributes of an individual to arrive at (i.e., predict) the sensitive attribute, using rules which are trained on similar individuals (occurring in previous released data). In parsimonious downgrading, a cost measure is assigned to the potential downgraded information that is not sent to Low. The idea is to determine whether the loss of functionality (to Low) associated with (High) not downgrading this data is worth the extra confidentiality. Decision trees assist in analyzing the potential inference channels in the data that one wishes to downgrade. The authors assign penalty functions to this parsimonious downgrading in order to minimize the amount of information that is not downgraded, and compare the penalty costs to the extra confidentiality that is obtained.

Other approaches covered by our inference engine include the following.

- *Handling inference during database design:* This approach is considered rather static. It depends mainly on schema design and integrity constraints. It was also pointed out that it is not very convenient to keep changing the database schema in response to each user's query.
- *Handling inference during query processing:* The bulk of the research mostly focuses on query modification mainly because queries are dynamic.

18.5.3 INFERENCES IN PROVENANCE

A user can infer sensitive information from the results returned from performing frequent queries over a provenance graph. We are particularly interested in any conclusion formed from premises, where the conclusion is formed without any expressed or prior approval from anyone or any organization that controls or processes the premises or information from which the conclusion is formed. Furthermore, our goal is to examine the inference problem that occurs with provenance data. We need automated software tools to discover and evaluate the interesting patterns and semantic associations in a provenance store. The amount of information generated by recording fine-grained provenance is an important but time-consuming work for security analysts. We can record the provenance using a semantic web language so that intelligent agents and reasoners can automate the inference without compromising the semantics of the underlying provenance.

18.5.3.1 Implicit Information in Provenance

A provenance document contains both data items and their relationships formulated as a directed graph. An intermediate node on a path in this graph may contain sensitive information such as the identity of an agent who filed an intelligence report, and so we need efficient tools for querying and inference as well. Also, we need to support large provenance graphs, and the ability to query this graph so that we can build user views that filter user queries.

Security policies (i.e., security constraints) are used to determine who can access a document and under what conditions access is to be granted. In intelligence, it may be necessary to guard one's methods and sources; hence, an access control policy could limit access to the source of a report to sister agencies. However, these policies are limited to creating views and do not take into account implicit information in the provenance and we need to develop policies that scale with the provenance data. We need to build large data stores for provenance. Provenance can be recorded in any knowledge representation language, for example, RDF, RDFS and OWL. Using these languages allows us to later perform inference over the provenance graph. Therefore, we could determine the implicit information over the provenance graph.

18.5.4 USE CASES OF PROVENANCE

The use cases for provenance can be found at: UseCases For Provenance Workshop (http://wiki.esi.ac.uk/UseCasesForProvenanceWorkshop)

Another useful source for use cases can be found at http://www.w3.org/2005/Incubator/prov/wiki/Use_Cases. This gives the initial use cases gathered by W3C incubator group.

For a list of security issues in provenance by the W3C group, see http://www.w3.org/2005/Incubator/prov/wiki/Security_issues_in_provenance_use_cases.

Use cases are also available at the url

http://lists.w3.org/Archives/Public/public-xg-prov/2010Jan/0014.html
http://arxiv.org/PS_cache/arxiv/pdf/1002/1002.0433v1.pdf

We construct use cases involving who/why/when/where queries. We may not know the answers to these queries for a particular domain, so revealing the provenance could be our best source for these answers. On the other hand, we may need to protect the who/when/where/why of a particular resource or node in a provenance graph. We present case studies in this section in order to illustrate what we want to achieve when we apply semantic web technologies to provenance information. In particular, we discuss some of the use cases using a toy hospital example. While we try to keep these use cases as close to our medical domain as possible, we also discuss use cases in other domains.

Data discovery encompasses the provenance of observing and capturing patient's activities at all stages in a visit and operations:

> A physician must rely on the historical information of a patient's record, such as who or what causes a record to be in its current state. Also the contents of the record can change with time which can result in a temporal fine-grained capture of the provenance information for decision processes.

18.5.4.1 Dataset Documentation

This allows physicians to retrieve the current and most up-to-date snapshot of a patient's record as well as its origin. This documentation supports further processing of the record by emergency personnel and drug dispensory units.

18.5.4.2 Pinpoint Errors in a Process

A where query for a patient would be useful if we need to pinpoint where in the process a possible risk could occur as a result of performing a surgery on the patient. For example, a where-provenance query could be used to identify at which phase in the flow any medication administered to the patient had a negative interaction with the ones the patient is already taking. By using where queries, we could compare the information in an earlier version of the record (which is generated prior to surgery) with that in a later version of the record (which incorporates the recording of events during the surgery).

18.5.4.3 Identifying Private Information in Query Logs

There are pieces of information that can also be used in identifying private information. Queries for phone numbers, addresses, and names of individuals are all useful in narrowing down the population, and thus increases the chance of a successful attack. From the query logs, it is possible to generate the distribution of queries for a user, the query timing, and also the content of the queries. Furthermore, it is possible to cluster users and to some extent augment the query responses with the user behavior. Finally, we can also correlate queries (e.g., those who query for X also query for Y).

18.5.4.4 Use Case: Who Said That?

The scenario is based on a financial architecture being done for a government agency. This is a large architecture involving information, services and processes. Most of the stakeholders are non-technical, many are accountants. As with any such architecture, it is based on a successive set of inputs and meetings with stakeholders - not all at the same time. While this architecture was not being done with semweb tooling (it was UML), the same situation arises despite the formalism used. Near the end of the project, one of the stakeholders was reviewing an information model for orders. This was not the first time this stakeholder had seen this part of the model, but they had not reviewed it in some time. The stakeholder pointed to a property on part of the model dealing with orders and asked: "Where did that come from? Who told you to put it in?" Certainly a reasonable question, but one we could not answer without a long dig through manual notes. There was nothing in the model to say where that property came from, when it was added or under what authority. In addition, the stakeholder noted that something they thought was in the model had been removed and wanted to know where it had gone. Again, the tooling could not help. *Conclusion:* The source (both the person entering the data and who told them to put it there), the situation (such as a meeting) and the time of each assertion in the model needs to be tracked. This should be part of the core knowledge management infrastructure and leads directly to the trustworthiness of the knowledge base as it evolves over time.

18.5.4.5   Use Case: Cheating Dictator

It seems that certain intelligence activities look at things like the college transcripts of interesting people and use these to draw conclusions about their capability and character. The story (and it may just be a story) is that "Saddam Hussein" attended a college in Australia decades ago. The transcripts for that college were obtained and made part of his personal profile. This profile impacted important political and military activities. It became apparent that for propaganda purposes these transcripts had been modified. Analysts wanted to know what inferences had been made by human and automated means, what information was inferred and how that could change Saddam's profile and potential actions. There was no way to trace this information path, making many of the opinions questionable. This is, of course, only one small example in the world where information may be intentionally falsified or obscured and where the resulting conclusions are critically important.The source and down-stream impact of information is critical, particularly when sources and information quality are re-evaluated. *Conclusion:* The track of inferences may span decades and this track may be of critical strategic value. In addition, inference is a combination of human and automated activities that affect down-stream conclusions.

In this use case, we show that by annotating the entities in our generated workflow with actual attributes taken from the web, we can verify qualifications of physicians and also point the querying user to appropriate URLs. These URLs could be part of the annotations about entities in our provenance graph, but they mainly serve to point to actual sources that verify the credentials of physicians.

Other uses cases include the following:

Aerospace engineering: maintain a historical record of design processes, up to 99 years.

Organ transplant management: tracking of previous decisions, crucial to maximize the efficiency in matching and recovery rate of patients

Below are some examples that illustrate policies relevant to the healthcare domain:

Example 18.7: Protecting the name of the physician.

In this case, any query that is issued should generate a response that does not divulge the name of the physician.

Example 18.8: For each patient, we generate workflows which capture the steps of various procedures generally performed in a hospital. In particular, we described surgery, general check-ups, post-care operations, etc.

18.5.5   Processing Rules

The inference rules can be encoded and processed in more than one format. These include encoding the rules using SPARQL queries, encoding the rules using description logics and finally the most expressive rules can be encoded as SWRL rules. There are differences in these approaches. A particular choice depends on the size of the knowledge base, the expressiveness of the rules and decidability. A query processing engine does not handle inference rules, but is still powerful. For example, we can query for entailments in an RDF graph encoding of provenance. These queries can also be used to discover paths in a provenance graph (i.e, using regular expression path queries). The results of these queries can be combined to provide answers to complex inference problems. Also, where scalability is a factor, the best option is to query for the pieces of information and combine the relevant parts in a smaller knowledge base. On the other hand, there are cases where it may not be feasible to enumerate all the possible queries that will answer a particular inference problem. Therefore, we may need automated reasoners enriched with enough expressive power to do the inference for us. These reasoners may also produce new deductions that were previously unseen by a query engine alone. However, with this power comes a price: decidability.

Rules are normally inherently more complex than the logic in the situation without rules. For example, in an RDF query engine, only the simple principles of entailment on graphs are necessary. RuleML is an important effort to define rules that are usable for the world wide web. The inference web is a recent realization that defines a system for handling different inferencing engines on the semantic web [MCGU2003].

18.6   IMPLEMENTATION DETAILS

18.6.1   ARCHITECTURE

Figure 18.5 presents the implementation of an inference controller for provenance. This inference controller is built using a modular approach, therefore it is very flexible in that most of the modules can be extended or replaced by another application module. For example, an application user may substitute the policy parser module that handles the parsing of the high-level policies to a low-level policy object. This substitution would allow the application user to continue using his/her business policies independent of our software implementation of the provenance inference controller. Essentially, we have followed a "plug-and-play" approach for implementing the inference controller. We have used open source products as much as possible in our implementation.

The products we have used in our implementation include Jena and Pellet. Our policies and data are represented in RDF. Jena is used to manage the RDF data. Our reasoner is based on Pellet. That is, our inference controller reasons about the policies and the data utilizing Pellet. We built additional inference strategies utilizing Pellet. When a user poses a query in SPARQL, the inference controller will examine the policies, rewrite the query based on the policies, query the Jena RDF store and retrieve the data that the user is authorized to see. In the next several sections, we will give examples of how our inference controller functions based on a healthcare applications.

18.6.2   PROVENANCE IN A HEALTHCARE DOMAIN

The healthcare domain sees provenance as a critical component of its operations. The provenance can be used to facilitate the communication and coordination between organizations and among members of a medical team. It can be used to provide an integrated view of the execution of treatment processes, to analyze the performance of distributed healthcare services, and to carry out

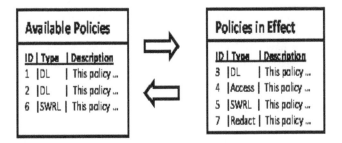

FIGURE 18.5   Implementation architecture.

audits of a system to assess that, for a given patient, the proper decisions were made and the proper procedures were followed [KIFO06].

We describe a medical domain with respect to sources available online such as http://www.webmd.com/. Our medical domain is made up of patients, physicians, nurses, technicians, equipments, medical procedures, etc. We focus on one example of the medical domain, a fictitious hospital. This is a toy example of a hospital that carries out procedures described at credible websites such as http://www.nlm.nih.gov/. These procedures include heart surgery procedures, hip replacement procedures, etc. Since the procedures are described by actual documents on the web, our generated workflow structures typically follow a set of guidelines that are also known to the user. However, the workflows generated by our system may not reflect exactly what goes on in a real hospital. We take into consideration that real hospitals follow guidelines related to a patient's privacy, therefore, our fictitious hospital generates workflows so that the entities in the provenance graph are known only internally. This ensures that the content of a record (i.e., an artifact), the agent who generated a version of a record, the time when the record was updated and the workflow processes are only revealed to a user via queries. Furthermore, the laws governing the release of the provenance (i.e., the contents of the generated workflow) are enforced by policies which are implemented by translating them into a suitable format for use internally by our system.

18.6.2.1   Populating the Provenance Knowledge Base

The provenance knowledge base is updated using a set of generators. There are background generators which are responsible for extracting background information that is normally available online. There is also a workflow generator that produces the actual provenance. The workflow generator produces synthetic provenance data that is not available online. It is this provenance data that has subsets which we must protect. We populate the provenance store by extracting information related to a healthcare domain. The healthcare domain is suitable in two ways. First, this domain actually records provenance and second, data about this domain is partially available online [KIFO2006].

18.6.2.2   Generating and Populating the Knowledge Base

We create a set of seeds which consists of a first name, a last name, a state and city. Each seed is used to create a query which is issued against the http://www.yellowpages.com/ or the http://www.whitepages.com/ website. These websites are useful for locating businesses and individuals via search terms. In order to extract information from these websites, we employ the services of a web crawler. A web crawler is a computer program that browses the world wide web in a methodical, automated manner or in an orderly fashion. Web crawlers are sometimes referred to as automatic indexers, bots, ants, harvesters, web spiders, web robots, or Web scutters. These crawlers are computer programs that follow the link structure of the world wide web and perform some tasks on the web pages they visit.

After the pages matching our initial query seed are crawled, we store the results in an appropriate format in a text file. Because this process is expensive, we build all our web crawl routines off-line, and load the text file contents into memory during the test cycles of our experimental phase. The first crawl gathers our assumed lists of patients. We use the zip codes of the patients to create queries for hospitals, doctors and their specialties. The results of these searches are also stored in text files, which have predetermined formats. These predetermined formatted text files allow us to build object classes with properties for entities such as persons, hospitals, doctors, and nurses.

18.6.2.3   Generating Workflows

For each patient in our toy knowledge base, we initiate workflows that update the records for the patient. The recorded provenance is the only confidential data we assumed in our system. The intent is to give the querying user an opportunity to guess the patient's disease, medications, or tests associated with the record. Provenance data are more interesting than traditional databases, because the controller not only has to anticipate inferences involving the users' prior knowledge, but also the inferences associated with the causal relationships among the provenance data objects.

18.6.2.4   Properties of the Workflow

We observe a few properties of the workflows we generated:

- Our provenance workflows are generated using the OPM toolbox [OPEN]. This toolbox captures the skeleton of a workflow generated by using the predicates in V_G^P, where

$$V_G^P = \{WasControlledBy, \; Used, \; WasDerivedFrom, \; WasGeneratedBy, \; WasTriggeredBy\}.$$

   That is, the initial workflows we generate are typically not annotated with RDF triples that are related to the entities in our workflow; for example, triples which make assertion about an agent name, address or age. Therefore, we avoid clutter, which makes it easier to visualize the medical procedures.
- Each entity in our workflow graph, G, can be annotated by RDF triples, which makes assertions about the entities. Our workflow is typically stored in its full form. That is, we add annotations to each workflow by transforming it into one that has relevant background information corresponding to the entities in the workflow.
- Each entity in G has attributes which were derived from either the yellow pages(http://www.yellowpages.com) or the white pages (http://www.whitepages.com/) website. These attributes are the ones that are a part of the user background knowledge. We also add other fictitious attributes to the entities in our provenance graph. These fictitious attributes allow us to scale the size and complexity of a provenance graph so that we will have some experimental data about the scalability our system.
- The workflow graph G contains the private information, i.e, the provenance of the activities performed on a patient's record. This is the information our inference controller is protecting. The primary methods we employ for protecting this information are provided by the reasoning services available in semantic web reasoners and policies that operate over G.

18.6.3   POLICY MANAGEMENT

We discussed several aspects of policy management in the design. We will repeat some of the information in this section.

18.6.3.1   Policy Screen

A policy screen provides the user with options to load and execute policies against the provenance graph database. The user has the option of executing any policy type, for example the default ones (access control, redaction, DL rules, or policies encoded as SWRL rules) or another policy type. The default policies are provided with a set of parsers that translate them to an internal policy representation. New policy types are compatible as long as a suitable parser is provided to translate each policy type to an internal representation. The internal representation can be any technology that operates over an RDF graph, for example, SPARQL query, DL, or SRWL rule. The policy screen has two panels. The left panel displays a list of policies loaded but not in effect, while the right panel displays the list of loaded policies which are in effect. Policy screens are illustrated in Figure 18.6.

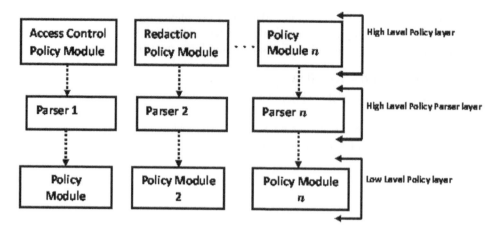

FIGURE 18.6   Policy screen.

18.6.3.2 Parsing Process

A high-level policy has to be translated to a suitable format and representation in order to be processed by a provenance inference controller. This often involves the parsing of a high-level policy to a low-level representation. Our design makes use of an extensible language for expressing policies. This language has been used successfully to write access control policies [MOSE2005, NI2009]. Our policies are written as XML documents which reside on disk until they are requested [BRAY2000]. XML is also equipped with features for writing rules [GROS2003, GOVE2005, HORR2004]. In addition, RDF and OWL can be represented in a XML syntax [BECH24, HORR04]. Our choice of an XML language allows us to take as input any high-level policy specification and an associated parser that maps it to a low-level policy format. The high-level application user also benefits from our use of a XML language, because XML is an open standard that is widely used and many data exchange formats are based on XML.

Figure 18.7 provides us with an overview of a policy parsing process. When a XML policy file is loaded, each policy in the policy file is parsed using a compatible parser. The parser is responsible for ensuring that the policies are well-formed. The default policies (i.e., access control, redaction, inference rules) are written in a XML file and the parser evaluates the XML file against a XML schema file. The policies in a successfully parsed XML file are then translated to a low-level representation.

18.6.3.3 High-Level Policy Translation

In this section, we discuss how a correctly parsed high-level policy is translated to an internal low-level policy. We first discuss two inference assemblers, the SWRL rule assembler and the description logics rule assembler. Then, we discuss two policy assemblers which translate the assess control and redaction high-level policies, respectively.

18.6.3.4 SWRL Rule Assembler

This module maps a high level XML file onto a set of SWRL rules. A SWRL rule has a head and a body. The body is used to encode a condition that must be satisfied before the information encoded in the head is applied to the provenance knowledge base.

18.6.3.5 A SWRL Policy Translation

The following is a policy which states that if a doctor has (or is attending to) a patient, then that doctor can also read the patient's record.

FIGURE 18.7   Parsing process.

```
<policies>
<policy ID="1" >
<description>…some description....</description>
<body>
<atom>?x rdf:type provac:Doctor</atom>
<atom>?y rdf:type provac:Patient</atom>
<atom>?y provac:patientHasDoctor?x</atom>
<atom>?y provac:hasRecord?r</atom>
</body>
<head>
<atom>?x provac:canReadRecord?r</atom>
</head>
</policy>
</policies>
```

This policy could be represented internally as

$$Doctor\,(?x) \wedge Patient\,(?y) \wedge patientHasDoctor\,(?y,\,?\,x) \wedge hasRecord\,(?r)$$
$$\rightarrow canReadRecord\,(?\,x,\,?\,r)$$

18.6.3.6   Description Logics Rule Assembler

This module maps a high level XML file onto a set of OWL restrictions. The OWL properties are used to create restrictions which are then used to restrict the individuals that belong to a class. These restrictions can be placed into three main categories:

1. Quantifier Restrictions
2. Cardinality Restrictions
3. hasValue Restrictions

Quantifier restrictions Quantifier restrictions consist of three parts:

1. A quantifier, which is either the existential quantifier (∃), or the universal quantifier (∀).
2. A property, along which the restriction acts.
3. A filler that is a class description.

For a given individual, the quantifier effectively puts constraints on the relationships that the individual participates in. It does this by either specifying that at least one kind of relationship must exist, or by specifying the only kinds of relationships that can exist (if they exist). An example of an existential quantifier can be used to define a physician as someone with a medical degree:

$$Physician \sqsubseteq \exists\ has.\ MedicalDegree.$$

Universal restriction states that if a relationship exists for the property then it must be to individuals that are members of a specific class. An example of a universal quantifier can be used to define a happy physician as one whose patients all have insurance:

$$HappyPhysician \sqsubseteq \forall hasPatients. (\exists hasCoverage. Insurer).$$

18.6.3.7 Cardinality Restrictions

OWL Cardinality restrictions describe the class of individuals that have at least ($\le$), at most $\le$ or exactly a specified number of relationships with other individuals or datatype values. Let P be a property, then

1. A minimum cardinality restriction specifies the minimum number of P relationships that an individual must participate in.
2. A maximum cardinality restriction specifies the maximum number of P relationships that an individual can participate in.
3. A cardinality restriction specifies the exact number of P relationships that an individual must participate in.

18.6.3.8 hasValue Restriction

A hasValue restriction describes the set of individuals that has at least one relationship along a specified property to a specific individual. The hasValue restriction is denoted by the symbol $\in$. An example of a hasValue restriction is $hasCountryOfOrigin \in Italy$(where Italy is an individual). This describes the set of individuals (the anonymous class of individuals) that has at least one relationship along the hasCountryOfOrigin property to the specific individual Italy.

18.6.3.9 Supporting Restrictions

We currently supported the following OWL restrictions:

1. **SomeValuesFromRestriction**
   SomeValuesFrom restrictions are existential restrictions which describe the set of individuals that have at least one specific kind of relationship to individuals that are members of a specific class.
2. **AllValuesFromRestriction**
   AllValuesFromRestriction are Universal restrictions which constrain the filler for a given property to a specific class.
3. **MinCardinalityRestriction**
   MinCardinalityRestriction are cardinality restrictions which specify the minimum number of relationships that an individual must participate in for a given property. The symbol for a minimum cardinality restriction is the 'greater than or equal to' symbol ($\ge$).
4. **MaxCardinalityRestriction**
   MaxCardinalityRestriction are cardinality restrictions which specify the maximum number of relationships that an individual can participate in for a given property. The symbol for maximum cardinality restrictions is the 'less than or equal to' symbol ($\le$).
5. **DataRange**
   This is a built-in property that links a property (or some instance of the class rdf:Property) to either a class description or a data range. An rdfs:range axiom asserts that the values of this property must belong to the class extension of the class description or to data values in the specified data range.

6. **Domain**
This is a built-in property that links a property (or some instance of the class rdf:Property) to a class description. An rdfs:domain axiom asserts that the subjects of such property statements must belong to the class extension of the indicated class description.

18.6.3.9.1 A DL policy translation
The following is a policy which states that any process that is controlled by a surgeon is a sensitive process.

```
<policies>
<policy ID="1" >
<description>...some description....</description>
<rule>
<restriction>AllValuesFromRestriction</restriction>
<property>opm:WasControlledBy</property>
<class>provac:Surgeon</class>
<label>provac:SensitiveProcess</label>
</rule>
</policy>
</policies>
```

This policy is converted internally as

$$\forall\ WascontrolledBy.\ Surgeon \sqsubseteq SensitiveProcess.$$

18.6.3.10   Access Control Policy Assembler
This module maps a high-level access control XML policy file to a low-level access control policy.

18.6.3.11   An Access Control Policy Translation
The following is a policy which states that any user has permission to access Doc_2 if it was generated by a process that was controlled by a surgeon.

```
<policies>
<policy ID="1" >
<description>description</description>
<target>
<subject>anyuser</subject>
<record>provac:Doc_2</record>
<restriction>Doc.WasGeneratedBy == opm:Process</restriction>
<restriction>process.WasControlledBy == provac:Surgeon</restriction>
</target>
<effect>NecessaryPermit</effect>
</policy>
</policies>
```

This policy could be translated to a query that retrieves the part of a provenance graph that this policy is allowing a user to view. A corresponding SPARQL query would then be

```
Select ?x
{
med:Doc1_2 gleen:OnPath("([opm:WasGeneratedBy]/
    [opm:WasControlledBy])" ?x
    ?x rdf:type provac:Surgeon).
}
```

18.6.3.12   Redaction Policy Assembler

This module maps a high-level XML redaction policy file to a low-level redaction policy.

18.6.3.13   A Redaction Policy Translation

The following is a policy which states that if there is a path which starts at Doc_4 and Doc_4 was derived from an artifact which was generated by a process that was controlled by a physician, then we should redact this path from the provenance subgraph containing the path.

```
</policies>
<policy ID="1">
<description>description</description>
<lhs>
<chain>
<start> provac:Doc_4</start>
<path>
     [opm:WasDerivedFrom]+ artifact AND artifact [opm:WasGeneratedBy] pro-
cess AND
   process [opm:WasControlledBy] physician
</path>
</lhs>
<rhs>_:A1</rhs>
<condition>
<application>null</application>
<attribute>null</attribute>
</condition>
<embedding>
<pre>null</pre>
<post>(provac:HeartSurgery_1,opm:Used, _:A1)</post>
</embedding>
</policy>
</policies>
```

This policy would evaluate over a provenance graph replacing any path that starts with a node labeled Doc_4 and connected to a process via a WasGeneratedBy link followed by a WasControlledBy link which has an end node labeled as physician (or is of type physician). Each such path would be replaced by a blank label _:A1 and :_A1 would be joined to the original provenance graph to some node labeled provac:HearthSurgery_1 using a link with the label opm:Used.

18.6.4   EXPLANATION SERVICE LAYER

A good feature to have is one where the reasoner derives new knowledge and then explains how it derived that new knowledge. The Pellet reasoner can explain its inferences by providing the minimal set of facts or other knowledge necessary to justify the inference. For any inference that Pellet computes, we exploit Pellet inference service which will explain why that inference holds. The explanation itself is a set of OWL axioms which, taken together, justify or support the inference in question. There may be many (even infinitely many) explanations for an inference; Pellet heuristically attempts to provide a good explanation.

Our provenance inference controller (discussed in detail in [THUR2014]) can then provide information about the classification of the knowledge base. For example, we may be interested in why a set of RDF triples were classified as sensitive, or why a concept is considered sensitive. The answers to these questions are left to the explanation service layer. This layer is built on top of the

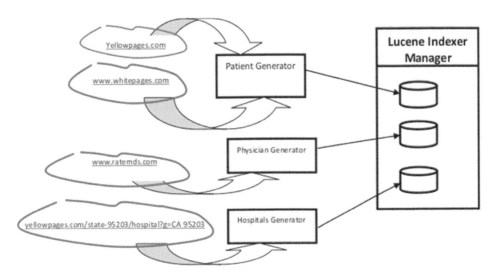

FIGURE 18.8 Explanation service layer.

Pellet explanation service and displays the set of axioms used to derive the concepts that are subsumed by another class.

The explanation service layer users pellet service to provide justifications (also warrants) for each piece of the provenance that is sensitive. The explanation service layer is useful for providing feedback to the application designer. The explanations are displayed using the low-level descriptions and may reveal details of how the internal classification works. This may be a bad feature of the system, since the application user may not understand description logics or OWL. Nevertheless, this service provides a desired feature, whereby the application designer can view the how his/her policies are interpreted by the low-level inference services. For example, since a high-level description logic rule may be applied differently from what the author intended, the policy designer now has an opportunity to tweak the high-level policies for the desired outcome. The explanation service layer is illustrated in Figure 18.8.

18.7 GENERATORS

We now explain the process whereby the knowledge is added to a provenance store. We build a set of generators. There is a set of background generators which are responsible for extracting background information that is normally available online. These is also a set of miscellaneous generators which builds synthetic data about diseases, medication, tests and treatments. The miscellaneous generator uses online sources to guide it in associating the the diseases with the related tests, treatment and diseases, and thus there is additional background information produced by these miscellaneous generators. Finally, we discuss the workflow generator that produces the actual provenance. The workflow generator produces synthetic provenance data that is not available online. It is this provenance data that has subsets which we must hide.

18.7.1 SELECTING BACKGROUND INFORMATION

We use real information that actually exists on current web pages so that we can demonstrate the effectiveness of the inference controller with respect to a set of prior knowledge of the querying agent. We identify a city and state in the United States. For this city, we target a set of zip codes. The information is downloaded from freely available websites such as yellow pages and white pages. We crawl these web sites and extract the name, address, telephone numbers, age, sex, relatives of various individuals, by setting a seed for a list of popular first and last names. This would allow us to capture similar attribute values for each individual patient in our toy hospital. For the hospitals, we select only those hospitals within the zip codes for the patients. Each hospital has a name, address and telephone numbers. Because many hospitals do not release the names of their staff, we perform searches for doctors and their specialty within the same zip codes. This is normal, since most specialists are affiliated with a particular hospital close to their practice. Some insurance companies do provide a list of the doctors and their affiliation on their websites, but many of these websites require a login id, or different verification code each time it is accessed. Due to these obstacles, we satisfy with a less accurate picture of the actual hospital. Also, since our system is user driven, automation and efficiency become a greater priority. This does not preclude a client from populating the knowledge base with their own data. Generating data this way makes the system more realistic than if we had used complete synthetic data. A querying user can combine the responses from the system with accessible background information to draw inferences. The querying user could then issue new queries to verify there guesses about the data in the knowledge base.

18.7.2 Background generator module

Figure 18.9 is a diagram of the different background generators. Each generator is built to target specific websites (or pages) which contain some information of interest. For example, www.ratemd.com provides structured information about doctors at a specific zip code.

18.7.2.1 Patient Generator

The Patient Generator extracts the attributes of a person from a set of web pages. Algorithm 18.1 details the job of the patient generator.

http://www.yellowpages.com/findaperson?fap_terms%5Bfirst%5D="fname"

```
&fap_terms%5Blast%5D=" Lname "
&fap_terms%5Bstate%5D=" State "
&page=1"
```

Figure 18.10 shows the result when *fname=John*, *lname=Smith* and *State=CA*. We then extract the address and telephone number from the result page. Figure 18.11 shows the result of executing Algorithm 18.1 when the base uri is www.whitepatges.com and the parameters are *fname=John*,

FIGURE 18.9 Background generator.

ALGORITHM 18.1   *findPersons* ()

1: *baseUri* ← *yellowpages. com*;
2: *uri* ← *baseUri + name + zip*;
3: *Link* [] ← *Spider* (*uri*);
4: **for all***r* ∈ *RS***do**
5: *Contents* ← *Extract* (*Link* [*i*]);
6: *Person* ← *Parse* (*Contents*);
7: *AddToDatabase* (*Person*);
8: *end for*

---

lname=Smith and *State=CA*. We then extract the address and age from the result page. Figure 18.12 is a list of attributes we collect for each patient in our provenance knowledge base.

18.7.2.2   Physician Generator

The Physician Generator extracts information as attribute values for a doctor. We modify the line 1 of Algorithm 18.1 by replacing the value of the base URI to base rateMd.com. Figures 18.13, 18.14, and 18.15 display the user interface for searching a doctor and the results, respectively.

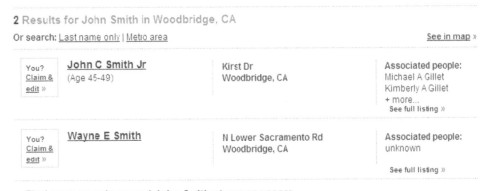

FIGURE 18.10   Partial page – Yellowpage.com.

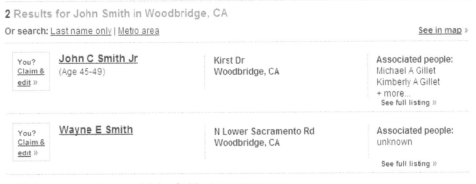

FIGURE 18.11   Partial page – Whitepage.com.

Find and Rate Doctors and Dentists

Over a million free doctor reviews since 2004

Doctor's **Last** Name: [smith]
Enter **last name** or last name, first name (include comma)
City or Zip: [95258]   State: [CA ▾] [USA ▾]
Specialty: [All ▾]

[Clear]   [Find Doctors in USA]   **FIGURE 18.12**   Patient attributes.

Dr. Peter Hickox
doctor
Lodi, CA

Gender: **M**
Specialty: **Gynecologist (OBGYN)**
Webpage:
Hospital:
Answers Email:
Online Appt. Scheduling:
Accepting New Patients: **Y**
Phone Number: ▾ **209-466-8546** ⊙
Med. School: **Albany Med Coll, Albany Ny 12208**
Grad. Year: **1981**

FIGURE 18.13   Partial page – ratemd.com.

Dr. Peter Hickox
doctor
Lodi, CA

Gender: **M**
Specialty: **Gynecologist (OBGYN)**
Webpage:
Hospital:
Answers Email:
Online Appt. Scheduling:
Accepting New Patients: **Y**
Phone Number: ▾ **209-466-8546** ⊙
Med. School: **Albany Med Coll, Albany Ny 12208**
Grad. Year: **1981**

FIGURE 18.14   Single Result page (obtained from rate-md.com).

18.7.2.3   Hospital Generator

We also generate hospital information from *yellowpages.com* website. Figure 18.16 shows the results returned from searching for a hospital. Figure 18.17 is a list of attributes we extracted for each physician in our provenance knowledge base.

18.7.3   Miscellaneous generators

This module uses www.webMD.com to determine the relationships between a disease, a medication, a test, and a treatment. Therefore, this allows us to add semantic association among these

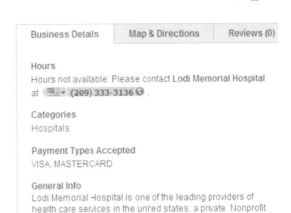

FIGURE 18.15   Multi-result page – ratemd.com.

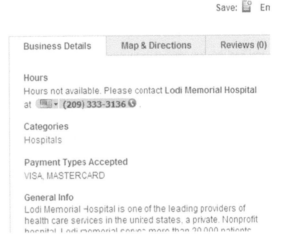

FIGURE 18.16   Partial page (Hospital) – yellowpages.com.

```
<id> 3 </id>
<firstname> Peter </firstname>
<lastname> Hickox</lastname>
<address></address>
<city> Lodi </city>
<state> CA </state>
<zip></zip>
<telephone> 20
```

```
66-8546 </telephone>
<speciality>Gynecologist </speciality>
<age></age>
<sex> Male <sex>
<school> Albany Med Coll, Albany NY 12208
<school>
<sex> Male <sex>
```

FIGURE 18.17   Physician attributes.

entities to our knowledge base. Since the relationships are background information that is also available to any user, we build rules that takes these semantic relationships into consideration when disclosing provenance information.

18.7.4 WORKFLOW GENERATOR

We build a set of standard workflows, which are taken from existing procedures (e.g., mercy-healthcom). As these procedures are freely available, we build rules to protect some sensitive components in the generated workflows. Furthermore, the relationships among the entities in these workflows can be explicit or implicit. Therefore, our inference controller utilizes a mixture of policies and inference rules to protect the information in these workflows.

18.7.5 ANNOTATING THE WORKFLOW

We annotate our workflow using the data produced by the background generator. Therefore, the associations between the attributes of a patient are the ones gathered from www.yellowpages.com and www.whitepages.com. Similarly, the hospital and physician attributes are in fact the ones gathered from www.yellowpages.com and www.ratemd.com.

18.7.6 GENERATING WORKFLOWS

As stated earlier, for each patient in our toy hospital example, we initiate workflows that update the record for the patient. The recorded provenance is the only confidential data we assumed in our system. The intent is to give the querying user an opportunity to guess the patient's disease, medications or tests associated with the record. Provenance poses more challenges than that of traditional data. The controller not only anticipates inferences involving a user's prior knowledge, but also considers the inferences associated with the causal relationships among the data items as well as the provenance entities (Algorithms 18.2).

18.7.7 INCOMPLETE INFORMATION IN THE DATABASES

We generated our data from various web pages, each contributing a part to the knowledge base. This represent a classic case of our knowledge base containing partial or incomplete information.

An incomplete database is defined by a set of constraints and a partial database instance. Answering conjunctive queries over incomplete databases is an important computational task that lies at the core of many problems such as information integration, data exchange, and data warehousing. A common example of partial information over a relational database is a view. A view can be defined so as to hide important data in the underlying database and thus restrict access to a user. This is usually done to satisfy some constraints; for example, employees in the accounts department can view the accounting records but not the human resources records. Given a query and an incomplete database, the task is to compute the set of certain answers. The certain answers are tuples that satisfy the query in every database instance that conforms to the partial instances

---

ALGORITHM 18.2 *generateworkflow* ()

patient ← getPatient();
graph ← generateOpmGraph();
annotateGraph (*graph*);

and satisfies the constraints. Answering queries under general constraints is undecidable. Therefore, the expressivity of the constraint language considered is typically restricted in order to achieve decidability. An analogy to incomplete information in databases is an OWL ontology. In an OWL ontology, the TBox can be seen as a conceptual schema containing the set of constraints, and the ABox as some partial instances of the schema.

An incomplete database has an important property that an inference controller can use when answering queries over the RDF database. When a query returns a negative response, the user must decide whether the query was attempting to access confidential information or whether the query was not entailed in the RDF database.

18.8 USE CASE: MEDICAL EXAMPLE

In this section, we provide examples of provenance queries. These queries can be used to identify resources for a policy or identify the answer for a user query.

The provenance graph in Figure 18.18 shows a workflow which updates a fictitious record for a patient who went though three medical stages at a hospital. In the first phase, the physician performed a checkup on the patient. At checkup, the physician consulted the history in the patient's record, med:Doc1_1 and performed the task of recording notes about the patient. At the end of the checkup, the physician then updated the patient's record, which resulted in a newer version, med:Doc1_2. In the second phase, the patient returned for a follow-up visit at the physician's request. During this visit, the physician consulted with the patient's record for a review of the patient's history and then performed a series of tests on the patient. At the end of this visit, the physician then updated the patient's record, which results in a newer version, med:Doc1_3. In the third phase, the patient returned to undergo heart surgery. This was ordered by the patient's physician and carried out by a resident surgeon. Before the surgeon started the surgery operation, a careful review of the patient's record was performed by both the patient's physician and surgeon. During the surgery process, the surgeon performed the task of recording the results at each stage of the heart surgery process. At the end of the surgery, the patient's record was updated by the surgeon, which resulted in a newer version, med:Doc1_4.

We assume that a hospital has a standard set of procedures that govern every healthcare service that the hospital provides. Therefore, each patient that needs to use a healthcare service will need to

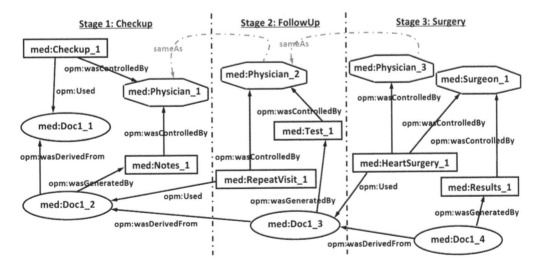

FIGURE 18.18   Provenance graph.

TABLE 18.2
RDF Annotations

Entity	RDF Annotation
Process	PerformedOn
Agent	Name, Sex, Age, and Zip Code
Artifact	UpdatedOn

go through this set of procedures. We use a fixed set of notations in Figure 18.18 to represent an entity in the provenance graph, for example,

```
<med:Checkup_n_1> .
```

The "n" denotes a particular patient who is undergoing a procedure at the hospital. Therefore, n = 1 identifies a patient with id = 1, n = 2 identifies a patient with id = 2, and so on. A larger number in the suffix of each process, agent and artifact signifies that the particular provenance entity is used at a later stage in a medical procedure. In practice, "n" would be instantiated with an actual patient id; this leads to the following set of RDF triples for a patient with id = 1 at stage 1,

```
<med:Checkup_1_1><opm:WasControlledBy><med:Physician_1_1>
<med:Checkup_1_1><opm:Used><med:Doc_1_1>
<med:Doc_1_2><opm:WasDerivedFrom><med:Doc_1_1>
<med:Doc_1_2><opm:WasGeneratedBy><med:Notes_1_1>
<med:Notes_1_1><opm:WasControlledBy><med:Physician_1_1>
```

The sameAs annotations on the light-shaded arrows are meant to illustrate that the reference to physician is meant to be the same person in all the three phases.

This is not a complete picture of the provenance graph; it would be further annotated with RDF triples to indicate for example, location, time, and other contextual information. Each entity in the graph would have a unique set of RDF annotations based on its type. Table 18.2 shows a set of compatible annotations for each type of provenance entity. A usage of these annotations in RDF representation for a physician associated with a patient with id = 1 would be,

```
<med:Physician_1_1><med:Name> "John Smith"
<med:Physician_1_1><med:Sex> "M"
<med:Physician_1_1><med:Age> "35"
<med:Physician_1_1><med:Zip> "76543"
```

18.8.1 SEMANTIC ASSOCIATIONS IN THE WORKFLOW

We identified various semantic associations such as, if X is an heart surgeon who updates patient Y record, then patient Y procedures and medications are related to heart surgery. This would allow the querying user to determine the disease of Y after querying for Y, X, and Y and X on the same path in the provenance for Y's record.

18.9 IMPLEMENTING CONSTRAINTS

Constraints are generally rules, but may have additional conditions as well. The conditions may specify circumstances for applying the rules (e.g., some temporal or location criteria).

One of our approaches is to use regular expressions to write our constraints. Therefore, we could specify the LHS of a rule by using regular expressions so that the constraint is enforced whenever a pattern exists in a provenance graph. We have examined the following approaches to constraint processing. We discuss the query modifcation process.

- DL concepts
- Query implementation
- SWRL rules
- Graph grammar/graph rewriting

18.9.1 QUERY MODIFICATION FOR ENFORCING CONSTRAINTS

We propose two approaches for modifying the graph patterns in a SPARQL query. These approaches use SPARQL filters and property functions. To determine the type of triple with respect to a security type (or label), the inference engine would use the domain ontology to determine the concept of each data item found in the subject or object of a triple or the classification of the property found in the TBox. This approach however fails when a triple pattern contains only variables and literals. We assume that either the subject, object or predicate is a URI in any triple in the graph pattern. Special provisions could be made to determine the security type for kinds of literals occurring in the object of a triple; for example, identifying a nine-digit SSN or a sixteen-digit credit card number.

18.9.1.1 Query Filter

Graph pattern matching produces a solution sequence, where each solution has a set of bindings of variables to RDF terms. SPARQL FILTERs restrict solutions to those for which the filter expression evaluates to TRUE. The SPARQL specification [PRUD2006] provides different techniques for modifying a graph pattern.

- **SPARQL FILTERs can Restrict the Values of Strings with regex**.

```
PREFIX dc: <http://purl.org/dc/elements/1.1/>

SELECT?title
WHERE {?x dc:title ?title
FILTER regex(?title, "^SPARQL")
}
```

- **SPARQL FILTERs can restrict on arithmetic expressions**.

```
http://purl.org/dc/elements/1.1/
PREFIX dc: <
>
http://example.org/ns#
PREFIX ns: <
>
SELECT ?title ?price
WHERE { ?x ns:price ?price.
FILTER (?price < 30.5)
?x dc:title?title . }
```

- Constraints in Optional Pattern Matching, for example.

```
http://purl.org/dc/elements/1.1/
PREFIX dc: <
>
http://example.org/ns#
PREFIX ns: <
>
SELECT?title?price
WHERE {?x dc:title?title .
OPTIONAL {?x ns:price ?price. FILTER (?price < 30) }
}
```

18.10 NEXT GENERATION INFERENCE CONTROLLERS

Social media data as well as highly linked data can be represented as RDF graphs. Therefore the ideas presented in the previous sections apply for such social graphs. The security policies may also be represented as RDF or in a language such as SWRL. These policies include access control policies and information sharing policies. For example, if a person divulges his religious beliefs then his political affiliation would be inferred. Therefore is a person wants to keep his political affiliations private, then his religious beliefs should not be posted on his social media website.

We can build the inference controller on top of the access control architeture that we described in Chapter 15. We illustrate such an inference controller in Figure 18.19. The inference engine is essentially the policy engine that controls access as well as handles unauthorized access via

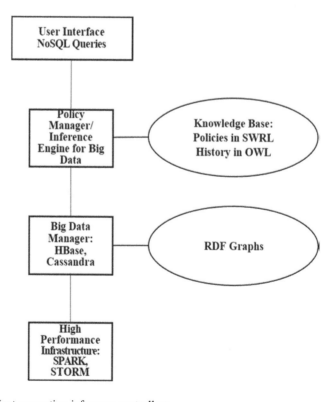

FIGURE 18.19 Next generation inference controllers.

inference. The social media data are respresented as RDF graphs and the policies and knowledge may be specified using a combination of SWRL, RDF, and OWL. When a user queries say in SPARQL, the policy engine examines the knowledge base which could include provenance data, the policies and modify the query. The modified query is posed against the RDF-based social media database. Much of the discussion in the previous sections as well as the implementation of the inference controller apply for RDF-based social media data.

More recently, the concept of knowledge graphs for representing and reasoning about knowledge has become very popular. As stated in [FENS2020], "Since its inception by Google, Knowledge Graph has become a term that is recently ubiquitously used yet does not have a well-established definition." The knowledge graphs have essentially evolved from the semantic networks and conceptual graphs of the 1970s and 1980s. They integrate the semantic networks and conceptual graphs with the more recent work in semantic web and ontologies. These knowledge graphs capture the knowledge and reason about the knowledge using various reasoning techniques built into them.

With respect to security and privacy, the challenge is can you aggregate different knowledge graphs and infer highly classified or private information? We have carried out a lot of research and developed tools to address this problem in the early 1990s with semantic networks and conceptual graphs [THUR1991]. That is, we use these networks and graphs to represent the knowledge and subsequently apply the reasoning techniques to determine whether sensitive information can be inferred. Much of our focus at that time was on logical inferences such as if A implies B and B implies C and if C is sensitive then should A be sensitive? If the knowledge is incorrectly classified, then the idea is to inform the application designer that there could be potential security violations via inference.

While the representation and reasoning techniques were limited in the 1970s and 1980s, with the advent of the semantic web and ontologies together with the traditional knowledge representation and reasoning schemes such as semantic nets have resulted in powerful knowledge graphs. Therefore, our challenge is to represent the knowledge and reason about the knowledge to determine whether there could be security and privacy violations. More details are given in [THUR2020].

18.11   SUMMARY AND DIRECTIONS

In this chapter, we first described the design of an inference controller that operates over a semantic web-based provenance graph and protects important provenance information from unauthorized users. Since our social networks discussed in Chapter 19 and 20 are also represented by semantic web technologies, the techniques we have developed apply for such social media data. Previous work to build an inference controller to protect data confidentiality was described in the late 1980s and early 1990s; however, this work was mainly in the area of multi-level secure databases and supported limited reasoning capabilities. Our current work is a substantial improvement over prior efforts with more sophisticated reasoning and policy representation techniques through the use of semantic web technologies. We used RDF as our data model as it supports the interoperability of multiple databases having disparate data schemas. In addition, we expressed policies and rules in terms of semantic web rules and constraints, and we classify data items and relationships between them using semantic web software tools.

Next, we discussed inference control through query modification. Query modification has also been referred it as query rewriting. In this approach, the inference controller takes a user query and modifies the query according to the policies and gives a sanitized result to the query. We provided background information on query modification for relational data as well as aspects of modifying SPARQL queries. While moving to SPARQL queries from relational queries is the first step toward handling inferences for next generation inference controllers, our ultimate goal is to process queries with sophisticated logic-based reasoners that use machine learning approaches. This way we can handle many more inference strategies than we have discussed in this book. As stated earlier, as the inference strategies become more complex, we need to keep scalability of the query processing techniques in mind. That is, while the data management system should release only authorized responses, users will require performance requirements to be met. Therefore, developing scalable inference controllers is one of our major goals.

In this chapter, we described the implementation of an inference controller for data provenance. The inference controller is built using a modular approach, therefore, it is very flexible in that most of the modules can be extended or replaced by another application module. For example, an application user may substitute the policy parser module that handles the parsing of the high-level policies to a low-level policy object. This substitution would allow the application user to continue using his/her business policies independent of our software implementation of the provenance inference controller. Essentially, we have followed a "plug-and-play" approach for implementing the inference controller. We have used open source products as much as possible in our implementation. The techniques we have implemented for inference control for provenance data can be applied for social media data represented using semantic web technologies.

This implementation is the first of its kind with respect to next generation inference controllers. We have migrated from the relational database approach in the 1980s and 1990s to a semantic web-based approach. The reasoning capabilities of the semantic web technologies make this approach more powerful. Our next step is to adapt this inference controller for knowledge and social graphs represented in RDF. We are also investigating more powerful reasoning strategies using machine learning techniques. Furthermore, we need to take into consideration the risks of unauthorized disclosure of provenance data. In addition, we can model the inference strategies as games where the players are the inference controller and the user of the system who could also be an adversary. That is, a game is played between the two parties and each party's goal is to win the game. Essentially, the inference controller would try and prevent any unauthorized information from getting into the hands of the adversary while the adversary will attempt to extract as much information as possible from the system.

REFERENCES

[BECH2004] S. Bechhofer, F. Van Harmelen, J. Hendler, I. Horrocks, D. McGuinness, P. Patel-Schneider, L. Stein, OWL Web Ontology Language Reference, W3C recommendation, 10, 2004.

[BIZE2003] C. Bizer, D2R MAP–A Database to RDF Mapping Language, Proceedings of the Twelfth International World Wide Web Conference-Posters, WWW, Budapest, Hungary, 2003.

[BRAU2008] U. Braun, A. Shinnar, M. Seltzer, Securing Provenance, *Proceedings of the 3rd Conference on Hot topics in Security*, USENIX Association, San Jose, CA, 2008, pp. 1–5.

[BRAY2000] T. Bray, J. Paoli, C. Sperberg-McQueen, E. Maler, F. Yergeau, Extensible markup language (XML) 1.0, Review VersionW3C Recommendation, 6, 2000.

[CARR2004] J. Carroll, I. Dickinson, C. Dollin, D. Reynolds, A. Seaborne, K. Wilkinson, Jena: Implementing the Semantic Web Recommendations, *Proceedings of the 13th international World Wide Web Conference on Alternate Track Papers & Posters*, 2004.

[CHAN1998] L.W. Chang, I.S. Moskowitz, Parsimonious Downgrading and Decision Trees Applied to the Inference Problem, *Proceedings of the 1998 workshop on New security paradigms*, 1988.

[DETW2008] L. Detwiler, D. Suciu, J. Brinkley, Regular Paths in SparQL: Querying the NCI thesaurus, *AMIA Annual Symposium Proceedings*, American Medical Informatics Association, 2008.

[DWYE1987] P. Dwyer, G.D. Jelatis, B.M. Thuraisingham, Multilevel Security in Database Management Systems, Computers & Security, Volume 6, #3, 1987, 252–260.

[EHRI1991] H. Ehrig, M. Korff, M. Lowe, Tutorial Introduction to the Algebraic Approach of Graph Grammars Based on Double and Single Pushouts, Graph Grammars and Their Application to Computer Science, H. Erhig, H.-J. Kreowski, and G. Rozenberg (eds.), Springer-Verlag, Berlin, 1991.

[EHRI2006] H. Ehrig, Fundamentals of Algebraic Graph Transformation, Springer-Verlag, New York, 2006.

[FENS2020] D. Fensel, U. Şimşek, K. Angele, E. Huaman, E., Kärle, O. Panasiuk, L. Toma, J. Umbrich, A. Wahler, Knowledge Graphs, Springer, 2020

[FIKE2002] R. Fikes, P. Hayes, I. Horrocks, DQL–a query language for the semantic web. Knowledge Systems Laboratory, Report DR-05, Stanford University, 2002

[GALL1978] H. Gallaire, J. Minker (Eds.), Logic and Data Bases, Symposium on Logic and Data Bases Advances in Data Base Theory, Plenum Press, New York, 1978.

[GOVE2005] G. Governatori, Representing business contracts in RuleML, International Journal of Cooperative Information Systems, 14, 2005.

[GROS2003] B. Grosof, T. Poon, SweetDeal: Representing Agent Contracts with Exceptions Using XML Rules, Ontologies, and Process Descriptions, *In Proceedings of the 12th International Conference on World Wide Web*, 2003.

[HORR2004] I. Horrocks, P. Patel-Schneider, H. Boley, S. Tabet, B. Grosof, M. Dean, SWRL: A Semantic Web Rule Language Combining OWL and RuleML, W3C Member submission, 21, 2004.

[KARV2002] G. Karvounarakis, S. Alexaki, V. Christophides, D. Plexousakis, M. Scholl, RQL: A Declarative Query Language for RDF, *ACM WWW,* 2002, 592–603.

[KIFO2006] T. Kifor, L. Varga, J. Vazquez-Salceda, S. Alvarez, S. Willmott, S. Miles, L. Moreau, Provenance in Agent-Mediated Healthcare Systems, IEEE Intelligent Systems, Volume 21, #6, 2006.

[KNUB2004] H. Knublauch, R. Fergerson, N. Noy, M. Musen, The Protege OWL Plugin: An Open Development Environment for Semantic Web Applications, ISWC, 2004.

[MCGU2003] D.L. McGuinness, P.P. Da Silva, Inference Web: Portable and Shareable Explanations for Question Answering, *The Proceedings of the American Association for Artificial Intelligence Spring Symposium Workshop on New Directions for Question Answering*, Stanford University, Stanford, CA, 2003.

[MCGU2004] D. McGuinness, P. Pinheiro da Silva, Explaining answers from the semantic web: The inference web approach, Web Semantics: Science, Services and Agents on the World Wide Web 2004, Vol 1, No. 4.

[MOSE2005] T. Moses, et al. Extensible Access Control Markup Language (XACML) version 2.0. Oasis Standard, 2005.

[NI2009] Q. Ni, S. Xu, E. Bertino, R. Sandhu, and W. Han, An Access Control Language for a General Provenance Model. Secure Data Management, LC NS 5766, 68–88, Springer Verlag, Berlin Heidelberg, 2009.

[OPEN] http://openprovenance.org/

[ORAC2012] Fine-Grained Access Control for RDF Data. available at http://docs.oracle.com/cd/E11882_01/appdev.112/e25609.pdf (2012).

[OULM2012] S. Oulmakhzoune, N. Cuppens-Boulahia, F. Cuppens, Stephane Morucci: Privacy Policy Preferences Enforced by SPARQL Query Rewriting, ARES, 335–342, 2012.

[PRUD2006] E. Prud'hommeaux, A. Seaborne, et al., SPARQL Query Language for RDF, Working Draft, W3C Recommendation, 20, 2006.

[REIT1977] R. Reiter, On Closed World Data Bases, Logic and Databases, H. Gallaire and J. Minker, Plenum Press, New York, 1977.

[ROZE1997] G. Rozenberg and H. Ehrig, Handbook of Graph Grammars and Computing by Graph Transformation, Volume 1, World Scientific Publishing, Singapore, 1997.

[SIRI2007] E. Sirin, B. Parsia, B. Grau, A. Kalyanpur, and Y. Katz, Pellet: A Practical OWL-DL Reasoner. Web Semantics: Science, Services and Agents on the World Wide Web, Volume 5, #2, 2007, pp. 51–53.

[STON1975] M. Stonebraker, Implementation of Integrity Constraints and Views by Query Modification, SIGMOD Conference, 1975.

[THUR1987] B. M. Thuraisingham, Security Checking in Relational Database Management Systems Augmented with Inference Engines, Computers & Security, 6(6), 479–492, 1987.

[THUR1990] B. Thuraisingham, Recursion Theoretic Properties of the Inference Problem, Presented at the Computer Security Foundations Workshop, Franconia, NH, June 1990 (also MITRE Report, June 1990).

[THUR1991] B. M. Thuraisingham, The Use of Conceptual Structures for Handling the Inference Problem, DBSec, Shepherdstown, West Virginia, 333–362, 1991.

[THUR1993] B. Thuraisingham, W. Ford, M. Collins, J. O'Keeffe, Design and Implementation of a Database Inference Controller, Data & knowledge engineering, Vol 11, # 3, 1993, 271–297.

[THUR2014] B. Thuraisingham, T. Cadenhead, M. Kantarcioglu, V. Khadilkar, Secure Data Provenance and Inference Control with Semantic Web, CRC Press, Boca Raton, FL.

[THUR2020] Cyber Security Meets Big Knowledge: Towards a Secure HACE Theorem. IEEE ICKG, 2020.

19 Emerging Applications for Secure Data Science: Internet of Transportation Systems

19.1 INTRODUCTION

The increasing complexity of cyberspace due to the development of the Internet of Things (IoT) Systems with heterogeneous components, such as different types of networks (e.g., fixed wired networks, mobile cellular networks, and mobile ad hoc networks), diverse computing systems (e.g., sensors, embedded systems, smart phones, and smart devices), and multiple layers of software (e.g., applications, middleware, operating systems [OSs], and hypervisors) results in massive security vulnerabilities as any of the devices or the networks or the data generated could be attacked. Adversaries will increasingly move into the cyberspace for IoT, and will target all cyber-based infrastructures, including energy, transportation, financial, and healthcare infrastructures. Providing cyber security solutions for managing cyber conflicts and defending against cyber attacks for IoT in such a complex landscape is thus a major challenge.

There is an urgent need to design and develop a cyber defense framework for IoT systems based on a layered architecture. The goals are to (i) develop techniques for secure networks (both wired and wireless), hardware, software, and systems as well as data sources when faced with attacks; and (ii) develop analytics solutions for detecting the attacks. However, developing such an integrated framework required developing solutions to numerous security problems for IoT systems including access control, adversarial machine learning for cyber attacks to the IoT system, and securing special kings of IoT systems such as the Internet of Transportation Systems.

While security is a major aspect of IoT systems, privacy should also be a critical consideration. Massive amounts of data are collected by the IoT systems including healthcare data, financial data, and other data such as driving patterns and the data is analyzed using sophisticated machine learning (ML) techniques to help the society. However, the machine learning techniques may uncover patterns that are extremely sensitive and private. Therefore, we need to develop privacy-aware machine learning techniques for the IoT Systems.

In this chapter, we focus on one type of IoT systems and that is Internet of Transactions Systems. In the recent years, there has been an explosion of AVs (Autonomous Vehicles). Companies are investing heavily in AVs. AVs evaluate their environment using a variety of sensors (e.g., camera, GPS, Inertial Measurement Unit [IMU], LiDAR, RADAR, and ultrasonic sensors). While there is great potential in AVs and the improvements it can do to the transportation industry, security, and privacy concerns pose new challenges that need to be addressed. The sensors are susceptible to malicious tampering (e.g., IMUs are susceptible to sound waves and GPS receptors are susceptible to spoofing signals). Vehicles should verify the veracity of sensor signals before acting on them [QUIN2020].

The IoT systems consisting of a collection of AVs have come to be known as the Internet of Transportation Systems. The Internet of Transportation Systems are subject to attacks (like any cyber physical system). Streaming data are being collected from such systems including autonomous and in the future driverless vehicles. As transportation systems go electric, they need energy conservation. Threats to the security of such systems could cause massive damage including

DOI: 10.1201/9781003081845-30

accidents, loss of lives as well as being stranded on lonely highways due to attacks on energy management.

Data Science/ML techniques are being applied to analyze the data of AVs and a challenge is to apply the stream analytics/learning techniques for transportation data. For example, how can the ML techniques be applied to the massive amounts of sensor data emanating from the AVs? [MASO2011]. The Internet of Transportation Systems will also depend heavily on Data Science/ Artificial Intelligence (AI)/ML techniques for various applications including optimum directions, driving without a human in the loop and many more. The adversary will learn the machine learning models that we use and try and thwart our models [ZHOU2012]. Finally, while massive amounts of data are collected by the Internet of Transportation Systems, the privacy of the individuals has to be protected. We envision that much of the data sharing and analytics will be carried out using the services running in the cloud integrated with the Internet of Transportation System [THUR2020].

This chapter explores how Artificial Intelligence, Security, and the Cloud can be integrated to develop Intelligent Internet of Transportation Systems. We first discuss the integration of cyber security and AI in Section 19.2. Section 19.3 discusses security and privacy for Internet of Transportation Systems. In Section 19.4, we discuss AI and Cloud-based Internet of Transportation Systems. Summary and directions are discussed in Section 19.5. Figure 19.1 discusses the concepts discussed in this chapter.

19.2   INTEGRATION OF CYBER SECURITY AND AI

Parts II and III have addressed the topics of integrating cyber security and AI. In this section, we will review the key points. There are three aspects to integrating cyber security and AI. One is to apply AI for cyber security, the second is to apply cyber security for AI and the third is to detect privacy attacks due to AI. Research began on applying AI for cyber security around the mid-1990s. The idea is to apply ML techniques for detecting unauthorized intrusions. This research was expanded in the 2000s to include malware analysis and insider threat detection [THUR2017]. Massive amounts of attack data are being collected. These data have to be analyzed so that malicious attacks can be detected. Furthermore, we also need to predict how the malware could mutate so that the attacks can be prevented [HAML2009]. In addition, streaming data are being analyzed to detect malicious insiders.

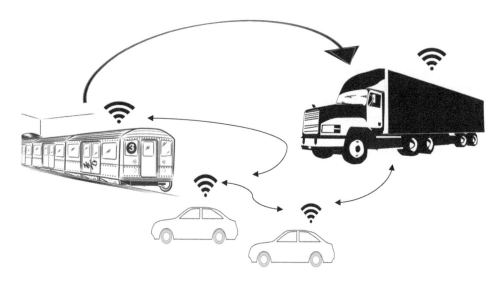

FIGURE 19.1   Emerging applications for secure data science: Internet of Transportation Systems.

FIGURE 19.2   Security for Internet of Transportation Systems.

The second area is securing the AI techniques. This area, now come to be known as adversarial machine learning, has become quite prominent over the past decade. We are increasingly depending on ML techniques for every aspect of our lives from healthcare to AVs. These ML techniques could be attacked and could result in catastrophic situations. Therefore, we need to examine the types of attacks and adapt the ML techniques. For example, in our work, we have examined support vector machines (SVM) and adapted the SVM techniques to detect some of the attacks. The adversary will learn about our models and adapt its behavior. Our adversarial support vector machine technique is able to learn what the adversary is doing and adapt itself so that it can detect the attacks. Over the time, it becomes game playing between the adversary and us.

The thirst aspect is the privacy violation that could occur to do the ML techniques. For example, it is now possible to integrate massive amounts of data and analyze the data and obtain various properties of individuals. This could result in the privacy of the individuals being compromised. Many privacy-aware machine learning (data mining) techniques have been developed [LIU2008]. The challenge is to enforce appropriate policies so that we can carry out policy aware data collection, storage, integration, analysis, and sharing [THUR2018]. Figure 19.2 illustrates the aspects of integrating cyber security and AI.

19.3   SECURITY AND PRIVACY FOR THE INTERNET OF TRANSPORTATION SYSTEMS

One of the approaches to the security and privacy of the Internet of Transportation Systems is to build a reference monitor using a Physics-Based Anomaly Detection (PBAD) algorithm for ground and aerial AVs [QUIN2020]. The algorithm will consist of three parts: (i) building a model offline of the AV's physical invariants, (ii) implementing an online tool to monitor expected and observed behavior to detect anomalies, and (iii) raising an alarm if significant residual difference exists between executions. The techniques have been applied both for ground and Ariella AVs. Later, we provide more details of the steps.

(i) Offline pre-processing: the AV's invariants are calculated using a well-known nonlinear model for aerial and ground vehicles. Accelerometer, gyroscope, and magnetometer sensor data on the x, y, and z axis is used for the aerial vehicle. Vehicle position and steering angle is used for the ground vehicle. (ii) Online stage: an Extended Kalman Filter (EKF) is used to predict AV's physical behavior by estimating unknown parameters from noisy sensor input. The algorithm is divided into two sections that predicts and corrects the estimation before it is compared against the sensor data. (iii) Anomaly detection: A CUSUM (cumulative sum control chart) algorithm is then used to detect persistent attacks. An alarm is raised if the residual difference is larger than a predefined threshold. Figure 19.3 illustrates our process.

Beyond the security of individual vehicles, the transportation sector could greatly benefit from a supporting infrastructure that allows communication between vehicles, motion sensors on lamp posts, and surveillance cameras (to name a few) to help identify traffic jams, re-route vehicles, and increase vehicle safety. From the user's perspective, privacy concerns arise from all the information needed by such system that could lead to private information being exposed such as vehicle identification and driving patterns. Legislators, engineers, and scientists should keep privacy concerns in mind as advances in IoT become more prominent in day-to-day activities. This will aid in improving the public perception, reduce hesitation from consumers and increase the adoption rate of new technologies [THUR2019]. Policy-based privacy-aware transportation systems are shown in Figure 19.3.

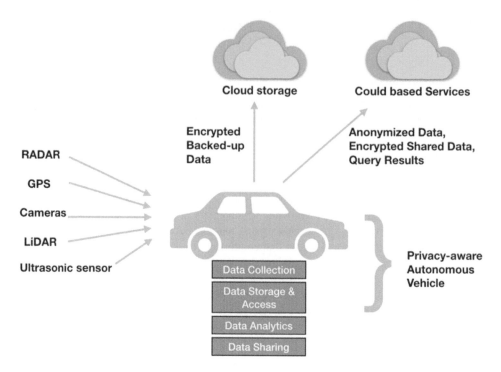

FIGURE 19.3   Privacy-aware policy-based Internet of Transportation Systems.

While handling security attacks and privacy-aware policy-based transportation systems are critical to providing secure and private IoT systems, we cannot forget about data confidentiality. For example, in Chapter 5, we discuss various types of access control policies for data confidentiality. We will revisit them here for Internet of Transportation Systems. Several data confidentiality techniques and mechanisms exist, the most notable being access control systems and encryptions. Both techniques have been widely investigated. However, for access control systems for big data in general and Internet of Transportation Systems in particular, we need approaches for the following:

- *Merging large numbers of access control policies:* In many cases, big data entail integrating data originating from multiple sources (surveillance cameras, sensor data from other vehicles); these data may be associated with their own access control policies (referred to as "sticky policies") and these policies must be enforced even when the data is integrated with other data. Therefore, policies need to be integrated and conflicts solved.
- *Automatically administering authorizations for big data and in particular for granting permissions:* If fine-grained access control is required, manual administration on large datasets is not feasible. We need techniques by which authorization can be automatically granted, possibly based on the user digital identity, profile, and context, and on the data contents and metadata.
- *Enforcing access control policies on heterogeneous multimedia data:* Content-based access control is an important type of access control by which authorizations are granted or denied based on the content of data. Content-based access control is critical when dealing with video surveillance applications that are important for security. As for privacy, such videos have to be protected. Supporting content-based access control requires understanding the contents of protected data and this is very challenging when dealing with multimedia large data sources.

- *Enforcing access control policies in big data stores:* Some of the recent big data systems allow its users to submit arbitrary jobs using programming languages such as Java. For example, in Hadoop, users can submit arbitrary MapReduce jobs written in Java. This creates significant challenges to enforce fine-grained access control efficiently for different users. Although there is some existing work [KHAN2014, ULUS2014] that tries to inject access control policies into submitted jobs, more research needs to be done on how to efficiently enforce such policies in recently developed big data stores.

- *Automatically designing, evolving, and managing access control policies:* When dealing with dynamic environments where sources, users, and applications as well as the data usage are continuously changing, the ability to automatically design and evolve policies is critical to make sure that data are readily available for use while at the same time assuring data confidentiality. Environments and tools for managing policies are also crucial.

19.4   AI AND SECURITY FOR CLOUD-BASED INTERNET OF TRANSPORTATION SYSTEMS

We envision that much of the data collected from the AVs will be sent to a cloud for further processing including carrying out analytics. That is, the massive amounts of data including attack data may be analyzed in the cloud using various ML techniques. Therefore, it is important that the cloud itself be secure especially if it has to carry out security critical operations.

We have designed and developed a layered architecture for a secure cloud [HAML2010]. At the lowest layer is the VNM (Virtual Network Monitor). Then, we have the VMM layer (Virtual Machine Monitor) that carries out virtual machine introspection. Above that is the cloud storage layer based on technologies such as Hadoop/MapReduce. The data may be encrypted which means querying and analytics will have to be carried out on the encrypted data. Above this layer is the query layer for querying the cloud data. Finally, we have the application layer and in our example the applications are those that support the Internet of Transportation Systems. Figure 19.4 illustrates our approach.

Data Science/ML techniques are being applied to analyze the data and a challenge is to apply the stream analytics/learning techniques for transportation data. The main question is to understand the nature of the complex transportation data and adapt the stream analytics techniques and apply them on the massive amounts of heterogeneous sensor data being collected. Such data will often emanate as data streams. Therefore, many of the techniques for stream-based machine learning need to be examined [LI2019]. In addition, deep-learning based techniques developed for IoT systems need to be examined [QIU2020].

The Internet of Transportation Systems will depend heavily on Data Science/AI/ML techniques for various applications including optimum directions, driving without a human in the loop and many more. The adversary will be learning the models used by the vehicles as well as learn about the data used in the training of the models. The adversary will attempt to thwart the vehicle's learning process. Therefore, the learning algorithms have to adapt to thwart the adversary's actions. Eventually it becomes game playing between the adversary and the vehicle's machine learning algorithms [ZHOU2012].

While massive amounts of data are collected by the Internet of Transportation systems, the privacy of the individuals has to be protected. As more and more sensor data are collected, the storage on the AVs will not be sufficient to store all of the data. We envision an encrypted cloud storage component where older data and/or less frequently accessed data are pushed to the cloud. Based on the access control policies, local applications running on the AVs will be given access to some of the collected data. When needed, these AVs will be allowed to access some of the encrypted data stored in the cloud via a simple query interface. We envision that much of the data sharing and analytics will be carried out using the services running in the cloud [THUR2018].

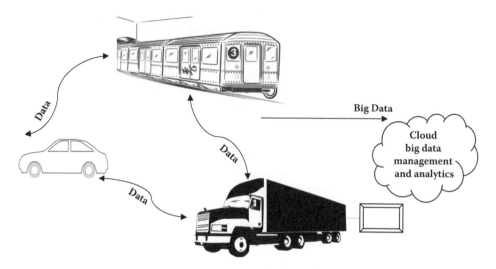

FIGURE 19.4   Cloud for secure Internet of Transportation Systems.

Another direction for enhancing security and at the same time ensure high performance computing is trustworthy analytics [AYOA2018]. Computations over big data may require massive computational resources and, organizations (e.g., automobile companies) may use a third-party service to outsource some computations to be cost-effective. When a third-party server is used for computation, data inherently becomes available in untrusted environments, that is, either observed by a man-in-the-middle during data transmission, or insider threat from adversaries at the third-party location where computation is performed. In these cases, data owners may need to protect their data and require cryptographic guaranties about data security and integrity of computational output from these third-party services. We are conducting research in Secure Encrypted Stream Data Processing and Trustworthy Analytics using advancements in embedded hardware technology (e.g., Intel SGX) to support trusted execution environment (TEE). We need to explore the applications of TEEs to Internet of Transportation and Infrastructures.

19.5   SUMMARY AND DIRECTIONS

The IoT has major implications in the transportation industry. Autonomous Vehicles (AVs) aim at improving day-to-day activities such as delivering packages, improving traffic, and the transportations of goods. AVs are not only limited to ground vehicles but also include aerial and sea vehicles with a wide range of applications. The IoT systems consisting of a collection of AVs have come to be known as the Internet of Transportation systems. While such IoT systems manage large quantities of sensor data, much of the data is also sent to a cloud for offline analysis. While there is great potential in AVs and the improvements, it can make to the transportation industry, security, and privacy concerns pose new challenges that need to be addressed as we move forward. In addition, AI techniques are also becoming crucial for such IoT systems to be able to intelligently manage the AVs. This chapter discusses AI and security for cloud-based Internet of Transportation Systems.

This chapter has discussed the characteristics of the Internet of Transportation Systems with respect to AVs as well as the security and privacy concerns of such systems. Next, we discuss how AI and Security may be integrated. Cloud-based Internet of Transportation Systems were also discussed. Finally, we discussed how AI, Security, and the Cloud may be integrated with the Internet of Transportation Systems.

We have only scratched the surface with respect to securing the Internet of Transportation Systems. We have to understand the various types of tracks and develop ML techniques to detect and prevent the attacks. We also have to examine how to handle the attacks on the ML techniques that are needed for the development of Intelligent Internet of Transportation Systems. Finally, we need to determine the types of data to send to the secure cloud for carrying out analytics.

REFERENCES

[AYOA2018] G. Ayoade, V. Karande, L. Khan, K.W. Hamlen, Decentralized IoT Data Management Using Block Chain and Trusted Execution Environment *Proceedings of the Information Reused and Integration, Salt Lake City, Utah*, 2018, pp. 15–22.
[HAML2010] K.W. Hamlen, M. Kantarcioglu, L. Khan, B.M. Thuraisingham, Security Issues for Cloud Computing, IJISP, Volume 4, #2, 2010, 36–48.
[HAML2009] K.W. Hamlen, V. Mohan, M.M. Masud, L. Khan, B.M. Thuraisingham, Exploiting an Antivirus Interface,Computer Standards and Interfaces, Volume 31, #6, 2009, 1182–1189.
[KHAN2014] L. Khan, K. Hamlen, M. Kantarcioglu, Silver Lining: Enforcing Secure Information Flow at the Cloud Edge, *Proceedings of the 2014 IEEE International Conference on Cloud Engineering, Boston, MA, USA*, 2014.
[LI2019] Y. Li, Y. Gao, G. Ayoade, H. Tao, L. Khan, B.M. Thuraisingham, Multistream Classification for Cyber Threat Data with Heterogeneous Feature Space, 2019. Proceedings of the World Wide Web Conference, WWW 2019, San Francisco, CA, USA.
[LIU2008] L. Liu, M. Kantarcioglu, B.M. Thuraisingham, The Applicability of the Perturbation Based Privacy Preserving Data Mining for Real-world Data, Data & Knowledge Engineering, Volume 65, #1, 2008, 5–21.
[MASO2011] M. Masood, L. Khan, B. Thuraisingham, Data Mining Applications in Malware Detection, CRC Press, 2011.
[QIU2020] H. Qiu, Q. Zheng, G. Memmi, J. Lu, M. Qiu, B.M. Thuraisingham, Deep Residual Learning based Enhanced JPEG Compression in the Internet of Things, accepted by *IEEE Transactions on Industrial Informatics*, Volume17, #3, 2020, pp. 2124–2133.
[QUIN2020] R. Quinonez, J. Giraldo, L. Salazar, E. Bauman, A. Cardenas, Z. Lin, Securing Autonomous Vehicles with a Robust Physics-Based Anomaly Detector, *29th USENIX Security Symposium (USENIX Security 20)*, Boston, MA, August 2020.
[THUR2019] B. Thuraisingham, SecAI: Integrating Cyber Security and Artificial Intelligence with Applications in Internet of Transportation and Infrastructures, Clemson University Center for Connected Multimodal Mobility, Annual Conference, Clemson University, Clemson, South Carolina, October 2019.
[THUR2020] B.M. Thuraisingham, SecAI: Integrating Cyber Security and Artificial Intelligence with Applications in Internet of Transportation and Infrastructures, Clemson University Center for Connected Multimodal Mobility, *Annual Conference*, October 2020.
[THUR2018] B.M. Thuraisingham, M. Kantarcioglu, E. Bertino, J.Z. Bakdash, M. Fernández, Towards a Privacy-Aware Quantified Self Data Management Framework, Proceedings of the 23nd ACM on Symposium on Access Control Models and Technologies, SACMAT 2018, Indianapolis, IN, USA, June 2018.
[THUR2017] B.M. Thuraisingham, P. Pallabi, M. Masud, L. Khan, Big Data Analytics with Applications in Insider Threat Detection, CRC Press, 2017.
[ULUS2014] H. Ulusoy, M. Kantarcioglu, E. Pattuk, K. W. Hamlen, Vigiles: Fine-Grained Access Control for MapReduce Systems, *2014 IEEE International Congress on Big Data (BigData Congress), Anchorage, Alaska, USA*, 2014, pp. 40–47.
[ZHOU2012] Y. Zhou, M. Kantarcioglu, B.M. Thuraisingham, B. Xi, Adversarial Support Vector Machine Learning, *Proceedings of the 18th ACM SIGKDD International Conference on Knowledge Discovery and Data Mining, Beijing, China*, 2012, pp. 1059–1067.

Conclusion to Part IV

Part IV, consisting of five chapters, described access control and data science. In particular, we discussed some of the experimental systems we have developed.

In the case of Secure Cloud Query processing based on access control (Chapter 15), we discussed an access control model for big data systems. A future direction includes improving query optimization as well as exploiting the Hadoop/MapReduce framework to improve performance. We also need to investigate improved indexing to enhance performance. In the case of cloud-centric assured information sharing (Chapter 16), we discussed how information may be shared securely in the cloud. We need to enhance the system by implementing more complex policies as well as implementing the distributed version CAISS++. We also need to carry out a formal analysis of the execution of the policies.

In the case of access control for social media systems (Chapter 17), we discussed an access control model for social media systems represented using semantic web technologies. We intend to extend this work by supporting flexible admin policies. In our framework, social networks' resources could be related to different users according to the supported ontology. To enforce access control, the framework has to decide how the specified access control policies have to be combined together. As such, a first important extension of the framework will be the support of a variety of policy integration strategies. In the case of inference control for big data systems (Chapter 18), we discussed the design and implementation of an inference controller for big data systems. Our next step is to adapt the inference controller for knowledge and social graphs represented in RDF. We are also investigating more powerful reasoning strategies using machine learning techniques.

Finally, in Chapter 19, we discussed AI and security for cloud-based Internet of Transportation Systems. In particular, we discussed the characteristics of the Internet of Transportation Systems with respect to AVs as well as described the security and privacy concerns of such systems. We also showed how AI and Security may be integrated into such systems. Cloud-based Internet of Transportation Systems was also discussed. Finally, we discussed how AI, Security, and the Cloud may be integrated with the Internet of Transportation Systems. We have only scratched the surface with respect to securing the Internet of Transportation Systems. We have to understand the various types of tracks and develop ML techniques to detect and prevent the attacks. We also have to examine how to handle the attacks on the ML techniques that are needed for the development of Intelligent Internet of Transportation Systems. Finally, we need to determine the types of data to send to the secure cloud for carrying out analytics.

DOI: 10.1201/9781003081845-31

20 Summary and Directions

20.1 ABOUT THIS CHAPTER

This chapter brings us to a close of *Secure Data Science: Integrating Cyber Security and Data Science.* We discussed several aspects including data science for cyber security problems such as malware analysis and insider threat detection, adversarial machine learning to handle cyber-attacks, privacy-aware data science, and access control for data science systems. The experimental systems are the ones that we have developed at The University of Texas at Dallas and include secure cloud query processing based on access control, cloud-based assured information sharing systems, secure, and private social media applications which are considered to be data science applications and inference control for big data systems. We also discussed several directions for secure data science.

The organization of this chapter is as follows. In Section 20.2, we give a summary of this book. This summary has been taken from the summaries of each chapter. In Section 20.3, we discuss directions for secure data science. In Section 20.4, we give suggestions as to where to go from here.

20.2 SUMMARY OF THIS BOOK

We summarize the contents of each chapter essentially taken from the summary and directions section of each chapter. Chapter 1 provided an introduction to this book. We first provided a discussion of big data, data science, and machine learning as well as supporting technologies for secure data science including secure data systems, data mining for cyber security applications, cloud and semantic web and big data security and privacy. Following this we discussed the various topics addressed in this book including data science for cyber security, security and privacy for data science and access control for data science. Our framework is a four-layer framework and each layer was addressed in one part of this book. This framework was illustrated in Figure 1.8. We replicate this framework in Figure 20.1.

This book was divided into four parts. Part I, which described supporting technologies, consisted of Chapters 2, 3, 4, and 5. Chapter 2 provided an overview of discretionary security policies in database systems. We started with a discussion of access control policies including authorization policies and role-based access control. Then, we discussed administration policies. We briefly discussed identification and authentication. We also discussed auditing issues as well as views for security. Next, we discussed policy enforcement. The major issue in policy enforcement is policy specification, policy implementation, and policy visualization. We discussed SQL extensions for specifying policies as well as provided an overview of query modification. In Chapter 3, we first provided an overview of the various data mining tasks and techniques and then discussed data mining for security applications. Chapter 4 introduced the notion of the cloud and semantic web technologies. We first discussed concepts in cloud computing including aspects of virtualization. We also discussed the various service models and deployment models for the cloud and provided a brief overview of cloud functions such as storage management and data management. Next, we discussed technologies for the semantic web including XML, RDF, Ontologies, and OWL. This was followed by a discussion of security issues for the semantic web. Finally, we discussed cloud computing frameworks based on semantic web technologies. Chapter 5 discussed the challenges and directions for big data security and privacy.

DOI: 10.1201/9781003081845-32

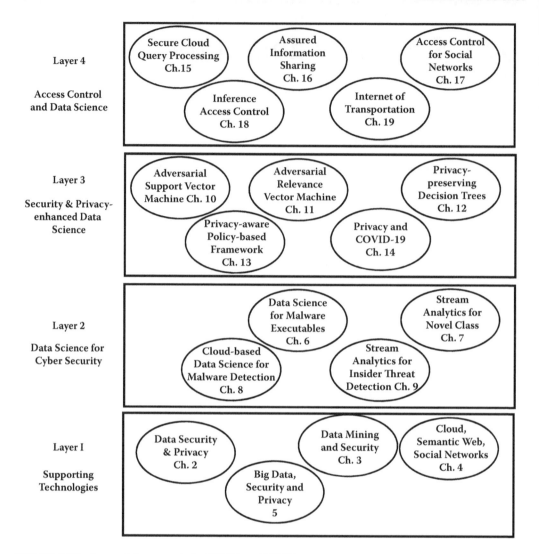

FIGURE 20.1 Layered Framework for BDMA and BDSP.

Part II, consisting of four Chapters 6, 7, 8, and 9, focused on data science for cyber security. In Chapter 6, we discussed the design and implementation of a data mining-based model for malicious code detection. Our technique extracts three different levels of features from executables, namely, binary level, assembly level, and API function call level. These features then go through a feature selection phase for reducing noise and redundancy in the feature set and generate a manageable-sized set of features. These feature sets are then used to build feature vectors for each training data. Then, a classification model is trained using the training data. This classification model classifies future instances (i.e., executables) to detect whether they are benign or malicious. We have shown how to efficiently extract features from the training data. We also showed how scalability can be achieved using disk access. We have explained the algorithm for feature extraction and feature selection. Finally, we showed how to combine the feature sets, and build the feature vectors. We applied different machine learning techniques such as SVM, J48, and Adaboost for building the classification model.

Part III, consisting of five Chapters 10, 11, 12, 13, and 14, discussed security and privacy-aware data science. In Chapter 10, we discuss adversarial support vector machine learning. We consider two attack models: a free-range attack model that permits arbitrary data corruption and a restrained attack model that anticipates more realistic attacks that a reasonable adversary would devise under penalties. We then develop optimal SVM learning strategies against the two attack models. The learning algorithms minimize the hinge loss while assuming the adversary is modifying data to maximize the loss. Experiments are performed on both artificial and real data sets. In Chapter 11, we discussed adversarial relevance vector machine learning. In particular, we presented a sparse Bayesian adversarial learning model. The algorithm sets individual kernel parameters to model adversarial attacks in the feature space by minimizing the log-likelihood of the positive instances in the training set. The learning models trained under this setup are more robust against attacks including the very aggressive ones. In Chapter 12, we discussed privacy-aware data mining. In particular, we described a modified C4.5 decision tree classifier which is suitable for privacy-preserving data mining. The classifier is built from the perturbed data set, and the model can be used to classify the original data with high accuracy. In the scenarios where many parties are participating to perform global data mining without compromising their privacy, our algorithm decreases the costs of communication and computation compared with the cryptography-based approaches. Our algorithm is based on the perturbation scheme, but skips the steps of re-constructing the original data distribution. Our technique has increased the privacy protection with less computation time. In Chapter 13, we discussed a privacy-aware policy-based data management framework for quantified self applications. In particular, we described a general framework, whereby users cannot only specify how their data are managed, but also restrict data collection from their connected devices as well as the storage and analysis of this data. More precisely, we discussed the use of data collection policies to govern the transmission of data from various devices coupled with policies to ensure that once the data have been transmitted, it is stored and shared in a secure and privacy-preserving way. In other words, we discussed a framework for secure data collection, storage, and management, with logical foundations that enable verification of policy properties. In Chapter 14, we presented a framework capable of handling enormous amounts of RDF data that can be used to represent big data systems such as social networks. As our framework is based on Hadoop, which is a distributed and highly fault-tolerant system, it inherits these two properties automatically. The framework is highly scalable. We also developed security models based on access control on top of the query processing framework.

Part IV, consisting of five Chapters 15, 16, 17, 18, and 19, discussed access control and data science that included the experiential systems we have developed. In Chapter 15, we described our design and implementation of a cloud-based assured information sharing system called CAISS. CAISS utilizes several of the technologies we have developed as well as open-source tools. We also described the design of an ideal cloud-based assured information sharing system called CAISS ++. We discussed a series of implementations of CAISS, CAISS+, and a demonstration system. In Chapter 16, we discussed the design and implementation of an extensible fine-grained online social network access control model based on semantic web tools. In addition, we propose authorization, administration and filtering policies that are modeled using OWL and SWRL. The architecture of a framework in support of this model has also been presented. We also described the implementation of an extensible fine-grained online social network access control model based on semantic web tools. In particular, we discussed the implementation of the authorization, administration, and filtering policies that are modeled using OWL and SWRL. In Chapter 17, we described the implementation of an inference controller for data provenance. The inference controller is built using a modular approach, therefore, it is very flexible in that most of the modules can be extended or replaced by another application module. For example, an application user may substitute the policy parser module that handles the parsing of the high-level policies to a low-level policy object. This substitution would allow the application user to continue using his/her business policies independent of our software implementation of the provenance inference controller. Essentially, we have followed a "plug-and-play" approach for implementing the inference controller. We have used open-source products as much as possible in our implementation. The techniues we have

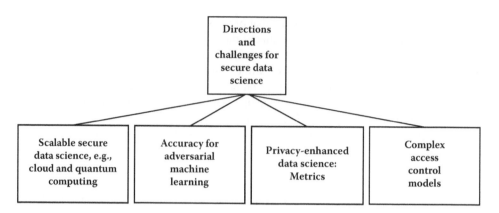

FIGURE 20.2 Directions and challenges secure data science.

implemented for inference control for provenance data can be applied for various types of big data systems.

This book's Appendix provides the broad picture for data management and discusses how all the books we have written fit together.

20.3   DIRECTIONS FOR SECURE DATA SCIENCE

There are many directions for Secure Data Science. We discuss some of them for the topics addressed in this book (Parts II, III, and IV). Figure 20.2 illustrates the directions and challenges.

In Part II, we discussed how data science could be applied to cyber security applications. Some of the directions include the following. In the case of data science for malicious executables (Chapter 6), we like to extend our work in multiple directions. First, we would like to extract and utilize behavioral features for malware detection. This is because obfuscation against binary patterns may be achieved by polymorphism and metamorphism, but it will be difficult for the malware to obfuscate its behavioral pattern. We would like to add more features to the feature set, such as behavioral features of the executables. This is because binary features are susceptible to obfuscation by polymorphic and metamorphic malware. But it would be difficult to obfuscate behavioral patterns. We would also like to enhance the scalability of our approach by applying cloud computing/big data framework for the feature extraction and selection task. This way feature extraction and classification would be more scalable. Cloud computing offers a cheap alternative to more CPU power and much larger disk space which could be utilized for much faster feature extraction and selection process. Besides, we are also interested in extracting behavioral features from the executables to overcome the problem of binary obfuscation by polymorphic malware.

In the case of stream data analytics for novel class detection (Chapter 7), we would like to extend our approach in multiple directions in the future. First, we would like to extend the technique we have developed to real-time data stream classification. To achieve this goal, we will have to optimize the training, including the creation of decision boundary. Besides, the outlier detection and novel class detection should also be made more efficient. We believe a cloud computing framework can play an important role in increasing the efficiency of these processes. Second, we would like to address the real-time data stream classification problem. Real-time data stream mining is more challenging because of the overhead involved in data labeling and training classification models. Third, we would like to utilize the cloud computing framework for data stream mining. The cloud computing framework will be a cheaper alternative to more efficient and powerful computing that is necessary for real-time stream mining. Due to the streaming nature of the data, we expect massive amounts of data to be collected and analyzed. Therefore, in addition to a cloud computing framework, we expect to use big data technologies for storing and managing the data. This way larger and real-world data streams can be analyzed and our approach can be extended to address the real-time classification and novel class detection problems in data streams.

In the case of cloud-based malware detection (Chapter 8), we propose two directions. First, our current feature selection procedure limits its attention to the best S features based on information gain as the selection criterion. The classification accuracy could potentially be improved using work on supervised dimensionality reduction techniques for improved feature selection. Second, the runtime performance of our approach could be improved by exploiting additional parallelism available in the cloud computing architecture. For example, the classifiers of an ensemble could be run in parallel as mappers in a MapReduce framework with reducers that aggregate the results for voting. Similarly, the candidate classifiers for the next ensemble could be trained and evaluated in parallel.

In the case of stream analytics for insider threat detection (Chapter 9), we plan to extend the work in the following directions. For unsupervised learning, we assume that no ground truth is available. In fact, over time some ground truth may be available in terms of feedback. Once a model is created in an unsupervised manner, we would like to update the model based on user feedback. Right now, once the model is created, it remains unchanged. When ground truth is available over time, we will refine all our models based on this feedback immediately. Also, when we update models, collusion attack may take place. Our goal is to identify a colluded attack. For this, during victim selection of models, we will take into account agreement of models over time. If agreement of models persists for a long time and survives, we will choose the victim from there.

In Part III, we discussed security and privacy-aware data science. Some of the directions include the following. In the case of adversarial support vector machine learning (Chapter 10), a future direction for this work is to add cost-sensitive metrics into the learning models. Another direction is to extend the single learning model to an ensemble in which each base learner handles a different set of attacks. We would also like to include an investigation of other adversarial machine learning techniques as well as different types of attacks. Also, we would like to consider additional game theoretic models. In the case of adversarial relevance vector machine learning (Chapter 11), the open problem is to discover an efficient approach to simultaneously update the kernel and the learning parameters. The solution would help find the optimal learning model against the worst-case attacks in the sample space. As in the vase of adversarial support vector machine learning, another direction is to consider different types of attacks.

In the case of privacy-preserving data mining (Chapter 12), a future direction is to build the classifiers which can be used to classify the perturbed data set. As we have mentioned before, with a better bound of the random noise data R, using the probability as weighting is an approach that needs further investigation. Also, as novel machine learning techniques are being developed such as deep learning approaches, we need to explore privacy-preserving machine learning for these approaches. In the case of privacy-aware policy-based data management framework (Chapter 13), the next step is to carry out a detailed design and implementation of the framework. We also have to design the formal framework so we can specify and reason about the policies regardless of the solutions implemented. We also need to take the behavioral aspects of the users into consideration. We need to adapt the framework for applications such as the Internet of Transportation Systems. Finally, in Chapter 14, we discussed the application of data science for COVID-19 related applications and discussed the privacy violations that could occur. We also discussed the various frameworks being proposed by organizations such as the American Civil Liberties Union.

Part IV, consisting of five chapters, described access control and data science. In particular, we discussed some of the experimental systems we have developed.

In the case of Secure Cloud Query processing based on access control (Chapter 15), we discussed an access control model for big data systems. A future direction includes improve query optimization as well as better exploiting the Hadoop/MapReduce framework to improve performance. We also need to investigate improved indexing beachboys. In the case of cloud-centric assured information sharing (Chapter 16), we discussed how information may be shared securely in the cloud. We need to enhance the system by implementing more complex policies as well as implement the distributed version CAISS++. We also need to carry out a formal analysis of the execution of the policies.

In the case of access control for social media systems (Chapter 17), we discussed an access control model for social media systems represented using semantic web technologies. We intend to extend this work by supporting flexible admin policies. In our framework, social network's resources could be related to different users according to the supported ontology. To enforce access control, the framework has to decide how the specified access control policies have to be combined together. As such, a first important extension of the framework will be the support of a variety of policy integration strategies. In the case of inference control for big data systems (Chapter 18), we discussed the design and implementation of an inference controller for big data systems. Our next step is to adapt the inference controller for knowledge and social graphs represented in RDF. We are also investigating more powerful reasoning strategies using machine learning techniques.

Finally, in Chapter 19, we discussed AI and security for cloud-based Internet of Transportation Systems. In particular, we discussed the characteristics of the Internet of Transportation Systems with respect to AVs as well as described the security and privacy concerns of such systems. We also showed how AI and Security may be integrated into such systems. Cloud-based Internet of Transportation Systems was also discussed. Finally, we discussed how AI, Security, and the Cloud may be integrated with the Internet of Transportation Systems. We have only scratched the surface with respect to securing the Internet of Transportation Systems. We have to understand the various types of tracks and develop ML techniques to detect and prevent the attacks. We also have to examine how to handle the attacks on the ML techniques that are needed for the development of Intelligent Internet of Transportation Systems. Finally, we need to determine the types of data to send to the secure cloud for carrying out analytics.

20.4   WHERE DO WE GO FROM HERE?

This book has focused on Secure Data Science. In has explored both data science for cyber security as well as security and privacy enhanced data science. We also discussed some of the experimental systems we have developed in secure data science. We need to continue with research and development efforts if we are to make progress in this very important area. The question is where do we go from here? First of all, those who wish to work in this area must have a good knowledge of the supporting technologies including cloud, data management and analytics, semantic web, and security. For example, it is important to understand the technologies that comprise data analytics and how they scale for handling massive data.

Next, since the field is expanding rapidly and there are many developments in the field, the reader has to keep up with the developments including reading about the commercial products and prototypes as well as the emerging systems. Finally, we encourage the reader to experiment with the products and also develop analytics and security tools. This is the best way to get familiar with a particular field. That is, work on hands-on problems and provide solutions to get a better understanding. The developers should be familiar with technologies such as Hadoop, MapReduce, HBase, Storm, and Spark as well as security technologies including various types of cyber-attacks and privacy considerations. The cloud will continue to have a major impact on handling massive amounts of data and processing for many big data systems including social media data systems and therefore security for the cloud will be an important aspect. Finally, data science is a broad term that includes data mining, data management, statistics and also includes the learning techniques in machine learning. Therefore, we need to include some of the emerging technologies such as deep learning and integrate it with cyber security. There are numerous applications of the technologies discussed in this book from healthcare, epidemiology, finance, to retail and marketing.

We need research and development support from the federal and local government funding agencies. Agencies such as the National Science Foundation, National Security Agency, the US Army, Navy, Air Force, the Defense Advanced Research Projects Agency, the Intelligence Advanced Research Projects Activity, and the Department of Homeland Security are funding research in security and machine learning. We also need commercial corporations to invest research and development funds so that progress can be made in industrial research as well as be able to transfer the research to commercial products. We also need to collaborate with the international research community to solve problems and promote standards that are not only of national interest but also of international interest. In summary, we need public/private/academic partnerships to develop breakthrough technologies in the very important areas of Secure Data Science.

Appendix: Data Management Systems – Developments and Trends

A.1 INTRODUCTION

The main purpose of this appendix is to set the context of the series of books we have written in data management, data mining and data security. Our series started back in 1997 with our book on *Data Management Systems Evolution and Interoperation* [THUR1997]. Our subsequent books have evolved from this first book. The purpose of this appendix is to provide an overview of data management systems as well as to show how the field has evolved over the years: from data to information to knowledge and now to big data. We will then discuss the relationships between the books we have written.

As stated in our series of books, the developments in information systems technologies have resulted in computerizing many applications in various business areas. Data have become a critical resource in many organizations and therefore, efficient access to data, sharing the data, extracting information from the data, and making use of the information, have become urgent needs. As a result, there have been several efforts on integrating the various data sources scattered across several sites. These data sources may be databases managed by database management systems or they could simply be files. To provide the interoperability between the multiple data sources and systems, various tools are being developed. These tools enable users of one system to access other systems in an efficient and transparent manner.

We define data management systems to be systems that manage the data, extract meaningful information from the data and make use of the information extracted. Therefore, data management systems include database systems, data warehouses, and data mining systems. Data could be structured data such as that found in relational databases or it could be unstructured such as text, voice, imagery, and video. There have been numerous discussions in the past to distinguish between data, information, and knowledge. We do not attempt to clarify these terms. For our purposes, data could be just bits and bytes or it could convey some meaningful information to the user. We will, however, distinguish between database systems and database management systems. A database management system is that component which manages the database containing persistent data. A database system consists of both the database and the database management system.

A key component to the evolution and interoperation of data management systems is the interoperability of heterogeneous database systems. Efforts on the interoperability between database systems have been reported since the late 1970s. However, it is only recently that we are seeing commercial developments in heterogeneous database systems. Major database system vendors are now providing interoperability between their products and other systems. Furthermore, many of the database system vendors are migrating toward an architecture called the client–server architecture which facilitates distributed data management capabilities. In addition to efforts on the interoperability between different database systems and client–server environments, work is also directed toward handling autonomous and federated environments.

It should be noted technologies have evolved over the past 24 years since we published our first book in 1997. With the advent of the world wide web, the importance of data was beginning to be realized. Over the past 24 years increasingly massive amounts of data are being collected, stored, processed, and analyzed. While the challenge was to manage petabyte-sized databases, which was called "the massive data problem" at that time has now evolved into zettabyte- and even exabyte-sized databases which is now called the "big data problem." Furthermore, while machine leaning

411

techniques used to work on what was called "toy problems" at that time is now used to work on "real-world problems." This is because of the tremendous advances in hardware as well as advances in understanding data as well as more sophisticated learning techniques, especially in the field of what is called "deep learning." Therefore, as long as organizations (commercial, academic, government) collect data and analyze data, big data analytics is here to stay. It also means we have to ensure that security and privacy policies are enforced at all stages of the data lifecycle. We have addressed some aspects of the challenges in this book.

The organization of this appendix is as follows. Since database systems are a key component of data management systems, we first provide an overview of the developments in database systems. These developments are discussed in Section A.2. Then we provide a vision for data management systems in Section A.3. Our framework for data management systems is discussed in Section A.4. Note that data mining, warehousing as well as web data management are components of this framework. Building information systems from our framework with special instantiations is discussed in Section A.5. It should be noted that Sections A.2 to A.5 have been taken from our first book and duplicated in each of our subsequent books. The relationship between the various texts that we have written for CRC Press is discussed in Section A.6. Section A.7 summarizes this appendix.

A.2   DEVELOPMENTS IN DATABASE SYSTEMS

Figure A.1 provides an overview of the developments in database systems technology. While the early work in the 1960s focused on developing products based on the network and hierarchical data models, much of the developments in database systems took place after the seminal paper by Codd describing the relational model [CODD1970] (see also [DATE1990]). Research and development work on relational database systems was carried out during the early 1970s and several prototypes were developed throughout the 1970s. Notable efforts include IBM's (International Business Machine Corporation's) System R and University of California at Berkeley's INGRES. During the 1980s, many relational database system products were being marketed (notable among these products are those of Oracle

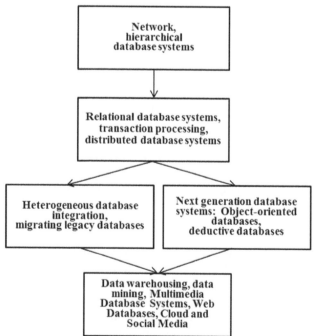

FIGURE A.1   Developments in database systems technology.

Corporation, Sybase Inc., Informix Corporation, INGRES Corporation, IBM, Digital Equipment Corporation, and Hewlett Packard Company). During the 1990s, products from other vendors emerged (e.g., Microsoft Corporation). In fact, to date numerous relational database system products have been marketed. However, Codd has stated that many of the systems that are being marketed as relational systems are not really relational (see e.g., the discussion in [DATE1990]). He then discussed various criteria that a system must satisfy to be qualified as a relational database system. While the early work focused on issues such as data model, normalization theory, query processing and optimization strategies, query languages, and access strategies and indexes, later the focus shifted toward supporting a multi-user environment. In particular, concurrency control and recovery techniques were developed. Support for transaction processing was also provided.

Research on relational database systems as well as on transaction management was followed by research on distributed database systems around the mid-1970s. Several distributed database system prototype development efforts also began around the late 1970s. Notable among these efforts include IBM's System R*, DDTS (Distributed Database Testbed System) by Honeywell Inc., SDD-I and Multibase by CCA (Computer Corporation of America), and Mermaid by SDC (System Development Corporation). Furthermore, many of these systems (e.g., DDTS, Multibase, Mermaid) function in a heterogeneous environment. During the early 1990s, several database system vendors (such as Oracle Corporation, Sybase Inc., Informix Corporation) provided data distribution capabilities for their systems. Most of the distributed relational database system products are based on client–server architectures. The idea is to have the client of vendor A communicate with the server database system of vendor B. In other words, the client–server computing paradigm facilitates a heterogeneous computing environment. Interoperability between relational and nonrelational commercial database systems is also possible. The database systems community is also involved in standardization efforts. Notable among the standardization efforts are the ANSI/SPARC 3-level schema architecture, the IRDS (Information Resource Dictionary System) standard for Data Dictionary Systems, the relational query language SQL (Structured Query Language), and the RDA (Remote Database Access) protocol for remote database access.

Another significant development in database technology is the advent of object-oriented database management systems. Active work on developing such systems began in the mid-1980s and they are now commercially available (notable among them include the products of Object Design Inc., Ontos Inc., Gemstone Systems Inc., Versant Object Technology). It was felt that new generation applications such as multimedia, office information systems, CAD/CAM, process control, and software engineering have different requirements. Such applications utilize complex data structures. Tighter integration between the programming language and the data model is also desired. Object-oriented database systems satisfy most of the requirements of these new generation applications [CATT1991].

According to the Lagunita report published as a result of a National Science Foundation (NSF) workshop in 1990 (see [SILB90] and [KIM90]), relational database systems, transaction processing, and distributed (relational) database systems are stated as mature technologies. Furthermore, vendors are marketing object-oriented database systems and demonstrating the interoperability between different database systems. The report goes on to state that as applications are getting increasingly complex, more sophisticated database systems are needed. Furthermore, since many organizations now use database systems, in many cases of different types, the database systems need to be integrated. Although work has begun to address these issues and commercial products are available, several issues still need to be resolved. Therefore, challenges faced by the database systems researchers in the early 1990s were in two areas. One was next generation database systems and the other was heterogeneous database systems.

Next generation database systems include object-oriented database systems, functional database systems, special parallel architectures to enhance the performance of database system functions, high-performance database systems, real-time database systems, scientific database systems, temporal database systems, database systems that handle incomplete and uncertain information and intelligent database systems (also sometimes called logic or deductive database systems). Ideally, a database system should provide the support for high- performance transaction processing, model complex applications, represent new kinds of data, and make intelligent deductions. While significant progress has been made during the late 1980s and early 1990s, there is much to be done before such a database system can be developed.

Heterogeneous database systems have been receiving considerable attention during the past decade [MARC1990]. The major issues include handling different data models, different query processing strategies, different transaction processing algorithms and different query languages. Should a uniform view be provided to the entire system or should the users of the individual systems maintain their own views of the entire system? These are questions that have yet to be answered satisfactorily. It is also envisaged that a complete solution to heterogeneous database management systems is a generation away. While research should be directed towards finding such a solution, work should also be carried out to handle limited forms of heterogeneity to satisfy the customer needs. Another type of database system that received some attention is a federated database system. Note that some have used the terms heterogeneous database system and federated database system interchangeably. While heterogeneous database systems can be part of a federation, a federation can also include homogeneous database systems.

The explosion of users on the web as well as developments in interface technologies has resulted in even more challenges for data management researchers. A second workshop was sponsored by NSF in 1995, and several emerging technologies were identified to be important as we entered into the 21st century [WIDO1996]. These include digital libraries, managing very large databases, data administration issues, multimedia databases, data warehousing, data mining, data management for collaborative computing environments, and security and privacy. Another significant development in the 1990s is the development of object-relational systems. Such systems combine the advantages of both object-oriented database systems and relational database systems. Also, many corporations are now focusing on integrating their data management products with web technologies. Finally, for many organizations there is an increasing need to migrate some of the legacy databases and applications to newer architectures and systems such as client–server architectures and relational database systems. We believe that there is no end to data management systems. As new technologies are developed, there are new opportunities for data management research and development.

A comprehensive view of all data management technologies is illustrated in Figure A.2. As shown, traditional technologies include database design, transaction processing, and benchmarking. Then there are database systems based on data models such as relational and object-oriented. Database systems may depend on features they provide such as security and real-time. These database systems may be relational or object-oriented. There are also database systems based on multiple sites or processors such as distributed and heterogeneous database systems, parallel systems and systems being migrated. Finally, there are the emerging technologies such as data warehousing and mining, collaboration, and the web. Any comprehensive text on data management systems should address all of these technologies. We have selected some of the relevant technologies and put them in a framework. This framework is described in Section A.5.

A.3   STATUS, VISION, AND ISSUES

Significant progress has been made on data management systems. However, many of the technologies are still stand-alone technologies as illustrated in Figure A.3. For example, multimedia systems are yet to be successfully integrated with warehousing and mining technologies. The ultimate goal is to integrate multiple technologies so that accurate data, as well as information, are produced at the right time and distributed to the user in a timely manner. Our vision for data and information management is illustrated in Figure A.4.

Traditional technologies:	Database systems based on data models:	Database systems based on features:
• Data modeling and database design • Enterprise/business modeling and application design • DB MS design • Query, metadata, transactions • Integrity and data quality • Benchmarking and performance • Data administration, auditing, database administration • Standards	• Hierarchical • Network • Relational • Functional • Object-oriented • Deductive (logic-based) • Object-relational	• Secure database • Real-time database • Fault-tolerance database • Multimedia database • Active database • Temporal database • Fuzzy database

	Multi-site/processor-based Systems:	Emerging technologies:
	• Distribution • Interoperability • Federated • Client-server • Migration • Parallel/high performance	• Data warehousing • Data mining • Web and cloud data • Collaboration • Mobile computing • Social media

FIGURE A.2 Comprehensive View of Data Management Systems.

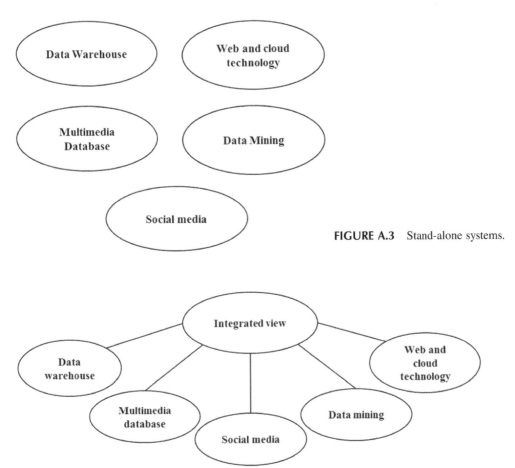

FIGURE A.3 Stand-alone systems.

FIGURE A.4 Vision.

The work discussed in [THUR1997] addressed many of the challenges necessary to accomplish this vision. In particular, integration of heterogeneous databases as well as the use of distributed object technology for interoperability was discussed. While much progress has been made on the system aspects of interoperability, semantic issues still remain a challenge. Different databases have different representations. Furthermore, the same data entity may be interpreted differently at different sites. Addressing these semantic differences and extracting useful information from the heterogeneous and possibly multimedia data sources are major challenges.

A.4   DATA MANAGEMENT SYSTEMS FRAMEWORK

For the successful development of evolvable interoperable data management systems, hetero-geneous database systems integration is a major component. However, there are other technologies that have to be successfully integrated with each other to develop techniques for efficient access and sharing of data as well as for the extraction of information from the data. To facilitate the development of data management systems to meet the requirements of various applications in fields such as medical, financial, manufacturing and military, we have proposed a framework which can be regarded as a reference model for data management systems. Various components from this framework have to be integrated to develop data management systems to support the various applications.

Figure A.5 illustrates our framework which can be regarded as a model for data management systems. This framework consists of three layers. One can think of the component technologies which we will also refer to as components belonging to a particular layer to be more or less built on the technologies provided by the lower layer. Layer I is the database technology and distribution layer. This layer consists of database systems and distributed database systems technologies. Layer II is the interoperability and migration layer. This layer consists of technologies such as heterogeneous database integration, client/server databases and multimedia database systems to handle heterogeneous data types and migrating legacy databases. Layer III is the information extraction and sharing layer. This layer essentially consists of technologies for some of the newer services supported by data management systems. These include data warehousing, data mining [THUR1998], web databases and database support for collaborative applications. Data manage-ment systems may utilize lower level technologies such as networking, distributed processing and mass storage. We have grouped these technologies into a layer called the supporting technologies layer. This supporting layer does not belong to the data management systems framework. This supporting layer also consists of some higher-level technologies such as distributed object man-agement and agents. Also, shown in Figure A.5 is the application technologies layer. Systems such as collaborative computing systems and knowledge-based systems which belong to this layer may utilize data management systems. Note that the application technologies layer is also outside of the data management systems framework.

The technologies that constitute the data management systems framework can be regarded to be some of the core technologies in data management. However, features like security, integrity, real-time processing, fault tolerance, and high-performance computing are needed for many applica-tions utilizing data management technologies such as medical, financial, or military, among others. We illustrate this in Figure A.6, where a three-dimensional view relating data management technologies with features and applications is given. For example, one could develop a secure distributed database management system for medical applications or a fault-tolerant multimedia database management system for financial applications.

Integrating the components belonging to the various layers is important to developing efficient data management systems. In addition, data management technologies have to be integrated with the application technologies to develop successful information systems. However, at present, there is limited integration between these various components. Our books have addressed concepts related to the various layers of this framework.

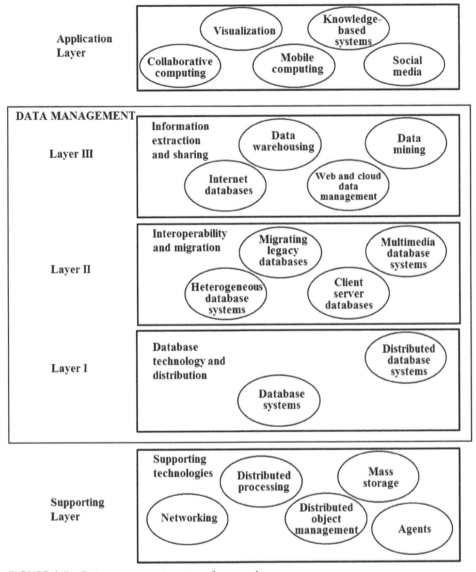

FIGURE A.5 Data management systems framework.

Note that security cuts across all the layers. Security is needed for the supporting layers such as agents and distributed systems. Security is needed for all of the layers in the framework including database security, distributed database security, warehousing security, web database security, and collaborative data management security.

A.5 BUILDING INFORMATION SYSTEMS FROM THE FRAMEWORK

Figure A.5 illustrated a framework for data management systems. As shown in that figure, the technologies for data management include database systems, distributed database systems, heterogeneous database systems, migrating legacy databases, multimedia database systems, data warehousing, data mining, web databases, and database support for collaboration. Furthermore, data management systems take advantage of supporting technologies such as distributed

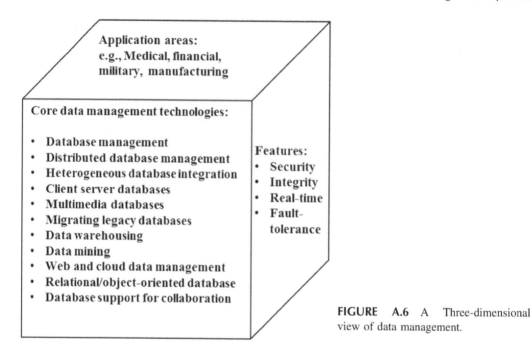

Application areas:
e.g., Medical, financial,
military, manufacturing

Core data management technologies:

- Database management
- Distributed database management
- Heterogeneous database integration
- Client server databases
- Multimedia databases
- Migrating legacy databases
- Data warehousing
- Data mining
- Web and cloud data management
- Relational/object-oriented database
- Database support for collaboration

Features:
- Security
- Integrity
- Real-time
- Fault-
  tolerance

FIGURE A.6 A Three-dimensional view of data management.

processing and agents. Similarly, application technologies such as collaborative computing, visualization, expert systems, and mobile computing take advantage of data management systems.

Many of us have heard of the term information systems on numerous occasions. These systems have sometimes been used interchangeably with data management systems. In our terminology, information systems are much broader than data management systems but they do include data management systems. In fact, a framework for information systems will include not only the data management system layers but also the supporting technologies layer as well as the application technologies layer. That is, information systems encompass all kinds of computing systems. It can be regarded as the finished product that can be used for various applications. That is, while hardware is at the lowest end of the spectrum, applications are at the highest end.

We can combine the technologies of Figure A.5 to put together information systems. For example, at the application technology level, one may need collaboration and visualization technologies so that analysts can collaboratively carry out some tasks. At the data management level, one may need both multimedia and distributed database technologies. At the supporting level, one may need mass storage as well as some distributed processing capability. This special framework is illustrated in Figure A.7. Another example is a special framework for interoperability. One may need some visualization technology to display the integrated information from the heterogeneous databases. At the data management level, we have heterogeneous database systems technology. At the supporting technology level, one may use distributed object management technology to encapsulate the heterogeneous databases. This special framework is illustrated in Figure A.8.

Finally, let us illustrate the concepts that we have described above by using a specific example. Suppose a group of physicians/surgeons wants a system where they can collaborate and make decisions about various patients. This could be a medical video teleconferencing application. That is, at the highest level, the application is a medical application and more specifically, a medical video teleconferencing application. At the application technology level, one needs a variety of technologies including collaboration and teleconferencing. These application technologies will make use of data management technologies such as distributed database systems and multimedia database systems. That is, one may need to support multimedia data such as audio and video. The

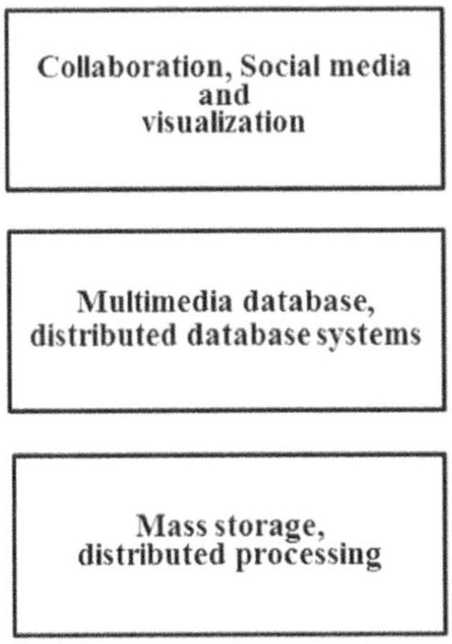

```
┌─────────────────────────┐
│  Collaboration, Social media │
│            and            │
│       visualization       │
└─────────────────────────┘

┌─────────────────────────┐
│   Multimedia database,    │
│ distributed database systems │
└─────────────────────────┘

┌─────────────────────────┐
│      Mass storage,        │
│   distributed processing  │
└─────────────────────────┘
```

FIGURE A.7 Framework for multimedia data management for collaboration.

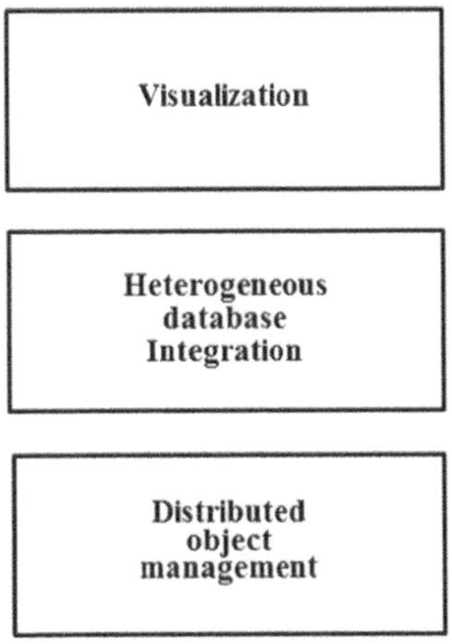

```
┌─────────────────────────┐
│       Visualization       │
└─────────────────────────┘

┌─────────────────────────┐
│      Heterogeneous        │
│         database          │
│        Integration        │
└─────────────────────────┘

┌─────────────────────────┐
│       Distributed         │
│          object           │
│        management         │
└─────────────────────────┘
```

FIGURE A.8 Framework for heterogeneous database interoperability.

data management technologies in turn draw on lower level technologies such as distributed processing and networking. We illustrate this in Figure A.9.

In summary, information systems include data management systems as well as application layer systems such as collaborative computing systems and supporting layer systems such as distributed object management systems.

While application technologies make use of data management technologies and data management technologies make use of supporting technologies, the ultimate user of the information system is the application itself. Today numerous applications make use of information systems. These applications are from multiple domains such as medical, financial, manufacturing, telecommunications and defense. Specific applications include signal processing, electronic commerce, patient monitoring and situation assessment. Figure A.10 illustrates the relationship between the application and the information system. The evolution from data to big data is illustrated in Figure A.11.

A.6 RELATIONSHIP BETWEEN THE TEXTS

We have published two book series. The first series is mainly for technical managers, while the second series is for researchers and developers. The books in the first series are the following: *Data Management Systems: Evolution and Interoperation* [THUR1997], *Data Mining: Technologies,*

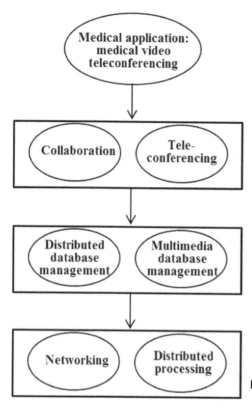

FIGURE A.9   Specific example.

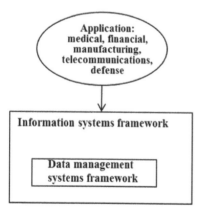

FIGURE A.10   Application framework relationship.

Techniques, Tools and Trends [THUR1998], *Web Data Management and Electronic Commerce* [THUR2000], *Managing and Mining Multimedia Databases for the Electronic Enterprise* [THUR2001], *XML, Databases and The Semantic Web* [THUR2002], *Web Data Mining and Applications in Business Intelligence and Counter-terrorism* [THUR2003], *Database and Applications Security: Integrating Data Management and Information Security* [THUR2005]. *Building Trustworthy Semantic Web* [THUR2007], and *Secure Semantic Service-Oriented Systems* [THUR2010]. Our last book in these series titled: *Developing and Securing the Cloud,* [THUR2014] has evolved from our previous book on *Secure Semantic Service-Oriented Systems.* All of these books have evolved from the framework that we illustrated in this appendix and address different parts of the framework. The connection between these texts is illustrated in Figure A.12.

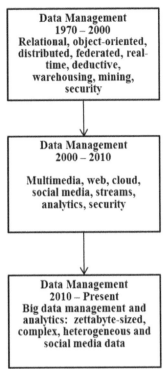

FIGURE A.11 From data to big data.

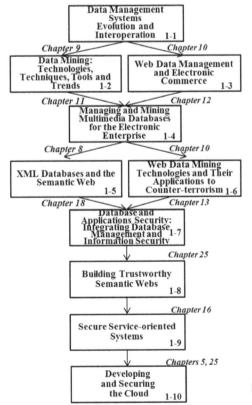

FIGURE A.12 Relationship between texts – series I.

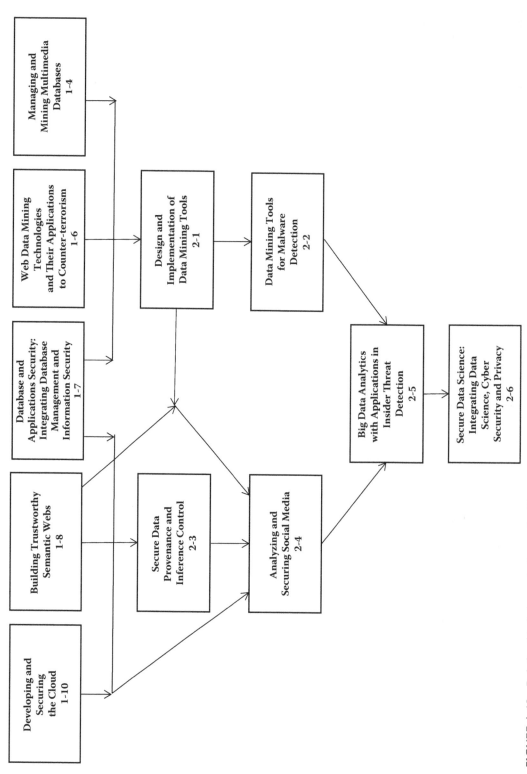

FIGURE A.13   Relationship between texts – series II.

We have published six books in the second series. The first is titled *Design and Implementation of Data Mining Tools* [AWAD2009] and the second is titled *Data Mining Tools for Malware Detection* [MASU2011]. Our book, *Secure Data Provenance and Inference Control with Semantic Web* [THUR2015] was the third in these series. Our book *Analyzing and Securing Social Networks* is the fourth in these series [THUR2016]. Our previous book *Big Data Analytics with Applications in Insider Threat Detection* is the fifth in these series [THUR2017]. Our current book *Secure Data Science: Integrating Cyber Security and Data Science* is the sixth in these series [THUR2021]. The relationship between these books as well as with our previous books is illustrated in Figure A.13.

A.7 SUMMARY AND DIRECTIONS

In this appendix, we have provided an overview of data management. We first discussed the developments in data management and then provided a vision for data management. Then, we illustrated a framework for data management. This framework consists of three layers: database systems layer, interoperability layer, and information extraction layer. Finally, we showed how information systems could be built from the technologies of the framework.

We believe that data management is essential to many information technologies including data mining, multimedia information processing, interoperability, collaboration and knowledge management, as well as data science which integrates data management, data mining, machine learning, and statistical methods to process massive amounts of heterogeneous data. This appendix stresses on data management. Security is critical for all data management technologies and we rely on these technologies for applications such as social media and insider threat detection. While the latter part of the 20th century was about the computer revolution, the early part of the 21st century is about the data revolution.

REFERENCES

[AWAD2009] M. Awad, L. Khan, B. Thuraisingham, L. Wang, Design and Implementation of Data Mining Tools, CRC Press, Boca Raton, FL, 2009.
[CATT1991] R. Cattell, Object Data Management Systems, Addison- Wesley, MA, 1991.
[CODD1970] E.F. Codd, A Relational Model of Data for Large Shared Data Banks, Communications of the ACM, Volume 13, #6, 1970, 377–387.
[DATE1990] C.J. Date, An Introduction to Database Management Systems, Addison-Wesley, MA, 1990 (6th edition published in 1995 by Addison-Wesley).
[KIM1990] W. Kim (Ed.), Directions for Future Database Research & Development, ACM SIGMOD Record,, Volume 19, #4, 1990, 4–5.
[MARC1990] S.T. March (Ed.), Special Issue on Heterogeneous Database Systems, ACM Computing Surveys, 1990, Volume 22, #3.
[MASU2011] M. Masud, B. Thuraisingham, L. Khan, Data Mining Tools for Malware Detection, CRC Press, Boca Raton, FL, 2011.
[SILB1990] A. Silberschatz, M. Stonebrakerm, J.D. Ullman (Eds), Database systems: Achievements and Opportunities, The "Lagunita" Report of the NSF Invitational Workshop on the Future of Database Systems Research, February 22–23, Palo Alto, CA (TR-90-22), Department of Computer Sciences, University of Texas at Austin, Austin, TX (also in ACM SIGMOD Record, December 1990, 1990.
[THUR1997] B. Thuraisingham, Data Management Systems: Evolution and Interoperation, CRC Press, Boca Raton, FL, 1997.
[THUR1998] B. Thuraisingham, Data Mining: Technologies, Techniques, Tools and Trends, CRC Press, Boca Raton, FL, 1998.
[THUR2000] B. Thuraisingham, Web Data Management and Electronic Commerce, CRC Press, Boca Raton, FL, 2000.
[THUR2001] B. Thuraisingham, Managing and Mining Multimedia Databases for the Electronic Enterprise, CRC Press, Boca Raton, FL, 2001.
[THUR2002] B. Thuraisingham, XML, Databases and The Semantic Web, CRC Press, Boca Raton, FL, 2002.

[THUR2003] B. Thuraisingham, Web Data Mining Applications in Business Intelligence and Counter-terrorism, CRC Press, Boca Raton, FL, 2003.

[THUR2005] B. Thuraisingham, Database and Applications Security: Integrating Data Management and Information Security, CRC Press, Boca Raton, FL, 2005.

[THUR2007] B. Thuraisingham, Building Trustworthy Semantic Webs, CRC Press, Boca Raton, FL, 2007.

[THUR2010] B. Thuraisingham, Secure Semantic Service-Oriented Systems, CRC Press, Boca Raton, FL, 2010.

[THUR2014] B. Thuraisingham, Developing and Securing the Cloud, CRC Press, Boca Raton, FL, 2013.

[THUR2015] B. Thuraisingham, T. Cadenhead, M. Kantarcioglu, V. Khadilkar, Secure Data Provenance and Inference Control with Semantic Web, CRC Press, Boca Raton, FL, 2014.

[THUR2016] B. Thuraisingham, S. Abrol, R. Heatherly, M. Kantarcioglu, V. Khadilkar, L. Khan, Analyzing and Securing Social Networks, CRC Press, 2016.

[THUR2017] B. Thuraisingham, P. Praveen, M. Masud, L. Khan, Big Data Analytics with Applications in Insider Threat Detection, CRC Press, Boca Raton, FL, 2017.

[THUR2021] B. Thuraisingham, M. Kantarcioglu, L. Khan, Secure Data Science: Integrating Cyber Security and Data Science, CRC Press, Boca Raton, FL, 2021.

[WIDO1996] J. Widom, Ed., Proceedings of the Database Systems Workshop, Report published by the National Science Foundation, 1995 (also in *ACM SIGMOD Record*, March 1996, Vol 25 (1), Database Research: Achievements and Opportunities into the 21st Century.

Index

Note: *Italicized* page numbers refer to figures, **bold** page numbers refer to tables

For Product Safety Concerns and Information please contact our
EU representative GPSR@taylorandfrancis.com Taylor & Francis
Verlag GmbH, Kaufingerstraße 24, 80331 München, Germany